The Science of
Teaching Swimming

The Science of Teaching Swimming

Mervyn L. Palmer, DSTA, AIST

Illustrations by the author

PELHAM BOOKS
London

To
Maureen who began it all
and
Shirley who had the patience and understanding
to see it through

First published in Great Britain by
PELHAM BOOKS LTD
44 Bedford Square
London WC1B 3DU
1979

ISBN 0 7207 1117 7

Filmset in Great Britain by
D.P. Media Limited, Hitchin, Hertfordshire

Printed by Hollen Street Press
and bound by Dorstel Press, Harlow

Contents

Preface

Mervyn Palmer has realised a lifetime's ambition in publishing this book, which will undoubtedly become a standard reference work for all serious students concerned with the teaching of swimming. It is a complete statement, based on many years of experience as a swimmer, on his careful observations and the testing of hypotheses. It explains very clearly the underlying principles, gives detailed analyses of skills and offers a wealth of carefully considered activities for the practising teacher.

His training as an engineer is much in evidence. The work is logical and the statements are supported by rational explanations, whilst the illustrations are meticulous.

This is no hotch-potch of previous publications but a most original and sensibly reasoned examination of the problems of teaching swimming, which continually returns to first principles. It will be of great value to our sport and countless boys and girls all over the world will benefit from Mervyn's efforts, which I know will give him great pleasure – a pleasure that will be shared by his former rivals and many friends in the world of swimming.

J.A. Holmyard,
Lecturer in Physical Education,
University of Bristol.
(Former National Technical Officer to ASA.)

ACKNOWLEDGEMENTS

I extend grateful thanks to all my many friends in the world of swimming for their help, encouragement and advice during the preparation of this book.

My special thanks go to June Whitehouse, DSTA, and Tony Holmyard, ASA coach and university lecturer, for their constructive comments; to Professor Colin Andrew of Bristol University Mechanical Engineering Department for his invaluable assistance; to George Rackham, FSTA, whose invaluable comments on the arts of swimming, synchro and diving have helped tremendously; to Mr C. Abercrombie of the Northern College of Chiropody, Salford; to swimmers of Bristol Central and Bristol North Swimming Clubs for their assistance in the water; to Leonard J. Kitt, MIMech.E, lecturer in mechanical engineering at Brunel Technical College; to Gordon Pancott, DSTA, for his help and encouragement throughout the project; to Helen Elkington, FIST, FISC, whose infectious enthusiasm unwittingly laid the foundations for the book many years ago; to members and staff of both the Swimming Teachers' and Amateur Swimming Associations for their kindness and help; to Allyson and her faithful typewriter; and finally to my wife Shirley who was a constant source of encouragement, and without whose patience and understanding the book would never have been possible.

I am also indebted to Gray's *Anatomy* which has helped me greatly in my researches for Part II of this book.

Introduction

This book has been written primarily for those entering the swimming teaching profession. It is designed also to provide a reference for established teachers who wish to further their careers by examination. It also gives general information on the many and varied swimming skills.

Most aspects of the teaching of swimming are covered, starting with methods of handling beginners with the emphasis on their safety in the new environment. The first visit to the pool and the associated hygiene requirements are dealt with in detail.

There then follows a syllabus of progressive aquatic activities, culminating in instructions on the teaching of the four basic competition strokes, together with their associated starts and turns. An analysis of faults and their corrective practices is to be found at the end of each chapter.

The basic teaching elements of diving, life-saving and survival are covered, together with practices leading to the actual performance of the activities associated with each skill. Also included is an introduction to synchronised swimming and waterpolo, in an attempt to foster these activities in schools.

Descriptions of the leisure and utilitarian strokes are provided for swimmers not interested in the competition aspects and wishing to swim merely for pleasure.

Most of the exercises are illustrated in order to assist the teacher in his or her endeavours.

The second part of the book is devoted to the anatomy and physiology of the human body with reference to the swimmer and aquatic activities.

'What we have to learn to do,
we learn by doing.'

ARISTOTLE (384–322 BC)

PART I
Swimming and Diving

1 Teaching Environment and Equipment

Numbers in the class

The ideal number for a class of swimmers is difficult to define, there being many factors to be taken into account. For beginners and non-swimmers, however, the fewer in the class the better. Numbers are sometimes dictated by the expanse of shallow water. Alternatively, should the shallow end be rather deep for beginners, the availability of artificial aids and equipment may decide how many may enter the water at one given time. As a general rule, the ideal number of non-swimmers is from six to twelve, although experience teaches us to cope quite satisfactorily with more.

If the majority of the class are swimmers of some standard or other, and suitable pool division equipment is available, the teacher should be able to manage a class of twenty to twenty-five pupils without too many problems. Classes in excess of this number may be quite successfully dealt with by suitable lesson planning and, providing that the necessary pool equipment such as dividing ropes, floats and submersibles are available, useful and productive lessons can be staged.

The frequency and regularity of lessons is also quite important. It has been found quite conclusively by experiment that, for instance, a concentrated course of, say, ten lessons over a two-week period during various national 'learn to swim campaigns' are far more productive than ten lessons which take place at one per week over a period of ten weeks.

This type of information should be utilised in lesson planning if only limited time and resources are available.

The pool

The shape, size and depth of the pool are all factors to be taken into account when planning the lessons. Beginners and non-swimmers need shallow water with room to play and experiment. For tiny beginners, the learner pool with a depth of 450–600 mm (18–24 in.) is ideal. Learners (those who are at the paddle stages) need enough depth to swim, but should also be able to stand on the bottom. Swimmers and improvers need room and sufficient water depth to dive, swim, turn and practise many other aquatic skills. The non-swimmers should therefore be allocated the very shallow water, the adept performers the deep end, with the improvers spaced safely between the two extreme groups.

Physically dividing the pool up into sections with ropes and floats (figs. 1.1 and 1.2) not only has the advantage of segregating the various

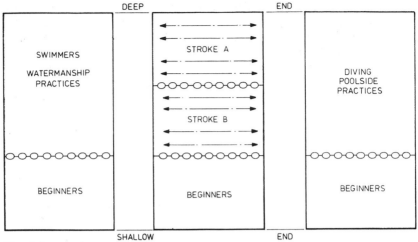

Fig. 1.1

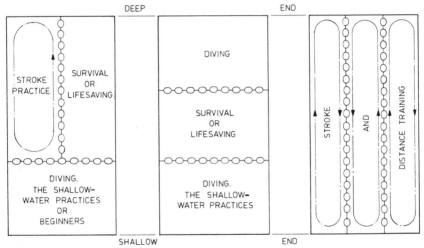

Fig. 1.2

activities, but also, in the case of the beginners and non-swimmers, denotes the safe and shallow area. Where the full length of the pool is available for class practices, the swimmers may carry out practices across the width of the pool in 'controlled waves'. Should space be limited, relay or staggered starts may be used across the width.

Relay swimming denotes swimming across or across and back the width of the pool and touching the side to send off a partner on a similar journey. Staggered swimming describes single-width practices only. With the class divided into pairs, one swimmer sets off across the pool to be followed at pre-determined distance by his or her partner. The initial distance between the two swimmers is best judged by the second member of the partnership: a push-off or dive is made as the first swimmer reaches or passes the half way point.

Where bathside diving practices are to be carried out, the necessary safety precautions regarding water depth should be observed. These are fully described in chapter 27. Should sufficient depth of water not be available, the entries should either be suitably modified or not carried out. As a safety precaution, wherever ropes are used, the teacher should ensure that they are in good condition and not liable to break. The end attachments should also be inspected before hooking them on to any existing poolside fittings. The swimmers often use dividing ropes to hang on to when they become tired or distressed; it is therefore essential that they are securely fastened and able to withstand such treatment.

TEACHING EQUIPMENT
Visual aids
A blackboard is useful for transmitting information during group sessions. Schedules of work may be tabulated and, while the teacher attends to one group, the others may continue practising according to the written instructions on the board. Charts which display various activities, such as the life-saving rescues or the survival antics are very revealing to children. Sequences of the various stroke movements may also be illustrated by charts and this should assist the teacher to explain certain activities.

Plastic models showing the sequences of movement have become a standard visual aid in the teaching of diving and synchro skills. When teaching resuscitation, dummies which react to thumping and blowing are excellent for portraying the function of the heart and lungs during an emergency situation. Demonstrating the use of floating objects during the survival practices enables the swimmers to appreciate the value of utilitarian objects, in an aquatic survival situation.

If facilities are available, feature films, film loops and slides relating to various aquatic activities are quite fascinating to young swimmers and such sessions are usually enthusiastic ones. Finally, the finest visual aid of all is probably that of actually witnessing some skill or other being demonstrated by an expert. This, accompanied by a verbal explanation of the demonstration, tends to embed itself in the minds of young swimmers. The sessions will be enhanced if the audience are able to get into the water and try out the particular movements themselves immediately after the show.

Ropes
As previously mentioned, ropes are invaluable for dividing up the teaching pool. Shorter ropes, suitably coiled and ready for use, are also

extremely useful items of safety equipment. A swimmer in difficulties may be hauled to the security of the poolside by deftly dropping the free end of a carefully coiled rope over or near one shoulder, so that he or she may grab it. Practising the art of rope throwing is a very useful water safety exercise for both pupils and teacher.

Poles

Long and short poles may be used for both safety and teaching purposes. The short pole held by the teacher while walking along the poolside and dangled in front of a swimmer attempting his first length can be most comforting. The long pole is extremely valuable in extracting a swimmer in difficulties from the central area of the pool.

Artificial aids

For many years, the swimming world has been divided about the use of artificial aids during the teaching of swimming. The argument as to whether aids are a good or bad thing will no doubt continue for many years to come.

From the earliest times of recorded history, drawings, paintings and writings have indicated that our ancestors used various forms of aids in order to assist their aquatic endeavours. There are drawings in existence of Egyptians around 3000 BC swimming with aids. There are pictures of Assyrians of 880 to 650 BC using inflated skins called *mussuks* to cross a river or lake. One wonders how long it took these ancients to learn to swim without the use of artificial buoyancy, or if they ever persevered. However, back to the present, let us examine the advantages and disadvantages of artificial aids in teaching the beginner to swim.

General advantages

1. The main advantage of the artificial aid is to allow instant water mobility and freedom. When the beginner has no need to worry about sinking, his attention may be concentrated on learning to swim.
2. The teacher is able to keep a group of learners fully occupied and experimenting with methods of propulsion and generally having fun.
3. Artificial buoyancy gives a feeling of safety and enables the fearful pupil to take part in the communal activities.
4. 'Tinies' may be safely waterborne in water which is deeper than their own height.
5. Pupils may rest or stop their movements and still remain afloat.
6. Specially designed aids, such as inflatable armbands may be slowly deflated in stages, until they merely become psychological boosters.
7. With such advantages, artificial aids may be termed 'educationally sound' types of equipment.
8. The availability of aids greatly enhances a competitive training programme.

General disadvantages
1. Equipping a large class is time-consuming.
2. Failure of an inflatable aid may cause a drowning accident.
3. Young children sometimes bite holes in inflatables.
4. Wrongly fitted and incorrectly designed, the aids can restrict movement.
5. Both children and adults tend to become too reliant on aids if not controlled.
6. Inflatables are dangerous if fitted to the legs – some children do this if left unsupervised.
7. Aids cost money to buy.

There are many types of artificial aid. Taking both the advantages and disadvantages into consideration, the teacher should endeavour to utilise them as he or she considers necessary.

Buoyancy aids now make up a valuable part of the equipment used during the teaching of swimming, but they should not be regarded as indispensable. However, it is important that buoyancy aids such as inflatable armbands and rings should not be confused with teaching aids such as polystyrene floats and kick boards: these latter items are indeed essential for the teaching progressions and part-practices.

2 Teaching Technique

It is the aim of this chapter to help the teacher develop a good and sound teaching technique.

Above all, *safety* must be the paramount factor, whatever swimming or diving activities are being performed.

Establishing a good teacher/pupil relationship
Sometimes this is rather difficult when you remember what little so-and-sos they were during the last lesson, but it is worth trying once more. You can often 'beat the system' by just rising above it. Be firm in your decisions but, on the other hand, don't be too restrictive, as this tends to incite mutinous feelings among the older pupils. Don't 'look down' on your class, 'look *at*' them. Keep a sense of humour flowing through the lesson. Remember, swimming is fun: let it be so at all times.

With the younger swimmers, the teacher must develop a rapport with the class, always encouraging, coaxing, gently chiding, kindly mocking and generally creating a light and enjoyable atmosphere, ensuring finally that they want to come back again.

Teaching positions (fig. 2.1)
It is always necessary for the class to be able to see the teacher (by rolling over in the water or by turning around), and it is always advisable for the teacher to be able to see every member of the class. When giving a demonstration, the teacher must be positioned in such a way that all the pupils are able to see his or her movements and, at the same time, they should be able to hear clearly what is being said.

The position the teacher takes on the poolside when the class is in the water is largely dependent on the size of the class. For instance, with a small class of six or seven, the teacher can stand near to them and above them, while they are in the water either standing or holding the rail. On the other hand, if the class is large enough to stretch the whole length of the pool, it is best that the teacher stands on the opposite side of the pool. The only disadvantage in taking up this position is that the swimmers must always return to the far side of the pool, away from the teacher, before the next instruction can be successfully given.

Another popular teaching position is at the end of the pool, with the pupils standing, or in the water holding the rail, along the length of the pool. A disadvantage of this position is that the pupils at the end of the pool farthest away from the teacher stand less chance of hearing the

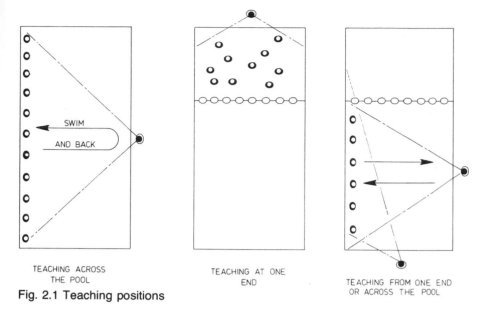

TEACHING ACROSS
THE POOL

TEACHING AT ONE
END

TEACHING FROM ONE END
OR ACROSS THE POOL

Fig. 2.1 Teaching positions

instructions. On the other hand, the teacher is able to wander across the end of the pool, back and forth, always being in the position to stop the exercise and deliver the next instruction. This position is ideal for a medium or small class and where there is an unobstructed walkway across the width of the pool.

With beginners in the shallow end, the teacher may stand to the side or at the end of the pool, taking care to stand well back from the edge, in order that the class may be addressed with a minimum of head turning or lifting.

The teacher should always stand erect when delivering instructions and never squat or kneel or lie down flat! This upright stance gives all the pupils a chance to see and hear what is about to take place. Never turn your back on the class: keep looking at them when talking to them. Also, resist the temptation to talk to the backs of their heads. Often, one sees a teacher sending a class swimming away from where he is standing at the poolside, delivering unheeded instructions to the backs of their heads. (Learners rarely take any notice of instructions while they are actually swimming: they are usually too intent on surviving or they genuinely cannot hear.)

Another bad practice is that of delivering an oration to the class while walking away from them across the end of the pool. This often happens when the teacher is anxious to get on with the exercise in hand.

It is very important for the teacher to assume the correct posture when carrying out a stroke demonstration (fig. 2.2). For instance, when the

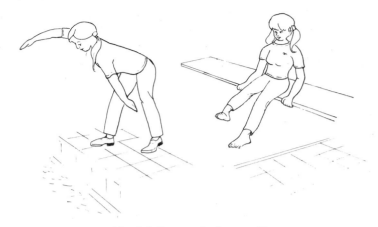

Fig. 2.2 Demonstration positions

front-crawl arm action is being demonstrated to the class by the teacher on the poolside, in order to emphasise the path of the hands as they move under the body, she should bend forward at the hips, thus placing the top half of her body in the correct swimming position. The swimmer's likely body roll may also be shown while the teacher is in this attitude. Equally, the stroke leg actions may be seen more readily when the demonstrator is seated with her legs completely free to carry out the movement.

Generally speaking, the teacher must choose a teaching position according to the size of the pool, the size of the class and the particular topic being taught. Experience will show where and how to stand and how to deliver instructions to the best advantage.

Finally, when addressing a class, talk to the whole class and not to a small group or individual, except, of course, if someone is misbehaving. Try not to show favouritism, and avoid sacrificing the whole of the class for the sake of a few. Each pupil or group of pupils must constantly be kept constructively and gainfully occupied.

Delivering the instructions
When addressing a class of swimmers, the teacher should speak slowly and clearly, using words and phrases suited to the standard of the children.

The amount of instruction given at one single time should be limited. It is absolutely useless to issue a class with a multitude of teaching points all in one breath, like: 'Put your hands in the water in front of your nose, fingers together, hands flat, then pull down in the water, underneath your body and, at the same time, bring your other arm out and over the water, elbow high and hand low,' etc. Could you take this in yourself at one go and think about each individual point during the ensuing swim? Keep each individual instruction short and simple.

It is important to avoid issuing instructions in a negative way, saying 'Do *not* do this' and 'Do *not* do that.' By giving positive instructions, you are suggesting to the pupils only one way – the *right* way.

Visual and spoken accuracy
One of my golden rules of the teaching of swimming is: 'Be visually and orally correct.' Children are the best imitators in the world and, if a particular demonstration is incorrect, so will be their performance. If you are in doubt as to the visual correctness, stand in front of a mirror and practise the motions until you are sure that you have it right. Enlist the aid of a colleague in order to check, if you are still unsure.

Probably the prime examples of incorrect movements are to be found in the front- and back-crawl arm actions. One often sees the teacher demonstrating the 'high elbow' recovery of front crawl, waving his hands high in the air, then wondering why the class are also waving their hands higher than their elbows on the recovery. Similarly, when demonstrating the recovery movement of the back crawl, best performed with the arms in a straight and vertical mode, quite a high percentage of teachers seem to carry out the action with anything but a straight arm. Needless to say, the children copy the movements beautifully.

As a teacher of swimming, become knowledgeable about swimming and all its associations, and always *sound* authoritative. At all times be in complete control of your voice in order that you may say what you mean and mean what you say.

Frequently, throw a little humour into your teachings; this helps to build up a good working relationship with the class.

Be enthusiastic and try to inject some form of competition into the lesson: children are great competitors.

Talk to the whole class as a group, look at them *all* in turn while you are talking to them. Make each individual feel as though he or she is an integral part of the class.

Use your sense of imagination in your instructing. For instance, back-crawl leg kicking may be likened to the class swimming like little boats with propellers churning merrily away at the back ends. Children are also great ones at the imagination game, as we all nostalgically recall.

Never be hesitant in encouraging any individual in the class. But in contrast, never encourage individuals who are successful in their endeavours to the detriment of those who try very hard, but just cannot make the grade. Conversely, if there is a group of keen and enthusiastic swimmers, be sure to set them a full programme of work to keep them busy and involved. Never neglect those who can for those who cannot. Remember, encouragement for trying is as important as encouragement for getting it right.

The syllabus

For every educational course of swimming instruction, there should be a planned syllabus of activities.

The programme itself may be defined by the local education authority, or alternatively it may be left to the teacher to establish a suitable plan of campaign.

The ultimate aim of any syllabus must be to promote the art of swimming and to foster all its many associated skills.

Throughout the syllabus, the water-safety feature must predominate, but, as secondary features, the demanding skills of watermanship, competition swimming, diving, life-saving, personal survival, synchro and waterpolo are all important aquatic activities which may be included. The teacher must therefore be equipped with adequate knowledge to deal with most, if not all, of these.

An outline of a basic educational swimming syllabus is illustrated in fig. 2.3. From this plan, the teacher should be able to design a programme to suit both the standard of pupils to be taught and the conditions under which instruction is to take place.

The value of games

All children love playing games. So if each little activity is treated as a game, an exercise which in the cold light of day is a chore becomes quite pleasurable. A fine example of this is a game of 'tag' or 'touch'. Walking through the water in order to catch his or her 'victim', the prospective swimmer unwittingly develops a feel for the water and how it affects movement. The 'victim' also learns to walk forward or sideways during the pursuit and, when contact has been made, both participants need to turn around in the water in order to reverse the situation and continue the fun. What a fine way to establish mobility and the feeling of balance and control. There are many other games to be played, some with apparatus such as a ball, a piece of rope or a hoop. They may be graded according to the age and ability of the swimmers and should always be supervised. A list of suitable water games is given on page 89.

What to teach first and when to teach it

Opinions vary widely as to which aquatic-based activity should be taught first. Perhaps we should first acknowledge the fact that when we plunge into water, we enter an alien environment. Therefore our first concern must be to teach people to survive in the water.

Just being able to swim a basic stroke is not really enough to make one safe in the water. For instance, consider someone who has been taught how to perform a version of breast stroke (or any other stroke) during their first lesson. Nothing else, just that!

How can they start off? A push and glide would help, but they haven't been through the rituals! How do they stop? They probably can't regain

Fig. 2.3

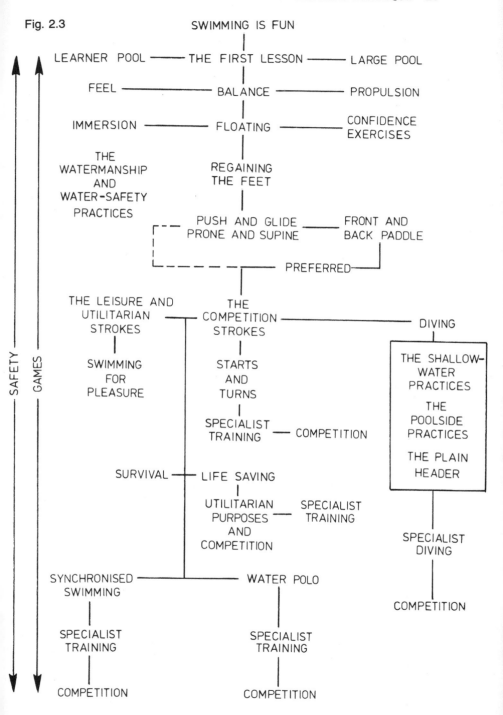

their feet. What happens if they wander accidentally or, through a false sense of security, into deep water and are then forced to stop? They probably can't tread water in order to remain stationary. If someone swam across their path or got in their way, how could they manoeuvre their way around them, if they've never been taught to swim other than in a straight line?

So perhaps there is a little more to swimming than merely being able to swim, and perhaps we should give consideration to some of the basic watermanship activities before attempting to teach the more formal styles.

This does not mean that any basic stroke teaching should be entirely neglected until all are able to push and glide or twist and turn. Indeed, if any stroke-related limb movements or combinations of movements can be practised in pursuit of some other activity, this can only enhance the teaching. For instance, our little swimmers playing shallow-end 'tag' would probably find that an alternate arm-paddling action (not unlike a front-crawl movement) assisted them in their endeavours to catch one another.

The planned lesson

Each individual lesson should have a definite objective and a carefully planned progression of activities by which this objective can be achieved. The activities must be practised in their correct sequence, for attempting to perform activities for which the swimmers are not ready may result in everyone just going round in circles and getting nowhere.

So, before taking a lesson, we must ensure that we have a definite plan in mind, and to formulate this plan the following facts must be ascertained:

1. The number of pupils in the class.
2. The ages of the pupils.
3. Whether it is a mixed group of boys and girls who may need segregating: teenage boys and girls sometimes lose concentration when they are mixed.
4. Their watermanship abilities: there may be a need for an assessment and grading session.
5. The pool requirements, availability of facilities and water temperature.
6. What equipment is available, such as robes, armbands, floats, diving blocks, submersed rings for survival practices, etc.

Now to the lesson itself. The individual practices should not be beyond the swimming abilities of the children, but, at the same time, they should become progressively more difficult so that the pupils are always slightly stretched. As previously mentioned, for new classes a grading session will probably be necessary.

As has already been stated, each individual lesson plan should form an integral part of an overall educational teaching syllabus containing a series of definite objectives. Each objective should be directed towards improving the children's watermanship and their swimming skills.

The basic lesson plan
The lesson may itself be divided into several parts, each part fulfilling a purpose. The basic constituents are outlined and, after a very brief poolside description of what is about to take place, the following format may be adopted.

1. *Introductory activity*
This brief and controlled activity is introduced mainly as a warm-up to the lesson. It allows the pupils to 'get themselves wet' and can set the tone of the ensuing lesson. The teacher may decide on a specific theme for this initial burst, or elect to give the pupils freedom of choice.

2. *Recapitulation of the previous lesson* (if it is related to the current one)
A quick recap on the main theme or objective of the preceding session will serve as a useful link between the two.

3. *Main activity* (based on the main theme or objective of the lesson)
This is the major feature of the whole programme and should be allocated the maximum amount of time. This particular feature may not be quite so evident during the initial lessons for beginners. The associated practices should be progressively phased and accompanied by the relevant teaching points. (See the various chapters on teaching the strokes.) The teacher should be aware of any faults which may occur during the practices and be able to apply the necessary corrective measures. Faults and their correction are to be found at the end of the chapters relating to the various skills.

4. *Contrasting activity*
In order to give the pupils a break from intensive learning, a short activity may be introduced into the lesson which, while being a complete contrast to the major theme of the lesson, bears some relationship (however slight) to the practices that have been performed.

5. *Supervised free time*
The lesson should end with a short free period in which the pupils can 'do their own thing'. This part of the lesson should be supervised, because, when they are released from the restrictions of the compulsory part of the lesson, children sometimes become a little wild. Strict control is necessary, therefore, in order that any dangerous activities may be curtailed. (See chapter 3.)

Times should be allocated to each part of the programme according to the importance of each activity, although circumstances may often cause the teacher to adjust the length of each period.

Teaching the skills

For the purpose of teaching, the elements of each basic swimming skill may be categorised in the following manner:

	EXAMPLE
1. *The complete skill*	Front crawl
2. *The associated activities* These are the component skills or part-practices which may be performed individually and, when combined, form the total skill.	Legs only
3. *The teaching practices* These are the various methods of practising the activity. They are usually progressive in terms of difficulty and are designed to establish the basic stroke movements or combinations of movements.	(i) With two floats (ii) With one float (iii) Unassisted
4. *The teaching points* Each teaching practice should be accompanied by a set of definite instructions as to how the various movements are to be performed.	(i) Kicking movement originates at the hip (ii) Loose ankles

By sub-dividing each skill in this fashion, the teacher should be able to plan a lesson constructively. The activities, together with their attendant teaching practices, may be used during fault analysis and correction sessions and also during periods of training.

The teaching system

When learning a new aquatic skill, pupils will benefit greatly from watching it being performed. If the main theme of the lesson is the teaching of some new skill, it is advantageous to commence the activities with a visual demonstration of that particular skill, whilst describing it verbally.

The class may then be invited to attempt the skill themselves, and the resulting performance should enable the teacher to assess precisely what kind of task he or she is faced with.

Following the initial whole-skill performance, the programme of individual part-practices should be carried out. These may be itemised as follows:

1. Leg-kicking practices   2. Arm-stroke practices

3. Breathing practices
4. Timing, rhythm and stroke
   co-ordination practices

5. Variations of the whole stroke
6. Return to part-practices for fault
   correction whenever necessary

The teaching therefore follows a whole/part/whole pattern, repetition of the various skills and part-skills being necessary throughout.

Which stroke first?

The pupils having attempted the two basic mobility strokes, namely front and back paddle, the teacher must now decide which particular style should be taught as the next major activity in the syllabus.

Probably the paramount stroke feature which dictates progress in the watermanship skills is the act of breathing. After all, if a swimmer cannot breathe adequately in proportion to the energy being used, he or she cannot possibly proceed very far without becoming very quickly exhausted.

Many traditionalists choose breast stroke as the starting stroke (even before the two basic mobility strokes) because it may be performed in a leisurely fashion with the head held high and face clear of the water. Consequently, providing conditions are favourable, a swimmer is able to breathe quite easily regardless of the overall stroke timing. Similarly, a swimmer may perform the back crawl stroke with the face clear of the water and again breathing presents no problem. Timing the breath is of no real consequence during the very early teachings.

Proceeding to front crawl, we encounter a problem. In order to perform the stroke correctly in its flat and horizontal mode, the swimmer's face must be placed into the water and some breathing discipline becomes necessary.

The butterfly stroke, with its particular breathing technique, is usually attempted after one or more of the previously mentioned skills have been accomplished.

Let us examine a few of the other factors that should be taken into account if the teacher adopts the 'easy breathing' approach. First, consider the breast-stroke leg action. What an odd combination of movements this is! To the learner, there is nothing natural about the limb tracks whatsoever. Good breast strokers are rare: it may be that good breast strokers are born rather than made and that they achieve the required symmetry of kick through natural ability. There is a school of thought which suggests that if the breast-stroke leg kick is taught as a first water movement, the swimmer stands much less chance of developing the 'dreaded screw kick'. This is very difficult to prove or disprove.

If we condemn the leg actions of front and back crawl as being detrimental to a good breast-stroke kicking movement, we must also take into account the fact that the natural walking action itself is very similar to the alternating and vertical movements of the crawls. This being so, most swimmers will have articulated their joints in this *natural walking* fashion, many times before they even enter the swimming pool. Consequently, if the movement were *really* detrimental, the number of good breast strokers would be much less than at present. Considering these arguments, perhaps breast stroke is not after all such a good 'starter' as it has been made out to be.

The back crawl also has its problems as a starting stroke, despite the 'natural' leg kick and face-up attributes which are considered to be advantageous. The vertically biased arm-recovery action tends to sink the less adept swimmer, and a large majority of learners feel insecure lying on their backs in the water. The teacher therefore must also have reservations about back crawl being the first stroke.

We have now systematically ruled out teaching every formal style as a starter! So where do we go from here?

There remains what might be described as a 'democratic alternative'. This is to allow the swimmers to try out three, or even four, different strokes successively and to let them make their own particular choice regarding which style (or styles) suits them best. The amount of instruction during such an exercise may be quite minimal. This popular method of teaching is known as 'multi-stroke' and is generally considered to be highly successful. Of course, it does not in any way absolve the teacher from teaching the related stroke progressions, but it does provide opportunities to divide the classes (and the pool) into sections, whereby differing styles may be simultaneously practised. As stated above, basic watermanship exercises up to and including the front and back paddles will already have been attempted, and these two skills readily adapt themselves to the front and back crawl strokes respectively.

It should be stressed, however, that the four competition strokes, i.e. the front and back crawls, butterfly and breast strokes, should not be regarded as the ultimate in stroke teaching. There are other styles that should be included in the syllabus, such as the various forms of back and side strokes (chapters 23 and 24). These movements may be practised in connection with life-saving and survival, or performed simply for pleasure.

Swimming is one of the most pleasurable and beneficial activities that exists and it is for this reason that the ancillary strokes should form an integral part of the overall programme.

Analysing the strokes
It is rare for a skill to be performed reasonably correctly by the whole class during their first attempt. Aquatic techniques are very exacting and demand considerable practice and concentration. It is an essential part of teaching therefore to be able to identify stroke faults, analyse their

causes, and apply the necessary remedies. Technique can be analysed according to the following guidelines:

First impressions

Does the stroke look right? Is the movement disjointed and unco-ordinated? The swimmer may seem to be working extremely hard and getting precisely nowhere. The effect may be picturesquely described as 'having no feel' for the water.

On the other hand, there are the gifted ones who make it all look so very simple and, apparently without effort, glide through the water with ease and grace. These performers seem to be in complete harmony with the water, caressing rather than fighting it. But, should the former situa-tion prevail, as is more than likely, we must learn to examine each of the various stroke features in order to discover precisely what is wrong.

Body position

The swimmer should lie as flat and horizontal in the water as the stroke technique will permit. His position should be observed first from the side, and then from the front, from behind and also from above. Only then do you gain a total appreciation of the swimmer's basic body position. Of course, a swimmer may vary his body position slightly during the stroke cycle in accordance with the style being swum. (The undulating effect in the butterfly movement is a good example.) His faults may be related to a characteristic of the stroke.

Leg action

Each stroke displays a different pattern of leg movement. The observer must decide whether the particular action is propelling, stabilising or elevating. Or does the leg movement contribute a proportion of each characteristic towards the overall effect? Are the various contributions sufficient?

If the stroke is of the simultaneous and symmetrical variety, is the movement being performed correctly and within the requirements of the stroke law?

If there is a definite recovery and propulsive phase, is the recovery movement being carried out with a minimum effect on propulsion? Remember that the recovery movements of both arms and legs contri-bute nothing towards propelling the swimmer forwards.

Any incorrect movement may affect the swimmer's basic body position in the water.

Arm action

In most swimming strokes, the arm movements provide the major con-tribution towards propulsion. Each complete arm cycle may be divided into two basic phases, recovery and propulsion. Recovery must be performed economically in terms of energy dissipation and with a minimum effect on propulsion. As soon as a limb has finished its propulsive phase, its profile should be minimised. Alternatively, it may be removed from the water so as not to create unnecessary resistance. If the recovery is over the water, the inertia effect of the swinging arms should not disturb the swimmer's natural body alignment causing him to zig-zag.

Are the arms being lifted completely clear of the water during their forward movements?

Are the hands entering the water in the correct position or are they too wide or too near to the face? Is there a 'cross-over' taking place?

Is the swimmer over-reaching and contributing in this way towards distorting the body alignment? As the result of an excessively fast, over-the-surface recovery, does each hand crash into the water setting up unnecessary turbulence? This is not conducive to propulsion.

Is the propulsive phase being carried out efficiently? Are the swimmer's fingers together or almost together? Are the hands flat or cupped? Is the propulsive pressure being directed backwards or is there too much sideways tendency? Is the propulsive phase too short or do the hands tend to 'feather'? It must be remembered that for the best results in stroke efficiency, the thrust which is generated by the arm movement must be projected directly backwards for as long as possible during the propulsive phase.

Breathing
Breathing out into the water is not a natural function, but is sometimes necessary. Lifting the head to breathe when it should be turned, or vice versa, can cause streamlining problems to the swimmer. (It usually results in sinking of the legs.) If there are obvious breathing difficulties, the method, type and rate of respiration should be investigated.

Is the swimmer using the best method of respiration for the stroke being performed? Sometimes it is best to exhale simultaneously through both mouth and nose into the water *explosively*. Sometimes a slower ejection is required, perhaps through the nose only, in a *trickle* fashion. Beginners sometimes find it easier to breathe out through their mouths, but there may be a problem of water entering the nostrils. A good point to remember here is that, if air is flowing down the nose, water cannot be flowing up it!

Is the type of breathing appropriate? There are many kinds of stroke-related breathing:

unilateral   –   breathing to one side only
bilateral   –   breathing on alternate sides
regular   –   a constant respiratory rhythm
irregular   –   unevenly spaced intakes of breath
frequent   –   once every one or two stroke cycles

infrequent   –   the breath is held for periods
variations   –   breathing either early or late
in timing   in the stroke cycle

Each individual type or combination has its own particular merits. For instance, a swimmer who is fresh and swimming front crawl with a rapid cycling rate does not necessarily need to take a breath at every stroke. At the start of the swim, the type of breathing that would most probably be used would be infrequent and explosive. He may breathe to one side only on the first lap in a unilateral fashion. On the second lap, he may wish to view the opposition in adjacent lanes, so he breathes bilaterally in order to have a quick glance to both sides. Towards the end of the swim, he is requiring more oxygen to cope with the sustained effort and therefore requires to breathe more often. The pattern then becomes more frequent and regular, but he is still probably using the explosive method.

During a training swim, breathing will probably be regular and in trickle fashion.

Breath-holding, owing to a fear of breathing out into the water, should not be confused with any of the above types. It is very common amongst beginners and can easily be identified by severe breathlessness, the occasional blue face and popping eyes!

Co-ordination
In every swimming style, the arm, leg and breathing movements should be in complete harmony with each other. The swimmer's stability, balance and propulsion in the water depend on the co-ordination and synchronisation of the arm and leg movements.

Similarly, if air is taken in at the wrong time, the timing and rhythm of the stroke may well be affected, giving it a jerky and less aesthetic appearance.

These are the basic stroke features and each should be examined carefully when forming an opinion of an individual's performance. It is worth remembering also that we are all built differently, both physically and mentally. Therefore, something which occurs when a particular swimmer carries out a certain action may not necessarily happen when someone else performs an identical movement. Be prepared to judge each stroke performance on its own individual merits in order to make the final analysis.

Stroke correction
At the end of each chapter relating to specific strokes, competition and otherwise, will be found a comprehensive section on faults and analysis relating to that particular style.

Individual stroke faults can often be difficult and sometimes even impossible to correct. A case in point is the 'dreaded screw kick' among aspiring breast-stroke swimmers. Patience, perseverance and concentration on the part of both swimmer and teacher, are needed to overcome this problem. More often than not, if the screw has developed, it stays for good. A swimmer who swims or trains regularly, can repeat a recently developed stroke fault many thousand times in a very short period so that it becomes deeply integrated into the overall movement and hence extremely difficult to correct. This problem shows the importance of correct initial teaching, together with the ability to recognise quickly the many and various stroke faults and understand their causes.

One tried and tested method of remedying faults is 'over-correction'. For example, a swimmer doing front crawl and entering his hand into the water too near to his face is instructed *incorrectly* to over-reach. He then attempts to stretch his arm further forward at the end of each recovery movement. He feels he is over-reaching but in reality he is probably entering his hand somewhere near the correct point.

Many other faults, such as excessive rolling, head lifting and recovery defects, may be corrected in the same way.

Fault correction is important and requires an extensive knowledge of the behaviour of the human body in the water. The teacher should attempt to gain experience in this field whenever possible.

Grouping the class
Unless they have been specially pre-selected, a class of swimmers will usually exhibit a fairly wide range of aquatic capabilities. The teacher may choose to sub-divide the class into manageable groups to do ability-related tasks in order that each swimmer's interest and enthusiasm can be maintained. Boredom during a lesson usually leads to distraction and disorder. The number of groups will depend on the range of ability and the number of pupils in the class.

There are various methods of employing the group system. For instance, at the commencement of a lesson, it may be advantageous to teach the class as a whole before resorting to group teaching. Alternatively, if the class has been working in groups it may sometimes be desirable to bring them together in order to point out and correct some common underlying fault.

Group teaching may also be employed at particular stages during the planned lesson. For instance, during the 'contrasting activity' period, several variations on the life-saving or survival themes may be practised simultaneously in group form.

Should unqualified but knowledgeable help be available during the swimming lesson, such assistance may be quite usefully employed in group work. The assistant should, with the help of some verbal and/or written instruction, be able to manage a group of swimmers and keep them occupied during the lesson. The teacher, of course, should always be in complete control of such an arrangement and frequent visits to such organised groups around the pool should be made during the lesson. It must be realised that an unqualified assistant will often be unprepared for an emergency situation calling for rescue or resuscitation.

Group work has many advantages, a few of which are summarised as follows:

1. A class of varying abilities may be taught more effectively.
2. With good planning the whole class may be kept fully occupied and interested for the entire lesson.
3. Progress of the more capable swimmers is not inhibited by the less skilful performers.
4. Special and personal attention may be directed when and where it is most needed.
5. No individual need be neglected.
6. By relating individual capabilities to the depth of the pool, a certain degree of safety may be ensured.
7. Many differing aquatic skills may be practised during one single period.
8. When suitable poolside assistance is available, it may be utilised effectively.
9. Upgrading (and downgrading) may be carried out by simply transferring swimmers from group to group, and, of course, changes of practice may also take place by the transfer method.
10. Smaller groups of swimmers present fewer problems to the teacher where instruction is concerned.

Partner assistance (fig. 2.4)
It is sometimes helpful and always enjoyable for children if they share their water work with a friend or partner. In the shallow end of the pool one partner supports the head, shoulders or feet of the other. It is often a useful activity where both physical and moral support are necessary initially to establish some kind of swimming movement.

The carrier can learn from watching the performer, but the main disadvantage of the system is that when one member of a partnership is working, the other is resting and hence effective lesson time is halved. There is also the problem of the resting partner getting cold.

The teacher must, from personal experience, assess the value of partner assistance by taking into account class standards and current environmental conditions. However, if partner work is to be introduced into a lesson, it is advisable to restrict it to short periods in order to avoid inactivity and boredom.

The grading session
Children are quick learners and, especially if they attend the swimming pool in their own time as a recreational activity, their watermanship abilities will soon manifest themselves.

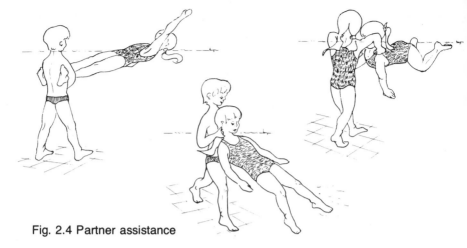

Fig. 2.4 Partner assistance

In order to assess their progress, the teacher should arrange frequent grading sessions related to the skills that have been taught. Systematic records should be kept of the results that are achieved by individual swimmers at each session. Good organisation is essential during these assessment sessions and it is useful if some form of poolside assistance is available.

1. *Watermanship skills*
With the pool divided up into suitable areas, the class may be split into groups, and each group allocated an area in which to carry out some pre-determined watermanship activity. The teacher or assistant may then assess and record the standard of each performance. A list of suggested watermanship skills follows.

(i) The push and glide on both front and back on the surface and submerged, then with variations such as to the bottom and up, standing on hands or somersaulting from the push.
(ii) Treading water, with and without clothes, and also with arms or legs immobilised.
(iii) Directional movement ability, i.e. forwards/backwards/sideways.
(iv) The surface dives, head first/feet first.
(v) Recovery of a submerged object.
(vi) Swimming through or under submerged objects.
(vii) Floating in various ways, i.e. on the back, the front and a mushroom float.
(viii) Sculling – support and propulsive, head-first and feet-first.
(ix) Stroke transition, i.e. from front to back crawl then rolling over on to breast stroke, smooth and elegant transition being the aim.
(x) Somersaults on the surface and submerged.

An appropriate watermanship, survival or distance award may be taken at this stage.

2. Competition skills

These are related to the strokes, their starts and turns. For the starts and turns, the teacher will find it advantageous to work across the width of the pool, so that several skills may be assessed during a short swim. The swimming skills may be assessed under two headings: style and efficiency. Body position, leg movement, arm action, rhythm, timing and turning all come under the scrutiny of the assessor of style, who must be knowledgeable. Time/distance or distance/time systems of measurement are used to assess efficiency.

The time/distance test simply involves timing the swimmers with a stop-watch over a set distance, the distance to be swum varying according to the ability of the pupils. Any of the four competition strokes may be used, and the time taken to swim the stipulated distance will reveal the efficiency of an individual's stroke.

The distance/time assessment, while also testing stroke efficiency, is at the same time a test of fitness and endurance, for the swimmer has to cover as much distance as possible in a given time.

Once more, the teacher will stipulate the stroke or strokes to be performed and also the manner in which they are to be carried out, i.e. one stroke or two different strokes, each for a set time, and whether the swimmers are to be clothed or unclothed. (A whistle may be sounded at times of stroke change.) Division of the pool may be made according to the number of group variations. The swimmers may use the 'elongated circuit', moving down one side of a lane and returning the other side. Figure 2.5 illustrates two configurations; overtaking may take place on the straight portions only.

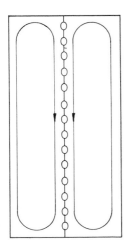
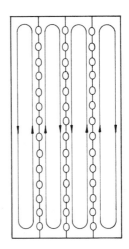

Fig. 2.5 Pool division for time/distance and distance/time swimming

3. *Life-saving and survival skills*

The skills in this category, some of which may have been assessed during the watermanship tests, are as follows:

LIFE-SAVING SKILLS

1. Back stroke (life-saving style)
2. Side stroke
3. The two styles of surface dives
4. Towing in the three approved methods
5. Support at the rail
6. Assisted exits from the water
7. In-the-water and bathside resuscitation
8. Questions on water safety in general

SURVIVAL SKILLS

1. The two styles of surface dives
2. Treading water (with various limbs immobilised)
3. Swimming while clothed
4. Removing clothing while treading water
5. Using clothing to assist floatation both on and off the body

This, then, is an outline of the grading session content. It must be understood by the teacher that the emphasis during such a session will be on assessment rather than instruction. These sessions should take place at least once a term, and it is essential for records relating to each swimmer's ability at each grading to be conscientiously maintained.

3 Safety in the Pool

Of all the amenities available to the general public, the swimming pool is perhaps the most dangerous if it is not used correctly and sensibly.

The swimming teacher must at all times be aware of the dangers associated with the pool and be able to cope with the situations that can arise within its confines. Safety of the pupils is of paramount importance and information relating to their safety must be instilled in them for their own protection.

Communicating this essential knowledge to the swimmers, together with the simple elements of pool hygiene, may be carried out in several ways:

1. By carefully prepared handouts outlining and illustrating the 'dos and don'ts' of swimming-pool behaviour, which may be distributed at the schools.
2. By a visit of the swimming teacher to each school, where a short and possibly illustrated talk may be given to future pupils.
3. By a talk given during the first visit to the pool.

The third method is probably the easiest and most practical, because the pupils are actually able to see the hazards and risks.

The following section outlines the main pool-safety features. The majority of these items are common to most pools and pool users.

Environmental safety

A thorough knowledge of the layout of the building, its shape, dimensions and surroundings is essential. You should know how to locate anything or anyone with the minimum of delay. A check on the emergency exits and fire-fighting equipment is a very useful exercise. One rarely hears of a swimming pool burning to the ground, but small fires do often occur.

Knowing the state of the walkways surrounding the pool when both wet and dry provides the teacher with an awareness of how quickly he or she is able to move around the pool.

It is useful to know the number of pool attendants on duty at any one time during a teaching period, and also their life-saving capabilities. Their assistance in an emergency may be invaluable. With this in mind, it is a good idea to maintain friendly relations with members of the pool staff: their co-operation will always be useful.

37

The whereabouts of *all* the pool safety equipment and first-aid kits, and how to use them, must be known. If there is any manual resuscitation equipment available, a short instruction on its use may help to save a life, as might a short course on first aid. Be fully conversant with all up-to-date aspects of life-saving, life-preservation and resuscitation.

Emergency warning sirens or other such devices are fitted as standard equipment in most pools, and their whereabouts, effectiveness and use should be known. Ropes, poles, life-belts and other such life-saving equipment should be in abundance around the poolside. The teacher should memorise the location of each piece of equipment, so that it can be used quickly and effectively should the need arise.

The telephone is also regarded as an emergency item and its availability, in case of emergency, should be assured at all times. The teacher must know the procedure for contacting the emergency services.

The ability of the teacher to make him or herself heard at least across the width of the pool when it is full of children is important. He or she must know the acoustic characteristics of the pool area, with varying numbers of swimmers present.

If the teacher feels that some vital piece of equipment is missing or not serviceable, notification of the matter to the pool staff must be immediate and effective.

Finally, all accidents should be recorded in an accident book.

The following points relate to the safety and behaviour of the classes that visit the swimming pool.

Shallow end/deep end

Remember that at least some of the class have probably never seen the inside of a swimming pool before and such an awesome stretch of water can be frightening to a child. So, to tell them which is the deep end and which is the shallow end of the pool is a good start. It may be written on notices, but not everyone can read, and it is also a good idea to tell the class precisely what, *in relation to their own height*, deep and shallow means. For their safety, and your own peace of mind, they should not attempt to venture beyond your designated boundary until you have given them permission.

Moving around the pool

When the area surrounding the pool gets wet it can become very slippery and accidents can happen extremely easily. Some pool floors are treated or tiled with non-slip materials, but they can still be dangerous if people run on them. Movement around the pool must therefore be undertaken at walking pace at all times.

Entering and leaving the water

It is necessary to ensure that no swimmer enters the water before you, the teacher, are completely ready and able to devote your full attention to them throughout the entire lesson.

When the class is ready, make a quick count, then, at the end of the lesson, count them once more. If there is someone missing, don't panic, but look on the bottom of the pool first! This may sound rather frivolous, but is quite practical, especially with young tots. It can be alarming to find that the class is suddenly one short. Therefore, make sure that anyone who wishes to leave the water to go to the toilet has your permission to do so. Similarly, get them into the habit of letting you know when they return to the pool. Make sure that any late-comers to the class report to you before joining in the activities. A youngster could slip into the water unnoticed, and then, by some terrible turn of fate, be left lying on the bottom of the pool as you count out of the water the same number as when the lesson began.

The whistle

The whistle is an essential part of the swimming teacher's equipment but it should not be over-used. The pupils must understand that whenever the whistle is blown, they must immediately 'stand down' or swim to the side, if they are in the water, or stop moving around on the poolside, be quiet and look at the teacher. With everyone's full attention focused in his or her direction, the teacher can issue the necessary instructions. Whistling by members of the class must be discouraged, in order to avoid confusion.

Noise level

Swimming pools are notorious for being noisy. A certain noise level is unavoidable and can be tolerated without too much discomfort, but excessive din caused by unnecessary screaming and shouting should be discouraged. From the safety aspect, a genuine shout or scream for help can easily be lost in a very noisy atmosphere and there are accidents on record which have proved to be attributable to this factor. Allowing the members of the class to work in pairs or small groups is one way of overcoming the effects and dangers associated with a high noise level.

Crying 'Wolf'

Pretending to be drowning just for fun is extremely silly and can some-times have unforeseen and tragic results. A weak swimmer or someone who may be in bad health might automatically try to rescue a drowning person by jumping in the water after them. The would-be rescuer is quite incapable of performing a rescue operation and in certain circumstances could himself quite easily drown. Pupils should be told in no uncertain terms that to pretend to be in trouble could end up by someone actually drowning, and *it would be their fault!*

Jewellery

Bodily contact in the swimming pool is far more likely to occur than on dry land. Sharp objects worn on hands, arms or legs may therefore touch another swimmer's body, resulting in accident and injury. The wearing of such items of finery should therefore be banned in the pool.

Spectacles in the water
A swimmer should be allowed to wear spectacles in the water if he or she feels safer in doing so and if the pool staff have no objection. However, they should be securely held in position by an elastic tie. An occasional glance to make sure that the bespectacled members of the class are coping without mishap is recommended.

Long nails
As people swim around the pool with their heads in the water and their eyes usually shut, collisions are inevitable, and more often than not it is one swimmer's hands in contact with another's face or body. Long nails can cut the skin, which in most cases is not too painful, but a scratched eyeball is another matter entirely. Anyone who has played waterpolo will confirm that long nails can hurt, sometimes seriously, so insist that the members of the class, especially adolescent girls, attend the lessons with trimmed nails, so that this type of accident may be avoided.

Fighting
No one on this earth will ever stop boys fighting, but the swimming pool is really not the place, especially during your lesson. Of course, the same rule applies to girls who may become too boisterous. Also, make sure that any warfare is not continued in the dressing-rooms or cubicles.

Eating in the pool
Chewing sweets and gum while in the water is often done, but in the interests of safety and hygiene it should be discouraged. Make a quick check and be sure that all eatables are duly disposed of before the class enters the pool.

A sweet or lump of chewed gum is easily washed to the back of the throat with an unwanted mouthful of water; if it gets stuck there we have 'panic stations' until, with a sharp slap on the shoulders, it should come free.

If the offending substance is not dislodged in this way the child should be put over one knee and slapped again on the back.

If this still does not do the trick the following method may be tried. Encircle the casualty from behind with both arms, making a 'balled up fist' with one hand and grasping the wrist of the 'fisted' hand with the other. Both thumbs should be innermost and in contact with the casualty's soft area below the rib cage and above the navel. Now, by applying a quick lifting hug, the sweet should be dislodged. If the first hug is not successful try again. The compression must be suddenly applied for it to be successful and, whenever such treatment has been given, the casualty should consult a doctor immediately after. This precaution is necessary due to the fact that the offending object may have disintegrated and some tiny particles have found their way into the air tubes of the lungs. This 'hug of life' was invented by Dr Henry Heimlich and there is evidence that one can successfully apply the method to oneself.

Eating before a swim

It is a good idea to tell your class regularly that they should not eat a meal, or anything approaching a meal, for at least an hour and a half before they swim. Heavy exertion just after eating can induce stomach cramp or bring on an attack of sickness.

Goggles

Goggles are very useful if your pupils' eyes become affected by the chemical content in the water. They can be dangerous, however, if they are badly designed and easily damaged. The best ones are those which extend above and below the bony ridge which can be felt around each eye.

If goggles need to be worn, make sure that they fit properly and make a good water-seal, otherwise it will be found that a large proportion of the lesson is taken up by the pupils having to stop and drain the water from them.

Removing the goggles to drain the water out is often the cause of accidents. Children pull them away from their eyes and let them slip from their fingers to snap back on to their face. Usually no damage is done, but there have been many cases of eyes injured in this way.

The situation may be aggravated by a faulty seal. The soft band often detaches itself, thus exposing the sharp edge of the transparent plastic from which the eyepieces are manufactured. When this crashes back into the eye, owing to the force created by the stretched elastic strap, severe damage to the eye is caused. The danger may be reduced by *rolling* the eyepieces back on to the forehead rather than *lifting* them away.

Goggles should be positively discouraged during diving from anywhere higher than the poolside or starting blocks. The force of the water easily dislodges them and renders them useless.

Polystyrene floats

Pupils must be taught to use properly all types of apparatus. Floats are excellent swimming aids, but when they are thrown 'edge on' across the pool they become very dangerous missiles. Another favourite pastime is for the children to bite chunks out of the floats, damaging the apparatus and sending particles of polystyrene floating off to be swallowed by some unfortunate swimmer. Placing the floats inside the swimming costume can upset a swimmer's buoyancy, apart from doing nothing whatsoever for her (or his) figure! Jumping on to the floats from a height is also a favourite trick usually resulting in a broken float. Diving in with the floats held in the hands is a rather dangerous procedure, the sudden upward thrust of the water on the floats during entry tending to wrench the arms and wrists. So insist upon using the floats for swimming purposes only, although sitting on them and playing gentle games does no harm whatsoever. In fact in most cases it enhances a child's watermanship capabilities.

Armbands
Placing armbands around the legs is a dangerous activity. The buoyancy characteristics of the swimmer are drastically changed, the effect being to raise the legs to the surface and make it difficult to raise the head, if the swimmer is in the prone position. Even in the supine position, the increase in leg buoyancy makes standing down almost an impossible task for the weaker swimmer. Young swimmers often bite holes in the inflatables and, apart from rendering the equipment useless, pieces of the material may be swallowed. So, once again, instruct your pupils in the correct use of this particular piece of apparatus and make sure that it registers.

Ducking and pushing in
Holding a person under the water, even for a short time, can be frightening for the poor unfortunate soul concerned. For a person who is wary of the water or someone who has claustrophobic tendencies, being forcefully submerged can set off a chain of unthought-of events which can lead to injury, sometimes serious.

Pushing in is a universal pastime around the swimming pool. In most cases, if carried out gently and without malice, it goes unnoticed by all but the unfortunate victim. But if there happens to be someone swimming past, minding their own business, having a body suddenly land on their back can put them off swimming for life. The person who has been pushed in can of course also end up in hospital.

Finally, how often have we heard of or seen non-swimmers being hurled into the water: this is downright lunacy. So, warn your pupils not to push other people in the water at any time: the consequences are always unknown and can sometimes be quite serious.

Balancing tricks on the poolside
A favourite trick among youngsters is that of walking tight-rope fashion along the handrail around the pool. This is fine sport until someone gets his foot caught behind the rail. Children also like to play on the steps leading down into the water. If these are of the fabricated type (usually aluminium or stainless steel) there is a gap between the steps and the wall just wide enough for a child's foot to get trapped. So both these games should be discouraged.

The diving area

Divers must make sure that the water area below is clear before launching themselves into space. This also applies of course to the more simple dives which take place from the bathside.

Dangerous tricks performed on the diving-boards, such as double dives, leap frog and leaping from board to board are to be discouraged.

Diving from the balcony (if there is one) is known to be a fine sport, but even so it is extremely dangerous.

It is essential that divers are able to swim reasonably well before they attempt their high springboard antics. One often sees a body enter the water quite respectably, then just about make it to the poolside once more with a last gasp.

Entering the water from a height, and near to a swimmer below is a dicey business – for both people concerned. 'Bombing' – leaping off the stage in a tucked attitude to make an enormous splash on impact with the water – also creates havoc. The risks involved here place the 'game' high on the danger stakes. Trick dives, carried out by novices without adequate and expert supervision, often result in injury. Pushing another swimmer in from any height is dangerous as is any form of play in this area, including the trick of heading a ball or catching a float thrown from the side while in mid-flight.

So, during a lesson, the diving area must either be placed out of bounds or provided with adequate supervision.

Discipline during the lesson

Gentle persuasion, minimal use of the whistle, together with the cultivation of a glare designed to freeze the most blatant offender, are perhaps the basic discipline techniques. However, serious and persistent offenders should be ordered from the pool. Suspension from the pool should be kept as an ultimate deterrent, tucked up your sleeve. To a great extent, discipline is a game of bluff and the teacher must learn from experience.

Roping off the shallow end

When you have a class of young beginners or learner swimmers they tend to drift off into 'distant' waters, especially if they are wearing armbands, or are supported by rings or other buoyancy gadgets. A rope, suitably anchored, slung across the shallow end of the pool, will prevent them wandering into the deep end. Similarly, any danger areas should be roped off and placed out of bounds.

Foreign objects in the water

The teacher must be very observant when children enter the water to spot if any harmful toys or gadgets are being smuggled in with them. Metal objects can obviously cause harm if walked on with bare feet. Glass objects can break and spread splinters over the pool floor. Plastic objects are also quite dangerous when they break or shatter into pieces. Most plastic toys are denser than water and consequently sink to the bottom, so can be harmful if stepped upon.

Balls and such like can be a good source of fun outside the main lesson, but their use should be strictly controlled. Small rubber balls can be quite hurtful if thrown at people across the pool. Older and bigger swimmers must be kept away from the beginners when a ball appears on the scene, as they tend to become very boisterous.

Inflatables such as small boats, air beds, etc., are usually banned from swimming pools.

It is best for the teacher to be sure that all the charges have been through 'customs' before they enter the water, just to be on the safe side.

Private pools
It is most important that entrance to a private or school swimming pool is controlled at all times. Whenever it is not in use, the pool should be locked and placed 'out of bounds'.

Supervisory assistance
School classes attending the swimming pool should always be accompanied by a responsible adult, preferably a member of the teaching staff. Wherever possible, this person should be responsible for the supervision of children when they enter the building and also while they use the changing-rooms or cubicles. Mixed classes sometimes pose a problem if such assistance is limited and separate rooms are used, but some form of help is usually available from the pool staff.

It is useful if the attending supervisor is able to notify the swimming teacher if there are any new pupils in the class. It is then possible to ascertain the newcomer's watermanship abilities before allocating him a suitable place in the line-up. Apart from taking an active part in the lesson, the person in charge of the class should be encouraged to wander around the poolside in order to keep an eye on things in general.

Leaving the class unattended
When a class of swimmers is in the water, never leave them unattended. If you have to leave the poolside, always leave some competent person in charge. A senior member of the class will serve this purpose for a short while. In the event of no one being available, the pupils should leave the water and sit away from the poolside for a few moments. Remember, *never* leave your class in the water completely unattended, even for a short while. If in doubt at all, get them out and make them dress while you are away.

Be seen and heard
When teaching a class of swimmers always stand in a position where you

can easily be seen and heard by everyone. Never turn your back on the class when they are under your supervision. During the lesson, get into the habit of regularly glancing around, so that you know what is happening all over the pool area. (See teaching positions, p. 18.)

Life-saving and resuscitation ability
A swimming teacher must be able to swim to, collect and tow a drowning person back to safety, land him without injury, then administer efficiently and quickly any life-saving techniques which may be necessary. He must also be able to administer resuscitation while in the water.

The unseen dangers
A teacher cannot be expected to be aware of the physical condition of all the pupils that are taken throughout the week. It is wise, however, to find out if anyone suffers from such things as heart complaints, respiratory diseases or epilepsy. These ailments should not automatically preclude their sufferers from swimming. Indeed, swimming is known to be of value to some people with respiratory disorders, and the gentle movements and water support that accompany the exercise are recommended by doctors as 'body menders' in many other cases. However, to obtain written permission from a doctor for a child to swim, if there is any doubt in your mind regarding his health, would seem to be a prudent move. Such members of the class must not be treated as outcasts, but at the same time a careful watch must be kept on them during the lesson. A protective friend taken into the teacher's confidence, with instructions to notify the teacher of any sudden attack or sickness, can be of great assistance on such occasions.

If during a lesson it is noticed that a pupil is getting unduly breathless, looking pale and showing signs of distress, he or she must be taken from the water and carefully and calmly dried and dressed; it is essential that he be kept warm during this period. Further action should then be taken by the attending school teacher, if it is considered to be necessary. If the swimming teacher is at all uncertain about how to treat the child on subsequent occasions, his headmaster should be contacted and the incident duly reported.

These are the major safety aspects of which a teacher should be aware. In addition, there may be special considerations, such as slippery steps and surfaces, designed to catch the unwary, or overhead structures which must not be used for playing Tarzan-like games. There may also be special rules which have been drawn up by the pool management for the safety and welfare of the swimmers.

There is too much information regarding safety and hygiene for the class to absorb at once. Let them have it in manageable quantities. For instance, a class of very young school children visiting the pool for the first time needs to be told not to run and which is the deep and the shallow end of the pool. They are not really interested in the fact that leaping from the balcony of the pool is taboo, or that they should not deliberately drown each other! If you give them too many instructions all at once they may forget why they came to the pool in the first place.

Summary
Below are suggestions as to what should be said to the children on safety, and when.

During early visits to the pool, instructions to beginners should be given in relation to the following:

The location of the deep and shallow ends
To walk and not run around the poolside and to keep away from the water's edge
Entering and leaving the water
The whistle
Chewing sweets

After a short while, apparatus such as armbands and floats may be used. The correct handling of these items of equipment should be made clear to the children, prior to their use.

On subsequent visits to the pool, reminders of the early safety rules should be given if considered necessary. The class should be warned about the following:

Crying 'Wolf'
Wearing jewellery
Wearing long nails
Fighting
Eating before a swim – this becomes more important as the activities become more vigorous
Ducking and pushing in
The diving area (*Note*: Water depth in relation to diving is covered in the chapter on diving)

You may find it necessary to make restrictions in addition to those mentioned above. If you do, make sure that they are genuine and do not arise merely because you are being fussy or bad-tempered.

4 Swimming-Pool Hygiene

Let there be no doubt about this particular topic, pool hygiene is extremely important but very difficult to control. For instance, you can tell the class to use the toilet before they enter the water, but you cannot guarantee that they do so. Again, you can tell them to come with clean swimsuits but you won't have time to check that they do. These are just two of the factors which affect the general standard of hygiene in the pool.

The teacher should carefully set standards which he or she wishes to be maintained during each class visit to the pool, and continue to insist that they are strictly adhered to until the proper procedure becomes automatic. Assistance may be needed during this initial training period, and discipline may have to be stricter than usual. But the end will justify the means.

Let us now examine the various aspects of hygiene in the swimming pool.

Walking around the pool area
Some pool authorities very sensibly prohibit the use of outdoor footwear on the pool surrounds. Shoes pick up a lot of filth in the street, and transferring this to an area where people are walking around with bare feet, then entering a pool where swimmers frequently take in great mouthfuls of water, is unpleasant and unhygienic. So try to keep your class away from the poolside while they are wearing their outdoor shoes.

Clothing
Most modern-day pools have somewhere for the swimmers to store their clothes while they are in the water, ranging from clothes-hanging frames to individual lockers. Sometimes, however, a group of people may be obliged to use a communal room and it is here that the children must be trained to fold their clothes tidily and keep all their possessions together. Such pastimes as hurling underwear and socks at each other must be firmly put down – great fun, but thoroughly unhygienic. Changing-room supervision by a school teacher or guardian is desirable in most instances.

The toilets
Swimmers, both young and old, are sometimes too lazy to leave the water to go to the toilet. You should therefore make it a strict rule that before anyone enters the water they must use the toilet. It is obviously essential that toilet paper is available. The class must understand that the proper toilet facilities must be used at all times.

Blowing the nose
Before leaving the changing-rooms the class must be encouraged to adopt
the habit of having a 'good blow'. This will reduce the unpleasant necessity to do so in the water!

The footbaths and showers
Few people are absolutely clean when they enter the pool establishment.
The normal secretion of sweat glands during the walk to the pool is
enough to make the body unclean.

   Children coming to the pool at the latter end of the day are particularly
likely to have dirty hands and faces. Therefore, the need for both the
showers and footbaths to be used is obvious. It helps, of course, if these
pool facilities are supplied with warm water rather than cold, so that the
cleaning operation can be carried out in comfort.

Sweets and chewing-gum
The matter of eating while in the water has been covered in the previous
chapter, but it is worth repeating that chewing while swimming is a
dangerous habit. Leaving used chewing-gum around the pool is most
unsanitary and, if it gets stuck to people's clothing, it is a great nuisance.

Plasters and bandages
The fact that a child is wearing a plaster or a bandage on some part of his
or her body must always be a cause for investigation. Generally speaking,
a bandage is worn to protect something which is too large to be covered by
a plaster. A bandage becomes useless in the water, so unless inspection
reveals there is next to nothing to hide, bandage wearers should be gently
but firmly told 'No swimming this week.'

   Plasters should always be carefully removed and the underlying
wound, abrasion or skin sore inspected. If it has healed or is of minor
consequence, there is no problem. Often, however, there is an open
wound under the plaster and here the teacher must make a decision
whether to allow the pupil to swim or not. If the wound is small and clean,
re-covering it with a waterproof plaster would seem to be in order before
allowing the child into the water. But if there is a boil or suppurating
wound, a new covering should be applied and the child told not to swim
while the infection is in this open state.

   A supply of plasters is a necessity if such inspections are to be carried
out correctly. If the teacher has no access to replacement plasters, it is
best not to remove any which the children may be wearing. Just tell them
kindly, 'Sorry, no swimming this week.'

   If a child has permission from the doctor to exercise gently a mending
limb after a sprain or fracture, any covering bandage should be carefully
removed and stored, then replaced after the swim. Special care should be
taken of this child during his water activities.

Foot inspections
Foot inspections should be an integral part of the early class swimming lessons. After a while it may be hoped that pupils will become conscientious enough to admit to having an infectious condition of the foot (or anywhere else for that matter). Young swimmers must be trained to be responsible for their own personal hygiene, because they will not always be visiting the pool in an organised class. Mandatory foot inspections should quickly cease therefore, and the pupils put on trust.

The existence of a contagious ailment in the pool environment can almost always be traced to someone's feet. So identification of foot infection is of prime importance. There are two main types of foot ailment, the foot wart, or verruca, and athlete's foot; both are contagious.

VERRUCA is another name for a simple wart. Verrucae can occur on any part of the skin and differ in appearance according to their type. The type in which we are most interested is also the one which gives most trouble, namely verruca pedis ('pedis' meaning 'of the foot').

Foot warts are considered to be the result of a virus infection of the skin. They seem to be acquired mainly where communal bare-foot activities take place, such as the swimming pool, communal showers, school gymnasiums, etc. A verruca will usually appear as a tiny black dot on the sole of the foot. If treated early enough it will be no bigger, but if left untreated, it tends to increase in size and becomes quite painful. As it gets bigger, a verruca takes on a brownish, rough and crumbly appearance, or it may be covered by a layer of hard skin. The infected person should seek the advice of a doctor as soon as possible.

The swimming teacher is advised to learn to recognise a verruca at any of its various stages of development. The Society of Chiropodists recommends that verruca sufferers should not use a swimming pool, or communal shower, or indeed any amenity where the contagion may be transmitted to other people. However, some authorities allow sufferers into the swimming pool if the verruca is covered with a plaster and the foot covered with a special sock. Anti-verruca socks are now available in plastic waterproof material, and these are very useful in checking the spread of foot infections.

ATHLETE'S FOOT This disease of the skin is very prevalent in this country and is not, as the name suggests, confined to those who participate in athletics. It probably acquired this name because, as the disease is contagious (i.e. spread by contact or conveyed by clothing, towels, socks, etc.), its incidence was found to be greater in places where sportsmen changed their clothes in communal places such as dressing-rooms and pavilions. Where athlete's foot is suspected, inspection should reveal that the skin between the toes appears white and sodden, and when it is dry it easily scales. Location of the disease is sometimes made easy for the teacher by the fact that the infected area can become very irritating and itchy. Athlete's-foot sufferers often give the game away therefore by having a good scratch between their toes. Until the trouble is completely cleared up, swimming-pool visits should be postponed.

Medical treatment and advice regarding the use of clothing and towels which have come into contact with the infected area should be sought as soon as the condition is discovered.

Skin rashes

The teacher is advised to make a quick inspection of the class for any other infectious ailments. Skin rashes and spots are always suspect, the spots especially if they appear in any great number.

Sores on a child's face could be impetigo, another contagious disease which may be easily spread by the inadvertent use of the infected person's towel. In cases of impetigo, swimming should be discouraged.

Psoriasis is a sometimes embarrassing skin condition which appears as red patches and white scales, usually on the knee caps and the backs of the elbows. It is not a contagious disease and sufferers should be allowed to swim if they so desire.

Experience will help the teacher to recognise most of the various skin complaints and to know what action should be taken in each case. But if in doubt, keep the sufferer out of the water until a medical opinion has been given. It is worth remembering also that some rashes are brought about merely by the excitement of the occasion. These 'nerve blotches' usually appear about the face and neck and disappear once the excitement has faded. (Swimming can, of course, be the cause of this excitement.)

Respiratory troubles

For the sake of everyone's health, a person suffering from a bout of bronchitis should not be allowed to swim. His tendency to cough and spit into the water is anything but hygienic. To a large number of young sufferers, bronchitis is seasonal, but the condition may be accelerated by a cold or cough. Therefore the importance of ensuring that young swimmers are thoroughly dry after a swim must be underlined.

Asthma sufferers can be affected by the excitement of the occasion, and may be seen fighting for breath; they should not be allowed to get in the water while this short-of-breath condition prevails. It should be remembered, however, that the bout could have been brought on merely by excitement and, by the next swimming lesson, all will be well.

Coughs and colds

People suffering from coughs and colds do not usually feel like swimming, but, if they should want to have a splash about, for the sake of their own health and community hygiene they should be discouraged from doing so.

Drying after a swim

Children are very negligent when it comes to drying themselves. They must be encouraged to dry thoroughly especially under the arms, between the legs and between the toes. Ears should receive special attention too (see chapter 36). Going out into a cold atmosphere with wet hair is probably the easiest way of catching a chill, so children must be told to give their heads a 'jolly good rub' before leaving the pool.

Costumes should be rinsed in tap water if possible and wrung out at the pool, although those pupils who wring them out in the swimming pool itself will face the wrath of the pool attendants. Swimming costumes should be hung on an outside line to dry! Drying them indoors tends to make the costumes smell rather musty after a while.

Menstruation

Menstruation begins when girls reach the age of puberty, usually between the ages of ten and fourteen, although there may be exceptions. It occurs approximately every twenty-eight days and lasts between three and five days, during which the heaviest discharge occurs in the first two days. Menstruation is a perfectly normal physiological process and every encouragement should be given to the girls to carry on with their usual swimming activities during their period if they feel like doing so. It is most unlikely to do them any harm. Some girls do, however, prefer to stay out of the water on the first day, and they should be allowed to do so. Any feeling of embarrassment or anxiety should be treated with understanding by the teacher.

Bathing caps

Bathing caps should preferably be worn over long hair. There is a growing tendency in swimming pools today for caps to be worn by both male and female swimmers, and the availability of the lightweight rubber caps with national flags and emblems printed on them makes the teacher's task of enforcing the appropriate rule a little easier. However, caps are an additional expense and this should always be considered before any hard and fast rules are made.

5 Hydrostatics

Hydrostatics is the study of buoyancy and floatation. Buoyancy is the ability of float: if a swimmer possesses good or positive buoyancy characteristics, he or she will float well in the water. Conversely, if a swimmer tends to sink readily below the surface, he is said to possess poor or negative buoyancy characteristics.

An object will float in a fluid only if its density is less than the density of the fluid. The fluid which we are concerned with is, of course, water, and in order to examine the meaning of this statement, we must define weight, mass and density.

Weight

Every material thing, including our own bodies, possesses the characteristic of weight. The air that we breathe may be weighed – it is very light, of course, but for any given volume, air definitely possesses weight (.001 kg/m^3 at 52°F and at sea level). Weight is related to the gravitational pulling force towards the centre of the earth (gravity) and the more *substance* that there is to an object, the greater is the gravitational pull and hence the greater the *weight*.

Mass

Mass is the quantity of substance or matter that is packed into an object. Therefore, a highly concentrated mass of substance will weigh more than a loosely concentrated mass contained in the same volume.

Density

It is the relationship of mass to volume of an object that defines its density and also dictates its particular buoyancy characteristics in the fluid in which it is required to float. The density of an object is thus its weight divided by its volume:

$$\text{density} = \frac{\text{weight}}{\text{volume}}$$

It may be measured in metric units, e.g.

$$\frac{\text{kilograms}}{\text{cubic metres}} \quad \left(\frac{\text{kg}}{\text{m}^3}\right) \quad \text{or} \quad \frac{\text{grams}}{\text{cubic centimetres}} \quad \left(\frac{\text{g}}{\text{cc}}\right)$$

or in imperial units, e.g.

$$\frac{\text{pounds}}{\text{cubic feet}} \quad \left(\frac{\text{lb}}{\text{ft}^3}\right) \quad \text{or} \quad \frac{\text{pounds}}{\text{cubic inches}} \quad \left(\frac{\text{lb}}{\text{in}^3}\right)$$

The density of fresh water in actual units is 1000 kg/m^3 or 62.4 lb/ft^3. If an object has a density of less than this, it will float: if its density is greater than that of water, the object will sink. There are certain materials which sink when placed in water, like steel and lead (see the table on page 55), and there are floatables like wood and expanded polystyrene which are in common use in the pool as teaching and training aids.

Sea water is denser than fresh water (1026 kg/m^3 or 64 lb/ft^3) and therefore gives more buoyancy.

Specific gravity
It will now be seen that by comparing the density of a material with that of water, its buoyancy is quite easily established. It is also the relationship of a particular material density to the density of water that establishes its specific gravity (or relative density). The specific gravity of a substance is equal (providing the units of weight are compatible) to:

$$\frac{\text{weight of a given volume of the substance}}{\text{weight of an equal volume of water}} \quad \text{or} \quad \frac{\text{substance density}}{\text{density of water}}$$

The specific gravity of water is 1.0 and if the specific gravity of an object or substance is greater than 1.0 it will sink, if less than 1.0 it will float. The effective specific gravity of the human body is generally in the region of 0.98. Consequently, if we ask our swimmers to assume a tuck or mushroom position in the water, they will probably exhibit buoyancy characteristics similar to that illustrated in fig. 5.1. The word 'effective' is used because the human body contains substances (bone and muscle) whose individual specific gravities are more than 1.0. However, the weight of the displaced volume of water is more than sufficient to support the floater. A surface ship displays similar buoyancy characteristics.

Water pressure
Water pressure increases with the depth of submersion. Pressure is defined as the force exerted by a fluid on the surface with which it is in direct contact. Intensity of pressure at any point is the force exerted on a net area. (Intensity of pressure is usually denoted simply as pressure.)

A submarine below the water surface is subjected to a greater intensity of pressure (pressure) than a submarine on the surface. This applies equally to our swimmers, and the effects of pressure can sometimes be harmful.

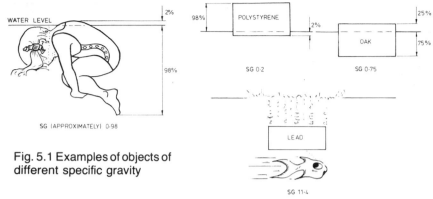

Fig. 5.1 Examples of objects of
different specific gravity

The buoyancy business

Archimedes (287–212 BC), a Greek mathematician, is reputed to be the discoverer of the fundamentals of floatation. It is said that, reclining in his bath one day, he started thinking about buoyancy and why, when he lay back, the water took his weight and he floated. Suddenly, the answer came to him. '*Eureka!*' ('I have found it!'), he cried and leaped from the bath to gallop down the road stark naked. His legendary reasoning is outlined as follows: when he entered the water he noticed that it rose up the sides of the bath; he then realised that this increase in depth was due to the bulk, or mass of his body, displacing a certain quantity of water; he reasoned that this quantity or volume of displaced water was equal to the portion of his body that was actually submerged below the surface; as he sank lower into the bath, the water moved further up the sides until suddenly he floated and the water stopped rising. He was almost completely submerged – only his head was clear.

TABLE OF SPECIFIC GRAVITIES AND DENSITIES

		DENSITY	
FLOATABLES	SG	lb/ft³	kg/m³
Fresh water at 25°C	1.00	62.4	1000
Sea water at 15°C	1.025	64	1026
WOODS			
Ash	0.70	44	705
Balsa	0.16	10	160
Boxwood	0.93	58	947
Oak	0.75	47	750
Teak	0.91	57	914
HUMAN			
Body whole (male)	0.982	61	978
Body whole (female)	0.971	60	962
Fat	0.938	59	946
MISCELLANEOUS			
Cork	0.21	13	208
Expanded polystyrene (training floats)	0.02	1.25	0.32
Fat (animal)	0.92	57	914
Rubber	0.92	57	914
Ice	0.875	55	875
SINKABLES			
WOODS			
Ebony	1.19	74	1186
Lignum vitae	1.25	78	1251
HUMAN			
Muscle	1.052	66	1058
Bone	1.80	112	1801
MISCELLANEOUS			
Gold	19.32	1206	19335
Lead	11.37	709	11375
Steel	7.83	489	7840

As he lay floating in this 'water mould', he deduced that the mass of water he had displaced had originally been supported by the water that now surrounded and supported *him*. This, then, was the vital clue. The original, and now displaced, Archimedes-shaped water mass must have been exactly the same weight as Archimedes himself, simply because the surrounding water had, in turn, supported both 'quantities' in complete equilibrium. The weight of the volume of displaced water was equal to the weight of the body floating in it. This is the theory behind buoyancy and floatation.

Actually, this astute Greek gentleman had found a method of checking the density of a crown, which the king, Hiero, had ordered to be made of pure gold: he was able to confirm the king's suspicions regarding the craftsman who had designed and made it.

Centre of gravity (CG) and centre of buoyancy (CB)

The centre of gravity of an object is the point at which, if the object were suspended, it would be perfectly balanced in all directions. Considering three different types of object, let us see precisely what this means.

Fig. 5.2 shows a line (which in theory has no thickness) on which there is a measured or geometrically constructed centre point. This point is the centre of gravity of the line, and if the line were of material form and could be picked up, this would be the point of balance.

The illustrations in fig. 5.3 show a series of objects of uniform thickness. By drawing a succession of geometrically related lines, the centre of gravity may be determined *on that particular surface only*. In other words, if the objects were made of cardboard of uniform thickness and we pinned any one of them (with freedom to rotate easily) through their relative CG positions, to a backing board, they would balance in any rotational position if spun around and allowed to stop. However, the objects do possess thickness and this dimension in each case displays its own CG characteristics. Collectively, we now have a three-dimensional or total CG and, in order to balance the objects freely, not pinned to the board, we must take into account the positions of both centres of gravity in the horizontal plane. Therefore, to balance the objects completely, we must suspend them directly above *both* centres of gravity (fig. 5.4). Although the point of suspension is outside the objects, a line drawn directly downwards passes right through the true centres of gravity. Also, the position of the CG in the vertical plane does not matter in this particular instance.

If we shift the point of suspension in certain directions, each object will swing to another balance position. However, if a vertical line is drawn from the new position of equilibrium, it will still pass through the true CG of the complete object.

It is only when an object becomes irregular in shape and its composition more complicated (like the human body) that the centre of gravity

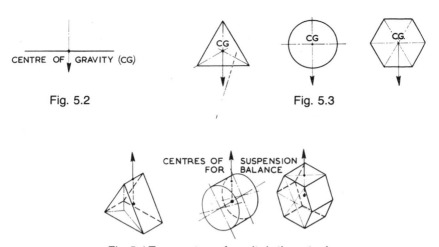

CENTRE OF GRAVITY (CG)

CG

CG

CG.

Fig. 5.2

Fig. 5.3

CENTRES OF SUSPENSION
FOR BALANCE

Fig. 5.4 True centres of gravity in the actual
centres of objects

becomes difficult to pin-point. It can be located by systematic mathematical computations or by experiment. If the profile of an object is symmetrical about a central plane in one direction and irregular in the others, the problem becomes slightly less complicated. The *stationary* floating human body may be compared with this. But if there are movable elements like arms and legs, the problem is of a complicated and variable nature.

How important is the position of the centre of gravity of the human body in swimming? The answer is: very important. We must remember that the swimmer is moving relatively unrestricted in a fluid which allows him to move backwards, forwards and sideways and also to twist and turn. Each change of movement will probably be accompanied by a change in the attitude of his body and limbs, and, when these movements of arms and legs take place, his equilibrium or stability in the water also changes, owing to the consequent *re-positioning* of his *centre of gravity*. Earlier in the chapter, we discussed buoyancy and how its effects serve to keep certain objects, like the human body, afloat. Remembering that a swimmer displaces a volume of water and that this displaced mass was originally the same shape as the submerged part of the swimmer, this swimmer-shaped volume of displaced water also has a centre of gravity. But, as the effect of water is to support the swimmer, the buoyancy forces are directed *upwards* unlike the gravitational forces that act *downwards*. Bearing these facts in mind therefore, as we have termed the downward-acting centre the centre of gravity (CG) we shall term the upward-acting centre the centre of buoyancy (CB). As the CB is related to the homogeneous mass of displaced water, its position will not necessarily be in the same location as the non-homogeneous human body.

When a body is floating in complete equilibrium or state of balance, the CG and the CB lie one above the other, the CG acting downwards and the CB acting to support the body. In ships, the centre of gravity lies above the centre of buoyancy, which is why a ship is only able to cope with a limited amount of roll before it becomes unstable and capsizes.

The human body, however, may float with its CG above or below the CB, while always maintaining a state of equilibrium. If a limb or limbs are moved in such a way, however, that stability characteristics are changed, the swimmer will roll or rotate in the water until a new state of equilibrium is attained or some corrective measure taken. Moving his body and limbs in certain ways can affect a swimmer's attitude in the water when he is merely floating and also when he is actually moving through the water. Let us consider some simple water experiments which demonstrate some aspects of variation of weight distribution and floating attitudes.

The centres of gravity and buoyancy of the human body
There are differences between the male and female anatomical and physical structure which contribute towards positioning the relative centres of gravity in different regions of the body (fig. 5.5). For instance, female bones are generally smaller and more slender than those of the male. The male chest tends to be deeper and his shoulders wider than those of the female. The female tends to be proportionately wider around the hips. A man's legs and feet are usually larger and heavier than those of a woman.

These various features form a pattern whereby the male centre of gravity tends to be proportionately slightly higher up the body, than that of the female. For a male of average build, approximately 68 kg (150 lb), the centre of gravity of his body would be just forward of the second sacral vertebra. For a woman of similar height, the centre of gravity would be approximately 25 mm (1 in.) lower.

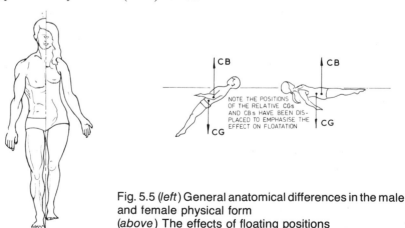

Fig. 5.5 (*left*) General anatomical differences in the male and female physical form
(*above*) The effects of floating positions

It is probable, however, that the respective centres of buoyancy tend to influence human buoyancy characteristics more than the centres of gravity. The *generally* larger chest and wider shoulders of the man, combined with his narrower hips, tend to create more displacement higher up his body. Hence, the CB will be higher than in the woman with her smaller chest and rounded hips. The female swimmer with her low CB tends to float naturally in a horizontal position. The male swimmer, however, with his heavier legs and less lower-body displacement tends to float more vertically. The teacher should recognise these natural physical features and make necessary allowances when asking swimmers to perform antics which require them to float.

Equilibrium and lateral stability
There are three possible conditions of equilibrium.

1. *Stable equilibrium* (fig. 5.6)
Where a small displacement from the equilibrium position produces a righting or correcting moment which restores the body to its original state. Most swimmers floating in a *horizontal* position display these characteristics; the CB lies below the CG and creates a righting moment for a slight body roll.

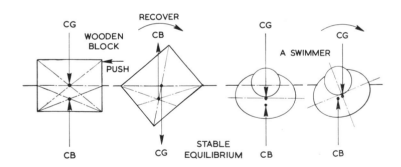

Fig. 5.6 After being displaced, the upward-acting CB tends to rotate the body back to the balanced condition

2. *Unstable equilibrium* (fig. 5.7)
Where a small displacement causes an overturning moment which tends to displace the body even further from its stable position. Very buoyant swimmers often display this toppling effect by turning over onto their backs during a front glide and vice versa. The denser sea water tends to magnify this effect by lifting the swimmer and the associated CG higher above the surface.

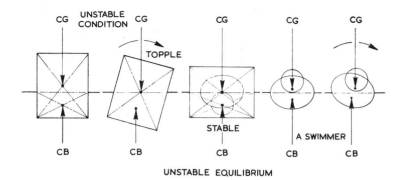

UNSTABLE EQUILIBRIUM

Fig. 5.7 After being displaced, the downward-acting CB continues to topple the tilted body until a new equilibrium position is established

3. *Neutral equilibrium* (fig. 5.8)

Where the body remains at rest in any position after being rotated or tilted. A waterpolo ball exhibits these particular features in all planes of movement, while a cylinder will balance in any position if rotated laterally.

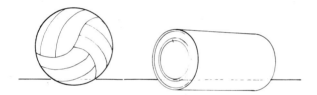

Fig. 5.8 Neutral equilibrium

Equilibrium and longitudinal stability

Fig. 5.9 shows a swimmer floating in a semi-horizontal and completely balanced attitude. The centres of gravity and buoyancy lie one directly below the other. Now, by gently moving his hands beyond his head, the centre of gravity moves towards his head. The centre of buoyancy moves in the same direction but, owing to the overall greater density of the arms than the displaced water, the shift of CB is not so pronounced as the CG. (Arms are heavily boned and muscled and consequently heavier than a corresponding volume of water.)

With CG and CB in new positions, the swimmer rotates (in a clockwise direction) in order that they both return to their original relative positions, one lying directly below the other. This re-establishes the balanced but now horizontal surface-floating position. By moving the arms back to their original position, the semi-horizontal float may be re-assumed.

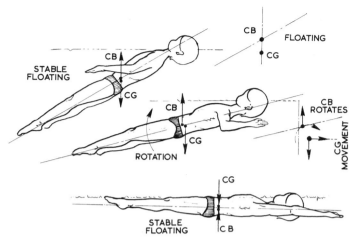

Fig. 5.9 An illustration of the rotation of a floating swimmer by arm movement

Fig. 5.10 shows a swimmer floating motionless in a *controlled* vertical position. Here, the attitude of the head, being heavy unsupported by the water, assists in manoeuvring the swimmer's body into various positions and controlling the vertical floating mode. By tilting the head forward, its CG moves forward, unbalancing the swimmer in such a way that her whole body swings slowly backwards and up towards the surface. Now, by tilting the head backwards, the swing may be arrested and re-directed so that the swimmer's body moves in the opposite direction. By tilting the head slowly back and forward in this way, a pendulum action may be developed. The swimmer's CB lies below her CG and this is basically an unstable situation, but the vertical position may be controlled by adjusting the head as described.

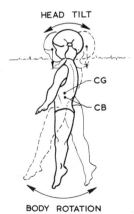

Fig. 5.10 Body movement caused by head movement

A deep breath should be taken and held for as long as possible, in order to enhance the swimmer's buoyancy characteristics while carrying out this exercise. The buoyancy effect of such an inhalation can be demonstrated in the following way. The swimmer, floating in a controlled upright mode, first of all breathes normally; a water-level measurement is taken relating to his head. Then he takes a deep breath and holds it; the swimmer should rise out of the water by a small but definite amount, perhaps 40 mm (1½ in.) (fig. 5.11). The increase in buoyancy is brought about by an increase in chest capacity without a noticeable increase in body weight.

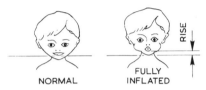

NORMAL   FULLY
                INFLATED

RISE

Fig. 5.11

In other words, by breathing in and expanding the chest, more water is displaced, and consequently the upward supporting forces are increased. This increased buoyancy, however, is not accompanied by an increase in body weight, so the swimmer floats higher in the water.

Demonstration of the effects of limb movement on floatation in the moving swimmer is rather complex. This is due to the fact that other features, such as *force reactions* to movement and *inertia forces*, need to be considered. However, the surface-diving section in chapter 25 shows how, by lifting the limbs from the water, it becomes easier for the *apparently* heavier swimmer to submerge. In the chapters on the strokes, the action/reaction principles are often mentioned. These indicate just how a performer's swimming mode may be affected by various limb movements.

6 Hydrodynamics

This is the study of moving (dynamic) bodies through the water or fluids in motion.

Propulsion
The dictionary definition of propulsion states that it is a 'driving or pushing forward'. In swimming this propulsion is necessary in order to overcome the natural resistive nature of the water (drag). If a swimmer wishes to move forward, backward or sideways, or merely to keep himself afloat, he must, by some means or other, develop a driving or supporting force in order to achieve this aim. He does this by articulating one or both sets of limbs in such a way as to create the necessary propelling or float-maintaining forces.

How then are these propulsive water forces created? Sir Isaac Newton (1642–1727), the eminent English mathematician, astronomer and philosopher, defined three laws of motion. Each of these laws may in some way be associated with the mechanics of swimming and explain how the various aquatic skills and manoeuvres are feasible.

First law of motion
A body continues in its state of rest, or of motion, in a straight line with constant velocity, except in so far as it is compelled by external forces to change that state. This means that a swimmer may float still in the water, or swim at a regular speed, until he does something to change that particular condition. For example, the floater may use his arms to create a rolling-over force and the swimmer may either increase or decrease his stroking rate (propulsive forces) in order to speed up or slow himself down.

Second law of motion
The rate of change of momentum of a body is proportional to the unbalanced force exerted on it and takes place in the direction of the straight line in which the force acts. (Momentum is the product of mass × velocity.) Simplifying this slightly, when our swimmer *accelerates* forward he does so by increasing the driving forces (stroke rate) which were originally created by his arms and legs to propel him at *steady* speed. The law states that the swimmer's rate of change of forward momentum is proportional to this required increase in developed backward thrust. The increase in power is necessary to overcome an accompanying increase in the resistive water forces (drag).

63

Third law of motion
To every force, or action, there is an equal and opposite force, or reaction. This means that, if our swimmer pulls or pushes on the water with his arms or legs, he will move or tend to move (react) in the *opposite* direction to the pulling or pushing action. It is this third law of motion which readily identifies itself with propulsion and also with the associated limb recoveries. In fact this law is involved in the mechanics of any aquatic manoeuvre or contortion.

The methods of propulsion
There are three basic forms of propulsion which affect swimming, namely, paddling, sculling and finning or flippering. A swimmer often uses combinations of these propelling actions, such as a hand-sculling action which is integrated with an arm pull or push movement.

Paddle movements (fig. 6.1)
A paddle-like action may be created by the pulling or pushing actions of the hands and arms (mainly), in a direction opposite to the required body movement (reaction), i.e. if the swimmer wishes to go forward, he should pull, push or paddle *directly backward* for as long as possible while his arms are in the water. Any sideways-, downward- or upward-directed forces will tend to reduce forward speed. (A canoeist uses a similar paddling action in order to propel and manoeuvre his canoe.)

Fig. 6.1

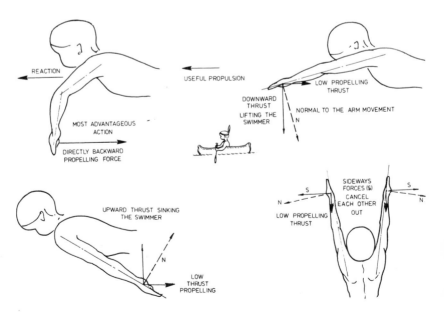

Sculling movements (described and illustrated in chapter 28)
These are limb movements which propel 'indirectly' by motion approximately at right angles to the direction of required travel. The action may be created by the hands, for instance, during back paddle and synchronised swimming, or by the feet as they close together during the whipping action of the breast stroke. The reaction is for the swimmer to move in an opposite direction to that in which certain elements of the thrust force are created. The backward movements of the hands are often combined with a sculling movement to produce a most effective form of propulsion. This is very evident in the butterfly stroke. In fact, a propulsive arm-pattern technique which combines the directly-backward movement of the arms with a rapid hand scull would be extremely useful where speed swimming is concerned.

Finning or flipper-like movements (fig. 6.2)
These types of wave-like motion are used by fish to propel themselves through the water, sometimes at phenomenal speeds. The best human-swimming examples are the leg actions of front crawl (up and down beats), back crawl (up beats only) and, of course, the dolphin butterfly, in which the complete undulating leg motion resembles and derives its name from the dolphin's mode of propulsion. A similar undulating form of movement may also be seen in the very effective and speed-creating use of sub-aqua flippers.

Fig. 6.2

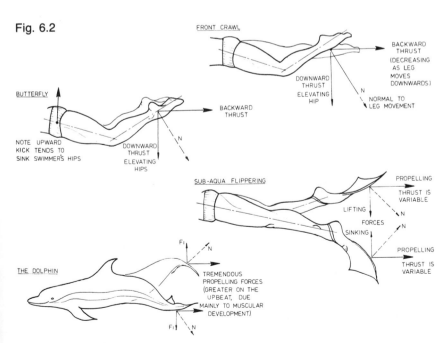

We have thus established that the reactive force acts in direct opposition to the acting or generating force and is exactly equal in its magnitude. Therefore it must be to a swimmer's advantage, in order that he may be driven forward, to direct his propelling forces immediately backward.

If we examine this statement a little more closely we can see how a stroke technique may develop and improve by knowledge of some simple mechanics. Figure 6.3 shows a swimmer's arm swinging in an arc about his shoulder joint (not necessarily the *correct* technique). The arm is moving down through the water with pressure already built up on the 'driving surface'. The resulting forces pushing against the water are directed perpendicularly to the long axis of his arm.

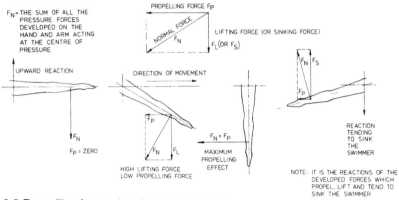

Fig. 6.3 Propelling forces developed by arm movement

Now, returning to basic mechanics, it is a fact that a single force may be resolved into two components acting at right angles to each other as illustrated. If we relate this theory to the swimmer's arm we can see that the total force generated by the angular movement may be resolved into average horizontal and vertical components, the vertical force tending to *lift* the swimmer and the horizontal force tending to push him *forward*.

Following on through the complete cycle, we can see that when the arm is in the plane of the shoulder there is no lifting force and the horizontal force is at its greatest to push the swimmer forward. At the end of the cycle the horizontal force has disappeared and the downward-directed force is tending to sink the swimmer.

From this analysis of an arm movement it can be seen that, for the maximum propulsive thrust to be maintained, the most effective part of the arm, i.e. the hand and lower arm, must be directed backwards for as long as possible during the underwater part of the cycle. In any stroke technique we can see that if an arm action is to realise its full effectiveness the following points must be remembered:

1. The hand and lower arm (the paddle area) must be directed mainly backwards as soon as the hand enters the water or commences its pull.
2. The length of this underwater action must be as long as possible within the confines of stroke technique and timing and also in accordance with the physical capabilities of the swimmer.
3. Any water forces which are developed in the vertical plane do not contribute towards forward propulsion.
4. Any sideways-directed forces do not contribute towards forward speed.
5. A decrease in arm (or leg) rate of movement will subsequently result in a reduction in swimming speed. Conversely, an increase in stroke rate should cause the swimmer to accelerate.

An important factor in swimming-stroke technique is the physiological law that the energy usage of a muscle or set of muscles approximately cubes (multiplies itself three times) with the speed of contraction. This means that if the arm is pulled a certain distance through the water in, say, one second and it uses ten energy units, if the time of the pull is then decreased to half a second, the energy dissipation in the muscles is a thousand energy units. Economy of movement must therefore be considered.

We have now established the *basic* mechanics of movement in the water and also that there are several methods of directing the arms and legs in order to create propulsion.

The physical characteristics of a swimmer and the effects on propulsion
On dry land, a swimmer's legs can exert far greater force than his arms, because in the average human being they are larger in size and physically stronger. In the water, however, they become less effective than the arms. This is due to their lack of flexibility and the relative smallness of the feet. The effectiveness of larger and more flexible feet can be demonstrated by comparing swimming speeds with and without the use of flippers.

Generally, male swimmers are stronger in the legs than females, and have larger feet, both of which factors tend to make their leg-propulsion movements more effective.

Ankle-joint flexibility is also important in swimming. For instance, in the crawl styles, for the best results, the feet should become flipper-like extensions of the legs. The ankles should therefore be capable of articulating freely and being plantar-flexed. In contrast to this, the breast stroker requires the ability to dorsi-flex his ankles or rotate his feet towards his shins during the propulsive stage of the leg movement. Then, during the ensuing glide, he should be able to plantar-stretch his ankles in order to create the streamline effect which enhances speed. Any deviation from this particular pattern of movement will be evident in the effectiveness of the leg action.

A swimmer's shoulders and arms should also be flexible and, as with the leg characteristics, constant repetition and training will improve this particular feature. The extent of possible shoulder-joint articulation is far greater than that of the hip joint, and it is mainly this characteristic, which enables the swimmer to develop more propulsion from his arms than from his legs.

The propulsive effects of large hands are similar to those of large feet and, providing the swimmer possesses or can develop the necessary muscular strength, they become a distinct advantage where speed is concerned.

Resistance to propulsion (drag)

As already discussed, a swimmer, or vessel, travelling through water meets resistance. Because of its 'dragging back' effect, this phenomenon is known as 'drag' and, as we shall see, it manifests itself in several ways. The size and shape of the swimmer or the vessel has a direct bearing on drag and its various forms.

As a general observation, the fastest human aquatic performers usually have broad shoulders, and deep chests that converge to narrow hips and legs. The leading parts of the swimmer, namely the head and shoulders, are rounded and the body tapers, giving an overall impression of stream-lining and low resistance.

A conventional fast-moving surface vessel on the other hand has its bows designed in such a way that they form a sharp wedge-like shape to slice through the water surface. This knife-form, combined with a parallel-sided hull and rounded stern, is ideal for surface travel and minimises the amount of energy that is dissipated in the formation of waves. Conversely, the modern submarine is designed with a rounded or bulbous nose since the motion of such a vessel through the water is a displacing rather than a cutting one. (The most effective shape of an underwater vessel is generally accepted to be that of an elongated tear-drop.) On some modern surface vessels, the leading underwater part of the hull also displays a rounded or bulbous profile, while at water level the bows are sharp in order to provide a cutting action. These combined features are found to improve bow-wave formation and enhance the general performance.

Relating these hydrodynamic facts back to our swimmer, it may be argued that, as the leading parts of his body are of a rounded character, he is best equipped for submersive rather than surface travel. However, results of experiments in this field are conflicting and will probably continue to be so with so many variables to consider. For instance, the leading shape of the swimmer is constantly changing as the arms reach forward in the water then pull backward. With the arm(s) stretched forward, the leading profile is tapered, but if the shoulder is exposed, the leading profile is a rounded one. These configurations display differing hydrodynamic characteristics.

Regarding high swimming positions it must be remembered that to elevate oneself in the water requires energy and this energy may well be better utilised in propelling oneself forward.

As previously mentioned, the drag phenomenon manifests itself in several ways and the various forms in which it affects swimmers are now described.

Profile drag
When a swimmer is observed from directly ahead he is seen to possess a submerged profile or silhouette which represents the area of body actually below the surface. As he moves forward he moves the mass of water directly in front of his projected area along with him. In other words, he transmits momentum to it.

Mathematically, an equation may be derived that states that this particular component of drag is equal to

water density $\times$ projected area $\times$ swimming speed^2 $\times$ a constant

or

$$D = KpAV^2$$

This is the Newtonian or so-called V-squared law of fluid resistance. It means that the drag forces increase as the square of the speed. Thus, if the swimmer doubles his speed, the water resistance is increased four times, and if he trebles his speed, the drag forces increase by nine times. Hence he has to work nine times harder to go three times as fast. Fig. 6.4 indicates, by the shaded area, the approximate profile drag area of an approaching swimmer rolling towards his pulling arm. The lower part of the propelling right arm is unshaded, because it is moving away from the direction in which the swimmer is travelling and faster than the rate at which he is swimming. Water resistance is therefore set up on a part of the trailing surface of the arm and the palm of the hand and it is the reaction of this resistive force which assists in propelling the swimmer forward.

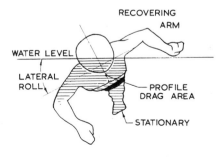

Fig. 6.4

With the rolling-stroke technique, part of the swimmer's head and the whole of his left arm is above the water level and therefore do not in any way affect profile drag. It has been shown that up to certain speeds (in the region of 1.6 m per second – say, a sixty-second 100-m swim), the overall drag is lower when the swimmer is rolled in this fashion, and in the front crawl stroke, a rolling action is considered by leading coaches to be one of the essential features of a good technique.

Obviously the horizontal and flat body position considerably enhances the profile drag characteristics of a swimmer.

Skin-friction drag
All liquids possess a characteristic known as viscosity, which may be defined as the fluidity of a liquid. For instance, it is easier to swim through water than it would be through treacle, because the viscosity of water is less than that of treacle.

Viscosity affects a swimmer in such a way that the water molecules in direct contact with him actually adhere to his skin, the next layer slipping in turn past the last one. This slipping action gradually decreases as the layers of molecules get further away from the swimmer's skin surface until it becomes non-existent in water which surrounds him. The slipping of one layer of molecules over the next causes friction.

Friction is caused when two objects rub against each other; for instance, if a heavy box is pushed along the floor, the friction between the box and the floor causes a 'dragging back' effect. There are several kinds of friction: static friction relates to the force required to start the box moving; once the box is moving there is still sliding friction to be overcome; if the box is put on wheels rolling friction is present; if the box is floated in water the resistance can be called fluid friction. It is this kind of friction which inhibits the fastest swimmers.

The effect of fluid friction becomes more critical as water speed increases; however, at the speeds which even the fastest competitive swimmers attain, the effect on their performance is quite small. But with the introduction of sophisticated timing equipment, fractions of a second become vital at the higher levels of competition. Shaving the skin, as some competitive swimmers do, may be a psychological booster but has a doubtful effect on speed unless of course body hair is excessive. The removal of head hair may be of some consequence for the fast swimmer whose head is carried low in the water. It is illegal in competition to rub the body with oil or any other preparation, but it would seem that this is the only way to reduce the effects of friction on the skin. With international competition being so very keen, it is more than likely that someone, somewhere, will concoct an undetectable skin-friction reducing balm.

It is worth mentioning here that high-speed surface vessels have very smooth polished hulls to reduce friction drag. But here of course we are considering speeds greater than those of the fastest swimmer.

Eddy drag and streamlining

If a hand is placed in a fast-moving stream with the palm facing the direction of flow, it will be found that the smoothness and continuity of the current becomes disturbed in that place. Behind the hand the water will become turbulent and whirls of water will appear. These whirls are known as eddies. A similar effect is created by sweeping a hand, partly submerged and facing forward, along the surface of still water. The whirls occur because the streamline characteristics of the flat and forward-facing hand are poor. They also appear in varying degrees of intensity behind swimmers.

A streamlined object is one which, by design or by its natural features, offers minimum resistance as it travels through a fluid medium such as air or water. When streamlining is good, the flow of fluid around the object is smooth and undisturbed, while a badly streamlined object creates disorder and eddies are formed. Examples of good and bad streamlining and the resulting eddy formation are shown in fig. 6.5. It will be seen that a swimmer's attitude in the water is also an important factor, with more eddies being formed as the flat and horizontal body position is lost.

By its very whirling nature, the direction of rotation of the water in each individual eddy either crosses or opposes the direction of motion of the object and tends to suck it backwards. The more prominent the eddy formation becomes, the more intensive is the sucking-back effect. Hence the need for swimmers to maintain their flat, horizontal and streamlined positions when swimming for speed and economy.

DIRECTION OF MOVEMENT

GOOD STREAMLINING

Fig. 6.5

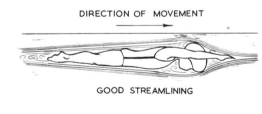

EDDIES —

THREE EXAMPLES
OF BAD
STREAMLINING

Wave drag
Waves possess energy, by definition, and the larger the wave, the more energy it possesses. Obviously a swimmer requires more energy to negotiate choppy water than flat and calm water. It may be a useful tip for racing swimmers to get in front and stay there in order to avoid the backwash of their rivals.

Architects of modern swimming pools have recognised the wave problem and have designed accordingly, the 1972 Munich Olympic pool being one example. The pool construction allows the water surface to be at the same level as the pool surround. Therefore as waves approach the side they are absorbed by a discreetly placed floor-mounted grille, instead of rebounding across the pool.

As far as swimming technique is concerned, the less surface disturbance that a swimmer makes, the less energy is used in the formation of waves which tend to drag him back. It may also be argued that an elevated swimmer generates more waves than one who swims low in the water.

Costume drag and drogue effect
Contemporary lightweight materials used in the manufacture of good-quality racing costumes are excellent with regard to minimising drag. Indeed some manufacturers claim that the friction properties of their products are lower than that of human skin. Heavyweight cloth which was once used in making swimsuits had a disastrous effect on speed through the water owing to its absorbent quality and coarse texture. The absorbency characteristic of a swimsuit is very important as swimmers tend to carry with them water which has been soaked up by the material.

Equally important is the fit of a pair of trunks or swimming-costume. If there are gaps between the swimmer and his or her costume, water tends to flow into and enlarge the space to form a 'drogue'. The action is similar to that of a sea anchor which old-time sailors used to throw overboard in order to restrict a ship's movement. Figure 6.6 shows how a drogue effect is created on badly fitting costumes. Streamlining is interfered with and the costume acts as a water scoop to slow the swimmer down.

Competition-swimwear designers have created styles to alleviate the problem, the high neckline of the modern woman's swimsuit being one example. Manufacturers are taking full advantage of lightweight synthetic materials to produce what must now be the ultimate in efficient racing swimwear.

However, it is worth mentioning that recent scientific experiment has shown that whan a woman divests herself of her modern, close-fitting, high-necked swimsuit, her swimming drag resistance is decreased by approximately nine per cent.

Having been made aware of the various problems that exist, the teacher should now be equipped to approach the teaching of the competitive strokes in a slightly scientific way.

Fig. 6.6 Drogue effects

The pulling hand: flat or cupped, fingers open or closed?
Asking young swimmers to cup their hands, or *slightly* spread their
fingers, usually brings forth quite a wide selection of profiles. The
intended hand spread is usually accompanied by a nervous finger twitch,
and the cupped hand may be anything from a waterpolo ball-like profile
to a balled-up fist.

To examine the effect of the cupped hand or spread fingers on the
pulling movement, experiments were carried out in an open water channel in the hydraulics laboratory of Bristol Polytechnic. These simple tests
related to water flowing past simulated models of hands in various positions. The three models were of an aluminium flat hand, the same profile
formed into a cup, fitting the profile of a 220-mm diameter ball, and a
wooden hand fitted with movable fingers. All the models were full-scale
adult reproductions (fig. 6.7).

Fig. 6.7 The test hands: (*left to
right*) flat aluminium, wooden
and cupped aluminium

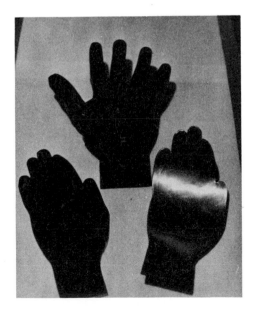

The test was set up as illustrated in fig. 6.8, whereby the 'hands' were each attached in turn to the pivoted and balanced beam. Water was made to flow past the three models at several different rates, and readings of force moments (or leverage) against corresponding water velocities were recorded. These recordings are set out in graphical form in figs. 6.9 and 6.10.

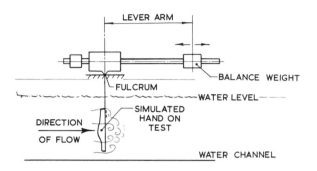

Fig. 6.8 Water test apparatus

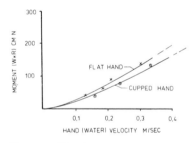

Fig. 6.9 Simulated wooden hand with movable fingers

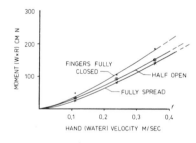

Fig. 6.10 Flat and cupped aluminium hands

Although not conclusive by any means, the results show some definite trends. For instance, the curves for the wooden model with variable fingers indicate that the hydrodynamic forces on the hand were definitely more when the fingers were closed together than when they were spread apart. However, the effect of half-closing the fingers was not very pronounced. One significant observation made during initial tests was that the passing water tended to open the *slightly* parted fingers a little wider. This would seem to indicate that the fingers should be controlled by muscular tension, rather than be left to assume the slight natural spread which is evident during relaxation of the hand.

Doc Counsilman, in his *Science of Swimming* 'bible', states that 'the cupping of the hand does reduce the pull considerably'. The curves relating to this particular aspect seem to corroborate his statement.

In order to relate some of these laboratory experiments to the swimmer, speed tests were carried out in the pool with the co-operation of three young swimmers.

The tests consisted of each swimmer passing two markers (towels) on the poolside, swimming at full stretch with fingers either fully open or fully closed, and recording the time taken in each instance. Each swimmer performed each test three times, taking a short recovery period between each dash. The various individual swimming speeds were then calculated and averaged out. The distance of the test swim was 14 m.

The results of the tests are graphically illustrated in fig. 6.11 in the form of percentage reductions in individual swimming speeds. It may be seen that there was considerable depreciation in performance when the swimmer's fingers were opened.

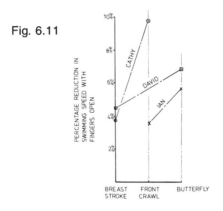

Fig. 6.11

Cathy is very strong-shouldered and her front crawl is predominantly arm-propelled. The effect on this stroke when she swam with fingers open was consequently very pronounced (9.8 per cent). She uses her arms and legs about equally in breast stroke; consequently, the finger-spreading effect, although quite noticeable, was much less than when she swam front crawl. David is a specialist breast stroke swimmer with a very powerful leg kick. The results indicate that, while swimming breast stroke and opening his fingers, the effect is not as great as with Cathy's arm-dominated front crawl. Perhaps David should make more use of his arms! David's butterfly stroke is arm-dominated and consequently the effect of open fingers is more pronounced (6.8 per cent). Ian is a front crawler but his legs produce quite reasonable propulsion. The effect of his finger spread while swimming front crawl was 3.5 per cent. Ian and David swim butterfly in a similar fashion, and produced comparable times using this style. The effects of finger spreading are consequently very similar (5.6 per cent and 6.8 per cent respectively).

Conclusions

In the various style-associated teaching points throughout the book, it is repeatedly stated that 'swimming hands' should be flat with fingers together or almost together. Fingers that are slightly apart would seem to be acceptable, providing they can be maintained in this mode. Experimental evidence showed that, even at low water speeds, the developed water force tended to spread the fingers apart. The teacher should, however, avoid creating a 'stretched-hand situation' whereby the fingers tend to bend backwards. This tendency seems to be more prominent in girls.

Finally, the analogy of drinking soup with a spoon instead of a fork often assists in getting the 'closed finger' message across to young swimmers.

7 An Introduction to Swimming

The most important swimming lesson that a child ever receives may well be the very first one. This first excursion into a new and exciting world may have a lasting effect. The teacher must play the paramount role in making sure that this initial 'baptism' is enjoyable as well as being *gently* instructive. It is up to the teacher to show that swimming is fun. When the whole class are eager to come back next time, the first lesson has indeed been a success both for the pupils and for yourself.

THE FIRST LESSON

AIM: To prove that swimming is fun
APPARATUS: A safety rope across the shallow end
A long pole and short pole
Armbands (in reserve)

As previously mentioned, the first swimming lesson will probably be the most important one that the children will receive. It must therefore be a successful one, full of fun, constant encouragement, praise and repartee. The number of early activities which the class may carry out are many and varied and you will without doubt eventually formulate your own ideas as to what the introductory lesson should consist of.

The depth and temperature of the water, the size of the pool, the number and ages of the participants and the length of the lesson are the major factors for consideration. For instance, an exercise of kneeling in one metre of water will be most unpopular with a class of children only a metre tall! Similarly, if these same tinies are unable to stand because the water is too deep, armbands will be required in order to keep them afloat. If the water is on the cool side, the activities will need to be vigorous to keep the children warm. The size of the pool and the area of shallow water in relation to the number of pupils will dictate the extent of free movement possible.

The ages of the pupils will dictate the standard and description of the activities to be performed. The very young will love walking along in the water pretending to be 'little men and women' but a group of older children may find this a rather babyish way of getting them to immerse their shoulders in water. In this case the instruction may be given in a different way, such as a warning that they should 'keep their shoulders down in the water, otherwise they will fly out through the roof!' Such statements usually raise a giggle but produce the right effect.

The first visit to the pool should begin with some kind of introduction from the teacher. The changing-room is a good place in which to broach matters of hygiene, safety and poolside behaviour. Then perhaps a brief guided tour of the establishment to show the class where such important facilities as the toilets, showers and footbath are located and how and when they should be used. (It is worthwhile mentioning at this stage that some of the children may never have seen or used a shower and may find it quite alarming; so make sure they all know and are prepared for what happens when the button is pressed.) Next, the teacher should outline once more as many rules relating to safety, hygiene and discipline as are appropriate at this stage.

Before entering the water, a physical inspection of the class should be carried out. This must be accompanied by an explanation to the chilen why it is necessary to subject them to this kind of treatment (see page 39).

If there is any possibility of a visual demonstration of what is required of the children, it should be used. This applies to even the simplest tasks such as getting in and out of the water and moving about. If someone is less timid than the others or has previously visited the pool, he may be used as a demonstrator.

It will undoubtedly give the pupils a little extra confidence if they can see how the long and short poles are used. The teacher must show that by holding the end of the poles the pupils are completely safe in the water. The use of the rope dividing off the shallow area of the pool can also be shown at this time. The 'ways of the water' should be carefully explained and if possible demonstrated. This should include an idea of how propulsion is created and a short land exercise to demonstrate the best way to walk along in the water, using a skiing leg movement assisted by a paddling hand action. When these short preliminaries have been happily tried and tested, it is time to get wet.

Before taking the plunge into cold water, such as the pool or the sea, the less adventurous among us like to sample the temperature by dipping our big toe in first. The best way for beginners to get used to the temperature is for them to sit along the pool's edge and dangle their feet in the water. The natural thing to do then is to kick and splash. Seeing who can 'make the most splash' or 'splash the roof', or even 'splash teacher', usually dispels any initial inhibitions. This fun activity can set the tone of the whole lesson. One word of warning here: make sure that the children sit well back from the edge if possible; the ensuing excitement may well see some of the more vigorous participants falling in!

Most of the class will now be fairly wet, so it is time for the first entry into the pool. If there are any children who cannot touch the bottom or are extremely timid, armbands should be used. If there are narrow steps leading down into the water, a forward-moving single file is most appropriate, using any handrail which may exist as a steadier. If the steps are wide, similar to a wide staircase, the children may like to sit on the steps, slowly descending, one by one, until they are in the water.

In most modern pools, a vertical step-ladder arrangement is installed in each of the four corners. Often the steps themselves will be formed in the side wall of the pool. (This is a good feature of pool design, providing obstacle-free end lanes.) Both types of fitment are accompanied by two handrails, one each side of the steps. The safest method of entry is by descending slowly backwards (facing the steps) into the water, at the same time maintaining a firm sliding grip with each hand on the rails. A wise move by the teacher is to tell the class how many steps there are.

Once in the water, the pupils will probably not need telling to grab hold of the pool rail with both hands. Then, in order not to cause congestion at the foot of the steps, a sideways-sliding foot movement will see them parading across the pool, sliding their hands along the handrail.

Getting safely out of the pool is as important as getting in, so, after the initial trip across the width or around the pool, an unhurried exit can be made. If there are two sets of steps in the shallow end a walk across the end of the pool from one set to the other before re-entry will help the children to get used to the safety rules relating to wandering too near to the poolside and moving at a steady pace rather than running. If there is only one set of steps available a simple adjustment to the queue-forming procedure will be required.

Where there are no steps down into the water, the children should remain seated along the poolside after having their initial fun-splash. Then, placing both hands flat and side by side on the edge of the pool to the right or left of them, they can slip unceremoniously into the water, at the same time turning to face the side and grasp the handrail. Even where there are steps for getting in and out of the water, this 'sitting and sliding in' method should be tried at the first lesson; it is quicker and allows more water time. Climbing out over the side will come naturally to most children, and those who are a little too tiny to clamber out in this fashion will use the steps.

The next stage is to persuade the children by bending their knees to immerse their shoulders completely below the water surface. Telling them that, with shoulders under, they won't fall over when they walk should do the trick. With shoulders immersed, the children may practise the floor-contact ski-walking action that they tried on the poolside before entering the water. The exercise may be a rail-holding one or, if the water is shallow enough, a free-moving activity. If the water is very shallow, a 'kneeling-walk' may even be tried.

It is these early exercises that give the children a feel for the water. They discover the resistance to movement which is created by the medium. Using the hands as paddles or oars, or even carrying out some elementary sculling movements, children quickly learn how to use the resistive character of the water to propel or support themselves.

If it has not happened already, the children are certainly going to get their faces wet sooner or later, whether they like it or not. So, rather than wait till it happens accidentally, it is good practice to carry out some specific face-wetting tricks. (Being taken unaware by cold water suddenly splashing on to the face usually causes the recipient to gasp; if the gasp coincides with an oncoming wave, the result may be disastrous.) The value of play and imagination may be seen when the teacher tells the children that 'all their faces are dirty' and need a quick wash. The exercise has a two-fold use: not only does it encourage each child to get his or her face wet, but the creation of imaginary soap-suds requires the use of two hands, and therefore they must let go of the handrail completely. There are of course many other ways of encouraging the children to release their grip on the rail, such as clapping their own efforts or singing an action song.

Taking the face-wetting exercise one step further, an experiment in face immersion and breath holding may now be introduced. By making a noise like sea lions (blowing and 'noising' into the water), a first attempt at breath control may be made. Even at this early stage it is helpful to mention that blowing out through the mouth and nose will reduce coughing and spluttering: if air is being blown down the nose water cannot be inhaled.

The timid ones will only pretend to put their faces into the water, and the act of face immersion may take weeks or even months for some to achieve. Remember, this is only the first visit and even to get into the water is a monumental act of courage for some children. Make light of any such minor shortcomings and enthusiastically applaud their efforts, however feeble they may seem.

This is probably enough direct instruction for one lesson so perhaps some kind of game designed to increase mobility would be in order. There are many appropriate games that may be played and these have been itemised on page 94 in accordance with the ages and abilities of the participants.

Finally, if there is enough time left, the lesson may end with a short period of *supervised* free play. The more robust characters in the class will have the chance to repeat a few of the tricks they have learnt in the new environment, while their less keen classmates will probably wish to get out and dressed.

Ensure that the steps are used correctly as the class leaves the water and that there is the same number of children at the end as there was at the beginning of the lesson. The first few drying and dressing sessions should be supervised, in order to make absolutely sure that all are thoroughly dried and dressed properly.

THE SECOND LESSON

AIM: Shallow-water mobility and regaining the feet

APPARATUS: Rope, poles, armbands, floats

This time you will want to get the class into the water right at the beginning of the lesson. While they are changing, a quick reminder may be given regarding the use of the toilets and whereabouts in the pool the children should assemble prior to the actual lesson, and a short poolside inspection session must be carried out in case of infection, wounds, etc.

Entry into the water may be via the steps for those who feel a little unsure, while the more intrepid ones may enter by the 'sitting and sliding' method. Whichever type of entry is used, the children should in the first instance hold the handrail with one or both hands once they are in the water.

To set a light-hearted tone to the lesson, a warming-up activity, such as jumping or bobbing at the rail, may be carried out, possibly singing to help the 'show' along. The teacher will do well to get into the swing of things by performing a few little jumps or bobs in time with the children. The children should be encouraged to sink lower in the water after every jump, until perhaps some of the less inhibited members disappear below the water surface for a brief instant. At this stage the teacher should be prepared for a little coughing and spluttering and wiping of eyes.

The next activity, of breath-holding, should ensure that most faces are immersed. This breath-holding exercise should perhaps be a little more prolonged than that which was carried out during the first lesson. Gradually increasing an 'immersion count' from one (a quick dip) up to three or even five makes the exercise progressive. A little encouragement should be given to the swimmers to open their eyes under the water by trying to count the outspread fingers on their partner's hands, or to see the tiles on the floor of the pool.

Mimicking sea lions as a breath-control exercise may now also be used in a progressive form, with a rhythmic pattern of short sub-aqua roars up to perhaps a count of five or six.

Further exercises in relation to balance should be incorporated into this second lesson. These may be jumping up and down while holding each other's hands or individual jumping, using outstretched arms and slightly spread-apart feet as aids to stabilisation and balance. The movements should initially be carried out in a gentle fashion, then with a little more vigour as confidence begins to soar. The teacher should watch out for the over-enthusiastic jumper who may slip on landing.

The next stage in the programme may be an attempt to assume a handrail-supported, face-down, prone, floating position. The horizontal mode may be achieved by the swimmers merely placing their faces in the water while grasping the rail firmly, either allowing their legs to float to the surface or kicking their feet up and down (front-paddle fashion) to bring them to the surface. This exercise naturally leads to a brief interlude of leg kicking at the rail. The finer points of technique can be dispensed with at this initial stage, the main aim of the exercise being to 'splash the roof with straight legs and floppy feet'.

Those who have difficulty in elevating their feet to the surface should try undergrasping the handrail and applying a little pressure between the elbows and the wall.

A partner-assisted kicking exercise may be performed by arranging the class in small groups and joining hands in chain fashion. The 'anchors' at the ends of the chains may each hold the handrail with their free hand, thus forming a half-circle away from the rail and back again. Alternate 'links' in the chain now attempt to raise their legs to the surface and kick on either front or back, their adjacent partners standing to provide the necessary support. A further development of the exercise is for the two 'anchors' to join hands, thus forming a full circle.

Leg kicking to the untrained can be rather exhausting: thirty seconds of kicking at a single spell would be adequate, this being followed by a short period of rest. (Supporting struggling partners also tends to make the shoulders ache.)

Regaining the feet after performing a short kicking exercise will be achieved by most children without really thinking about it. Those experiencing difficulty in elevating their legs will find little trouble in standing once more, while the swimmers whose limbs display some degree of buoyancy (probably the girls), may easily regain a standing posture once more by applying a downward pressure on the handrail or on their partners' hands and assuming a slight tuck at the same time.

This is an introduction to the skill of regaining the feet and, before any free and unassisted kicking or swimming exercises are carried out, the particular prone or supine-related standing-down procedure must be taught. The teaching practices are fully illustrated and described in chapter 10 (prone) and chapter 13 (supine). They include the use of floats and the methods of holding them correctly. The teacher must make a special point of emphasising how this is done every time the floats are used in these initial lessons.

Before using the floats as a practice aid to regaining the feet, however, they may be utilised in order to provide some degree of physical and moral support during a few 'shoulders-submerged' walking or sliding movements. Some of the more adventurous members of the class may even be inspired to 'take off' for a few brief moments. The more timid children may be fitted with armbands at this stage if they are not already wearing them.

Practice in regaining the feet from a prone position may now be carried out with the intention of learning the front glide in the next lesson. The standing-down skills are necessary before an attempt is made to introduce this new feature in the syllabus.

Towards the end of the lesson, a short game should be a popular move, followed by a similar period of supervised free play before the class climb out of the water (preferably over the side).

THE THIRD LESSON

AIM: Watermanship skills including the prone push and glide leading to front paddle
APPARATUS: Rope, poles, armbands, floats

After the inspection and detection session, the class may enter the water either down the steps or over the poolside; some brave ones may even feel like jumping in by now, and a brief warning should be given to them to bend their knees before landing in the water.

Once they are all in, a quick 'jumping bean' activity will serve to accustom them to being in the water. The first exercise may be a brief interlude of rail-supported face-down floating. This is a repetition of one of the second-lesson activities and is carried out in preparation for the ensuing theme.

Armbands may be used at this stage and the class may be grouped into perhaps two ability sections.

The glide activities may commence with a little jump from the bottom of the pool in order to perform a float-assisted glide to the handrail before standing down. (Before the exercise, the method of holding the floats should again be stressed.)

The next exercise is similar to the first, except that the swimmers push off the wall before carrying out the glide and standing down once more. Where the swimmers are unsure or inhibited, the exercise may be a partner-assisted one: the partner, standing a short way from the wall, assists the swimmer by grabbing the float as it arrives and holding it firmly while a standing position is regained. Both these activities may be tried in head-up and head-down modes.

The push-and-glide progressions may then continue as outlined in chapter 11.

After these important practices the swimmers should be sufficiently confident to attempt their first swimming stroke, namely the front or dog paddle. The practices should be carried out in a logical sequence as described and illustrated in chapter 12.

The lesson can again end with a game followed by a few minutes of supervised free play.

As already stated, a plan of campaign is always useful, and a few suggested plans for thirty-minute periods are given in the table below. The teacher is advised to formulate a personal set of lesson plans and be prepared to modify them according to circumstances. It is worth remembering that ideal lesson circumstances are very rare indeed and the times that are given are simply a guide. It may be necessary, for instance, to repeat an exercise many more times than anticipated, thus throwing the whole schedule out of gear. On the other hand, you may get a class of budding champions! So keep an open mind and be prepared to change your plans.

TYPICAL LESSON PLANS

2 MINS *	5 MINS *	12-15 MINS *	
INTRODUCTION AND WARM-UP ACTIVITY	RECAP OF PREVIOUS LESSON	MAIN LESSON THEME DESCRIPTION	TEACHING PRACTIC
A game	Submersion practices and regaining the feet – prone	The push and glide prone Explanation and demonstration	1. Pushing-off techniques 2. Surface prone glides 3. Underwater prone glides 4. Methods of surfacin
Width swims: free choice with dive start	Front crawl Short assessment swim Grouping the class	Improvement of the front-crawl leg action Explanation and demonstration	1. At the rail 2. With one float 3. Demonstration and short rest 4. Fully stretched 5. Full front crawl stroke
Team swim	Complete movement of breast stroke also legs-only-with-float practices	Introduction to breast-stroke arms Full-stroke demonstration and explanation	1. Standing in shallow water 2. Walking 3. Walking with breath 4. Full stroke movements with extended glide and competition style
Various ways of entering the water: 1. Jumping 2. Diving 3. Sliding	Outline of survival award scheme and practices with demonstrations	Survival swimming Explanations and demonstrations: 1. Treading water 2. Surface diving 3. Underwater swimming	1. Support sculling 2. Various leg movements. 3. Feet-first surface diving practices 4. Head-first surface diving practices 5. Diving for blocks and through hoops
Front-crawl width swims for assessment	No recap Group the class according to ability	Introduction to butterfly swimming Demonstration by proficient performer with commentary Part of a multi-stroke sequence	1. Pupil version of stroke (whole practice) 2. Legs only at the rai 3. Legs only with float 4. Arms only, standing 5. Arms only, walking (Introduce breathing 6. Attempt full stroke

* These times are approximate and are intended only as a guide.

5 MINS *	3 MINS *
NTRASTING ACTIVITY	SUPERVISED FREE TIME
ames involving main- eme activities pushing between partner's legs, hand stands etc.	games
eestyle team swims	and
rface diving blocks and ough hoops mpetitions	fun
me of waterball or nchro practice	Safe
tended supervised free time	

8 The Learner Pool

With a class of very young swimmers-to-be, the use of a shallow pool, i.e. about 600 mm (24 in.) deep is invaluable. Here, they are able to stand, sit, kneel, crawl, float or walk on hands with legs trailing in complete safety and even swim, to prove beyond all doubt that 'swimming really is fun' (see fig. 8.1). These convenient little exercises, when added to those which are carried out in slightly deeper water, will substantially augment the teacher's overall repertoire of early activities. Demonstrations by the more adept children should be used whenever possible. One note of warning when using shallow learner pools: jumping in is dangerous and should be discouraged; the depth is not sufficient to cushion the swimmers as they enter the water in this fashion.

Fig. 8.1 The learner pool

Confidence activities for the learner pool
1. Kneeling, stretching and kicking (on the front), tucking and kneeling again (fig. 8.2)
2. Hand walking and kicking (fig. 8.3)
3. Float-assisted kicking (fig. 8.4)
4. Float-assisted pushing and gliding (fig. 8.5)
5. Front paddle
6. Floating on the back (fig. 8.6)
7. Pushing and gliding on the back (fig. 8.7)
8. Float-assisted leg kicking on the back (fig. 8.8)
9. As a continuation of the previous exercise, the back-kicking movement may be upgraded.
10. Faces in and blowing bubbles (fig. 8.9)

Fig. 8.2 Kneeling, stretching and kicking

Fig. 8.3 Hand walking and kicking

Fig. 8.4 Float-assisted kicking

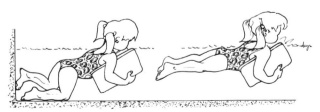

Fig. 8.5 Float-assisted pushing and gliding

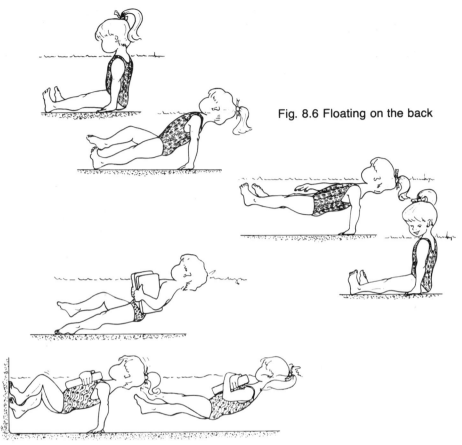

Fig. 8.6 Floating on the back

Fig. 8.7 Pushing and gliding on the back

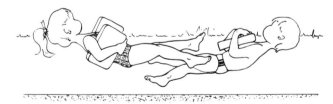

Fig. 8.8 Float-assisted kicking on the back

Fig. 8.9 Faces in and blowing bubbles

9 Confidence Exercises for the Beginner

One of the most difficult tasks for a swimming teacher is that of *safely* instilling a sense of 'water confidence' into young children. Probably one of the best ways of doing this is by allowing the swimmers-to-be simply to play in the water. Through play they will learn sub-consciously the need to overcome and also to use the resistive nature of the water. However, in addition to play, a series of exercises which are illustrated and described in this book have been designed to assist the teacher in planning a safe introductory phase of the syllabus.

The young swimmers may be fitted with armbands if they are too small to reach the bottom of the pool, if they are genuinely afraid, and on any other occasion when the teacher considers it appropriate.

1. Sitting on the poolside and splashing with the feet (fig. 9.1)
2. Safe entry and exit (fig. 9.2)
3. Walking forwards holding the rail (fig. 9.3)
4. Walking backwards holding the rail (fig. 9.3)
5. Jumping up and down holding the rail (fig. 9.4)
6. Face splashing and 'washing' the face (fig. 9.5)
7. Blowing bubbles and making sea-lion roars while holding the rail (fig. 9.6)
8. Crocodile walking (fig. 9.7)
9. Holding the floats (fig. 9.8)
10. Walking with the floats (fig. 9.8)
11. Jumping into shallow water (chest depth) (fig. 9.9)
12. Handrail swinging and crab walking (fig. 9.10)
13. Blowing ping-pong balls
14. Alternately kicking and supporting (fig. 9.11)

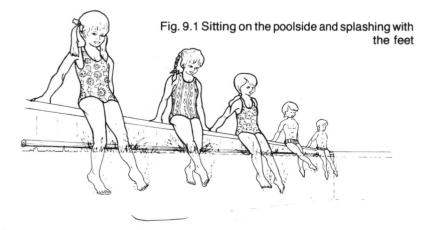

Fig. 9.1 Sitting on the poolside and splashing with the feet

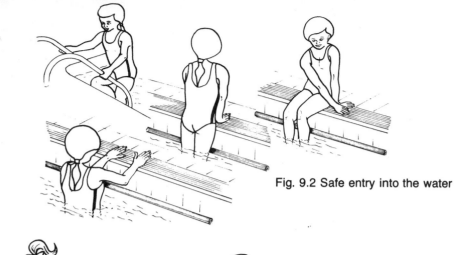

Fig. 9.2 Safe entry into the water

Fig. 9.3 Holding the rail while walking forwards or backwards

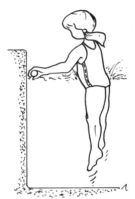

Fig. 9.4 Jumping up and down

Fig. 9.5 'Washing' the face

Fig. 9.6 Blowing bubbles and making sea-lion roars

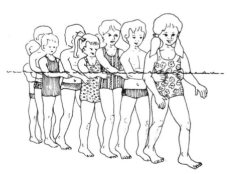

Fig. 9.7 Crocodile walking

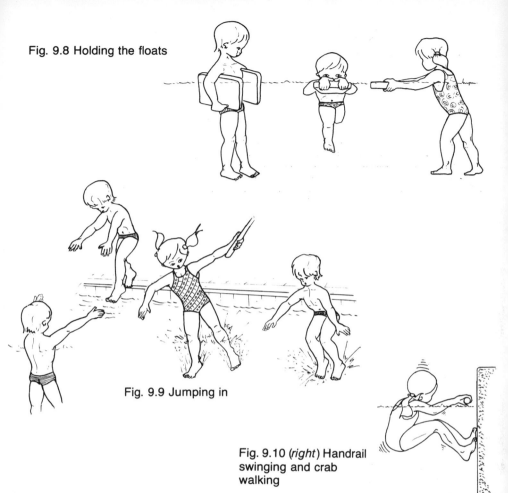

Fig. 9.8 Holding the floats

Fig. 9.9 Jumping in

Fig. 9.10 (*right*) Handrail swinging and crab walking

Fig. 9.11 Alternate kicking and supporting

Floating

Most young Caucasian children are able to float in some attitude or other. There seem to be fewer floaters among negroid children. The reasons behind this phenomenon are still subject to investigation, but it could well be due to the greater density of the latters' bone structure.

Experiment has shown that girls tend to float more readily in a horizontal mode than boys, because of the difference in their anatomical and physiological make-up. (The relative positions of the centres of gravity and buoyancy seem to be the major influencing factors here). There is also evidence to suggest that after the age of twelve the ability to float tends to decrease among the male population.

Floatation and buoyancy and their effects on the swimmer are discussed in chapter 5.

Potential swimmers are considerably assisted in their endeavours if their buoyancy characteristics are of a positive nature. When a person sinks while static and with lungs fully inflated, he is said to possess negative buoyancy. Retaining a lungful of air enhances a swimmer's ability to float. Therefore a quick puff out immediately followed by an inhalation is the type of controlled breathing necessary during the head-up floating practices.

Remember, there may be young swimmers (or older ones) who just cannot float under any circumstances. These people must be allowed to use some kind of limb movement in order to provide support. Another important point is that swimmers should *not* be encouraged to hold their breath for extended periods. A count of ten is quite sufficient.

The mushroom float

This is the basic floating test attitude. If a swimmer possesses positive buoyancy *with* a lungful of air, he will be able to float in this head-down tucked position. The back should be clear of the water surface in most cases.

The mushroom position (so called because of its likeness to the head of a mushroom) is assumed by tilting the chin forward on to the chest and tucking the legs, so that the knees are near to, or touching, the head. The arms are then wrapped around the lower legs. Care must be taken that the tuck is not too tight, thus tending to squeeze the air out of the lungs. The activity is best performed in shallow water initially, where the swimmer may take a breath and gently jump off the bottom into the tuck mode. The body will roll and bob about into a stable floating position.

One of the advantages of the mushroom float, besides deciding whether a swimmer is able to float or not, is that it is a fully submersive exercise. It gives the teacher an opportunity to persuade the swimmers to get their heads wet and open their eyes in order to orientate themselves. The tuck position is also, of course, a basic dive mode. Regaining the feet from a prone position is a natural movement to follow from a mushroom float and this is yet another advantage of the exercise.

Tucking up with head down is also closely allied to the front somersault movements which are used during the synchro skills and front-crawl flip turns. When using partner assistance during the practices related to these activities, the mushroom position is a good starter for both the front and back somersault-assisted flip-overs.

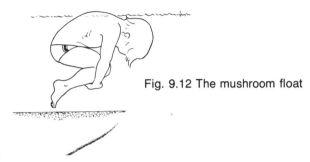

Fig. 9.12 The mushroom float

The prone float

The prone float layout may be taken up by simply taking a breath and leaning forward in shallow water. The face should be placed down and the arms relaxed forwards or out sideways. If both legs and arms are allowed to take up a natural outspread position, the pose may be likened to that of a starfish.

Lifting the head just enough to take a breath then returning once more to a face-down position is a survival activity called drown-proofing. The swimmer, with minimal effort and controlled submersive exhalation, can float in this relaxed mode for some considerable time.

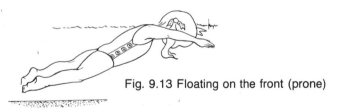

Fig. 9.13 Floating on the front (prone)

The supine float

This is the most popular floating attitude in which the face may be maintained clear of the water.

In taking up the position, the swimmer lies on his back with lungs inflated and arms outspread and relaxed. The legs are then allowed to take up their natural floating position. As previously mentioned, boys' feet tend to sink. Consequently, the head requires to be tilted right back in order to keep the face clear of the water. Girls seem to experience less trouble in this direction. The difficulty in assuming the position in the initial stages is in controlling the breathing as small waves wash over the face.

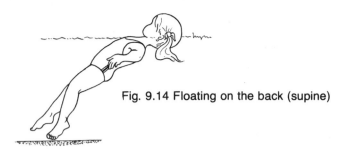

Fig. 9.14 Floating on the back (supine)

Shallow-water games

Swimming is fun, so games must be played. There follows a list of games which the teacher may add to or modify to suit the class and the environment.

·1. *Follow my thumb* The teacher points a thumb in either direction; the pupils have to make haste in the direction of the thumb.

, 2. *Ring o' roses* Complete submersion on the 'All fall down'.

3. *Shadow boxing* A good warming-up exercise.

4. *Rats and rabbits* Two lines of pupils side by side face the teacher who stands on the poolside at the shallow end. One line is code-named Rats, the other Rabbits. The teacher calls 'Rr-r-r-rats' or 'Rr-r-r-rabbits'. If 'Rats' is called the Rats rush to seek sanctuary by touching their nearest side before being caught by a Rabbit, and vice versa.

5. *Out of the circle* Half the class form a circle by clasping hands. The other half stand inside the circle. The children inside the circle try to escape under or over the 'boundary fence'.

·6. *Submarine* Holding the nose with one hand, the pupils sink, then stretch their other hand into the air to simulate a periscope.

7. *Goldfish* Putting the face into the water and opening the eyes, counting each other's fingers, etc.

8. *Jumping in* With or without teacher or pupil assistance.

9. *Simon (or O'Grady) says* Pupils must only do what Simon says they are to do.

10. *Bunny hops* The children imitate rabbits and hop across the shallow end.

11. *Number game* Give each particular exercise a number, then the class performs according to whichever number is called. This is a memory game which is great fun.

10 Regaining the Feet from the Prone (Front-Lay) Position

Regaining the feet, regaining a standing position, standing down, standing up, putting the feet down: each of these phrases describes the same movement, and, as long as teacher and pupil are on the same wavelength, any one or more of the descriptions may be used.

Before carrying out too many 'mobile and free' movements in the shallow ed of the pool, the teacher should make absolutely sure that his or her charges are able to regain a standing position from both the back (supine) and front (prone) swimming positions.

There are two different methods of performing the feet-regaining movements from both prone and supine modes. In each individual skill, the feet may either be rotated under the body or the body may be moved forward over the feet. The arm movements for each are completely opposite. The methods described and illustrated are probably the easiest and most widely used. There are individual instances, however, where the 'reverse actions' are more appropriate and the teacher may find advantages in using them.

The overall movement, technically speaking, involves the action/reaction principle, which is referred to in previous chapters. The downward-acting arms create an upward water force. It is this total action force that the swimmer uses to react against, in order to rotate his legs towards the pool floor.

THE MOVEMENT (fig. 10.1)
Regaining the feet in shallow water, from a prone swimming or floating attitude, is performed by sweeping the straight and forward-stretched arms palms facing the pool floor) vertically downwards. At the same time the legs are tucked and the head is tilted back. As body rotation takes place and an upright position is achieved, the legs are again straightened and the swimmer stands upright with both feet on the bottom of the pool. Should one arm-sweeping movement not be sufficient to rotate the swimmer into an upright mode, both arms may be recovered to the forward psition and a further downward sweep carried out. This may be done until the swimmer becomes proficient in performing the skill with just one arm sweep.

95

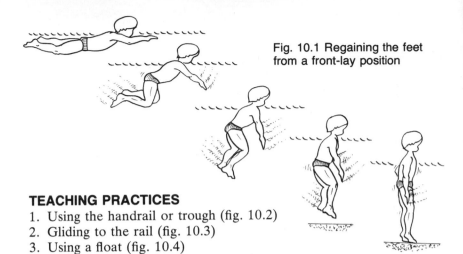

Fig. 10.1 Regaining the feet
from a front-lay position

TEACHING PRACTICES
1. Using the handrail or trough (fig. 10.2)
2. Gliding to the rail (fig. 10.3)
3. Using a float (fig. 10.4)
4. Partner-assisted standing (fig. 10.5)

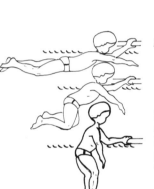

Figs. 10.2, 10.3
and 10.4
Regaining-the-feet
practices from a
front-lay position

Fig. 10.2

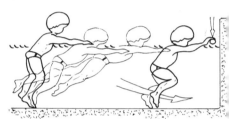

Fig. 10.3

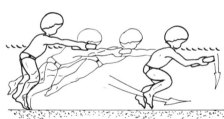

Fig. 10.4

Fig. 10.5 Partner-assisted regaining the feet

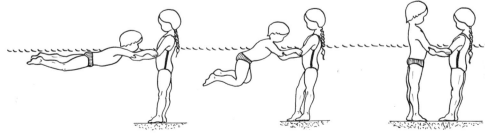

11 The Prone Push and Glide

This is probably one of the most commonly used combinations of movement in swimming and consequently a fair amount of importance should be attached to it.

Before any of the mobile swimming exercises are carried out, the pupils usually need to push off on their fronts or backs from the poolside. The prone or supine glide modes are very reminiscent of the normal swimming positions, with the swimmer adopting a stretched and streamlined attitude for the best results. Pushing and gliding movements are also, of course, a fundamental part of the competition starts and turns.

A dive from the poolside usually ends with a glide to the surface and the pupils must also be taught this re-surfacing technique.

Waterpolo players are usually experts in the skill of pushing off, but they usually use some part of an opponent's anatomy, rather than the poolside, from which to push off.

Before attempting the practices, it is essential that the pupils are able to regain their feet from the prone or supine mode of each exercise.

TEACHING PRACTICES
A successful glide needs to be performed with the exponent in a fully stretched and streamlined attitude. In assuming this position, the pupil needs to put his or her face into the water in order that the head may blend in with the tapered shape of the arms and thus enhance the streamlining. It is expedient, therefore, for the teacher to introduce some simple bubble-blowing or similar face immersion exercises before the pupils actually become mobile.

1(a) Glide to the rail (fig. 11.1)
  (b) Glide away from the rail (from a jump off the bottom) (fig. 11.2)
2. Pushing off from a two-handed grip along the water surface (fig. 11.3)
3. Standing push-off and glide along the water surface (fig. 11.4)

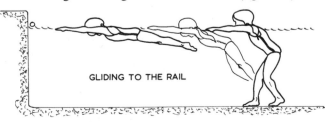

Fig. 11.1

GLIDING TO THE RAIL

97

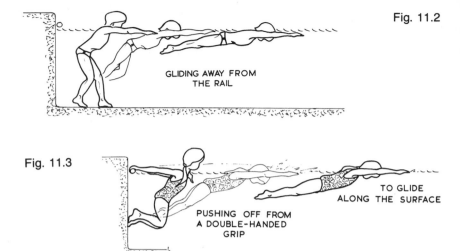

Fig. 11.2

GLIDING AWAY FROM
THE RAIL

Fig. 11.3

PUSHING OFF FROM
A DOUBLE-HANDED
GRIP

TO GLIDE
ALONG THE SURFACE

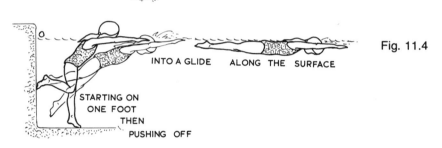

INTO A GLIDE   ALONG THE SURFACE

Fig. 11.4

STARTING ON
ONE FOOT
THEN
PUSHING OFF

The importance of the face-down glide

The importance of placing the face down in the water during the glide so that the water line is approximately at the centre of the head may be demonstrated by a simple experiment. The pupils are instructed to push off from the side as in this last exercise but at the same time lifting their heads so that they are clear, or almost clear, of the water and looking forward. The length of their glide should be measured by the pupils themselves. (The floor markings or tiles are suitable for this.) The exercise is repeated with their heads lowered into the water so that the waves wash over them throughout the movement. They will no doubt find that the second more streamlined mode has the advantage of creating fewer waves and allowing them to glide a greater distance.

Manoeuvring during a glide (fig. 11.5)

A submarine travelling under water may change its direction of movement either towards or away from the water surface by use of·elevators mounted on its hull. Similarly, a swimmer may change the direction of a glide by using his hands as elevators and tilting them in the direction in which he desires to travel. Also, by manipulation of the head, the same

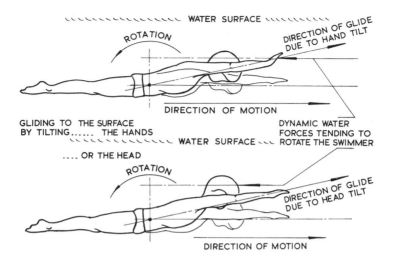

Fig. 11.5

steering effect may be experienced. Probably the most important point for the teacher to remember when teaching the pupils how to manoeuvre during a glide is that for the manipulation of either hands or head to take effect, the swimmer must be gliding at a reasonable speed. A reasonable speed may be described as that which results from a vigorous push-off or from a dive from the poolside.

Obviously, the movement of both hands and head in the same direction will magnify the steering effect, but it must be remembered that elevation of both hands and head will increase the swimmer's profile and slow him down, the effect of the head being more predominant in this respect than the hands.

Manoeuvring by use of the hands
Assuming an athletically stretched mode as illustrated in fig. 14.5, the swimmer continues to glide along a horizontal path. This direction may now be changed by pivoting both hands so that they are tilted upwards. The dynamic water forces (forces due to movement in the water) now act on the elevated hands to rotate the swimmer upwards and direct him towards the surface. Similarly, if his hands are tilted downwards, he changes the direction of his glide towards the bottom of the pool. (This is more difficult because deeper submersion requires more effort to overcome the swimmer's natural buoyancy characteristics.) Further tricks may be played by tilting the hands to the left or right. But it must be emphasised once more that a reasonable glide speed must exist for these diversions to be successful.

Manoeuvring by use of the head
The same effect on the direction of glide may be obtained by tilting the head. An upward tilt will produce the most effect, but will probably require a little more movement in order to produce the same directional effect as the hand tilt (the hands being further from the swimmer's centre of gravity than the head).

4(a) Standing push-off and glide below the water surface (fig. 11.6)
  (b) Glide to the bottom and up again
5. Push-off and glide more allied to the competition style (fig. 11.7)

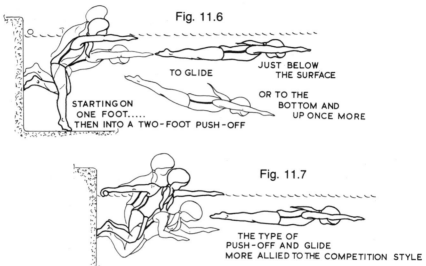

Fig. 11.6

TO GLIDE

JUST BELOW
THE SURFACE

STARTING ON
ONE FOOT.....
THEN INTO A TWO-FOOT PUSH-OFF

OR TO THE
BOTTOM AND
UP ONCE MORE

Fig. 11.7

THE TYPE OF
PUSH-OFF AND GLIDE
MORE ALLIED TO THE COMPETITION STYLE

Many games and contests may be created where each activity relates in some way to the push-and-glide movement. These may include fun exercises such as finding and recovering objects and gliding between each other's legs (fig. 11.8). As originally stated, the particular combination of movements involved in the push and glide are to be found in many, if not all, the various aquatic skills. Therefore, the practices are well worth any extra time that a teacher may care to spend teaching them.

Fig. 11.8 Pushing and gliding – between one or more partners' legs

12 The Front Paddle

Having now performed quite a number of confidence exercises, the pupils should be quite at home in the shallow end of the pool. They have practised the skills of regaining the feet from a prone position and should be able to carry out a reasonable head-down glide on the water surface.

There is a very good chance also that most of the would-be swimmers are able to open their eyes while their faces are immersed. Breathing out under the water surface should again not create any real problems for the majority of class members.

However, before proceeding to attempt further skills, the teacher should be fully aware of any discrepancies in the overall class ability and, if it is considered necessary, a return to a particular set of exercises should be carried out. This is especially important in the instance of regaining the feet from a prone attitude. The pupils are now about to become truly waterborne, with feet up and kicking along the surface. Therefore, being able to place their feet firmly on the pool floor once more, after a quick, initially exhausting aquatic excursion, is a most necessary requirement.

The teacher may have utilised armbands in order to give the more timid or tiny pupils some degree of confidence during the introductory exercises. These may still be used during the front-paddle practices, but an effort must be made towards the end of the series of exercises gradually to reduce the amount of supporting air in the aids, eventually removing them completely so that the swimmers are moving through the water completely unaided. Where armbands have not been used during the lessons to date and the would-be swimmers seem confident enough in the water, the teacher is advised to attempt the front-paddle practices without initially using the inflatable aids. If, however, certain pupils seem to be experiencing difficulties, armbands may be introduced.

Difficulties should not arise, however, in the early part of the programme where floats are used for carrying out the leg exercises.

DESCRIPTION OF THE STROKE
Body position
From the side, the swimmer should appear as horizontal and flat in the water as possible. (This is, of course, excellent positional training for the later proper stroke practices.) The arm stroke is a shorter and quicker version of the front-crawl underwater arm movement; consequently the shoulders tend to remain in the lateral plane. The performers are novices

who probably still do not enjoy getting their faces splashed, in which case their heads will be held well up in order to avoid the oncoming waves.

Leg kick
The leg kick is an alternating and continuous movement, performed in the vertical plane. The action originates from the hips; the knees, while not held rigid, are not deliberately flexed. The ankles should be relaxed throughout ('floppy feet') and the feet themselves should assume a slight but natural extension.

Further leg-kick descriptions may be found in the chapter on front crawl.

The arm movement
The whole movement is performed under the water surface, and any water disturbance which may occur in front of the swimmer's face, owing to hand movement, must be avoided. The main object is to 'push the water backwards' from a fully stretched-forward position for each arm cycle, then recover once more below the surface. The arms move alternately and the action is continuous. The fingers should be held together throughout and the hands held flat – not cupped – with the wrists slightly flexed.

Breathing
The style of the preliminary stroke is such that the swimmer's head is held up clear of the water. Therefore, in the relatively calm conditions that prevail in a normal teaching pool, there should be no difficulties with breathing. However, it is advisable for the teacher to create some form of respiratory discipline. This should take the form of inhaling through the mouth and blowing out through the nose. The swimmers should be encouraged to breathe as normally as possible and not adopt the habit of holding their breath for long periods.

Co-ordination
The whole stroke movement should display a rhythmical and continuous character. The leg-kicking action should be neatly integrated with the arm movement in such a way that there are four to six beats to every complete arm cycle.

The relationship between the skilfully performed front paddle and the front crawl stroke is very close. In fact, the transition from one to the other may be carried out fairly easily providing the pupils are capable of underwater exhalation.

Teaching the front paddle
Before attempting the front paddle, the teacher should ensure that his or her charges are reasonably 'at home' in the water. There may be a few

who are still addicted to the armbands, and if the class is large, or the pool is deep, a few members may still require a slight morale booster in the shape of a pair of these inflatable aids. This should not deter the teacher from pressing on with the early stroke practices.

The standard of the pupils at this stage should be that:

1. They are mobile with feet off the bottom, 'artificially aided' or unaided.
2. They are able to regain their feet from a prone swimming position (if the water depth allows this).
3. They have carried out, with some degree of satisfaction, the face-wetting and submersive bubble-blowing activities.
4. They can carry out, with some degree of skill, a head-down push and glide along the water surface.

Having established that the majority of the class have reached this standard, the front-paddle practices may commence. The style of teaching follows the 'whole-part-whole' pattern which has been adopted throughout the book, whereby the complete stroke is attempted, followed by part-practices and finally the whole stroke once more.

THE TEACHING PRACTICES (fig. 12.1, overleaf)
Activity: full-stroke demonstration by an able performer
Practice: observation of demonstration by pupils
TEACHING POINTS
1. The reasonably flat and horizontal body position should be highlighted.

2. The continuous arm movement reaching back to the hips, and the consequent underwater recovery, should be seen quite easily when viewed from the side.

3. During both the propulsive and recovery parts of the arm cycle, the hands will be seen to remain flat with fingers closed.

4. The legs should be reasonably straight and beat rhythmically with the swimmer's heels just about breaking the water surface at the peak of each upbeat.

Activity: full stroke
Practice: first attempt at the whole stroke
TEACHING POINTS
1. The general characteristics of the stroke technique should be outlined as described in the previous teaching points.

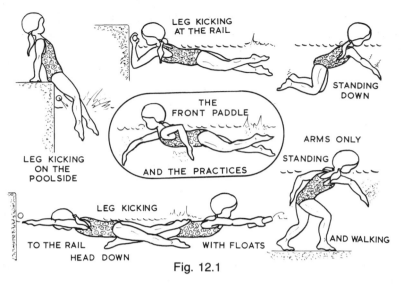

Fig. 12.1

2. There is usually a predominance of short high-speed hand movements to be seen during this first attempt. A longer and slower underwater action should be the eventual aim.

3. A short mention of a four- or six-beat rhythm should be made: some children may appear to kick with one leg and pull with one arm all at the same time.

The teacher will probably witness quite a considerable number of faults and failings during this practice. The class should proceed to the *part-practices* associated with the stroke, to improve matters wherever necessary.

Some of the part-practices are described in greater detail in chapter 16, relating to the front crawl.

Activity: leg action
Practice 1: sitting on the poolside
TEACHING POINTS
1. The leg movement should originate from the hips rather than the knees.

2. *For this particular exercise only*, the teacher should encourage the pupils to *stretch* their legs. This should alleviate any *deliberate* knee bend. There will probably be in most cases, however, some degree of knee bend when the kicking rate is slow, occurring just after the change of direction from back to forward leg movement. This flexing is a natural trait and, when transferred to the water, it will be accentuated and become an integral part of the kick.

3. The feet should assume a natural extension and the ankles should be loose ('floppy feet'), slight 'toeing-in' should occur and the legs should move with only a slight lateral gap between them.

4. The depth of kick (a rather loose term in this particular instance) should not be more than 300 mm (12 in.) and the rate of movement should not be too rapid, say, one per second, or thereabouts. (If the kicking rate or depth becomes excessive, the pupils tend to fall into the water!)

5. The sitting position for the practice is with the bottom planted firmly on the poolside, but forward enough for the lower legs to be in the water. By leaning back slightly on their arms, the performers may balance quite easily in order to carry out the kicking movement.

The exercise has the advantage of the performers being able to see their leg movements. They are therefore able to make, and at the same time observe the effect of, various adjustments to the kick. As the exercise is a static one, it should not be prolonged for too long a period. As soon as the teacher can see that the majority of his pupils have got it right, they should proceed to the next practice which, although again static, is at least in the water.

Practice 2: at the handrail
TEACHING POINTS
1. The rail should be held correctly as described. Where particular swimmers are more buoyant and more proficient at the skill, it may be found that a handrail (and trough) overgrasp combined with extended arms can be used. (A third method of handrail support, using one hand with the other placed on the wall, is to be found in the chapter which describes the front-crawl teaching practices (chapter 16). This technique requires a little more skill than the methods already outlined here. Consequently, establishing the supporting mode could supplant the leg kick as the major feature of the exercise.)

2. The movement should be alternating and continuous and carried out in the vertical plane.

3. The kick should originate from the hips and the legs should be straight during the upbeat. The downbeat should display a partial flexing of the knee joint during the initial stage of the movement. The leg should then extend vigorously throughout the remainder of the beat, to finish up straight and stretched at kicking depth. (The *individual* leg motion should resemble that of the undulating swimming movement of a dolphin.) If the lower leg joints are relaxed at the start of the downbeat, the initial knee bend should occur naturally. The swimmer should not deliberately bend the knees. Let the water bend the knees – not the swimmer.

4. The ankles should be relaxed and floppy and the feet naturally extended and slightly inverted. During the downbeat, the water forces will tend to extend the ankle joint even further, thus enhancing the propulsive effects of the feet.

5. The heels should just break the water surface, and the depth of kick is closely related to the rate of the movement. If, therefore, a depth of approximately 300 mm (12 in.) is achieved, the kicking rate should automatically sort itself out. Excessive or deliberate knee bending will cause unnecessary and undesirable splashing as the swimmer's feet rise out of the water at the end of each upbeat.

6. This exercise can be a tiring one, especially for non-water-fit young swimmers. Consequently the teacher should not be tempted to prolong the practice unnecessarily.

These are the two static leg exercises and, as previously mentioned, the practice time should be just long enough for the teacher to ensure that the pupils perform the movement with some degree of correctness.

We now move on to the float-assisted mobile activities. Here the effectiveness of each individual leg action may be assessed very simply, by observing whether the swimmers move forward smoothly and at a reasonable speed.

Practice 3: with floats
TEACHING POINTS
1. Holding the floats: in each case, the floats must be held firmly and, in the first instance, they should be held one in each hand at approximately the centre of the long edge, then tucked under the armpits. In the second part of the exercise, the single float should be grasped with both hands, in the centre of the long edge – fingers underneath and thumbs on the top, or alternatively, with both hands lapping over the short end of the float and forearms over the length of it. In both cases, the arms should be straight.

2. A definite leg-kicking rhythm should be established in order that the movement provides propulsion and body elevation.

The remainder of the teaching points are the same as for the previous practices.

Practice 4: in the athletically stretched position
TEACHING POINTS
All the relevant teaching points have been covered in the previous paragraphs.

The breathing sequence may cause a few problems at first, but if the pool is not too wide and the 'propellers' are effective, some swimmers usually manage to navigate the width without too much trouble. Where difficulties are encountered, however, a return to the float-related practices is advised. The whole exercise is enhanced by a strong initial push-and-glide movement, and if the class have been well versed in this particular skill, many continuous full-width swims should be in evidence.

This completes the leg practices relating to the front paddle. The overall efficiency of the leg movement is very important. Consequently, the teacher should persevere with the various activities until there is easy progression through the water, using the legs as the only propelling source.

Activity: arm action
Practice 1: while standing
The teacher should be able to demonstrate to the class the correct arm movement while standing on the poolside. The demonstration should be accompanied by an adequate but brief verbal description of the motion and the teacher should position himself correctly to perform it.

The pupils should stand in the water, ranged across the shallow end of the pool facing the teacher.

TEACHING POINTS
1. The correct under-the-body hand movement should be adequately described and demonstrated.

2. Elbows should be slightly flexed, hands flat with fingers together during the propulsive part of the cycle. The wrists should be quite flexible in order that the hands may be faced directly backwards (towards the feet when actually swimming) for as long as possible during the pull/push phase.

3. The hand/arm recovery should take place under the water surface and, as the hand moves forward to the re-start position, it should be faced palm down in order to minimise water resistance.

4. Any water surface disturbance due to the hand movement is unnecessary and should be avoided.

5. The teacher should not be tempted to subject the class to too much verbal stroke terminology. With a simple phrased description and correct visual demonstration, the swimmers should easily be able to understand precisely what is required of them.

6. Standing in the half squat – one-foot-forward posture – with shoulders immersed in the water is desirable in order to maintain balance.

7. As the head is held clear of the water during front paddle, any reference to breathing may be omitted.

Practice 2: while walking (or sliding) forward
TEACHING POINTS
The previously outlined stroke-teaching points, together with the necessary instructions for sliding the feet forward, are applicable to this exercise.

Activity: complete stroke
Having established what the pupils *should* be doing with both their arms and legs, the whole stroke can be attempted again. Armbands may still be retained if the teacher judges it necessary.

Practice 1: short swims to the poolside and
Practice 2: full-width swims
Short shallow-water swims (say, 2–3 m/2–3 yds in length) to the handrail are a good way to begin the exercises. Then, as confidence and ability improves, the distances may be lengthened until full-width swims can easily be performed.

TEACHING POINTS
All the previously mentioned stroke-teaching points are relevant as the whole movement is knitted together. In addition:

1. Some attempt may be made to relate the rates of arm and leg actions. A four- or six-beat rhythm is popular.

2. The whole action should not be too hurried. The rate of movement may easily be controlled by the length of the arm-pull. If a swimmer seems to be moving his arms too quickly, he is probably pulling too short. It is therefore advisable for the teacher to attempt to lengthen the underwater arm movements in such instances.

The front paddle stroke is essentially a beginner's movement (although in a racing form, it is often used as a front crawl-related training exercise), and as such it should be practised and used mainly over the shorter (width) distances. The limb movements are natural: the kicking action is very closely allied to walking or running; the arm movements similar to those of a child crawling about the floor. As previously mentioned and illustrated, the paddling swimmer's head is held aloft with face normally clear of the waves, so there should be no breathing problems. Taking all these points into consideration, front paddle is a good stroke with which to commence an aquatic career. Also, if the swimmers are able to overcome the fear of immersing their faces and subsequently blowing out under water, the front crawl stroke is a natural sequel whereby longer swimming distances may be attempted.

13 Regaining the Feet from the Supine (Back-Lay) Position

THE MOVEMENT (fig. 13.1)

As with the prone regaining-the-feet sequence, the supine movements are related to the mechanics of the action/reaction principle. The arc-like downward and forward arm-sweeping action enables the swimmer to react or rotate her tucked body towards the floor of the pool. Then, when she is in a suitable upright position, simply by stretching her legs she is able to regain the standing position once more. Rotation is enhanced by nodding the head forward during the activity. (This head movement tends to shift the swimmer's centre of gravity forward.) Should a single arm-sweep not be sufficient, a further one or more circular pressure-creating hand movements should eventually create the rotation required in order that the swimmer may stand down.

The water for the following exercises should be approximately chest-deep.

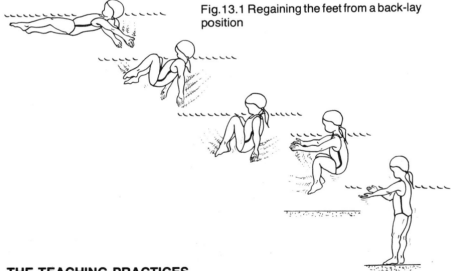

Fig. 13.1 Regaining the feet from a back-lay position

THE TEACHING PRACTICES

1. Using the handrail or trough (fig. 13.2)
2. Float-assisted standing (using two floats) (fig. 13.3)
3. Jumping backwards (fig. 13.4)
4. Partner-assisted standing (fig. 13.5)
5. Hooking both feet under the handrail (fig. 13.6)

109

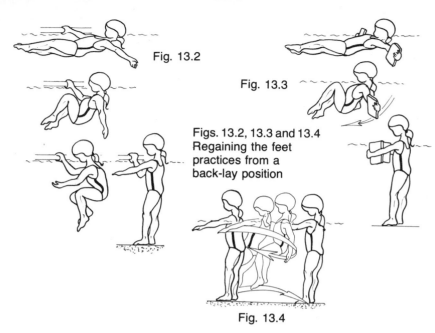

Fig. 13.2

Fig. 13.3

Figs. 13.2, 13.3 and 13.4
Regaining the feet
practices from a
back-lay position

Fig. 13.4

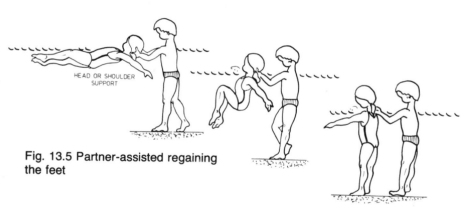

HEAD OR SHOULDER
SUPPORT

Fig. 13.5 Partner-assisted regaining
the feet

Fig. 13.6 (below) Regaining the feet
from a rail-hooked position

14 The Supine Push and Glide

The swimmers should now be able to regain a standing position in shallow water from a back-lay swimming mode. In carrying out these particular practices, they will probably have performed their own versions of the back paddle and the push-off and glide from the wall. The back paddle and its relevant practices are to be found in the following chapter, but this is preceded by a series of progressions aimed at producing a reasonable push-off and glide on the back. With this skill, coupled with the recently gained ability to regain the feet, the pupils can approach swimming on the back with some confidence.

THE TEACHING PRACTICES
1. From the handrail (fig. 14.1)
2. Start-related push-off and glide (fig. 14.2)
3. Underwater push-off and glide (fig. 14.3)

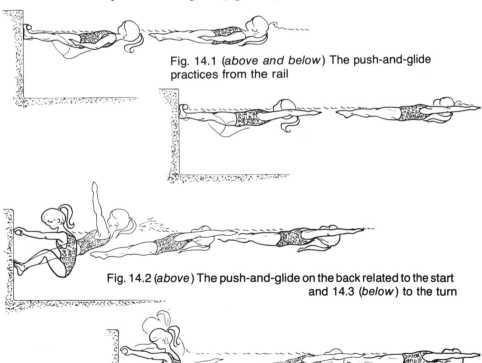

Fig. 14.1 (*above and below*) The push-and-glide practices from the rail

Fig. 14.2 (*above*) The push-and-glide on the back related to the start and 14.3 (*below*) to the turn

15 The Back Paddle

The pupils should by now be gaining confidence in the water. They should have carried out the practices relating to the back glide and regaining the feet from a supine position. The two sequences should have familiarised them with the back-lay or supine swimming mode. The wise teacher makes absolutely sure that all the swimmers are able to regain a standing position *by demonstration* before attempting to carry out the next sequence of practices leading to the back paddle. If there are members of the class who cannot perform the movement, the teacher must return to the relevant practices before proceeding further. Dividing the class into various ability groups may be necessary in order to carry this out.

There may be a need for armbands to be worn by the less able swimmers and those who feel uncertain about swimming on the back. The fact that water sometimes tends to wash over the upturned face and into the ears causes a certain amount of distress; also, not being able to see where one is going, or what is happening around one, can undermine a swimmer's water confidence. The extra buoyancy that the armbands provide should dispel some of this uncertainty. The teacher should not be averse to using them, therefore, if necessary.

A DESCRIPTION OF THE STROKE
There is a part-stroke relationship to the competition back crawl, this being in the leg movement only. The arm action takes the form of a hand-sculling pattern rather than the long pull/push propelling movement which is accompanied by an over-the-water recovery.

Body position
The swimmer should be as flat and horizontal as possible: most swimmers tend to 'sit' slightly in the water. At this stage of teaching, where speed is not essential, a *slight* hip bend is permissible. The head should be pillowed on the water so that the water line is in the region of the ears. By looking upwards and very slightly towards the feet, the swimmer should be able to place his or her head in the right position.

Leg kick
The leg kick is similar to that of the front-paddle action. The movement is alternating and continuous and takes place in the vertical plane. The leg should rise to just below water level at the peak of the cycle and neither

toes nor knees should break the surface. The foot should then sink to approximately 200–300 mm (8–12 in.).
A more detailed description of the leg kick is given in chapter 17.

Arm movement
The arm action is that of a predominantly support-sculling movement. (A complete description of this particular arm action and its teaching practices is to be found in chapter 28.) The skill is rather difficult to perform with perfection unless practised regularly. Indeed, many of our synchronised swimmers fail to reach the pinnacle of achievement simply because they do not appreciate and carry out the simple rudiments of the sculling movement. However, when dealing with beginners, the skill should be presented and practised in its simplest form in order to provide support rather than propulsion.

Breathing
The head-back/face-up swimming mode automatically positions the face clear of the water. This being so, there should be no breathing problems, and a natural breathing rhythm, dictated by the amount of exertion taking place, should be adopted.

Teaching the back paddle
There may be quite a high proportion of the class who, although they are able to perform a reasonable front paddle, will feel a little safer on the back initially if wearing a pair of armbands. Once more, the teacher should be prepared to compromise for a short while as long as progress is maintained.

Before attempting the exercises, it is desirable that the pupils have reached the following standard:

1. They are mobile, preferably able to perform a reasonable front paddle.
2. They are able to regain their feet from a supine position.
3. They are able to perform the supine push and glide with some degree of skill.

THE TEACHING PRACTICES
Activity: full stroke demonstration by an able performer
There will probably be one individual keen and able enough to perform the skill in front of the class, although while the natural kicking motion should be done well, the hand scull may leave something to be desired. At this initial stage, it may be advisable for the teacher to gloss over this particular skill and concentrate the attention of the class on the leg movement. The verbal description should be brief, as should the demonstration swim, the activity taking the form of a few widths of the pool.

Practice: observation of demonstration by pupils
The class should be suitably arranged around the poolside in order to witness the demonstration and hear the accompanying description. A performance of the standing-down procedure may also be useful while the whole class have their attention focused on the demonstrator.

TEACHING POINTS
1. The reasonably flat and horizontal swimming position should be underlined. The particular mode is dictated mainly by the position of the swimmer's head which should be pillowed back in the water. The performers should look upwards at the roof of the pool.

2. The swimmer's legs should be moving continuously with a relaxed, alternating beat. The knees should always be below the water surface and the toes should just break through to cause minimum splash.

3. The hands should be continuously oscillating outwards and inwards in a horizontal plane with palms biased towards the bottom of the pool.

4. A quick review of the standing-down procedure should highlight the sweeping arm/hand motion combined with the tuck and the forward-tilted head.

Activity: full stroke
Having made sure that all the class are able to regain their feet from a back-lay swimming mode, the teacher may now arrange and, if necessary, equip the class with armbands for their first attempt at the back paddle.

Practice: first attempt at the whole stroke
For obvious safety reasons, this first practice is best carried out in shallow (chest-deep) water.

TEACHING POINTS
1. Keeping the tummy to the surface (bottoms up).
2. Avoiding excessive splash.
3. Heads back in the water thus reducing the tendency to 'sit' in the water.
   Besides giving the pupils a chance to try out the stroke themselves, this activity will enable the teacher to assess the ability of the class in relation to the forthcoming part-practices.

Activity: leg action
Practice 1: sitting on the poolside
Practice 2: with two floats
Regaining the feet using the floats should be performed to the teacher's satisfaction before proceeding.

TEACHING POINTS
1. The leg kick should be rhythmic and originate from the hips with no deliberate knee bend.

2. Legs should be straight but not stretched: let the water bend the knees *not* the swimmer. The feet should be partially and naturally extended with the swimmer's ankles loose ('floppy feet') and rotated slightly ('toed-in').

3. The toes should just about break the surface on the peak of the upbeat but the knees should never emerge above the water line. (If this happens, 'cycling' is probably taking place: this is a kicking fault.)

4. Kicking depth should be 300–450 mm (12–15 in.).

5. Holding the floats correctly: this may need several reminders.

6. A reasonably horizontal and flat body position should be maintained. The floats have a tendency to make the swimmers 'sit' in the water. (A repeated cry of 'bottoms up' may be necessary!)

Practice 3: starting with two floats, then releasing one
Practice 4: 'cuddling' a single float
Practice 5: unsupported
The practices may continue until the teacher is satisfied that there is some propulsive leg movement among the majority of the swimmers. Wherever possible, the exercise should be eventually performed without the use of aids of any description, and when the swimmers appear to be sufficiently skilled the arm practices may commence.

Activity: arm action
The hand movement in the back paddle is that of a simple hand scull. The technicalities of the action and the teaching practices are fully explained in chapter 28.

Activity: arm action and full stroke
Practice: flat scull with feet hooked under the rail, then letting go into the back paddle
TEACHING POINTS
All the previously mentioned, part-stroke teaching points are applicable.
   By facing the palms of the hands *towards* the direction *from* which the swimmer is moving, the flat scull should have more of a propulsive nature.

A successful performance of the back paddle is quite an achievement for a swimmer. In carrying out the stroke, he has probably overcome any fears he may have had about lying on the back in the water. Once the sculling movement is established, the skill is transferable to many other watermanship activities, such as treading water and the more precise art of synchronised swimming. It also gives the swimmer a sub-conscious feel

for the water and assists in general moving about in all directions at will.
    An elementary version of the back crawl stroke is quite an easy step
from the back paddle, with no breathing problems.

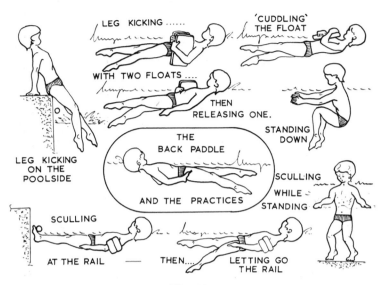

Fig. 15.1

THE COMPETITION STROKES

Children love to compete with each other. What sport offers more scope for competition than swimming?

The formal strokes, namely front and back crawl, breast stroke and butterfly, are presented in the following chapters in an educational teaching pattern based on ASA competition laws. This is sound reasoning when one considers, for instance, the precise nature of the breast stroke and its performance, together with the possible eventuality of children joining swimming clubs and competing under ASA jurisdiction. Both the back crawl and butterfly strokes also fall into this 'law abidance' category.

The technicalities of each of the styles are analysed and discussed in a logical fashion, and the major features of the various movements have been injected into the teaching practices and included in the associated teaching points. Before attempting to teach each stroke, the teacher is advised to study the set of preparatory standards which, while not essential, are a useful basis from which to start off. At the end of each teaching section, a set of stroke faults and their possible corrections are to be found.

16 The Front Crawl

The front crawl stroke has evolved as the fastest of the competition styles. The Fédération Internationale de Natation Amateur (FINA) does not mention front crawl by name in its rule book, but it does mention freestyle. (In fact, up to the year 1900, all competition events were of a freestyle nature.) In contemporary freestyle events, however, the performers are invariably front crawl swimmers.

STROKE TECHNIQUE
Body position
As stated earlier in the book, in order to obtain a true picture of a swimmer's body position during his stroke performance, he must be viewed from the side, from above, from in front and from behind. It must also be remembered that in all styles, the body position relates to the individual physical characteristics of the swimmer.

When viewed from the side, the front crawler should be seen to be swimming in a flat and horizontal attitude, shoulders, back and legs no more than a few centimetres below the surface. Any deviation from this basic horizontal position will increase the profile area, amplifying the drag forces already created by the movements.

Increase in profile area is most commonly caused by the legs sinking too deeply in the water as a result of lifting the head too high or not kicking hard enough to elevate them towards the surface. Poor inherent buoyancy characteristics may also contribute towards the swimmer moving with his legs in a depressed attitude. In endeavouring to rectify the 'see-saw' effect of lifting his head, the swimmer may try kicking his legs harder. This action will probably in turn cause his back to arch with the final result looking very similar to the crawl stroke used in waterpolo. This is a very exhausting stroke with bad streamlining characteristics. So, as far as speed swimming is concerned, the elevated-head-and-shoulders type of stroke must be avoided.

The position of the swimmer's head should be viewed from directly in front: the still water line should be approximately at the natural hair line. Raising the head higher increases the drag forces: raising his head approximately 70 m above the water-line/hair-line position and moving at a speed of 1.5 m per second, a swimmer under observation increased his body drag forces by as much as fifty per cent.

It must be understood, however, that the head tends to be higher when swimming fast: when travelling slowly only the crown of the head may be in view. It can therefore be seen that lifting rather than turning the head to take a breath can have a considerable effect on body drag as well as disturbing stroke rhythm.

In chapter 6, on drag and its effects on propulsion, it was mentioned that the front crawler increases his efficiency with a body roll. The roll also assists in directing the leg movements towards stabilising the arm-recovery reaction. Roll should be equal from side to side.

As the swimmer moves away, the view from the rear should show that his heels are just breaking the surface. His hips should be rolling slightly less than his shoulders, and his buttocks should be just below water level.

The hip roll will be transmitted to the leg kick so that the beat does not take place in the *true* vertical plane. As swimming speed increases, the kick tends to be more biased towards the vertical plane, owing to the smaller angle of body roll associated with the increase in stroke rate.

Viewed from above, it is essential that the swimmer's long body axis is in line with the general direction of motion. Any deviation from this course can probably be traced to incorrect breathing-in technique or faulty arm-stroking. If the swimmer's long body axis swings out of the true directional alignment, there will be an increase in profile as well as wave drag.

It may be seen that, in general, faulty body positioning is related to stroking or breathing technique. Therefore, in assessing a swimmer's attitude, all stroke movements should be taken into account, together with any physical characteristics and, possibly, fear of putting the face in the water. Only when this analysis has been made can corrective practices be put into operation.

Leg action

The leg movement is an alternate and continuous action in the vertical rather than the horizontal plane. The action maintains the body in a horizontal position, creates propulsion, and balances the stroke by reacting against the action of the arms.

Owing to physiological limitations, the leg kick is nowhere near as mechanically sound an action as the arm movement. Throughout the kicking cycle, the feet are extended, like a ballet dancer's on tip-toe. Failure to achieve this extended position results in a loss in propulsive foot area and less thrust (fig. 16.1). During the upbeat, the feet are held in this plantar-flexed attitude by contraction of the soleus and gastrocnemius (calf) muscles. On the downbeat, the ankle-joint extension is assisted by the hydrodynamic pressure forces developed during this high-speed movement. The toes are also slightly pointed inwards in order to present a larger propelling surface to the water (fig. 16.2). This, to most swimmers becomes a natural movement after practice, if indeed it is not already in evidence at the start.

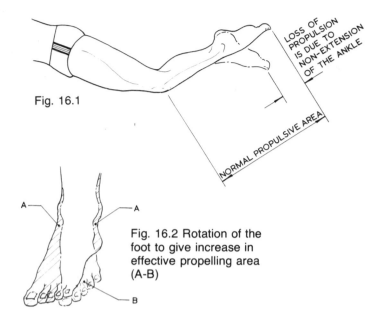

Fig. 16.1

LOSS OF PROPULSION IS DUE TO NON-EXTENSION OF THE ANKLE

NORMAL PROPULSIVE AREA

Fig. 16.2 Rotation of the
foot to give increase in
effective propelling area
(A-B)

The kicking movement originates from the hips with no conscious
flexing at the knee joint. The depth of movement should be no more than
450 mm (18 in.), but depends on the swimmer's height, the shorter-
legged swimmers usually kicking shallower than the taller ones.

On the downbeat (fig. 16.3) the knee tends to lead with the lower leg
and extended ankle *initially* rotating in an *opposite* direction towards the
swimmer's bottom. It is the subsequent rapid contraction of the quadriceps group of muscles which moves the leg swiftly downwards, the
extended foot acting rather like a flipper, the generated water pressure
acting on the instep tending to press the foot backwards. Let the water
bend the knees: this instruction helps produce the *initially* controlled but
relaxed rotation of the lower leg on the downbeat.

It can easily be seen why a swimmer's legs should not be kept rigid
during this vertical type of kick. Knee extension or leg stiffness during the
initial downbeat would prevent any propulsive forces being generated at
all; indeed they would tend to be directed forward rather than backward.

It is also obvious that a proportion of the thrust created on the downbeat is directed downwards, elevating the hips and maintaining the
swimmer's body in the horizontal and flat mode.

A high rate of leg kicking demands a considerable amount of muscular
energy. Consequently, the circulatory system is required to channel more
blood into the massive leg muscles than it normally would, because of the
greater oxygen usage. This use of blood and oxygen is detrimental to the
muscles which move the more efficient arms. The legs themselves are

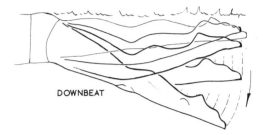

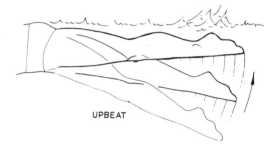

Fig. 16.3 The front-crawl leg action

heavy in relation to the arms, and the rapid accelerating and decelerating movement of such large masses against the generated water pressure is exhausting for even the fittest of swimmers. The frequency of leg kick usually varies between two and six beats per complete arm cycle, depending on the swimmer's technique and the distance being swum. Generally, the leg kicks are more frequent and deeper over shorter distances. There may also be a decrease in the depth of kick, which in turn gives the appearance of a leg 'flutter'. The middle- and longer-distance techniques tend to economise in energy by maintaining a shallow leg movement, say to 300 mm (12 in.), and at the same time decrease the rate to perhaps a two-beat action. There is, however, no reason why the two-beat kick should not be used in the sprints and the higher-rate kick used in the longer distances, provided that in each case they perform their designated tasks efficiently and correctly.

It is generally accepted that a swimmer who produces a 100-m time of about sixty-seven seconds uses his leg kick with reasonable effectiveness. However, at faster speeds, the legs tend to play less part in the propulsion and tend to create drag. This is like hanging on to a fast-moving motor boat and kicking the legs to make it go faster: no matter how quickly the legs were moved they would not increase the boat speed but could well reduce it by creating more drag.

Stroke balance may be partially achieved by the application of the Newtonian action/reaction law previously described. For instance, a downward action of the right arm has a lifting reaction tending to raise the swimmer's front end and sink his legs. However, if at the same time as this arm movement the left leg is acting downwards, the reaction is to lift the left hip, thus counterbalancing the depression of the legs. Generally, the effect of the leg action in maintaining balance can be seen more readily when the legs are not being used and supported by some suitable training aid. The movement of the arms will tend to contort a swimmer's body in many ways, as they perform their stroke cycle with no accompanying leg reaction to balance out the propulsive forces that are set up.

Thus, when body streamlining and stroke balance has been achieved, if there is enough propulsion to overcome the inherent drag characteristics of the legs themselves, the leg action may be termed effective. If further propulsion can be gained without undue exhaustion, the action may be termed efficient and economic.

Arm action

The arm action is predominant and produces by far the most propulsion in the front crawl.

The arm cycle may be divided into two phases: the underwater propulsive part of the stroke, and the recovery which takes place over the water surface. The action is continuous and alternating, with one arm moving under the swimmer to create propulsion while the other recovers over the water to the start or entry position.

In order to analyse each individual part of the propulsion and recovery actions, the whole movement has been broken down as follows (fig. 16.4):

PROPULSIVE PHASE	RECOVERY PHASE
catch	release
pull	recovery over the water
push	entry

Propulsive phase: catch

The catch may be justifiably described as the foundation of the propulsive phase of the stroke. As soon as the hand has entered the water and moved below the surface, the catch commences. By a constant speed or an accelerating downward and backward movement, water pressure is created on the hand and lower arm and the swimmer begins to 'feel' the water. For maximum effect, the fingers should be together (or almost together), the hand flat and the wrist very slightly flexed (see chapter 6). The depth of movement required to create the desired pressure is usually about 300 mm (12 in.). The fingertips should be directly in line with the vertical central plane of the swimmer's body. At the entry stage, the elbow should be slightly higher than the hand and it should remain so during the catch. The propulsive pressure on the palm of the hand and lower arm may be established by the speed of movement at entry.

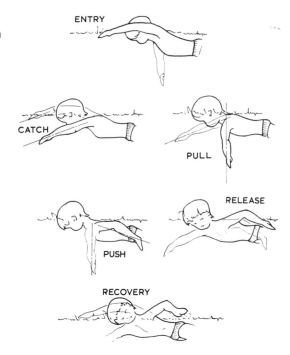

Fig. 16.4 The front-crawl arm action

However, it is not desirable that the entering hand crashes into the water, thus creating excessive turbulence and drag.

The catch movement is therefore an *accelerating* movement following a *controlled* entry.

Propulsive phase: pull

The arm pull follows on from the catch and continues until the pulling hand and arm lie in the same lateral plane as the shoulder.

Arm propulsion, in the true sense of the word, can only take place when there is sufficient pressure created on the propelling surfaces of the hand and lower arm to sustain swimming speed. This propulsive pressure is dependent on the speed of the arm movement in relation to that of the water. This means that if the swimmer is travelling at V metres/second, his propelling arm must be moving at something more than V metres/second in the opposite direction in order that the propulsive pressure is maintained.

If the swimmer is not accelerating (i.e. he is moving at a constant speed), the pressure build-up on his hand and arm must be sufficient to overcome all the various forms of drag created by the water. If he increases his speed, he must overcome these drag forces and also the inertia of his body. The increase of propulsive power must be developed by an even faster stroking rate.

There is one other point worth mentioning here: if the arms move too quickly through the water, excessive eddies are set up in the wake of the limb movement, thus reducing the effective power. This may be termed *over-pulling* or *slipping*. So the optimum speed of the arm throughout the pull must be found by good and knowledgeable teaching and by the swimmers themselves appreciating the 'feel' of the water. ('Feel' of the water is very difficult to define and it is only by personally 'stroking and caressing' the water that the teacher can begin to experience this phenomenon.)

During the pull, the palm of the hand should be facing, as near as possible, immediately backward, thus directing the propulsive forces in the most advantageous manner. The fingers must be together, or almost together, and the hand itself should be flat. To establish this backward-facing palm, the wrist will initially need to be slightly flexed and, in order to achieve a good purchase on the water, the elbow should also be flexed and remain elevated above the hand. Excessive bending of the elbow brings the hand nearer to the swimmer's body and, while the pull is mechanically easier owing to the shorter lever arm (over-pulling can take place easily here), it is less effective. A weak-shouldered swimmer may make things easier (but less effective) for himself by, amongst other things, pulling close to the chest.

The fingers are positioned so that they move in the vertical and central plane of the body. Excessive movement of the hand across this central plane in either direction tends to introduce longitudinal body rotation and increase profile drag.

Lateral body roll begins towards the start of the pull and reaches its maximum as the hand and arm pass through the shoulder plane.

Propulsive phase: push
Transition between the pull and the push should be smooth and unnoticeable; it takes place at the shoulder plane. At this phase change-over, the fingers lie approximately in the central body plane and the arm is flexed at the elbow. The hand faces directly back and lies in line with the forearm. As the arm moves, for the first time in the underwater part of the stroke, the hand leads the elbow. Extension of the wrist ensures that the palm continues to face towards the feet. As the hand approaches the waist line, it starts to track outwards and upwards until, at almost full rearward extension, the hand lies very close to the hip and in line with the forearm.

The body will now be rolling to the opposite side to facilitate lifting of the hand from the water in preparation for the recovery phase of the arm cycle.

Recovery phase: release
Arm recovery takes place as soon as the catch/pull/push phases are complete. In order to commence the movement, the hand and arm need

to be lifted or 'released' from the water. This action takes place while the body is rolled to the opposite side, and the elbow precedes the hand on leaving the water.

If the push phase has been carried out correctly, the hand will be close to the hip or the top of the thigh when release takes place. If a shortened version of the push has taken place, the hand will probably leave the water in the region of the waist. This is a very common fault in learners, and indeed in more adroit swimmers when they begin to tire.

As the release takes place, the hand should be close to the body and relatively relaxed, the little finger is usually the first to emerge and the hand lies in line with the forearm. As soon as it is free from the water, the arm has to be recovered over the water to the entry position in preparation for the next underwater part of the cycle.

Recovery phase: recovery over the water
A recovery action, by its very nature, does not contribute towards propulsion. If it is carried out incorrectly, the movement can be detrimental to the swimmer's overall performance. It is therefore essential that recovery technique is not neglected, and that a smooth, efficient and comfortable movement is established at an early stage of the stroke development.

The swimmer's shoulder flexibility will probably be the paramount factor affecting his arm recovery. Should the 'rotational freedom' of the shoulder joint be great, the swimmer will be able to achieve the desired elbow-high and hand-low swinging trajectory, with little body roll (fig. 16.5). A 'tight-shouldered' individual, however, will need to roll further, but not necessarily excessively, in order to maintain a high elbow action while at the same time just clearing the water with his hand. The hand trajectory will more than likely be a wide sweeping one.

Fig. 16.5 The elevation of the elbow just prior to entry during the front-crawl arm recovery

Muscular energy is needed to lift the arm from the water and set it in motion then, once sufficient speed is achieved, the anterior shoulder muscles may be partially relaxed and allow the limb to swing, under its own momentum and a little guidance, into the re-entry position. This partial muscle activity thus allows a controlled but relaxed arm recovery movement to take place.

The hand traces a path just above the water surface, moving in an arc about the shoulder joint. The wrist and finger joints are relaxed. At the points of release and (re-)entry, the elbow is slightly flexed. This angle of flexion varies during the arm movement and reaches a maximum (approximately ninety degrees) as the arm and hand pass simultaneously through the plane of the shoulder.

It is not uncommon to see a competition swimmer recovering his or her arms with no elbow flexion whatsoever. In this method, the hand, being further from the source of rotation, i.e. shoulder joint, has to travel further than it would if the elbow were bent; the path of the hand is often elevated above that of the elbow. This usually means that the speed of the hand is faster than it would be in the conventional bent-arm type of recovery, and that consequently there is less control over the movement; the hand thus crashes into the water creating unnecessary commotion, and may sometimes enter the water on the wrong side of the central body plane. The effect of this crossed-over entry action is to bend the swimmer into a banana shape as he swims: this of course increases the drag and interferes with the definite and smooth rhythm which the swimmer is attempting to establish.

The higher rotational speed of the arm also generates a greater centrifugal force, which is proportional to the rotational arm speed (squared). This force acts directly along the axis of the arm and away from the swimmer, tending to pull his shoulders in the direction of the hand. Excessive rotational speeds also necessitate high acceleration which in turn introduces unwanted inertia forces which tend to contort and retard the swimmer.

Recovery phase: entry
The hand enters the water finger tips first and forward of the shoulders in a controlled mode. The lateral* point of entry lies between the central body plane and a parallel plane passing through the shoulder joint. The fingers should be together, or almost together, and the hand flat; there should also be slight flexion of the wrist. The elbow should also be flexed and elevated a little higher than the hand, in order to achieve this finger tips-first entry.

---

* Lateral is defined as 'across the body', as opposed to axial which signifies 'along the length of the body'.

The high-elbow/low-hand entry has several important advantages. Firstly, an elbow-first entry would create excessive wave drag. Secondly, it establishes the hand and arm position in preparation for the subsequent catch phase. Thirdly, the flexed elbow helps to reduce the tendency for the swimmer to over-reach. This fault has an adverse effect on the deltoid-dominated muscular action, by increasing the effective radius from the shoulder joint to the centre of (propulsive) pressure. The swimmer may not be strong enough to cope with this extra leverage and may tire quickly.

Entering the hand laterally outside or across the desired entry point (or area) can have the effect that the subsequent catch and pull movements rotate the swimmer across the line of progress.

This concludes the description of a single arm cycle. The opposite arm moves in a similar fashion to that described above, but as one arm propels, the other recovers. The whole action may be described as alternating and continuous.

Hand trajectory
When viewed from directly below, the complete pattern of arm movement may be similar to that shown in fig. 16.6. The trajectory of the hand during the propulsive phase usually takes the shape of an elongated S or ogee. However, its path of movement may be affected by the degree of lateral roll of the swimmer's body beyond or away from the central plane.

Fig. 16.6 A typical front-crawl hand trajectory

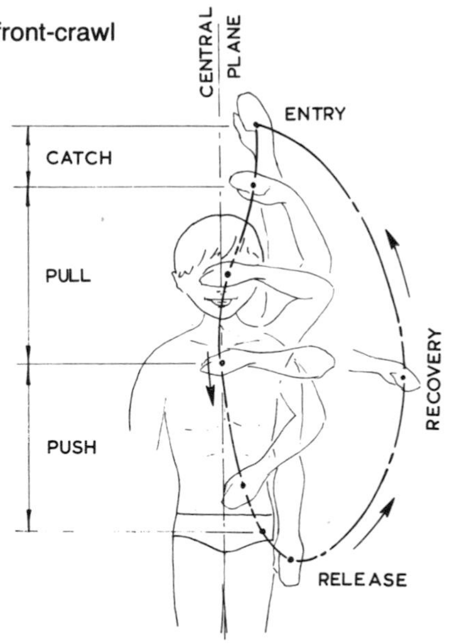

Breathing

Breathing movements should be carried out in such a way that they blend rather than interfere with the general stroke pattern. It is better to let the stroke technique dictate the breathing pattern rather than vice versa.

A breath is taken on the arm-recovery side as the swimmer's head is rotated in the same direction as the body roll, thus enabling him or her to inhale as the mouth clears the water.

Assisting the inhalation sequence is the fact that, due to the water speed, the swimmer sets up a bow wave around his head. This in turn creates a 'breathing trough' around the face and reduces the amount of head rotation that is necessary in order to snatch a quick breath.

As soon as air has been inhaled, the face returns to the water and, at the same time, the recovery arm swings around towards the entry point. The head now resumes its approximate hair-line/water-line relationship in preparation for the breathing-out process.

As the swimmer's body rotates in the opposite direction to that of the breathing side, the head may roll smoothly with it or remain facing forward and downward.

Methods of breathing out into the water and the associated timings are many and varied. Probably that which has least effect on the stroke technique is 'breath holding', whereby the complete air intake is retained for a short period before exhalation takes place explosively into the water in preparation for the next breath.

This particular method is often used during short swims up to, say, 100 m, but is not advised for the untrained swimmer for longer distances as it becomes rather exhausting after a while. Constant training in breath holding is reputed to increase the blood-capillary network and enable competition swimmers to hold their breath for long periods during racing swims, without apparent ill effects.

Exhalation into the water may be of the trickle or explosive pattern, taking place through the nose and/or mouth. *Trickle* exhalation through the nose only is probably the best method during a slow or medium-paced swim. During a sprint or rapid-arm-cycling swim the *explosive* method of exhalation will most likely be the favourite. Here, breathing out should take place just prior to the face leaving the water in order to snatch the next intake of air.

Whichever method is adopted, it is always good practice when learning to allow a slight trickle of air to escape from the nose as it passes through the water surface. This prevents water droplets finding their way to the back of the throat, causing coughing and spluttering.

A breathing technique may be used whereby the swimmer takes a breath at every stroke or every other stroke, etc., *on the same side* (unilateral). Alternatively, the swimmer can take a breath on *alternate sides* (bilateral technique) every one and a half arm cycles. The trickle or explosive technique may be used with either of these methods.

It is advisable for the learner swimmer to adopt regular breathing patterns during his initial swims. These patterns should fit in unobtrusively with the overall technique to produce a natural and even rhythm.

Air must always be taken into the lungs whenever it is needed; the breathing rhythm should accommodate this. Excessive breath-holding is not advisable for the untrained as it tends to starve the lungs of oxygen and leads very quickly to fatigue. (Learner swimmers tire very quickly, and this is usually the main cause of their tiredness.) Also, if the breath is held, the breathing muscles themselves are tensed, thus requiring more oxygen than usual.

The nearer the swimmer can come to the track athlete in his breathing technique, the better. The runner is able to take a breath at the rate that he needs it. The swimmer should endeavour, as far as possible, to do the same.

Co-ordination

Co-ordination and stroke rhythm should develop naturally with practice. Early teaching faults are usually associated with the breathing technique.

To create a balanced and even stroke, the swimmer's legs must move in such a way as to react against any out-of-balance forces created by the arms during propulsion and recovery.

A rhythmic leg beat of six kicks per complete arm cycle produces good stroke-balancing characteristics. Using this timing, the swimmer is able to co-ordinate his limb movements to produce counter-balancing forces which maintain his body in a reasonable state of equilibrium.

The four-beat rhythm also provides reasonable stroke stabilisation, but, with the decrease in frequency, the amplitude of the kick may need to be increased.

The two-beat or cross-over rhythm is a pure stabiliser, being used mainly in distance swimming. Here, each complete arm cycle is accompanied by one beat from each leg. The leg movement is usually accompanied by a synchronised body roll and this results in the kick being biased towards the horizontal rather than the vertical plane.

The results of good stroke co-ordination are immediately apparent to the onlooker, but the smoothness of a swimmer's performance may be affected by speed. For instance, he may display jerky stroke movements at the lower end of his speed range but, as he increases his stroke rate, the whole movement evens out into a flowing rhythm.

Early teachings are best directed toward the six-beat rhythm with any special adjustments in technique and timing being left until later, should the swimmer decide to take up the sport in a competitive way.

Fig. 16.7 The stroke diagrams

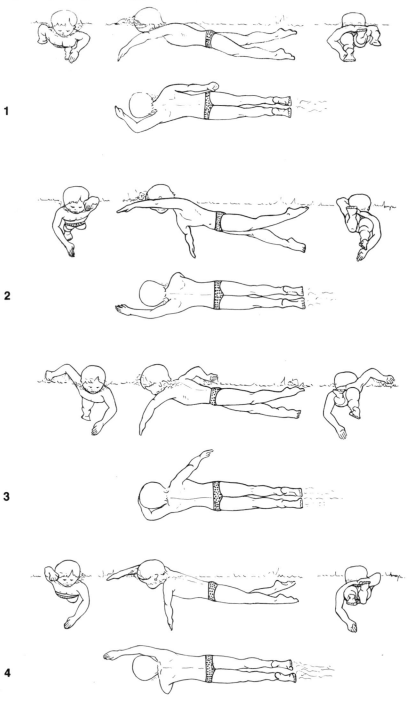

1

2

3

4

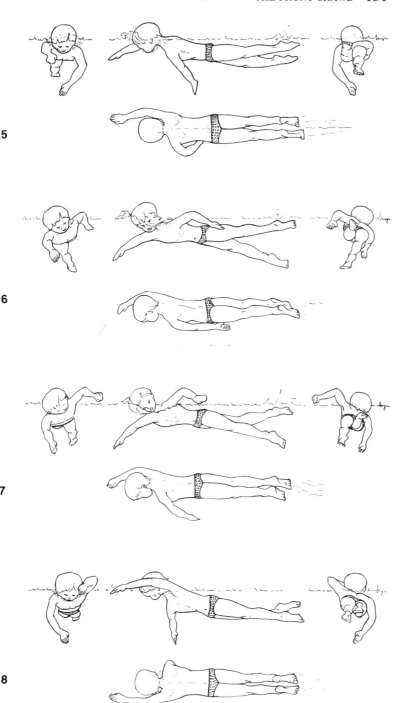

5

6

7

8

Teaching the competition strokes

Each feature of the competition strokes has been analysed and systematically broken down into what is considered a logical sequence of teaching progressions or part-practices. The teacher may not wish to use the sequences of activities exactly as they are presented. However, it is not advisable to omit too many of the progressions, otherwise the continuity of learning may be lost. On the other hand, the teacher may find his own favourite activities have been omitted from the series: if their inclusion is justified by their usefulness, by all means add such activities to the overall programme.

Each set of stroke-related practices has been presented in a continuous form, but in fact, with only a certain amount of lesson time available, the individual activities will need to be sub-divided and integrated into a sequence of lesson plans.

An important feature in teaching the activities is *repetition*. In the majority of instances it is only after returning to the part-practices many times that a particular movement or combination of movements establishes itself among the swimmers. As a teacher, never be reluctant to step backwards; it is not necessarily a backward step.

Preparatory standards for teaching front crawl

Before commencing the following programme of front-crawl practices, it is advisable that the pupils are able to perform the following activities with a degree of skill:

1. Confidence exercises – face-wetting, blowing bubbles and submersion. (The swimmers are bound to get their faces wet)
2. Regaining the feet from a prone position (should the shallow-end swimmers wish to stand up part-way across)
3. Push and glide from the poolside (for starting off)
4. Front paddle for at least twenty metres (as an introduction to elementary prone swimming)
5. Treading water (should the deep-end swimmers need to stop for any reason at any time)
6. General water-mobility exercises (swimmers may have to move sideways to avoid others; also they may have to stop and then start swimming once more)

TEACHING THE FRONT CRAWL

There will be few pupils in the average class who have not watched some variation of the front crawl stroke being performed. They may, of course, know it by some other name, such as the 'overarm' stroke, or describe it, sometimes quite picturesquely, by gesticulating their arms wildly. However, probably *none* of the pupils will have had the stroke technique actually demonstrated to them.

If an able performer can be found for the occasion, an excellent way to start the first front-crawl lesson is by staging such a demonstration.

Activity: demonstration swim with commentary
This visual approach has already been mentioned earlier and it will be found to be invaluable in the teaching of any stroke. A return to such demonstration of full- or part-stroke techniques is well worth consideration at any time. The demonstration swim need only be of short duration, with the pupils gathered around the poolside so that they have a good view and can at the same time see and hear the teacher without averting their eyes too far from the swimmer.

A simple descriptive text should be used without too many long words and technicalities, bearing in mind the ages of the pupils involved and also how much they are able to absorb at any one time.

Explanation may take the form of a description of the swimmer's body position in the water, followed by the main features of the leg action. The arm movement may be divided into two stages, namely the pull (underwater phase) and the recovery (over-water phase, including the entry).

A brief mention of the breathing technique may be made, pointing out that the swimmer is breathing out into the water. It is worth noting at this stage that probably the greatest hurdle that the pupils will have to overcome in learning the stroke is the breathing technique. The breathing-in phase of the sequence is precise and exhaling into the water is unnatural, so in order to get full concentration on style, it is advisable that initial full-stroke practices are carried out with the breath being held for short durations. (Most pupils will do this, whatever instructions they receive.) These early practices may take the form of short swims across the pool with the swimmer's head held in such a way that the face is immersed and the water line is approximately at the natural hair line.

The head position may be described as looking forward and slightly downwards. The early swims in this attitude will help to establish the desired horizontal position and at the same time provide a good foundation for future stroke work.

At the end of the demonstration, question time should be kept to a minimum. This is not usually difficult because the pupils are usually eager to have a go.

Having shown the pupils the stroke being performed and explained something about its technique, full-lesson participation may now commence.

Activity: initial full-stroke swims (fig. 16.8, overleaf)
Without any further instruction, the class now have the chance to demonstrate their skills, such as they are, by swimming a short, pre-determined

distance under the watchful, and not too critical, eye of the teacher. A short dash back and forth across the pool will enable the teacher to assess the task in hand and give the class an opportunity for a warm-up.

Fig. 16.8

TEACHING POINTS

1. Achievement of the correct head posture is a very important feature of the stroke practices. The water line should be approximately at the swimmer's natural hair line, taking account of individual physical characteristics. Excessive lifting of the head in fear, or for any other reason, tends to elevate the chest and sink the legs, thus making it difficult for the swimmer to maintain the desired horizontal mode. In their depressed attitude, the legs tend to lose their rhythm and a regular kick becomes more difficult to achieve. A pedalling action is a common result, and this in turn of course does not lift the legs or propel the swimmer forward.

Countering the effect of the 'head-up' attitude may be carried out by a vigorous leg movement. This is very exhausting, and for novices and weak swimmers almost impossible. Waterpolo players swim in this position in order to observe the field of play. It takes, however, many hours of exhaustive practice to achieve a successful performance of this special head-up technique.

2. The legs must be elevated to provide lateral body stabilisation. An even rhythm in the leg beat provides the reactive balancing effect to the arm action. Uneven rhythm results, for instance, in excessive body roll to one side. If the swimmer's leg action gives propulsion at this stage, this is a bonus.

3. High elbow recovery and entry.

4. Continuity of the stroke movement is very important and is dependent on many inter-related factors within the stroke technique. At this early stage of learning it is advisable not to spend too much time endeavouring to correct faults in the overall technique, but rather to proceed to part-stroke practices and concentrate on obtaining good results there before returning to the full stroke.

Activity: leg action
When performing prone leg practices, pupils will often turn their heads and try to look behind them in order to see how their legs are shaping up.

If they can actually see how their arms or legs are performing it invariably assists in achieving the required result.

Practice 1: sitting on the poolside and kicking the legs (fig. 16.9)

Fig. 16.9

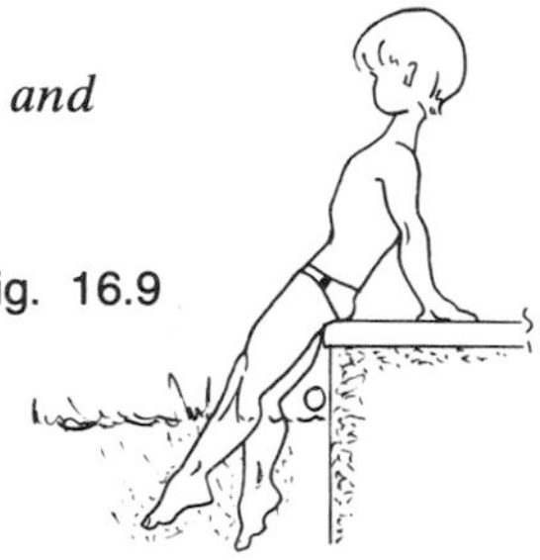

TEACHING POINTS

1. The kick is an alternating leg action.

2. The leg movement originates from the hip. Leg propulsion is based on the techniques described earlier in this chapter and it is essential that this hip-generated kick is emphasised right from the start of the practices.

3. The legs should be close together (in the lateral plane). This is more of a physical advantage than a hydrodynamic one. Spreading the legs unnecessarily brings into action the lateral leg-muscle groups not normally used in this action.

4. The kicking depth should be not more than 450 mm (18 in.). The depth of kick has a direct bearing on the rate of the leg beat. If the kick is deep, the mechanics of the action dictate that the rate of movement is slower.

5. Relaxation of the knee joint enables the whip-like movement, which produces the major part of the leg propulsion, to take place on the downbeat. (In this particular exercise the whip is on the upbeat.)

6. Relaxed ankles ('floppy feet') with 'toeing-in' is important. By relaxing the ankles, some people are able to shake their feet about quite loosely. The 'toeing-in' of the feet is, for some people, a natural physical attribute; for others this foot position has to be cultivated. The reason for 'toeing-in' is that it increases the effective propulsive area of each foot.

7. A smooth action. The whole leg action should flow smoothly, although without the resistive effects of the water to moderate the movements slightly, this land-based exercise may be jerky. Tensing the joints will also tend to produce incorrect movements and hasten the onset of fatigue. Cramp may even set in at this stage.

8. Good rhythm and timing. The timing should be regular with the teacher setting the pace by counting, say, a six-beat pattern: one-two-three/one-two-three, and so on. The six-beat rhythm will probably be the best one to use during the teaching of the stroke.

Practice 2: poolside rail-supported leg kicking
The pupils are in the water holding the handrail or channel to continue the kicking practices. This exercise may be a revisionary one from the earlier front-paddle teachings but, as this is not always so, the lesson is presented here as being for the first time. Perhaps a little more finesse will be accomplished on this occasion.

The method of holding on to the rail or channel will probably need a short explanation. Some learners find difficulty in raising their legs to the surface while holding the rail or channel; others use their natural buoyancy and kicking ability to elevate themselves quite easily. If they are using a handrail the pupils can undergrasp it and press their elbows to the wall; the lever action raises their outstretched bodies and legs to the surface (fig. 16.10). A certain amount of control is needed in order to keep the legs in the water when the kicking exercise commences. A slight relaxation at the elbow joint will lower the legs if they rise too high.

Where only a channel exists around the pool, there is another holding method which may be employed. Holding the channel with one hand, the child places the palm of the other hand, with fingers pointing downwards, flat on the wall; both arms should be reasonably straight. Then, by pushing with the lower hand, the outstretched body and legs will rise to the surface (fig. 16.11). The position on the wall of the pushing hand is important. For instance, if a pupil holds the channel with his right hand and places the left hand flat on the wall and too far to the left, his body will swing round to the right. Conversely, if the left hand is too far to the right the pupil's outstretched body will veer round to the left. By carefully positioning the hand under water, however, a happy medium can be found that aligns the swimmer correctly.

The exercise has a limited value because without the freedom of forward movement it is difficult to judge the efficiency of the leg action. It does however enable the teacher to talk to the pupils and attempt to make adjustments to their various techniques, while they are static and can see and hear him easily.

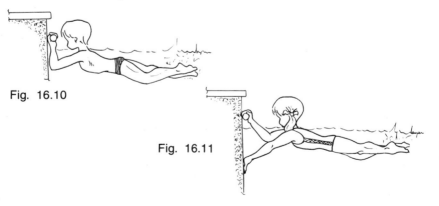

Fig. 16.10

Fig. 16.11

All the teaching points given for the first exercise are relevant here, together with the following:

9. The feet must be kept in the water at all times, with the heel in the uppermost part of the kick just breaking the surface.

Practice 3: leg kicking using floats (figs 16.12 and 16.13)
The exercise enables the pupils to become mobile in the water by using floats. A pair of these are tucked one under each arm, or, where a single float is used, it is held in the hands with the arms fully outstretched in front. The movement shows immediately whether the pupils possess anything resembling a propulsive technique.

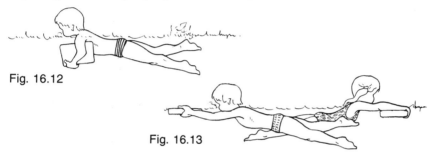

Fig. 16.12

Fig. 16.13

The afore-mentioned teaching points are all applicable to this exercise, and the following should now be added:

10. The pupils should once more be shown how to use two floats, by tucking them under the arms and grasping them firmly on the long sides, or one float which is grasped in the centre with thumbs on the top and fingers underneath. Alternatively, they may rest their forearms over the top of the float and curl their fingers over the end, the water lifting the float up against the forearms. When swimming with one float, arms must be kept fully stretched in front, with the float riding flat on the water surface. If a float is brought in close to the body by bending the arms, the swimmer tends to lean on it and force it below the surface, rendering it less effective.

Practice 4: fully stretched kicking (fig. 16.14)
This is a leg-kicking exercise carried out in the fully stretched position with the face in the water. The water line should be at the hair line and the breath is held while width practices are carried out. With this exercise we have now reached the true flat and horizontal swimming attitude which should be emphasised strongly.

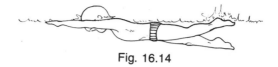

Fig. 16.14

The teaching points have all previously been mentioned, except that of maintaining a fully stretched and streamlined position, and also the following:

11. The swimmers should be shown the method of head lifting and breathing, should they not be able to hold their breath for a full width.

Activity: breathing
Practice 1: standing in the shallow end of the pool near the side and holding the rail (fig. 16.15)

Fig. 16.15

The main aim of this first breathing exercise is to give the swimmers enough confidence to put their faces in the water – then breathe out. Some of the pupils may have performed this exercise at an earlier stage and for them this is a recapitulation, but, for others, the practices may be completely new.

The most troublesome and off-putting part of this early exercise is when water is allowed to enter the nasal passages during exhalation. The results can be distressing and sometimes painful. Let us, therefore by careful coice of practices, attempt to minimise the coughing and splutterings which can take place. Working on the theory that, if air is flowing down the nose, water cannot be going up it, the pupils are instructed to hold the rail, take a breath through the mouth (not too deep), then place their faces in the water and gently trickle the air out through their noses. (Turning the head in order to inhale at this stage is not important, so the pupils may simply lower their faces into the water in a straightforward fashion.) The important feature to emphasise here is that nasal breathing must continue as the face leaves the water. If the children all adhere to this simple instruction there will be minimal distress.

Rubbing the water from the eyes will probably be common practice during these early breathing exercises. The teacher should attempt to discourage this as the lesson progresses.

The exercise should be continued until the pupils are able to repeat this face-ducking movement several times. The teacher should look for complete face submersion and the tell-tale sign of bubbles surfacing around the ears.

Variations in the methods of breathing out into the water may now be introduced. A straightforward nodding action rather than turning the head can still be used.

The pupils may experiment with a nose-and-mouth and a mouth-only trickle exhalation with the accent on breath control. If trouble with water ingress ino the nasal passages during the latter exercise is experienced, the pupils should return to nose-only or nose-and-mouth breathing until they have learned to control their respiration.

Sprint swimming necessitates an explosive delivery of air into the water, so the pupils may now try this method of breathing out. They should take a breath, then place their faces into the water and quickly exhale through mouth and nose. A short pause between the submersion and explosion relates the movement to actually swimming the sprint front crawl stroke. (A brief mention of this fact can motivate the class into greater effort and stimulate imaginations.) As soon as the air is expired, or at the 'tail end' of the blow, faces are lifted clear of the water in preparation for the next intake.

After a short while, the pupils will probably have acquired some skill in submersive breathing, and may now proceed to the next series of exercises. These relate not only to the methods of breathing out into the water, but also to the technique of inhalation.

During the performance of the front crawl stroke, the swimmer's face is turned to one side to enable a breath to be taken, and this is brought about by rotating the head. Therefore, we should now introduce head rotation, rather than head lifting, into the breathing cycle.

The pupils hold the rail and stand in the same way as in the previous exercises; they then place their faces into the water and breathe out by a method that may be stipulated by the teacher or be left to each individual pupil's discretion. In order to take the next breath, the pupils rotate their heads until their mouths are just clear of the water for a gasp of air to be taken. As soon as inhalation has taken place, they return their faces into the waer and then breathe out. A breathing rhythm may now be established as the exercise is repeated.

Turning the head to breathe while static is slightly different from inhaling while moving through the water with reasonable speed. The forward motion tends to create a bow wave around the head, and it is in the trough formed by the wave that the swimmer inhales. There is therefore no need for the head to be rotated quite so far when swimming.

Emphasis on the head position should, at this stage, be brought into the teaching. The water line should be approximately at the hair line and, if the eyes were open, they would be looking forward and downward at about thirty degrees.

A development in the practices is for the pupil to withdraw the arm which is on the 'breathing side' away from the hand rail and place it down by his side. This allows more freedom for the head roll to take place and may accommodate a slight shoulder roll, thus bringing the movement nearer to that of actually swimming. Care must be taken, however, to ensure that the head still rotates in relation to the shoulders and not, in a stiff-necked fashion, with them.

A further practice may be employed, whereby the pupils are encouraged to breathe in on the opposite side to their first choice. This introduces a bi-lateral quality into the sequence and may be related to competition swimming.

TEACHING POINTS

1. The breath must be taken in through the mouth and exhaled through the nose and/or the mouth.

2. The water line should be at the natural hair line during the exhalation phase of the cycle.

3. The head must be rotated and not lifted.

4. If trouble with the ingress of water into the nasal passages is experienced, the technique of breathing out through the nose as the face breaks the surface should be emphasised.

5. Rubbing the eyes after submersion must be discouraged as this is impractical when actually swimming.

Fear of putting one's face in the water is quite common and, should the teacher encounter such inhibitions among members of the class, due consideration must be shown and the teachings adjusted accordingly. It takes considerable courage for anyone with this type of phobia to submerge his face in the water and even more to breathe out while still there. It must be further understood that some individuals *never* overcome this fear, and it is therefore advisable not to enforce these practices on a pupil who is genuinely frightened of immersing the whole of his face. Instead, treat the whole matter lightly; encourage him, for instance, to take a warm shower and look up at the stream of water as it cascades down, or tell him to try blowing bubbles in the sink at home; the security of a warm bath at home could also be a good place to attempt the exercise.

Tne final point: as the practices develop, suggest opening the eyes in the water. Encourage this, but again do not enforce it. Some pupils find no difficulty in looking around under the surface, while others may be affected by the water additives and end up with sore eyes. As time progresses and games are played, most young people will learn to put their faces in the water in order to see something or other and will probably breathe out during the process, and difficulties which may have arisen earlier will gradually disappear.

The previous set of exercises has been carried out in a static manner; we now attempt to integrate the breathing pattern with the leg action and, in doing so, re-introduce some mobility into the programme.

Practice 2: float-assisted leg kicking

TEACHING POINTS

All the teaching points emphasised during the static practices are relevant, and the following may be added:

6. The flat horizontal swimming position should be maintained at all times. The exercise will probably display how lifting the head rather than turning it tends to sink the legs. A class demonstration of this fault, and its remedy, might be useful at this stage.

7. A regular breathing rhythm, synchronised with the leg beat, should be established. This may take the form of one breath for every four or six kicks.

If the practices have been carried out with reasonable success, the class should now be traversing the pool with confidence and be ready to proceed to the arm practices. However, should the teacher feel that a little more practice is required, he or she should persevere a little while longer.

Activity: arm action
Practice 1: standing (fig. 16.16)
The first exercise relating to the arm movement may take place while the pupils are standing in the shallow end of the pool and facing the teacher as he or she demonstrates the actions from the poolside. (The water should be approximately chest-deep.)

Fig. 16.16

1. Entry of the hand into the water must be finger tips first. The elbow should be flexed and slightly higher than the hand, which in turn must be flat with palm facing downwards.

The flexed and elevated elbow should allow the hand to enter the water at approximately thirty degrees to the horizontal. Laterally, the fingertips must enter at a point somewhere between the central plane of the body and the outside of the shoulder. This places the arm in a mechanically sound position in order to commence the pull. Over-reaching must be avoided at all costs as the fault tends to distort the swimmer's shoulders and the long axis of the body. It also places the pulling muscles at a mechanical disadvantage prior to the pull.

The excessive stretching forward of the arm also causes the elbow to drop, which in turn can result in an incorrect elbow-first entry.

2. After entry, the hand must initially move fairly rapidly so that pressure may be built up on the palm and lower arm. The technical term for this part of the stroke is the catch, and if the teacher feels he must single it out for mention, it may be described as being the point where the swimmers 'catch and feel' the water on the palms of their flat hands before pushing it back behind them. (The water is not really pushed back, of course, but the phrase is descriptive.)

3. Throughout the pull-and-push phases, the hand must not move beyond the body's central plane or wander excessively outside the width of the shoulders or hips (whichever is the wider). Moving too far away in a lateral direction from the central plane tends to introduce 'snaking' into the stroke and this causes all sorts of problems.

4. The hands should be flat and the fingers together, or almost together, at all times during the propulsive phase of the stroke.

5. The palm of the hand must face directly back towards the feet for as long as possible during the underwater phase of the cycle. This is necessary in order to ensure maximum forward propulsion throughout the full arm sweep.

6. The elbow should leave the water before the hand, and it should also be forward of the hand when this release takes place. If the reverse situation occurs, it usually means that the push phase is non-existent or that excessive body rolling is taking place.

7. The recovery hand must follow an outward-swinging arc, just clearing the waves. The elbow must be higher than the hand throughout. Straight arm recoveries have the effect of distorting the long body axis. Relaxation is the key word during recovery, which should be accompanied by a slight body roll.

8. The co-ordination between the arms seems to come automatically to young swimmers. If any description is needed, it could be something to the effect that the arms are almost opposite each other as they move. (If the teacher's demonstration has been correct and clear, there should be no doubt about this point.) Some teachers call it a windmill style but this tends to conjure up a straight arm-recovery movement in the minds of young swimmers.

9. The whole arm movement should be continuous and alternating and the shoulders must remain submerged throughout.

Practice 2: walking in shallow water
TEACHING POINTS
All the previous teaching points are relevant here, together with the point that a horizontal back position should be maintained as far as possible.

This is made somewhat difficult by the fact that the swimmers' heads are lifted. Therefore to add some breathing technique to these practices is the next step.

Practice 3: standing or walking with breathing, with or without a float (fig. 16.17)

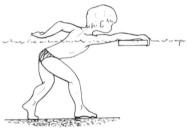

Fig. 16.17

Practice 4: float-assisted single-arm practice (fig. 16.18)
This practice is carried out with a float held by one hand in front of the swimmer, while he or she performs single-arm stroke cycles accompanied by the leg action. The movement may be performed with or without breathing and can be used both as a progression or as a corrective exercise.

Fig. 16.18

TEACHING POINTS
All teaching points previously mentioned are relevant, together with the method of holding the float.

Activity: stroke co-ordination
Dog paddle (fig. 16.19)
Most of the pupils will probably have started their swimming careers by learning front or dog paddle. (Front paddle and dog paddle are very similar movements, although the name front paddle seems to be more allied to beginner teaching.) So, having improved the leg action and body position and introduced stroke-related breathing, we may return to this simple stroke. We can also introduce into it some of the new techniques that have now been learned, thus bringing the swimmers one step nearer to the ultimate goal of front crawl.

The arm pull should be slightly modified for this new dog-paddle exercise so that it becomes longer and consequently slower than the earlier version. The recovery is still an underwater one, however, with a minimum of profile resistance. The action should also include a slight body roll in the direction of the pulling arm.

Fig. 16.19

TEACHING POINTS

1. A horizontal body position must be maintained at all times, with water-line/hair-line relationship being of paramount importance.

The less able swimmers in the class will initially try to breathe in by lifting the head as one hand presses down into the catch. This lifting action will have the effect on the legs of making them sink deeper than required and upsetting their rhythm. Continual emphasis must therefore be made on rotating rather than lifting the head in order to inhale.

A slight body roll should be integrated into the stroke; this is one of the essential features of a good front crawl and assists with the breathing technique.

2. The leg movement must be continuous, with all the previously mentioned teaching points being observed. The beat should be a shallow flutter or a six-beat pattern. This kicking rate is ideal for the long arm pull and the subsequent slow recovery.

3. The arm stroke should be a long one rather than the shortened version that was used in the earlier front-paddle practices, in order to accommodate the timing of the leg beat.

The hands should pull alternately under the swimmer's body with each palm facing directly backward for as long as possible throughout the movement.

Arm recovery is carried out under the water surface and, in order to minimise resistance during this part of the stroke, each elbow should be brought close to the body as it moves forward. Also, during this forward movement, the hands must be flat, with the finger tips pointing ahead. (The swimmer's elbow may tend to break the surface at the end of the pull: this does not really matter.)

4. Breathing methods should conform to those that were practised earlier. It is most important that the stroke rhythm and timing are not interrupted by any movement associated with respiration.

Breathing in should be accompanied by a lateral head roll and breathing out should be into the water.

The teacher must be careful not to venture into the realms of coaching. As long as the pupils have tried to carry out the various methods of breathing, it is probably best left, for the time being, to each individual to adopt his or her own technique, as long as it is reasonably correct.

5. The head should be swivelled independently of the shoulders to prevent excessive rolling to the breathing side.

Activity: full front crawl stroke
The exercises may be carried out initially as a fully integrated style, then with the pupils concentrating on a single skill at a time within the overall technique while still *performing the full stroke movement*.

This method of full-stroke teaching has the advantage that each swimmer is devoting full attention to an individual practice, but at the same time performing it in relation to all the other unique stroke factors which affect it.

Individual limb practices tend to be carried out in isolation and, as overall technique improvers, they leave much to be desired. As body exercises and muscle developers they are, of course, ideal, and are used constantly during a training programme.

They form a vital part of learning the strokes from the beginning, and are also invaluable during fault correction. However, only when the complete stroke is practised can a single stroke feature be assessed. One example of these shortcomings has already been given: the front-crawl leg practices using floats fail to introduce body roll into the movement which is, of course, an integral part of the overall stroke technique. The legs therefore do not work in the variable plane that they experience during full stroking. However, for leg and tummy muscle development, float-assisted leg practices are ideal. Similarly, with the various breathing practices carried out at the rail, the static mode does not produce the bow wave or body roll which are present during complete stroke performance, hence the head needs to be rotated further in order to inhale.

Full stoke practices may commence with short swims to the rail with the breath being held. The distance can then be gradually increased until a full width is being completed.

Breathing action may then be introduced using an infrequent pattern, i.e. one or two breaths per width, taken at will. The frequency may then be increased until the pupils are able to manage one breath per arm cycle.

The width exercises may take place in 'waves' whereby one set of swimmers takes off at the teacher's signal to follow the first set of swimmers.

If it is convenient, longer distances should be attempted by the more adroit members of the class. This gives a chance for each individual stroke to develop, although the teacher must be constantly looking for technique faults. Remember, the longer a fault is practised, the deeper it becomes integrated into the stroke, and the more difficult it is to remove.

It may be advantageous now for the class to be split yet again into ability groups, in order that more specialised instruction may be given to the less able pupils and more demanding practices performed by the more adept swimmers.

If an attending class teacher is willing and able to assist, he or she could watch over an activity that does not need specialist knowledge.

TEACHING POINTS

All the previously mentioned teaching points apply during full-stroke practices. General stroke co-ordination should be encouraged with emphasis on a smooth rhythm and regular breathing habits. The teacher must always be prepared to return to part-stroke practices in order to concentrate on one specific teaching point. Remember the earlier statement regarding individual exercises and their necessary integration into the whole stroke.

The series of exercises are meant to form the foundation for a set of lesson plans. Alteration and addition to the sequence may be necessary, according to the standard of the pupils, the time available and the environmental conditions.

Diving in and pushing off from the side are also important and can be related to general stroke technique. These points are covered in later chapters.

A comprehensive set of faults associated with the stroke, accompanied by relevant corrective practices, now follows.

FAULTS AND THEIR CORRECTION

Feature: BODY POSITION

FAULT	EFFECT ON STROKE	CORRECTION
1. Head too high caused by: (a) fear of placing face in water (b) incorrect idea of head position (fig. 16.20) (c) head lifting instead of turning to breathe	1. Chest tends to lift 2. Legs tend to drop or need to be kicked harder in order to counter the rotation 3. Slow and ponderous action or highly energetic leg kick with arched back 4. High resistance created by low legs	1. Shallow-water breathing practices 2. Supine push-and-glide practices in order to attain correct head position 3. Full- or part-stroke practices with no breathing; concentration on water-line/hair-line relationship 4. Sufficient leg movement to keep legs to the surface 5. Resort to full-stroke practices by introducing and increasing frequency of breathing 6. Practise blowing bubbles in sink or bath at home
2. Head too low	1. Shoulders tend to bunch during recovery 2. Breathing rather difficult	All practices as before
3. Excessive body roll caused by: (a) Over-reaching, or could be *result* of over-reaching (b) Too-high recovery (c) Excessive head turn to breathe (fig. 16.21) (d) Stiff neck – hence head and body turn together (e) Pulling too deeply	1. If roll is one-sided, which is usual, uneven stroke rhythm 2. Leg rhythm may be affected; usually accompanied by a rhythmic 'thump' at every arm cycle	1. Full-stroke practices with no breathing 2. Introduce breathing by requesting a snatched intake by *head rotation*, followed by an immediate face back into water movement 3. Breathing on the opposite side to the roll 4. The individual faults are all covered in other stroke phases
4. Snaking, caused by wide fast arm-recovery movements	Body distorts in 'banana' fashion when viewed from above	Arm-recovery fault section covers this problem

Feature: LEG ACTION

FAULT	EFFECT ON STROKE	CORRECTION
1. Too deep	1. Can cause excessive profile drag 2. Energy expenditure high – very tiring	1. Aim for shallower beat by speeding up kicking rate 2. Float-assisted exercises and full-stroke movement

Fig. 16.20 Fault: head too high

Fig. 16.21 Fault: excessive turning of the head in order to breathe. Note how the swimmer has rolled too far to the right, introducing an element of over-reaching with the right arm

| 2. Straight leg movement (no knee bend) | 1. Reduced propulsion due to backward thrust developed on upbeat only
2. Muscular energy wastage due to lack of relaxation | 1. Float kicking with *relaxed* knee and ankle joints
2. Emphasise the importance of the knee leading the foot initially on the downbeat |
| 3. Kicking from knee instead of hip | Reduced propulsion | 1. Legs-only practices with floats
2. Emphasis on kicking basically from the hip, with relaxed knees and ankles |

FAULT	EFFECT ON STROKE	CORRECTION
4. Flutter-kicking (a shallow fast beat)	1. Provides stability (not a fault) 2. Creates limited prpulsion 3. Usually accompanied by energy-wasting splash 4. Elevates body (not a fault)	1. Emphasis on trying to get propulsion from leg kick by kicking deeper 2. Legs-only practices with floats where effectiveness of kick may be assessed
5. Legs and feet leaving the water at the end of upbeat	1. Excessive splash. (Some degree of splash or water disturbance is inevitable, but must be minimal) 2. Turbulence which is caused resists propulsion 3. Wasted energy in creating the splash	1. Emphasis on kicking from the hip 2. Reduce kicking rate 3. Lift head slightly in order to submerge legs slightly 4. Straight legs throughout the upbeat
6. Maintaining stiff ankle joints	Reduced propulsion	Legs-only float practices, emphasis on relaxed ankles ('floppy feet')
7. Alternating beat completely abandoned in favour of a hybrid breast side-stroke kick: non-appreciation of leg action	1. Reduced propulsion 2. Interference with a smooth rhythm 3. Aesthetically wrong	1. Plenty of legs-only float practices 2. Full-stroke practices in fast, short sprints

Feature: ARM ACTION
Phase: ENTRY

FAULT	EFFECT ON STROKE	CORRECTION
1. Too wide or too narrow	1. Propulsive force tends to divert swimmer from intended direction 2. Decreased muscular advantage 3. Interference with the natural roll of the swimmer	1. Direct hand(s) towards space between shoulders 2. Over-correction may be of use: if entry is too wide, swimmer attempts to 'cross-over'; if there is 'cross-over', a wide entry should be attempted
2. Too far forward (over-reaching)	1. Elevates shoulder girdle excessively; puts pulling muscles at mechanical disadvantage 2. Disturbs natural stroke rhythm 3. Excessive rolling	1. Attempt entry in elbow-high and slightly flexed mode 2. Over-correction: swimmer attempts the entry too near to the face

3. Too near the face (glide entry)	Forward motion of hand and arm creates unnecessary resistance	1. Attempt entry in elbow-high and slightly flexed mode 2. Over-correction: swimmer attempts to over-reach
4. Hand slap	1. Waste of energy 2. Creation of waves 3. Setting up of resistive and turbulent underwater conditions	1. Controlled entry with elevated elbow, forearm and hand approximately in line and slightly inclined to water surface 2. Slow recovery down slightly
5. Wrist excessively flexed (right-angles to forearm), sometimes known as 'digging'	1. Mechanically incorrect in relation to next (catch) phase 2. Resistance to motion by back of hand	1. Controlled entry with elevated elbow, forearm and hand approximately in line and slightly inclined to water surface 2. Slow recovery and catch phases down slightly
6. Wrist excessively extended (hand bent backwards)	Forward-directed splash at entry, setting up unnecessary resistance	Streamlined and controlled entry with elevated elbow, forearm and hand approximately in line and inclined to water surface
7. Too vigorous an entry	Resulting from an excessively fast recovery	Slow recovery down to a more controlled one
8. Elbow entering before hand	1. Unnecessary drag created 2. May be due to an incorrect body position (legs too low or head too high) 3. Insufficient body roll 4. Fault may be due to a physical tightness of the swimmer's shoulders: loosening exercises required	1. Concentration on a high-elbow/low-hand recovery movement; finger-tips must enter the water before the elbow 2. See body position corrections
9. Hand entering sideways, little finger or thumb first	Subsequent phases of catch and pull may take place using a sculling rather than a direct full-hand-area propulsive action. Loss of power and 'hand wander' may also result	1. Hand must enter water finger-tips first. Shallow-water standing practices 2. Use of hand paddles accelerates fault if continued into other propulsive phases

10. Pausing at point of entry	1. Action of stopping arm tends to sink shoulder 2. Momentum is lost: more energy needed to create it once more – waste of energy	1. Momentum of recovery must be used to drive hand and arm into catch position smoothly 2. Part- and full-stroke practices

Phase: CATCH

FAULT	EFFECT ON STROKE	CORRECTION
1. Hand cupped	Decrease of effective propulsive area –loss of speed and waste of energy	1. Hand should be slightly flexed at the wrist with fingers straight and together 2. Single arm – with float practices or shallow-water standing 3. Part- and full-stroke practices
2. Excessive acceleration, may be result of excessively fast entry	Fast-moving hand creates high turbulence and excessive drag effects – loss of power	1. Swimmer must 'feel' the water rather than fight against it 2. Entry and catch movement must be slowed down and controlled
3. Fingers spread apart, due to lack of control or swimmer's tenseness	Loss of propulsive area and efficiency	1. Fingers must be together, or almost together 2. Concentration on this single aspect
4. Dropped elbow	Effective propulsive area reduced	1. Elbow must be elevated above the hand at all times: shrugging the shoulder assists this 2. Shallow-water or single-arm/float practices
5. Palm directed downwards	A press is created which tends to lift the swimmer: this is unnecessary	Catch must be directed towards the feet, rather than the bottom of the pool

Phase: PULL

FAULT	EFFECT ON STROKE	CORRECTION
1. Dropped elbow	Hand and forearm tend to slide rather than create propulsive pressure	1. Elevation of elbow above hand must be emphasised 2. Hand and elbow must reach shoulder plane together, *not* elbow first. Minimal dry-land or shallow-water practices 3. Part- and full-stroke practices
2. Feathering (not to be confused with sculling)	1. Hand wanders from side to side, finding the easiest path 2. Lack of control due to weak muscles	1. More control needed 2. Pull must be firmer 3. Arms-only practices enabling concentration on correct limb track and shoulder development to take pl

3. Fingers spread	Loss of propulsive area and efficiency	Concentration on this aspect alone
4. Pulling too wide	Tendency to turn away from the arm which is pulling wide	1. Concentration on the hand moving directly under the swimmer 2. Opening the eyes (using goggles if necessary) assists in establishing the limb track 3. Over-correction: pulling across the body
5. Pulling across the body excessively	1. Excessive rolling 2. Tendency to turn towards pulling arm 3. Uneven stroke rhythm	1. Return to shallow-water practices 2. Single-float practices 3. Arms-only-with-feet-supported exercises 4. Full-stroke practices 5. Opening the eyes under water (with goggles if necessary) to observe action 6. Breath-holding 7. Bilateral or opposite-side breathing 8. Over-correction: attempting to pull wide
6. Pulling too deeply (usually a single-arm fault)	1. Excessive rolling 2. High opposite-arm recovery 3. Uneven rolling motion 4. Uneven arm pull 5. Interference with leg movement 6. Interference with smooth stroke rhythm	1. Breath-holding 2. Bilateral or opposite-side breathing 3. Arms-only with floats 4. Speeding up the whole stroke cycle 5. Shallow-water practices 6. Establishing or increasing elbow flexion 7. Over-correction: pulling closer to body
7. Hand(s) pulling too close to body (mechanically easier, owing to decreased leverage)	1. Loss of power 2. Pull becomes mechanically 'over-strong': turbulence created 3. Pull shortens: may be due to weak shoulders. Swimmer's strength will develop with practice	1. Shallow-water practices 2. Feet-supported practices 3. Full-stroke practices 4. Slow stroke timing down to accommodate deeper/longer pull 5. Increase body roll 6. Over-correction: swimmer attempts to reach for the bottom
8. Pulling too short; push phase non-existent	1. Push phase lost 2. Arm-stroke propulsion almost halved	1. Shallow-water standing and walking practices with emphasis on pushing past shoulders 2. Feet-supported practices 3. Full stroke with extension of arm pull to push phase
9. Hand not directed backwards (slipping or slight sculling), mostly to be found in beginners	Reduction in propulsive efficiency	1. Appreciation of the maximum propulsive area principle 2. Shallow-water standing practices in order to observe movement 3. Resort to hand paddles (if available) in order to accentuate fault

Phase: PUSH

FAULT	EFFECT ON STROKE	CORRECTION

Generally, all the faults, their effects and corrections found in the pull phase are relevant here, plus:

Completion of the propulsive effect too soon, by not directing the hand fully backwards for as long as possible during the push	Loss of power and efficiency	1. Concentration on this single feature during shallow-water arm practices of standing and walking 2. Feet-supported arm practices 3. Concentrate on a slight hand 'flip' just prior to release 4. Breath-holding while performing part- and full-stroke practices

Phase: RELEASE

FAULT	EFFECT ON STROKE	CORRECTION
1. Hand-first release instead of elbow-first	1. Unnecessary muscle tension initiating a stiff-shouldered instead of relaxed arm recovery 2. Wrist is stiff rather than relaxed	1. Standing shallow-water practices concentrating on an elbow-out-first relaxed release 2. 'Flinging' the arm forward into a relaxed recovery 3. Ensuring that the wrist is relaxed and that finger tips are last to leave the water
2. Release too wide of the body	1. Result of an incorrect push 2. Loss of propulsion due to reduced backward-hand movement	Ensure that hand brushes thigh during release. Correction as for Fault 1

Phase: RECOVERY

FAULT	EFFECT ON STROKE	CORRECTION
1. Hand-high/ elbow-low movement	1. Recovery usually a high-speed one, with hand crashing into water causing much splash at entry 2. Tendency to distort swimmer's body by the movement reaction 3. Unnecessary muscular tension 4. More control required at entry in order to avoid excessive splash, hence more energy usage	1. Shallow-water practices, standing and walking, with emphasis on relaxed elbow, low recovery, and 'flinging' the arm forward 2. Arms-only practices with breathing 3. Full-stroke practices concentrating on flinging action

FAULT	EFFECT ON STROKE	CORRECTION
2. Hand leading elbow at shoulder plane	1. Probably result of an incorrect release 2. Unnecessary muscular energy usage	Correction as for Fault 1
3. Hand swinging too wide	1. Action/reaction effect tends to distort body (snaking) 2. Danger of cross-over at entry 3. Body too 'square' in water	Correction as for Fault 1
4. Arms and hands too stiff	1. Stroke appears to be jerky 2. Unnecessary muscular energy usage	Correction as for Fault 1
5. Too fast	High amount of splash at entry	1. Slow the arm stroke down slightly 2. Introduce some slight control during recovery movement
6. Finger tips ploughing through water surface	1. Excessive drag 2. Loss of power and energy 3. Usually accompanied by too wide an entry	1. Elevate hand and elbow slightly 2. Introduce slightly more body roll
7. Hand recovering *directly* below elbow	1. Too much elbow flexion and hence unnecessary muscular energy usage 2. Hand probably brushes water surface and enters short or elbow-first	1. Shallow-water practices, standing and walking with emphasis on outward and forward hand swing 2. Part-stroke and full-stroke practices with emphasis on fault

Note The degree of shoulder flexibility has a profound effect on arm recovery. The teacher should therefore make allowances for 'tight-shouldered' swimmers who do not possess the ability to perform a relaxed and easy recovery.

Feature: BREATHING

FAULT	EFFECT ON STROKE	CORRECTION
1. Holding the breath for too long	1. Tiring 2. Rhythm existent only in short bursts	1. Breathing should be as rhythmic and natural as possible 2. Handrail breathing practices as described in various chapters 3. Breathing with float-assisted leg kicking 4. Full-stroke practices, gradually working up to regular cyclic breathing 5. Emphasis on breathing in through the mouth and out through the nose/mouth and nose – trickle breath

2. Lifting head to breathe	1. Increased resistance to propulsion 2. Interference with stroke rhythm 3. Tendency for legs to drop 4. Interference with leg-kick rhythm	1. Handrail practices in shallow water, holding rail with one (non-breathing side) hand; emphasis on head rotation instead of head lift; eyes looking forward and down during trickle breath out 2. Float to full-stroke practices emphasising fault correction
3. Failing to breathe out some air from nose	Coughing and spluttering	Correction as in Fault 2
4. 'Flicking', due to hair covering the eyes during the intake movement	Jerky stroke as the head flicks the hair away	1. Haircut 2. Wearing a cap

Feature: CO-ORDINATION

FAULT	EFFECT ON STROKE	CORRECTION
1. Recovering one arm before the other has commenced the pull (catch-up stroke)	Continuity of motion is not smooth; extra energy is required to accelerate the body at the beginning of each stroke	1. Speed up the whole stroke movement 2. Maintain arm-stroke continuity, windmill-style 3. Full-stroke practices only
2. Breathing too late in the arm cycle	1. Tendency to glide with extended arm forward 2. Good chance of taking in water 3. Breathing action may be rushed and inadequate 4. Extra load put on the respiratory system	1. Sequence breathing in with arm recovery: as arm releases, head should turn to take an inward breath 2. Full-stroke practices only

17 The Back Crawl

The back crawl, as its name suggests, is performed with the swimmer lying in a supine position. The arms alternate continuously with each other, by recovering clear of the water then re-entering to carry out the propulsive stage of the stroke. The legs kick with an alternating rhythm, which is biased towards the vertical plane and is synchronised with the arm movement.

The swimmer does not encounter any breathing problems as a rule while the stroke is being carried out, owing to the fact that his face is clear of the water, although, as will be suggested later, some form of respiratory discipline is advised.

The stroke performance of back crawl is governed by ASA laws which state that '. . . the swimmers shall swim upon their backs throughout a race. . . . Any competitor leaving his normal position on the back before the head, foremost hand, or arm has touched the end of the course for the purpose of turning or finishing shall be disqualified.'

STROKE TECHNIQUE
Body position
The side view of a back crawler's attitude in the water should reveal that the chest is lying flat and horizontal and just level with the water surface. Due to the mechanics of the leg kick, the swimmer's hips must ride slightly lower than those of the front crawler. However, the tendency to 'sit' in the water allowing the hips to sink lower than required must be avoided. The effect of the 'sitting' position on the swimmer's forward progress is to bring about an increase in both profile and eddy drag forces, thus down-grading the performance.

The head should be approximately in line with the body and the eyes should be looking up very slightly towards the feet. The created bow wave should pillow the swimmer's head and may wash over her forehead and on to her face. (The experienced swimmer deals with this overwash naturally, but for the learner water washing over the face, in the eyes and up the nose can be quite distressing.) With excessive tilting of the head the swimmer will assume the chin-forward, 'sitting' position.

When viewed from ahead, the swimmer's shoulders should be seen to be rolling towards the direction of the pulling arm; they should reach a maximum deviation from the horizontal, as the hand and arm pass through the shoulder plane.

156

The law states that the swimmer should remain on the back during the actual swim. This may be interpreted as limiting the body-roll angle to a maximum of forty-five degrees, which is compatible with the mechanics of the arm action. Unlike front-crawl technique, in which the swimmer's head rolls in a similar respect to that of the body, the back crawler's head tends to remain relatively still, while the shoulders carry out the rolling motion which is brought about by the arm movements.

The shoulders should not be laterally displaced as a result of the arm action, but should be always co-axial with an imaginary straight line stretching from one end of the pool to the other.

As the swimmer moves away from the observer, her toes may be seen to be *just* breaking the water surface. Her hips should move with a slight rolling reaction, which in turn is associated with leg action.

Taking an overhead look at the swimmer, her 'long axis' should be in line with the intended direction of movement. There should also be no bending of the body due to incorrect limb movements, which will tend to increase the profile and eddy-drag characteristics of the stroke.

In conclusion, as with any stroke, the swimmer's body position in the water is closely related to the efficiency of her arm and leg movements and their co-ordination with each other.

Leg action

The legs move alternately in a plane which is biased towards the vertical. (The movement does not take place in the true vertical plane owing to the transmission to the hips of the swimmer's shoulder roll.) Part of their function is to stabilise and balance the stroke. The downbeat movements also contribute quite substantially towards elevating the hips and maintaining the desired body position. Basically, the back-crawl leg action is similar to that of the front crawl, the main difference being, of course, that the movement is inverted or upside down.

Considerable propulsion can be developed during the upbeat (as opposed to the downbeat in the front crawl), while the downbeat contributes very little towards moving the swimmer forwards. During the downbeats, the ankles are semi-relaxed while, during the upward sweep of the feet, the extension of the ankles (plantar flexion), is effected by calf muscle (triceps surae) tension. This 'bending back' of the feet during the upbeat is assisted by the generated water pressure on the insteps.

During the stroke-learning period, this variation in muscular tension cannot really be taught: if the swimmers are required to maintain the extended-toe (ballet-toe) position, attacks of cramp are very likely. Therefore, although eventually not desirable, 'floppy feet' are probably more advisable in the initial stages of instruction, allowing the technique to develop naturally with further practice.

The leg movement is generated from the hip joint and the upbeat is initiated by rotation of the thigh. The lower-leg extensor muscles (quadriceps femoris) are semi-relaxed during this early stage of the upward movement, then, as the knee nears the surface, the extensors swiftly contract to accelerate the lower leg in a vigorous and propulsive upward arc. (The muscular action is similar to that described in the front-crawl leg movement.)

The inward-pointing toes do not necessarily break the water surface although they can rise above the water level owing to the speed and inertia of the leg. The upward motion of the foot causes a turbulent reaction and the 'local water' is lifted. It is below this water mound that the foot should remain. The foot only splashes as it passes excessively through the water surface. The knees should at all times remain below the water surface and, if they do appear during the performance, the swimmer is probably using a 'cycling' motion, which reduces the effectiveness of the movement.

Owing to the downward-pointing lower leg, the generated propulsive forces at the start of the upbeat are almost in the horizontal plane and being directed backwards in the most advantageous manner.

As the upward movement progresses, however, the backward forces are transferred into vertical downward-acting reactions and propulsion diminishes. When teaching this upward-kicking movement, it may be described to the pupils as 'letting the water bend the knees rather than the swimmer deliberately bending them'.

The flicking movement of the foot, which results from a semi-relaxed ankle joint, is not unlike that of a footballer's action as he kicks the ball with his instep (minus the follow-through). This is a good demonstration point.

Ankle flexibility together with the ability to hold the feet in a plantar-flexed position, is of great importance in achieving a worthwhile leg kick. Learner swimmers sometimes tend to keep their ankles stiff and held at right angles to the shin, a foot position which cannot possibly produce any worthwhile propulsion.

The downbeat provides stabilisation and body elevation, but no measurable propulsion. The depth of kick should be from 450 mm (18 in.) to 600 mm (24 in.) and will vary with the physical characteristics of the swimmer. The tall, strong and rangy individual will probably drive his or her legs deeper into the water than a swimmer with short legs or less flexibility.

The big toes should pass very close to each other as they alternate. This excludes any unnecessary contraction of the thigh abductor muscles and retains the feet in the most advantageous position for propulsion.

All other circumstances being equal, the back- and front-crawl leg-kicking movements are capable of producing comparable degrees of propulsion, although the arm movements contribute the greater share of the propulsion in both strokes. In fact, the front crawl is the faster of the two strokes: assuming that this higher speed is attributable to the more powerful arm action, it may be said that the possible percentage of leg-to-arm participation in the front crawl is less than that of the back crawl.

Therefore it may be argued that, in relation to the overall stroke, the back-crawl leg action may be more efficient than that of the front crawl.

Arm action

As in the front crawl stroke, the motion of the arms is alternating and it is from this movement that the major propelling forces are developed. The arm cycle may be divided into two main phases, the underwater or propulsive movement and the recovery, which is carried out over the water surface.

In order to analyse the complete movement, these two phases will be sub-divided in the following manner (fig. 17.1, overleaf):

Propulsive phase	Recovery phase
catch	release
pull	recovery over the water
push	entry

Fig. 17.1

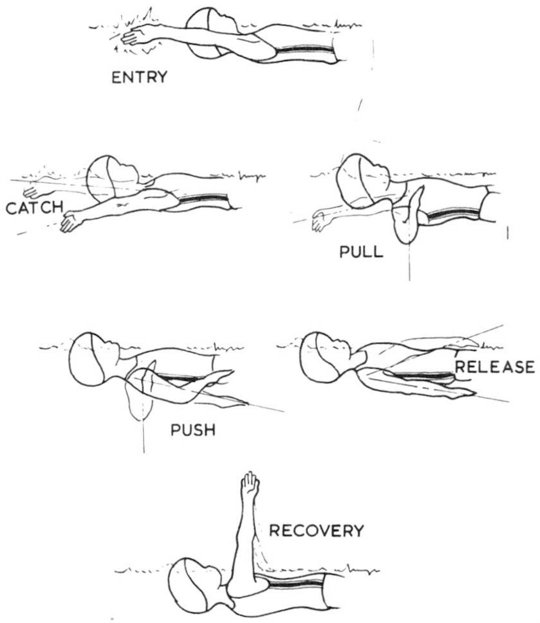

ENTRY

CATCH

PULL

PUSH

RELEASE

RECOVERY

Propulsive phase: catch
To reiterate an earlier statement: the catch may be justifiably described as the foundation of the propulsive phase of the stroke. The movement

commences immediately the hand has entered the water directly in line with and ahead of the shoulder joint. The hand, with fingers flat and together, sinks to a depth of between 150 mm (6 in.) and 300 mm (12 in.). The pulling arm remains straight at this stage, but the wrist maintains a slightly flexed attitude in the direction of the little finger (initiated at the entry stage) and also in the natural direction of the palm. The path of the hand is downward and beginning to move outwards away from the line of the swimmer's shoulder.

The catch movement is a flowing continuation of the entry but, in order to establish propulsive pressure on the hand and lower arm, it is a rapid and accelerating one. It is at this point that the swimmer establishes her feel of the water.

The shoulders should, at this early stage of propulsion, have commenced their lateral roll, thus assisting in the correct positioning of the arm for the start of the pull.

Propulsive phase: pull
The back-crawl pull (and push) has been the subject of much controversy for many years. Should the movement be executed with a bent or straight arm? The straight-arm supporters cite the famous Adlop Kiefer, probably the father of the modern back-crawl style. Kiefer's underwater action showed that his pull/push movement was executed with his arms absolutely straight, and using this style he won the 1936 Olympic 100 m back stroke title in a time of 1.05.9.

Contemporary exponents of the stroke, almost without exception, use the bent-arm pull/push. This type of action is used by Roland Matthes, probably an even more famous back stroker than Kiefer, who won the 100 m back stroke at the 1972 Olympic Games with a time of 56.58, although exactly how much of the improvement in time may be attributed solely to the differing movements will never be known.

With young children, it may be advantageous for them to begin learning the stroke by sweeping their arms in a semi-circle from the point of entry to the position of release. For some obscure physiological reason, many children, when asked to bend their arms during the pull, find it necessary to bend the recovery arm as well. (Rather like patting the top of the head with one hand and rubbing the tummy with the other, it tends to get a little confusing.)

It must be stated, however, that the bent-arm pull/push has been scientifically proved to be the more mechanically sound movement, with the swimmer's arm flexed at elbow and wrist for the underwater sweep.

For teaching purposes, to obtain maximum propulsion for the maximum time, the swimmer's hand and lower arm should be facing towards her feet for as long as possible during the propulsive sweep. Coupled to this is the simple feature of maintaining the hand below the water surface and elevated above the level of the elbow for the major part of the time.

Observing these simple rules, the correct limb tracks tend to sort themselves out reasonably well in the initial stages of learning.

After the catch has been completed, the swimmer's hand starts to move downwards, outwards and in the direction of the feet. The elbow starts to bend and drop below the level of the hand. The wrist is flexed so that the palm of the hand faces towards the feet as early as possible during the underwater journey.

The finger-tips are submerged to an approximate depth of 230 mm (9 in.) at this stage and the hand continues to move below the water surface in a horizontal elongated 'S' pattern (see part 1 of fig. 17.2).

The angle between the forearm and the upper arm decreases to almost a right-angle as it reaches the shoulder plane. Shoulder strength tends to dictate the magnitude of this angle, with stronger swimmers able to cope with the increased leverage resulting from greater angles up to, say, 120 degrees. The shoulders continue to roll to the pulling side. This lateral movement assists in maintaining the propelling hand below the water surface and also serves to keep the shoulder of the recovering arm clear of the water.

The pull continues until the hand and arm simultaneously reach the lateral shoulder plane. It is at this point that the hand is laterally furthest away from the body and at its shallowest depth.

Propulsive phase: push
Throughout the pulling phase the elbow leads the hand, but now, as the hand itself passes the shoulder into the push, it takes up the leading position with the palm still facing towards the feet and the finger tips still approximately 230 mm (9 in.) below the water surface. The palm faces backwards for a short distance, and the elbow and hand start to move in towards the body once more.

At about the level of the swimmer's waist, the forearm moves in a vertical arc about the elbow joint, and the hand, with palm now facing downwards, passes close to the hips, thus creating a final thrusting action towards the bottom of the pool.

The arm, in completing the propulsive stage of the cycle, assumes a straight mode with the hand eventually facing palm-downwards some 230 mm (9 in.) below the swimmer's hips.

Recovery phase: release
This is rather a long movement.

From the completion of the push, the arm, remaining straight, moves vertically upwards, close to the body. The hand may either be retained in the palm-downwards mode, or, by axial rotation of the arm, it may be turned to face inwards thus ensuring a thumbs-out-first release from the water. The back-of-the-hand-first and thumb-first releases from the water both form part of the accepted stroke technique, and the phrases should be used during the teaching of the stroke. It does not matter which method is used as long as the wrist is reasonably relaxed as the hand leaves the water.

There is a further school of thought which advocates a little-finger-out-first technique. This movement tends to place the medial rotator muscles of the arm into unnecessary tension and seems to have no advantage over the more natural and relaxed methods.

Recovery phase: recovery over the water
This takes place in the true vertical plane. The elbow is maintained straight and the wrist is held in a semi-relaxed position.

During this semi-circular movement, the arm is medially rotated so that, at the end of the recovery, the hand faces outwards, thus facilitating a little-finger-first entry.

The speed of recovery should be controlled to synchronise with the slower propulsive movement of the other arm. The arms should remain at approximately 180 degrees out of phase with each other throughout the whole cycle. Controlling the speed of the recovery, and entry, ensures that the arm does not crash heavily into the water, creating water turbulence and consequent drag.

A 'high' recovery of the arm in the true vertical plane avoids bending the body which occurs if the arm is swung sideways during recovery. This distortion of the body about its long axis often occurs if the backward swing of the arm is low and wide. The low and wide recovery also has a tendency to tip the swimmer to that side owing to the weight of the arm acting downwards.

Shoulder flexibility is an important factor during the recovery movement, with the loosely-muscled swimmers able to achieve the high swinging action more readily than the weight-lifters and gymnasts.

Recovery phase: entry
During the recovery over the water, the swimmer's arm should have been medially rotated so that, at re-entry, her arm is straight and facing outwards with fingers together and straight.

Just prior to her little finger entering the water, her wrist should be flexed to the side of the little finger.

The lateral point of entry should be directly in line with the shoulder plane and the distance ahead of the swimmer is automatic, providing the straight-arm mode is maintained. At the point of entry the shoulders should be laterally horizontal with the water surface. Once more shoulder flexibility is important in achieving the shoulder-in-line entry. The 'less flexibles' may probably have to be content with a wider (say 'ten to two') entry.

As previously mentioned, it is important that the entry of the hand into the water is controlled and that its speed is unchanged from that of the recovery over the water, thus preventing it from crashing into the water and setting up unnecessary turbulence for the body to pass through. In turbulent conditions, local eddy patterns and air bubbles form pockets of 'negative' pressure which, when the hand moves into the catch, make it difficult for the swimmer to build up 'positive' pressure or get the feel of the water on the palm and lower arm as propulsion commences.

A continual 'flowing' movement during the transition from the recovery into entry is also necessary in order to prevent the transmission of unnecessary mechanical forces that would be developed by the sudden acceleration or deceleration of the arm on entering the water. These forces, reacting at the back crawler's shoulders, tend to make her bob up and down as she swims.

Breathing
Respiration should present no major problems to back crawlers because their faces are clear of the water most of the time. An aquatic breathing pattern should be as natural and as closely allied to that of a comparable land exertion as possible.

In practice, it is found that back crawlers use a normal 'I need a breath' reflex action and think no more about it. Indeed, many back-crawl specialists at all levels of competition, when questioned about their breathing habits while swimming, all found it difficult to say, without first experimenting, exactly how and where they breathe during the stroke cycle. However, it seems that most swimmers breathe regularly and inhale as one arm recovers over the water. The breath is expelled either gently through pursed lips, or through the mouth and nose in a semi-explosive fashion during the recovery of the opposite arm.

Co-ordination
As in front crawl, the timing of the leg beat usually follows a natural pattern based on the formula of six leg beats to one complete arm cycle. This rhythm results in a smooth and flowing movement.

The mechanical actions of the legs balance out the reactions that are developed during the arm cycle. For instance, for most of the time that the right arm is recovering, the acceleration of the arm after release and the fact that the arm is out of the water tend to make the swimmer roll to the right. If we now examine the leg kick during the same short period, we should see that the right leg is moving down, thus lifting the right hip and countering the tendency to roll to that side. Contra-rotating forces tend to cancel each other out and stabilise the swimmer in a flat and horizontal attitude in the water. It is, in fact, unusual to see the back crawl being performed with anything other than a six-beat stabilising rhythm.

Fig. 17.2 The stroke diagrams

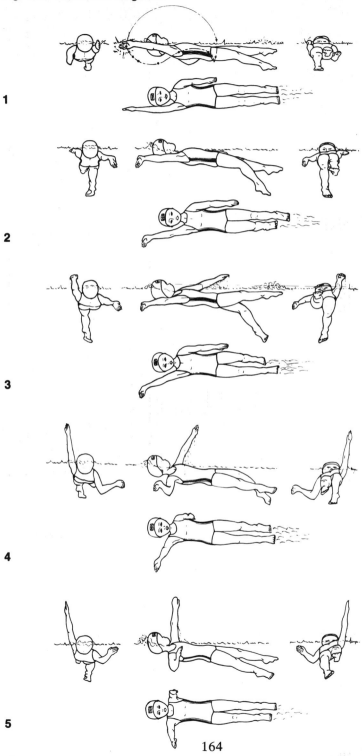

1

2

3

4

5

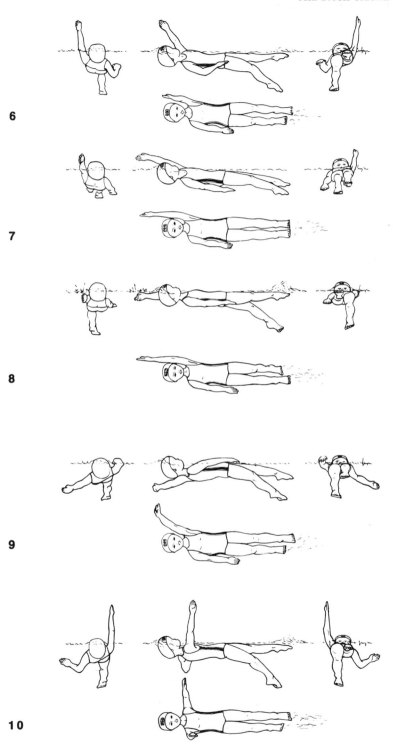

6

7

8

9

10

Preparatory standards for teaching the stroke
Swimming unaided and unassisted on the back can sometimes be alarming for beginners. Therefore, before the teacher commences to teach the back crawl (proper) stroke progressions, there are a few watermanship skills which the pupils should be able to perform with some degree of confidence and alacrity. These are as follows:

1. Confidence exercises: face wetting, blowing bubbles and submersion. (Although on their backs, the swimmers are bound to get their faces wet and water up the nose)
2. Regaining the feet from a supine position
3. Pushing and gliding from the poolside
4. Back paddling at least 20 m (22 yds): this is an ideal introduction to back crawl swimming
5. Treading water
6. General water mobility exercises: in back crawl the peformers are swimming 'blind' and collisions in deep water are likely. Stopping, starting, rolling over, reversing and moving sideways in deep water are therefore necessary skills

TEACHING THE BACK CRAWL
The back crawl is a natural progression from the back paddle, a stroke which should have been attempted by the pupils at some time in their swimming careers.

Back crawl is a popular stroke with younger pupils because it can be performed without them having to put their faces in the water. The fact that some members of the class may not yet have relinquished their armbands does not exclude them from taking part in the practices.

Probably the greatest initial difficulty to be overcome by learners is that of remaining afloat while they recover their arms over the water. The change in buoyancy experienced as each arm leaves the water and its full weight is transferred to the swimmer's body tends to make him sink.

The usual reaction to this 'sinking feeling' is for the prospective back crawler to 'sit' in the water or simply panic and struggle to regain the feet after one brief attempt at the arm stroke. It is therefore necessary, before starting this new set of exercises, that every one of the pupils is able to regain his feet from a supine position without too much difficulty.

Activity: demonstration swim with commentary
As an introduction to the first back-crawl lesson, the pupils should be treated to a visual demonstration of the stroke. This may be carried out by one of the more adept swimmers in the class or preferably by a back crawler of some distinction, if one is available. This visual demonstration is a really important feature of the lesson and a little forethought and

planning is well worthwhile, to enable the class to witness the stroke being performed in a substantially correct manner.

The teacher will now have the chance to point out all the major features of the stroke and describe where, how and why they should take place.

It is worth repeating that the teacher should position himself strategically on the poolside and arrange the pupils so that they can see and hear clearly.

The main teaching points of the stroke may be categorised and applied as previously described.

The swimmer's flat and horizontal body position should be emphasised, showing how his head is pillowed against the water and that his eyes are gazing upwards and slightly towards his feet.

The fact that the toes rise to the surface and do not create too much water disturbance should also be underlined, as should the fact that the swimmer's knees are submerged throughout the kick.

The arms are recovered high over the water in an arc and, throughout this movement, they are held straight but not stiff. Another point worth highlighting is the fact that, during the arm recovery, the thumb (or the back of the hand) leaves the water first, and the little finger is always leading as the re-entry takes place.

The long underwater phase can be described, showing how the palm of the hand faces the feet for as long as possible during the pull and that the hand stays below the water surface aided by a slight shoulder roll.

The teacher should point out how easy and rhythmical the stroke looks when it is performed correctly, with the leg beat blending in smoothly with the arm movement.

The swimmer is seen to be breathing quite easily and naturally and this fact is also worth a mention.

Activity: initial full-stroke swims
This short demonstration now sets the scene for the first exercise whereby the class show just how good they are at performing the back crawl. It may take the form of width swims, in which the pupils attempt the complete stroke before going on to, concentrate on individual aspects of the stroke action.

TEACHING POINTS
1. The body position in the water may be affected by the positioning of the swimmer's head or by the effectiveness of the leg kick. A back crawler who lies back in the water, with his ears just below the water surface, stands a good chance of maintaining himself in the flat and horizontal mode. The swimmers should be encouraged to look up at the roof of the pool, rather than in the direction from which they are swimming. Excessive backwards head tilt sometimes tends to 'over-correct' a swimmer's sinking hips. The effect of this is to raise the legs too high in the water,

thus causing unnecessary splash which reduces the effectiveness of the leg kick.

Another feature of an excessive backwards head tilt is that the water tends to wash over the face and enter the nose, causing, at this early stage of learning, some distress. 'Sitting' in the water has already been mentioned and, where this occurs, the 'bottoms-up' instruction, or something similar, should be given.

The swimmer's legs should be terminating their whip-like upward beats with the extended feet lying just below the water surface. The downbeat should be with straight legs which will assist in raising the hips and maintaining them in this elevated position.

Body roll should be limited to approximately forty-five degrees with any increase in this probably being due to the swimmer's hand pulling too deeply in the water.

2. The leg-beat rhythm should be regular and the depth of kick should be limited to 600 mm (24 in.). With pupils of short stature, the depth of kick should be limited to, say, 300–450 mm (12–18 in.). Kicking depths may be changed by varying the rates of beats.

The kick should always originate from the hip joint with the knee joint extending rapidly during the upbeat. Flexibility of the ankles is necessary for effective propulsion and the term 'floppy feet' adequately describes the required condition.

3. During the arm movement the thumb-out-first and little-finger-in-first features should be emphasised. Elbows should be straight but not necessarily stiff during the high over-the-water recovery.

The propulsive phase should take place from the position where the hand enters the water, behind and in line with the shoulder, then continue on to where it brushes the thigh before commencing the recovery movement once more.

It is unnecessary to emphasise the bent-arm pull at this particular stage; merely sweeping the hand around to the side should be adequate.

The swimmer's hands should remain relatively flat with fingers together throughout the movement.

Each arm should remain approximately opposite the other (windmill-fashion) during the cycle.

4. The breathing cycle needs no mention at this stage, as the face should remain clear of the water at all times during the stroke performance.

5. A six-beat rhythm should be the aim of each pupil, but during this early attempt at the stroke such refinements may well be absent.

In order to assist in establishing and maintaining a stroke rhythm, a one-two-three/one-two-three count may be made silently by the swimmers as they traverse the width of the pool.

6. Premature glancing back over one shoulder, in order to avoid a collision with the poolside, may be prevalent during these early practices. The movement usually produces a longer-than-usual roll towards the head-turning side. This peculiarity may be avoided by the pupils identifying a part of the overhead structure which appears in their sight, just before they touch the side.

Another method of gauging the proximity of the poolside is by counting the number of arm strokes across the pool prior to the touch.

Activity: leg action
The following set of practices are designed to develop the back-crawl leg kick, the movement being essential in establishing the flat and horizontal body position together with propulsion and stability.

The first exercise is identical to that which was performed at the start of the front-crawl leg practices; however, the description and related teaching points are repeated here so that the reader may follow the suggested sequence without having to refer back.

Fig. 17.3

Practice 1: sitting on the poolside kicking the legs (fig. 17.3)
TEACHING POINTS
1. The kick is an alternating leg action.

2. The leg movement originates from the hip. Leg propulsion is based on the technique described in chapter 19 and it is essential that this hip-generated kick is emphasised right from the start of the practices.

3. The legs should be close together in the lateral plane. This is more for physical comfort rather than for hydrodynamic reasons. Spreading the legs unnecessarily brings into action the abducting leg muscles not normally used in this action.

4. The kicking depth should not be more than 450 mm (18 in.). The length of a child's legs has a direct bearing on the rate of the leg beat and the depth of kick. If the kick is deep, the rate of movement will be slower than that of a shallower flutter-like action.

5. An initially semi-relaxed knee joint enables the whip-like movement, which creates propulsion, to take place on the upbeat.

6. Relaxed ankles ('floppy feet') and 'toeing-in' are essential for back crawl; some pupils are able to shake their feet about quite loosely, while others show less flexibility. The 'toeing'in', or inward rotation of the feet, is a natural function for some people, but as it is most unlikely that the whole class will be 'pigeon-toed', this point is worth stressing. The reason for medial rotation of the foot is that it increases the effective propulsive area.

7. The whole leg action should flow smoothly and not be jerky in any way. Stiffening the joints requires muscular energy, therefore such action not only produces incorrect movements, it also tends to hasten the onset of fatigue.

8. The rhythm of the leg kick should be regular, with the teacher setting the pace by counting out a six-beat pattern, one-two-three/one-two-three, and so on, which will probably be the best and most natural one to use during the teaching of the stroke.

Practice 2: leg kicking in the water – holding the rail (fig. 17.4)
This second exercise is also a static one with the limited usefulness which this always implies. The main purpose of the practice is for the pupils again to observe the action of their legs but this time to be more or less in the supine swimming position.

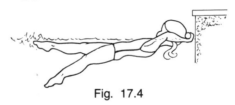
Fig. 17.4

It is useful too in that the teacher is able to stand immediately above the pupils in order to observe and give advice where needed. The best teaching position, however, is where the pupils are able to see as well as hear the teacher. This may be at the end or, as in this particular instance, on the opposite side of the pool.

The main disadvantage of this exercise, and that which limits its use, is the uncomfortable position which the pupils may be required to adopt while holding the rail. This point should be borne in mind when carrying out the practice.

TEACHING POINTS
All the teaching points mentioned in the first exercise will be relevant to this practice. In addition to these, the following may be included:

9. While holding the rail or channel correctly, the pupils should be encouraged to extend their arms in order to bring the head away from the pool wall. This extension of the arms should make the exercise a little more comfortable should the pupils find that their necks are cramped or hunched up.

10. The leg movement should be an accentuated upward flick of the feet (similar to kicking a football), generated from the hip. The toes should just rise to water level but not break the local, slightly turbulent water surface.

If the hip-originated movement is being performed fairly correctly, there may be no need to emphasise the submerged knee position at the peak of the upbeat. However, if any members of the class are 'cycling', some over-correction may be necessary in the form of an instruction to maintain straight legs throughout the kick.

11. When the head is in contact with the rail and the pupil is pulling himself close to the wall, he may tend to sit in the water. If this should happen, the 'bottoms-up' or 'tummies-up' instruction must be given.

In this anchored position, a slight increase in kicking speed and a conscious effort on the part of the pupils to straighten out is usually sufficient to attain the desired flat and horizontal attitude. The previously mentioned extension of the arms also assists in maintaining the correct mode.

By this time, the pupils should be performing a relatively correct leg kick; we may therefore progress from the static to the more useful mobile forms of practice.

A general check on regaining the feet from a supine position should be made before the new exercises commence. If any members of the class are unsure about the procedure, a brief session of standing-down practices should be carried out both with and without floats, until the teacher is satisfied with the standard of proficiency.

Practice 3: leg kicking with two floats (fig. 17.5)

Fig. 17.5

TEACHING POINTS
The following teaching points may be added to those given for the previous practices:

12. The correct and secure method of holding the two floats while swimming on the back is essential because, when held in this vertical mode, the upward water buoyancy forces tend to snatch them from the

swimmer's grasp. A firm hand grip, combined with tucking the elbows in to press the floats against the body, must be emphasised.

13. Positioning the head is important, and the desired horizontal and flat mode can be enhanced by the pupils pillowing their heads back in the water so that their ears are just in line with the surface.

Looking up at the overhead structure while swimming on the back should now be an established part of the teacher's instruction. Excessive backward tilting of the head may cause choppy water to wash over the swimmer's face. If this occurs, a *slight* forward tilting of the head towards the feet should remedy the problem.

14. This being the first mobile exercise, it is worth reiterating yet again that the leg movement should originate from the hips, and the ankles should be relaxed with the feet extended and 'toed-in'.

Practice 4: leg kicking with one float
We may now progress to the next standard of practice, which is that of using less buoyancy support during the kicking exercise.

A single float may be held across the chest (fig. 17.6), on the tummy (fig. 17.7) or behind the head (fig. 17.8). Once more, the exercise should commence with instruction on how to hold the float. In the case of the cross-chest grip, the float is hugged or cuddled to the chest by placing the arms over the upper surface and gripping it securely on opposite (long) sides with both hands.

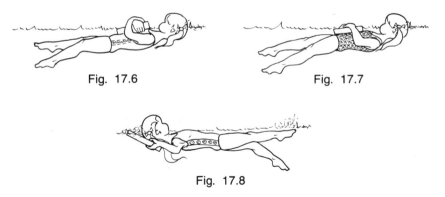

Fig. 17.6   Fig. 17.7

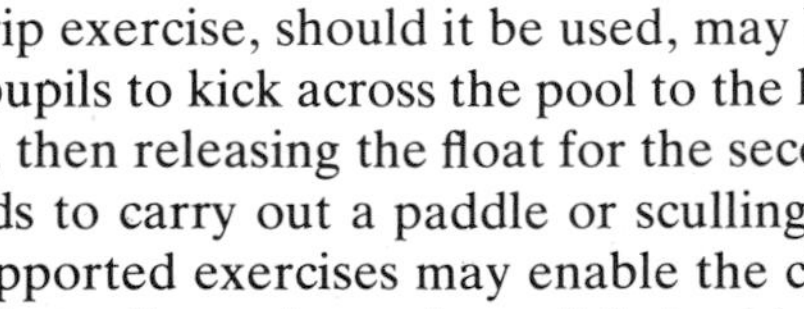

Fig. 17.8

The tummy-grip exercise, should it be used, may be upgraded slightly by allowing the pupils to kick across the pool to the half-way stage in the supported mode, then releasing the float for the second half of the swim and use the hands to carry out a paddle or sculling action.

These float-supported exercises may enable the children who are still wearing armbands to divest themselves of their aids or allow them to be partially deflated. The final exercise of support-to-unsupport may require some armbands to be worn once more and the teacher should be alert to make any adjustments that may be needed.

It is important that these children carry out the practices in a water depth which is shallow enough for them to regain their feet without much difficulty.

TEACHING POINTS

All the teaching points relating to the leg-kick technique are applicable during these practices.

Practice 5: leg kicking with scull (fig. 17.9)
During the previous exercise, the pupils were introduced to leg kicking with no assistance from the floats. If, during some earlier lesson, they have carried out the back-paddle practices, this swimming exercise should present no problems to them. If, on the other hand, the class have no previous experience in the use of their hands while paddling on the back, some brief explanation of the sculling action should be given (see chapter 15).

Fig. 17.9

The kicking exercise is now performed utilising the sculling movements to swim across the pool.

TEACHING POINTS

All the previously mentioned teaching points relating to the actual stroke technique are applicable here with the following addition:

15. The method of sculling, although necessary to the exercise, should not become a major part of the teaching. The amount of instruction relating to this particular movement should be minimal, bearing in mind that the paramount feature of the exercise is the back-crawl leg action.

Practice 6: leg kicking with hands resting on the upper thighs (fig. 17.10)
TEACHING POINTS
All the previously mentioned teaching points are relevant, with perhaps most emphasis being placed on the flat and horizontal swimming mode with head well back in the water.

Fig. 17.10

Practice 7: leg kicking in a fully (athletically) stretched position (fig. 17.11)
For this final exercise in the leg-action practices, the swimmer takes up a
fully stretched attitude with arms stretching back behind the head.

The arm-stretch mode is closely allied to that of actually swimming. It is
also similar to the submerged position that a swimmer adopts after a start,
or push-off following a turn, during a back-crawl race.

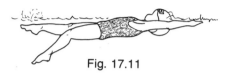

Fig. 17.11

TEACHING POINTS

All the teaching points previously mentioned are applicable here, with
the following addition:

16. The arms must be fully stretched to maintain streamlining. They
should also be fully supported at all times by the water. Clasping the
hands together gives the appearance of the converging bows of a boat,
and has a slight effect in reducing the swimmer's frontal resistance.

Activity: arm action
Useful back-crawl arms-only practices are very limited in number. This is
due to the fact that, when actually performing the stroke, the swimmer
utilises the stabilising forces that are developed by the leg kick to coun-
terbalance the turning forces created during the width-of-the-body arm
pull which tend to make her zig-zag.

In general, mobile arms-only exercises are used only as a training aid
with both legs being supported by some floating device. Even here,
however, the exercise has its limitations, in as much as neither body-roll
nor leg-movement reactions are present.

With these facts in mind, we will restrict our practices to three static
forms of exercise aimed solely at establishing the correct limb tracks.

*Practice 1: standing in the shallow end of the pool and rotating the arms in
the back-crawl manner* (fig. 17.12), *the teacher demonstrating the action
from the poolside*
TEACHING POINTS
1. The arms must be kept straight but not stiff throughout this exercise.

2. The hands should remain flat and the fingers together. A slight flexion
of the wrist may take place at the start of the pulling action.

3. Each arm should remain approximately 180 degrees out of phase with
the other at all times, windmill-style.

4. The pulling movement should commence just after the little finger has entered the water. (This is an imaginary entry owing to the fact that the pupils are in a standing position.) The position of the hand at entry must be directly in line with the shoulder joint. Shoulder flexibility is an important factor in the correct placing of the hand and arm directly behind the shoulders. Should a swimmer's shoulder girth be tightly

Fig. 17.12

muscled (boys are generally less flexible about the shoulders than girls), he may find it rather difficult to achieve the desired arm-entry position.

Where this physical limitation occurs, the teacher must make allowances and accept whatever the pupil or pupils can achieve. Indeed, the teacher may himself find difficulty in demonstrating the correct action because of this flexibility problem. If this is so, the problem should be worked on and improved by exercises and, in the meantime, one of the pupils should be used as a demonstration model.

Termination of the pull should be with the hand facing the outer thigh and adjacent to it. The hand should be approximately 230 mm (9 in.) behind the lateral shoulder plane when the outstretched arm is horizontal. This would be equivalent to a water depth of 230 mm (9 in.) if the swimmer were lying in the horizontal mode.

Practice 2: feet hooked under the rail (figs 17.13 and 17.14)

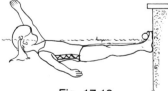

Fig. 17.13   Fig. 17.14

TEACHING POINTS
The previously mentioned teaching points may be adjusted to apply during this exercise, the main difference being, of course, that the move-

ment is being performed in the correct horizontal swimming mode rather than in the standing position. In addition,

5. The depth of pulling movement is the most important feature during this practice and care should be taken that the hands do not sink too deeply. The depth of 230 mm (9 in.) is just about right for good results.

Practice 3: full-stroke movement, preferably across the width of the pool (fig. 17.15)

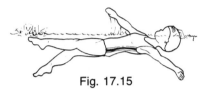

Fig. 17.15

The pupils may now become mobile once more by carrying out the full-stroke movement but using the legs in the form of a shallow flutter-kick.

The emphasis will be on the arm action with the leg movement assisting to maintain a good swimming position. This full-stroke practice is recommended rather than one whereby the legs are supported by some artificial means. The reasoning behind this suggestion is that:

1. The sideways arm pull tends to distort the natural alignment of the swimmer (snaking), owing to the absence of any leg-balancing forces at this stage.

2. Using the float while swimming in this supinated position, by holding it between the legs, demands a little more skill than the swimmers may possess at this stage in the practices. Consequently, time may be wasted in retrieving rather than actually utilising the floats.

3. Using the float tucked under one arm while swimming with the other tends to make the pupils 'sit' in the water. The practices outlined here, however, are not by any means mandatory and, if the teacher finds that selective use of the floats produces the results he desires, such activities should be included in the programme.

The teacher should ensure that the weaker swimmers are nearer the shallow end of the pool. Starting with their feet hooked under the hand-rail, and lying back in the water, the pupils perform the arms-only movement.

After a couple of warm-up cycles, the pupils, with their arms continuing the motion, gently push away from the rail. They perform a shallow flutter-kick in an attempt to swim across the width of the pool.

TEACHING POINTS

The main teaching points have been referred to in the preceding arm-action practices. It will probably be necessary, however, to stress some of the points, such as the correct body and head position. The hips should be riding high ('bottoms up') in the water and the pupils should look up at the roof. The emphasis should be placed on a thumb-out-first/little-finger-in-first arm movement incorporating a vertical or near-vertical semi-relaxed straight-arm recovery. The arm cycle should be without pause. Arm entry should be directly in line with the relative shoulder, the upper arm brushing the ear. The pull/push movement should still be carried out at this stage using a semi-circular arm sweep. The depth of pull should be maintained at a maximum of 230 mm (9 in.) and body roll should be minimised.

It is not usually necessary to mention the breathing during the early performances of the stroke, due to the fact that the face is held clear of the water most, if not all, of the time. It might be worth recalling, however, the fact that the swimmers should be breathing in through the mouth and out mainly through the nose and *not* holding their breath.

The full-stroke exercise, with limited leg movement, leads naturally on to the next activity.

Activity: stroke co-ordination

The leg kick was largely ignored in the previous exercise, but now the complete movement as well as the rhythm and timing will be fostered.

It will be found that it is necessary to link the leg timing to the arm movement rather than vice versa and it is best to teach a six-beat movement (six leg beats to one complete arm cycle). In practice, if the pupils are instructed to aim for a one-two-three/one-two-three leg rhythm as the arms carry out the complete movement, the stroke timing will evolve as a natural process.

Stroke variation

As previously mentioned, the whole stroke is now ready for analysis and, before the straight-arm action becomes too deeply integrated, a slight variation in the pulling movement should be introduced. The teacher will be aware of the fact that better propulsion characteristics are attained by facing the palms of the hands directly backwards for as long as possible during the arm stroke (see chapter 6).

With this fact in mind, and with the pupils at a stage where they are able to absorb a slight variation in the initially taught technique, the straight-arm pull may be modified to the technically superior bent-arm pull/push movement.

The swimmers are now shown, by a practical swimming demonstration if possible, the technique of the bent-arm action. A short explanation of the advantages of the movement should also be given, underlining the fact that the palms are facing towards the feet for a longer time during the underwater cycles, thus providing more propulsion.

Teaching practices
The pupils now revert to a previous static exercise, namely that of hooking the feet under the rail and carrying out the arm movement while lying in a supine mode. This time, however, instead of the straight-arm pull, the bent-arm action is substituted.

When this new movement is more or less established, the pupils may once more carry out full-stroke practices incorporating the modified arm stroke.

TEACHING POINTS
1. Immediately the hand and arm enter the water, the catch is made, with the arm initially remaining straight. The elbow then bends and, with wrist held firm, the pull/push movement is carried out with the palm facing towards the feet for as long as possible during this underwater arm sweep.

2. The finger tips must remain sufficiently deep so as not to cause bubbles or any water-surface disturbance.

3. At the conclusion of the push phase, the hand should be just wide of the thigh with palm facing down.

4. The release may be carried out by either the thumb or the back of the hand leaving the water first.

5. Arm recovery is as previously described with the arm held straight.
Further full-stroke work may be carried out, introducing the correct underwater push-glide-stretch into swim sequence. This in turn may lead to back-crawl starting and turning practices.

FAULTS AND THEIR CORRECTION

Feature: BODY POSITION

FAULT	EFFECT ON STROKE	CORRECTION
1. 'Sitting' in the water (too low): probably related to head being held too high, due to fear of water washing over the face or merely being in a supine position	1. Increase in profile drag 2. Difficulty in performing correct limb actions	1. Appreciation of horizontal body position 2. Supine surface push-and-glide practices 3. Legs-only practices unassisted, preferably in fully (athletically) stretched position 4. 'Bottom-up' or 'tummy-up' 5. Head well back – look up 6. Reassure and coax

2. Too high: head may be held too far back	1. Legs tend to break the water surface 2. Loss of efficiency in leg action 3. Probable breathing problems due to water washing over the face	1. Lift head very slightly in order to drop legs 2. Legs-only practices as before 3. Full stroke, eyes looking up and slightly towards feet
3. Excessive roll (beyond 45°), probably related to digging the arms too deeply during pull	Effect on general rhythm and leg action	1. Mobile arms-only practices with feet supported 2. Emphasis on maintaining shoulders laterally stable by reducing pulling depth 3. Speed up the arm movement 4. Full-stroke practices
4. Arching the back	1. Head probably too far back and even submerged 2. Back muscles in unnecessary tension 3. Tummy and legs out of the water 4. Breathing problems associated with submerged head	1. Float-assisted leg practices, float in 'cuddle' position to encourage slight sitting (over-correction) 2. Legs-only practices with scull – head looking towards feet (over-correction) 3. Full stroke with feet in view at all times (over-correction)

Feature: LEG ACTION

FAULT	EFFECT ON STROKE	CORRECTION
1. Feet breaking the surface	1. Excessive splash leading to increased eddy resistance 2. Loss of power	1. Emphasis on correct body position and appreciation of leg kick and its attendant errors 2. Legs-only, unassisted practices: emphasis on toes just reaching water surface on the upbeat 3. Slow the kicking rate down and increase depth slightly
2. 'Cycling', i.e. bending the knees at the peak of upbeat	1. Ineffective kicking action 2. Excessive leg splash	1. Float-assisted leg practices with emphasis on the hip-orientated upward foot kick, appreciation of movement 2. No 'Knees up Mother Brown' actions 3. Unassisted leg practices to measure the effectiveness of corrections 4. On to full stroke with minimal leg splash
3. Flutter-kick (very shallow and fast movement)	1. Reduced effectiveness of leg kick 2. Sometimes excessive splash	1. Slow the action down and increase depth of kick 2. Float-assisted practices 3. Full-stroke practices: slow down stroking rate and attempt to establish a six-beat rhythm, originating from the hips

4. Feet in dorsi-flexed mode	1. Ineffective kick and lack of propulsion 2. Hips and legs drop in the water due to lack of elevation forces	1. Sitting on the poolside and observing foot movement (limited practice) 2. Ankles must be relaxed ('floppy feet') 3. Kick from hips with partial relaxation of knees 4. Mobile legs-only and full-stroke movement with concentration on 'floppy-foot' flicking movement
5. Legs too wide apart – usually accompanied by sitting	1. Completely ineffective movement 2. Action akin to 'egg-beater' action used in treading water	Return to 'square one', and proceed through the whole leg practice sequence once more, stressing all teaching points

Phase: ENTRY

FAULT	EFFECT ON STROKE	CORRECTION
1. Across the line of the body (beyond the head)	1. 'Snaking' 2. Elbows probably bent as hand enters 3. Initial propulsion lost due to direct sideways hand movement	1. Handrail- or partner-supported arm movements 2. Emphasis on straight-arm recovery with hand entering in line with related shoulder, little finger first 3. Action should be 'swinging', rather than stiff 4. Full-stroke practices with visual assistance regarding hand-entry position 5. Over-correction may help
2. Too wide: this may be due to lack of shoulder-girdle mobility (usually found in boys and men), or lack of appreciation of arm action	1. If due to shoulder stiffness, arm stroke is jerky and usually splashy 2. Loss of propulsion due to reduced length of pull	1. Shoulder mobility exercises such as free arm swings (land) and back-crawl arm movements (water) 2. Otherwise, handrail- or partner-supported practices 3. Visual assistance regarding hand-entry position 4. On to full-stroke practices 5. Over-correction may help. The teacher should realise that some swimmers may never reach the standard of shoulder flexibility that accompanies a good back-crawl arm action, and adjust their efforts accordingly
3. Back of the hand first	Initial entry creates braking effect	1. Emphasis on little-finger-first entry with arm straight: slight sideways wrist flexing (towards little finger) helps 2. Assisted and free swimming
4. Stopping the hand at entry	1. Momentum transfer results in shoulders sinking into water 2. Swimmer may bob slightly	Full-stroke practices with emphasis on continuation of movement from the recovery

FAULT	EFFECT ON STROKE	CORRECTION
5. Uncontrolled entry – probably due to high-speed recovery	Excessive splash created and consequent loss of power due to local water turbulence	Full-stroke practices with emphasis on slow and controlled recovery movement: controlled entry will follow
6. Over-reaching	Excessive stretching forward tends to distort the swimmer's alignment	Rail practices under supervision: pupil attempts to maintain the shoulder joints in line with each other

Phase: CATCH

FAULT	EFFECT ON STROKE	CORRECTION
1. Fingers spread: may be continuation of relaxed recovery	1. Extended catch 2. Loss of power	1. Fingers together during recovery, then transferring this into catch 2. Rail/partner-assisted practices into full-stroke movements 3. Emphasis on fault
2. Hand directed sideways	Initial propulsive force	1. Slight flexing of wrist in order to direct propulsive forces towards feet 2. Rail/partner-assisted practices into full-stroke movements 3. Emphasis on fault
3. Catch movement too slow: remember, this initial accelerating hand movement is the foundation of the whole propulsion. Hand pressure must be established quickly and maintained	Loss of power due to shortened pull, resulting from extended catch	Full-stroke movements with increased arm stroke rate

Phase: PULL

FAULT	EFFECT ON STROKE	CORRECTION
1. Hands and/or arms too near water surface	1. Excessive water-surface disturbance 2. Loss of power	1. Emphasis on maintaining hand at least 100 mm (4 in.) below surface 2. Float-supported single-arm movement 3. Full stroke
2. Too deep	1. Excessive body roll may result 2. Muscular effort may be too much for the swimmer	1. Handrail- or partner-supported arm movement 2. Concentrate on shallow pull (see above) and maintaining shoulders square with surface. (Latter point – over-correction) 3. Full-stroke practices trying to maintain steady head and shoulder position 4. Single-arm practices (float-assisted)

3. Straight arm pull: this type of pull is essentially for learners to establish the back-crawl movement. The bent-arm (palm facing feet) pull should be established as soon as supine mobility is attained	Loss of power: this was quite a useful method of back-crawl pull before the technique of the bent-arm movement was developed. For non-competitive swimmers, it is still quite a satisfactory mode of propulsion	1. Appreciation that the hand should be directed towards the feet for as long as possible during the underwater movement 2. Handrail- or partner-supported arm movement with emphasis on above point 3. Full-stroke movement 4. Single-arm practices (float-assisted)
4. Turning the hand palm upwards or downwards	Loss of propulsive power	Correction as for Fault 3
5. Elbow leading hand into the push phase	1. Slipping takes place 2. Loss of propulsion	Correction as for Fault 3
6. Too rapid: hand may be too near body, swimmer over-strong	1. Excessive turbulence created 2. Hand tends to move without effect	1. Slow the whole stroke movement down. 2. Emphasis on a long and effective pull 3. Single-arm float assisted practices 4. Full-stroke practices: mobility exercises are more advantageous

Phase: PUSH

FAULT	EFFECT ON STROKE	CORRECTION
1. Non-existent push: arm recovers from just beyond shoulder plane	1. Greatly reduced propulsion 2. Hurried stroke	Full extent of movement with hand continuing to the thigh to be emphasised All as Fault 3 corrections shown in pull phase
2. Shortened push: slightly extended version of above	1. Reduced propulsion 2. Hurried stroke	Correction as for Fault 1
3. From a deep pull, an upward-sweeping hand movement to the surface	Tendency to sink the hips, (action/ reaction effects)	Emphasis on completing push by an in-sweeping arm/hand or a down-sweeping forearm and hand
4. Too rapid	1. Excessive turbulence 2. Hand tends to move without effect	Correction as for Fault 6, pull phase

Phase: RELEASE

FAULT	EFFECT ON STROKE	CORRECTION
1. Not in the upper thigh region: result of an incomplete or non-existent push phase; may be too wide	1. Slight reduction in propulsion may result 2. Effects may be transferred into recovery movement, giving it a bent-arm or wide appearance	Emphasis on completing the push and brushing the thigh during release Correction as for Fault 1 of push phase
2. Too rapid	1. Action/reaction effects tend to sink the related shoulder 2. Water tends to be lifted and washed over the swimmer's face	1. Emphasis on a slower and controlled release 2. Full-stroke practices in order to integrate arm movement into complete cycle
3. Hand and arm too tense: remember, release is essentially a shoulder movement; the head and arm should follow in a semi-relaxed mode	1. Waste of energy 2. Recovery tends to have a jerky and stiff appearance	Full-stroke practices (preferably lengths, in order that swimmer can settle into a rhythm) with emphasis on relaxed release and recovery
4. Hands stopping at release	1. Disturbance in rhythm and stroke continuity 2. Waste of energy	Correction as for previous fault

Phase: RECOVERY

FAULT	EFFECT ON STROKE	CORRECTION
1. Too wide	1. Outward swinging movement gives action/reaction effect – swimmer's body tends to distort, 'banana' fashion 2. Increase in profile drag 3. Interference with leg rhythm	1. Emphasis on a vertical recovery movement, thumb or back of the hand out first, little finger in first 2. Handrail- or partner-assisted arm movement 3. Full-stroke practices
2. Too rapid	See effect 5 in entry phase	Correction as for Fault 5 in entry phase

3. Bent-arm recovery (not to be confused with slight arm relaxation)	1. Stroke loses its smooth aesthetic appearance 2. Arm is very rapidly straightened again as elbow passes shoulder – may result in splashed entry 3. Wastage of energy if straightened by effort	Correction as for Fault 1
4. Too tensed (elbow and wrist held very stiff)	As effects shown in Fault 2, release phase	Emphasis on relaxation. Correction as for Fault 2 in release phase
5. Hand and arm moving across body	1. Water tends to splash over face 2. Unnecessary arm movement 3. Entry usually behind or beyond the head	Correction as for Fault 1

Feature: BREATHING

FAULT	EFFECT ON STROKE	CORRECTION
Ingress of water up the nose due to the head being held back too far	Swimmer tends to cough and splutter and loses concentration	1. Breathing discipline to be adopted: inhale on one arm stroke, exhale on the next 2. In through the mouth, out through the mouth and nose. (Nasal exhalation is important)

Feature: CO-ORDINATION

FAULT	EFFECT ON STROKE	CORRECTION
Disunity of arm stroke: action should be a continuous 'windmilling' movement	1. Non-continuity of propulsion 2. Excessive energy usage due to slowing down and speeding up again	Full-stroke practices with emphasis on 'windmilling' movement: a little arm tenseness may creep in, but in this instance let the priority be stroke continuity. Attend to other faults later

Note Generally, co-ordination may be affected by individual faults as previously mentioned. Therefore, a return to part-practices may be necessary in order to co-ordinate the whole movement.

18 The Breast Stroke

The formal performance of the breast stroke is rigidly controlled by Amateur Swimming Association laws. These laws appertain to the competition style only, but it is considered to be good general teaching practice to adhere to them. The main reason for this, is that many children at some time or other enter a race at school or at a club gala. Disqualification from the breast-stroke event because of incorrect stroke technique could be a bitter and unnecessary disappointment.

The breast-stroke laws state that:

> The swimmer's body shall be kept perfectly on the breast and both shoulders shall be in line with the water surface. All movements of the legs and arms shall be simultaneous and in the same horizontal plane without alternating movements.
>
> The hands shall be pushed forward together from the breast and shall be brought back on or under the surface of the water.
>
> In the leg kick, the feet shall be turned outwards in the backward movement. A 'dolphin' kick is not permitted.
>
> A part of the head shall always be above the general water level, except that at the start and at each turn the swimmer may take one arm stroke and one leg kick while wholly submerged.

As can be seen, the two main restrictions are that the stroke movements must be carried out in a simultaneous fashion, and that the corresponding parts of each limb must be in the same horizontal plane at all times. In other words the movements of the limbs on the left-hand side of the swimmer's body must be a mirror image of those on the right-hand side and, at the same time, each part of each limb on the left-hand side must be the same distance from the general water level as the corresponding parts of the limbs on the right-hand side.

The breast stroke is the slowest of the competition strokes and, with the restricted limb movements and underwater recoveries, it is likely to remain so.

There is another form of breast stroke which may be termed the 'leisure style'. Here, while the basic mechanics of movements are similar to that of the competition stroke, the rate at which the limbs articulate, as the name suggests, is much slower.

Informal swimmers usually perform in a continually head-up, easy-breathing mode and, where the leg kick is reasonably strong, the stroke cycle often terminates in a prolonged glide. Learners are often taught in this 'glide-emphasis' fashion in order to demonstrate and develop the efficiency of their leg kicks.

Another version of the leisure style is with slow but continually 'revving' arms and legs, providing the swimmer with a steady but not too rapid rate of progress.

The basic mechanics of propulsion are similar in all the styles, but the movements of the formal or competition stroke demand more discipline and finesse. Consequently, it is this precise pattern of movement that we teach.

STROKE TECHNIQUE
Body position
Viewed from the side, the swimmer's body should be as streamlined and horizontal as the technique of the leg kick will permit.

If the hips should be too elevated, there is a possibility that the feet, when they are in the fully recovered position, will break the surface of the water, thus decreasing their effectiveness during the propulsive stage of the movement.

The position of the swimmer's head, as the reader no doubt remembers from earlier chapters, can have a profound effect on body position. This is especially so in the breast stroke where the hair line should be in the region of the water line except during a breathing intake. Lifting the head too high tends to elevate the upper part of the chest, and in turn the swimmer's body is rotated so that the legs sink lower in the water. This upright swimming position can often be seen among learners and people who do not like getting their faces wet.

The fault whereby the swimmer's heels break the surface if the hips are riding too high in the water *may* be counteracted by slightly lifting the head. It is worth mentioning that a 'leg' swimmer's hips usually ride lower in the water than those of an 'arm' swimmer.

The angle of the upper legs in relation to the long body axis is important to overall body streamlining. Should the hip joint be flexed excessively during the recovery of the legs in preparation for the kick, a considerable amount of resistance is set up by the resulting profile of the thighs.

Accompanying this overflexing of the hip, there is a tendency also for the swimmer's bottom to bob up and down with each leg cycle.

From the front, the swimmer's shoulders should lie in line with the water surface; in other words, the lateral shoulder plane must be horizontal. The head should not bob up and down excessively in order to accommodate the breathing pattern. (Excessive lifting means anything more than 100 mm (4 in.).) The movement of the arms, as will be seen later, has the effect of raising the swimmer's head above the water level as well as propelling him forward. This elevating effect should itself bring the mouth almost if not completely clear of the water, whereby an inward breath may be taken. In some instances, a slight head lift may be needed to augment the natural shoulder rise.

As the arms perform their cycle there should be no water-surface disturbance created by the recovery or catch movements. Neither should the feet ever break the water surface.

From above, the swimmer should be seen to be proceeding in a straight line with his long body axis parallel with the direction of movement, with no tendency to side stroke.

The whole symmetrical and simultaneous pattern of movement can easily be seen from this angle and any deviation from the correct technique readily identified.

Leg action

For many years people have debated two alternative theories about the propulsion in the breast-stroke leg action. The first is the 'wedge' action theory concerning the vigorous inward movement of the legs from the astride position. Experts were convinced that water was squeezed backwards as the legs closed, the reaction of which propelled the swimmer forward. The second theory is that the swimmer is driven forward by the pressure of the soles of the feet on the water, similar to the action of a frog's kick.

Consider first the 'wedge' action theory. The initial fact to remember when dealing with a 'low viscous' fluid such as water is that when pressure forces it to escape from a confined space it will always find the easy way out or, in other words, it will seek the path of least resistance. Fig. 18.1 shows a swimmer completing the final movement of a wedge kick.

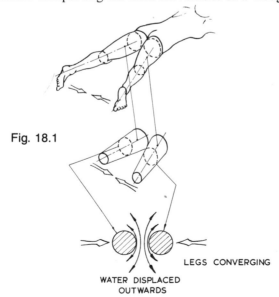

Fig. 18.1

LEGS CONVERGING

WATER DISPLACED
OUTWARDS

Comparing the legs with two similarly shaped sections, we can see that by making the two near-cylinders converge the majority of the trapped water is displaced in directions which are at right-angles to the long axes of the section, this being the line of least resistance. Some water escapes from the extreme ends of the sections, but the amount is minimal.

It can now be seen that for any considered section of the swimmer's legs (similar to that shown in fig. 18.1), the larger amount of water will always be displaced from between them in an upward and downward direction (away from the long axis) rather than along the length of the legs as they are closed together. Consequently the water pressure which is developed in the direction of the leg axis is minimal and has no propulsive effect.

The second theory, relating to a frog-like kick whereby propulsion is gained by the sole of the swimmer's foot pushing directly backwards, would seem to be rather unlikely. The limited amount of propulsive power that can be generated by the sole of the human foot, compared with the mass of the body to be moved through the water and the drag to be overcome, is insignificant.

The frog is able to swim quite successfully by pushing *directly* back on the water. However, if a brief study is made of the frog's anatomy and the relationship between the size of its body, the strength of its legs (used for jumping quite long distances) and the sole area of its feet, it can easily be seen how the animal is able to move so quickly and efficiently through the water using a straight-back kick. With our relatively tiny feet we cannot compare ourselves with the frog.

So, if the kick is not developed by either of these actions, how do breast strokers generate the thrust from their legs which is sometimes quite considerable?

The answer to this question is that, during the propulsive phase of the kick, the soles of the feet are positioned in such a way (by dorsi-flexion and opening) that they perform what may loosely be described as a uni-directional sculling motion as they sweep together – uni-directional because the movement is in *one* direction always towards the inside of the foot, as compared with a true sculling motion which is oscillatory.

Let us examine the foot carefully in order that we may see how its anatomical shape assists in developing this thrust to propel the swimmer forward.

Fig. 18.2 shows a normally shaped human foot viewed from the front, together with a picture of the sole area. Also shown in the view of the sole is the approximate area that is normally in contact with the floor, when a person is standing. (This may be checked quite easily by wetting the sole of the foot and standing on a dry surface: the normal foot shape will be similar to that shown in the photograph.)

An imaginary cutting plane X–X is passed through the foot and the shape of the resulting section is shown in the top right-hand picture.

It may be seen that the under shape of the foot is slightly inclined

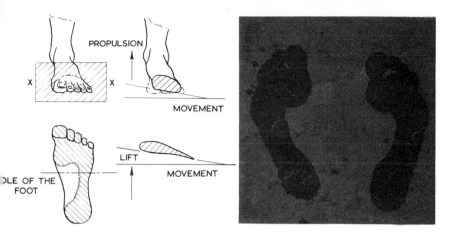

Fig. 18.2

inwards and produces an aerodynamic form similar in shape to the true one as illustrated. If the aerodynamic shape is moved in the direction of the arrow, pressure is built up on the under surface to create 'lift'. Similarly, by moving the foot (in the water) in the same fashion, propulsion may also be created. Also, as the angle of the sole of the foot and its speed through the water increases (up to a point), the propulsive effect increases. Hence the necessity of the whip-like movement of the feet. This is the theory of the scull (analysed further in chapter 6) applied to the feet.

If the feet are moved inwards simultaneously, as in the breast-stroke leg kick, twice the amount of propulsion is developed. The propulsion increases approximately as the square of the speed that the feet move together (i.e. at twice the speed, the feet produce four times the amount of propulsion).

It may also be noted that at the beginning of the kick the feet point outwards and at the end of the movement they point backwards. They therefore *rotate* through approximately ninety degrees, rather like the action of a propeller blade. The feet, throughout the 'whip' part of the kick, move so that the soles of the feet are inclined towards their direction of movement, thus augmenting the 'sculling angle' already existing in the anatomical form of a normal foot. (A flat-footed person does not possess this natural foot arch, but this does not mean he cannot make a good breast-stroke swimmer.)

So, it may be seen that if the breast stroker is able to perform this foot scull in an efficient manner, good propulsion may be gained from the leg kick.

Howard Firby in his fine book on competitive swimming mentions an experiment in which he fashioned a pair of 'back-to-back feet' in the form of a propeller. When fitted to a simple boat the 'feet' rotated and propelled the boat through the water.

A few years ago I too carried out a similar investigation, in order to demonstrate the unilateral sculling action at the feet during the breaststroke whip-kick. For the purpose of this text, the simple (and not too scientific) experiment was repeated and a description now follows.

I sculptured a pair of quarter-scale right feet from a solid piece of timber. The feet were modelled in a heel-to-heel fashion and when completed the profile resembled that of a boat's propeller, the contour of the instep combining with the natural arch of the sole to produce a hydrodynamic shape. (The *general contour* of the feet was examined by a local chiropodist who said they 'weren't bad'!) The propeller was then fitted to a simple elastic-powered boat as shown in fig. 18.3.

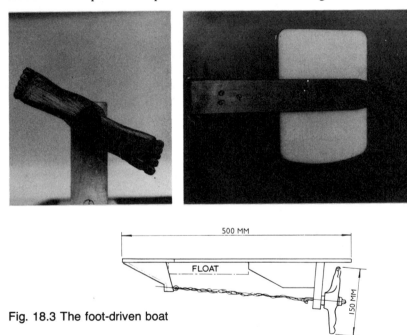

Fig. 18.3 The foot-driven boat

When first tested in the bath at home, the foot-propelled boat demonstrated rather unladylike qualities by turning over on her back, showering her constructor with water in the process. However, by the deft use of a polystyrene float, the stability problems were quickly rectified.

The wooden feet were fashioned as though they were in contact with the floor (as if in a standing position). Consequently for the first water test, it was the natural arch-dominated characteristics of the feet which were to be responsible for propelling the boat forward.

When wound up and placed in the water, the boat moved steadily but slowly forward. The test was repeated several times at various propeller speeds but the forward speed seemed to be limited.

In order to pursue the investigation further, the feet were remodelled in order to produce a more definite angle between the soles of the feet and the floor (when standing). This angle of *inversion* was set at approximately fifteen degrees. (Inversion of the feet means inclining the soles inward to face towards each other – see fig. 30.31.)

Replacing the reshaped and 're-charged' boat into the water, it now moved at a considerably increased speed with the propeller churning away at about the same rotational speed as during the previous tests. When related to the breast stroke, the demonstration seemed to indicate that, although dorsi-flexion of the feet is vital throughout the kicking movement, propulsion is enhanced by inverting both feet as they close together.

The additional medial flexing of the ankle joint seems to add considerably to the unilateral sculling effect of the natural foot arches. Underwater observations of good breast-stroke swimmers seem to confirm this.

Recovery
Due to the position that the legs are required to assume in preparation for the propulsive part of the kicking cycle, the profile drag effect related to leg recovery is greater in the breast stroke than in any of the other three competitive strokes. However, by good technique and teaching this may be minimised.

The kicking cycle commences with both legs in a fully stretched and streamlined attitude, the feet being together, or almost together. (This is the position the legs should have assumed at the end of the last kick.)

The body attitude ensures that the swimmer's heels are approximately 200 mm (8 in.) below the water surface.

At the appropriate moment in the complete stroke cycle, the hips and knees are flexed and the heels are drawn up towards the swimmer's seat. During this movement the knees are spread apart to approximately the width of the swimmer's shoulders, and the heels, as they near the seat, may also move apart a short distance.

During this drawing-up movement, the toes should maintain a backward-pointing mode in order to assist in the general streamlining characteristics, although in reality they lie within the forward profile of the swimmer, i.e. looking from the front, the feet cannot be seen and therefore do not add to the swimmer's profile.

Care must be taken in order that the forward movement of the thighs is not excessive, thus increasing the profile drag more than is necessary.

Figure 18.4 shows how the effective forward thigh profile varies with the angle of leg recovery, and also how the streamlining characteristics of the legs are affected. It can be seen that in illustration A the swimmer's hips are elevated rather high in the water causing the feet to break the surface and reduce their effectiveness. Illustration B shows the swimmer's legs recovered so that they form the same approximate angular relationship with the surface but this time the hips are riding lower in the water and the feet are submerged.

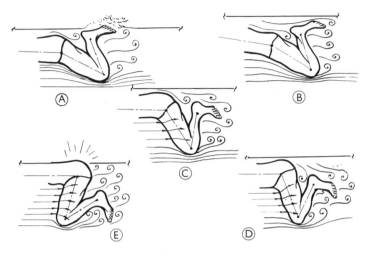

Fig. 18.4

Basically both these examples exhibit good streamlining characteristics due to the shallow angle of the thighs with the water surface. The hips form an angle of approximately 150 degrees with the body axis and the seat is about 200 mm (8 in.) below the water surface. Streamlining is quite good at this angle with the area of turbulent eddies reduced as far as possible for the recovery position.

This limb attitude is very near to the ideal position required to accelerate the feet into the propelling part of the cycle.

Mechanically, the lower-leg extensor muscles (the quadriceps) are at a disadvantage at this recovery angle, but the forces required to overcome the inertia of the lower leg and created water pressure are well within the capabilities of these very strong activators.

Illustrations C and D show that, by progressively drawing the knees up under the hips, the streamlining characteristics tend to deteriorate.

At position E not only are the drag effects very severe, but also the seat is above the water surface. The effect here is that the swimmer progresses through the water with a 'bobbing bottom'.

Now let us suppose that our swimmer has taken up a leg-recovery position as illustrated in B, and is ready to perform the propulsive part of the kick.

The propulsive part of the cycle

The competitive stroke law states that 'the feet shall be turned outwards in the backwards movement'.

This compulsory 'toeing-out', as we have seen, assists in developing an efficient leg thrust. Combined with this outward turn, both feet are moved into the dorsi-flexed position. It is important that this 'flat-foot' mode is maintained throughout the kick in order to generate the uni-directional foot scull described earlier.

The propulsive part of the leg movement commences with a vigorous extension of both the thighs and the lower legs. The feet, still in the dorsi-flexed and 'toeing-out' mode, accelerate outwards and backwards.

At almost full-limb extension, the feet start to sweep inwards and together. During the final part of the movement and as the legs decelerate and close together, the feet are stretched into the plantar-flexed attitude for a streamlined glide, if one is to be incorporated into the stroke, or subsequent leg recovery.

Figure 18.5 shows the path of the feet during the propulsive movement together with an approximation of the way in which they accelerate into the whipping phase.

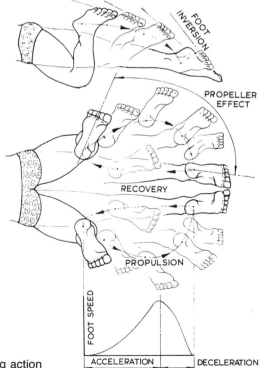

Fig. 18.5 The breast-stroke leg action

It is also important that the soles of the feet are inclined or angled towards each other (foot inversion) for full propulsive effect (see fig. 18.3).

It should also be noted how the feet act as 'partial propellers' by rotating through almost a right-angle during the kick.

Arm action

Too many breast strokers rely solely on their leg kick for propulsion, with their arms performing only a short, sideways, almost symbolic pull in keeping with the general rhythm and timing of the stroke, but contributing nothing towards moving the swimmer forward.

If any stroke is to be reasonably efficient, limb movement must provide propulsion for as long as possible within the overall cycle.

Breast-stroke arm movement is the shortest one of the competitive group of strokes. It is also the least efficient mainly because of this limited travel and also its underwater recovery.

Many breast strokers terminate their arm propulsion at the end of the backward movement, then thrust their hands forward to the start position once more.

There is, however, some extra propulsion to be gained by the swimmer carrying out a sculling movement with the hands as they travel inward towards the central body plane, prior to the forward thrust. Figure 18.6 shows a typical limb track of the arm cycle, illustrating this sculling feature.

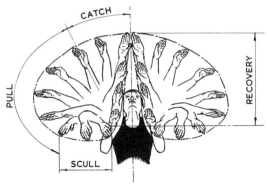

Fig. 18.6 The breast-stroke arm action

As mentioned previously, the underwater recovery of the arms is detrimental to the overall stroke efficiency. Bearing this point in mind, as soon as the propulsive movement is completed the elbows should be drawn close to the swimmer's body in order to minimise their profile drag area. To reduce drag, as soon as the hands have completed their task they should be positioned flat and streamlined and should remain in this position as they are pushed forward.

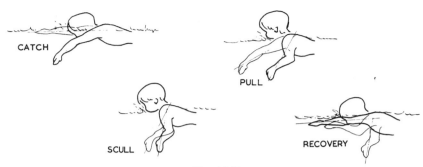

Fig. 18.7

Catch (fig. 18.7)

At the commencement of the movement, both arms should be fully stretched ahead of the swimmer with the palms of the hands approximately 100 mm (4 in.) below the water surface and facing directly downwards, fingers together and thumbs touching. As with all propulsive limb movements, the initial phase of the cycle is a catching action whereby pressure is built up on the hands and lower arms and the swimmer 'feels' the water.

To accomplish the catch, the hands should be rotated to face outwards and downwards at a 'palm angle' of approximately forty-five degrees. At the same time the wrists are slightly flexed in order that the palm may face square to the intended direction of movement.

The hands are now moved in an accelerating mode – outwards, backwards and downwards. The extent of the catch movement depends mainly on the rate of acceleration of the hands which, in turn, should not be too rapid, otherwise cavitation and eddies will develop behind the hands and lower arms, leading to 'overpull'. Another feature of the initial hand movement is that, if there is any surface turbulence, the hands are too high in the water. The propulsive hand trajectory must be out, back and downwards, with no noticeable water-surface disturbance occurring at any time.

Pull (fig. 18.7)

Normally, the catch will take place during the first 300 mm (12 in.) of hand movement, to be followed immediately by the pull.

During the pull, the elbows may become slightly flexed and remain elevated above the hands, the palms directed so that they face backwards.

At a position slightly ahead of the shoulder plane, the hands should be at their widest distance apart and, when viewed from head-on, theoretical lines drawn between the palm centres and the front of the swimmer's head should form at least a right-angle (see fig. 18.8). (This is only an approximation which may be used to effect when teaching beginners. As their stroke techniques develop, this arm configuration may change.)

It is at this point forward of the shoulders that the arc of movement of the hand changes direction to move inwards and, at the same time, a lateral rotation of the forearm takes place to incline the downward-pointing hand inwards, in preparation for the scull. This is the termination of the pull, and the swimmer's hands should be slightly forward of and below his elbows.

Scull (fig. 18.7)
The forearms, being now medially rotated, ensure that the palms are inclined inwards in order to perform the uni-directional sculling movement.

The scull takes place just below the shoulders and continues until the hands pass under the shoulder joints on their way into the recovery.

During the performance of the less formal styles and also during the initial stroke-learning period, the scull will be non-existent. It is only later as techniques are improved that this characteristic becomes a feature of the arm stroke.

Recovery (fig. 18.7)
Recovery of the hands takes place with them being pushed forward in a flat and streamlined mode below the surface of the water. The direction in which the palms face during the forward push is unimportant, just as long as the fingers point forwards and the hands are flat. The technique varies from swimmer to swimmer.

During the recovery movement the elbows should be tucked in close to the body in order to minimise the profile drag effects, although this feature tends to vary with the speed of the arm cycle.

At the termination of the movement, the swimmer's arms should be stretched ahead, the hands should be flat with fingers together. The palms should face downwards and be at an approximate depth of 100 mm (4 in.).

A rather common fault which takes place during the push forward is that the hands are not held flat, consequently the swimmer tends to push himself backwards. Recovery is an 'evil necessity' in swimming and therefore must take place with the minimum of interference to forward movement.

If a glide is to be included in the technique, it should be performed with the arms in this fully stretched position and held until the start of the next arm cycle.

Breathing
Most breast strokers breathe during every stroke because it is convenient and simple to do so.

The downward-moving arms tend to elevate the shoulders so that, with a slight backward tilt of the head, the face emerges clear of the water at approximately the end of the pulling movement. It is at this point in the stroke cycle that a breath is taken through the mouth (see part 5 of the stroke diagrams).

Immediately following the intake of air, the swimmer's shoulders tend to sink as the arms are pushed forward. The head is now tilted forward into the 'normal' swimming position whereby the hair line is approximately at the water line. (If the eyes were open at this stage, the swimmer would be looking forward and downward at approximately thirty degrees to the water surface.)

Exhalation should take place through the mouth or mouth and nose. The latter technique is probably the more practical, thus ensuring that the nasal passages are maintained clear and preventing the ingress of water to the 'uncontrollable' region at the back of the throat.

The timing and method of exhalation depends mainly on the swimmer's technique. A fast-stroking action will dictate that the swimmer exhales in an explosive fashion mid-way through the pull.

A slower 'revving' stroke will enable the swimmer either to hold the breath for a very short while, then exhale in an explosive manner prior to the next intake, or to exhale by a controlled trickle through mouth and nose or mouth only, so that complete exhaustion of air occurs just before the head is raised for the next intake.

The latter method is probably a more natural system of respiration. A simple method of teaching the exhalation part of the breathing cycle is to persuade the learner to 'blow his hands away' as he pushes them forward during the recovery.

The leisure forms of breast stroke display an elevated head position and breathing out usually takes place above the surface in a less disciplined manner than that of the competition style.

Beginners carrying out early breast-stroke practices also tend to maintain a head-high posture, breathing in and out at will. It is advisable, with competition in mind, for the teacher to introduce some breathing discipline at an early stage of the stroke teaching, thus ensuring that there will be less likelihood of faulty breathing habits developing at a later stage.

Finally, some success may be gained in the teaching of the breathing technique by concentrating on the exhalation part of the cycle rather than the inhalation phase. A swimmer may breathe in and hold his breath for some considerable time, but, if exhalation has occurred, the subsequent intake of air must take place almost immediately. Bearing this fact in mind, the breathing practices may focus on 'blowing the hands away' rather than breathing in at the end of the arm pull.

Co-ordination
Synchronisation of the arm, leg and head movements is an important feature of the breast stroke and, should the timing of the individual

actions be even slightly out of phase with each other, a jerky and inefficient action will result.

Probably the major feature of the relationship between the leg and arm movements is that the arms should be fully extended in front of the swimmer before the peak of the kicking thrust is reached. In order to achieve the correct sequence of movements, the arms should begin their pulling action while the legs are in the stretched position. Then, at the end of the pull and the beginning of the inward hand scull, the legs begin their recovery cycle. If this initial timing is achieved, the arm will be fully stretched in front of the swimmer when the propulsion peak of the leg kick occurs. If a breath has been taken at the correct stage, it enables the head to be lowered into the normal swimming position as the arms are thrust forward, thus enhancing body streamlining during the leg kick.

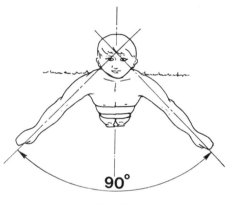

Fig. 18.8

At the end of the leg kick, there may be a glide introduced into the stroke. The length of this glide is dependent on the power of the swimmer's leg kick and the rate at which he is stroking. If a leisurely style is being performed, the glide can be (according to the strength of the leg kick) quite a long one. Another factor affecting the glide length is the swimmer's natural buoyancy. Should the legs have a tendency to sink readily, his ability to glide will consequently be less.

Competition swimmers tend to swim with a constantly 'revving' action and no apparent glide, because, of course, the glide is a slowing-down process.

When teaching the stroke, I tend to think of the arms, legs and breath all 'shooting out' at the same time, and encourage the swimmers to 'let it all hang out' at once.

Fig. 18.9 The stroke diagrams

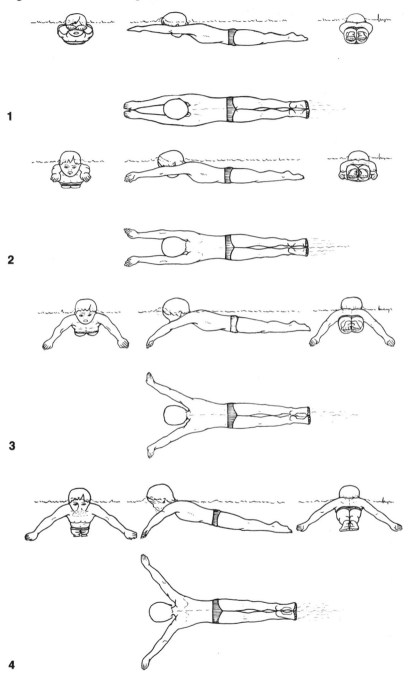

1

2

3

4

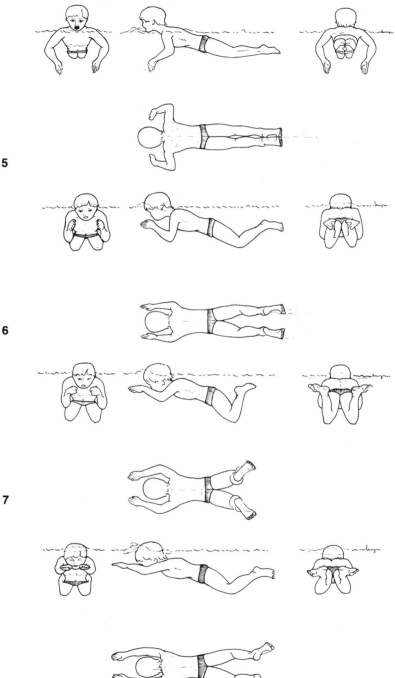

5

6

7

8

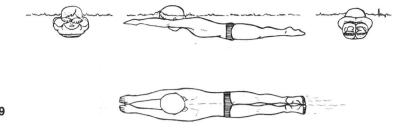

9

Preparatory standards for teaching the stroke
The preparations for teaching breast stroke are identical with those required for teaching the front crawl: before commencing the following programme of breast-stroke practices, therefore, it is advisable that the pupils are able to perform the following activities with some semblance of skill.
1. Confidence exercises – face wetting, blowing bubbles and submersion
2. Regaining the feet from a prone position
3. Pushing and gliding from the poolside
4. Front paddling at least 20 m
5. Treading water
6. General water mobility exercises

TEACHING THE BREAST STROKE
The breast stroke is a popular first teaching stroke, especially where adults are concerned. The main reasons for this are that the stroke is performed in the 'natural' prone position and also that, during its performance, the exponent may keep his or her face clear of the water. As mentioned earlier, it is also a leisure stroke and, swimming being so universally popular, the stroke will probably be seen in this guise more often than in any other.

The arm cycle is not a complicated action, but the leg movement is rather alien in its nature, compared with that of the other three strokes whose swinging motion is closely allied with walking or running.

Breast-stroke leg kick is essentially a movement of co-ordination, flexibility and control, with the ability to perform the action being almost inherent, rather than one which is acquired. I firmly believe that true breast strokers are born rather than made, and as far as the leisure swimmers are concerned, it is not essential that perfection is achieved.

Breathing during the performance of the stroke does not usually present any problems. As mentioned earlier, the swimmer is able by design to keep his or her face clear of the water quite easily throughout the whole movement. It should be noted, however, that some kind of breathing discipline must be introduced during the early practices, in order that young swimmers are able to progress naturally into the competitive style. This demands a lower position of the head in the water.

Most of the class will probably have tried swimming a version of the breast stroke in their paddling days. Many hybrids may be evolved at this early stage, such as a wide-sweeping arm pull with a front-paddle leg kick, or a downward simultaneous pull combined with the infamous 'screw-kick'. The true breast strokers will be seen displaying not necessarily an absolutely correct movement but a *sense of symmetry* which is one of the main ingredients of a correctly executed style.

It has been mentioned before that children are expert mimics. With this fact in mind, therefore, it is sensible to give them something to copy. So, if at all possible, before letting them loose on the exercise treat them to a visual demonstration of the stroke accompanied by a clear and concise explanation of all the main features of the style. Needless to say, the demonstration must be carried out by someone who is able to swim the breast stroke using correctly timed and skilfully executed movements.

When the teacher has made sure that all the class are well positioned to see and hear the demonstration, the show may begin.

Activity: demonstration swim with commentary
The demonstration is best performed lengthways down the pool because one of the stroke features that needs highlighting is the powerful leg kick and the resulting glide. Swimming widths does not exhibit this feature to advantage.

The stroke may be performed in a leisure fashion initially, then as a racing style. Here the teacher will be able to point out the main differences between the two techniques, such as the lower head position and the stroke continuity which produces a shorter, almost non-existent glide in the racing stroke.

Adhering to the previously established sequence of explanations, the swimmer's body position may be singled out as the initial feature, showing how the hips are slightly lower in the water than when the other strokes are performed. It should be quite obvious how this lower swimming position enables the feet to be submerged during the latter part of the leg recovery and the early propulsive phase.

It will be seen also how dominant is the swimmer's leg kick and how noticeable is the sudden surge forward, which is caused by the rapid 'whipping' movement of the feet. This whip-like leg movement should be highlighted as one of the most important features of the stroke.

The pattern of the downward and backward arm pull will need to be viewed from the side and from ahead of the swimmer, and the class should be encouraged to change their positions in order to make these observations.

The demonstrating swimmer should show how the breathing movements are carried out in both the leisure and racing strokes. The pattern of breathing in through the mouth, as the shoulders are elevated by the downward arm movement, then the breathing-out motion through the mouth and nose as the hands are thrust away into the recovery, should easily be seen by the class.

A further note on the 'flat hand-low resistance' recovery may also be made by the teacher when referring to the push forward. Timing the stroke may be memorably described as 'letting it all hang out' at the same time. In other words, pushing the hand *out*, kicking the feet *out* and breathing *out*, all at the same instant in the stroke cycle. This combination of movements will easily be seen to be happening each time the swimmer kicks into the glide. It should be suggested to the class that if they concentrate on these simultaneous actions, the timing of the stroke is inclined to look after itself.

As the breast stroke is very law-restricted, the teacher should briefly explain the ASA laws, pointing out how the performer is adhering to them.

After witnessing the demonstration, the class may be invited to perform their version of what they have just seen.

Activity: full stroke
Practice: initial full-stroke swims
TEACHING POINTS
Right from the outset, the ASA laws which govern the performance of the stroke should be introduced into the teachings. There is no need for these stroke laws as such to be mentioned to the class; the children probably will not absorb such technicalities during the early stages of learning. The teacher, however, should be thoroughly aware of the peculiarities associated with the various limb movements and, consequently, be able to include these features in the instructions which are given.

1. The points relating to the symmetrical and simultaneous aspects of the stroke performance must be the major teaching features. Each arm or leg movement must be a mirror image of its corresponding limb and the swimmer's shoulders and hips should be square and laterally parallel with the water surface.

2. The feet should remain below the surface at all times and, during the propulsive part of the kick, they must be retained in the cocked and 'toed-out' position. (The term 'cocked' must be carefully explained as 'the toes are brought up towards the shins'.)

3. The arm actions should be directed towards attaining the backward and downward patterns of movement, with no water-surface disturbance being in evidence at any time.

The shoulder line should be the limit of backward arm movement and any tendency to over-pull should be highlighted.

4. The swimmer's head may be kept high during this exercise, and consequently there should be no breathing problems in evidence.

These few teaching points would seem to be adequate at this early stage, more precise instruction being given during the part-stroke and later full-stroke practices.

Activity: leg action
Practice 1: land exercise – sitting on the pool surround and carrying out an 'inverted' leg movement (fig. 18.10)

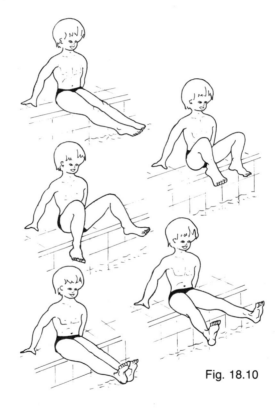

Fig. 18.10

In order to demonstrate the leg movements to the class, there is a choice of several positions that the teacher may take up. For instance, by sitting on the edge of some convenient elevated poolside seat and raising his or her legs above the floor, the teacher should be able to carry out this land exercise quite satisfactorily for all to see. If there is a 1-m diving-board, this makes an ideal base for the demonstration.

Alternatively, the pool surround may be used if it is dry or if there is something suitable to sit on. Here, the teacher is able to assume a position similar to that which the pupils will take up during the exercise. (It will be better for the children to stand, should this latter position be taken up, in order that they may witness each movement clearly.)

A further method of demonstration is for the teacher to stand on one leg (suitably supported, of course) and demonstrate the kicking motion with the other leg. The movement itself, however, may not be quite so clear to the pupils, and is not really recommended as an initial choice for class display purposes. (After such a one-legged demonstration it has been known for the mimics in the class to swim using one leg only!)

A method of demonstration that has been used successfully is to select a suitable member of the class and, with the others gathered around so that they may all see, the pupil sits on the floor in the correct position. By grasping one of the pupil's feet in each hand, the teacher manipulates them in such a way that they perform the correct pattern of movement. The advantage of this system is that the teacher is able to interrupt the movement at any stage in order to point out precisely why the legs or feet are working in some particular fashion.

In the initial stage of the practice, the pupils should perform the pattern of movement in a sequence of separate phases as follows.

THE FIRST MOVEMENT Starting in the sitting position with feet outstretched and together, the heels are now drawn up towards the seat. As the knees bend in order to accomplish the movement, they also move away from each other until they reach a distance of approximately shoulder-width apart.

Perhaps the paramount feature of this recovery part of the movement is that the feet should have taken up a cocked or dorsi-flexed attitude by the time they have reached the end of the drawing-up movement, the heels being some 150–200 mm (6–8 in.) from the seat.

THE SECOND MOVEMENT The legs are now straightened and the feet are moved outwards, so that the pupils are all sitting with their legs astride and in contact with the floor. The cocked-foot position should be maintained with the toes pointing outwards.

THE THIRD MOVEMENT The legs, still straight, should now be closed together. (During the normal in-the-water swimming movement, both feet should attain a stretched and streamlined attitude only at the end of the closing movement, but this is not really necessary in the land exercise.)

The pupils may initially carry out several individual cycles of the movements to numbers, in an attempt to master the pattern. Once the action has been established in their minds, it may be performed without a pause, in a similar manner to that of actually swimming.

TEACHING POINTS

1. Emphasis should be placed on a slow recovery (knee bend) followed by a vigorous straightening and closing of the legs. Continuity of movement should also be a feature of the final versions of the exercise.

2. Outward pointed feet flat and at right-angles to the shins (cocked) must be in evidence throughout the exercise.

The duration of the exercise should be short and, in order to retain its value, it should be followed immediately by repetition of the pattern of movement in the water.

Practice 2: leg-kicking practice at the rail (figs 18.11 and 18.12)

TEACHING POINTS

1. The pupils should display a definite whip-kick, an accelerated out-round-and-together propulsive movement compared with the slower recovery.

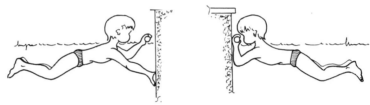

Fig. 18.11   Fig. 18.12

2. The teacher must be persistent regarding the 'flat-foot' or 'Charlie Chaplin' stance (see fig. 18.13) being maintained throughout the propulsive phase, but culminating now in both feet taking up an athletically stretched mode at the end of the kick.

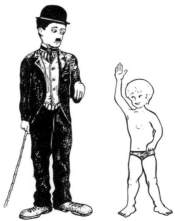

Fig. 18.13 Feet in the 'Charlie Chaplin' position

3. The heels should be together or almost together as they are drawn up to the buttocks.

4. The observance should be made throughout the whole motion of the ASA law whereby 'The feet shall be turned outwards in the backward movement. A "dolphin" kick is not permitted.'

5. The slower recovery movement should be limited to a position whereby the angle between the thighs and the trunk does not exceed 150 degrees. (An angle of 150 degrees is shown as a teaching guide.) The effect of excessive leg recovery, i.e. when the knees retract below the swimmer's hips, is for the bottom to bob up and down and, because of this distinct feature, the fault is easily identified.

6. The mirror-image effect of one leg compared to the other must be maintained, with the hips, knees and ankles of each leg being retained in the laterally horizontal mode throughout the whole cycle. Where this simultaneous and symmetrical image is not attained, the movement results in producing some version or other of the dreaded screw-kick.

SCREW-KICK The ASA law relating to the breast-stroke leg kick states that: 'All movements of the legs shall be simultaneous and in the same horizontal plane without alternating movements.' The screw-kick occurs when there is non-observance of these rules. Movements of the legs are out of phase with each other, with one foot usually lower in the water and travelling in a different direction from its companion.

Invariably one of the swimmer's feet is pointed throughout the kick, and propulsion – if there is any – is developed by the instep and shin rather than the sole of the foot. The 'screw' may be caused by the lowering of one shoulder, but it is not always accompanied by this fault.

7. From the stretched position and back again, the leg movement should remain continuous.

8. The swimmer's hips should be low enough in the water to prevent the feet from breaking the water surface as they are drawn up to the seat, or again, at the start of the backward kick. (If the feet have a tendency to break the water surface, it will be when they are near the swimmer's seat.)

9. The heels should be drawn up to within approximately 150–200 mm (6–8 in.) of the swimmer's seat during the recovery.

10. Holding the rail or scum channel in such a way that the swimmer is elevated to a suitable depth for practice is a fairly simple operation and the teacher should therefore make sure that the pupils are able to perform this feature of the exercise satisfactorily, rather than adopt the partner-support system.

Practice 3: leg movement with partner (carrier) support (fig. 18.14)
TEACHING POINTS
All the teaching points previously mentioned relating to the leg kick are applicable to this exercise, together with the extended-arm method of holding each other, as described.

The pupils should by now be displaying a movement allied to the correct breast-stroke kick. In order to get some idea of how effective the movement is, the next exercise is a mobile one.

It has been said earlier that if the pupils are able actually to witness their limb movements, correction of any faults that may be present is made easier. In the following practice, the swimmer is able to observe his leg movements while at the same time being supported by one or two floats.

Fig. 18.14

Practice 4: leg movements in a supine float-supported position (fig. 18.15)
TEACHING POINTS
The general pattern of the kick is the same as when it is performed in the prone swimming position. All the appropriate features of the kick will therefore be relevant.

A repeat of the exercise may now be performed with the swimmers lying on their fronts.

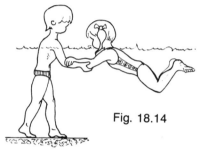

Fig. 18.15

Practice 5: prone swimming legs-only movement, first with two and then with a single float (figs 18.16 and 18.17)

Fig. 18.16   Fig. 18.17

Probably one of the most common faults will be too much reliability on the floats. The pupils should therefore be encouraged to stretch their arms in front of them and not lean on the floats for support. The correct methods of holding the floats should be continuously stressed during the exercises.

The rest of the related teaching points are all as previously mentioned.

The establishment of a glide is the only new point to arise in the exercise and this must be carried out with the swimmers assuming a fully stretched position.

Practice 6: unsupported push and glide to the rail with one or more kicks (fig. 18.18)

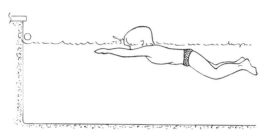

Fig. 18.18

TEACHING POINTS
All the leg-movement teaching points are as previously described.

If the swimmers are able to maintain a fully stretched face-in-the-water mode, this will assist them in establishing a good body position for the exercises.

Practice 7: unsupported leg kicking across the pool width
TEACHING POINTS
All the teaching points relating to the leg movement are now recalled once more, and are as follows:

1. The appreciation of the whip-kick whereby the pupils display a definite accelerated out-round-and-together propulsive movement compared with the slower recovery.

2. The teacher must be persistent about the 'flat-foot' or 'Charlie Chaplin' stance being maintained throughout the propulsive phase but culminating now in both feet taking up an athletically stretched mode at the end of the kick.

3. The heels may be together or a short distance apart when they are drawn up to within 150–200 mm (6–8 in.) of the buttocks.

4. The ASA law should be observed throughout the motion: 'The feet

shall be turned outwards in the backward movement. A "dolphin" kick is not permitted.'

5. The slower recovery movement should be limited to a position whereby the angle between the thighs and the trunk does not exceed 150 degrees. The effect of excessive leg recovery is for the swimmer's bottom to bob up and down and, because of this distinct feature, the fault is easily identified.

6. The mirror-image effect of the movement must be maintained, with the hips in the laterally horizontal mode. Where this simultaneous and symmetrical action is not attained, the movement results in a version of the screw-kick

7. From the stretched position and back again, the leg movement should remain continuous.

8. The swimmer's hips should be low enough in the water to prevent the feet from breaking the water surface as they are drawn up to the seat, or again at the start of the thrust. (If the feet have a tendency to break the water surface, it will be when they are near the swimmer's seat.)

Having now completed a full set of breast-stroke leg practices, the pupils should be ready to absorb some new activities concerning the arm stroke movement.

Activity: arm action
Practice 1: standing in shallow water (fig. 18.19),
the teacher demonstrating
the action from the poolside

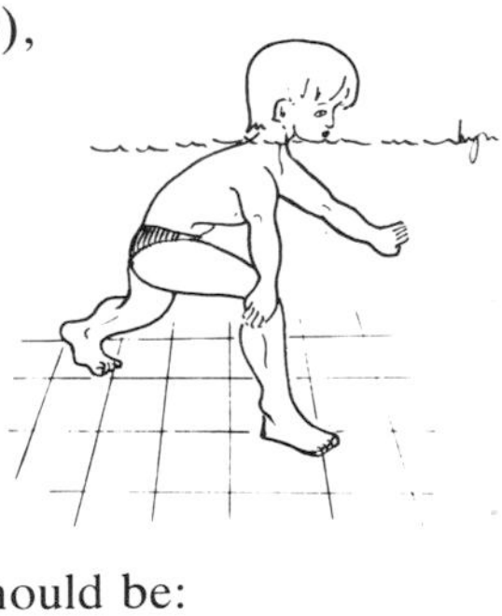

Fig. 18.19

TEACHING POINTS
1. The starting (static) position for the arms should be:
   (a) hands – with fingers together, straight and flat
   (b) thumbs – touching
   (c) palms – facing directly downwards
   (d) wrists – unflexed with the flat hands in line with forearms
   (e) elbows – straight but not stiff
   (f) shoulders – upper part just below the water surface. (It is advisable for the teacher to tell the pupils to keep their shoulders in the water throughout the movement)
   (g) arms – generally stretched forward parallel with the water surface.

2. The hands must be kept flat throughout with fingers together.

3. In order to face the palms directly backwards for as long as possible during the actual pull, the wrists should be flexed for most of the movement.

4. The elbows should be maintained relatively straight during the pull.

5. The movement should be downwards, outwards and back: if there is any surface disturbance, the path of the arms is incorrect.

6. The hands should not travel back beyond the plane of the shoulders. It is advisable for the teacher to insist that they definitely.terminate their backward movement, say, 150 mm (6 in.) forward of the shoulders.

7. As the pulling movement commences, the hands still maintained in a flat mode are faced diagonally downwards and outwards accompanied by a slight flexion of the wrist.

Practice 2: pulling and sliding or walking
TEACHING POINTS
All the teaching points mentioned in the previous static arms-only exercise are relevant.

Some, if not most of the pupils, will tend to move with their shoulders raised well above the water surface. Pointing out that this is 'flying rather than swimming' and that they should 'be fish, not birds' usually helps. Also, they will probably tend to push their arms back further than the plane of the shoulders in order to assist themselves along, their main objective being to produce forward movement rather than the correct breast-stroke arm action. With this in mind, it is best to avoid any reference to speed, otherwise the whole purpose of the exercise will be lost.

Initially, the leisure style of breast stroke should be performed so that the swimmer's head is held high enough above the surface to avoid any breathing problems. However, with competition and rough water conditions in mind, it is advisable to introduce some breathing discipline during these part-practices. Also, as the breathing sequence is more closely allied to the arm movement than to the leg movement, it is considered to be advantageous to include some breathing instruction at this particular stage.

Practice 3: pulling and breathing while standing, then while walking or sliding (fig. 18.20)
TEACHING POINTS
1. Inhalation must be through the mouth and exhalation is best carried out through the mouth and nose in a trickle fashion. It is worth reminding the class that breathing out through the nose is advisable because, if air is coming down the nose, water cannot go up it.

Fig. 18.20

2. Inhalation, when coupled with 'blowing the hands away' takes place towards the end of the arm pull.

3. During the exhalation, the swimmer's mouth and nose should be lowered into the water while he continues to look forward. (Jutting the chin forward helps to maintain this position.) Exhalation may continue into the early phase of the arm pull.

We should by now be in a position to bring all the breast-stroke movements together. Concentration may therefore be centred on co-ordination and timing of the individual actions in order to produce a synchronised and aesthetic performance.

Activity: stroke co-ordination
Practice: width swims
The full-stroke movements may take place across the width of the pool. An instruction to make the pupils understand and remember the movement is, 'Let it all hang out at once': i.e. kick the legs out (backward and inward kick), push the arms out (recovery forward) and breathe out – all at the same time.

This description of the overall movement is simple for learners to understand and, although to the pure technician it leaves a little to be desired, it has proved to be quite successful in teaching breast-stroke co-ordination. The teacher is advised to refer to the earlier stroke diagrams, in order to familiarise himself or herself with the movements if at all unsure.

A rhythm of pull/breathe in, then kick/breathe out and glide should be established. Introducing a glide at the end of the cycle will tend to avoid any hurried and jerky movements.

Continuation with the full-stroke movements may now proceed with a return to part-practices as the need arises. Grouping the class will probably be necessary if such action has not already been taken.

FAULTS AND THEIR CORRECTION

Feature: BODY POSITION

FAULT	EFFECT ON STROKE	CORRECTION
1. Head too high	1. Hips and legs drop lower than necessary 2. Increase in profile drag effect	1. Head lift synchronised with arm pull 2. *Minimum amount*, in order to inhale through mouth 3. Maintain water-line/hair-line relationship beyond this 4. Surface prone push-and-glide practices

5. Float-assisted legs-only practices
6. Extended-arm leg practices with breathing
7. Full stroke – emphasis on head position

FAULT	EFFECT ON STROKE	CORRECTION
2. Head too low	1. Feet break the surface 2. Danger of disqualification during competition	All corrections as above
3. Bobbing, caused by over-flexing hips, incorrect timing, lifting head excessively	1. Wastage of energy 2. Increase in profile drag area	1. Attention to leg kick (see leg-action faults) 2. Attention to co-ordination (see co-ordination faults) Corrections as shown in Fault 1
4. Shoulders not parallel with water surface	1. Tendency towards side stroke 2. One shoulder dropped 3. Tendency to screw-kick 4. Danger of disqualification during competition	1. Attention to arm stroke and its symmetrical movement (see arm-action faults) 2. Breathing practices: swimmer may be attempting to avoid oncoming waves and turning head (see breathing faults)

Feature: LEG ACTION
Phase: RECOVERY

FAULT	EFFECT ON STROKE	CORRECTION
1. Excessive flexion of hips	1. Knees move to position vertically below hips, or beyond 2. Bobbing takes place 3. Excessive profile drag created	1. Attention to extent of thigh recovery 2. Inverted breast-stroke legs-only practices with float 3. Prone legs-only practices with float 4. Emphasis on knee bend rather than hip flexion
2. Excessive thigh abduction (knees too wide apart)	1. Excessive strain on abductor muscles during propulsive phase 2. Slight increase in profile drag	1. Emphasis on narrow kick 2. From behind, thighs making an approximate angle of sixty degrees with each other or knees approximately shoulder-width apart 3. Inverted breast-stroke legs-only practices with float 4. Prone legs-only practices with float
3. Asymmetric movement	1. Tendency towards asymmetric kick 2. Disqualification during competition	1. Leg practices at the handrail with emphasis on *slow* symmetrical recovery 2. Set up circular heel movement at constant speed 3. Distinguish between slow recovery and higher-rated kick 4. Proceed to supine and prone float-assisted practices

FAULT	EFFECT ON STROKE	CORRECTION
4. Failure to rotate the feet outward and dorsi-flex at the end of recovery	Failure to develop the sculling action with the soles of the feet	1. Visual demonstration 2. Partner assistance at the handrail: partner holds swimmer's feet and positions them correctly, i.e. rotates both feet outward and presses them towards the related shin 3. Handrail leg practice by numbers, then continual emphasis of the 'preparation-for-kick' position 4. Float-assisted leg practices supine and prone
5. Insufficient recovery, i.e. failure to position the heels near enough to the seat prior to the kick	Loss of power	1. Bathside sitting exercises: emphasis on bringing the heels near to seat during recovery 2. Handrail exercises, partner-assisted or free-moving 3. Proceed on through the logical leg-action practice sequences
6. Feet breaking water surface	Loss of power	1. Float-assisted practices with emphasis on body position, and keeping feet submerged 2. Full-stroke practices keeping head elevated sufficiently to enable feet to remain submerged
7. Asymmetric recovery: legs not recovering together or in the same lateral plane	1. Creating screw-kick 2. Loss of power 3. Danger of disqualification during competition	1. Handrail practices slowly and rhythmically, then gradually speeding up 2. Partner assistance by holding and manipulating both feet correctly 3. Proceed through logical sequence of leg practices, returning to handrail movements if necessary Rectification of this particular fault requires considerable patience, dedication and concentration from both teacher and pupil.

Phase: PROPULSION

FAULT	EFFECT ON STROKE	CORRECTION
1. Asymmetric movement (screw-kick)	1. Loss of propulsion 2. Danger of disqualification during competition	All as corrections for Fault 7 (recovery). Bear in mind that the fault is sometimes impossible to cure in the time available
2. Pushing feet directly backwards with no inward and circular 'whip'	1. Considerable loss of propulsion 2. Movement too rapid – swimmer tends to jerk	Demonstrate the ineffectiveness of pushing feet directly backward as compared with whipping action All as corrections for Fault 7 (recovery)

FAULT	EFFECT ON STROKE	CORRECTION
3. Allowing the feet to drop too low in water	1. Decreased effectiveness of leg kick 2. Closely allied with previous faults	As above
4. Failure to dorsi-flex the feet – usually an adult beginner method of kick due to lack of ankle flexibility	1. Loss of propulsion 2. Propulsion developed by fronts of feet instead of soles	All as for Fault 4 (recovery)
5. Straightening the legs before they are adducted	Loss of propulsion	1. Demonstration and explanation of whip-kick theory and ineffectiveness of wedge-kick 2. Logical sequence of float-assisted practices to full-stroke movements
6. Failure to close legs together and attain fully stretched mode	1. Loss of streamlining 2. Increase in resistance to forward momentum	Legs-only float-assisted practices, concentrating on streamlining aspect

Feature: ARM ACTION
Phase: CATCH

FAULT	EFFECT ON STROKE	CORRECTION
1. Hands directed sideways instead of sideways/ backwards and downwards	Catch is effective (i.e. pressure is built up on hand and lower arm), but in being directed sideways the propulsive force is ineffective	1. Wrists must commence movement by being slightly flexed 2. Movement must be side/back and down 3. Arm practices in shallow end, emphasis on initial movement
2. Hands directed directly downwards	1. As above but directed downwards 2. Head and shoulders tend to bob up and down	As above
3. Hands too near surface to begin with	1. Excessive water disturbance and turbulent drag 2. Loss of power	1. Commence catch with hands approximately 75 mm (3 in.) below water surface 2. Practise as above
4. Fingers apart: this fault and correction is applicable throughout propulsive movement	1. Catch will be ineffective and prolonged 2. Subsequent arm movement will be less effective	1. Shallow-water practices with emphasis on fingers together 2. On to full-stroke practices

Phase: PULL

FAULT	EFFECT ON STROKE	CORRECTION
1. Hands directed sideways and parallel with water surface	1. Pull becomes shorter 2. Increased profile drag at the end of pull 3. Probable water-surface disturbance – wasted energy 4. Failure to lift the body and head for breathing cycle 5. Pull probably beyond shoulder plane 6. Pull directed excessively sideways rather than backwards	1. Shallow-water practices: concentration on correct back/side and down movement 2. To full-stroke practices
2. Pulling with elbows bent and hands directed sideways	Ineffective pull due to geometry and arm/hand movement	Emphasis on a straight arm pull with flexed wrists Correction as for Fault 1
3. Pulling too steeply, continuation of catch (2)	1. Head-and-shoulders bobbing motion 2. Shortened pull	Correction as for Fault 1
4. Elbows dropped	1. Pull ineffective 2. Loss of power due to 'slipping'	Correction as for Fault 1 1. Emphasis on a straight arm pull with flexed wrists 2. Elbows should always be above the hands
5. Pulling beyond the shoulder plane	1. Longer pull, but recovery is subsequently longer and more resistive 2. Removal of forward body-balancing forces, hence head and shoulders drop 3. Rhythm of stroke is disturbed 4. Overall loss of power	1. Shallow-water practices, emphasis on keeping hands in front of shoulders at the end of pull: 'Keep hands in sight all the time' 2. Full-stroke practices: speed up whole movement so as not to allow the longer pull to take place
6. Uneven pull (tendency towards side-stroking action), usually	1. Swimmer tends to swim slightly on the side rather than on the front	1. Shallow-water practices, introducing breathing sequence 2. Full-stroke practices with breathing and a glide

| associated with fear of facing forward and incorrect breathing technique | 2. One shoulder drops – interference with leg movement 3. Danger of disqualification in competition | 3. Emphasis on keeping shoulders square and pull symmetrical |

Phase: RECOVERY

FAULT	EFFECT ON STROKE	CORRECTION
1. Elbows too wide	Increased profile drag and consequent wastage of energy	1. Shallow-water practices with emphasis on tucking the elbows in at the end of pull 2. Full-stroke practices
2. Hands not directed forward, i.e. inclined upwards rather than flat and streamlined, sometimes on the water surface	1. Increased (dynamic) drag and consequent wastage of energy 2. Usually accompanied by forward-directed splash	1. Full-stroke practices with hands in a flat and forward-directed mode during recovery 2. No water disturbance; hands below surface throughout
3. Hands too wide (shoulder-width) when being pushed forward and when recovery is completed	Disturbs the streamlining effects which are present when the thumbs are together	1. Full-stroke practices with emphasis on 'thumb-touching' recovery 2. Emphasise glide in streamlined mode
4. Recovery not fully completed and too low	1. Usually a circular or beginner's arm action with no forward stretch 2. When too low, swimmer tends to pull *up* and back rather than *down* and back, thus tending to sink the shoulders rather than life them	1. Shallow-water practices with emphasis on recovery just below water surface into fully stretched mode 2. Full-stroke practices starting the catch higher in the water

Feature: BREATHING

FAULT	EFFECT ON STROKE	CORRECTION
1. Breath-holding may be due to fear of the water	Swimmer quickly becomes fatigued	1. Breathing discipline to be adopted: in through the mouth, out through the mouth and nose 2. Return to shallow water and float-assisted practices
2. Failure to breathe owing to head being held too low or tilted forward (allied to Fault 1)	As above	As above

19 The Butterfly

The butterfly law* states that:

Both arms are to be brought forward together over the water and brought back together simultaneously and symmetrically.

The swimmer must remain completely on his front with both shoulders maintained parallel with the water surface.

All movements of the feet are to be performed in a simultaneous fashion. Simultaneous oscillating movements of the legs and feet in the vertical plane are permitted. The legs or feet need not necessarily be at the same level but there must be no alternating movements between them.

STROKE TECHNIQUE
Body position
It is difficult to define the butterfly body position precisely other than by saying that if the timing of the whole stroke is correct, a side view of the swimmer will show him carrying his hips high in the water with a minimum os undulation.

A flat and horizontal swimming mode is desirable in order to keep the profile drag characteristics at a minimum. The vertically biased movements of both the arms and legs contribute towards making the swimmer's shoulders and hips rise and fall about the centre of gravity of her body as she moves through the water. Here it can be seen that after the arms have entered the water, even though the elbows are elevated, the reaction of the downward forces on the hands and lower arms tends to raise the shoulders.

At the same time as this arm movement takes place, the legs are together, moved vigorously downward, in order to carry out the major propulsive phase of the kick. The result of this action is that the swimmer's hips are also raised.

Throughout the complete stroke cycle, therefore, the hips and shoulders tend to fluctuate in their relationships with the water surface.

As skill is acquired, the butterfly swimmer develops a stroke technique with a flowing rather than a jerky appearance, and at the same time the hips are maintained in a permanently elevated position with body fluctuation being held to a minimum.

*As given in the current *ASA Handbook*.

Breathing in requires the swimmer's head to be lifted by 'hyper-extension' of the neck resulting in the chin being thrust forward. This neck articulation provides more than just a head tilt; it also allows the head to be 'slightly isolated' in its movement. Consequently, the effect on shoulder and chest elevation in the water (both undesirable features) is minimal.

For the rest of the stroke cycle, the head should be positioned in the 'normal' attitude with the water line between the hair line and the top of the head.

When the swimmer is examined from head-on, the shoulders must be seen to be laterally in line with the water surface. Except for when breathing in, the top of the swimmer's head rather than his face should be seen by the observer.

During the recovery sweep, the arms, hands and shoulders should be completely clear of the water surface before re-entry takes place at some point ahead of the shoulders.

When moving away, the swimmer's shoulders and back should be visible during recovery and the arms should be seen to be lifting cleanly from the water in an elbow-high mode.

The soles of the feet should just be visible at the peak of the leg kick upbeat and, in maintaining this maximum kicking level, the amount of splash should be kept at a minimum.

Owing to the symmetry of the stroke's limb movements, the overhead observer should see the swimmer moving in a straight path. The arm movements should be seen to be mirror images of each other and the swimmer should not be obscured by excessive splash.

Leg action
The leg action which is now most widely used during the performance of the butterfly stroke is that of the 'dolphin' or 'fishtail' kick.

When this simultaneous double overarm stroke first made its appearance during the 1930s, it was used in the breast-stroke event and the accompanying leg kick was that of the lawful breast-stroke movement. In fact, for some time after the stroke segregation took place in 1952, butterfly swimmers continued to use the breast-stroke kicking style. The current swimming laws still permit the use of a breast-stroke leg action but, for competition standards, the more suitable dolphin kick has been widely adopted and the stroke teachings should be adjusted accordingly.

Dolphin kick
Both the legs move simultaneously in the vertical plane in a *similar* fashion to the singular leg action of the front crawl, the power emphasis being on the downbeat. However, as the legs move in complete unison, their effect on the body is somewhat different. They act to elevate the swimmer's 'tail-end', as in the front crawl, but the upward reaction is

more powerful and less frequent. The need to stabilise the body laterally does not arise due to the lack of body roll.

As both legs act together there is a strong possibility that the kick is propulsive as well as elevating.

The timing of the stroke is such that there are two relatively equal leg kicks to one arm cycle and, as may be seen from the stroke diagrams, the downbeats occur during the catch phase and again towards the end of the pull.

The downbeat, which occurs at the end of the arm pull, contributes towards prolonging the swimmer's arm-developed momentum. It also helps to counteract the backward reaction of the accelerating-forward arm-recovery movement.

It is during the recovery movement, and as the result of a combination of the powerful, propulsive arm movement and the leg kick, that the swimmer moves at his fastest *instantaneous* speed.

The next kick takes place during the catch phase, after the swimmer has 'dived' back into the water once more. It is this diving action following the arm recovery which tends to rotate the swimmer longitudinally so that the hips rise.

The 'nose-down' attitude which follows tends to cause the feet to rise above the water surface and return once more with a 'thump'.

The leg movement is generated from the hips, the upbeat taking place while the knees and ankles are extended and the downbeat commencing with initial knee flexion then ending with a final whip-like action of the lower leg.

Both beats are capable of creating propulsion. It is an important feature of the upbeat that the swimmer's legs should remain straight. Any flexion of the knees during this recovery movement tends to cause the pressure forces which are developed on the back of the lower leg to act against propulsion.

Throughout the whole movement, the feet should be held in a sometimes-water-pressure-assisted, stretched (plantar-flexed) position. They should also be rotated ('toed') inwards, so that the big toes are in close proximity to each other throughout the kick. The knees may be held a short distance apart in order to aid the foot rotation. The competition law states that the legs and feet need not necessarily be at the same level, but keeping the feet together tends to provide a better propulsive effect.

As already mentioned, the hips tend to fluctuate in their depth by moving up when the swimmer kicks down, then moving down once more as the legs are elevated towards the surface.

The optimum depth of the leg kick depends mainly on the physical characteristics of the swimmer and the skill with which she is able to perform the action.

Some swimmers develop a leg movement whereby the first kick (say, at the entry) is slightly more pronounced than the next. This may be due to the previously mentioned nose-down attitude. The second beat (at the end of the arm pull) in theory needs to be the more powerful, in order to assist the swimmer in lifting her arms from and over the water. The raising of the shoulders during this phase tends to sink the legs, giving the effect of a deeper kick.

Most teachers, however, teach a constant kicking-depth and leave further refinements to the swimming coach. Here the depth of kick may vary from 450–600 mm (18–24 in.) according to individual stature and strength.

Arm action

The arm action of the butterfly stroke may be described as taking place in a simultaneous and symmetrical fashion. It provides the major contribution towards propulsion.

The path of the hands during the propulsive phase of the stroke passes through an 'S'-shaped form. The shape is sometimes more picturesquely compared with a 'shapely and buxom wench'. However, variations in the underwater limb tracks are many and varied (as indeed are shapely wenches).

Underwater examination of butterfly swimmers shows that a great deal of the propulsive movement is that of a sculling action with the hand being slightly inclined towards the direction of movement.

The whole movement has been divided into the propulsive and recovery phases, then broken down further into component stages for analysis as follows (fig. 19.1):

Propulsive phase	*Recovery phase*
catch	release
pull	recovery over the water
push	entry

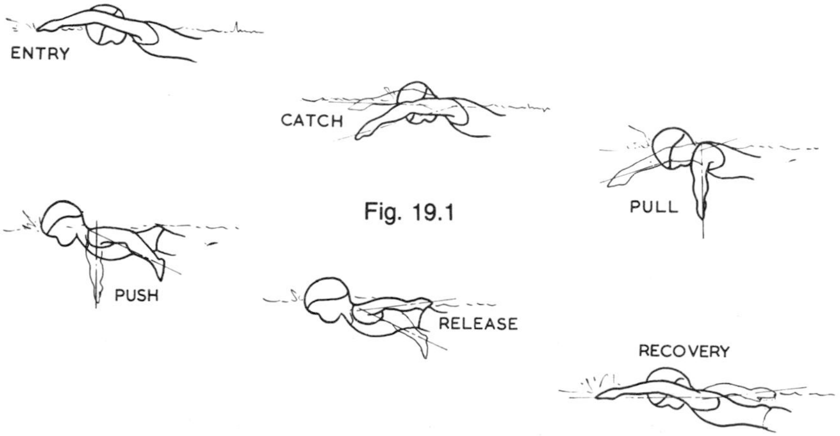

ENTRY

CATCH

PULL

Fig. 19.1

PUSH

RELEASE

RECOVERY

Propulsive phase: catch
As previously described, the catch forms the foundation of the succeeding propulsive movements and takes place immediately after the arms have entered the water.

The most important points relating to this pre-catch arm attitude are that the elbows should be slightly flexed and elevated above the hands, and that the arms should not be spread too wide apart. The elbow-high position enables the whole shoulder girdle to be postured in a mechanically strong fashion. It also allows the hands and the lower arms to be directed in the most advantageous manner in order to carry out the acceleration and pressure-generating catch. Too wide an entry and catch tend to place the pulling muscles at a mechanical disadvantage.

The catch movement should take place with the hands accelerating outwards and diagonally downwards. Movement which is biased excessively downwards should be avoided as it will tend to lift the swimmer's shoulders, thus causing her to move with a bobbing action. (Elevation of the elbows and the downward elevation of the swimmer's body help to avoid this fault.) The movement should take place smoothly and quickly, avoiding the tendency to 'snatch' the water.

The hands should be flat with fingers together or almost together, accompanied by a slight flexing of the wrists: this assists the swimmer in establishing the 'feel' of the water.

The catch continues for as long as the arms continue to accelerate, which is usually after the hands and lower arms have moved through a distance of 200–300 mm (8–12 in.) during the process.

Some swimmers tend to 'catch' the water, then immediately lose the 'feel' once more. They then find it necessary to integrate their catch into the pull phase, thus reducing the range of propulsive movement. It is vital therefore that the catch, pull and push phases should all be successive and continuous for economy and speed.

Propulsive phase: pull
Transferring smoothly on from the catch, the hands now feel the pressure of the water on them to commence the pull phase. They continue to move in the same, slightly outward direction as was initiated during the catch, the action resembling that of a uni-directional sculling action.

This outward (and downward) arm movement changes direction soon after the catch, however, and the hands, with the elbows still elevated and wrist flexed, are faced directly backwards to move for a very short distance parallel to the swimmer's body axis while continuing on slightly downwards at the same time.

As the hands approach the swimmer's shoulder plane, their direction of movement is changed again so that they now start to sweep inwards once more, towards the central plane of the body. The method of propulsion also changes from that of a directly backward-thrusting action back to that of a scull. At the shoulder plane, both arms are laterally in line and the hands, now at approximately their lowest depth, are starting to move in close to each other and once more face directly backwards.

This is the transition point from the pull to the push.

Propulsive phase: push
The transition should be smooth and undetectable.

The swimmer's hands continue to face directly backwards and remain in close proximity to each other during the first part of the movement. The forearms and extended fingers should be inclined inwards towards each other at an angle of approximately forty-five degrees to the water surface. Sideways-on, the forearms should remain in more or less the vertical plane, with the elbows elevated. From the transition point to the start of the release phase, the swimmer's upper arms (from shoulder joint to elbow), remain almost parallel with the water surface.

The push phase is a short one and there exists a close relationship between it and the release.

Recovery phase: release
The arms begin their release from the water towards the end of the push phase. The elbows are still flexed (and elevated) and the hands, having now moved out from beneath the swimmer's body, pass within close proximity of the hips.

Complete extension of the arms at the end of the push should be avoided. This stretching backwards tends to bunch the shoulder muscles and cause havoc with the timing and rhythm of the stroke.

The most important feature of the release is that the elbows should leave the water before the hands. In order to make this somewhat easier, the swimmer's wrists should be relaxed, and the palms turned to face partly inwards.

The hands, as they leave the water, should be comfortably wide of the swimmer's thighs and already moving forward into the recovery over the water.

Recovery phase: recovery over the water
The recovery-over-the-water movement should take place with the elbows slightly flexed and elevated above or in line with the hands.

The swimmer's shoulder flexibility is probably the predominant factor affecting the butterfly recovery movement with the 'natural' butterflyer possessing a high degree of freedom and flexibility in her shoulder girdle.

During the recovery movement, the arms are lifted completely out of the water and swung forward and round, towards the position of entry once more. This swinging movement may be regarded as being momentum-assisted, relying on the initially generated momentum to carry the arms over the water surface to the point of entry.

The speed of the recovery depends mainly on the amount of power which is put into the initial release movement.

As with all forward accelerating actions, there must be a corresponding set of opposing reactions. Therefore, as the arms are accelerated forwards into the recovery, the swimmer is subjected to reactions at his shoulders which tend to slow him down. The leg kick which takes place just prior to the recovery movement assists in counteracting these backward directional forces.

Recovery phase: entry
The hands enter the water in a semi-controlled fashion, the movement being a straightforward continuation of the momentum-assisted recovery.

The elbows should be in a slightly elevated mode and the extended hand should be in line with the forearm. A side view of the entry should show the swimmer's arms 'diving' simultaneously into the water at a shallow angle.

The distance between the hands as they perform their dive should not be excessively wide because not only does this put the pulling muscles at a mechanical disadvantage, but it also reduces the available pulling movement.

Probably the best area of entry is somewhere in the region directly ahead of the swimmer's shoulders. This enables her to obtain a long underwater propulsive movement, see fig. 19.2.

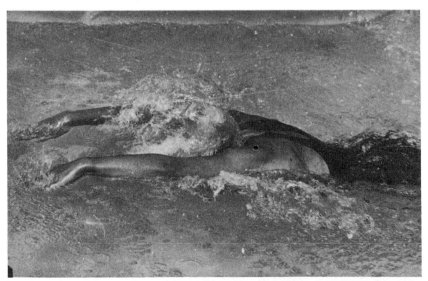

Fig. 19.2 A good butterfly arm entry. Note how the wrists are slightly flexed in preparation for the catch

PATTERNS OF HAND MOVEMENT From directly below, the swimmer may be seen to be describing a path of movement with the hands as they pass from entry to release. These hand patterns vary according to the physical characteristics of the swimmer and each one may well be correct when related to the performer. Some examples of the infinite number of variations are shown in fig. 19.3.

Fig. 19.3 (*left*) The keyhole patterns and (*right*) the hourglass patterns

Generally the patterns fall into two shapes, aptly nicknamed the 'keyhole' and 'hourglass' profiles.

The keyhole shape tends to be the better type of pull from both the physical and mechanical aspects, the reason being that the powerful arm depressors and rotators are at their mechanical best.

Breathing

As with all stroke-breathing patterns, there is a phase in the stroke cycle which is most advantageous for inhalation to be carried out. In the butterfly, this respiratory intake should occur during the period when the shoulder and head are elevated above the water surface.

If we examine the stroke diagrams (p. 227), it will be seen that this maximum shoulder lift occurs during the release phase, then continues on well into the first stage of the arm recovery over the water.

The swimmer's head is lifted by hyper-extension of the neck (jutting the chin forward) in order to inhale. This neck extension limits the amount of shoulder elevation required during recovery and avoids the need for the swimmer to increase her lift in order to breathe in through the mouth. After a breath is taken, the head is returned to the normal swimming position.

Seemingly, the most successful method of exhalation among butterfly swimmers is that of expiring the breath through mouth and nose into the water in an explosive fashion. The exhalation phase should be timed so that the swimmer is expelling the last vestiges of air as his face breaks the water surface. Emphasis should be placed on getting the final part of the exhalation phase correct; the starting point will then sort itself out automatically.

How often should the swimmer breathe? As often as necessary, provided that the movement is integrated as unobtrusively as possible into the overall technique. This may mean that the swimmer requires to take a breath at every arm cycle, or at every two strokes (as in the diagrams). A swimmer in a sprint race may not require to take a breath for some time during the early stages of the event, and will then vary the frequency of breathing for the remainder.

The matter is largely up to the individual and her skill, fitness and physical needs. However, it must be remembered that breathing is an important facet of the stroke technique, so it should be practised thoroughly during the stroke practices.

Co-ordination
Assuming that the swimmer is using a double-leg-kick-to-one-arm-stroke style (a typical competition style), the timing of the movements should be approximately as follows: taking the starting point of the stroke cycle as arm entry, the first downward-acting leg beat should occur almost immediately after the hands have entered the water and have proceeded into the catch movement.

The combined reaction of both the arm and leg downward actions is that the swimmer's shoulders and hips are elevated in the water.

The second leg beat occurs right at the end of the push phase, with the forward reaction of this leg movement assisting the swimmer to lift her arms from the water in order to carry out the recovery.

The breath should have been expired during the propulsive stage and it is during this second downbeat that the head is again lifted, in order that the next breath may be taken.

Using this double-beat co-ordination, the stroke rhythm should be of a kick-kick-throw/kick-kick-throw nature, with the breathing sequence slotted unobtrusively into the movement.

Should a swimmer adopt a single leg beat to one arm pull, the timing will be such that this single downbeat occurs at the start of the arm pull (the same point as the first downbeat in the double-beat style). The breathing pattern must fit in with the limb movements in a similar fashion to that previously described. The rhythm of the stroke will now be of a kick-throw/kick-throw nature.

The butterfly stroke may be compared to the classic jig-saw puzzle. When all the individual pieces are fitted together correctly the overall effect gives great satisfaction, but if just one small feature is missing or out of place, the aesthetic appearance of the picture diminishes considerably.

Fig. 19.4 The stroke diagrams

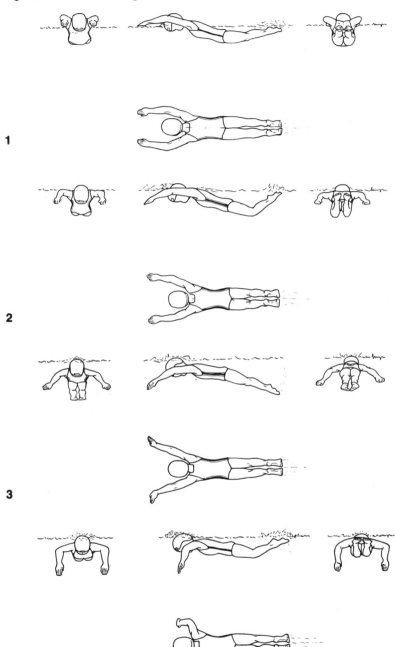

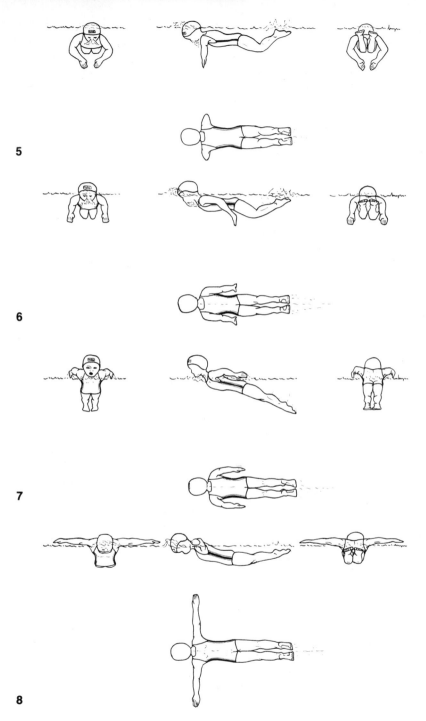

5

6

7

8

Preparatory standards for teaching the stroke
Butterfly requires just a little more strength, shoulder flexibility and water experience than the other styles, in order to perform the complete stroke with any finesse. (A brief attempt at the stroke during the earlier stages of teaching, however, can be quite enlightening for both teacher and pupils, and the sight of a line of tiny, bobbing bottoms traversing the pool width can be quite amusing.)

Before commencing the progressive butterfly activities it is advisable that the swimmers should have attempted at least two of the three previously described competition stroke-practice programmes. If this has been carried out as suggested, the preparatory standards for teaching the stroke will have been covered satisfactorily.

TEACHING THE BUTTERFLY
There are usually two different reactions from young learners when the butterfly stroke is mentioned: some shudder at the very thought, and some, unfortunately in the minority, are adventurous and keen to try it.

A great deal of apprehension can be dispelled by a positive approach to teaching the stroke. But there is no doubt about it, recovering both arms over the water surface at the same time with 'nothing to stand on' is rather difficult, to say the least. However, if the teacher is prepared to highlight the aesthetic nature of the stroke and the fact that its performance demands a high degree of skill, the majority of pupils will rise to the challenge out of sheer natural competitive-mindedness.

Successful performance of butterfly requires a fairly high degree of shoulder flexibility. If considerable freedom of movement is not present, learning and performing the stroke will be difficult and the teacher should take account of this during the instruction.

Again, a good point to remember is the fact that butterfly was once used in the breast-stroke competition events and, indeed, the stroke may still be performed quite successfully using the breast-stroke leg movement. If this previously attempted kick can be used initially in order to ease various individual problems, the teacher will be well advised to take advantage of this. It must be realised, however, that the breast-stroke type of leg kick is rarely used for contemporary speed swimming.

Activity: demonstration of the stroke with commentary
As with other strokes, a demonstration of the style, accompanied by a few 'pearls of wisdom' from the teacher, is the best way to begin.

There may be more difficulty in obtaining a suitable performer for the butterfly than for the other strokes, but taking the trouble to find one is well worth the effort in order that the pupils may witness the skill being performed and the various features being explained at the same time.

So with the class and teacher suitably positioned, the full stroke demonstration may commence.

The swimmer's body position may be best described as *slightly* undulating with the hips rising and falling in opposition to the leg movement. The symmetrical and simultaneous leg movements may be likened to that of a dolphin's tail, indeed the stroke is often described as the 'dolphin butterfly'.

The recovery of the arms over the water should be seen to be clean, with the finger tips entering the water first and the hands approximately shoulder-width apart. The arm pull/push is a fairly long one with the hands driving back towards the hips. (A short vertically biased pull which tends to lift their shoulders excessively will probably be prevalent among beginners.) The fact that the elbows start to leave the water before the swimmer completes the push should be highlighted.

For the sake of the demonstration, the swimmer should be instructed beforehand to breathe in on alternate arm cycles if at all possible, in order to illustrate the desired flat and horizontal body position as well as the technique of breathing.

The timing of the inhalation should be explained as being towards the end of the push or as the hands leave the water. The position of the head when breathing takes place should be emphasised. The swimmer's head will be raised and his chin jutting forward (hyper-extension of the neck).

Exhalation will be of the explosive type and should take place just prior to the swimmer's face breaking the water surface. The pupils will find difficulty in observing this unless they have the luxury of underwater viewing windows, so the point should be specially emphasised.

The exhibition in most instances will be necessarily short owing to the probable limitations of the demonstrator.

Activity: initial full-stroke swims
After watching the demonstration, the class may be lined up along the length of the pool and invited to 'do their own thing' across the width of the pool and back. As the style tends to deteriorate quickly with fatigue, the teacher is advised to use the width of the pool rather than the length for this first activity. Assessment and grouping may be carried out, if desired, after several attempts at the width.

The more adept performers, if there are any, will be easily identified and these may be positioned at the deeper end of the pool where they may be used for additional demonstrations if required. Gradation of the remaining pupils in relation to their particular abilities may then take place from here.

This early full-stroke exercise will not last long and the introduction of part-practices should take place as soon as the teacher is satisfied with the grading and positioning of the members of the class.

TEACHING POINTS
1. Trying to establish an over-the-surface arm recovery

2. Using a dolphin *or* breast-stroke leg kick initially

3. Lying flat and horizontal in the water

4. Holding the breath for short periods

Activity: leg action
In order to give the swimmers a better feel for the leg kick and its propulsive effect in the water, the mobile kicking practices may be performed in positions other than that of the correct prone surface swimming mode.

The leg movement may, for instance, be tried with the swimmers lying on their backs or on their sides. Further to this, performing the kick while submerged gives a whole new aspect to the undulating movement, relating it more closely to the dolphin's swimming movement.

Lengthy periods of isolated leg practices are not recommended, and as soon as some semblance of the correct movement is evident, full-stroke exercises should be introduced.

In order to establish the basic movement, a brief session of poolside rail-assisted kicking is advised.

Practice 1: leg kicking at the rail (fig. 19.5)
As a starter, a straightforward front crawl-type leg beat may be used to show the similarity in *individual* leg movement in the two kicks.

Fig. 19.5

TEACHING POINTS
1. The dolphin kick may be described to the class as being similar to a double front-crawl leg action, with the physical aspects of each individual leg movement being very similar to that of front crawl. Both legs must work together and in unison at all times.

2. The legs should preferably be together, the ankles should be loose ('floppy feet') at all times during the kick. (If the ankles are loose, the resistance of the water on the fronts of the feet will tend to extend and streamline them.)

3. The motion should be wave-like.

4. The hips must not bob up and down excessively. (An example of an excessive bob is for a swimmer's bottom to rise clear of the water surface.) The usual cause of this fault at the rail is that the legs are being held too stiffly.

5. The depth of kick is an individual thing, but generally the depth should not exceed 450 mm (18 in.), and during the movement tends to adjust itself automatically.

6. The kick should originate from a hip movement, and the foot lag at the start of the downbeat will be found, in most instances, to be a natural function.

7. The feet should remain in the water as much as possible. The usual thump of the feet on the water at the start of the downbeat must be minimised.

Practice 2: leg movement using a float (fig. 19.6)

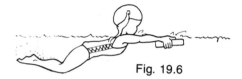

Fig. 19.6

TEACHING POINTS

All the previously mentioned teaching points are applicable, combined with the following:

8. A stretched and streamlined position should be maintained.

9. Variations in the rates of kicking should automatically bring about changes in depth of the kicks. Should there be instances of the 'thump-thump' beat and excessive hip undulation, varying the kicking rate should assist in rectifying these two faults.

10. Methods of holding the floats correctly should also be mentioned once again.

Any approximation of the correct leg actions will be evident to the teacher by the swimmer's ability to move across or along the pool without too much difficulty.

Practice 3: leg kicking in the athletically stretched position
The pupils may now abandon the floats for a while in order to carry out the leg-kicking movement in an athletically stretched, head-down mode with occasional breathing (fig. 19.7).

This practice may be performed first in a prone attitude on the surface from a push and glide. The swimmers, using the dolphin kick, move across the pool with hands touching and arms stretched ahead along the water surface. The upper arms should cover the ears and each performer, with face in the water, should look forward and slightly down (if the eyes are open), in order to position the head correctly.

In order to introduce some variety into the lesson, the teacher may experiment by letting the pupils perform the movement in different swimming modes.

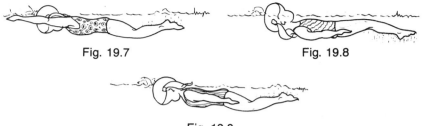

Fig. 19.7   Fig. 19.8

Fig. 19.9

Surface swimming on the back and on the side may be introduced (fig. 19.8), together with the performance of these variations while the swimmers are submerged.

Some swimmers may find the kicking movement easier to perform with their arms by their sides (fig. 19.9).

A little competition may be used to help the lesson along, such as discovering who is best at front or back or submerged swimming.

Nose clips may be used to some advantage during the underwater practices.

TEACHING POINTS

Most of the previously mentioned teaching points are relevant during these exercises. It will probably be discovered that the kick becomes more effective and thus the swimmers are able to move faster when they are submerged. It may therefore be argued that they gain a better appreciation of the movement when carrying out the leg beat underwater (fig. 19.10).

These practices should establish some degree of leg propulsion and this being so, the pupils may now proceed to the arm-action activities.

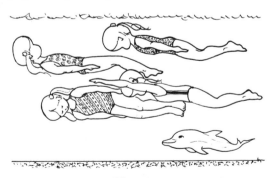

Fig. 19.10

Activity: arm action
Practice 1: standing in shallow water (fig. 19.11), *the teacher demonstating from the poolside*

Fig. 19.11

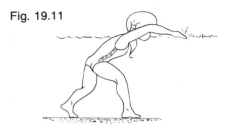

TEACHING POINTS

1. Fingers should be together during the underwater phase.

2. There must be a deliberate attempt to 'catch' the water and maintain the development pressure right through the pull/push phases.

3. The palms of the hands must face directly backwards for as long as possible during the underwater phase.

4. The elbows should be elevated just above the hands and slightly flexed at the entry stage. They should continue to maintain this elevated position right through the underwater phase. There will be a variation in the angle of elbow flexion, probably reaching a maximum under the swimmer's chest.

5. Hand entry should be finger tips first and approximately shoulder-width apart. The positioning of the arms and hands, i.e. elbows slightly flexed and hands shoulder-width apart, will automatically set the stretched-forward distance at which the swimmer's hands enter the water ahead of him.

6. At this practice stage, the hands are easily controlled to move in closer together as they pass below the shoulders. (Control of the hand-movement pattern becomes more difficult when the pupils actually begin swimming.) Describing the movement as being similar to that of a 'curvaceous girl' will give some idea of the limb track – to the boys at least!

7. The push phase should not be extended too far back. In fact, the elbows should start to release themselves from the water just before the push is completed.

8. The whole movement should be continuous with no pauses.

9. The recovery movement must take place with the arms and hands completely clear of but only just above the water surface.

10. Relaxation during the arm-recovery movement will be difficult at first, with the pupils tending to let their hands lead the elbows. Elbows lead – hands trail during the early part of the recovery. This must be emphasised, as must be the controlled throwing-forward of the arms.

11. The position of the head during this exercise is not really important since the pupils are probably watching the teacher perform his or her demonstration.

Note Shoulder flexibility may be a problem during the arm-recovery phase and the teacher must bear this in mind when asking swimmers to perform movements of which they are physically incapable.

Practice 2: arm movement while walking across the pool
The previous exercise may now be modified in such a way that the arm stroke is carried out while the pupils are walking across the width of the pool. The forward-bending body attitude should be maintained and the shoulders should remain just below the water surface during the propulsive movement.

TEACHING POINTS
All the teaching points outlined in the static exercise are relevant, together with the following:

12. The position of the head may now become lower than in the previous exercise. In fact the pupils, having practised other strokes, should be able to place their faces in the water with little trouble and hold their breath for at least half the width.
    If the hair-line/water-line position can be assumed, the pupils will move a little nearer to the actual swimming position. The swimmers should remember to continue breathing out through the nose as the face leaves the water.
    Attempting to bury the head too deeply in the water tends to inhibit the freedom of the shoulders during recovery.

Practice 3: arm movement to the wall (fig. 19.12)

Fig. 19.12

TEACHING POINTS
All the previously mentioned teaching practices are applicable to this exercise. Failing to clear the water surface during arm recovery will probably be the most prevalent feature in the movement. This fault may be remedied in some small way by lifting the head very *slightly*, thus allowing the shoulders a little more freedom of movement.

Practice 4: arm movement away from the wall
The next exercise is really a progression of the last ones, with a float being held between the swimmer's thighs. The pupil pushes and glides away

from the poolside, then performs the complete arm movement across the pool. Continuity of movement should be encouraged.

Breath-holding should be maintained wherever possible, but if pupils are forced to take a gulp of air, the correct timing should come naturally.

If some members of the class look confident, width swims may be attempted without using the floats and introducing some form of leg movement. The breast strokers of the class may prefer to use their own particular leg kick at this stage.

TEACHING POINTS

In addition to all the teaching points previously mentioned:

13. The flat and horizontal swimming position should be emphasised now that the pupils start to become mobile. (The use of the floats, of course, helps in maintaining the elevated body position but, as soon as the teacher is satisfied with the progress of the arm movements, leg action should be introduced in order that the swimmers may perform the stroke unassisted.)

Activity: breathing
Practice 1: arms only, with breathing, while standing in shallow water
TEACHING POINTS
1. Exhalation should preferably be just prior to release and should be explosive through mouth and nose.

2. Inhalation should take place during the arm-recovery movement.

3. The shoulders should be elevated in order to accommodate arm recovery only, *not* inhalation. Movement of the head should be in conjunction with this recovery movement, thus allowing the mouth to be sufficiently clear of the water for the swimmers to breathe in.

4. The head should be at approximately the hair-line/water-line position for breathing out.

5. Taking a breath during every recovery movement should be attempted.

Practice 2: full-stroke movement with breathing
TEACHING POINTS
1. Breath should be taken in through the mouth and exhaled through mouth and nose.

2. The swimmers should merely raise their heads to clear the local waves in order to breathe and not attempt to stand up in the water.

3. The timing of the breathing is important and should be precise in order to avoid any unnecessary pauses in the stroke cycle.

4. Exhalation must be into the water, culminating in a final burst as the swimmer's face leaves the water.

Activity: stroke co-ordination (fig. 19.13)
It will probably have been discovered by the pupils, by the time the teachings arrive at this stage, that the butterfly stroke is rather fatiguing! The teacher must make allowances for probable stroke deterioration with the onset of tiredness.

The stroke co-ordination practices should not be carried out at anything like racing or competition speed. In fact, the swimmers may find it advantageous to introduce a stretched glide into the stroke after the arms have recovered over the water.

Fig. 19.13

Assuming that a competition-type two-beat cycle is to be taught, it is best that the pupils are shown by visual demonstration exactly where the first and second kicks appear in relation to the arm movement. This can be done by the teacher using one arm and one leg to demonstrate the feature of the movement while supporting himself against some solid foundation.

The first leg downbeat should occur as the hands drive down into the water at the catch stage. The second kick should then appear at the end of the arm-push phase, thus assisting the swimmer to release his arms from the water.

If the teacher can display a 'kick there and there' action while moving his or her arms in the correct motion, it will provide the pupils with a recognisable pattern to work to.

After a few cycles, the 'kick there and there' is superseded by a 'kick-kick-throw' description. In reality, the two kicks perform somewhat different functions and world-famous coaches tend to differ in their opinion as to precisely what these functions are. If the teacher therefore omits to say that one kick should be more vigorous or deeper than the other, the pupils will tend to 'do their own thing', letting the natural stroke rhythm and technique sort things out for themselves.

Practice: stroke co-ordination without breathing
The exercise is best performed across the width of the pool with short periods of rest as necessary. This method of practice gives the pupils just enough time for them to adjust to the kicking rhythm, yet not get too fatigued. The breathing sequence, during the first of the co-ordination practices, has been omitted in order that the pupils may concentrate on carrying out one thing at a time.

TEACHING POINTS

All the previously mentioned teaching points relating to the arm- and leg-stroking techniques are relevant, together with the following:

1. The timing of each kick must occur at the correct point in relation to the arm cycle.

2. The swimmer must endeavour to swim in a flat and horizontal mode, keeping his head with hair line at the water line.

3. The arm stroke must be a powerful one and should terminate with a push.

Activity: full stroke with breathing

The final component of the whole-stroke movement – breathing technique – may now be added.

An intake should be taken at the appropriate time in relation to the arm stroke by raising the head as previously described. Blowing out should occur just prior to the intake.

The whole practice may now be carried out, and as the pupils get stronger and fitter, the distances that are swum may be gradually increased.

Part-practices should be returned to whenever necessary, which is likely to be very often. The related teaching points should be continually emphasised throughout the practices.

FAULTS AND THEIR CORRECTION

Feature: BODY POSITION

FAULT	EFFECT ON STROKE	CORRECTION
1. Legs too low due to weak leg action or elevated head. (Body must be as horizontal as possible within the required stroke movements)	1. Increase in profile drag and resistance to forward movement 2. Direction of leg propulsion upwards rather than forwards	1. Legs must be elevated and head must generally be lowered 2. Prone push-and-glide practices, in order to create horizontal swimming mode 3. Mobile leg practices with and without float assistance – rapid kicking rate 4. Full-stroke practice with breath-holding 5. Special attention to head position during inhalation phase 6. Emphasis on double beat
2. Excessive piking at the hips	1. Excessively undulating appearance of stroke (bobbing) 2. Leg kick too deep 3. Excessive usage of energy 4. Increase in profile drag and resistance to forward movement	All corrections as in Fault 1 Front-crawl leg movements may assist in rectifying fault

3. Excessive undulation due to arm movement (catch/pull and recovery) – shoulders may not be flexible enough for fluent recovery movement	1. Swimmer's head and shoulders bob up and down 2. May be related in Fault 1	1. Shoulder mobility exercises – preferably the stroke itself 2. Emphasis on head position and trying to relax the neck muscles: depressing the head tends to inhibit backward shoulder movement 3. General attention to arm action

Feature: LEG ACTION

FAULT	EFFECT ON STROKE	CORRECTION
1. Leg kick too shallow	Ineffectiveness may be shown up by: (a) Low body (legs) position (b) Loss of stabilisation (reaction to arm movement) (c) Lack of propulsion	1. Mobile legs-only practices with emphasis on smooth and slightly undulating propulsion at the correct depth, float-assisted and unassisted. 2. All the teaching points mentioned previously should be highlighted with main emphasis on kicking depth.
2. Failure to achieve full knee extension on downbeat	Loss of propulsive power	All corrections as in Fault 1
3. Excessive knee bending, probably due to lack of appreciation of wave-like total leg motion	1. Loss of propulsion 2. Feet will probably break the surface	All corrections as in Fault 1 1. Variations in body position, i.e. supine and side, together with surface and submerged practices 2. Emphasis on a hip-orientated leg movement
4. Excessive effort during the upbeat (recovery)	Tendency to sink the hips (bobbing)	Emphasis to be placed on downbeat with a semi-relaxed recovery movement All corrections as in Fault 1

Feature: ARM ACTION
Phase: ENTRY

FAULT	EFFECT ON STROKE	CORRECTION
1. Too wide (well beyond swimmer's shoulder-width) 'plain header' position, may be due to lack of shoulder flexibility or weakness	Slight reduction in available muscular force	1. Full-stroke mobility and strengthening arm practices 2. Emphasis on touching thumbs together at entry (over-correction)
2. Stopping the arms at entry, catch usually of a vertical nature	Shoulders tend to bob up and down	1. Emphasis on driving the hands into the water and then into a continuous and mainly backward-directed catch 2. Limited shallow-water practice 3. Full-stroke practices

3. Shoulders too low, probably due to overall stroke weakness	Elbows enter before finger-tips	1. Return to legs-only and body elevation practices 2. Full-stroke practices with emphasis on elevated-elbow entry
4. Entry too splashed, probably result of excessively rapid recovery	1. Splashing absorbs energy which could be used more efectively for propulsion 2. Increased resistance to propulsion	1. Emphasis on relaxed but controlled recovery and subsequent entry with elevated elbows. 2. Full-stroke practices

Phase: CATCH

FAULT	EFFECT ON STROKE	CORRECTION
1. Wrongly directed. (Elbows should be elevated, wrists partly flexed, hands flat and fingers together, in order to direct propulsive forces mainly backwards)	Loss of propulsion	1. Shallow-water practices with emphasis on entry and subsequent catch with elevated elbows. (Remember, the catch is an accelerating movement) The 'hourglass' or double elongated 'S' patterns of movement should be attempted 2. Full-stroke practices with emphasis on the catch direction and depth
2. Fingers apart	Loss of propulsive area	1. Concentration on closing the fingers after the (relaxed) recovery movement 2. Full-stroke practices
3. Catch too slow	1. Extended catch – subsequently a reduced pull 2. Loss of power	All corrections as in Fault 1, with full-stroke practices in which emphasis is on an accelerating and rapid initial hand movement

Phase: PULL

FAULT	EFFECT ON STROKE	CORRECTION
1. Dropping the elbows: instead of creating pressure on the palm and forearm, partial arm-streamlining or slipping takes place	1. Loss of power 2. Propulsive forces not created to the fullest extent due to slipping 3. Forces that are developed are directed mainly downwards	1. Emphasis on elevated and slightly flexed elbows as a continuation of the catch movement 2. Shallow-water practices (or in front of a mirror) 3. Full-stroke practices ('Try to push during the pull')
2. Straight arm pull	1. Initial forces directed downwards instead of backwards 2. Consequent shoulder bobbing takes place 3. Muscular/ mechanical disadvantage – leverage arm too great	All corrections as in Fault 1, with special emphasis on elevated and slightly flexed elbows

FAULT	EFFECT ON STROKE	CORRECTION
3. Too wide	1. Decrease in muscular effectiveness 2. Decrease in length of pulling movement	1. Concentration on directing the hands towards the central body plane 2. Shallow-water practices 3. Full-stroke practices: establish the hourglass or double-ogee movement
4. Feathering (not to be confused with sculling) probably due to general arm/shoulder weakness	Loss of power and elevation	1. Full-stroke practices in an attempt to control and correct the underwater arm movements and, at the same time, develop shoulder strength 2. Practices may be leg-kick predominant at first, then graduating to the normal two-beat turning
5. Pull too short, which probably means that there is no subsequent push phase	1. Loss of power 2. General incorrectness of whole stroke	All corrections as in Fault 1
6. Asymmetric limb movement	1. Incorrect stroking 2. Possibility of disqualification during competition	All corrections as in Fault 1
7. Hands crossing over	As in Fault 6	All corrections as in Fault 1
8. Hands too near the body	1. Lack of propulsion and leverage 2. Arm pull may be 'too strong', causing slipping	All corrections as in Fault 1, with emphasis on pulling a little deeper

Phase: PUSH

FAULT	EFFECT ON STROKE	CORRECTION
1. Non-existent push, release in the region of shoulder plane	1. Reduction in power 2. Increased rate of stroking	1. Full-stroke practices with emphasis on arm-stroke extension into the push phase 2. Attempt to terminate propulsive phase near the thighs 3. Breath-holding at first, then developing a regular breathing pattern
2. Too short, release too early	As above	All corrections as in Fault 1
3. Hands not directed backwards throughout the pull, may end facing inwards or upwards	1. Reduced effectiveness of pull if facing inwards 2. If facing upwards, tendency for hips to drop	Emphasis on backward-directed hand movement to a point prior to release All corrections as in Fault 1

| 4. Too wide | 1. Muscular effectiveness reduced
2. Reduced power and probably early fatigue | All corrections as in Fault 1 |

Phase: RELEASE

FAULT	EFFECT ON STROKE	CORRECTION
1. Too wide as the result of an incorrect push	Same as in Fault 4 in push phase	All corrections as in Fault 1 in push phase
2. Hands releasing prior to elbows	1. Incorrect underwater movement 2. Creation of excess profile drag 3. Loss of power 4. Unnecessary shoulder bunching	1. Shallow-water practices 2. Emphasis on correct release – elbow first, then followed by hand, and relaxed flinging recovery 3. Full-stroke practices without breathing 4. Normal full-stroke practices
3. Too soon, as a result of a short or non-existent push. (Remember, the arms commence their release during the latter end of the push)	Shortened arm cycle with consequent loss of power	All corrections as in Fault 1 of the push phase

Phase: RECOVERY

FAULT	EFFECT ON STROKE	CORRECTION
1. Shoulders and arms too tight: may be result of lack of flexibility or head pressed excessively forward	1. Early onset of fatigue 2. Jerky motion 3. When the head is pressed forward, the upper-limb muscles work against each other, giving the appearance of stiffness	1. Flexibility exercises such as land-based free arm swings or plenty of slow and relaxed front and back crawl 2. Head position should be such that the water line is at the hair line (or just above), except when breathing-in takes place 3. Full-stroke easy length practices
2. Hands and arms failing to clear the water surface: may be due to insufficient power from the legs or (as at the end of the butterfly race) sheer fatigue	1. Creation of unnecessary resistance 2. Onset of fatigue 3. Loss of power	All corrections as in Fault 1 1. Attention to leg kick (part-practices) and body position 2. Increase number of leg kicks to one arm fling 3. Concentration on elbow-high and relaxed (as possible) recovery
3. Too slow: probably due to lack of strength and/or shoulder flexibility	1. Entry probably too wide and short 2. Upright body position probable	All corrections as in Faults 1 and 2

Feature: BREATHING

FAULT	EFFECT ON STROKE	CORRECTION
1. Failure to take breath – breath-holding due to weak and ineffective stroking	Swimmer quickly becomes fatigued	1. Return to poolside and part-practices with an emphasis on breathing discipline 2. Explosive breathing is essential; concentrate on breathing out through mouth and nose 3. Full-stroke practices
2. Lack of neck flexibility	Swimmer tends to lift the shoulders excessively rather than utilise the full articulation of the spinal (atlanto-occipital) joint: this may be a physical disability	All corrections as in Fault 1
3. Holding the breath for too many stroke cycles	Inflexibility of the neck tends to make breathing a definite chore.The swimmer therefore tends to hold the breath for too long, thus inducing premature fatigue	All corrections as in Fault 1

Feature: CO-ORDINATION

FAULT	EFFECT ON STROKE	CORRECTION
1. Propulsive movement too short	1. Not enough time for the second leg beat 2. Due to lack of propulsion, hips tend to drop	Refer to the push-phase corrective practices
2. A single-beat leg movement – with the kick in the wrong place: should appear as the hands perform the catch phase	1. Swimmer usually has trouble in clearing the water during recovery 2. Stroke has an excessive undulating appearance	1. Leg-action practices with emphasis on rhythm and continuity of the movement 2. Full-stroke practices with emphasis on a kick-kick-throw rhythm
3. Fatigue	Untrained swimmer tends to tire quickly and the co-ordination and timing become erratic	1. Width practices with emphasis on clearing the water during arm recovery, and an elevated body 2. Start with one pull per width, then glide. Gradually increase number of arm pulls until a two-beat rhythm is achieved. The first leg beat should be as the hands catch the water and the second should be during the release phase

20 Medley and Relay Swimming

After all the competition strokes have been taught, the teacher may wish to introduce the swimmers to the fun and excitement of medley racing.

Medley events take two forms, individual and team, the former being very exhausting and demanding great fitness and skill. Individual medley demands that the competitor swims an equal distance, in each of the four competition styles, in an established sequence as follows:

first phase   – butterfly
second phase – back stroke (usually back crawl)
third phase   – breast stroke
fourth phase – freestyle

The individual phases may vary in distance from one width for beginners and for turn practices, right up to 100 m in the more serious competition events.

The team event requires four swimmers to complete the set distance, each swimming a different style, in the following sequence:

first phase   – back stroke
second phase – breast stroke
thire stroke   – butterfly
fourth phase – freestyle

The individual ASA stroke laws all apply during both forms of event, but the freestyle leg must be different from the other three styles.

Individual medley
The individual version of medley requires special attention to be paid to the transition of stroke turns.

For instance, the first stroke change from butterfly to back stroke requires a butterfly finish to be quickly translated into a back-crawl start. The transition from back stroke to breast stroke is best carried out by the swimmer executing a backward tuck somersault at the wall. The rotation will ensure that he or she surfaces on the front in order to perform the next leg. The last turn has to be of the breast-stroke touch-and-rotation type, probably with a front-crawl push-off and glide.

Team medley
The team event requires that the finishing competitor touches the end of the course before his or her team-mate dives in, otherwise team dis-

qualification will occur. The biggest problems that face competition are those of diving in too soon or too late. With beginners, an early start often occurs because of the sheer excitement of the occasion. In order to improve take-offs, the teacher should organise sessions of specialised medley relay swimming, concentrating on the skill of leaving the mark at precisely the right moment.

Relay swimming
Team relay racing is great fun both as part of the lesson, and as a competition feature during a school or club swimming gala. Team swimming of any description can usually add excitement to an organised swimming session. It may be used in either the 'warm-up' periods or during the 'contrasting activity' phase of the planned lesson. School swimming galas usually include 'house' team swims and it is here that the swimmers may exhibit their relay skills.

The paramount features to be practised are the same as for the medley events, that is taking off correctly without risking disqualification.

21 The Competition Starts

There are basically two ways of starting a race. The first, from the poolside, is a dive, and this method of entry applies to freestyle (front crawl), butterfly and breast-stroke races. The second method is to start from the water and is used during the back-stroke events. The aim of the start is to propel the swimmer away from the end of the pool as quickly as possible and with as much momentum as can be developed. The flight through the air should be as prolonged as possible because, immediately the swimmer enters or re-enters the water, drag forces are encountered which diminish his speed.

The body during flight should be fully stretched and straight with the head tucked in between the upper arms. Entry or re-entry into the water should be finger-tips first at a very slight incline so that the swimmer may steer a very shallow-dipping and curved glide path. Initial stroking should commence as the glide speed diminishes to normal swimming speed, with attention being paid to the aspects of stroke law relating to the particular style.

Generally, the requirements of a good starter are:

1. Quick reactions
2. Ability to generate instantaneous maximum power
3. A knowledge and appreciation of the relevant body mechanics, together with the ability to put them into practice
4. Understanding of the general hydrodynamic principles related to moving through the water

THE DIVE START
Preparatory position
The relevant law states that, on a signal from the starter (usually a whistle), the competitor should step on to the rear of the starting blocks or stand a short pace back from the edge of the starting line.

Standing in this position she should be relaxed but mentally aware and concentrating on her intended swim.

Approach
On the starter's command, 'Take your marks', the swimmer should step forward on to the edge of the pool or starting block. It is essential that, for this instant of time, the competitor is looking downwards in order to see

exactly where and how the feet are to be placed. Often one sees an inexperienced swimmer gazing around the pool at friends or the starter while moving forward, finally taking up the starting position by feel. This is incorrect and unnecessary.

Stance or starting position for the conventional dive (fig. 21.1)
Having looked to see exactly where she is stepping, the swimmer should ensure that the position of her feet is such that the toes are curled around the edge of the starting base, ensuring a good grip. The heels *must* be flat. Standing on the base with the heels in this mode provides a firm foundation for the stance and minimises any tendency to topple into the water prematurely. The toe grip may be enhanced by moving the heels apart slightly in order to allow more of the toes to curl over the edge (fig. 21.2). The feet should be placed a short distance apart to provide lateral stability and ensure that a mechanically sound take-off is achieved.

Fig. 21.1 The conventional dive start

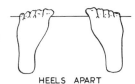

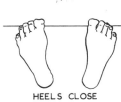

Fig. 21.2 (*left*) Two-toe grip and (*right*) four-toe grip

HEELS CLOSE

HEELS APART

Viewed from ahead, the best stance is with the ankle joints vertically below the hip joints (fig. 21.3), so that on take-off the thrust is directed straight into the starting platform with no element of sideways thrust. The knee joint is slightly flexed and the hips sufficiently bent to allow the back to be almost in a horizontal position. The most mechanically advantageous angles of limb flexion are as shown in fig. 21.4. The head is angled to enable the eyes to look forward and downward at approximately thirty degrees to the horizontal. This head position has the advantage of providing the good viewing angle necessary in a team race prior to take-over.

The arms should be hanging down and directed very slightly outwards

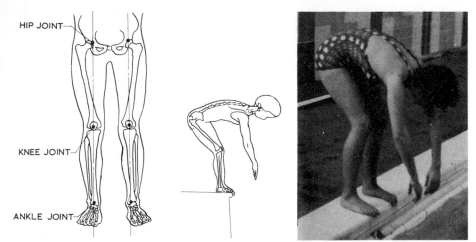

Fig. 21.3 The stance (front view)   Fig. 21.4 The stance (side view)

in semi-relaxed attitude. When viewed from the side, the arms may vary between being just ahead of the shoulders to a position back by the thighs.

For absolute stability and balance, the centre of gravity of the body should be positioned directly over the region between the balls of the feet and the heels.

The swimmer must be fully aware of the imminence of the starting signal, but concentration should be directed towards actually leaving the mark rather than on the signal itself. The starter should wait until all the competitors are absolutely still before giving the signal to commence the race and, should there be a prolonged pause before the signal, the swimmer must resist any temptation to look up or raise the heels.

Take-off
Drop
The take-off should be explosive!

As soon as the competitor hears the starting signal, the take-off movements commence with no delay. The centre of gravity of the body shifts forward and the heels lift, this movement being brought about by contraction of the anterior muscles of the lower leg.

At the same time, the arms begin to swing forward (if they were positioned in a backward-biased position), then upward and outward in an arc.

The head starts to lower and the breath will be expired. (Breathing is a natural function of survival and should not really need to be taught.)

There is no extension of the legs at this early stage.

The swimmer continues to move forward and the heels continue to rise as the arms reach the uppermost part of the swing. Continuation of the movement sees the arms now moving in a backward, inward and downward arc. The head continues to lower and the swimmer sinks into more of a crouch position.

Drive

The swimmer is now in a position to commence a vigorous leg extension to drive her powerfully away from the start.

The arms complete their swing to lie fully outstretched ahead of the shoulders with hands flat and palms facing downwards; the thumbs should be touching or almost touching. The head should be down between the arms with the biceps covering the ears.

The legs should now be completely straight with a final extension of the ankles, to power the swimmer into flight.

A breath is taken at approximately this point. As mentioned earlier, the timing of the inhalation is usually a natural one.

Flight

The flight through the air should be directed outwards and very slightly upwards away from the starting position, as far as possible. The body should be fully stretched and streamlined with avoidance of any tendency to 'jack-knife'. If the flight is correctly performed, the path will be in the form of a flattened parabolic arc and directed in such a way that termination of the flight finds the swimmer slightly inclined downwards with his outstretched and touching hands leading.

Entry

Entry into the water is made fingers first with the body slightly inclined to the surface. The swimmer should continue to remain perfectly streamlined and stretched. It should be noted that a front crawl stroke demands a shallower entry than breast stroke and butterfly styles due to the subsequent related swimming speeds and underwater actions.

Glide

Once under the surface, a glide takes place at approximately 600 mm (2 ft) depth, with the swimmer maintaining her fully stretched attitude. Glide speed is faster than swimming speed due to the momentum developed during the take-off, and this accumulated power should be used to the swimmer's advantage.

Any attempt to commence stroke activity before the glide speed has diminished to the stroke-related surface swimming speed will tend to slow a competitor down.

Initial strokes

The glide time interval and the initial stroking techniques will be dependent on the style to be performed and related governing laws. The front-crawl surface speed being faster than the others, stroking must be started at an earlier stage, while breast strokers glide for longer due to their slower swimming speed. Butterflyers commence stroking somewhere between these two glide lengths.

Some teachers insist that swimmers commence their leg beat before the arms start to pull (part-practices being the exception). If we accept the fact that in the three fastest strokes, namely front crawl, butterfly and back stroke, the arm stroke is the paramount feature in relation to propulsion, we must also accept that the arm stroke has the most effect on the swimmer's speed. Therefore, introducing the less effective leg beat on its own at something like surface swimming speed will serve to retard speed rather than enhance it.

Front crawl – initial strokes

There are no laws dictating the performance of the underwater technique. At the appropriate time the legs commence their drive, and simultaneously one hand commences the vertically biased catch and the other arm continues to stretch ahead.

The action will tend to elevate the swimmer towards the surface where normal stroking practices may commence. A slight body roll in a direction away from the initial pulling side may assist in releasing and recovering the arm over the water surface. The number of strokes the swimmer takes on the surface before carrying out a breathing cycle is dependent on her technique and the distance she is about to swim.

Breast stroke – initial strokes

The governing law states that the swimmer may perform one complete arm stroke and one complete leg kick under the water surface. The kick should bring the top of the head to the surface.

The arm stroke is a long rearward-directed pull, right back to the thighs. The recovery is carried out by keeping the hands and elbows tucked in close to the body, thus reducing profile drag effects.

While the arms are recovering, the legs perform a normal breast-stroke kick, and at the same time the head is lifted to assist the swimmer to the surface in accordance with the stroke law requirements.

Explosive exhalation takes place through mouth and nose as the swimmer's face breaks the surface.

Normal stroke procedure commences immediately.

Butterfly – initial strokes

Butterfly law states that only one arm pull but unlimited leg kicks may take place while the swimmer is completely submerged. If the legs do start to kick before the arms start to pull, however, the advantage of the glide speed may well be lost, as previously mentioned.

The long arm pull is compatible with the normal stroke technique with the hands ending up back by the thighs. The head is lifted during this pull, thus assisting the swimmer to the surface where a normal over-the-surface recovery may take place. Normal stroking now commences.

THE GRAB START (fig. 21.5)
This dive is only possible if suitable starting facilities are available, namely, something to grab hold of in the correct place during the dive.

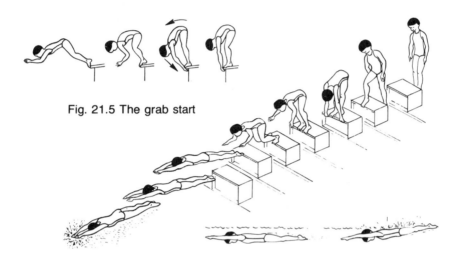

Fig. 21.5 The grab start

The drive away from the side is essentially the same as for the arm-swing dive, when the arms are near the end of the forward swing.

The flight through the air, entry, glide and initial strokes are very similar. The only really different part of the overall activity is the arm action. Understanding that the swimmer pulls herself forward by flexing her arms to overbalance, and hence drives herself forward by vigorous extension of the legs, is essential in order to teach the dive.

The trajectory is lower than that of the arm swing due to the fact that there is less lift available as a result of the lack of arm swing. Consequently, the entry into the water is usually shorter.

But again, due to the shallower entry, the time to, say, 5 m (16½ ft) may be faster.

THE MODIFIED TRACK START STANCE
Until sets of suitably constructed starting blocks become legal, there is little value in this start. The main reason for this is that at the moment it is essentially a one-legged take-off providing half the 'drive-off' power.

SUMMARY OF STARTS

General starting (Rule 118): The starter shall take up a position at the side of the course, the competitors, on a signal from the starter (or referee) shall step on to the rear of the starting blocks or stand a short pace back from the edge of the starting line or enter the water as required by laws 121–124. On the preparatory command 'Take your marks', the competitors shall immediately take up a starting position either on the front of the starting block or line or as required to conform to the relevant parts of ASA laws 121, 122, 123 and 124, and shall remain stationary until the starter gives the starting signal (shot, whistle, 'Go' or klaxon).

PHASE	PREPARATORY POSITION	STARTING POSITION ('TAKE YOUR MARKS')			
		FEET	KNEES	HIPS	HEAD & EYES
FRONT CRAWL	Behind the mark in the appropriate lane. Relaxed but attentive	Slightly apart with toes gripping edge of pool May be together for grab start Hip, knee & ankle joint, all in one line best mechanical advantage	Slightly apart and flexed slightly less flex for grab	Flexed	Head slightly raised eyes looking fwd and down. This position is essential for relay take-overs head slightly lower for grab start
BACK CRAWL	In the water facing the start hands holding starting rail feet on the wall – relaxed but attentive	Slightly apart – balls of feet on wall (not gutter) toes under surface feet as high as comfortably possible not necessarily on the same level	Well flexed and apart Mechanical advantage comments as	Flexed	Head bends forward towards wall
BREAST STROKE	As front crawl		All as front crawl		
BUTTERFLY	As front crawl				

ARMS	LEAVING THE MARK (GO)	FLIGHT & ENTRY	GLIDE	INITIAL STROKES
By the sides, fwd, level or behind shoulder plane – or gripping the the ledge over which the toes are curled inside or outside the feet	Hips & knees straightened, arms swing back out & forward – or the body is pulled down & forward by flexing the arms	Flight with body straight entry to be shallow. Body straight feet and arms athletically stretched Entry for 'grab' will probably be nearer to take-off than for conventional arm swing	Just below surface. Athletically stretched	Maintain glide until its speed equals swimming speed. Leg kick then commences and one hand moves into catch, leaving other extended until surface stroking commences. Breath held for initial strokes
Hands holding rail or trough about shoulder width apart front crawl	Hips & knees straighten. Arms flung back in an outwards sweep to a thumbs touching position – palms facing up arms straight	Back should be clear to the water during flight. Re-entry in athletically stretched position, fingers first, back slightly arched upwards	Shallow breathing out through nose to clear air passages as face breaks surface, Athletically stretched	Maintain glide until speed equals swimming speed. leg kick commences and one hand moves into catch, leaving the other extended until stroking commences
		Flight with body straight entry slightly deeper than F.C. to take advantage of under-water action – body athletically stretched.	Below surface, athletically stretched	Maintain glide until speed equals swimming speed – armsweep right back to thighs recover as legs kick. Head breaks surface stroke commences breathing cycle commences at same time
All as front crawl				Maintain glide until speed equals swimming speed leg kicks and long arm sweep commence approx. together.

PRACTICES LEADING TO THE STANDING STARTS

In carrying out these practices, it is assumed that the pupils have been taught:

1. The early shallow-water diving practices
2. Elementary poolside practices
3. The plunge
4. Both surface and submerged prone push-off-and-glide practices

STANDING START WITH CONVENTIONAL ARM SWING

ACTIVITY	TEACHING PRACTICES	TEACHING POINTS
1. The arm-swing movement (fig. 21.6)	Standing away from the poolside, pupils practise the arm swing and jump-up. Starting in a semi-crouch position, this is similar to a diving start	1. The arm swing is a natural forward-upward and backward movement. If the pupils are told to jump up and reach for an overhead object, the natural arm swing is made. 2. Pupils to jump and reach up on the up-swing 3. Achieving height is the main aim of the exercise, together with establishing the correct direction of the arm swing

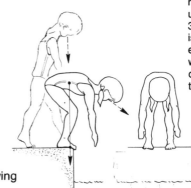

Fig. 21.7 Taking up the starting position

Fig. 21.6 Practising the arm swing

| 2. Taking up the stance for the conventional arm-swinging movement (fig. 21.7) | Swimmer to take up position on poolside
(a) Feet hip-width apart
(b) First and second toes (at least) curled over the edge of the pool
(c) Heels flat on floor
(d) Knees flexed
(e) Hips flexed
(f) Arms hanging by sides and slightly forward
(g) Head lifted slightly with eyes looking forward and down
(h) Swimmer mentally alert
(i) Swimmer must look down at the pool edge in order to see where she is stepping |

| 3. The take-off, flight, entry and glide (fig. 21.8) | 1. The stance and arm swing are now combined. The swimmers dive in on 'Go' and glide to surface
2. Repeat for increasing glide distances
3. Introduce some distance competition. It is important that the teacher gives a *sharp* and *loud* signal in order to instil a sense of urgency into the pupils | 1. Continuity and correct limb track of arm swing
2. Vigorous extension of legs
3. Body straight during flight
4. Emphasis on getting 'out' rather than 'up'
5. Arms extended, hands flat with palms facing down at entry – finger-tips first
6. Aim for shallow entry
7. Glide to surface |

Fig. 21.8

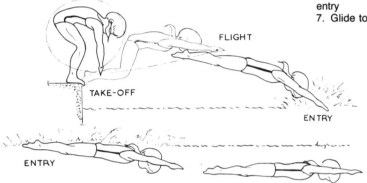

GLIDE INTO INITIAL STROKE MOVEMENTS

| 4. As 3, but with initial strokes introduced | The dive start with individual stroke practices

For the initial stroke movements, refer to chapter 22 | As before (see turns) |

THE STANDING STARTS: FAULTS, ANALYSIS AND CORRECTION

FAULT	ANALYSIS	CORRECTION
1. Incorrect arm swing	Swimmers sometimes get themselves tied in knots regarding the rotational direction of the arm swing. The result is that of a butterfly-like movement	The swimmers must ensure that the initial arm movement is a forward one
2. Incorrect stance – slipping may occur	Legs too wide or feet too close together	It may be necessary for the teacher physically to place the swimmer in the correct position.

3. Raising the heels	The swimmer moves forward on to the balls of the feet and lifts the heels. Falling into the water prematurely usually occurs	The swimmer must be completely steady with heels firmly planted on the poolside prior to the starting signal. Holding the stance is good practice for curing this fault
4. Anticipating the starting signal	The swimmer dives in before the starter's signal	As for Fault 3
5. Flopping into the water	Insufficient leg extension or speed of extension; head may be raised too high; swimmer may be fearful of diving in general	1. Return to push-and-glide practices with emphasis on glide length 2. Return to poolside practices leading to plunge 3. Emphasis on leg extension and distance away from take-off point
6. Starting to swim too early	From the dive, the initial glide speed is faster than swimming speed, hence premature stroking will slow the swimmer down	Fault can only be assessed by an onlooker, usually by timing the swimmer over a short distance then making adjustments
7. Always commencing the swim with a breast stroke-like arm sweep, regardless of stroke to be performed (usually front crawl)	This is a beginners' fault whereby they swim to the surface then start to swim along it instead of making the sequence continuous	If front crawl is to be swum, one arm should pull while the other temporarily remains outstretched. Normal stroking then follows
8. Excessive glide length	The swimmer maintains the glide position too long, therefore requiring to accelerate to swimming speed. This requires extra energy	This again is an observable fault. Rectification can only be applied on poolside assessment and instruction

Generally starts are neglected in competition swimming. One often hears of swimmers performing many many lengths, but it must be remembered that they only had to dive in the water just once in order to complete them. For competition swimming, starting practices from the poolside and (for back crawl) in the water are necessary. Therefore the teacher should hold special one-width starting sessions in order to improve this important feature of racing. Practices related to the different competition styles should also be carried out.

THE BACK-CRAWL START (fig. 21.9)

The relevant law states that the competitors should line up in the water facing the starting end with both hands on the end rail or starting grips. The feet, including the toes, should be under the surface of the water. Standing in or on the gutter or curling the toes over the top of the gutter is prohibited.

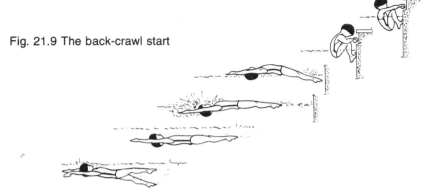

Fig. 21.9 The back-crawl start

Preparatory position

On direction from the starter, the swimmer enters the water and takes up a position facing the start. She grasps the bath rail, trough or other fitting such as hand grips on the starting blocks which may be provided for the purpose of starting a back-stroke race. The hands should overgrasp the rail and be spaced approximately shoulder-width apart. The feet should be placed on the wall with toes beneath the water surface. The feet need not necessarily be on the same level; indeed some swimmers prefer to position one foot slightly higher in the water than the other in order to obtain a better foundation for take-off.

The same mechanical features as those outlined for the front-crawl stance (fig. 21.4) are applicable. On the command 'Take your marks', the arms are flexed, thus lifting the swimmer forward and upward to bring body and head near to the wall or starting block. By flexing her elbows, the swimmer uses the balls of her feet as a fulcrum to lever her back as clear of the water as she can. This action will enable her to attain a position whereby she is able to drive herself backwards over the water surface at the appropriate moment.

Take-off

As in the standing start, the take-off should be explosive.

On hearing the starting signal, the swimmer performs a simultaneous set of movements. She throws her head back, vigorously extends her legs and swings her straightened arms outwards and round in an arc so that the hands finally come together behind the head, palms uppermost and thumbs touching. It is important that the arms move with a lateral 'action' in order that their respective 'reactions' are self-cancelling. The body should be directed away from the wall and inclined very slightly upwards, the back will be laterally square and facing the surface. The swimmer's head will be tipped right back so that she looks 'down the course'. At the same time as these movements take place a breath is taken although, as in the standing start, this is a natural function which need not be actually taught.

Flight
The swimmer should endeavour to elevate herself as clear of the water as possible during flight. Her body should be streamlined, stretched and slightly arched with head held right back.

Re-entry
The finger-tips should enter the water first, followed by the head then the lower parts of the body. The entry must be at a slight angle so that the swimmer is directed forward into a shallow glide.

Glide
The glide under the water takes place at a depth of approximately 450 mm (18 in.) with the body in a horizontal, athletically stretched, supine mode. If the start is performed correctly, the speed of the glide is faster than that of the swimmer when she is on the surface. She must therefore maintain this streamlined attitude until swimming speed is reached in order to gain full advantage from the start.

Initial strokes
There are no restrictions regarding underwater strokings as long as the swimmer maintains her back-swimming position. When the glide speed has diminished to that of normal swimming speed, the legs commence their beat and simultaneously one arm starts to pull. The stroking action, combined with a slight lifting of the head, should bring the swimmer to the surface where normal stroking may commence.

As the limb action begins, the swimmer may start to breathe out, trickle-fashion, through mouth and nose and continue to do so as the face breaks the surface. This continuous exhalation while the swimmer's face emerges through the surface eliminates water ingress into the nasal passages.

PRACTICES LEADING TO THE BACK-CRAWL START
In carrying out these practices, it is assumed that the pupils have been taught:

1. The early shallow-water diving practices
2. Both surface and submerged supine push-off-and-glide practices

ACTIVITY	TEACHING PRACTICES	TEACHING POINTS
1. The push and glide (see chapter 14)	1. A supine push-off: facing the rail and taking up a position similar to that of the correct start, the pupils commence the movement with a slight pull-up, then sink to below the water surface to approximately 300 mm (12 in.). At the same time as the pull-up, a breath is taken. Once below the surface, each swimmer lets go of the rail, puts his or her head back and assumes a back-lay position. Then, by stretching the legs, the push-off from the wall is made while at the same time both arms are fully extended beyond the head. During the glide to the surface, the swimmer is instructed to slowly exhale through the nose and continue to do so until his or her face is clear of the water	1. Firm push-off: the feet need not necessarily be laterally level 2. Head well back 3. Fully stretched and streamlined attitude during glide, arms covering the ears 4. Palms of hands should be facing upwards. (These may act as elevators) 5. Ensure that pupils breathe out through the nose as face clears the water 6. Push-off must be below water surface
	2. Exercise as before but, after a short glide, introduce a leg-kicking movement to surface. Continue across the width of the pool (fig. 21.10)	All as before
2. The pre-starting position in a relaxed pre-race attitude. (This is the position taken up by the swimmer when he or she comes under starter's orders)	1. Pupils take up a relaxed correct pre-starting position as follows: (a) Feet hip-width apart and placed firmly on the wall (b) Feet not necessarily on the same level (c) Toes must be below the surface. (This is competition law) (d) 'Balance' on the balls of the feet and the toes (e) Feet as near to the surface as possible while at the same time maintaining control and comfort (f) Hands overgrasping the rail at approximately shoulder-width apart (g) Arms straight and relaxed	1. The importance of the position of the feet must be emphasised in order to avoid slipping at take-off. This is related closely to the physical characteristics of the swimmer, i.e. the length of legs and arms, flexibility of the hips and any excess weight around the waist.
3. The starting position: on the command 'Take your marks', the arms are flexed to draw the swimmer towards the wall and upwards. The head bends forward to be near the wall	1. Taking up the starting position from the relaxed attitude may be carried out several times; each time the swimmer returns to the relaxed mode 2. The starting command should be sharp, loud and authoritative	1. Elevation *above* the water surface 2. The correct position of the feet will be evident here – if they are too low, or incorrectly spaced, the swimmer will tend to slip 3. The head should be brought near to the wall or starting surface

| 4. The take-off with glide | 1. An early practice may be tried in the shallow end of the pool. Swimmers standing in chest-deep water, facing the wall, take up semi-crouch attitude with arms stretched forward along the water surface. They jump up from the bottom and backwards, swinging the arms out, sideways and back, to assume a backward glide in water
2. An intermediate practice may be carried out, if the class is small, from the steps leading down into the water
3. Taking-off from the wall may now be practised. The swimmers should be aiming to project themselves *over* the water rather than *through* it | 1. Emphasise the outward and semi-circular movement of the arms, rather than a vertically biased arc.
2. Arching the back
3. Throwing the head well back to look at the other end or side of the pool
4. Finger-tip re-entry
5. Aim for long streamlined and stretched glide
6. Breathing out rough the nose towards the end of the glide or (in the cases of better-quality starts) as the face clears the water |

5. Leg movement   1. Introduce leg kick towards the end of the glide (fig. 21.10)
(This is only a teaching progression: normally arm and leg movements would start together)
2. Full starting procedure, into full stroke must commence

Use of the hands and/or head in order to surface
1. A *single* arm stroking (fig. 21.11) the cycle, followed by complete sequence
2. The first arm stroke should bring swimmer to surface
3. A slight body roll may assist this initial recovery movement

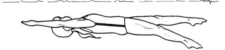

Fig. 21.10

Fig. 21.11

Once more, the starting commands should be sharp, loud and authoritative.

THE BACK-STROKE START: FAULTS, ANALYSIS AND CORRECTION

FAULT	ANALYSIS	CORRECTION
1. Incorrect arm swing	The movement should be an outward swing, thus cancelling out any unwanted reactions	Concentration on the direction of swing during take-off
2. Incorrect starting position: slipping may occur	Feet must be below the surface and hip-width apart. If they are too low or too wide the feet will slip	Teacher must ensure the correct feet placings prior to take-off
3. Insufficient take-off momentum: the swimmer must get as clear of the water at take-off as possible	May be due to: (a) insufficient leg extension (b) inability to stretch backwards (c) failure to tilt the head back far enough, hence swimmer 'sits' in the water, and pushes it backwards in a wave	1. Return to supine push-and-glide practices with emphasis on distance 2. Swimmers must look for the opposite side during take-off
4. Gliding too deeply	Swimmer tends towards a backward somersault through excessively arching the back	1. Return to push-and-glide practices 2. Swimmer should attempt to straighten out at take-off 3. Swimmer should raise the head slightly
5. Surface push-off, usually accompanied by excessive wave formation	Swimmer's angle of take-off is probably too steep, or the back is not arched enough	1. Return to push-and-glide practices 2. Head must be tilted back at take-off, looking for the opposite side 3. Emphasis on arching the back

22 The Competition Turns

During competition events, if a race is longer than the length of the pool, the swimmer must perform a turn (or turns) in order to complete the designated distance.

Swimmers who are able to turn quickly and efficiently at the end of a lap can enhance their overall performance quite considerably. A good turn is dependent on several skills and these are formulated below:

1. A fast approach to the wall
2. A well-judged touch or point of rotation
3. A speedy transition from linear to rotational movement
4. A balanced, well-directed and streamlined push-off glide
5. The correctly-timed commencement of the initial strokes
6. The correct restarting-to-swim technique to ensure continuity of propulsion

For each stroke there is a set of competition laws which must be adhered to during the period between reaching the end of the pool and starting the return swim.

For the purpose of analysis, general turning technique has been sub-divided into phases, as follows:

1. Approach   4. Push-off
2. Touch   5. Glide
3. Rotation   6. Initial strokes

1. Approach

When any turn is about to be performed, a fast approach to the wall is essential in order that a fast linear speed may be translated into a rapid rotational speed.

A swimmer who makes a slow approach into a turn must generate turning speed at the wall and during the turn: this is difficult to do and loses valuable time and energy.

Should the turn not require the touching of the wall with the hand, a slow swimming speed is even more difficult to translate into a speedy rotation.

When the approach is being made, the distance to the end of the course must be viewed or judged accurately by the swimmer. Any necessary adjustments can then be made to the timing of the stroke, thus ensuring that the touch or turning point is reached at precisely the correct moment in the stroke cycle.

In a freestyle event, a hand touch is not necessarily required and, if a 'flip turn' is used, it becomes imperative that the swimmer judges his speed and distance from the end of the course with precision.

Good initial positioning and timing during the approach will ensure that both feet are finally planted on the wall accompanied by sufficient flexion of the hip, knee and ankle joints to provide a sound basis for a powerful push-off.

The back-stroke approach requires a backward glance of some description in order to ascertain the position in relation to the end of the pool. Care must be taken at this stage not to roll excessively from the normal back swimming position, thus inviting disqualification.

It is important for turns to be practised at racing speeds. The swimmer continues to approach the end of the pool after the turn movements have commenced. He must therefore get used to pin-pointing the correct spot at which to turn during an actual race, as this will be different from when carrying out a training swim.

2. Touch

As previously mentioned, in a freestyle race the stroke law stipulates that the touch may be made with any part of the body. Freestyle exponents have taken advantage of this law by the development of the high-speed flip turn. In this turn, the actual rotation of the body is performed some distance away from the wall, with only the feet coming into contact prior to the push-off.

The breast-stroke turn laws state that the swimmer must touch the end of the course with 'both hands simultaneously at the same level either at, above or below the water level'. Just prior to the touch, the swimmer must maintain his shoulders in a horizontal position.

A butterfly touch is made in a similar fashion to that of the breast stroke, the style being subject to almost identical law requirements.

The back-crawl law requires a touch to be made with the hand or, in the case of bad timing, the arm or the head! The swimmer must remain in the 'normal back swimming position' until such a touch is made.

Most swimmers possess a favourite turning arm. However, practices must be carried out using either arm as the touching one, with subsequent rotation in the related direction.

3. Rotation

Generally, the rotational phase of a turn must be carried out as rapidly as possible and it is worth remembering that if a swimmer's body is contracted into some form of a tuck, a faster rotation is possible than if he is in a semi-flexed attitude. This basic mechanical principle is closely allied to the ability of a high-board or spring-board diver to perform faster somersaults in a tuck position than when 'piked'.

Further improvements in rotational speed may be achieved by elevating some parts of the body clear of the water. For example, the arc of movement of the feet and lower legs during a back-crawl turn can be speeded up by traversing them *over* rather than *through* the water.

The reaction of the hand pushing on the wall assists the swimmer to rotate the body in the instances when a hand touch is required.

In the case of a flip turn, rotation may be assisted by the downward action of the hands and lower arms from the region of the swimmer's hips. This movement, combined with the forces built up on the submerged back due to dynamic water pressure, serves to create the necessary rotation.

In all instances, a full 180 degrees of rotary movement must be achieved before push-off is attempted, in order to return directly back along the course. Failure by the swimmer to position himself correctly, will cause him to slip or push sideways with valuable time being lost while corrections are made.

4. Push-off
A firm and powerful push-off is essential and in all cases there is advantage to be gained by pushing off under the water, thus avoiding any resistance to motion caused by water-surface disturbance.

The feet should be placed firmly and evenly on the wall about shoulder-width apart, the leg joints being sufficiently flexed to effect a good recoiling action. Both arms should be stretched ahead of the swimmer in the direction of the intended swim. The trunk should be lying horizontal and flat with the head tucked down between the upper arms for good streamlining.

The push-off takes place by vigorous extension of the legs propelling the swimmer forward.

5. Glide
The glide takes place directly from the push-off with the swimmer's body in a fully stretched and streamlined attitude. The initial direction of motion is horizontal, with any bias towards surfacing being brought about by natural buoyancy or by movement of the head or hands during the initial stroking phase.

If performed correctly, the glide speed is initially faster than the swimming speed in most cases. The depth of glide should be such that the swimmer's back is *approximately* 450 mm (18 in.) below the water surface. This, however, will finally be dependent on the swimmer's individual physical characteristics, and the stroke to be subsequently performed.

6. Initial strokes
It is important that stroking does not take place too soon during the glide away from the wall. As previously mentioned, a well-performed glide is

initially faster than the swimming speed and full advantage must be taken of this fact. It is only when the speed of the fully submerged and stretched swimmer starts to diminish that stroking should commence.

The initial movement techniques are largely dependent on the strokes which are being performed and the laws which govern these activities. These will be discussed at a later stage during the descriptions of the individually styled turns.

Generally speaking the fastest stroke, front crawl, dictates that the transition from glide to swim takes place at the swimmer's highest speed. Therefore, the associated glide will be necessarily shallow and short. The butterfly and back-stroke glides will be relatively longer because of their slower swimming speeds. Finally, with breast stroke, generally considered to be the slowest stroke, the glide will be the longest and, in relation to the other strokes, the deepest.

FRONT-CRAWL TURNS

The law regarding freestyle swimming states that the competitor shall touch the end of the course with any part of his body. Taking into account the natural speed of the stroke and the advantage of performing the turn without having to touch the wall with the hand, a front-crawl flip turn is undoubtedly the fastest.

Grab-throwaway and the pivot turns are easier for less able swimmers to perform and they can probably turn faster using a reasonable version of either of these methods than a badly executed flip.

During the learning period, and in many instances beyond this, the grab-throwaway turn is often used. Here, the swimmers may take a quick gasp of air during rotation and set themselves up prior to the push-off and glide. The grab-throwaway turn is similar to the breast-stroke and butterfly turns.

The flip turn (fig. 22.1)
Approach
The approach is made at high speed. The position of the end of the course must be judged extremely carefully because there can be no adjustment made at the wall should the rotation be performed in the wrong spot.

There is no hand touch and it must be realised that the developed momentum will continue to propel a swimmer on towards the wall after stroking ceases and the turn commences. A breath is taken at a convenient time before the turn is started.

Rotation
The initial axis of rotation is parallel to the water surface with the swimmer commencing the flip sequence in a horizontal attitude with feet and legs stretched. Both hands should be moved back and positioned

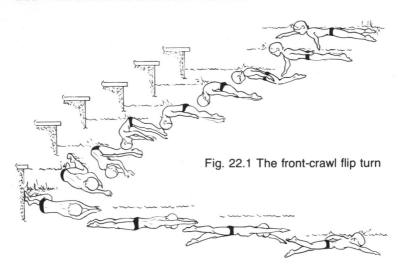

Fig. 22.1 The front-crawl flip turn

adjacent to the thighs with palms facing downwards, and the chin is tucked into the chest.

The next part of the sequence is for the swimmer to assume the pike position with the head directed downwards.

Then, by pressing down with the hands, a rotating force is developed, and it is by combining this turning moment with the water forces which are developed by the swimmer's momentum that the swimmer rotates both legs over the water surface and towards the end of the pool. An accentuated and cross-body movement of one hand also provides a quarter-twist in a direction opposite to the hand movement. She changes from a pike to a semi-tuck position during the process and it is this contracted body mode which enhances the speed of rotation.

The forward movement of the swimmer, combined with her 'piked' position, contributes greatly towards assisting rotation. Here, the water forces developed on her back act in the opposite direction to her forward momentum, thus assisting her to flip her legs over (fig. 22.2).

Fig. 22.2

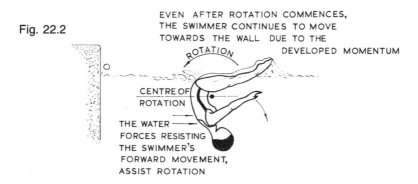

EVEN AFTER ROTATION COMMENCES, THE SWIMMER CONTINUES TO MOVE TOWARDS THE WALL DUE TO THE DEVELOPED MOMENTUM

ROTATION

CENTRE OF ROTATION

THE WATER FORCES RESISTING THE SWIMMER'S FORWARD MOVEMENT, ASSIST ROTATION

Touch
Completion of the rotation and semi-twist should find the swimmer with feet planted firmly and slightly apart on the wall with adequate flexion of the leg joints to facilitate a powerful push-off. The quarter-twist produces a somewhat 'side-lying' attitude, with the arms positioned in front of the head prior to being fully stretched towards the direction of the intended motion.

Push-off
A vigorous straightening of the legs, combined with a further quarter-twist, enables the now fully stretched and streamlined performer to push away from the wall and at the same time assume the desired swimming mode. The depth of push-off should be approximately 300–450 mm (12–18 in.) below the surface. During both the push-off and the glide, the head should be tucked down between the upper arms, thus minimising profile drag.

Glide
The swimmer continues in this athletically stretched attitude, making full use of the speed and momentum developed at the push-off. The depth of glide may be gradually decreased by *slightly* tilting the hands or head upward. (This movement will be found to be essential if the push-off is too deep.)

Initial strokes
As the swimmer's glide speed starts to diminish, the legs commence their beat and one arm simultaneously commences the catch. The other arm remains fully stretched in front of the head. The initial downward motion of the hand tends to bring the swimmer to the surface. (It may be advantageous for the swimmer to retain some of the body roll which is brought about during rotation, thus assisting her to clear the recovering arm from the water.) Exhalation may take place just before the head breaks the surface, or the breath may be held until some later stage. Normal stroke actions may commence as soon as the surface swimming mode is regained.

The pivot turn (fig. 22.3)
Approach
The approach is made at maximum speed with sufficient observation at the end of the course being made by the swimmer while not interrupting the stroke rhythm. A breath may be taken just prior to the touch being made. Any adjustment to stroke length and timing must be carried out to ensure a good start to the turn.

Touch
Contact is made about 150–250 mm (6–10 in.) below the water level

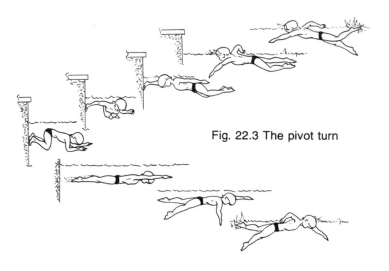

Fig. 22.3 The pivot turn

with the leading hand. Fingers should be pointing downwards *and* towards the direction of turn, with the hand almost if not completely flat on the wall. The elbow should be slightly flexed, thus allowing the body to move in towards the wall.

Simultaneously with the touch, the legs, held close together, begin to draw up under the body and the chin is tucked into the chest.

(Attention is drawn to the fact that, although a hand touch is not obligatory in competition, it is necessary here in order to carry out the rotation.)

Rotation

After the touch, the touching arm plays the major role during the turn by straightening vigorously to direct the shoulders away from the wall, causing the lower body to pivot around so that the tucked legs move near to the wall. This rotating movement may be assisted by a lateral sweep of the other arm, although most swimmers rotate without using this movement. The pivoting action takes place about a vertical axis (centre of gravity) with the swimmer's back lying almost parallel with the water line. When rotation is complete, the feet are firmly and evenly planted on the wall and the arms assume a position in front of the swimmer; the head is still in its lowered position between the arms. The whole rotary motion takes place with the back at a depth of 150–200 mm (6–8 in.).

Push-off

By vigorously straightening the legs and extending the arms, the swimmer drives away from the wall to carry out the glide and initial stroking techniques as previously described in the flip turn.

The grab-throwaway turn (fig. 22.4)

Approach

The approach is made at the relevant swimming speed in the same way as for the pivot turn.

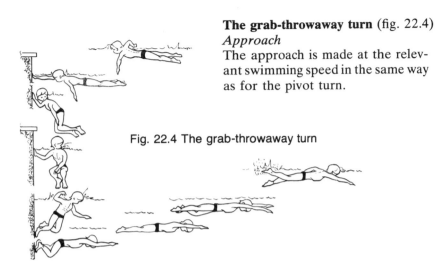

Fig. 22.4 The grab-throwaway turn

Touch

During the learning period and again during training, if there is a handrail or trough, the swimmer may grab this in order to commence rotation. If no such fitting is installed, the touch should be made on the wall. (As for the previous turns, the hand touch is not obligatory.)

Rotation

(A turn to the right is described: the left-hand turn is identically opposite.)

Rotation is carried out in a very similar way to that used in the breast stroke and butterfly. Here, the swimmer is assisted in making a speedy rotation by assuming a semi-tucked position, with trunk almost vertical.

The turning movement is initiated with a push by touching with, say, the left arm. The hand presses on the wall and the body continues to pivot to the right about an almost vertical central turning axis. The right arm does not play a very important part in the actual rotation.

The head is above the water surface during rotation and a breath may be taken during this period. The left arm, after leaving the wall, may be brought forward over and back into the water in preparation for the push-off. The completion of rotation should find the swimmer with feet firmly and evenly planted on the wall, with the trunk in a near-horizontal mode. The arms should be preparing to push forward with elbows tucked well in and hands approximately 200 mm (8 in.) in front of the eyes with palms facing downwards. The whole body, including the head, should be completely submerged to a depth of about 300 mm (12 in.).

The push-off and glide are identical to those of the pivot turn.

THE BACK-CRAWL TURN (fig. 22.5)

The relevant law states that there shall be no deviation from the normal back-stroke swimming position until the foremost hand or arm (or head!) has touched the end of the course.

Probably the fastest of the back-stroke turns is the one which is performed by amalgamating a half-backward somersault with the suggestion of a twist; it is this technique which is described in this section.

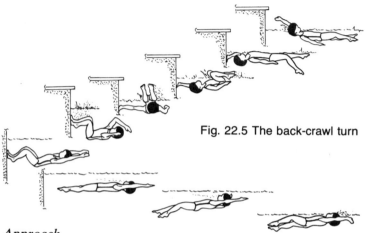

Fig. 22.5 The back-crawl turn

Approach

As in all turns, the approach must be made in the normal swimming attitude without slackening speed. The distance from the wall can be judged by a backward or sideways glance or, if the surroundings are familiar, a look at the overhead building structure of the pool. The length of the arm stroke must be adjusted so that one arm is fully stretched forward to make contact. Care must be taken not to drop one shoulder excessively in order to look towards the end of the course as this is a fault which may result in disqualification in a competition event.

Touch

The leading arm is stretched forward in a direct line with the shoulder joint, and the touch is made just below the water line with the fingers or palm of the hand. When contact is made, the fingers should be pointing downwards. Immediately after the touch the body is allowed to drive on towards the wall a short distance by allowing the touching arm to flex slightly.

A breath is quickly taken at this stage and the head is tilted well back.

If a swimmer should mistime the touch, the other hand may be quickly moved back to the wall in a 'rescue bid'. The turn may be then completed with both hands in contact with the wall.

Rotation

The actual rotation is brought about by the swimmer using the generated linear momentum and directing it to cause the body to pivot while using the leading shoulder joint as the centre of rotation. Direction of rotation is towards the touching arm.

During rotation the head is kept tilted well back; for a speedy turn, the knees and lower legs should be lifted clear of the water (fig. 22.6), the touching arm remains flexed. The other arm does not necessarily take any active part in the performance and may be kept tucked into the body.

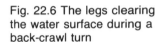
Fig. 22.6 The legs clearing the water surface during a back-crawl turn

As the legs swing towards the wall, the swimmer rolls *slightly* into the turn and her flexed arm extends to push the upper part of the body in the opposite direction. This action enables the tucked and slightly twisted swimmer to pivot about the vertical centre, bringing the feet into contact with the wall at about 180–200 mm (6–8 in.) below the water surface. The arms, meanwhile, take up a flexed attitude, with the hands a few inches apart and slightly in front of the head prior to being stretched forward. The head assumes a natural position with the face being directed upwards.

During rotation the swimmer may find trouble with ingress of water up the nose. This may be alleviated by a slow outward trickle of air through the nose throughout the whole underwater sequence. This procedure, however, takes a little practice to carry out successfully.

Push-off

The balls of the feet must be planted firmly and evenly on the wall and slightly apart with the leg joints flexed ready to extend and drive the swimmer away. There is no necessity for the feet to be laterally level. During leg extension the arms assume a fully stretched attitude in front of the head and pointed towards the intended direction of movement.

Push-off is made by a vigorous stretching of the legs, thus propelling the completely submerged and streamlined swimmer back along the course.

Glide

The supinated glide is in the streamlined and stretched mode and continues under the surface until the speed begins to diminish to that of
swimming speed.

As previously mentioned, trickle breathing through the nose may be
carried out during the glide phase should ingress of water prove
troublesome.

Initial strokes

As the swimmer begins to slow down, the legs commence their beat and
one arm begins a normal pull; this action tends to elevate her in the water
and it is at this point that the breath is exhaled.

Unless trickle breathing has already commenced, breathing out mainly
through the nose as the face surfaces ensures that the nasal passages
remain free from the ingress of water. Once on the surface, the swimmer
continues the normal stroking actions.

THE BREAST-STROKE TURN (fig. 22.7)

The stroke law* states that:

When touching at the turn, or on finishing a race, the touch shall
be made with both hands simultaneously on the same level, with
shoulders in horizontal position.

Swimming under the surface of the water is prohibited except one
arm stroke and one leg kick after start and turn.

A swimmer may take one stroke to assist him in returning
promptly to the surface. Either the complete or incomplete movement of the arms and legs shall be considered as one stroke or kick.

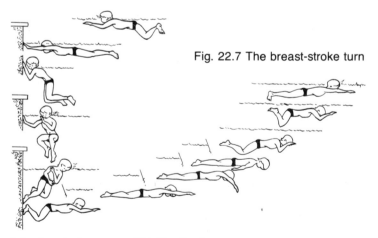

Fig. 22.7 The breast-stroke turn

* As given in the current *ASA Handbook*.

From the moment when a swimmer, after start or turn, begins the second stroke, one part of the head shall always break the surface of the water.

The teacher must be observant of all these features during the teaching practices.

Approach
The breast stroke is the style which permits the best view of the end of the course, due to the fact that the head is carried in a slightly elevated position. The stroke length should be adjusted in such a way that, with a final leg kick, the arms are outstretched together in front of the swimmer. This final kick and glide will ensure that the wall is reached with maximum speed and momentum.

Touch
The touch should be made with both hands simultaneously; they must be on the same level (ASA law).

The hands should be placed on the wall at about 200 mm (8 in.) apart with the fingers pointing upwards. The wall, *not* the handrail, should be the point of touch. At the same time as contact is made with the hands, the legs start to draw up under the body.

The swimmer's speed will tend to bring him closer to the wall and the elbows are subsequently flexed to allow this to happen. The head is held in the normal position.

Rotation
(A turn to the right is described: the left-hand turn is identically opposite.)

To assist the swimmer to make a speedy rotation, the heels are tucked well up towards the buttocks with the trunk almost vertical. Rotation is brought about by a turning movement initiated with a push by the right arm. The left hand presses on the wall and the body continues to pivot to the right about an almost vertical central turning axis. The right arm does not play a very important part in the actual rotation after providing the initial push. The head is above the water surface during the early stages of the turn and a breath should be taken during this period. The completion of rotation finds the swimmer with feet firmly and evenly planted on the wall with the trunk in a horizontal mode. The arms should be preparing to push forward with elbows tucked well in, hands should be approximately 200 mm (8 in.) in front of the eyes, with palms facing downwards. The whole body, including the head, should be completely submerged to a depth of 450–600 mm (18–24 in.).

The speed of rotation may sometimes be enhanced by swinging the trailing arm over the water towards the forward-stretched push-off position.

Push-off
The push-off should take place while the swimmer is fully submerged. His back should be about 300–450 mm (12–18 in.) below the surface, and the initial direction of motion should be horizontal.

The movement is brought about by a vigorous extension of the legs during which the swimmer assumes a fully stretched and streamlined attitude, with the head tucked down between the upper arms.

Glide
In the athletically stretched position, the swimmer is now probably travelling faster than swimming speed. In order to gain full advantage from the momentum developed, the glide must be maintained until the speed diminishes to that of the swimmer's surface speed.

Initial strokes
The law states that, after a turn, only one arm stroke and one leg kick shall take place while the swimmer is submerged.

At the appropriate time, the arms perform a simultaneous extended sweep so that the hands end up adjacent to the thighs (fig. 22.8). When they have completed this sweep, the arms are recovered, during which time the hands and elbows are hugged as close to the body as possible throughout, in order to minimise profile drag.

During the arm recovery, the legs perform their powerful drive so that, as the kick reaches its zenith, the arms become fully stretched. It is at this point that the head is lifted. The lifting action, combined with the

Fig. 22.8 The underwater extended arm sweep after the breast-stroke turn

developed speed, serves to bring the swimmer to the surface, and it is only when the head breaks the surface that normal stroking can recommence.

Forced mouth and nose exhalation takes place as the swimmer breaks through the water surface.

THE BUTTERFLY TURN (fig. 22.9)
The stroke law* states that:

> The body shall be kept perfectly on the breast, and both shoulders in line with the surface of the water.
>
> When touching at the turn, or on finishing a race, the touch shall be made with both hands simultaneously on the same level, with shoulders in the horizontal position.
>
> After the start and turns, a swimmer is permitted one or more leg kicks and one arm pull under the water, which must bring him to the surface.

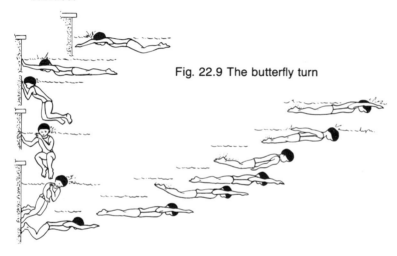

Fig. 22.9 The butterfly turn

Approach
The approach to the point of turn must be at full speed. The swimmer should endeavour to judge his stroke timing so that the final movement, prior to the touch, results in the arms being fully outstretched in front.

Touch/rotation/push-off and glide
All these movements are identical to those described for the breast-stroke turn.

The glide length will be shorter, however, due to the generally faster speed of the butterfly stroke.

* As given in the current *ASA Handbook*.

Initial strokes

Butterfly law states that the swimmer may make one or more leg beats but only one arm pull under the water surface, the subsequent recovery being over the water.

Summary of
(ASA Stroke Laws numbers 66
69 (Back Stroke) all

		APPROACH	TOUCH	ROTATION
FRONT CRAWL	PIVOT	Very fast turn starts short distance from wall – judgement very important	Leading hand, palm on wall fingers pointing towards direction of turn. Under surface	In fully tucked position, with back barallel to water surface
FRONT CRAWL	FLIP	Very fast. speed has direct relation to rate of somersault. Distance judgement very important in order to achieve good push	Hand touch not necessary	Vertical action combined with half or full twist – starts in pike position knees bend at end of turn for push
BACK CRAWL	HALF SOMERSAULT	Fast. Timing of arm stroke to achieve good hand placing very important. Head held well back looking for wall.	Leading hand touches below surface – fingers pointing towards pool floor and inwards. Head tilted back legs beginning to tuck must be on the back	On back with *part* twist – as much of the legs as possible above water. Tight tuck for speedy rotation
BREAST STROKE		As fast as the stroke timing allows. Head up to look up at wall. Stroke lengthened or shortened. Touch at the end of the leg kick	Two hands on the same level and simultaneously (law) fingers pointing up or towards turn. Allow elbows to bend, thus bringing the body closer to wall head rotated towards turn. Body beginning to tuck	Body in a fairly upright position. Legs tucked. Free hand may assist rotation
BUTTERFLY		As above	As above	As above

The arm pull is similar to the sweep used in the breast-stroke turn, but it is an initial downward movement of the hands that brings the swimmer to the surface. The same type of breathing technique as that described in the performance of the breast-stroke turn is also used.

Turns
(Freestyle), 67 (Breast Stroke), 68 (Butterfly) and apply)

PREPARATION FOR PUSH	PUSH OFF	GLIDE	INITIAL STROKES
Feet firmly on wall not necessarily on same level below water surface	Head down between arms. Hips and knees vigorously extended under water	Under surface in athletically – stretched position not too deep. Elevation to surface automatic after practice	As glide speed diminishes to swimming speed legs commence and one hand moves into catch – other arm remains extended. Stroking commences
Feet firmly on wall probably in a diagonal setting	As above	As above	As above
Feet firmly on wall not necessary in line. Swimmer must be on the back (law) hands positioning themselves beyond the head	Square and on the back (law) – in an athletically stretched position. Under surface push. Slightly elevated to assist surfacing	As above	As above
Feet firmly on wall on the same level. Head down. Hands stretched beyond the head. Legs flexed at knees and hips for maximum push off force	As front crawl	As above	Maintain glide until its speed equals swimming speed. Arms then sweep right back to thighs. Recover as legs kick and head breaks surface. Stroke and breathing cycle commences
As above	As front crawl	As above	Maintain glide speed until it equals swimming speed. Legs and arms commence stroking

TEACHING PRACTICES LEADING TO THE TURNS

The practices leading to the final performance of the various turns have been initially broken down into individual movements, then gradually assembled until the turn is complete. By carrying out the exercises in this fashion the swimmers are able to concentrate on the more difficult aspects of each skill.

Each introductory lesson may commence with a visual demonstration of the turn accompanied by a descriptive commentary. The pupils may then be invited to try the particular movement out for themselves before attempting the part-practices that follow.

FRONT CRAWL : THE FLIP TURN

ACTIVITY	TEACHING PRACTICES	TEACHING POINTS
1. Push-off and glide (see chapter 11)	1. Push-off using single-handed grasp of rail or channel, no stroking 2. Using the outstretched hands to elevate during the glide to surface, no stroking; after pushing and gliding, return to side and repeat. Glide depth to be 300–450 mm (12–18 in.)	1. The push-off should be under water 2. The correct depth of push-off 3. Feet should be planted firmly, evenly and the correct distance apart on wall, not necessarily on the same level 4. Correct distance from the wall in order to ensure a powerful drive away 5. Head down between the outstretched arms, upper arms over ears 6. Hands flat, thumbs together, palms facing downwards 7. Push-off force to be *equally* distributed between the feet 8. Push-off must be on the balls of the feet 9. Direction of push – horizontal, with any depth adjustment during glide being made by using the hands as elevators
2. Push off and glide, then introduce leg movements (fig. 22.10). This is only a progressional exercise. Legs-only movement from the glide would not normally occur following the glide	1. Push off, using single handed grasp. After short glide begin leg movement, glide to surface using hands as elevators and legs to give propulsion along the surface in the fully stretched mode 2. Half-width practices to commence with, leading to full-width practices	All teaching points above are applicable, together with: 10. Short counts of two or three seconds before starting leg movements. This is to emphasise that the initial push-off speed is normally faster than the legs-only swimming speed.

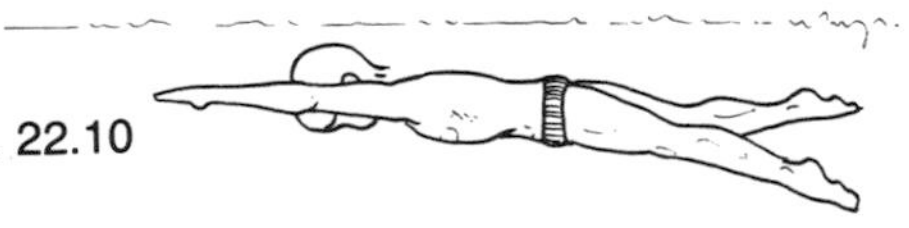

Fig. 22.10

3. Push off and glide into initial full-stroke movements (fig. 22.11)

1. As before but introducing arm movements
2. Introducing a slight roll: the swimmer will later tend to push off on his side from the turn. The roll will assist the swimmer in clearing his arm from the water during its initial recovery over the surface

11. Single arm pull, the other arm remaining outstretched until required to move (the uppermost arm to pull first)
12. Swimmer should almost be surfaced in order to recover over the water

Fig. 22.11

4. A tuck somersault from a push-off (fig. 22.12)

Push from the side on the surface, then into a stretch/tuck forward somersault. (Push from wall to give momentum.) At the end of somersault, attempt to regain a stretched supine attitude

1. Push on the surface, head down; stretch, *pike*, then quickly into *tuck somersault*-stretch
2. Hands will move back towards the hips then move downwards, thus providing an action. The reaction will be to assist the swimmer in rotating (The swimmer will come up in a back-lay (supine) position. This final attitude will be changed later)
3. Eyes retained open in order to orientate
4. Head down, chin tucked to chest
5. The swimmers may use a 'mechanical' sequence such as push-straight-pike-tuck-over-straight

Fig. 22.12

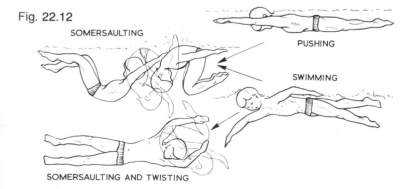

SOMERSAULTING

PUSHING

SWIMMING

SOMERSAULTING AND TWISTING

5. Somersaulting from a swim (fig. 22.12)	1. Push off underwater, leg and arm movements as previously taught. Swim to centre of width, perform a tuck forward somersault then stretch	1. Swim into somersault to be fast 2. The pre-tuck stretch should be automatic
	2. As above, but introducing a half-twist so that the swimmer ends up on his front (prone) facing the direction he came from During the final performance of the turn, the swimmer will probably rotate laterally only a quarter-twist, ending up on his side	3. Likening of the movement to a 'cartwheel' in the water gives the pupils an idea of the twist required. (After several attempts the twist usually appears to come naturally)
6. Somersaulting and pushing-off from the side Full-width swims, attempting the turn at each change of direction Introduce races to give swimmers competition experience	1. Swimming to the poolside (width-swims, or from the centre of the pool to side), putting the whole movement together *near* the wall; no pushes away from the wall to begin with, concentration on the rotational movement 2. Beginning the somersault movement in a position obviously too far away from the wall (chosen by the teacher), the swimmers move gradually in closer to the wall with each attempt	All the push-off teaching points already mentioned, and 4. Emphasis should be placed on speed of approach

FRONT CRAWL: THE PIVOT TURN

As an interim measure this may be taught and used should the swimmers not be too adept at the flip turn. As with the flip, the essential part of the overall turn is the push-off and glide. So the lesson would commence with the same type of activities and teaching practices (1, 2 and 3), then continue as follows:

ACTIVITY	TEACHING PRACTICES	TEACHING POINTS
1. The pivot	1. Standing in shallow end, facing wall, place one hand on wall by leaning forward, place head in water, jump/tuck. Push with hand on wall and swivel round to face opposite direction. Place feet on wall – *no push*. (No push is advised here so that full concentration may be centred on the pivot movement)	1. Full tuck required 2. Swimmer's back must be parallel with water surface 3. Touching arm must be used effectively 4. Other should assist turn by pulling across the swimmer's chest 5. Head down – turned in the direction of pivot 6. Eyes open in order to orientate
	2. Getting slightly back from the wall, push off from bottom of the pool to the wall. Practise the turn, by finally placing both feet on the wall (no push at this stage)	All as before, plus: 7. Aim for a finger-tip touch with semi-elbow flexion
	3. Swim in from a short distance away, ensuring that the touch is made with the favourite hand. (No push – feet on wall)	All as before, plus: 8. Aim for a speedy approach 9. Forward glance in order to judge correct touching distance
2. Pivot and push/glide	Introduce *slight push* away from wall and glide, after the pivot has taken place	All as before, plus: 10. Feet to be firmly and evenly planted, slightly apart; push-off on the balls of the feet 11. Symmetrical and directionally correct push-off
3. Pivot and push and glide and stroke	Introduce initial strokes. Then alternate arms to turn on	All as before, plus: 12. Correct initial stroking technique as for flip turn

FRONT CRAWL: THE GRAB-THROWAWAY TURN

The initial push-off-and-glide practices should precede the turn.

This turn is probably the slowest, but it is popular and most frequently used among beginners and during training sessions. The main reason for the turn's popularity is that breath may be taken during the movement. The main skill of the turn lies in the push-off-and-glide technique.

The practices may take place in the first instance by simply standing on the bottom in chest-deep water, holding the rail, then with a little jump the swimmer pivots to push off on the water surface in a glide, head down.

Developing this into an underwater push-off and glide is all that is now needed. (It is not necessary during a freestyle event to touch the wall with the hands, therefore the rail or channel may be used as a hand-hold.)

Points to remember about this turn are as follows:

1. The turn is essentially a single-handed affair – the pupils must be discouraged from climbing up the wall with both hands on the rail.
2. The swimmer need not necessarily be in a fully prone position before push-off.
3. Push-off will be as for the flip turn – then into initial strokes.
4. The importance of the action of the 'other hand' is secondary.
5. The head should be turned as quickly as possible in the direction of push-off.

THE BACK-CRAWL TURN

ACTIVITY	TEACHING PRACTICES	TEACHING POINTS
1. Push-off and glide (fig. 22.13)	1. A supine push-off, facing the rail and taking up a position similar to that of the start. The pupils commence with a slight pull-up, then sink to approximately 300 mm (12 in.) below the water surface. At the same time as the pull-up, a breath is taken. Once below the surface the swimmer lets go of the rail, puts the head back and assumes a back-lay position by stretching both legs evenly to push away from the wall, at the same time extending the arms ahead. During the glide to the surface, the swimmer is instructed to exhale slowly through the nose and continue to do so until the face clears the water	1. Firm and evenly balanced push-off: the feet need not necessarily be laterally level 2. Head well back 3. A fully stretched and streamlined attitude during glide 4. Palms of hands facing upwards: these may act as elevators 5. Ensure that pupils breathe out as face clears the water. This will reduce the amount of coughing and spluttering which usually accompanies such exercises
2. Push-off, glide, then add the leg kick, and finally arm and leg movements	2. Exercise as above, but after a short glide, introduce a leg-kicking movement to surface 3. As above, then introduce the arm movements	All as before pull 6. One arm pull, remaining arm outstretched until appropriate time to pull

Fig. 22.13 Back-crawl
push-off-and-glide practices

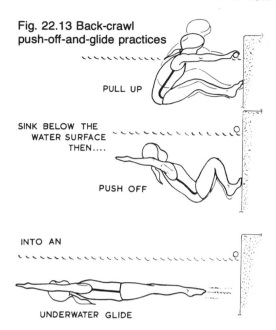

PULL UP

SINK BELOW THE
WATER SURFACE
THEN....

PUSH OFF

INTO AN

UNDERWATER GLIDE

| 3. Washing tub (fig. 22.14) | Swimmer 'sits' in water with bottom low, hips fully flexed and shins lying approximately level with the water surface. The arms stretched sideways, use a sculling action to pivot around. (The action is more fully described in chapter 28.) | 1. Ensure that the tuck position is as described
2. The head may be upright to begin with, but as the turn requires a backward head tilt, the pupils should attempt to look upwards as the rotational skill is acquired |

Fig. 22.14

| 4. Part 'washing tub' rotation near the wall, pushing off into a glide (fig. 22.15) | The swimmer stands in the shallow water then assumes the 'washing tub' position. She then pivots around placing both feet firmly and evenly on the wall, to push off in a fully stretched attitude on the water surface | 1. Feet to be firmly and evenly placed on wall
2. The distance away from the wall should be such that a push-off is possible
3. Both arms to be fully stretched backwards at push-off; the head should be between the arms with the face 'looking' upwards |

Fig. 22.15

5. Wall-assisted pivot, rotation (fig. 22.16)	1. The swimmer stands near to the wall with her back to it. She then reaches back, places one hand on wall below the handrail or trough. Then, with a *slight* push-off from the bottom, a semi-tuck is performed and the swimmer, by allowing the arm to flex, moves closer to the wall. As the head nears the wall, the arm is straightened out to provide an eccentric pivoting force thus rotating the swimmer in basically the same body-tuck attitude as the 'washing tub'. The feet should now be planted firmly and evenly on the wall. No push-off – simply *concentrate* on the pivot or rotation	1. The touching hand should be below the water surface 2. Fingers pointing downwards when the hand touches the wall to commence the pivot 3. The extension of the pivoting arm after the initial flexing must be vigorous in order to assist the pivoting action 4. The swimmer should be sufficiently near to the wall in order to allow a good push-off 5. The head should be well back 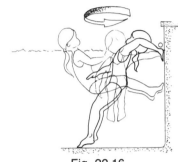 Fig. 22.16
6. Wall-assisted push-off and turn	2. As before, with push-off on the water surface	All as before, together with the push-off-and-glide-related teaching points
7. Legs only to wall with correct hand placing (fig. 22.17). This gives the swimmer a chance to gauge the proximity of the wall during the approach	Swimming to the wall legs only, one hand sculling, the other arm stretched ahead. Leading hand placed on the wall, legs continue to kick, position maintained for a few seconds. A good practice for 'glancing back' at the wall	1. Fully stretched swimming attitude to be maintained throughout 2. Leading arm close to the swimmer's head and stretched ahead 3. Minimal backward glance to observe touching point 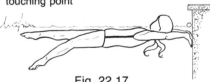 Fig. 22.17
8. Swimming to the wall on back using legs only – in the fully stretched position, then carrying out a complete turn	The swimmers start approximately half-way across the pool (or they may swim widths), moving by using a legs-only action in an athletically stretched position.	1. The kick must be vigorous 2. The swimmer may turn on either hand 3. Her head must be well back during rotation 4. There must be a firm finger touch on wall 5. An attempt must be made to traverse the lower legs *over* the water surface during pivot

Both arms are
stretched forward,
allowing the swimmer
to turn, on her
favourite hand. The
turn is carried out,
complete with push
and glide

6. Push-off and glide under the water
surface

9. Swimming in
towards the wall,
using the full
stroke, then
turning to swim
away once more

All teaching points as before, plus:
7. Push-off to be athletically stretched,
then into a *single* arm pull, followed by
normal stroke cycling
8. Breathing out during the short glide

All previously mentioned teaching points
apply

THE BREAST-STROKE TURN

ACTIVITY	TEACHING PRACTICES	TEACHING POINTS
1. The push and glide (under water)	Similar to the front-crawl turns: the activities should commence with push-and-glide practices. The push-off should be slightly deeper than the flip turn as a result of the initial stroking technique differences	The push-off and glide should be slightly deeper than for the front-crawl turns, being in the region of 450–600 mm (18–24 in.)
2. Push-off and glide, then pull and kick	The underwater stroke is now introduced. It is important that the stroke laws be strictly adhered to. The arm pull should be a full sweeping one, with the hands ending up in the vicinity of the thighs. The leg kick should be combined with a head lift. Pull, recovery, kick, head lift. *The head must break the 'surface' before the next stroke sequence begins.* As the face breaks the surface, the swimmer breathes out through mouth and nose	1. The pull should be a *long* sweep, the elbows being flexed sufficiently to allow the hands to be directed back for as long as possible 2. During recovery, the hands and arms must be in close proximity to body (see fig. 22.7) 3. Head positioned low initially 4. The leg kick and head lift should occur more or less together 5. The push-off must be deep enough to accommodate these movements before the swimmer finally breaks the water surface

3. The touch and pivot to the push and glide	Swimmer stands slightly away from wall, then leans forward and touches the wall with both hands. They should be shoulder-width apart with fingers facing upwards. Both hands must be on the *same level* and may be above or below the water surface. (These are the stroke law requirements.) This is the touch position at *all* times. With a slight push-off from the bottom of the pool, the swimmer pivots around by giving an eccentric push, first with both, then with one hand. The body rotates laterally and pivots to face downwards. Both feet should end up firmly and evenly planted on the wall. The push and glide under the surface immediately follows. Re-surface by tilting the hands upwards	1. Emphasis on the *two-handed touch* 2. The head must pivot in the direction of the turn 3. Body elevation during rotation must not be excessive 4. Rotation must be a complete 180 degrees so that the swimmer faces directly down the course 5. Push-off must be under water, and body perfectly on the breast
4. Push off the bottom or lean forward to touch/turn then swim (fig. 22.18)	The swimmer stands a short way from the wall, then leans forward or pushes off the bottom to touch both hands on the wall. He then executes the turn, pushes off and glides, then commences the initial strokes	All teaching points as before, with special attention to the stroke law

Fig. 22.18

| 5. Swim and turn, then swim | 1. The pupil may now swim using the full stroke towards the wall, execute the turn and resume swimming 2. Width practices carrying out the turn at each touch | All teaching points as before |

THE BUTTERFLY TURN

The butterfly turn is very like the breast-stroke turn, and the practices consequently are similar. The butterfly push-off is slightly shallower. The law states that there shall be one arm pull but as many kicks as the swimmer wishes to carry out. The arm pull is not quite the same as the breast stroke and the thrust is more in a vertical direction, thus elevating the swimmer.

The glide is still present, but not quite so long, the swimming speed of the butterfly being faster than that of the breast stroke.

TURNING FAULTS AND THEIR ANALYSIS

In most instances, turning faults may be generalised. However, the teacher must be aware of the ASA laws apertaining to turns, and should teach the skills within the confines of these particular restrictions.

FAULT	ANALYSIS	CORRECTION
1. Approaching too slowly. (The approach should be fast, providing the swimmer is able to swim fast!)	It is essential that the swimmer does not have to *generate* rotational speed during the turn. A fast approach is essential whereby the linear momentum already developed is merely transformed to rotational momentum	Swimmers are sometimes fearful of injury through impact with the wall. Goggles are a useful aid on such occasions. Otherwise a towel placed on the poolside, markings on the bottom of the pool, or some convenient overhead structure may be used as a marker
2. Approaching blind	The swimmer fails to judge the position of the end of the course, or make necessary adjustments in his stroke movements	As for Fault 1

3. Misjudging the touch or point of rotation, the swimmer crashes into the wall	Judging the point where the turn commences is an acquired art. The teacher and swimmer must remember that the swimmer will continue to move in towards the wall *after* the start of the turn	Constant repetition with poolside advice is the only real solution to the problem. It must also be realised that different speeds require different points of commencement
4. Failure to tuck or, where applicable, elevate the legs clear of the water	The act of tucking-up automatically increases the speed of rotation. This speed is also enhanced by elevating parts of the body above the surface	The teacher must convince the swimmers that tucking and elevating are essential for rapid turns. Practices must be directed along these lines
5. Slipping at push-off, or pushing off diagonally	The fault is probably due to partial turning or poor feet-positioning (or both) prior to push-off	Rotation must be complete and *both* feet *must* be firmly planted on the wall prior to push-off
6. Failing to push off because swimmer turns too soon	The swimmer turns too far out, consequently the feet fail to reach the wall for the push-off movement	Corrections as for Fault 3
7. Pushing-off too deeply	The swimmer directs the push towards the bottom of the pool	The teacher must demonstrate that travelling to the surface by a downward curve is *much* further than the desired straight-line path. Underwater push-off-and-glide practices to the surface are needed
8. Pushing-off on the water surface	The swimmer pushes off on the surface, probably with head too high. Creation of waves is a disadvantage in this instance	Corrections as for Fault 7
9. Failing to achieve the fully stretched position during glide	The swimmer may enhance his glide length by assuming a streamlined posture	Return to the push-off-and-glide practices with emphasis on streamlining and maximum glide distance

10. Commencing to swim too soon	An effective push-off is usually more rapid than swimming speed	Poolside assistance and advice is necessary. Timing a complete turn and swim sequence with a stop-watch is useful here
11. Turning in the wrong direction	This usually occurs during a back-crawl turn. The swimmer tries to rotate towards the turning arm instead of away from it	The direction of rotation is always away from the touching or turning arm. Special concentrated rotation practices are recommended

Races are often won or lost by the quality of turns. Therefore, as with starts, turning sessions should be planned as lesson main themes. Width practices should be used to give an opportunity for the highest number of turns to take place in a given period.

The competition strokes all feature different turning characteristics, therefore practices related to each of the individual styles should be carried out.

23 The Back Strokes

There are five different versions of back stroke, the definitions of which should not be confused with the contemporary competition-biased back crawl as described in chapter 17. The back strokes are as follows:

1. Elementary back stroke
2. Inverted breast stroke
3. Double overarm or English back stroke
4. Single overarm back stroke
5. Life-saving back stroke

The first four of these strokes form a pattern of evolution, each one at some time or other having been used in early competitive events. The back crawl can be identified as the final link in the competitive chain, being the fastest and most efficient method of swimming on the back.

However, the teacher will realise that, while speed swimming must be deemed important, many pupils, especially adults, are not interested in competition. Consideration must therefore be given to acquiring a teaching knowledge of the ancillary strokes as well as the competition strokes. All the strokes listed, together with side stroke and the 'head up' version of breast stroke, may be classed as leisure strokes. However, both the life-saving back stroke and side stroke serve more utilitarian purposes, when related to the life-saving skills.

Brief illustrated descriptions of the double-arm back strokes, together with the life-saving back stroke and side stroke, now follow. (The single overarm back stroke, whose arm action resembles the back-crawl pattern, has been omitted from the detailed stroke descriptions as, with the development of the more aesthetic back-crawl movement, it would be of merely historical interest.)

The back-stroke teaching progressions are very closely allied to the evolution of the stroke movements themselves, commencing with the basic breast-stroke kick in the inverted (supine) mode, then gradually developing and extending the arm movements.

The leg movement of the back strokes, while necessitating a simultaneous and symmetrical kicking pattern, is probably easier to perform than the alternating back-crawl movement, especially among adult swimmers. This is mainly due to the fact that the feet need not be extended into the plantar-flexed position which is essential for the vertically biased alternating kick. Most adults seem to find this foot extension rather difficult to achieve due to the inflexibility of their ankles. '

Except when performing the English back stroke, the swimmer's face should be clear of the water. Therefore, breathing should be as natural as possible. However, if the teacher encounters problems in this direction, a breathing rhythm may be introduced whereby inhalation takes place through the mouth at the start of arm recovery and exhalation occurs during the pull. Breathing out some if not all of the exhausted air through the nose is important, in order to prevent ingress of water and consequent distress to the swimmer.

Back-stroke leg movement
All the back strokes are performed using an identical leg-kick pattern. The swimmer's body position should be in each instance as flat and horizontal as the stroke pattern will permit, remembering that the feet and legs must never break the surface. The life-saving leg kick will demand the lowest swimming position, because the rescuer must avoid kicking the subject he is towing. There are obvious differences in the various arm movements, and each individual version of the stroke displays different co-ordination and timing of the leg and the arm movements.

As previously mentioned, the back-stroke leg kick is a supinated version of the breast-stroke whip-kick and it is propulsive in character. Full ankle extension at the end of the kick is not really important as swimming speed is not the paramount feature of the stroke.

Lying initially in a comfortably stretched supine-glide position with legs together, the recovery movement commences with the swimmer bending and opening his knees, thus lowering his feet in the water. The extent of the knee bend should be such that the heels lie approximately below (but not beyond) the knees. As the feet sink, they are dorsi-flexed (toes towards the shins), rotated outwards and, as in the breast-stroke leg recovery, the heels should be a short distance apart.

Propulsion is created in a similar fashion to that of the breast-stroke whip-kick whereby the feet are swept in an accelerating outward and closing arc-like movement, ending up once more in the comfortable stretched glide mode; by maintaining the feet in the cocked position, through the kick, the closing action of the soles creates a sculling effect which thrusts the swimmer forwards. The glide at the termination of the movement is related to the variety of stroke being swum. If the swimmer desires a leisurely effect, the glide may be maintained until forward motion diminishes or his legs begin to sink. The kicking movement may then be repeated. If a more continuous propulsive effect is required, however, as when a swimmer is executing a subject-supporting life-saving tow, the glide will be non-existent.

Elementary back stroke (fig. 23.1)
Arm movement
For the duration of the glide, the swimmer's arms should be near to his

sides in order to minimise his profile. The arm stroke takes place with the swimmer's arms and hands completely submerged throughout the whole cycle.

The recovery movement commences with both the flattened hands being drawn up close to the sides of the body to chest level. From here the arms are stretched sideways in cruciform style. The hands should be some 150–200 mm (6–8 in.) below the water surface and remain so during propulsion. In this outstretched position the swimmer's arms are acting rather like brakes, so for minimal profile resistance, there should be no prolonged pause between the termination of recovery and the start of the propulsive phase.

As soon as full sideways extension is achieved, the palms should be faced in the direction of the feet. Then, with hands flat and fingers together, the swimmer moves his arms in a propulsive sweeping arc towards his sides, where they remain throughout the ensuing glide and until the next arm recovery commences. This is the back-stroke arm action in its simplest form.

Fig. 23.1 Elementary back stroke

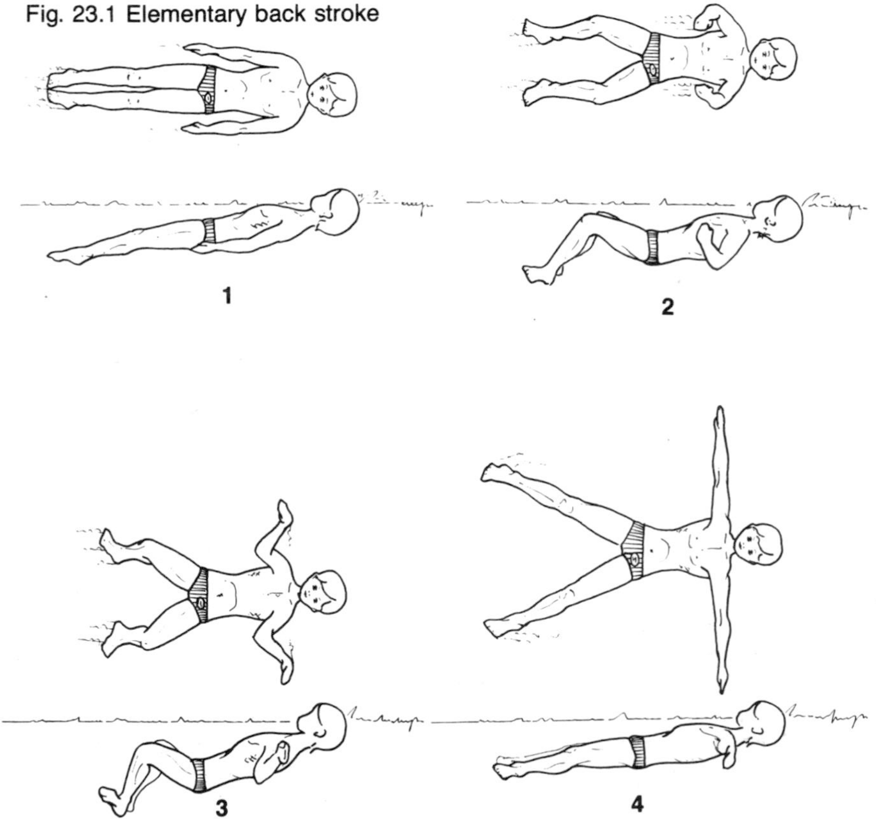

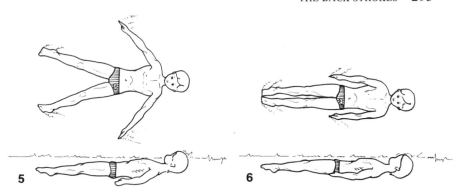

Synchronisation of leg and arm movements

There can be slight variations in the co-ordination between the individual arm and leg cycles. Most beginners seem to favour moving both sets of limbs in complete unison. (Fig. 23.1 illustrates this type of synchronous movement.) Another method is for the swimmer to commence his arm recovery in advance of the leg-recovery movement. Theoretically, this is more correct, for arm and leg propulsive movements should ideally commence at approximately the same time and, as the hands need to travel further than the feet during their recovery, they require to start their journey a little earlier. However, when teaching the stroke, either variation may be considered to be correct.

The swimmer sweeps both arms in to his sides and his feet 'whip' together simultaneously, and the resulting thrust from these combined movements creates propulsion and a subsequent glide, before the next stroke cycle commences.

Inverted breast stroke (fig. 23.2)

This is simply an 'extended pull' type of breast stroke, being performed in a supine mode with both sets of limbs remaining submerged at all times.

Arm movement

The arm stroke is similar in form to the extended pull which takes place after a breast-stroke dive or the push-off which follows a turn while the swimmer is still submerged. Another almost identical movement is that which is used during underwater swimming.

Commencing in a supine-glide mode, with both arms by her sides, the swimmer recovers both hands symmetrically and close to the body to a position beyond the head. In the resulting supine-stretch position, the swimmer's arms should be close to her ears and her hands should be approximately shoulder-width apart and inclined, so that the palms are facing obliquely outwards. After a short pause (glide), the arms are swept in a vigorous propelling semi-circular movement back to her sides. The depth of the pull should be approximately 150–200 mm (6–8 in.).

Fig. 23.2 Inverted breast stroke

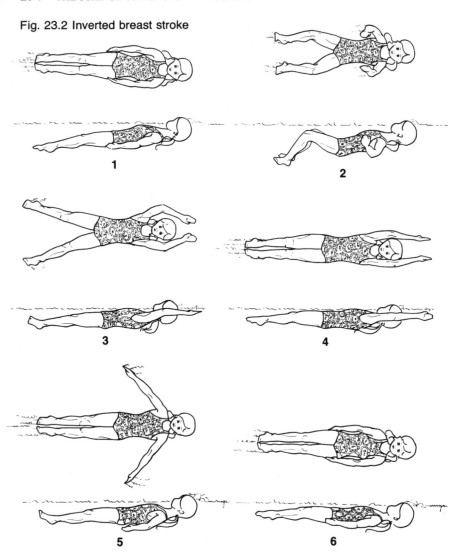

1

2

3

4

5

6

Synchronisation of leg and arm movements
The synchronisation of the limb movements is very similar to that of normal simultaneous and symmetrical breast stroke. The outward and backward arm pull is carried out while the legs remain stretched and the feet together. There is a short glide at this stage. The arms and legs then commence their recovery together and, as the hands pass the shoulders on their way to the stretch position, the leg kick takes place. It is here that the second glide occurs, while the swimmer maintains a fully stretched mode.

Double overarm or English back stroke (fig. 23.3)
This stroke was first developed as a racing stroke during the early 1900s. Competitive swimmers of the period started to realise that the under-water arm recovery of inverted breast stroke was slow and created excess resistance to motion. In their search for faster swimming, the pioneers began to experiment with over- rather than under-the-water arm recoveries and it is from the English exponents of this early style that the name is derived.

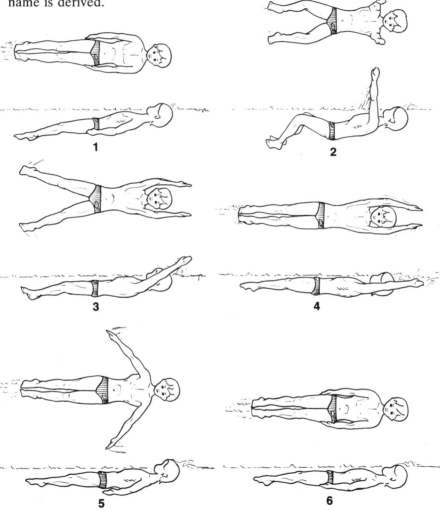

Arm movement
The recovery movement of the arms takes place out of the water. From the supine-glide position, both arms in a straight mode are lifted vertically and simultaneously from their position adjacent to the swimmer's sides.

Passing close to his ears they are then stretched ahead of the swimmer on completion of the movement. The hands, with fingers straight and together, should be approximately shoulder-width apart and facing obliquely outwards as they re-enter the water for a short glide.

The propulsive arm-sweeping movement is carried out in exactly the same way as in the inverted breast stroke.

In order to prevent water being washed over his face during the recovery, the swimmer should not be tempted to spread his arms out further, but should merely slow the initial part of the movement down; the water is then given sufficient time to run off his arms before reaching his face. Because of this wash over the swimmer's face, it is wise to introduce some breathing discipline into the movement.

Synchronisation of leg and arm movements with breathing
Starting in a fully stretched supine-glide position, the swimmer carries out his propulsive arm sweep. During his movement, the legs remain straight and athletically stretched and the breath is expelled. There follows a short glide. The arms and legs are now recovered simultaneously and, as the hands pass vertically above the shoulders, the leg kick is performed, thus driving the swimmer forward as his stretched arms re-enter the water in front of him. An inward breath should be quickly taken as the arms are lifted from the water and prior to any lifted water reaching the face.

Slight initial flexing on the wrists, culminating in slight extensions, may be introduced as an arm-stroke refinement. This is in order that the palms may be directed back towards the feet for as long as possible, thus creating maximum propulsion. A slight elbow bend may also enhance the pull.

Single overarm back stroke
The single overarm back stroke may be described as a supine trudgen movement. The arms are recovered alternately over the water in a similar fashion to the back-crawl recovery. Each single arm pull (or recovery) is accompanied by a back-stroke leg kick. The stroke was one of the many variations of competition back stroke eventually to be superseded by the back crawl of today.

Life-saving back stroke (fig. 23.4)
The life-saving back stroke is one of the two towing or carrying strokes used during aquatic rescue situations, the other carrying stroke being the side stroke.

The leg-movement pattern is identical to that described earlier. The only differing feature between the leisure back-stroke leg kick and the more utilitarian life-saving action is the rate and continuity of the movement. The higher kicking frequency is required because more effort is needed in order to tow a 'subject' through the water. Also, in an emergency, getting the casualty to safety and subsequently administering resuscitative treatment must be performed with the utmost speed and urgency.

The actual methods of rescue are fully covered at a later stage, together with other necessary life-saving practices and skills.

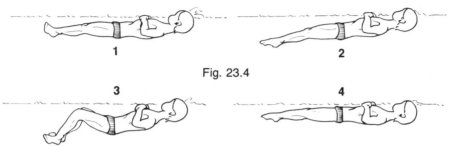

Fig. 23.4

TEACHING THE BACK STROKES

The leg-action practices will probably have been covered in some way during the breast-stroke teaching sequences. However, the following teaching practices and their accompanying teaching points will assist the teacher in formulating a plan of instruction. A demonstration with commentary is a useful way to begin.

Activity: back-stroke leg action
Practice 1: on the poolside
Pupils sit on the poolside near the water's edge with legs dangling. By placing both hands behind them and leaning back with arms straight, the legs may be lifted and an inverted breast-stroke leg movement may be carried out.

TEACHING POINTS
1. Feet should be cocked (toes towards shins) during whip.

2. Heels almost back to the seat.

3. Heels together or a short distance apart.

4. Propulsive movement to be vigorous circular pattern of feet ending with feet together.

Practice 2: in the water with two floats
Pupils to hold one float under each arm in order to carry out the leg movement.

TEACHING POINTS
1. Holding the floats in the centre of the long sides and tucking the opposite sides under the arms, squeeze elbows to sides to secure floats.

2. Lying back in the water rather than sitting – 'bottoms up'.

3. Feet and knees must be submerged at all times.

All other teaching points as before, with an emphasis on 'pushing the water back' with the soles of the feet as they quickly close together.

Practice 3: in the water, 'cuddling' or holding one float over the tummy
A single float may be held either to the chest or over the stomach.

TEACHING POINTS
1. Holding the float correctly and firmly: either method of holding the float is satisfactory, with perhaps a little more security in the 'chest cuddle', but more inclination to 'sit' in the water.
All the previous teaching points are relevant.

Practice 4: with finning or sculling
The swimmers now attempt the leg movement without artificial support. The hands are used to propel either by sculling or finning. The exercise may be attempted by holding one float then, after establishing the movement, letting go to continue across the pool unassisted.

TEACHING POINTS
1. A re-cap on sculling and finning.

All other teaching points as before.

Practice 5: without using the hands
The swimmers now attempt the leg movement without any other means of support or assistance.

Activity: back-stroke leg and arm action
Practice 1: back-stroke leg and arm action
Elementary back-stroke practice.

TEACHING POINTS
1. The shortened underwater arm movement fully explained.

2. Kick and pull simultaneously.

3. Breathing out on the pull/kick.

4. All leg-movement teaching points as before.

Practice 2: back stroke with lengthened underwater arm movement
The prone breast stroke may be performed for a few widths, then a direct transfer of the movement to the supine mode.

TEACHING POINTS
1. Normal breast-stroke teaching points (see chapter 18).

2. Extended arm pull introduced only after the swimmers have turned over on to their backs. (This does not introduce bad habits when the prone version is performed.)

3. Arms and legs in the water at all times.

4. Co-ordination: recover (arms and legs)-kick-glide-pull-glide-recover.

5. Breathing in through the mouth during leg recovery and out mainly through the nose during the arm pull.

All other relevant teaching points as before.

Activity: full stroke – Double overarm (English back stroke)
Practice 1: standing in the shallow end and establishing the movement
TEACHING POINTS
1. From the hips, arms should be parallel as they swing forward and up. From the upward-stretch position, the arms are moved downward and out in two semi-circular arcs to the sides once more.

2. Palms facing towards direction of movement

Practice 2: full back-stroke movement
TEACHING POINTS
1. Arm movement as previously described.

2. Co-ordination: recover (arms and legs)-kick-glide-pull-glide-recover.

3. Breathing: in through the mouth as the arms are lifted from the water and out mainly through the nose during the arm pull.

Note: If the leg-kick movements are weak, this over-water recovery may tend to sink the swimmers, in which case a return to legs-only practices may be necessary.

A further development may be introduced by encouraging the swimmers to carry 'diving block' or something similar.
TEACHING POINTS
1. The movement must now be propulsive.

2. The swimmers should try to elevate themselves in the water and lie as flat as possible (legs and feet in the water).

3. The water should pillow the swimmers' heads.

4. A definite rhythm of kick-glide-recover-kick-glide should be established.

5. The objects to be carried should not be too heavy to begin with.

As a diversion, the class may be divided into pairs and the 'straight arm carry' (see chapter 26) may be practised, the main aim being for the rescuers to save rather than drown their partners!

24 The Side Stroke

If we watch a mediocre breast stroker swimming in choppy water, we shall probably notice that in order to avoid the waves splashing or 'attacking' his face, he will turn his head sideways. On the other hand, the trained swimmer in the same situation will control his breathing and limb movements in such a way that the rough water makes no visible impression on his stroke pattern or attitude in the water. A further observation of the average swimmer will probably reveal that, if the wave-avoidance action continues, the shoulder opposite to the direction of head turn will drop in the water and he will tend to turn on to his side in order to maintain progress. Accompanied by this axial body rotation, the arm stroke loses its symmetry and the legs tend to cross over each other during the kicking movement.

This is one probable step in the evolution of the side stroke as a recognised swimming style. The side stroke was used in competitive freestyle events during the early 1900s and even before this. Exponents improved the speed characteristics of the movement by recovering the upper arm over the surface after each pull.

The side stroke has two main contemporary uses, leisure swimming and life-saving. Another important use of the side stroke is when the teacher accompanies one of his charges in their first attempt to swim a length of the pool. Swimming alongside the 'venturer' and using side stroke, the teacher is able to offer words of encouragement and watch for any sign of panic or distress. The adjacent side-swimming position also allows the teacher to give a little physical support or even to carry out a quick rescue should it become necessary.

DESCRIPTION OF THE STROKE (fig. 24.1)
Body position
The swimmer takes up a side-lying position (either side). The general free-swimming mode will be as flat, streamlined and horizontal as possible. When the stroke is used as a life-saving carry, however, the rescuer's position in the water will be lower due to the overlaying subject. (See the 'cross-chest' life-saving tow, chapter 26). The head will be pillowed on its side and rotated slightly so that the swimmer's gaze is directed to the side and slightly forward.

Fig. 24.1

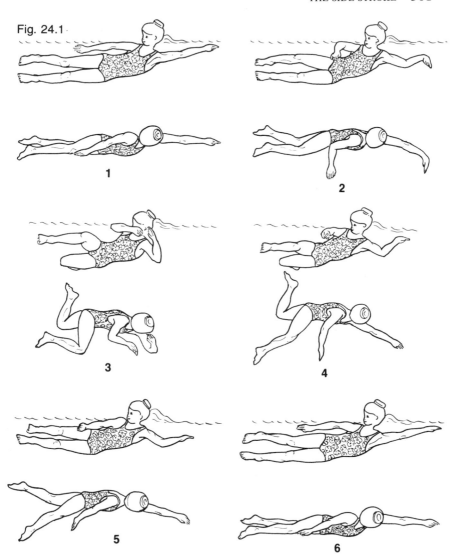

Leg movement

The action is picturesquely called the 'scissor-kick'. The legs move in unison with each other, one above the other, in opposing directions and parallel with the water surface. Commencing from a stretched and plantar-flexed mode, the heels are initially recovered up towards the seat together, by flexing both hips and knees. This initial symmetrical recovery part of the kick is short and is immediately followed by a forward and backward separation of the legs. The leg nearest the water surface moves forward with its foot becoming dorsi-flexed in the process, and the lower leg moves back with both knees becoming partly flexed during this movement. This is the completion of the recovery phase.

The propulsive part of the kick occurs by straightening the knees and closing the legs together in one continuous movement. The feet should assume the plantar-flexed or stretched mode as the legs sweep together in a scissor-like movement. The backward-directed thrust is developed from the back of the upper leg and the sole of its foot and from the front of both the foot and shin of the lower leg. The legs remain together, one above the other and in contact throughout the ensuing glide.

Arm movement
The arms work alternately below the water surface, one pulling while the other recovers.

Commencing in the stretch position – that is, with the lower (leading) arm reaching directly forward, palm facing downward and the other arm stretched down the side of the body, with palm adjacent to the upper thigh – the upper arm is now recovered to a *comfortable* forward extreme by moving the flat hand up the body, keeping it and the elbow tucked in close in order to minimise the swimmer's overall profile. The comfortable forward position should neither induce shoulder strain nor tend to rotate the swimmer into a prone position. During this upper-arm recovery movement, the lower arm carries out its pull by performing a vigorous downward- and backward-sweeping action. This movement takes place directly under the swimmer's body and the palm of the flat hand with fingers together should face directly backwards for as long as possible during the movement. The elbow should be flexed during the pull, which should reach approximately as far back as the swimmer's waist. From here, the arm is recovered once more to the forward-stretch position, at the same time keeping both the elbow and forward-pointed flat hand as close to the body as possible.

As this leading arm is being recovered, the upper arm carries out its pull by sweeping the hand back vigorously towards the thigh, where it remains throughout the ensuing glide. The palm should be faced backwards with fingers together and the elbow flexed throughout the major part of the pull.

Synchronisation of the leg and arm movements
As the lower or leading arm commences its pull, the legs commence their recovery movement. The scissor-kick then takes place at the same time as the upper arm pull and also as the leading arm (having completed its pull) is stretched forward. This is the position of the stretched glide.

Breathing
There may be a need for some degree of breathing discipline due to the fact that the swimmer's face is at some time during the stroke partly

submerged. As the leading arm commences its downward and backward motion, the tendency is for the swimmer's head to lift. This is as good a time as any to take an inward breath through the mouth.

Then, as this same arm recovers forward and assumes its glide position, the breath should be slowly exhaled in a controlled fashion from both mouth and nose.

Timing
The timing of the movement should be fairly continuous, with perhaps a short pause at the end of the cycle while the swimmer is in the glide position. The whole action may be carried out in a leisurely fashion or speeded up, according to circumstances.

TEACHING THE SIDE STROKE
Activity: visual demonstration
As with all strokes, a visual demonstration is a good way to start off. This should be accompanied by a verbal description which highlights the various stroke features. With a *small* class, the stroke may be successfully demonstrated and described by the teacher himself in the water, while the pupils wander up and down the poolside within hearing distance. Otherwise, an adept pupil will probably come to the rescue.

TEACHING POINTS

1. The side-lay position should show a horizontal body position with one ear pillowed in the water.

2. The fundamentals of the leg movement should be explained, emphasising the source of the thrust and the stretching of the legs during the kick, and the streamlined and close proximity mode of the feet and legs during the glide.

3. The arm pull should highlight the flat-hand and flexed-wrist pull with the fingers together. The extent of both the lower arm pull (to near the waist) and the upper arm pull (back to the thigh) should be underlined, as also should the paths of the respective recoveries.

4. The forward arm-recovery movements themselves should adequately demonstrate the streamlining features, whereby the elbows tucked into the sides and forward-pointing hands combine to reduce water resistance.

5. The breathing sequence should be obvious to the observers, both inhalation (during the leading arm pull) and exhalation (during the kick and glide) phases being clearly defined.

6. The stroke-synchronisation features may be best demonstrated by concentration on the simultaneous performance of the leg kick and the upper arm pull. The rest of the stroke normally falls into line.

7. Timing of the movement may be portrayed by the demonstrator speeding and slowing the stroke. The glide phase will be reduced as the stroke rate is increased.

8. A further variation on the theme may be attempted by lifting the upper arm *over* the water during its recovery, thus performing the over-arm version of the side stroke.

The demonstrator may show how a smooth transition from breast stroke to side stroke can be effected. Commencing the demonstration using the prone breast-stroke style, the swimmer gradually rolls over on to his side, at the same time letting the arm and leg movements adjust naturally to the new swimming mode. This rolling into the stroke may be used to some considerable advantage when teaching the stroke.

Activity: full-stroke movement
The class should be more than ready to attempt the stroke themselves and should now be invited to show just how good they are. The practices may be carried out across or up and down the pool as conditions dictate. As the stroke exhibits a distinct and, hopefully, long glide phase, length practices may be more advantageous in this instance. The pupils may go straight into the stroke or use the breast-stroke transition method.

TEACHING POINTS
All the teaching points listed previously may apply where necessary. A 'pull and kick-glide' rhythm should assist the co-ordination of the arm and leg movements.

Activity: side-stroke arm movement
Practice: while standing in shallow water
The arm movement should be carried out whilst the swimmer bends sideways, completely submerging the shoulders, and stretches the lower arm forward just below the surface of the water, palm facing downwards. The other arm should be by the side of the body, hand on thigh. The legs should be suitably astride (one foot forward) in order to maintain balance.

The arm movement is commenced by the forward arm sweeping down and backwards. The thumb should be uppermost with the palm facing backwards. To accommodate this hand attitude, the elbow should be flexed. The extent of the pull should reveal the hand reaching back as far as the forward thigh.

Recovery of the hand should be initially close to the body, then directed forward once more in a streamlined, hand-flat mode. The fingers should be biased towards facing forward and the elbow tucked in for minimum profile resistance. There should be no water-surface disturbance during this forward hand movement. The thrust of a correctly performed movement should tend to pull the swimmer forward on to the leading foot.

The action should be repeated in the singular fashion until some semblance of the arm pull is developed.

The second arm movement may be practised while the forward or lower arm is maintained in the forward-stretch or glide position. The first part of the upper arm action which, incidentally, is more of push than a pull, necessitates a recovery. The flat hand slides up close to the swimmer's body with the thumb leading. Then, when it is just ahead of the chin, the wrist flexes and the elbow is elevated so that the propulsive push may be performed.

In carrying out the push, the hand, with fingers together, should sweep right back to the thigh facing directly backwards for as long as possible during the movement. When the upper arm movement is being performed satisfactorily, the lower arm may be introduced and the complete arm cycle practised.

The sequence of movement is an alternate one whereby, as one arm recovers, the other carries out its propulsive activity.

TEACHING POINTS

1. The recovery movements should take place with the hands presenting minimum profile to the water and the elbows tucked well in to the swimmer's body.

The propulsive movements of each arm should be strong and powerful, with the full propulsive area of the hands being presented to the water for as long as possible during the catch/pull and push.

2. The extent of the hand movements should be as previously described.

3. At no time should the hands or arms appear above the water surface.

Activity: side-stroke leg movement
Practice: with a float
The scissor-kick may be carried out with the assistance of a float. The movement must be performed while the swimmer is in the basic glide position and lying fully on his side.

TEACHING POINTS

1. The correct method of holding the float – end grasp, with forearm resting on the float.

2. The fully stretched glide position should be maintained: leading arm holding the float, upper arm with hand resting on the outer thigh, head pillowed sideways on the water, eyes looking forward and to the side.

3. The kick should be carried out as previously described. Recovery should be slow with a vigorous whipping, scissor-like closing action.

4. The feet should not pass over each other at the end of the scissor movement. The legs should close together and then assume a fully stretched (feet plantar-flexed) attitude.

5. As with the blades of the scissors, the legs should remain close together (adducted) in the lateral plane of the swimmer's body.

6. The legs should always remain below the water surface and their movements should always be parallel with it.

As a further development of this basic leg exercise, the upper arm may be introduced into the movement, whereby the arm push takes place at the same time as the scissor-kick.

Activity: full stroke (with breathing)
The complete stroke may now be performed up and down (preferably) or across the pool. Emphasis should be placed on the kick-glide phase, thus highlighting the effectiveness of the propulsive features of the action.

TEACHING POINTS
1. All the individual limb-movement teaching points are relevant.

2. The synchronisation of the arm and leg movements should be as previously described. The arms must recover and propel alternately, with the legs performing their kick as the upper arm pushes backwards.

3. The breathing sequence should be in through the mouth and out (as a trickle) through mouth and nose or nose only. The timing of the intake should coincide with the slight upper-body lift, which is brought about by the initial part of the lower arm's pulling action. The breathing-out part of the phase should take place during the glide.

4. The glide should be a definite feature of the full-stroke practices. As previously mentioned, the effectiveness of the propelling movement may be measured by the length of the dwell. The next stroke should be performed, however, before too much momentum is lost.

5. Complete body streamlining should always be assumed during the glide for the most efficient results.

6. The head should be pillowed sideways on the water and face forward: this allows the swimmer to see ahead.

FAULTS AND THEIR CORRECTION

Feature: BODY POSITION

FAULT	EFFECT ON STROKE	CORRECTION
1. Head lifted too high	Body will rotate and legs will drop	Pillow the head lower in the water
2. Legs breaking the surface	Unnecessary splashing and loss of propulsion	Incline the body slightly upwards towards direction of motion by lifting the head or pressing down on the leadinvarm
3. Rolling from the side-lay position	Hybrid arm and leg movements result in a reduction in efficiency and increased fatigue	Rotation of the body is effected by the head position and also by the limb tracks. So, turning the head towards the desired direction of rotation and/or directing the arms or legs to assist rotation, the swimmer may achieve the correct side-lay mode

Feature: ARM ACTION
Leading (lower) arm

FAULT	EFFECT ON STROKE	CORRECTION
1. Pushing the hand forward in a non-streamlined mode	Usually creates a splash and develops propulsion in the wrong direction	Concentrate on a flat-hand/fingers-forward recovery, elbow tucked into the body
2. Pulling beyond the centre line of the body (across or to the side, breast-stroke fashion)	The swimmer tends to swim in a curve rather than a straight line	The hand should pull directly under the body so that the thrust-pressure centre lies near if not in the vertical control plane
3. Pulling too deeply (perhaps with a straight arm)	1. According to the individual's strength, the deep pull may tend to fatigue 2. Leading shoulder tends to drop	Flex the elbow slightly and moderate the pull
4. Over-reaching	Tendency to delay the catch movement due to the straight arm	Limit the arm-recovery movement so that the shoulder girdle is not over-stretched

Upper (trailing) arm

FAULT	EFFECT ON STROKE	CORRECTION
1. Failing to streamline the hand and arm during recovery	Creates unnecessary resistance	1. Emphasise that the narrow area of the flat hand (finger-tips) should be directed forwards during recovery 2. Keep arm tucked into body

2. Recovering the arm too far forward	Swimmer tends to roll towards the recovering arm, presenting slightly more profile to the water	Limit the recovery so that the swimmer does not roll over on to his front
3. Arm performing a sideways (breast stroke-like) movement during the pull	Swimmer tends to go round in circles	Keep the arm as close (laterally) to the body as possible
4. Top arm pulling in time with lower arm (breast-stroke type of movement)	1. Side-stroke style of movement is incorrect 2. Co-ordination and continuity is affected	1. Emphasise the simultaneous pull (top-arm) and recovery (lower-arm) movement 2. Shallow-water practices in order to establish co-ordination
5. Pushing back too far	Swimmer tends to 'bend in the middle'	Sweep the hand back to the upper thigh only

Feature: BREATHING

FAULT	EFFECT ON STROKE	CORRECTION
Failing to co-ordinate breathing with stroke cycle or breath-holding	The side stroke is a leisure stroke (life-saving excepted), therefore breathing must be as regular as possible	Full-stroke practices with an emphasis on a slow outward trickle from nose or mouth and nose: breathing in will follow automatically

25 Personal Survival Techniques

Within certain bounds, open water need not be feared, but it should *always* be respected. Every year brings an increase in participants in the many aquatic recreational activities such as sailing and boating. Unfortunately, there is also an annual increase in drownings and fatalities due to exposure in open waters. With this in mind, it is obvious that the recreational water user should endeavour to prepare himself for the unexpected. This preparation may be partly achieved by providing the necessary material life-saving and support equipment. However, in addition to these aids, it is extremely useful for the swimmer, sailor, canoeist, etc to possess a sound knowledge of *personal* survival techniques.

There are in existence, various personal survival tests and award schemes. These are designed to introduce swimmers and other aquatic sportsmen and sportswomen of all ages to some of the many skills and requirements which become very useful when faced with open-water situations. However, before dealing with these skills there follow some general recommendations relating to survival in open water.

1. When sailing, an approved style of life-jacket, properly secured, inflated if necessary and regularly tested, should be worn at all times.

2. Should your boat overturn and remain floating, stay by it and hang on. If it starts to sink, *swim away from it* as quickly as possible to avoid being sucked down with the resulting downwash. This applies to anything large that may sink.

Remember that most things which contain a volume of air float. Therefore hang on to articles such as empty bottles – a sealed lemonade bottle under each arm will keep most people afloat – or wellington boots, which make fine supports if upturned and full of air. An upturned bucket containing air is a fine buoyancy aid, and the eternal plastic bag is a ready-made life-saver.

3. Keep your clothes on while in the water *unless they are an encumbrance* or if they are useless in the current situation. Closely woven textiles permit a layer of water to be trapped between them and the body and this layer in turn acts as an insulator since water is a bad heat conductor. Nylon and cotton shirts and blouses are made of closely woven fabrics; most of the natural and man-made fibres from which trousers are made are also of a close-weave nature. Generally speaking, anything which is lightweight, fairly tight-fitting and of low porosity is a suitable

garment to retain in a water-survival situation. Knitted woollens are of no real value: their characteristic of soaking up water serves only to make them heavy and consequently they become a burden. Nylon sailing gear is usually an excellent insulator in a survival emergency.

The other important factor is that the layer of trapped water should be maintained as static as possible. This is brought about by sealing all the exits – trouser bottoms should be tucked into socks, cuffs and neck should be buttoned up if possible, shirts or blouses should be tucked into trousers. Remember, moving water carries heat away from the body much more quickly than static water.

However, should the 'survivalist' be a mediocre or poor swimmer, there may be a justifiable need for removal of a suitable garment in order to create a buoyancy aid.

4. It is a good thing to keep the head well covered, especially on a windy day. Once more, we have a heat-transfer problem: a chilly breeze can rob the swimmer of his bodily heat by extracting it through the top of his head and face. A hat pulled well down over the head and forehead helps in alleviating this.

Keep as still as possible. Unnecessary limb movement absorbs valuable energy which will be needed later should the emergency situation be prolonged. Loss of consciousness may be caused by the lowering of the body temperature (hypothermia), and in open water will most probably result in drowning.

Learn to tread water or swim with a minimum of limb movement. In the long term, speed is not usually as important as endurance. Remaining afloat and alive and using as little energy as possible for as long as possible is the real objective. For endurance, the best swimming styles to use are the leisure forms such as breast, back or side stroke and these should be practised over increasing distances. Changes of stroke may be made as often as necessary, and in all cases the swim should be performed without touching the bottom or sides of the pool. There may also be the odd occasion where speed is desired and a lively front crawl is useful.

Individual survival tests often have time limits imposed on them. These are *training situations only*, whereby endurance capabilities and general fitness ar developed by working against the clock. A real emergency situation could be of a long duration and, pool-hire expenses being what they are, long-term test conditions are very often difficult to arrange.

Some of the following activities are particularly allied to survival, but most are a part of an overall syllabus of watermanship and water safety. It has been mentioned that there may be wisdom in removing *some* clothes in an aquatic survival situation, therefore a few hints in divesting oneself of excess or unwanted apparel are included in the text. However, to begin with, let us deal with some of the watermanship skills which themselves relate especially to survival.

TREADING WATER

The act of treading water may be defined as 'not moving forward, backward or sideways by any substantial amount while at the same time, remaining afloat in an upright position'. The arms and legs are made to move in a relatively relaxed fashion in order to create an upward thrust and hence assist in keeping the swimmer afloat. This skill may be classified as being one of the essentials of watermanship and water safety.

In a small way, treading water may be compared with driving a car. Here, the driver often has to come to a controlled stop while someone passes in front of him. He then has to wait a short while, still in complete control, before smoothly moving away once more. Likewise, the swimmer often requires to stop swimming forward in deep water because of someone 'crossing his bows'. In order not to sink, he now has calmly to tread water for a short while before moving smoothly on towards the intended destination.

Here, then, is one of the many uses of the practice of treading water. The skill also forms an integral part of most of the aquatic disciplines, such as synchronised swimming, waterpolo, life-saving and, of course, survival.

As a result of their natural buoyancy characteristics, some swimmers find it easier to tread water than others. The good floater will not need to put quite so much effort into limb movements as the poor floater in order to remain afloat. In fact, some swimmers are able to sustain an upright and balanced mode and retain their heads above the water surface quite easily, by using only a very slight movement of the hands, feet or head.

One of the secrets of treading water is for the performer to keep as much of himself immersed in the water as possible. This is in order that the water may do the supporting, rather than his relying completely on limb movements.

The degree of head-and-shoulder submersion will depend on the calmness of the water surface. In an indoor pool where the water does not get too choppy, the swimmer may settle well down in the water, but again, in open sea with waves breaking all around, he or she may need to elevate a little higher in order to breathe freely. The sea, of course, assists in buoying the swimmer a little higher because of its greater density. (See chapter 5 on hydrostatics).

Another good point to remember when treading water is to keep the head well back. This articulation has a two-fold effect. Tilting the head backwards raises the mouth and nose a little higher above the water surface, and it has the effect of lifting the back of the tongue away from the posterior wall of the throat thus ensuring that the breathing channels remain unrestricted (fig. 25.1).

Arm movement (fig. 25.2)
The arm movement should take the form of a support-sculling pattern.

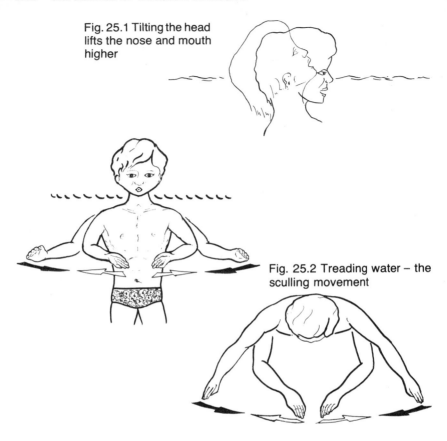

Fig. 25.1 Tilting the head lifts the nose and mouth higher

Fig. 25.2 Treading water – the sculling movement

The swimmer's hands should be working at a depth of approximately 200 mm (8 in.) with the active supporting forces being directed towards the bottom of the pool in order to react the swimmer upwards. (For sculling see chapter 28 on synchronised swimming.)

Each forearm should work in an approximate horizontal arc, from directly in front of the shoulder joint to a point roughly 300 mm (12 in.) outside it. The movement should be continuous and not too vigorous.

Leg movements (fig. 25.3)
There are a variety of leg movements which may be associated with treading water. They are described as follows:

1. An alternating, front-crawl type of kick
2. A cycling or pedalling action
3. A breast stroke-orientated movement
4. A side stroke or scissors-kick
5. An alternating breast-stroke (egg-beater) motion
6. A hybrid or permutation of two or more of the previous movements

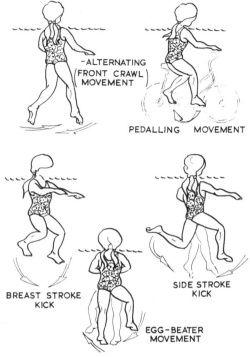

Fig. 25.3 Treading water – the kicking movements

Rhythm
The rhythm and co-ordination of the arms and legs are not really important. The frequency of each individual pattern of movement should be the minimum that allows the performer to stay comfortably afloat.

Breathing
Breathing should be as normal as possible in relation to the energy being used. The usual pattern of 'in through the mouth and out through the nose' should alleviate any distress except, of course, for that caused by the odd unexpected wave. An advantage may be gained, however, in the early practices by the swimmers holding a deeply taken breath. This enhances the buoyancy characteristics.

Variations on the theme
Once the swimmers have become adept at the skill they should try performing the movements by immobilising the various limbs in permutation style, i.e. treading water using both legs and one arm, or with both arms behind the back. Using both arms with no leg movement may also be tried, and, perhaps the hardest activity of all, that of keeping the head above water while raising one then both arms above the water surface.

Teaching practices
All the following practices may be carried out by pupils who are confident in deep water.

First practices: the leg movements in the horizontal swimming modes
The pupils should have previously carried out the various stroke practices. The basic leg movements of each of the strokes may now be isolated and practised as follows:

1. The front-crawl alternating movement
2. The breast-stroke simultaneous and symmetrical kick – this may be practised as a prone and/or supine exercise
3. The side-stroke kick (with arms if necessary)
4. The cycling or pedalling movement

Each of the surface practices may be performed using floats or, as an improved standard of progression, completely unaided and without the use of an arm movement. The breath may be held for short periods if the pupils swim with their faces in the water.

TEACHING POINTS
1. The movements should be as continuous as possible. This will help to alleviate any excessive bobbing action when the action is finally practised in the vertical position.

2. Normal breathing should be encouraged wherever possible. If a swimmer has his face in the water, there should be a slow and controlled underwater exhalation.

3. The non-alternating stroke kicks should display a definite surge forward at every cycle. This will enable the teacher to assess the strength of the individual kicks when they are called upon to act against gravity at a later stage in the practices.

Second practices: the leg movements in an upright mode, with floats (fig. 25.4)
Each of the previous leg movements may now be carried out while each pupil holds a float firmly up in front of or 'cuddled' to the chest.

TEACHING POINTS
1. The floats should be held correctly.

2. The floats should be kept on the water surface at all times, and not be relied on too much. (When the floats disappear from sight, the pupils are usually leaning too heavily on them.)

3. Bobbing should then be automatically minimised by keeping the leg movements as regular as possible.

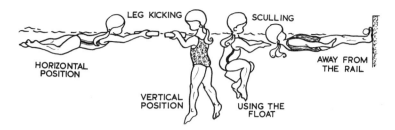

Fig. 25.4 Treading water – the teaching practices

4. Tilting the head back in order to bring the face clear of the water will assist breathing.

5. The body should be balanced in an upright mode at all times.

Third practice: arm action (a sculling movement in the supine position)
The pupils should line up in the water along the poolside, facing the wall. By hooking both feet under the rail, they then lie back in the water thus assuming a supine feet-supported position.

Practising the sculling movement in this static position is reasonably simple for most. It may be developed into a mobile exercise by releasing the feet and performing, if necessary, a gentle body-elevating kick accompanied by the scull, across the pool.

For pupils who find difficulty in keeping their legs up, a float held between the legs should be of assistance.

TEACHING POINTS
1. The main teaching points of the scull are covered in chapter 28.

2. Progress through the water should be mainly by means of the sculling action rather than by a leg kick.

Fourth practice: arm action (a sculling movement in an upright position, float-assisted)
The pupils now place a float between their upper legs and, by partially 'sitting' in the water and bringing their knees slightly forward, they assume a semi-upright floating position.

TEACHING POINTS
1. The scull is now a support rather than a propelling movement. Therefore the palms must be facing more or less downwards rather than in the opposite direction of propulsion.

2. The float and lower body should be positioned such that the sculling forces counteract any body rotation rather than assist it.

3. Using the floats as supports, the swimmers should all be fairly well elevated in the water. There should therefore be no problems with breathing.

4. Gripping the floats firmly between the legs is important, otherwise most of the lesson time is spent retrieving and re-positioning.

5. The smaller size of floats (300 × 200 mm: 12 × 8 in.) is the most useful for the exercise. The larger type provides too much buoyancy and control becomes rather difficult.

Fifth practice: treading water
Treading water may now be attempted, and the water for this exercise should be approximately chin-deep. Timid and weak swimmers will probably find comfort in being near the handrail or trough for their first tries. The whole skill is 'knitted' together with the chosen leg movement being combined with the supporting scull. Holding the breath for these early attempts will help bad floaters to keep their heads above water.

TEACHING POINTS
1. The attempt must be a genuine one rather than a 'quick kick then grab the rail'.

2. The head should be held well back in order to assist breathing.

3. A slight inclination towards a supine position may be allowed at first, but gradual support in the vertical position should be the aim.

4. The breath may be held at first, then quickly exhausted and a new intake made immediately. Holding the breath in this way enhances a pupil's buoyancy, but after a while can speed up exhaustion.

5. Arms and legs should be used in a regular and integrated pattern wherever possible.

The practices should continue until the swimmers are competent in the skill. Variations and permutations of limb movements as previously described may then follow.

THE SURFACE DIVE
The surface dive may be described as a controlled act of complete submersion from a surface-swimming mode. The activity may be used wherever surface-floating objects require to be negotiated by swimming beneath them. Alternatively, when an object (even a swimmer in distress) is lying below the water surface, perhaps on the bottom of the pool, river or sea near the shore, a surface dive may be used as a means of retrieving the object.

There are two recognised methods of performing a surface dive. One is a head-first submersion which is best carried out from a preceding breast-stroke swimming movement. The other is a feet-first submersion which may be performed most successfully from an upright treading water mode.

Submersion
One of the most important features of the many and various aquatic tricks and activities that the swimming teacher must recognise is that a swimmer is able to sink below the water surface more easily if he raises as much of his body above the water immediately before sinking. The upward body (or part of the body) movement, which may be created from some suitable motion of the hands and/or feet, contributes eventually towards a downward momentum which in turn allows the swimmer not only to return to the original starting level, but also to pass through and below it.

It is this sinking feature that we use to advantage when teaching both methods of the surface dive.

Head-first surface dive (fig. 25.5)
The swimmer approaches the point at which the dive is to be made while performing a normal breast-stroke action. If an object is to be retrieved or approached under water, the initial surface movements should be performed a short distance back from the object. This allows for the swimmer to glide or swim downward at a slight angle to the vertical.

The actual diving movement is performed in the following fashion. Selecting the spot for submersion, the swimmer starts a normal breast-stroke arm pull, but instead of ending the backward sweep at the shoulder plane, the hands continue back towards the region of the thighs. The legs remain straight and stretched. As they reach thigh-level, the palms are turned to face towards the bottom of the pool and the arms are swept in a vigorous and continuous downward movement.

The arm-sweeping action creates an equal and opposite upward reaction (fig. 25.6). (See also chapter 6.) This reaction enables the swimmer (after taking a medium-sized breath) to thrust head and shoulders downwards into the water and, at the same time, endeavour to rotate his legs into an upright or near-upright position. It is more than likely that a knee bend will occur during this movement. This is quite acceptable as long as the legs are relatively straight in the final upright position. The unsupported legs, now apparently weighing heavier in the air, then assist the swimmer in sinking down into the water.

After the initial downward sweep, the hands are moved forward once more thus enabling the swimmer to commence underwater swimming which will take him to an even greater depth, or propel him off in a horizontal direction. (Notes on underwater swimming are to be found at the end of this chapter.)

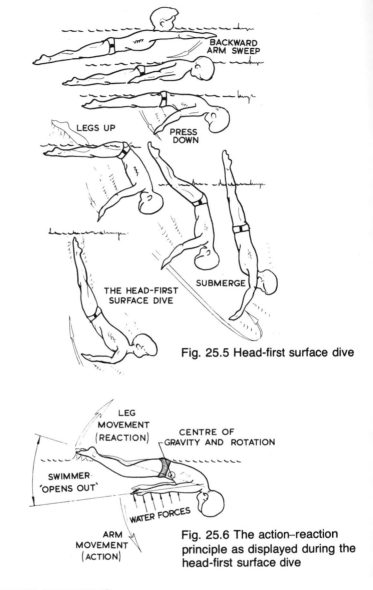

Fig. 25.5 Head-first surface dive

Fig. 25.6 The action–reaction principle as displayed during the head-first surface dive

UNDERWATER SWIMMING
1. Breast stroke (modified)
Probably the most successful underwater action is that of a modified breast stroke. The modification to the stroke is in the arm movement where, instead of the short shoulder-plane-limited pull, the swimmer sweeps the arms right back to the thighs. The normal timing of the stroke is maintained.

2. Hybrid breast-stroke/crawl movement

The previously described breast-stroke arm movement may also be combined with an alternating crawl-type leg kick. This type of movement is quite successful with the stronger swimmer.

3. Front paddle

A normal front paddle stroke is adopted, with both arms and legs performing the alternating and continuous movement exactly as described in chapter 12. This time, however, the swimmer is completely submerged.

The main difficulty of swimming under water (besides holding the breath) is simply being able to remain submerged. One often sees a so-called underwater swimmer firmly believing himself to be fully submerged, but actually performing with bottom and legs breaking the water surface at every kick. The swimmer with this difficulty should attempt to swim 'downhill' by pulling slightly up as well as backwards during the arm movement.

Holding the breath for even short periods may be a problem, but the process of trickling air gently through the nose enables the swimmer to extend slightly the time he can remain under water.

Practices which include both surface dives and underwater swimming may take the form of swimming through weighted hoops or under submerged poles. The game of retrieving a diving block can provide children with many hours of entertainment. When playing the inevitable game of tag in the pool, swimmers will come to realise that underwater swimming can be very fast. The long underwater pull and the absence of surface waves enhance a swimmer's speed over a short distance.

Safety

As with all other underwater practices, the teacher must be on a constant look-out for trouble. The main source of worry is that the competitive child may try to stay under rather too long. The teacher should limit the time of any submersive excursions by tapping the rail or side of the pool with a pole.

Feet-first surface dive (fig. 25.7)

Again, the swimmer takes advantage of the 'what goes up must come down' feature. Commencing in an *upright* treading-water position and a short distance away from the undecwater target (if there is one), the swimmer performs a vigorous downward-directed breast stroke-type kick and a simultaneous push down with the hands, which together should lift him out of the water. At the same time as this body elevation takes place, the swimmer adds to the unsupported weight by quickly raising both arms above the head. Complete submersion now takes place.

In order to assist the downward movement even more, the swimmer should stretch both legs and extend the feet, thus streamlining the body completely.

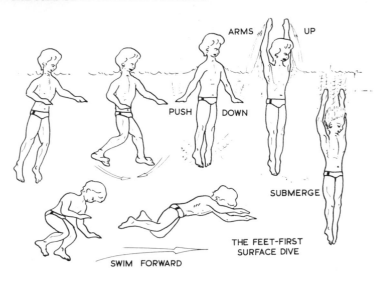

ARMS   UP

PUSH   DOWN

SUBMERGE

THE FEET-FIRST
SURFACE DIVE

SWIM FORWARD

Fig. 25.7 Feet-first surface dive

The downward momentum should submerge the swimmer well below the surface. (In shallow water, say 2 m (6½ ft), a surface diver can usually reach the bottom quite easily using this method.) When sufficient depth is reached or when vertical movement diminishes, the swimmer assumes a tuck position from where forward underwater swimming commences.

TEACHING THE SURFACE DIVE

The head-first surface dive may best be taught by starting off with a series of previously described practices. These earlier movements, such as the push and glide along the surface and then to the bottom of the pool, will prepare the swimmer for the forthcoming underwater activities, Also, from the push and glide, we may divert the pupil's attention to standing on their hands in order to get them used to being inverted in the water. Keeping their eyes open during these movements enables the swimmers to orientate themselves while submerged.

Head-first surface dive
Teaching practices (fig. 25.8)
1. During the initial practices, the emphasis is mainly on the push-and-glide skills. The fact that the push should be a vigorous one, and also that the swimmer should be stretched and straight with head down during the glide, should already have been established at an earlier stage of teaching.

2. Standing on the hands from a downward-directed push from the side is simply a case of lowering the head and shoulders and reaching for the

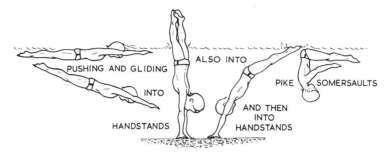

PUSHING AND GLIDING

INTO

HANDSTANDS

ALSO INTO

AND THEN
INTO
HANDSTANDS

PIKE

SOMERSAULTS

Fig. 25.8 Head-first surface dive – the teaching practices

bottom of the pool (in chest-deep water). Then, using the momentum of the glide to rotate the lower body (now uppermost) over the hands, the legs are stretched upwards, consequently achieving (with a little luck), the balanced handstand. If the pupils are not already accustomed to being inverted in the water, this exercise should do the trick.

3. Probably the most difficult part of the head-first surface-diving movement is that of raising the legs out of the water just prior to sliding below the surface. This particular part of the activity may be practised as a part-exercise by carrying out forward pike somersaults in the water from a push off the side. The downward action of the hands when they are initially placed adjacent to the thighs highlights the reactive effect required to raise the hips and rotate the swimmer.

4. The whole skill may be practised once more from a push and shortened glide along the surface, leading into a handstand. The swimmer sweeps both hands backward from the forward-stretched position to the region of the thighs to press down in an attempt to raise both legs out of the water. Continuing on from the forward sweep, the hands now reach for the bottom of the pool and the handstand may be completed.

The exercise is more difficult than simply directing the push-off towards the pool floor (practice 2).

It will be found that the deeper the water (within reason), the more successful will be the balance, the ideal depth being such that the inverted swimmer's knees are about at water level during the handstand.

5. The head-first surface dive may now be attempted in deeper water by approaching the submersion point using a head-up breast-stroke movement. It is good practice to approach the submersion point using a head-up stroke as it allows the swimmer (rescuer) to keep a floating object (or subject) in view. This technique is discussed in greater detail later.

The pupils (and the teacher) should by now be fully aware of the principles involved and be able to perform the hip-and-leg-elevating downward arm sweep effectively.

1. The hands should be back in the region of the thighs at the start of the dive.

2. Palms must be faced downwards in order that upward-reactive hip movement is created.

3. The arm sweep must be accompanied by a body pike and downward thrust of the head and shoulders.

4. The legs should be raised as far into the air as possible in order to assist the dive. It is desirable that they should also be straight, stretched and together (not kicking) as they submerge. The knees may be flexed, however, in attaining the stretched position.

5. The forward sweep of the arms automatically places them in a position such that they may move straight into the underwater swimming stroke.

6. A medium-sized breath should be taken just prior to making the dive.

7. Opening the eyes during the downward movement becomes necessary if an object is to be recovered.

Weighted and submerged devices, such as poles or hoops, provide the swimmers with definite objects to swim under or through directly from a surface dive. Diving blocks scattered on the bottom also enable them to perform the task of collecting an object and raising themselves and the object once more to the surface. This may be carried out by swimming or pushing off from the bottom of the pool.

Feet-first surface dive
Teaching practices (fig. 25.9)
1. In shallow water (chest-deep), the swimmers jump up, then submerge to sit on the floor of the pool. The exercise may be carried out initially without the swimmers deliberately raising their arms above their heads. As the exercise progresses, the arm raise may be introduced, which is required during the performance of the actual skill.

2. The swimmers should be reasonably adept at treading water before venturing into deeper water to attempt the next exercise. This practice is aimed at vertical submersion and is effected by the swimmer simply scooping both hands upwards. The swimmers tread water and then, in their own time, use an arm scoop-assisted vertical feet-first dive.
The arm propulsion is biased upwards, therefore the palms must be

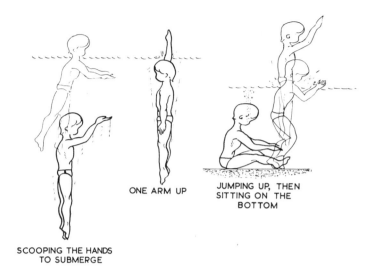

ONE ARM UP

JUMPING UP, THEN
SITTING ON THE
BOTTOM

SCOOPING THE HANDS
TO SUBMERGE

Fig. 25.9 Feet-first surface dive – the teaching practices

facing towards the water surface during the upward sweep and inwards (for least resistance) during the recovery. The scooping action is a continuous one and the swimmers should immediately cease any leg movement and assume a stretch as the submerging actions commence. A trip to the bottom of the pool should be attempted where a semi-tuck and push back to the surface may be performed.

3. The same initial practice situation is set up, namely that of treading water. The swimmers now attempt to submerge feet-first by raising one arm above the head immediately prior to disappearing below the surface. The other hand may assist with an upward scoop or it may be held by the side. Sinking to the bottom of the pool as before should be the aim.

4. The final practice is to raise both arms above the head before sinking. The whole movement may now be attempted and combined with a tuck and a short underwater swim. The bottom of the pool may be used initially to assist the swimmers perform their tucks, but if conditions are suitable, a complete semi-rotational movement should be carried out by the pupils without the assistance of the pool floor.

Recovering objects from the bottom and swimming under and through various submerged obstacles may now be performed. When these practices are performed, the teacher should ensure that the vertical submersion takes place a short distance away from the object or obstacle. This enables the swimmers to swim towards the target rather than descend directly on top of it and have to perform a series of aquabatic contortions.

TEACHING POINTS

1. The swimmers should appreciate how helpful the raised arms can be towards self-submersion.

2. A full stretch should be assumed during the descent.

3. A medium rather than deep breath should be taken just prior to submerging. (A deep inspiration increases the swimmers' buoyancy characteristics, thus making it more difficult to descend.)

4. In instances where a swimmer finds it difficult to submerge, the arm scoop as well as the initial arm raise may be utilised. In deeper water, the combination of both actions will almost certainly be necessary.

5. Tucking up to rotate and swim forward should eventually be attempted without contacting the floor of the pool.

6. Underwater swimming should be carried out in the manner previously described.

Taking off clothes in the water
If it is prudent to remove clothes while swimming, there are relatively easy methods of performing such antics. These are best practised initially in shallow water where the 'survivalists' are able to stand, and with as wide a choice of attire as possible. It may be useful to retain a grip on any removed clothing so that buoyancy aids may be made from them.

The first rule when taking off clothes in the water is to undo *all* buttons and fastenings. While practising the unfastening activities, the technique should be attempted using one hand only, with just occasional help from the other hand. In deep water the other hand may be used in order to remain afloat. The next rule is to remove each article of clothing quickly and cleanly without taking a mouthful of water or, if the garment is an upper one, 'blanketing' the face to cause suffocation.

Probably the easiest method of removing a short-sleeved woollen jumper or similar garment is to roll or gather the item up from the waist to the armpits then pull it over the head and free the arms. This also works with a light long-sleeved jumper (fig. 25.10).

The last movement should be carried out quickly and while the breath is held. This particular combination is necessary because the swimmer may tend to sink while manipulating a heavy water-logged garment above the water surface.

Where a sleeved pullover or jumper is to be removed, it is sometimes useful to ease one arm free from its sleeve then pull the garment off over the head and to one side (fig. 25.11).

Upper garments which undo down the front may be slipped off jacket-fashion after all the buttons are released.

Lower garments such as trousers or slacks should be fully undone then pushed down the legs as far as possible where they may be kicked off (fig. 25.12).

It may be useful to retain light footwear but experience has shown that, even with soft shoes on, swimming becomes rather difficult.

If such occasions do arise, shoes may be retained by securing them by the laces to the swimmer's belt or around the neck. They may even fit into a pocket or inside a shirt or jumper. As previously mentioned, long boots such as wellingtons may be utilised as buoyancy aids when inverted.

Fig. 25.10 Removing a jumper

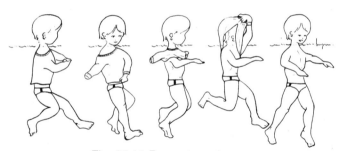

Fig. 25.11 Removing a jumper

Fig. 25.12 Removing trousers

Inflation of clothing

As mentioned earlier, light and tightly woven natural or synthetic materials tend to trap air quite readily when wet. Therefore, should the swimmer find the need for extra buoyancy, garments made of such materials are the most suitable for creating floats.

Probably the most important point in maintaining floats once they are made is not to drag them below the surface, otherwise the trapped air tends to be forced out through the weave.

Firstly, the outlets in the garment, such as the sleeves of a shirt or blouse or the legs of trousers or slacks, are best sealed by tying their ends into knots. These form natural air bags and are ideal as buoyancy boosters. Inflating the garments may be carried out in a variety of ways, all of which require the exponent to float or tread water during the 'blow up'. Lying on the back and gently kicking is often useful during such activities.

One obvious method of inflation is for the swimmer to puff air into the prepared garments in a balloon-blowing fashion. Trousers, for instance, may be gathered up just below the zip or fly opening. Then, by poking one finger into the gathered material, an access or 'blow hole' may be made in order to inflate the knotted legs. It is helpful if the hole is sealed in some way between the blows.

The legs of trousers may be knotted together and inflated to form a buoyancy aid or 'life jacket' when inflated (fig. 25.13), or knotted individually and inflated to make a pair of sausage-like air bags (fig. 25.13).

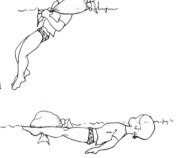

Fig. 25.13 (*left*) Blowing up trousers and (*right*) two ways of using trousers as a buoyancy aid

Lifting garments clear of the water then deftly bringing them down once more on to the surface usually serves to trap a volume of air in most garments, including shirts and blouses (fig. 25.14). There is, however, a knack in keeping the air confined in the space, and subsequent handling of the garment must be skilful. A girl's shirt, while still being worn, becomes an air trap when used in this way (fig. 25.15). (The result sometimes gives the impression of impending motherhood, as illustrated!)

Fig. 25.14 Alternative method of inflating trousers

Fig. 25.15
Using a dress
or a shirt as a
buoyancy aid

Spreading a garment out on the surface and blowing bubbles into it from underneath is yet another method of inflation. Once more, there is a knack in gathering the garment together without spilling the trapped air, and utilising it for a buoyancy aid.

Figure 25.16 shows the use of both clothes and a bucket as buoyancy aids.

These are a few more skills which may be practised in shallow water to begin with, before trying them out in water where the swimmers are unable to reach the bottom.

Fig. 25.16
Using clothes
and a bucket
as floating aids

26 Life-Saving

When treated with disrespect, water can be lethal, as both teacher and swimmer must remember at all times. Safety must always be the paramount factor in all activities, and if somebody is in danger and an aquatic emergency arises, always be ready and able to cope adequately with it.

The basic life-saving skills should not be treated as something to be *tried* in the supervised free-play period: they are important and should be treated accordingly.

The swimming teacher's ability to save life is essential. Learn the various skills thoroughly and practise them often, and when you have mastered them, teach them correctly in such a way that they will never be forgotten.

The basic life-saving skills are outlined in this chapter, together with teaching practices and teaching points. However, the teacher is well advised to obtain a copy of the Royal Life-Saving Society's *Life-Saving and Water Safety* manual, which contains a more detailed study of the subject.

Perhaps the most important feature in life-saving is to be an accomplished swimmer. It is pointless trying to rescue some poor unfortunate soul in difficulties if you are going to get into similar difficulties yourself. When teaching the various life-saving skills, make sure that a reasonable basic standard of swimming ability is achieved before proceeding with partner-related practices; i.e. it is pointless asking one pupil to tow another, if the potential rescuer can hardly swim himself. In a real situation, both would probably drown.

We shall, in this chapter, examine the swimming-pool environment only. Further situations related to open water are covered adequately in the RLSS handbook.

THE BASIC PERSONAL LIFE-SAVING SKILLS

The swimmers – and this includes the teacher – should have achieved a minimum standard of watermanship before attempting the more advanced life-saving practices. A suggested level of ability is as follows:

1. The ability to swim at least 400 m (440 yds) in a reasonable time, say fifteen minutes.
2. The ability to perform at least three of the four competition strokes in recognisable style, including breast stroke.

3. The ability to carry out the majority of the basic watermanship practices outlined in chapter 25.

4. The ability to jump and plunge into the water from the poolside.

Water fitness is also important. Knowing how to rescue and being capable of rescuing are two entirely different things. Water fitness can only be achieved by swimming, so swim often and encourage your charges to do likewise.

In addition, the swimmers should be able to perform the side stroke (see chapter 24), sculling (see chapter 28), the surface dives (see chapter 25) and be able to tread water (see chapter 25).

Leaving deep water without assistance is another important skill (see fig. 26.1). This is a movement which depends on the ability to combine and utilise the natural upward-buoyancy forces created by the water, together with the momentum generated by the arms and legs.

With both hands, slightly wider than the shoulders, the swimmer grasps some convenient ledge; in most instances this is the edge of the pool. Then, by fully extending both arms (if not already extended), she sinks into the water. When she is fully extended, she carries out a vigorous breast stroke-like kick and simultaneously heaves herself upwards by flexing her arms. From this point onwards, the action depends on the type of person carrying out the movement.

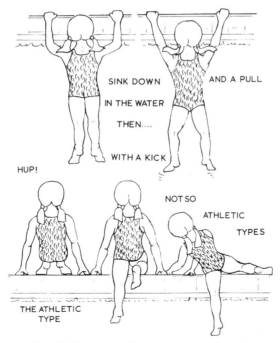

Fig. 26.1 Leaving the water unassisted

THE ATHLETIC TYPE These lucky people are able to place both feet on the poolside between the hands (similar to a gymnastic vault), stand up and simply walk away. This is how most of the story books illustrate the movement.

THE NOT-SO-ATHLETIC TYPE Here the pool rail might be used to provide one foot support, or the knee may be placed on the side before standing up.

THE OVERWEIGHT, WEAK-SHOULDERED AND ROTUND TYPES These are the unfortunate ones who have trouble in getting themselves out of the water even if a shark is nibbling at their toes! There is a way for them to negotiate an exit from the water – it is not elegant, but it is effective. The original heave-ho is the way: the object of the exercise is for the swimmer to lean forward on to the poolside and, if possible, on to her strongest elbow. Once the elbow is taking the weight, the next part of rolling over on to the tummy and getting to the feet is relatively easy. Sometimes this requires practice and it is best to start in the shallow end where, by jumping up from the pool floor in order to make the exit, the movement becomes slightly easier.

PERSONAL SAFETY SKILLS
In the following descriptions, the swimmer is termed the 'rescuer' and the person in difficulty is termed the 'subject'.

1. Entering the water safely in an emergency
When the water is murky and/or its depth cannot be readily assessed, a head-first entry can be dangerous and could kill! It is far less dangerous (although in no way desirable) to sustain damage to a leg by jumping in than to risk a head injury by colliding with some submerged and unseen object. Although we are dealing with the swimming-pool environment, such 'unknown conditions' entries must be practised in safe circumstances for obvious reasons. They are therefore included here.

Lowering
With the risk of personal injury uppermost, the first method of water entry for intended rescue should be to lower oneself slowly into the water if possible, at the same time endeavouring to keep the subject in view. (If he submerges you may have trouble pinpointing his whereabouts once more.) If the water is shallow enough, you can now wade to the subject; if too deep, you must swim with head up.

Jumping in
There are two life-saving related methods of jumping into the water, the first being the straddle jump and the second the compact jump.

Straddle jump (fig. 26.2)
During the straddle jump from the poolside the main aim of the rescuer is to keep his head above water on entry. This is achieved by presenting as much body area to the water surface as possible. The resulting profile then creates such resistance that the swimmer's 'instantaneous buoyancy' is considerably enhanced and, hopefully, his head remains clear of the water throughout the jump.

Fig. 26.2 The straddle jump

STARTING POSITION This may be with knees and hips slightly flexed and the toes of both feet curled over the edge of the pool. Alternatively, a semi-crouch track-start pose may be adopted with the toes of the front foot curled over the poolside. In either case, the arms should be stretched forward and sideways, each one forming an angle of forty-five degrees with the shoulder plane. The palms of the hands should be facing downward and the elbows slightly flexed. The swimmer should be looking forward with his eyes firmly fixed on the subject (or, in practice, some convenient eye-level object).

TAKE-OFF The swimmer should now spring forward (not upwards) with one leg leading the other, almost as if he were running. The resulting profile which is then presented to the water surface should be quite extensive. The trailing leg should remain in contact with the poolside or take-off station for as long as possible.

ENTRY The entry into the water will be quite a tumultuous one and, if it is carried out correctly, the swimmer's hair should stay dry!

Teaching practices
The teaching practices for the straddle jump are merely performing the action itself.

TEACHING POINTS

1. Ensuring a firm foot grip on take-off

2. Looking forward rather than down

3. A horizontal rather than upward-directed spring, the back foot remaining on the poolside as long as possible

4. Presentation of maximum profile to the water

5. Keeping the head above water at all times

6. A vigorous downward-directed hand scull may be introduced in order to enhance temporary buoyancy

7. Set off into a breast stroke swim immediately

8. Breathing usually occurs as a natural function, but usually it is best to breathe in at take-off and out through the nose as the splash subsides or as the swimmer surfaces

Compact jump (fig. 26.3)
This is used for entry from a height above the poolside.

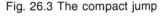

Fig. 26.3 The compact jump

STARTING POSITION This is usually a relaxed upright position with both feet firmly anchored over the platform. Both arms should be across the chest with each hand lightly grasping the opposite upper arm or shoulder. Alternatively, the arms may be at the sides. The former method enables the nose to be lightly pinched during the jump, should this be more comfortable. The swimmer should be looking forward after assessing the jumping height.

TAKE-OFF The swimmer should simply step forward and drop as vertically as possible into the water. It is important not to look down, otherwise facial impact with the water may be painful. The arms should be held tightly into the sides and the legs slightly flexed.

ENTRY This will be a fairly splashy one, but the swimmer should not change his position until submerged. He may then spread his arms to slow his descent and pull and kick to the surface once more. The breath should be exhaled through the nose during ascent and continued as he breaks the surface. He may now proceed towards the subject or to the poolside.

Teaching practices
These should begin at the poolside, and gradually progress to a safe height.

TEACHING POINTS

1. The jump must be out and away from the take-off point in order to avoid contact with the poolside.

2. The swimmer must ensure that the area below him is clear.

3. Looking forwards or slightly upwards is desirable.

4. The arms must remain tucked to the sides during flight and entry.

5. Breathing out through the nose during surfacing and as the face breaks the water will minimise coughing and spluttering.

2. Approaching the subject
The important features of approaching someone in difficulties are:

Speed – getting within contact range as soon as possible is absolutely vital.
Keeping the subject in view during the approach swim or being able to pinpoint, as near as possible, the position of submersion, should they have 'gone down': this is a continuation of the point mentioned in the water-entry skills. There are only two strokes with a head-up/looking-forward style. Front crawl, when swum in waterpolo fashion, permits a good view but, for the unfit, is extrememly tiring. It is useless reaching a subject and becoming exhausted in the process – the difficult part is yet to come. Breast stroke is generally slower than front crawl, but it exhibits the head-up position as a natural stroke feature. The style is not too exhausting and would seem to be the correct one to use.

3. Keeping a safe distance
In a real situation, a drowning person is always desperate for some supporting 'straw' to grab at. Also, the prevailing circumstances enable him to muster considerably more strength than usual. Considering both these factors, it is advisable when approaching a buoyant but struggling subject not to swim straight up to him, but to hold back briefly and quickly assess the situation. Perhaps a little verbal reassurance will help. Explain what is intended and reassure him. He may react favourably before you make contact, and this *may* make things a little easier.

If the subject is conscious and has submerged, contact must be made in order to bring him to the surface once more. This can be dangerous and needs considerable practice, skill and strength which only come with specialist life-saving instruction. If, on the other hand, the subject is unconscious, the rescuer's personal danger is slightly reduced, but the subject's risk of drowning is high. Both situations require the surface-dive skills to be used and in the second instance speed is vital.

Reversing (fig. 26.4) is one way of staying temporarily out of reach of a panic-stricken individual. The initial part of the movement is not unlike that of regaining the feet from a prone position. The arms are both pressed downwards and the legs are reacted downwards also. Finally, a sweeping arm movement (in the opposite direction of desired motion) drives the swimmer backwards in the reverse direction and the legs swing upwards. The whole movement resembles that of a pendulum. The 'single leg block' is a defensive method which may be used if the struggler gets within clutching distance. Here, the 'reverse' movement is carried out then, with one foot in contact with the subject's shoulder (or chest in a real situation), the rescuer should be able to push away and out of reach once more. It is important that the subject remains in view at all times.

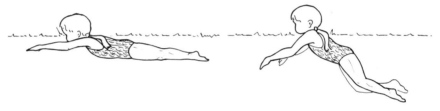

Fig. 26.4 Reversing

Ducking away (fig. 26.5) is another method of avoiding the too-close attention of some desperate soul in difficulties. The illustration shows that the swimmer has been grabbed around the neck, but with a quick lowering of the head and a timely push upwards and against the subject's body or arms, a safe distance is once more assumed. (The upward-directed push not only assists in escaping the clutches of the victim, but also provides him with a little extra temporary buoyancy.) Probably, the most important feature of this particular movement is that of ducking the head, on which the subject originally gained a hold.

In order to avoid unnecessary accidents and injuries, all the contact-

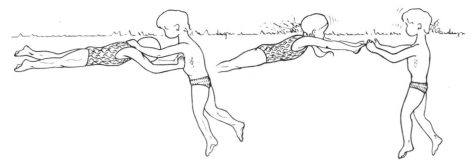

Fig. 26.5 Ducking away

avoidance techniques should be performed decisively and vigorously, *but without malice*. Life-saving is *not* a martial art and any over-enthusiastic actions on the part of rescuer or rescued can cause unnecessary injury. It is also necessary in the early stages of practice that life-saving partners are of comparable size and strength. The defensive techniques may initially be attempted against the poolside where no harm can be done, before proceeding further with a partner.

4. Releasing from a restrictive hold
The application of these particular skills should not really be necessary if the swimmer has been successful in blocking or ducking away or in keeping a safe distance, and by subsequent reassurance and manoeuvring has taken the subject safely in tow.

However, if the subject does succeed in grabbing and holding the swimmer, a quick and effective release must be made. It is important that, during the various release movements, the swimmer should endeavour not to lose contact or control over the subject. In a real situation where there are rough or murky waters, re-establishing lost contact may be difficult or even impossible.

Push-up breaks
A desperate swimmer will grab the first floating object that comes within his reach. If, due to some temporary lapse of vigilance, that floating object happens to be the potential rescuer, some counter-measures must be applied.

Should the unwary rescuer's head and neck be encircled by the subject's arms (fig. 26.6A) an effective method of escape is for the swimmer to tuck her chin in to her chest and push the subject upwards. This may be carried out by applying force under his elbows or armpits. The reactive force will cause the rescuer to sink below the surface where a suitable manoeuvre may be made by turning the subject to surface once more behind her.

A similar release may be carried out if the clutch is more substantial

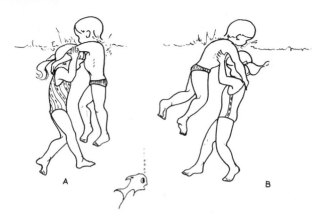

Fig. 26.6 The push-up breaks

and further down the body. Figure 26.6B shows the unwary rescuer securely pinioned by the subject's encircling arms. The method of release is somewhat similar to the previous one, except that, because the subject's grip restricts lower-arm movement by the rescuer, force must be applied to the subject's chest rather than to his elbows or armpits. If the grip is high enough up the rescuer's arms, an outward arm swing tends to shift the subject's grip further up, whereby the former method of release may be adopted.

Arm-pull breaks (fig. 26.7)
Should the subject grab with both hands one of the rescuer's wrists, a fist should be formed by the hand of the captured arm. With his free hand, the rescuer then grasps his own fist and pulls sharply up or down against the subject's thumb joint. The hand movement must be long and vigorous enough for the subject's grip to be completely relinquished.

Fig. 26.7 The arm-pull breaks down and up

The action will bring about a temporary loss of contact which must quickly be re-established. In order to carry this out, the rescuer must speedily grab the subject by the upper arm or shoulder and turn him to face in the same direction as herself. A suitable towing position may then be taken up.

If both the rescuer's wrists are grabbed, a downward and outward swing of both arms (against the subject's thumb joints once more), should be made in order to facilitate release. The subsequent turn and tow is then carried out.

In order to establish the correct direction of the rescuer's arm movements, the releases themselves are best carried out initially by the pupils working in pairs on dry land.

The RLSS handbook outlines further methods of breaking various and more alarming grips, which are beyond the scope of this chapter. The teacher is well advised to study these, however, and be ready and able to perform them if required, in the 'line of duty'.

5. Tows
There are four basic established methods of tow; each one has been developed to cope with certain specific conditions.

Non-contact tow
This is a tow which may be used when the subject is conscious and able to hang on to some makeshift towing aid. The aid may be a rigid one such as an oar, the branch of a tree or a piece of suitable flotsam. The main attribute of such an aid is that it should be reasonably light and buoyant. A non-rigid aid, such as a belt or some article of clothing, is quite satisfactory, and the subject may well find it is more convenient to float along on his or her back.

The essential factor in such a tow is speed. This is because the subject cannot rely on any direct buoyancy boost from the swimmer, but she must rely on movement through the water to assist floatation.

The swimming stroke should be either the life-saving back stroke (with one-arm assistance if necessary) or the side stroke.

Extended-arm tow (fig. 26.8)
The subject for this type of rescue should be passive or co-operative and prevailing conditions calm. The swimmer's grip is formed by cupping one hand (of the extended towing arm) under the subject's chin. One essential feature here is to ensure that the grip does not throttle the subject by slipping down on to her throat. It is best that the third and fourth fingers of the gripping hand be either curled or lifted (as though 'drinking tea with the vicar') in order to avoid this. For good manoeuvrability and control, the swimmer's arm should remain extended and he should be more or less directly ahead of the subject.

Fig. 26.8 The extended-arm tow

Once more, speed is essential, not only to maintain the subject high in the water, but also because, in the event of her being injured, medical aid may be urgently required. The swimming stroke should be either of the life-saving back-stroke or side-stroke styles. The free arm should be used to assist progress and the towing arm may be alternated as often as necessary. If the subject is conscious, constant reassurance should be given if at all possible.

Chin tow (fig. 26.9)
This is a close-contact type of tow where the subject needs a firm control-ling hand. The rescuer's grip is on the subject's chin, as previously described. In order to take up this hold, the swimmer's gripping arm (say, right) is passed over the subject's (right) shoulder. The grip is enhanced by the swimmer squeezing his arm into the subject's (right) shoulder. The remaining arm is used to assist the life-saving back-stroke style. The towing position should be with both participants in a cheek-to-cheek mode. This closeness enables the rescuer to talk quietly and calmly to the subject in an effort to reassure.

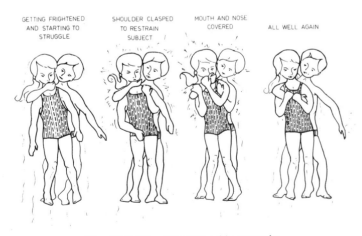

Fig. 26.9 The chin tow with struggle

Should the subject start to struggle, the free arm should be used to grip the adjacent shoulder as a restraint, remaining there for as long as necessary. If this hold fails, the rescuer should slide his gripping hand further up the subject's face in order to cover his mouth and pinch his nose. When he cannot breathe, the subject will probably grip the offending arm and drag it away towards his chest and, hopefully, hold it there. The tow may continue in this fashion with perhaps the rescuer's hand securing a firmer grip under the subject's armpit. The free arm should once more be utilised as soon as it becomes possible.

Cross-chest tow (fig. 26.10)
This is another close-contact towing method by which the rescuer is able to lift the subject reassuringly high in the water. The elevation of the subject in this way makes the rescue suitable for rough conditions, or if floating obstructions have to be seen and avoided.

The rescuer takes a grip under the subject's (say, right) armpit with his (left) hand, by passing the arm over the (left) shoulder and across the chest. By tucking the subject's (left) shoulder into his (left) armpit, and thrusting his upper (left) hip into the subject's back, the rescuer establishes a firm and reassuring hold on the subject.

The swimming style will be side stroke with the free arm assisting.

Fig. 26.10 The cross-chest tow

6. Landing
Having safety towed the unfortunate subject to the poolside, we have to ensure that they are landed safely.

A fully conscious and helpful subject (fig. 26.11)
This does not require much skill. The subject simply rests her hands on the poolside and the rescuer provides a stirrup in order to assist the landing. In deep water the stirrup is formed by one hand, but where the depth is shallow and the participants are able to stand, both hands may be used to perform the lift.

Fig. 26.11 Leaving the
water assisted

An incapable or unconscious subject
Should the subject be unconscious or unable to get himself out of the
water, the rescuer must achieve some safe supporting position from which
he may briefly rest or commence the next move.

At the end of the tow the rescuer should grab the pool rail or trough
with his free hand and carefully manoeuvre the subject between him and
the rail while at the same time maintaining a firm grip (fig. 26.12). This
movement is assisted by the rescuer providing some support to the
subject. In the illustration, the rescuer's knee may be seen being used as a
buoyancy aid during rotation of the subject.

When the subject is 'sandwiched' the rescuer's grip may be relinquished and the rescuer's arms are positioned one at a time under the
subject's armpits (fig. 26.13). The actual landing starts from here.

From the support position, the subject must be safely brought to dry
land ⅜fig. 26.14). The easiest method of performing this task is for the
rescuer to secure the subject's hands on the poolside and then climb out.
The illustrations show how this may be carried out.

Once on dry land, the subject may be landed by the straight-arm (fig.
26.15) or crossed-arm (fig. 26.16) method. Extreme care must be taken
in each instance, in order to ensure that the subject's head is not bounced
on the floor as it is lowered to the poolside.

In both methods of landing, the rescuer must avoid personal back
injury w ich may occur by lifting in an incorrect manner. The illustration
shows the rescuer crouched in an upright position prior to hoisting the
subject from the water. By straightening his legs and maintaining the
upright stance, the weight of the subject is transferred through his
shoulder girdle and *axially* down his vertebral column and into the lower
limbs. In this way, bending loads on the spine (the dangerous ones) are
minimised.

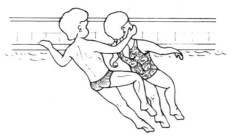

Fig. 26.12 At the end of the tow and into the support position

Fig. 26.13 The support position

SECURING
SAFELY

THEN
GETTING OUT

Fig. 26.14 Landing the unconscious subject

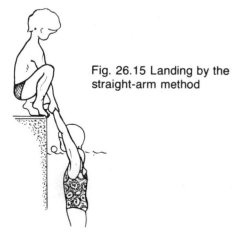

Fig. 26.15 Landing by the straight-arm method

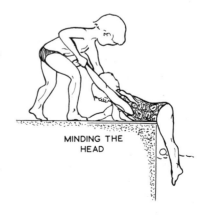

MINDING THE
HEAD

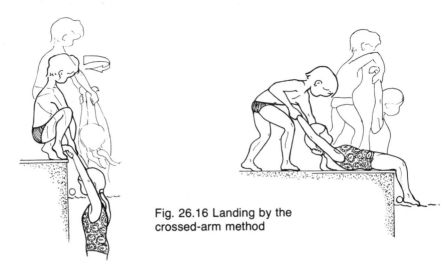

Fig. 26.16 Landing by the
crossed-arm method

The rescuer should at all times grip the subject's wrists for landing rather than her hands. The wrist grip is more secure and less likely to slip over the protuberance of the hand.

The actual process of hauling the subject out of the water varies according to water depth. In deep water, both the straight- and crossed-arm landing methods may be used, while in shallow water it is more advisable to use the straight-arm procedure only. The reasoning behind this is that the crossed-arm landing (and the straight-arm landing in deep water) is best performed after 'dunking' the subject several times in the water. This rapid lifting and lowering action enables upward momentum to be generated, thus assisting the landing. 'Dunking' can only be successfully performed in deep water. It must be emphasised also that the subject's head should remain above water at all times while being subjected to the 'dunking' process.

Probably the main advantage of the crossed-arm landing is the subject's positional readiness for expired-air resuscitation, should it be required.

7. Turning a casualty (fig. 26.17)
Should the subject be landed on to her front and require to be turned over for resuscitation purposes, the following method may be adopted.

The rescuer should first remove the casualty completely from the water, then take up a kneeling position by her side. The casualty's arm nearest the rescuer should be stretched forward. Now, by grasping the far shoulder and hip (clamping the wrist at the same time), the rescuer manipulates the casualty over towards him so that she rests on her lower thighs. Now, by carefully supporting both her shoulders and head, the

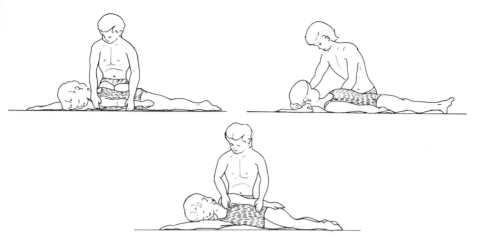

Fig. 26.17 Turning the casualty

rescuer should gently lower her into the supine position. The outstretched arm is then placed by her side. Artificial resuscitation may now be commenced is required. Crossing the casualty's foot over the nearest one before starting the turn is another variation of the theme.

8. Dealing with respiratory failure

When a casualty has stopped breathing, it is absolutely *vital* to re-start respiration immediately. The brain needs to receive a continuous supply of oxygen and, if deprived of its supply for more than about three and a half minutes, permanent damage is likely to result. In many unfortunate instances, mental capacity has been damaged by temporary oxygen starvation, even though resuscitation has eventually been carried out.

It therefore must be emphasised that the most important factor in any form of respiratory resuscitation is the speed with which the life-supporting oxygen can be pumped into the casualty's lungs.

In the same context, it is far more important to re-start respiration than to discover the root cause of the failure unless it is immediately evident. Although in the instances with which we are concerned the cause will be obvious, i.e. drowning, there are other causes of respiratory failure, such as food 'going down the wrong way' and blocking the upper airway. The teacher may have to deal with an instance of this if a sweet or chewing-gum has escaped 'customs clearance' when a child has entered the water. Other situations which may inhibit or stop breathing are:

1. An excess of smoke due to fire
2. Toxic fumes or gases (not unknown in swimming pools)
3. Suffocation – the nose and mouth entrances blocked
4. Electrocution

5. Compression of the neck, i.e. strangulation
6. Compression of the chest by crushing in some way

The *initial* treatment for all these states of emergency is either to remove the cause or remove the subject from the cause of asphyxia. (The word asphyxia describes the condition in which there is a lack of oxygen in the blood and consequently the tissues do not receive an adequate supply.)

Here we shall concentrate our attention on the casualty who has stopped breathing through drowning.

Expired-air resuscitation
Respiration is the process by which oxygen is transferred from the environmental air to the blood in our bodies, while at the same time carbon dioxide, a waste product, is expelled. The air we breathe in consists of approximately one-fifth (twenty per cent) oxygen and four-fifths (eighty per cent) nitrogen. The expired air consists of the complete nitrogen content and sixteen per cent oxygen, the remainder being carbon dioxide. In other words, we only use four per cent of our oxygen intake: the expired sixteen per cent can be breathed directly into a casualty's lungs in an attempt to save his or her life. This is the reasoning behind the expired-air resuscitation method, and it has been shown conclusively that this is the only really efficient method of artificial respiration.

How then should it be performed? Returning to the poor soul we earlier landed and, by some means or other manoeuvred into a supine position, we are now ready to apply respiration should it be needed.

First, check to see if the casualty is breathing:

Does the chest or abdomen rise and fall?
Can you feel any respiratory movement of the chest or abdomen?
Place your eye near the casualty's airways – can you feel any exhaled breath?
Is there blueness of the face, lips, conjunctivae and nail beds?

If there is no sign of respiration or if you have any doubts at all, apply resuscitation without delay – every second is vital. Remember, it is both safe and wise to commence artificial respiration while breathing appears to be failing. If there *are* signs of breathing, but it is noisy, this means that the airways are blocked in some way. Check the mouth for debris; this may be in the form of vomit, false teeth, loose teeth (after a collision), a sweet, seaweed (at the seaside) or just plain water. This may sound unsavoury, but remember, a life is at stake. If you want to be ill yourself, wait until later!

If breathing cannot be re-started by removal of any obvious blockage, a sharp slap between the shoulder blades with the casualty face down may remove some unseen offending obstacle. In the case of a child and a suspected sweet-like obstruction, place the child over one knee with his head down and give several sharp blows with the flat of the hand between his shoulders. This should dislodge the offending obstacle.

If there is still no sign of breathing after this quick initial survey and treatment, with the casualty once more on her back, tilt her head well back. This may be carried out by placing one hand on the subject's head, just above the forehead, and the other hand either under her neck or preferably gripping her chin. This movement of the head causes the root of the tongue to move away from the back of the throat (fig. 26.18). This removes another of the unseen obstructions.

Fig. 26.18 (*left*) Head forward – tongue at the back of the throat and (*right*) head back to clear the air passages

The casualty may start to breathe with a gasp and a splutter. If she does, hold her like this for a few seconds in order to re-establish and ease respiration. Then, if she is still unconscious, place her in the coma or recovery position, which is described on page 348. If she should recover consciousness, keep her still and warm and in a comfortable position, and summon medical assistance and advice.

Should she still not show any signs of breathing, apply artificial respiration (fig. 26.19). With the casualty's head held as previously described, the rescuer should:

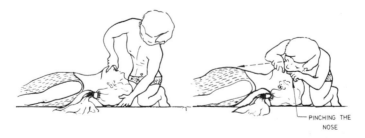

Fig. 26.19 Applying expired-air resuscitation (mouth to mouth)

1. Open his mouth wide and take a deep breath.
2. Pinch the casualty's nose with the fingers of the head-supporting hand.
3. Seal his lips around the casualty's mouth, or close the casualty's mouth and seal the lips over the casualty's nose.

4. Blow into the casualty's lungs until her chest rises.* (The rescuer should glance towards the casualty's chest in order to observe this.)
5. Remove his mouth and watch the chest fall.
6. Repeat and continue at the normal breathing rate, say one blow at about every five seconds.

It is advantageous to commence respiration with four quicker breaths, in order to inflate and build up the oxygen content within the casualty's lungs. If the heart is beating, there should be a return of colour to the patient's face. It may not be possible to slow one's own breathing down to a five-second cycle after an energetic rescue. This does not matter.

If the chest does not rise, the rescuer is either failing to make a proper lip seal around the casualty's mouth or the airway is still blocked. Check that the head is tilted back far enough, before searching for some other physical obstruction.

If the airway is clear, the pinkish skin tinge will soon reappear. Should the heart be stopped (cardiac arrest), cardiac massage should be adopted. (See *First Aid*, the authorised manual of the St John Ambulance Association and Brigade.)

As consciousness returns, the casualty will start to breathe on her own. This is the time to stop resuscitation. In order to assist respiration, the rescuer should continue to support the casualty's chin, and hence ensure that the airways remain open. If the casualty starts to breathe regularly but remains unconscious, he should be laid in the recovery or coma position. Probably, the best sign of a successful resuscitation attempt is for the casualty energetically to push the rescuer away!

It is worth noting that any ingress of water into the lungs cannot be removed, so do not try. Fresh water is quickly absorbed into the blood and duly despatched by the normal body functions. Sea water is less readily absorbed but is still unremovable by the rescuer. Maintaining the casualty in a head-low position allows any fluids to be despatched via the mouth and during unconsciousness prevents the ingress of such fluids into the lungs.

How long should artificial respiration be continued? Either until the casualty starts to breathe once more; until some qualified medical authority tells you to stop; or until it becomes impossible for you to continue. Remember, even when there are *no* visible signs of life, there *is* still hope.

How soon should artificial resuscitation be applied? Immediately it has been recognised that breathing is failing or has failed. It cannot be emphasised enough that *speed* of application is *vital*.

Deep-water resuscitation
If the subject has become a casualty before the rescuer manages to get

* During practice or demonstration, the breath should be blown down past the 'casualty's' far cheek.

him to safety, and the rescuer recognises that breathing has failed, deep-water resuscitation should be attempted immediately.

This method of resuscitation demands quite considerable swimming skill and ability. The swimmer positions himself alongside the subject, maintaining continual progress towards safety at the same time. Then, by holding the underside of the subject's head with one hand and at the same time holding his jaw closed and tilting his head back with the other hand, artificial respiration may be applied. The method of application should be mouth to nose. This avoids the likelihood of water entering the subject's gaping mouth. Resuscitation is applied while the swimmer elevates himself in the water using vigorous leg movements. (The actual kicking action may be any one of those described in the chapter on treading water.) Care must be taken to ensure that the casualty is not used as a form of aquatic support during the swimmer's attempts to elevate himself. The slightest downward pressure or release of manual support will cause the unfortunate person to sink once more beneath the waves.

The rescuer then leans over and forms a mouth seal around the casualty's nose in order to blow air into his lungs.* The initial multi-quick breath application is impractical on this occasion; consequently, the rate of one blow every five seconds (approximately) should be immediately established if possible. Breathlessness on the part of the rescuer, however, often necessitates some deviation from this timing.

It is possible to administer deep-water resuscitation even if the subject's head is temporarily submerged, provided a completely air-tight seal is created.

Resuscitation should continue, if needed, as the swimmer wades in shallow water supporting his charge (fig. 26.20). Alternatively, if the rescuer has opted to carry the subject to the poolside in deep water,

Fig. 26.20 Resuscitation while walking in shallow water

---

* During practice or demonstration, the rescuer's mouth should be applied to the 'casualty's' forehead or he should blow past the far cheek.

resuscitation may be carried out in a single-arm support mode (fig. 26.21). It is useful on such occasions to allow the casualty's body and legs to sink into the water thus enhancing the desirable head-back mode. This single-arm method of support may also be utilised at sea or in a river where some convenient floating aid may be found.

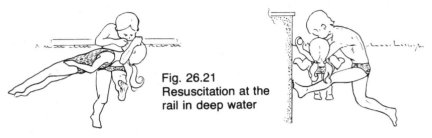

Fig. 26.21
Resuscitation at the
rail in deep water

9. After-care

In all situations where the subject begins to breathe but remains unconscious, he or she should be placed in the coma or recovery position while awaiting urgent medical attention.

Coma is a medical term denoting a level of consciousness. There are four levels:

1. FULL CONSCIOUSNESS – mental faculties normal
2. DROWSINESS – easily roused, but lapses into unconsciousness once more
3. STUPOR – may be roused with difficulty, aware of painful stimuli but not of sounds such as voices speaking to him
4. COMA – cannot be roused by any means

The recovery or coma position is illustrated in fig. 26.22. The patient should be kept warm and a watchful eye maintained on his or her breathing and pulse rate. (The normal adult pulse rate in a rested state is from sixty to eighty beats per minute. In children and young infants, this rate increases to some ninety to a hundred and forty beats.) The pulse rate may be checked either at the wrist (radial pulse) or on the neck (carotid pulse). Following resuscitation, every recovered casualty should be transferred (by ambulance if possible) to hospital or to a doctor for medical attention.

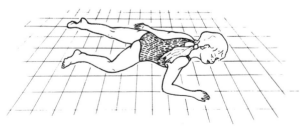

Fig. 26.22 The recovery or coma position

GENERAL LIFE-SAVING TRAINING

As already emphasised, some degree of water fitness is desirable, but skill in the art of watermanship is absolutely essential.

Entering the water from various heights should be practised regularly, as should the towing strokes and releases. The tows may be performed individually where partners are not available, using swimmers' heavy blocks or, for the super-strong, towing buckets! Releases may be initially practised on dry land in order to establish the movements, before carrying them out in shallow and finally in deep water. Remember, these are not martial-art skills and, while some degree of authenticity is desired, injury may result if the participants become too enthusiastic.

Breast stroke and side stroke, together with the life-saving back stroke, should all be practised regularly. Assisting partners to land in both deep and shallow water should also be included in any life-saving syllabus. Resuscitation techniques using special practice apparatus are also a necessity for those who frequent aquatic playgrounds.

27 Diving

Almost every child loves to dive head-first into the water, be it from the poolside, the diving platform, the springboard or from some other convenient take-off point. Also, a dive is necessary at the start of three of the four major competition stroke events (although the rules state that competitors may start a race by jumping into the water). Again, of course, there are the springboard and highboard skills which are classic sports in themselves, but it is not intended to go too deeply into this rather specialised subject here.

The main purpose of this chapter, is to provide teachers with the knowledge that is required in order that they may teach the basic diving skills to suitably proficient swimmers. This will be achieved by presenting a progressive sequence of practices. These are designed to guide the prospective divers carefully and safely through the simple shallow-water exercises and poolside practices and eventually to the performance of a satisfactory (and hopefully aesthetic) head-first entry into the water. But there are a few facts regarding the safety of the young divers that a teacher should know before commencing any diving activities.

The paramount concern in teaching pupils how to dive must be for their own safety, and the safety of others who happen to be in the vicinity. Divers must be taught to be safe before, during and after the event.

Before the dive
1. Probably the first question is whether the water is deep enough for a dive to be performed. Even from the poolside, a young diver rising to only half his or her height hits the water at a speed something like 4 m (13 ft) per second, which may be better understood as approximately 9 miles per hour.

The diver, hitting the water cleanly and almost vertically at this speed, will descend very rapidly to the bottom of a 1.98-m (6½-ft) pool. If the direction of the underwater glide remains unchanged, the performer will strike the bottom. This is not so dangerous, however, providing that he or she has assumed the correct arm-stretched and hand-clasped position in order to protect the head.

How can we make sure that the water is deep enough to carry out the safe performance of a particular entry? The answer is a complex one and involves many variables such as the weight of the individual, the entry angle into the water, the height of take-off, the cleanness of the entry and, of course, the skill and experience of the divers themselves. With the reader's indulgence, I will use myself as one example of how much 'skill and experience' have to be brought into the calculation.

My weight is approximately 111 kg (17½ stone), but after many years of diving into the water, I am able to negotiate safely a head-first entry from the side into the shallow end (1 m: 3¼ ft) of a local pool. To onlookers, the experience is not unlike a minor earthquake and seems to set up a tidal wave, but I always emerge completely unscathed.

The secret of my 'success' is that I perform a *shallow* entry and, *where shallow conditions prevail, this is the safe way to dive in.* There is, of course, a limit to the water depth any diver may safely negotiate and the teacher must, by experiment and experience, learn to judge this extreme.

To use one further illustration, I remember during my now distant childhood seeing a one-legged gentleman named Peg-Leg Pete safely dive from an extremely high tower at a local fairground into a tank of water not much more than 1.8 m (6 ft) deep. His skill and experience must have been phenomenal, especially at night, when he ignited himself and descended into the then flaming tank.

From these two examples, it may be seen that skill and experience in entering the water are two very important features of safe diving. We must, therefore, make sure that our teachings provide the prospective divers with a fair chance of surviving long enough to gain the necessary skill and experience.

Figure 27.1 illustrates the relationship between the angle of entry of a diver and the depth of water when he becomes completely submerged. The teacher must realise, however, that the diver will continue to move downward beyond these positions, and consequently safety margins must be allowed below these depths.

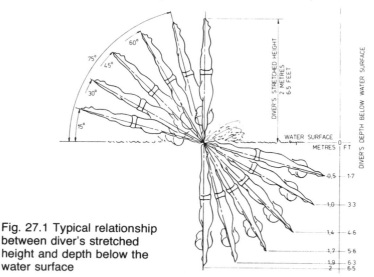

Fig. 27.1 Typical relationship between diver's stretched height and depth below the water surface

Having established what is a safe depth of water, we may now take into consideration some other safety features to be observed before the dive.

2. Has the diver taken up a safe and balanced starting position or stance? Many diving injuries are caused by the performer's feet slipping on take-off, so at all times make sure the diver's feet are correctly positioned. (This particular aspect will be covered more fully later in the chapter.)

3. Train your divers to adopt the habit of having a good look around in order to see that the entry locality is clear and free of approaching swimmers, before diving into the water. This is particularly important in relation to the back dives, where taking up the balanced starting position tends to take a little longer. Situations can change quickly in a pool, and while a diver is carefully taking up his or her stance, a previously clear space can, within a few seconds, become crowded with swimmers. If the teacher is working in controlled circumstances, this danger can be almost eliminated. But if swimmers other than those under the teacher's care and control are present, the problem can be serious.

In the instance of a back dive, a partner can be of great help by informing the diver whether the coast is clear or not, and helping him or her to balance prior to take-off. Another high-risk activity is diving from springboards or high platforms. Often the structure of the diving stage itself is a visual impediment to the diver, blocking the view of the locality in which he or she intends to land. Once more, the teacher must instil into every diver the importance of making sure the area of water directly below is completely free of swimmers, and is likely to remain so throughout the period of the dive. A good rule is to insist that divers swim away from the immediate vicinity of the stages as soon as they surface.

4. One of the important features about diving for the teacher (and in turn the divers themselves) to realise is that any rotation during the flight must be generated during take-off.

In order to define rotation in simple terms, if our diver leaves the take-off position from a standing position and enters the water head-first, he has rotated 180°. So, within the terms of safety, it must be understood that if the diver is to stand a chance of entering the water in some certain pre-determined attitude, i.e. head-first or feet-first, the decision must be made and the necessary physical adjustments carried out *before* he leaves the take-off point. This feature is just as important to the young beginner carrying out the sitting dive as it is to the more adept performer using the springboard or platform. (The mechanics of rotation are covered later in this chapter.)

During the flight through the air
Once the diver has left the side of the pool, the springboard or platform, the pattern of the line of flight through the air *cannot be changed*. This is

not to say that his body attitude cannot be altered, indeed he is able to tuck or pike or twist in the air. This fact may be difficult for beginners to understand, but the teacher should insist that if they start off right they stand a good chance of finishing right, despite what may happen in between.

Entry into the water should be clean and, according to water depth, at the correct pre-determined angle. If rotation has been too severe, the diver may 'go over', risking back injury in the process. (The theory of entry angles and 'going over' is examined later.) Maintaining the arms fully stretched with hands clasped is standard practice. (In the section on 'definitions' the reasoning behind this is illustrated.) The general aesthetic quality of the flight may well be enhanced by the physique of the diver himself. The ability to arch the back and hyper-extend the knees and ankles is indeed a most valuable asset in competition. It may be prudent to mention at this stage that to *enter* the water with an arched back is dangerous. When the arms, head and shoulders strike the water, they tend to begin slowing the diver down. However, the remainder of the body, that is the trunk and legs, just keep on going and something has to give way. If the diver is straight and stretched, the water yields and the impact is absorbed by the shock-proof qualities of the human frame. But if his back is arched, the strain of the momentum-generated lower body is transferred to the vertebrae (spinal column) which at the very least can prove to be extremely painful.

Following the dive
A head-first dive is deemed to have been completed when the toes have disappeared below the water surface.

If the entry angle is shallow the resulting glide is also shallow, and by suitably manoeuvring the hands or head, the diver may re-surface with little effort. Should the entry be a clean and steep one, the diver will plunge towards the bottom of the pool. As he does so he must take care to ensure that the direction of travel is not changed drastically by elevating the hands or head too soon. Such action may well result in the same back-rending effects as described earlier.

Providing the choice of water depth has been a sensible one, the diver should continue to the bottom of the pool where, by a suitable man-oeuvre, he may push off to surface once more. Alternatively, should the dive be a shallow one from the bathside or a low platform, a hand- or head-directed glide to the surface may be effected.

THE SHALLOW-WATER PRACTICES
There are many things a diver may learn in shallow water before attempting to enter head-first from the poolside. The first and most obvious is that of becoming accustomed to being under water. Being aware of the

immediate underwater surroundings is another useful acquisite for the diver. Therefore, a few short submersive interludes of opening the eyes will be found to be most valuable. The head-first entry necessitates being inverted or upsidedown. In order to adjust to this position in the water, a few handstand exercises are of great value.

The following poolside practices each terminate with a glide under the water surface. In order to control the direction of movement during the glide, the hands or head may be used as an elevator. Pushing and gliding from the poolside above and below the surface enables divers to practise the skill of manoeuvring in the safety of shallow water. There are other tricks to be tried and all are designed to prepare the prospective divers for their first poolside entry.

One important point for the teacher to remember is that diving from the water back into the water is safer than plunging in from the poolside. Therefore, besides acclimatising the divers to the underwater situation in which they will soon find themselves, the risk of injury by impact with the water is eliminated.

These practices may take place in water that is approximately chest-deep. The pupils should be able to regain the standing position from both a front- and back-lay position.

The first exercises are designed to accustom the pupils to being totally submerged. Similar exercises may have been carried out earlier in the syllabus of work. If this is so, the exercises may serve as a refresher.

1. Immersion while holding the poolside rail (fig. 27.2)
2. Free immersion (fig. 27.3)

Fig. 27.2

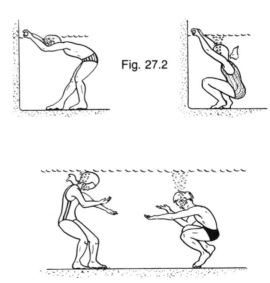

Fig. 27.3

3. Retrieving objects from the bottom of the pool (fig. 27.4). The purpose of this exercise is to encourage prospective divers to open their eyes
under water, mainly for orientation purposes.

The deeper the water, the more difficult is the task of getting down
to the bottom of the pool, because of the natural buoyancy characteristics
of the human body. The illustrations show that where the water depth is
greatest, the swimmer finds that she has to jump up from the bottom of

Fig. 27.4

the pool in order to gain some downward momentum on re-entry, then
swim down to the object. As the water becomes deeper than the
shoulder-depth shown, the swimmer will probably need to use a surface
dive in order to retrieve the sunken object.

4. Tucking, stretching and standing (fig. 27.5)

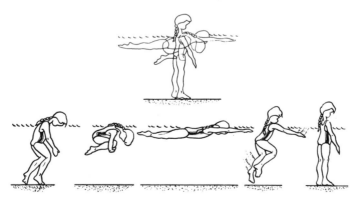

Fig. 27.5

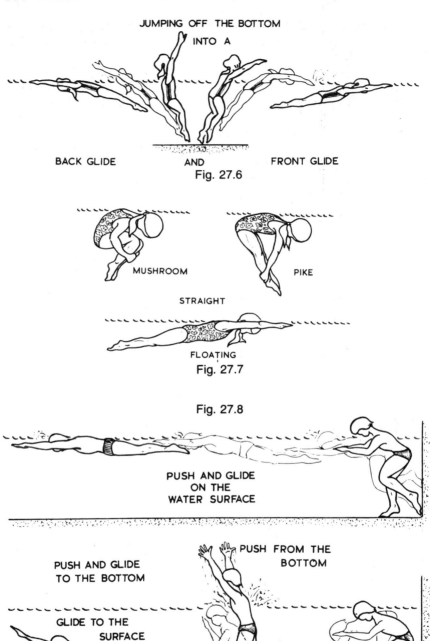

JUMPING OFF THE BOTTOM
INTO A

BACK GLIDE   AND   FRONT GLIDE

Fig. 27.6

MUSHROOM   PIKE

STRAIGHT

FLOATING

Fig. 27.7

Fig. 27.8

PUSH AND GLIDE
ON THE
WATER SURFACE

PUSH AND GLIDE
TO THE BOTTOM

PUSH FROM THE
BOTTOM

GLIDE TO THE
SURFACE

5. Jumping off the bottom into a back and front glide (fig. 27.6)
6. Assuming the three basic dive positions by face-down floating (fig. 27.7)
7. The push and glide (fig. 27.8). Here once again is one of the standard exercises which are used in both swimming and diving. The methods of pushing off and gliding, together with the use of the hands and the head in re-surfacing, have been fully covered in chapters 11 and 14. They are included here as revision exercises related to the forthcoming skills and practices. The push-off itself is of minor importance, being merely a means of developing the necessary glide momentum.
8. Pushing away from the side into a handstand (fig. 27.9)
9. Handstand from a surface dive (fig. 27.10)

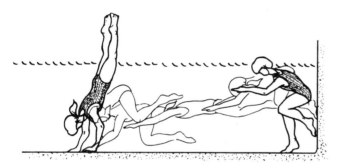

Fig. 27.9 Pushing away from
the side into a handstand

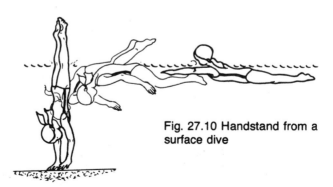

Fig. 27.10 Handstand from a
surface dive

10. Diving from a semi-crouch position in the water (fig. 27.11)

FRONT SOMERSAULT

HANDSTAND

FROM A
SEMI-CROUCH
POSITION

INTO A......

....THEN GLIDE TO
THE SURFACE

GLIDE TO THE
BOTTOM....

OR...... JUMP UP

Fig. 27.11

HEAD-FIRST ENTRY FROM THE POOLSIDE

The following descriptions cover some of the many diving activities which may be used to form the basis of an elementary diving syllabus. The shallow-water practices should have prepared the swimmers for the kind of experiences they will meet when they perform an entry into the water from the poolside. The sequence of diving exercises is progressive: they gradually increase in terms of difficulty.

The illustrations are designed to show the teacher how the pupils should position themselves at the start of a dive. The series of figure drawings show approximately the sequence of continuous movements that take place during the take-off, flight, entry and glide.

The features of each of the dives are discussed and the overall movement is then analysed as follows:

1. Starting position
2. Take-off
3. Flight through the air
4. Entry into the water
5. Underwater glide

Following the description of the actual movements, the safe minimum water-depth requirements are given.

Theoretically, there are two possible spheres of underwater activity which have been designated respectively the safe or 'desired glide area' and the 'error margin'. The diver's ideal underwater glide path lies within the imaginary boundaries of the desired glide area. If the performer stays within these boundaries during the underwater glide, the movement should be a safe one. The error margin is a proportion of the minimum safe water depth and lies below the desired glide area. This extra depth of water *must* be allowed in case the diver makes an error in judgement during the early part of the dive and plunges too deeply into the water. In this error margin, the diver is still able to avoid collision with the bottom of the pool.

The main teaching points of each dive are given briefly and may be linked with any descriptive notes the teacher requires during actual teaching or during the course of examinations. Finally, diving faults are described and analysed and corrective measures are suggested.

The reader should understand that certain faults and corrections are common in many dives and, in certain instances, a particular fault and appropriate correction(s) may apply for several different dives.

The minimum safe water depth in each dive sequence has been related to the actual performer's height. It may easily be seen that a child 3 ft (900 mm) tall will be able to negotiate a safe head-first 'sitting' entry into 3 ft of water, whereas an inexperienced child 5 ft (1500 mm) tall will probably collide with the floor of the pool in the same depth of water. It is worth remembering also that the springs require more water depth than the falls.

The minimum safe water depths have been determined experimentally, and it was found to be desirable that the error margin is *at least equal to one quarter* of the desired or estimated glide depth. This allows for errors in performance together with any physical features, such as extra body weight and long arms, which are not immediately evident to the teacher. In practice, the tallest and heaviest members of the class would take up positions in the deeper water, while the smaller ones would range along the poolside where the water is relatively shallow. If all divers are entering from the same spot, the depth should be chosen to accommodate the tallest and heaviest individual.

Where it is obvious that a pupil is failing to interpret the correct requirements of a dive, the teacher should return to some earlier related practice which the pupil is able to perform with reasonable skill. The pupil may then concentrate on the weak point, without having to pay much attention to other parts of the skill in which he or she is already proficient. It is in this way that the transfer of skill from one movement to the next becomes evident.

Even when the performance of a particular entry looks reasonable, it is usually wise to repeat the movement several times in order to establish the skill in the minds of the pupils.

It is helpful, during the initial stages of teaching the bathside practices, for towels to be draped over the poolside. The pupils may then position themselves for take-off on a towel and thus reduce the risk of slipping. This is an interim measure only and may be dispensed with as the divers become more proficient.

Divers should not wear goggles during the poolside practices (or indeed during the shallow-water practices). The force of the water on the face at entry (and push-off) is liable to rip the goggles off, causing injury to the face and eyes.

If bathing caps are not worn, long hair should be tied back. This avoids the problems of strands obscuring the diver's view or getting into her (or his) mouth.

Secure swimwear is essential during these high-speed movements. A loose pair of trunks or insecure shoulder strap can cause loss of concentration (and dignity) on the part of the diver. There is also the danger of loose straps getting tangled up, thus impairing limb movement.

Divers should be confident swimmers in deep water. It is one thing to negotiate a safe entry into the water, but quite another to reach the poolside safely once more.

Performing the glide at the end of the movement has been included as an integral part of the overall activity. A glide may only be performed if the swimmer is actually moving at speed through the water. The diver develops this movement as a result of falling from a height into the water. Being able skilfully to utilise the developed momentum is not only energy-conserving but also ensures an effortless and safe journey to the water surface once more.

Jumping off from the bottom of the pool in order to reach the water surface has been practised during the shallow-water exercises. This movement will become necessary and is indeed very useful should contact with the pool floor be made after a dive.

When the earlier poolside practices are carried out, the more fearful pupils may find a little consolation if an able colleague stands in the water near to where they perform their dive. Being able to hang on to 'something solid' on re-surfacing relieves the natural anxiety which may exist during these initial falls and dives.

The teacher should keep a careful watch at all times when diving pupils are submerged, especially during the early entries when they are unfamiliar with the required skills.

A series of aquabatics following the poolside exercises includes a few of the skills that are necessary before the divers proceed to the more complicated movements from the springboard and highboard.

THE POOLSIDE PRACTICES

An attempt has been made in this text to distinguish between the various entries from the poolside by naming them 'falls', 'dives' and 'springs', although *all* head-first entries are generally denoted dives.

The entries are not described in any significant order and the teacher should arrange the programme according to the situation, i.e. numbers and ages of the pupils, depth of the pool, abilities of the divers, etc. Some entries may even be omitted completely if desirable, providing the general teaching progression is maintained.

Falls
The diver overbalances into the water mainly as a rotating movement and simply falls into the water. The preparatory arm-and-head positions, together with a gentle extension of the trunk and legs during the fall, serve to create a gentle entry, almost as though the diver is 'pouring' himself into the water. The preparatory arm position for a fall is with the stretched arms and clasped hands pointing directly at the intended entry spot.

Dives
The diving movements take place with an extension of the legs which should send the diver outwards and away from the take-off point. The outstretched arms and clasped hands should once more 'spot' the point of entry during the preparatory stance.

Springs
These are movements which tend to highlight the flight through the air. The diver should attempt to spring *upwards* and *outwards* into a gentle curve, before entering the water in a clean head-first mode. The arms should initially be pointed upwards, approximately in the direction of the arc of flight. The diver's stretched and arched body should attempt to follow continuously through the line of flight as though passing through an imaginary curved tube which ends in the water. As already stated, the feature of the spring is to gain height, therefore the aim of the diver should be to direct the take-off thrust more upwards than outwards.

Sitting take-offs, falls and springs
Bunched sitting fall (fig. 27.12)
This may be performed from the poolside, although if suitable steps are available, an entry may be carried out from this slightly lower take-off point. It is usually the first of the bathside practices, and is a logical progression from the shallow-water practices.

The main feature of the activity is that it is a fall rather than a spring. This means that the diver falls forward, while gently unrolling from the bunched starting position. She then heads straight towards the water, rather than traversing up and out before entry as in the springing dives.

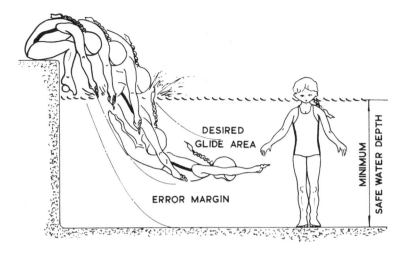

Fig. 27.12 Bunched sitting fall

The bunched starting position enables the diver to start off as near to the water surface as possible: this should eliminate some of the fears and uncertainties that may be present.

A poolside rail or trough is really essential for the performance of the dive. Where these do not exist, placing the feet flat on the wall at the start can sometimes produce good results. However, this starting position requires a little more skill than most beginners possess, and it may be expedient, should a good foot-hold not exist, to miss the sitting activities and move straight to the kneeling dives.

STARTING POSITION The diver sits on the poolside, well back from the edge, with both feet on the rail or trough. The feet should be together or almost together, and a firm foot-hold should be established. When the movement is to be performed where no foot-hold is available, the diver will need to sit well forward in order that the feet may be placed flat on the wall for take-off. Timid pupils will also prefer to sit forward towards the edge of the pool. The bathside activities may start from here, should the teacher consider it to be necessary.

The diver should bend forward so that the chest is in contact with the upper legs, thus establishing the bunched attitude.

The arms should be stretched and pointing down at the water surface, forming an angle of approximately sixty degrees with it. Both hands should be clasped together as shown in fig. 27.38. The head should be tucked well down between the upper arms, with the biceps covering the ears.

TAKE-OFF, FLIGHT AND ENTRY The diver falls forward using the foot-hold as a pivot (which is why the performance of the movement becomes difficult when there is no foot-hold available).

Although desirable, full extension of the legs rarely takes place to begin with, the divers tending to give the impression of 'pouring' themselves in to the water with little splash, providing the head is kept down between the arms. With practice, however, the pupils will improve their performances and the teacher should encourage them to push a little more vigorously away from the side, thus enabling them to enter the water cleanly but further away from the take-off point.

A controlled underwater glide to the surface should be the ultimate aim, though initially the pupils may tend to struggle to the surface gasping for air: this is to be expected. The shallow-water teaching practice of breathing out through the nose on surfacing should be repeated until the action becomes automatic.

MINIMUM SAFE WATER DEPTH This is the first of the bathside practices and consequently it is unwise to move away from a depth of water where the prospective divers can easily regain their feet after the dive. On the other hand, some performers do tend to plunge a little too deeply at first, therefore the recommended minimum safe water depth is approximately chin-depth.

TEACHING POINTS

1. Head down between the arms throughout the dive.

2. Arms to remain outstretched with hands clasped together.

3. Encourage gliding rather than swimming to the surface.

4. Start the dive with the hands pointing directly at the intended entry spot.

5. Sit well back from the poolside.

6. Breathe out through the nose on surfacing.

7. Encourage the divers to open their eyes under water.

FAULTS AND THEIR CORRECTION

FAULT	FAULT ANALYSIS	CORRECTION
Flopping	The diver, usually through fear, raises her head. This in turn elevates the chest and the result is a 'belly flop'	The head *must* be kept well down between the arms throughout the dive

| Landing in the water feet-first | Once more, this fault usually results from a fear of putting the head down, coupled with an upward and outward spring. The arms often point upwards or outwards instead of at the water | Again, the head must be kept down between the arms which in turn must remain pointing at the water. The dive is not a spring but a fall; consequently, the diver should unroll herself, endeavouring to fall neatly head-first into the water |

High sitting fall (fig. 27.13)
This is a continuation of the previously described bunched sitting fall practices and is performed from the poolside. The diver merely assumes a more upright starting position and enters the water a little further away from the wall. The overall mechanics of the movement are very similar.

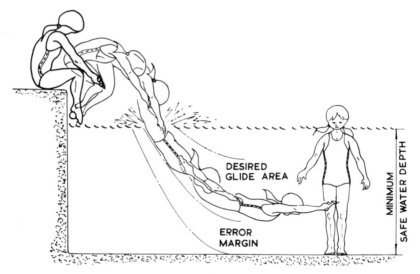

Fig. 27.13 High sitting fall

STARTING POSITION The diver sits well back on the poolside, with both feet on the rail or trough. The feet should be together or almost together in order to avoid slipping on take-off. The arms should be straight, with hands clasped, and pointing towards the intended point of entry. The head should be positioned in such a way that the eyes focus comfortably on the entry spot.

TAKE-OFF, ENTRY AND GLIDE In order to take off, the diver should lean forward and pivot about the foot support. The head should be tucked down between the outstretched arms and the body should open out slightly just before and during entry into the water. Comparing the entry point with the last exercise, the distance away from the poolside should be slightly greater. The angle of entry, however, should be very similar. Once more, the diver should try to carry out a glide in order to re-surface.

MINIMUM SAFE WATER DEPTH The minimum safe water depth will be approximately chin-depth as before.

TEACHING POINTS
1. Sitting well back before starting the dive will assist in making the fall just a little higher.

2. Firm positioning of the feet.

3. Arms and eyes 'spotting' the intended point of entry before taking off.

4. Hands clasped together and head tucked well down between the upper arms at entry; the arms should remain fully outstretched throughout.

5. The diver should endeavour to enter cleanly and produce a glide to the surface.

6. Breathing out through the nose as surfacing takes place.

The faults and their correction are as described for the bunched fall.

Sitting spring (fig. 27.14)
The aim of the movement is for the prospective diver to establish, from the sitting position on the poolside, more of an upward and outward movement rather than in the previously attempted falls. A springing take-off achieves this.

STARTING POSITION The diver sits upright and well back from the edge of the pool, with feet resting on the rail or trough a short distance apart. The arms should be fully stretched above the head with hands clasped together. The head should be positioned in such a way that the diver is looking straight forward or perhaps slightly downwards towards the water surface. In this attitude the upper arms will cover the ears.

TAKE-OFF, FLIGHT, ENTRY AND GLIDE The diver bends forward in order to initiate the take-off and, as she does so, her legs are straightened, thus lifting her hips. Her arms and head should remain in the same relative position as before take-off commenced.

    The proportions of the arc of flight will vary according to the amount of spring that is developed during take-off, and the more upward and

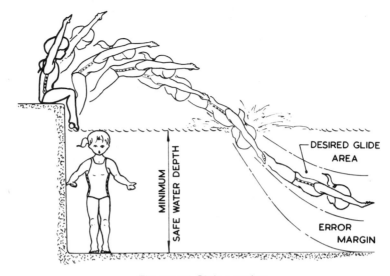

Fig. 27.14 Sitting spring

effective the spring becomes, the steeper will become the angle of entry. In this early dive, it is best to limit this angle to forty-five degrees in order to avoid too steep a glide and collision with the bottom of the pool. (Remember, this is only a bathside sitting practice and the pupils should feel safe at the pre-determined water depth.)

The diver should attempt to enter the water cleanly, finger tips-first and with a slight hip bend. During the movement through the air, the diver should follow the arc of flight as though passing through a curved tube into the water.

The stretched position should be maintained after the diver has fully entered the water, with the previously learnt techniques of surfacing being brought into action.

MINIMUM SAFE WATER DEPTH The minimum safe water depth should be approximately equal to the height of the diver.

TEACHING POINTS

1. Sitting well back to begin with.

2. Firm positioning of the feet in order to avoid slipping at take-off.

3. Forward and slightly downward starting position, with arms stretched upwards and hands clasped together at the start.

4. A definite upward spring, accompanied by a slight hip bend to assist in making a clean entry.

5. Head kept down between the arms.

6. Not more than a forty-five degree entry.

7. Glide to the surface using the nasal breathing-out techniques as previously described.

FAULTS AND THEIR CORRECTION

FAULT	FAULT ANALYSIS	CORRECTION
Flopping	The dive becomes a fall rather than a spring. It is more than likely that the diver's head position is one of the root causes	The spring take-off must be emphasised maintaining a head-down/arm-stretched attitude throughout the dive
Feet entering first	The diver fails to achieve the flight arc and falls feet-first into the water	The springing take-off and hip-bend attitude should be emphasised. The head should be kept well down. The diver should attempt to 'spot' the entry point before take-off then direct the arms at it during flight
Bending the legs on entry	The legs fold up on entry	The diver should attempt to stiffen and lock the legs straight immediately after take-off

Kneeling and squatting dives

Moving on from the sitting dives, our intrepid performers may now attempt to dive into the water using the poolside instead of the rail or trough as a take-off point. The following dives are classed as 'one-foot take-off' movements, with the diver systematically raising herself a little higher for each of the progressions. They form useful intermediate practices between the sitting and two-foot standing take-offs.

Kneeling dive (fig. 27.15)

As already mentioned, the take-off movement is initiated by one leg. The starting position is a balanced one and the diver is as close to the water surface as she can get without actually sitting on the poolside. Extension of the pushing-off leg during take-off will enable the diver to enter the water a little further away from the edge of the pool than if the movement were a fall. The resulting appearance of the movement will be something between a fall and a double-foot take-off spring.

STARTING POSITION The diver should kneel on one knee near the edge of the pool. The other leg should be positioned in such a way as to afford a firm curled-toe grip over the poolside. If a 'knee-adjacent-to-foot and spread-slightly-apart stance' is adopted, the diver should feel comfor-

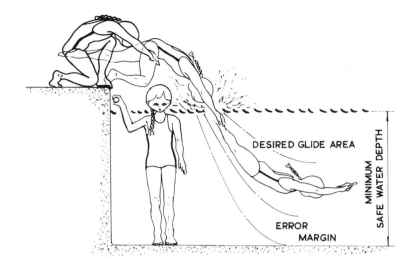

Fig. 27.15 Kneeling dive

tably balanced. The body should be bent forward so that the outstretched arms, with hands clasped, are pointed down at the intended point of entry. The degree of forward bend should be such that the position of the diver's armpit is adjacent to the knee of the take-off leg. (Figure 30.15 shows this as the left leg and armpit.) The head should be tucked well down between the outstretched arms which should cover the ears.

TAKE-OFF FLIGHT, ENTRY AND GLIDE The take-off is effected by the diver leaning forward to over-balance. The head is kept well down between the outstretched arms, and as pivoting takes place about the contact foot, the take-off leg is extended. The rate of leg extension may be increased over several performances of the dive in order to project the diver slightly further away from the point of take-off.

Bearing in mind that the take-off is at 'half-power', the effectiveness of the single-leg push will be limited.

The backward-placed foot should retain its contact with the poolside during the early part of the take-off movement. Then, as the diver's body passes beyond the support foot, the trailing leg should extend out behind, thus aiding the diver to affect a clean and stretched entry. There should be no reliance placed on the trailing foot to assist the take-off, owing to the risk of the diver slipping on the wet poolside.

Entry into the water should be fairly shallow, the maximum angle to aim for being forty-five degrees. A glide should then take place and the diver should use the techniques of surfacing and breath control that have previously been practised.

MINIMUM SAFE WATER DEPTH Any divers who appear rather timid while attempting this first movement from the poolside may tend to fall steeply rather than dive outwards to culminate in a shallow glide to re-surface. It is therefore wise for the teacher to arrange for the water depth to reach the diver's chin at least. Increasing the depth will, of course, depend on the individual diver's confidence and watermanship.

TEACHING POINTS

1. A well-balanced knee-to-foot starting position with the toes of the take-off foot curled over the poolside.

2. Head well down between the arms throughout the dive.

3. Arms fully stretched, hands clasped throughout the movement to re-surfacing.

4. A 'half-power' spring outwards should be attempted.

5. A clean entry should result from the slight spring outwards, with both legs finally stretching and coming together as they disappear below the surface.

6. The angle of entry should be between thirty and forty-five degrees. This will result in a shallow glide, providing the diver remains stretched. The glide should be extended at least until the diver's hands reach the surface.

7. Direction of underwater movement should be controlled by the diver's hands and/or head.

8. Breath control throughout the dive must be emphasised, especially at the moment of lifting the face from the water.

FAULTS AND THEIR CORRECTION

FAULT	FAULT ANALYSIS	CORRECTION
Falling over on the poolside	The diver finds difficulty in balancing on the poolside at the start of the dive	The knee-to-foot position, with a slight spread between the two, should be assumed. This provides a good base on which the diver is able to stabilise herself
Flopping	Head-up fall into the water	Emphasis on a head-down-between-the-arms mode coupled with extension of the support leg
Entering at too shallow an angle	The fault should not be confused with flopping. Leg extension is present, but the diver enters with a large splash	Most probably, the diver enters with head held high, therefore highlight the importance of keeping the head down, spotting the entry with the outstretched arms

Squat fall (fig. 27.16)
This is the first of the two-foot take-offs from the poolside. The toe-to-heel foot position is adopted in order that the diver is able to balance more easily in the starting position. This compares with the relatively unstable full crouch attitude, where the feet are in line with each other. The height of the diver's head above the water is slightly greater than in the kneeling dive.

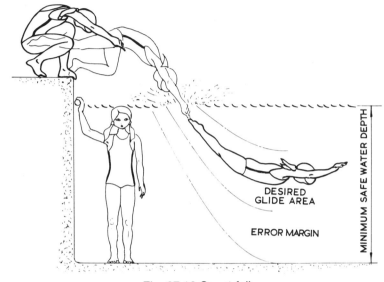

Fig. 27.16 Squat fall

STARTING POSITION The diver takes up the squat position with one foot forward. The toes of this leading foot should be curled over the side, providing a firm grip. The other foot should be placed so that the toes are level with or just behind the heel of the leading foot. A slight sideways gap between the feet also aids the diver's stability. The body should be bent forward towards the water with head tucked down between the upper arms. The hands should be clasped together and the outstretched arms should point directly at the intended point of entry.

TAKE-OFF, FLIGHT, ENTRY AND GLIDE The diver overbalances into the water by leaning further forward; at the same time both body and legs should gently extend so that she assumes a reasonably stretched mode as entry takes place. The take-off thrust should be concentrated at the leading foot. An angle of approximately forty-five degrees to the water surface should be aimed for.

The arms must remain outstretched with hands clasped and the head must be kept tucked well down between the arms. The diver should endeavour to bring her legs together in an athletically stretched and straight fashion as they disappear below the surface. She should attempt to glide to the surface once more by suitably manoeuvring her hands and/or head. Breathing out through the nose as the face leaves the water should be an integral part of the whole pattern of movement.

MINIMUM SAFE WATER DEPTH Although the movement is a fall, the diver is able to develop a little more height than before due to the two-footed stance. Consequently, the water depth is increased slightly to that of the diver's normal standing height.

TEACHING POINTS

1. A steady and balanced take-off position.

2. Arms fully stretched and pointing at the intended point of entry, hands clasped.

3. Head tucked well down at the start and on throughout the dive.

4. Extension of the legs and feet, in order to create a clean and aesthetic entry.

5. A forty-five-degree entry should be aimed for.

6. The glide should be a controlled one in order to bring the diver once more to the surface.

7. Breath control should be practised.

FAULTS AND THEIR CORRECTION

FAULT	FAULT ANALYSIS	CORRECTION
Flopping	Flopping uncontrollably into the water with no outward movement in evidence, often with the head: probably due to fear of falling into the water	The head must be tucked down between the arms, the take-off leg should be extended, the arms should point towards the intended entry point
Excessively bending the legs at entry	The legs are not stretched and impact with the water has the effect of snapping the lower legs into a knee-bend position	The diver should concentrate on extending the legs and keeping them stretched throughout

Landing feet-first in the water	The diver seems to stall in mid-air, then land ungracefully feet-first and rather flat in the water	The stretched arms must initially be pointed towards the water. The diver should then endeavour to follow in this same direction, thus performing a continuous arc of flight and entry

Squat spring (fig. 27.17)
This is a more adventurous and exacting variation of the last movement. The upward and outward spring is created by thrust from both feet rather than the limited 'half-power' take-off of the squat fall. Entry is steeper, resulting from the higher arc of flight.

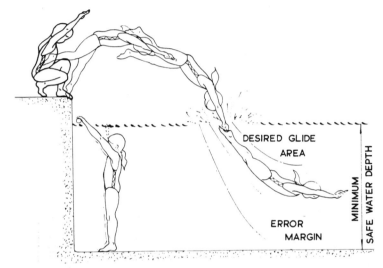

Fig. 27.17 Squat spring

STARTING POSITION The diver takes up the squat on the edge of the pool. One foot is forward with toes curled over the poolside and the other is placed slightly behind the heel of this leading foot. In order to maintain balance, the rear foot may have to be placed a little further back than for the fall. This is because the diver's stance is more upright, thus moving the body centre of gravity further back. Slight sideways spacing of the feet also enhances this balance position. The diver should lean slightly forward, with the angle of inclination to the vertical being between thirty and forty-five degrees.

Hands should be clasped together, with the arms fully stretched and pointing upwards in line with the body. The head should be upright, with the upper arms covering the ears. The diver should be looking forward and down at the intended point of entry.

TAKE-OFF, FLIGHT, ENTRY AND GLIDE By leaning forward, the diver unbalances. At the same time, the legs are extended to direct her upwards and outwards into an arc-like movement. During the movement through the air, the diver's body should assume a similar contour to that of the arc of flight. This gives the effect of her sliding around an imaginary curved shape.

The entry angle into the water should be approximately forty-five degrees, by which time the diver's legs should be fully stretched and together. Throughout the whole movement, the diver's arms should remain fully stretched and the head should continue to be tucked in between them. The hands should remain clasped together.

The movement should end in a glide, with the diver bringing herself to the surface.

MINIMUM SAFE WATER DEPTH The movement is a springing one whereby the diver visibly rises above the take-off point. This being so, the minimum safe water depth is slightly more than the diver's normal height.

TEACHING POINTS

1. A balanced starting position with feet comfortably placed on the poolside; the toes of the forward foot should be curled around the edge of the pool.

2. A fairly upright pose to begin with, arms stretching upward in a continuing line with the back, hands clasped together.

3. Head positioned so that the diver is looking forward and downward at the intended point of entry; upper arms cover the ears.

4. Take-off should be upwards and outwards in a clean arc. Entry should be at approximately forty-five degrees with the diver stretched and streamlined and with feet together.

5. A controlled glide to the surface.

FAULTS AND THEIR CORRECTION

FAULT	FAULT ANALYSIS	CORRECTION
Over-balancing at take-off	The diver is not steadily poised and attempts the dive before she is balanced	Attention to the position of the feet, ensuring that a firm foundation is established
Slipping at take-off	The diver's foot slips along the edge of the pool, causing a badly extended movement	Once again, the feet must be correctly positioned. The diver must not apply any sideways force to the leading foot. A steady and stabilised starting position must be created before take-off – a towel draped over the poolside may be used as an interim measure

Feet-first entry	The diver gives the appearance of performing a stall, falling back into the water without completing the arc of flight	Fear may be a cause here. If so, return to the fall or the sitting practices. The take-off angle may be too steep in relation to the force exerted by the diver's legs. If this is so, reduce the angle and increase the strength of the take-off
Too flat or too steep an entry	The diver may land flat in the water or enter too steeply	In both cases, attention must be centred on he angle of take-off and the consequent arc of flight. Once the diver leaves the poolside, the flight path is determined and cannot be changed

Lunge dive (fig. 27.18)

This is a dive which is a natural follow-on from the squat spring. The take-off is a standing one-foot affair, and the performer may be encouraged to streamline a previously faulty flight and entry by the teacher lightly guiding (not lifting) the front side of the diver's trailing leg as she takes off.

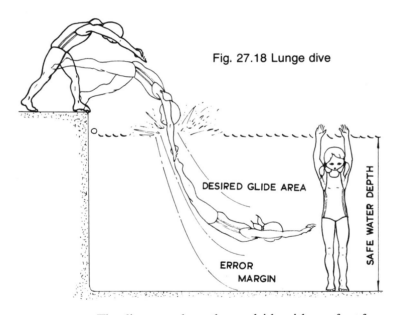

Fig. 27.18 Lunge dive

DESIRED GLIDE AREA

ERROR MARGIN

SAFE WATER DEPTH

STARTING POSITION The diver stands on the poolside with one foot forward, and slightly bent at the knee. The toes of this leading foot should be curled over the edge in order to afford a firm take-off. The trailing leg should also be slightly bent and its foot placed on the pool surround approximately 600 mm (2 ft) behind the leading foot. There should be a slight sideways spacing of the feet in order that the diver's poolside poise is a balanced one.

The diver's body should be inclined forward towards the water and the outstretched arms, with hands clasped, should be pointing towards the intended point of entry. The head should be tucked down between the upper arms with the eyes comfortably viewing the water-entry spot.

TAKE-OFF, FLIGHT, ENTRY AND GLIDE The diver leans forward over the leading foot and at the same time lifts the trailing leg in order to overbalance into the water. It is important that the take-off leg does not collapse. During the movement through the air, the diver raises the take-off leg to position it beside the trailing leg. The take-off movement must be smooth and continuous. The trailing leg must straighten out during its lift and, together with the leading leg, should assume and maintain a stretched mode until finally disappearing below the water surface.

The entry should take place at approximately forty-five degrees to the water surface. The arms must remain outstretched and the head tucked in between the biceps throughout the dive.

As previously mentioned, the lunge dive may be found useful in rectifying faults in take-off. This applies to some of the other standing dives where, for instance, a performer is failing to carry out the required upward and outward arc of flight. The teacher, by standing on the trailing-leg side of the diver, may lightly place the palm of his hand somewhere above the pupil's knee. Then, as the diver takes off, the teacher's hand guides the trailing leg upwards. This guidance must be applied *very gently* and there must be no attempt to lift the diver's leg into the air.

The diver should attempt to glide to the surface.

MINIMUM SAFE WATER DEPTH If the movement is performed correctly, the entry may be of a relatively steep nature. It is therefore expedient to carry out the dive in a water depth at least equal to the approximate height of the diver's upward-stretched hands.

TEACHING POINTS

1. Steady and balanced starting position as in fig. 27.18.

2. Toes of the forward foot firmly curled over the poolside.

3. Hands clasped together – arms outstretched, pointing towards intended point of entry.

4. Head tucked in between the hands, eyes looking towards the water.

5. Smooth take-off with the stretched rear leg lifting initially, to be joined by the take-off leg before final entry into the water.

6. Entry between thirty and forty-five degrees to the water surface.

7. A controlled glide to re-surface.

FAULTS AND THEIR CORRECTION

FAULT	FAULT ANALYSIS	CORRECTION
Toppling	The diver topples over sideways on or before take-off	This is probably due to there being insufficient sideways spacing of the feet, or too much backward spacing of the rear foot. Attention to starting poise is needed, bearing in mind the correct positioning of the feet
Low arc of flight and flat entry	The diver's take-off leg tends to collapse and the diving movement is relegated to that of a fall. The dive itself may be used as a 'corrective movement' in other standing poolside dives where the fault is collapsing into the water	The teacher should use the gently applied leg-lifting technique. This should enhance the diver's arc of flight and consequent entry
Bending the legs at entry	The diver 'back kicks' with one or both legs on entry	Emphasis must be made on a fully stretched and streamlined attitude as the diver performs the entry

Standing falls

These are also performed from the poolside.

Low crouch fall (fig. 27.19)

The low crouch fall may be interpreted as the starter for the standing dives. As the name suggests, it is a falling rather than a spring dive. The main features are the ability to keep the head well down between the upper arms at entry, together with terminating the take-off with a gentle push from the side of the pool in order to create a slicing entry rather than a flop.

STARTING POSITION This may be loosely described as a 'bottoms-up low crouch'. The feet should be together, with the toes gripping the edge of the pool and the heels down. The knees are slightly bent and the hips flexed so that the diver is bending forward over the edge of the pool with his bottom high. The head should be lower than his hips if possible and

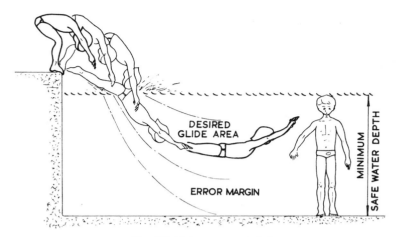

Fig. 27.19 Low crouch fall

tucked down so that the ears are covered by the upper arms. In this head-down position, the diver should be able to raise his eyes to glance towards the intended point of entry. The hands should be clasped together and the stretched arms should also be directed towards the intended point of water entry. The diver must be completely balanced, with his centre of gravity positioned approximately mid-way between the heels and the balls of the feet.

TAKE-OFF AND FLIGHT The diver leans forward to over-balance into the water. The legs should be gently extended to push him away from the side. The arms must remain extended, with the head tucked well down.

ENTRY Entry into the water must be finger tips-first. It is essential at this stage that the head is maintained in its lowered attitude in order to prevent a flop occurring. The push-away from the side, being a gentle outwards one, should ensure that the diver enters the water at not too steep an angle.

MINIMUM SAFE WATER DEPTH The dive, being a low fall without a great deal of gravitational momentum, results in a relatively shallow glide. Therefore, the minimum water depth should be approximately equal to the diver's own height.

FAULTS AND THEIR CORRECTION

FAULT	FAULT ANALYSIS	CORRECTION
Flopping into the water	Probably through fear (this is the first of the standing dives), the diver fails to extend his legs. The head may also be raised subconsciously to avoid a collision with the water	More vigorous extension of the legs, together with keeping the head tucked well down between the arms: gentle persuasion may be necessary here

Semi-crouch dive (fig. 27.20)

The movement is a progression which may follow on from the crouch fall or the lunge dive. The diver's starting position is slightly more upright and, while the outstretched arms are still pointing at the intended point of entry (as opposed to being directed upwards), a slight forward spring occurs at take-off. The diver enters the water a little further away from the poolside than he does in the crouch fall and the resulting glide path is shallower.

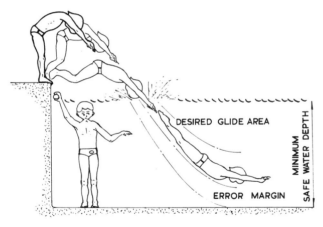

Fig. 27.20 Semi-crouch dive

STARTING POSITION The feet may be together or slightly apart. The heels should be flat on the poolside and the toes curled over the edge. The diver takes up the semi-crouch position with a very slight bending of the knees and his trunk inclined forward at approximately forty-five degrees. The arms should be outstretched and pointing towards the intended point of entry; the hands should be clasped together. The head is tucked down between the arms with biceps covering the ears. The diver's eyes may be directed forward so that he views the intended entry position. He should be balanced and steady before take-off.

TAKE-OFF AND FLIGHT The diver leans forward to over-balance and slightly bends his knees a little further. The aim of the performer should be to enter the water cleanly and at a shallow angle. Consequently, extension of the legs should be late in the flight, to direct the diver in a shallow arc *outwards* over the water rather than up. The arms must remain outstretched and the head tucked well down between them.

ENTRY AND GLIDE The diver should endeavour to enter the water in a fully stretched mode. His head should be kept buried between his outstretched arms and his ankles fully extended. The angle of entry should be fairly shallow, in the region of thirty degrees to the horizontal.

During the consequent shallow glide the diver should retain his arms in the fully stretched mode in order to guide himself through the water and also prevent injury should a collision occur.

MINIMUM SAFE WATER DEPTH The dive is of a relatively flat nature, therefore the minimum safe water depth should be equivalent to the diver's normal standing height.

TEACHING POINTS

1. Steady stance, toes curled over the edge, heels flat, slight knee bend.

2. Trunk bent forward at approximately thirty degrees to horizontal.

3. Head tucked down between the arms.

4. Hands clasped together, arms stretched forward with upper arms covering the ears and pointing directly at intended entry point.

5. Take-off by further knee bend then outward (rather than upward) spring to straighten the legs before entry.

6. Head remains low throughout flight, entry and the early part of the glide.

7. Entry at approximately thirty degrees to horizontal.

8. Glide position to be maintained – hands and/or head being used as elevators in order to re-surface.

9. Breathe out through nose as the face passes through the water surface.

FAULTS AND THEIR CORRECTION

FAULT	FAULT ANALYSIS	CORRECTION
Flopping	Fear may cause the diver to lift his head. There may also be a lack of extension of the legs	A return to the crouch fall may be necessary if the fault is persistent. Emphasis must be placed on keeping the head down. More extension of the legs may be necessary in order to develop a reasonable flight and entry
Bending the knees on entry, or opening the legs	As the diver hits the water, his knees bend. Similarly, through lack of muscular control, he may open his legs. Fear may be the cause once more	The diver may be told to concentrate his thoughts into extending and maintaining a legs-stretched position immediately after take-off. This form of concentration is very successful
Too deep an entry	The diver's legs collapse and the dive becomes a fall	The outward spring must be emphasised. Aim to enter at a pre-determined point, such as that marked by one of the lines on the pool floor

Pike fall (fig. 27.21)

This dive is an important exercise in a diving syllabus. The piked body position is one of the three basic body positions, and the angle of entry is closely allied to that of the plain header, being near to the vertical. When performed correctly, the dive displays a rather casual appearance, but in reality it requires a fair degree of control in order to produce a clean and aesthetic entry.

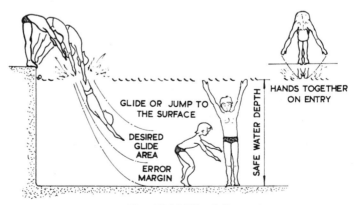

GLIDE OR JUMP TO THE SURFACE

DESIRED GLIDE AREA

ERROR MARGIN

SAFE WATER DEPTH

HANDS TOGETHER ON ENTRY

Fig. 27.21 Pike fall

STARTING POSITION The feet must be together, toes gripping the edge of the pool, heels flat and legs straight. The diver should bend at the hips to pivot the trunk forward and downward so that the head is positioned slightly lower than the hips. The arms should either be spread to form an angle of sixty degrees between them, or when stretched should be pointing directly towards the intended point of entry with hands clasped together. The head should be tucked down between the arms with the biceps covering the ears. The diver should be completely balanced before taking off.

TAKE-OFF AND FLIGHT The diver moves his weight forward to over-balance. The essential feature of the dive is to maintain the legs in their straight and stretched mode throughout. In doing this, the diver eliminates any spring from his legs and the movement becomes simply a rotating one, with the balls of the feet acting as the pivot point. The head remains tucked down between the arms which remain outstretched and directed towards the pre-determined point of entry.

ENTRY The entry of the diver's upper body is near to the vertical. As his hands enter the water, both feet are gently lifted upwards together from the take-off point. The legs remain stretched out straight with the ankles fully extended. The rotation of the legs about the hips should continue as the diver slides cleanly into the water. The arms must remain outstretched during the glide by means of which, with suitable manipulation of the hands, the diver may once more elevate himself to the surface. The outstretched hands also reduce the danger should a collision occur.

MINIMUM SAFE WATER DEPTH The dive is of a vertical nature so the minimum safe water depth should be equivalent to the diver's arm-stretched height.

TEACHING POINTS

1. Feet together, toes curled over the edge, heels flat, legs straight.

2. Head lower than hips to start with.

3. Arms straight, either forming an angle of sixty degrees with each other, hands flat facing downwards; or pointing directly at the intended entry point, hands clasped together.

4. Legs straight throughout dive, ankles extended on entry.

5. No spring from the side.

6. Head held down between the arms throughout.

7. Entry angle biased towards the vertical.

FAULTS AND THEIR CORRECTION

FAULTS	FAULT ANALYSIS	CORRECTION
Flopping into the water	Raising the head, or the legs collapsing at take-off	Keep the head down. Maintain the legs in their straight and stretched mode
Flat entry into the water	Insufficient initial flexing at the hips, raising the head, lifting the arms	The head-lower-than-hips position must be attained at the start of the dive. The stretched arms must remain directed at the original target and the head must remain tucked down between them
Springing, i.e. bending and straightening the knees	Lack of confidence in the ability to perform the movement	A more itemised approach by the teacher is needed, outlining the simplicity of the dive

All the above faults may evolve from a fear of falling and, if the teacher recognises the presence of this anxiety, a return to the springing dives is recommended.

Plunge dive (fig. 27.22)

A short time ago, the plunge was a regular competition event. The competitors, usually mountainous men, plunge dived into the water in order to see how far they could glide in a set time, the furthest plunger receiving the accolade.

Modern-day teaching standards, however, tend to include the plunge dive in the dive progressions and it has become one of the many stepping stones in most educational diving programmes.

The movements are very similar to those of the racing dive, the shallow underwater glide being common to both dives.

It is the first dive in the series in which an arm swing is utilised to assist the diver in projecting himself away from the poolside.

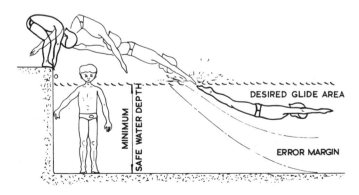

Fig. 27.22 Plunge dive

STARTING POSITION The diver takes up a 'bottoms-up' low crouch on the poolside. His feet should be a short distance apart with the toes of each foot curled over the edge. His arms should hang down so that the hands touch, or almost touch, the edge of the pool just outside each foot. The head should be positioned in such a way that the diver's face is directed comfortably downwards and he is looking at the water below him.

TAKE-OFF AND FLIGHT The diver over-balances towards the water and at the same time swings both arms backwards. As he continues to fall towards the water, his legs vigorously extend and both arms swing sharply forward once more to take up a fully outstretched, thumbs-touching attitude in front of his head.

ENTRY The entry into the water should be a shallow one. The diver's body should be almost fully stretched with just a slight curve in order to achieve a clean and aesthetic movement into the water.

GLIDE The glide is a shallow one and should take place at a depth of approximately 300–450 mm (12–18 in.) below the surface. The diver should remain fully stretched and, as a result of the shallowness of the entry, he should drift to the surface once more without manipulation of either hands or head. However, if the dive is deeper than usual, a slight upward tilting of the hands will ensure that re-surfacing is brought about quite quickly.

MINIMUM SAFE WATER DEPTH The dive is of an outward and relatively flat nature and, if performed correctly, the glide should take place just below the water surface. Consequently, the minimum safe water depth is at approximately chin- or shoulder-height.

TEACHING POINTS
1. Feet slightly apart, toes curled over the edge of the pool.

2. Knees bent, hips bent, body in a 'bottoms-up' crouch.

3. Head down with eyes looking forward and down.

4. Arms lying by the side to start with, then swinging backwards and forwards into a thumbs-touching, fully stretched mode during the flight.

5. Take-off should be vigorous with an energetic leg extension.

6. Direction of flight should be outwards over the water rather than upwards.

7. Entry and glide should be shallow.

FAULTS AND THEIR CORRECTION

FAULT	FAULT ANALYSIS	CORRECTION
Flopping	The diver lands too flat in the water. (This type of entry can be painful and repeated flat entries are usually revealed by 'glowing chests')	The diver's head must be kept low. Extension of the legs may be occurring too late in relation to the diver's take-off. There should be a slight bias towards an initial upward arc of flight
Too steep an entry	The diver's arc of flight is too high. Consequently, the entry is steep and the glide is too deep	Emphasis on the arm swing and leg extension should be made, together with the synchronisation of the two movements. The direction of travel should be more outward than upward

Standing springs

The standing springs are skills which are designed to prepare our divers for the exacting and aesthetic plain header, which follows this next set of practices.

Beginners often 'stall' just after take-off in attempting to achieve sufficient *lift*, an ingredient which is essential for a successful springing entry. The consequent impact with the water, often picturesquely described as a 'belly flop', can be most painful and undignified. In order to reduce the risk of such happenings, a series of water-based practices have been included. These exercises all take place in approximately chest-deep water, so that if the diver misjudges the take-off or fails to leap high enough, he simply falls back safely into the water and no harm is done.

Figures 27.23, 27.24 and 27.25 demonstrate some waterborne activities in which the young divers perform shallow dives back into the water, also diving over each others' backs, arms and over a pole. All begin from the 'Y' position. Such activities are quite safe, but fulfil the purpose of attempting to gain the height which is vital for the springing take-offs and the plain header.

Fig. 27.23 Shallow-water 'dives'

Fig. 27.24 Diving over a partner's arms

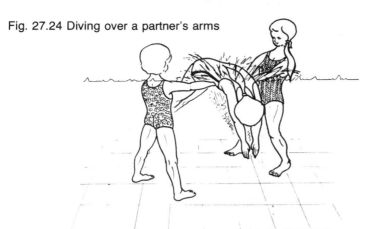

Fig. 27.25 Diving over the pole

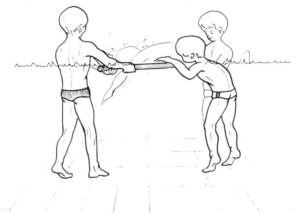

Where problems in gaining height from the poolside are experienced, a return to the water practices may be made or a series of formal straight jumps can be included in an attempt to improve the take-offs.

Low crouch spring (fig. 27.26)
This is the first approach to the plain-header series of dives.

The diver now begins to concentrate on obtaining an increase in height from take-off as opposed to the more outward-biased arc of flight previously practised in the plunge. As well as gaining height, the diver also starts to appreciate the real meaning of rotation: his body position changes during the flight from the perpendicular-biased starting position to that of being completely inverted for the vertical or near-vertical entry.

STARTING POSITION The diver takes up a balanced semi-crouch position on the poolside with feet together or almost together, and toes curled over the edge. His arms should be outstretched above his head and in line with his back. Both hands should be clasped together. The head position should be such that the diver is looking directly and comfortably forward and downward at the intended point of entry, 900–1200 mm (3–4 ft) away from the poolside.

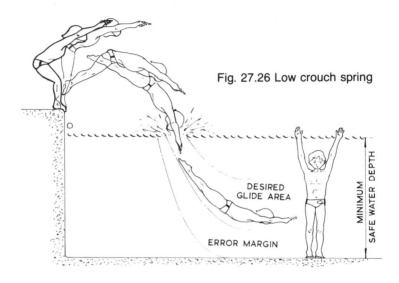

Fig. 27.26 Low crouch spring

DESIRED GLIDE AREA

ERROR MARGIN

MINIMUM SAFE WATER DEPTH

TAKE-OFF AND FLIGHT Take-off is initiated not so much by over-balancing, as in the previous dives, as by a vigorous extension of the legs. This leg thrust driving past the diver's centre of gravity creates the rotation he requires in order to enter the water in a head-first mode. The body remains bent at the hips during most of the flight and the head remains tucked in between the outstretched arms.

ENTRY The diver should, at this first attempt, enter the water at approximately sixty degrees to the water surface. As he disappears below the surface, he should endeavour to extend his hips in order to assume a straight and stretched position.

GLIDE By this time, the diver should be fairly skilled in any underwater activities which follow the entry. Descriptions and comments on these movements should therefore no longer be necessary and will be omitted.

MINIMUM SAFE WATER DEPTH Because of the upward spring, the water must be deeper than for the last movement. The minimum safe water depth is therefore designated as being approximately equal to the diver's stretched height.

FAULTS AND THEIR CORRECTION

FAULT	FAULT ANALYSIS	CORRECTION
Landing flat	The diver fails to create sufficient rotation, thus landing flat (and painfully) in the water	More attention should be paid to the diver's take-off and its timing. An upward thrust too early or too late can cause a flat landing. Raising the head during the flight is another cause, therefore the head should be maintained in a chin-low attitude
Going over on entry	The diver's hands and lower arms enter the water first and the water acts momentarily as a fulcrum. The diver consequently changes the rotation centre from his own centre of gravity (CG) to a point somewhere on his submerged arms. With rotation continuing, his body topples 'over centre': this is known as 'going over' on entry	Speed of rotation is too severe, and therefore must be reduced. The diver should try to move in an arc and not drop his head and shoulders quite so quickly, thus creating less of a somersault movement

High crouch spring (fig. 27.27)
This is a straight progression of the previous low crouch spring dive. The starting position is more upright and is now approaching the stance of the plain header. At take-off, instead of moving immediately outwards and upwards from the side, the initiated rotation should bring the diver's feet back over the poolside slightly before they rise upwards and out over the water. The reasons for this are that the rotation is becoming more complete (180 degrees for a vertical entry) and that the peak of the flight arc is getting higher.

STARTING POSITION The diver takes up a high-crouch position on the poolside: this is merely a more upright stance than that of the low crouch spring. The arms are outstretched and in line with his back. As a result of the more erect pose, the arms are near to the vertical and consequently the head is also raised a little more. The hands should be clasped together. The diver's feet should now be together, with the toes gripping the edge of the pool. In standing with feet together (they may be turned slightly outwards in order to enhance the balance), the diver is preparing himself for the plain-header stance, whereby the feet are positioned together before take-off.

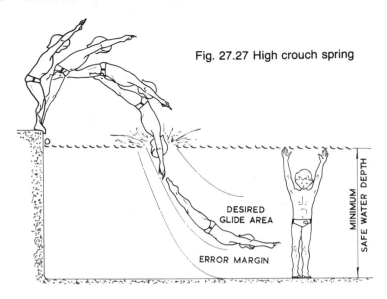

Fig. 27.27 High crouch spring

DESIRED
GLIDE AREA

ERROR MARGIN

MINIMUM SAFE WATER DEPTH

TAKE-OFF AND FLIGHT A rapid extension of the legs should propel the semi-piked diver into the flight. The feet should be fully stretched and in contact with each other. The semi-pike position should be maintained through the air, then the diver opens out as the hips disappear below the surface.

ENTRY Entry into the water should be near-vertical and clean. The diver should endeavour to streamline his entry by fully stretching himself as he submerges. It is essential that both legs and feet remain in contact with each other and that his knees do not 'snap back'.

MINIMUM SAFE WATER DEPTH The minimum safe water depth for the dive is approximately that of the diver's normal standing stretched height.

TEACHING POINTS

1. The correct feet-together stance with a semi-crouch.

2. Arms stretched upward and in line with the back, hands clasped together.

3. Eyes looking forward and slightly down at the water to begin with.

4. Take-off is a spring with no visible over-balancing.

5. Flight through the air should be in a semi-piked attitude.

6. The entry should be as near-vertical as possible without going over. The diver should open out from the semi-pike to a fully stretched mode as he disappears below the surface.

7. There should be minimal splash.

Faults and their correction are as for the low crouch spring.

Spring header (fig. 27.28)
This is the immediate forerunner of the plain header and its practices. The arm and body relationship now changes to that of the 'Y' configuration and the initial movement is an over-balancing one. The hip bend during flight is as before, and entry should again be as vertical as possible without going over.

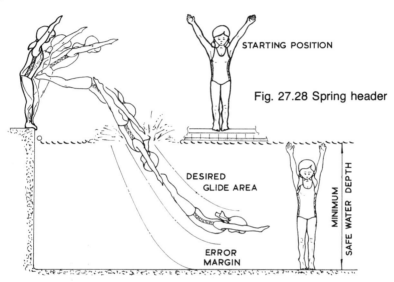

STARTING POSITION

Fig. 27.28 Spring header

DESIRED
GLIDE AREA

ERROR
MARGIN

MINIMUM
SAFE WATER DEPTH

STARTING POSITION The diver stands on the poolside with feet together or with heels together and toes turned slightly outwards. The toes should be curled over and gripping the edge. Both legs should be straight with the body leaning very slightly forward. The arms should be stretched above the head and, from the front, together with the body, they form a Y. From the side, the diver's arms should be a continuation of the line of the straight back. The hands should be flat with fingers together and palms facing forwards.

The head should be positioned comfortably so that the eyes are focused on the intended point of entry.

TAKE-OFF By contraction of the anterior lower-leg muscles, the diver moves forward on to the balls of the feet. At the transition between balance and unbalance, the legs are slightly flexed then, together with the ankles, vigorous extension takes place, propelling the diver upwards into flight.

FLIGHT The spring upwards should lift the hips and, combined with a forward movement of the shoulders, rotation takes place. The semi-pike position, which was in evidence at the start of the dive, is held throughout the major part of the flight.

At the peak of the flight, the diver initiates the movement that will bring both hands together; thumbs will be touching and arms fully outstretched as entry takes place. If the diver is sufficiently skilled to clasp the hands together, she should do so.

ENTRY Entry into the water should be as near to the vertical as possible without going over. As the diver disappears below the water surface, the body extends into the straight and streamlined mode which is essential for a clean and aesthetic completion of the movement.

MINIMUM SAFE WATER DEPTH The diver is now trying to gain height in order to enhance the performance of the movement. Consequently, the entry is at a greater speed and momentum than before and, if the path into the water is steep and near the desired vertical, submersion will be relatively deep. Taking these factors into account, the considered minimum safe water depth should be approximately equal to the diver's fully stretched height.

TEACHING POINTS
1. A completely balanced starting position is essential with heels together. The feet may be together or pointing slightly outwards and the toes should be curled over the edge of the pool.

2. There should be a slight bend of the knee and hip joints and the diver's back should be straight and leaning slightly forward from the hips.

3. The arms should be upstretched to form a Y with the body, the angle between the arms being sixty degrees. This angle may be measured approximately by making the distance between the two hands equal to one arm's length, thus forming an equilateral triangle. The palms should be facing forwards and fingers should be together.

4. Eyes should be focused on the intended point of entry.

5. Take-off should be initiated by leg movements only.

6. The aim should be to attain height during flight.

7. The arms should start to close together at or just after the peak of the flight is reached.

8. A semi-pike position should be in evidence during the major part of flight.

9. Entry should be as near-vertical as possible without going over.

10. The diver should extend into an athletically stretched position just prior to entry.

11. The head should blend in with general body streamlining as entry takes place.

FAULTS AND THEIR CORRECTION

FAULT	FAULT ANALYSIS	CORRECTION
Going over	The diver's rotation is too severe and, when the hands and lower arms are arrested in the water, the remainder of the body continues to rotate about a new centre. The fault is usually initiated by dropping the head and shoulders excessively at take-off, as if performing a somersault	Concentration on the upward spring must be emphasised. The head should be maintained in its semi-erect position and the arms should remain pointing upwards during take-off. Combined with the attitude of the head should be a slightly more upward gaze of the eyes
Entering too flat	The diver executes too much of an outward take-off and consequently lands rather flat in the water	There is probably an excessive lean forward at take-off and the diver's flight path becomes too elongated. The relationship between the leaning angle and the take-off movement should be adjusted with the leg extension taking place earlier and directed more upwards
Bending the knees at entry, and legs and feet not held together	This is a recurring fault whereby the diver's knees snap back, or her legs are apart as entry is made	Emphasis must be made on straightening the legs and holding them stretched. Pressing the feet together throughout the dive usually improves performance

Plain header (fig. 27.29)
The plain header may be regarded as the culmination of the forward entries from the poolside. However, besides being a poolside dive, it is used quite safely by competition divers at various heights up to 10 m (32½ ft).

The dive was introduced to school swimming by George Rackham in 1961, and replaced the more difficult English header whose arm swing introduced all kinds of problems to the diver which were often reflected in the far from aesthetic entries.

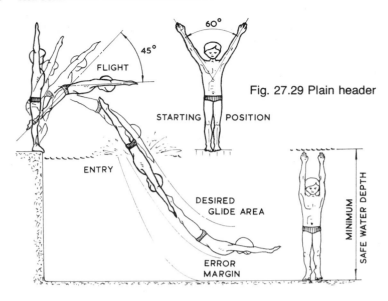

Fig. 27.29 Plain header

The main feature of the movement is that the diver is required to take up a 'Y' position at the start, after which the upstretched arms close together just prior to entry into the water. For the dive to be a successful one, the performer must attempt to gain as much height as possible during the flight through the air.

The previous standing springs should have adequately prepared the divers for this first formal dive.

STARTING POSITION The diver should stand erect on the poolside, his heels flat on the floor in line with each other and together. The fronts of the feet may be together (big toes touching each other), or they may be spread slightly apart. Either position is correct: the latter one probably affords better balance but allows less grip as the diver curls his toes over the edge of the pool (see fig. 21.2). The knees should be touching or close together.

The arms should be positioned straight and slightly stretched in the 'Y' position with palms facing forward, i.e. the arms are equally spread each side of the head forming an angle between them of approximately sixty degrees. From the side, the diver's arms, back and legs should display a contoured but vertical aspect. His centre of gravity (CG) will be poised above and between the balls of the feet and the heels to give complete stability. The head should be erect with eyes focusing on a point ahead and slightly above the diver. Respiration should be steady and shallow with no attempt to hold the breath at this stage.

TAKE-OFF By contraction of the anterior leg muscles, the diver's body weight is transferred forward. If the action is not restrained in any way, his heels will lift and his CG will move forward past the balls of his feet. It is at this point that the diver is committed to the dive. The original pose will be maintained to the 'commitment stage'.

Just beyond this 'point of no return', the diver bends his hips and knees very slightly. This movement is carried out in order that the upward and eccentrically directed thrust may be made and, when the legs are vigorously extended, drive him away from the poolside and enable him to rotate.

The diver's back and arms, during this transition movement, remain in line with head erect and eyes focused ahead and slightly up. The hip bend should create a slight forward lean.

At the precise moment of take-off (as the feet leave the poolside), the hips should be directly over the balls of the feet. The 'Y' position of the arms is maintained. Breathing in will be natural and will take place during take-off.

FLIGHT After the vigorous extension of the legs, they should remain in the fully stretched, toes-pointing mode. The feet should be pressed together and laterally in line with each other. The hip bend is increased slightly and the upper trunk and arms remain in the same position relative to each other.

This attitude is retained until just prior to the diver's entry into the water. At this point the hands are brought together, the arms remaining straight and stretched, and the hips start to extend once more.

ENTRY During the actual entry, the diver should be as close to the vertical plane as possible but not beyond it, with the toes finally disappearing into the water at approximately the same spot where the finger-tips entered. The diver should extend his body from the hip-bend attitude as he enters the water so that he becomes fully stretched and straight with feet still pressed tightly together. The dive is deemed to be complete when the toes disappear below the water surface.

MINIMUM SAFE WATER DEPTH The teacher should ensure that the minimum water depth for the plain header is at least and preferably more than the diver's fully stretched (on tip-toes) height.

TEACHING POINTS
1. The diver should assume a completely balanced starting position with heels together. The feet may be together or slightly outward-facing, with toes curled over the poolside.

2. From the side, the diver's arms, trunk and legs should be in a straight vertical line.

3. The arms should stretch upwards and outwards at approximately sixty degrees, with palms facing forward.

4. The eyes should be focused forward and slightly upwards.

5. At take-off the trunk and arms should remain in line with each other.

6. Take-off should be initiated by flexing of the hip and knee joints followed by vigorous extension of these together with the ankle joints.

7. The aim of the diver should be to attain as much height as possible.

8. The hips should be slightly bent (semi-piked) until just prior to their disappearance into the water.

9. At entry the trunk should be as near to but *not beyond* the vertical.

10. The hands should come together and the diver should be fully stretched as he enters the water.

FAULTS AND THEIR CORRECTION

FAULT	FAULT ANALYSIS	CORRECTION
Slipping on take-off	Due to a condition of unbalance or insecure foot placing, the diver slips as take-off force is applied to the poolside	The diver should carefully and in his own time, establish a steady and balanced stance before commencing the movement
Going over	The diver tips over beyond the vertical at entry. Probably due to dropping the shoulders excessively and consequently magnifying the rotation effect. Take-off movement tends to be jerky with perhaps too much hip flexion	Return to the plain-header shallow-water practices, and spring header. Avoid dropping the shoulders at take-off. Emphasise the slight upward gaze during the stance. The take-offs must be controlled with an emphasis on gaining height. The formal jumps in a 'Y' position are excellent practices for increasing elevation at take-off
Too shallow an entry	The diver over-balances excessively before applying the take-off force	The plain header is essentially an eccentric leg-thrust dive. Over-balancing should be minimal and just sufficient to direct the diver away from the poolside for reasons of safety. Emphasise elevating the hips and gaining height rather than distance. Return to spring-header practices

Entry too near to the poolside	The diver gains enough height, but take-off is too vertical	Return to the plain-header shallow-water practices in an attempt to establish the correct flight path. The spring header should then be used as a means of 'skill transfer', with emphasis on 'flowing through a curved tube'
Failure to gain sufficient height	The diver's legs collapse at take-off: this is usually due to fear	Return to the earlier dives in order to build confidence
Jack-knifing (bending excessively at the hips)	The diver flexes his hips and this, combined with a vigorous drive from the take-off point, causes the fault to occur	Return to the plain-header shallow-water practices and semi-crouch dives, emphasis on 'flowing through the curved tube'
Closing the hands together too early	From the 'Y'-positioned take-off, the arms should remain in this pose until just prior to entry. The angled form provides the diver with slightly more stability and control during flight	The plain-header shallow-water and bathside practices should be attempted while maintaining the 'Y' position during the actual entry. The closing action may then be adjusted gradually under observation

Jumps

Jumping into the water from the poolside can be great fun and children usually enjoy it. The feet-first entry may also be of a more formal nature and is to be found in many of the competition diving skills. The definition of a jump as far as we are concerned is simply that the performer leaves the take-off point feet-first, then lands feet-first in the water. Jumps are excellent confidence-builders in addition to being fun exercises. Should the jumper experience water entering the nose, a quick nasal blow as the face sinks below the water surface will prevent this from happening.

Free jumps (figs 27.30 and 27.31)
As the name implies, the jumps are informal and unrestricted entries into the water. They may be performed in many ways, such as standing, running, twisting, tucking, or by a small group holding hands. Some of the many and varied methods of informal entry are illustrated.

Safety and survival jumps (figs 26.2 and 26.3)
Jumping into water of unknown depth, or with unknown dangers lurking below the water surface, demands another facet of the jumping skill to be

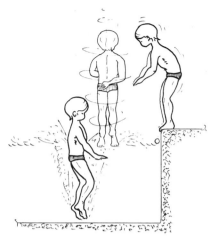

Fig. 27.30 Jumping in with a twist

Fig. 27.31 Free jumps and partner jumps

learnt. Life-saving and survival tests both include shallow feet-first water entries, whereby the swimmer is required to enter the water feet-first and, at the same time, restrict immersion to an absolute minimum. (These safety jumps are described and illustrated in chapter 26, together with jumping from a height – the compact jump.)

Formal jumps (fig. 27.32)
These movements are closely allied to competitive diving and are separate skills in themselves. The take-off, flight through the air and entry should all be strictly controlled by the performer.

It is essential that a slight upward gaze is maintained throughout the complete movement, especially in the reverse or backward jumps.

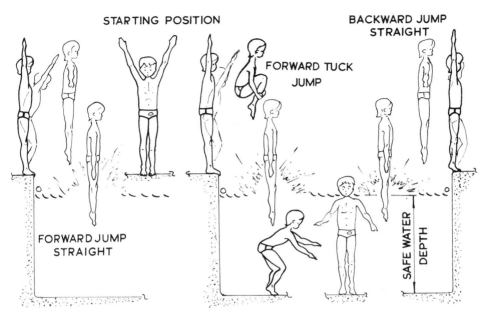

STARTING POSITION

BACKWARD JUMP
STRAIGHT

FORWARD TUCK
JUMP

FORWARD JUMP
STRAIGHT

SAFE WATER DEPTH

Fig. 27.32 Formal jumps

Aquabatics

There now follow a few aquabatic tricks allied to diving, which the teacher may care to use in order to maintain the spirit of fun and adventure in the lesson.

'Porpoising' (fig. 27.33), in which the exponents use the bottom of the pool as a push-off platform, is great fun. Leaping off the bottom of the pool and gliding between a partner's legs is essentially a shallow-end antic, but is a good group game (fig. 27.34). Tuck rolls involve one of the basic body positions and are excellent confidence-builders (fig. 27.35).

Fig. 27.33 'Porpoising'

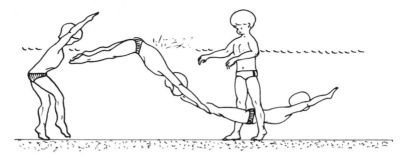

Fig. 27.34 'Porpoising' under a partner's legs

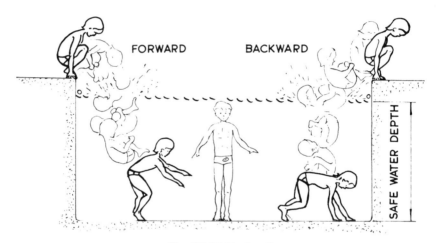

Fig. 27.35 Tuck rolls

The teacher should encourage the divers to maintain the tuck position for as long as possible during the movements. Depth of water is rather important, owing to the fact that the tucked diver tends to sink uncontrollably to the bottom of the pool.

DEFINITIONS
The 'Y' position (fig. 27.36)
This describes the diver's body with both upstretched arms diverging slightly from the shoulders, so that the included angle between them is approximately sixty degrees (the arms being equally spaced above the head). Laterally, the arms should be in a continuing line with the back and

the flat hands, with fingers together, should face directly forward and be in line with the forearms.

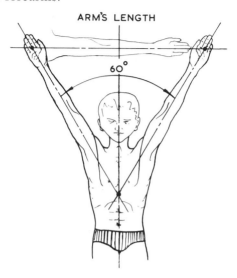

Fig. 27.36 The 'Y' position

The sixty-degree position may easily be estimated by the teacher by measuring the length of the diver's arm then spacing the hands apart by this amount (thus forming an equilateral triangle).

The 'Y' position is used primarily during the performance of the plain header and preceding spring header dives. It may, however, be used in any of the standing take-offs from the poolside, after the initial hand-clasp entries have been mastered. It may also be used during standing dives from higher take-off positions than that of the poolside.

The 'Y' position should be held for as long as possible in the air, then the hands are brought together with arms still outstretched just before entry takes place.

Stretched arms and clasped hands (fig. 27.37)
This is mainly a safety position whereby the diver stretches his arms fully above or ahead of him, clasping the hands together as he does so. The resulting anatomical configuration, being triangular in form, is mechanically strong and, if the diver locks his arms in this position, he has created a protective shield in front of his vulnerable head as he hits or glides through the water. Clasping the hands together improves the rigidity of the arms at the shoulder joints, compared with simply placing the hands together side by side. Also, by inclining the clasped hands towards the direction of the flight or glide, the palms of the hands are

better equipped to absorb the shock than the pointed fingers should a collision occur.

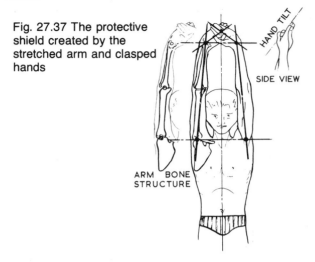

Fig. 27.37 The protective shield created by the stretched arm and clasped hands

Take-off angle (fig. 27.38)

This is the angle at which the diver leaves the take-off point in relation to the water surface. For the early, low-starting-position dives this take-off is of low dimensions, but for the springs and plain header it is relatively steep.

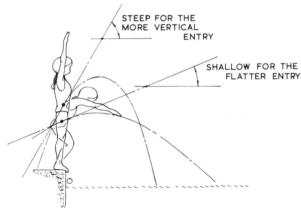

Fig. 27.38 Take-off angles

Arc of flight (fig. 27.39)

This is the path in the air along which the diver's body centre of gravity moves from the completion of take-off until her hands enter the water.

The arc of flight consists of two components of movement. One is horizontal and the other is vertical. The individual velocities of these two movements change in such a way that the horizontal velocity is constant and the vertical one varies in relation to the gravitational pull of the earth. Therefore, when a diver springs upward and outward, he continues upward until all the vertical momentum created by his legs (and the springboard) has disappeared, then he starts to fall towards the water.

Momentum is the product of mass × velocity and is a measure of the 'quantity of motion'. Related to the diver, it means that as he reaches the

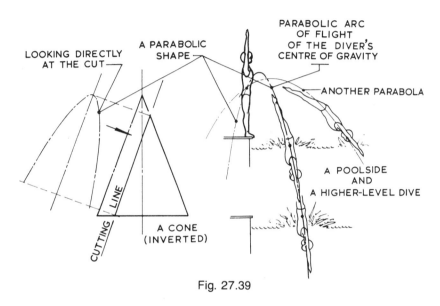

Fig. 27.39

peak of his upward movement, his vertical component of velocity drops to zero. Therefore his vertical momentum is also zero. As he begins his downward fall, the gravitational force increases his velocity (he accelerates), and hence his momentum increases once more. His mass (related to his body weight), remains constant, of course. As both the diver's mass and horizontal velocity are constant, the horizontal momentum remains constant also.

The arc of flight has a definite and symmetrical shape known as a parabola. A parabola curve may be mathematically calculated if certain factors are known. But as a simple illustration of what the shape looks like, fig. 27.39 shows an upside-down ice-cream cone: if we take a knife and slice anywhere through the cone with the cut being parallel to the sloping side of the cone, the resulting shape (viewed directly on the cut surface) is a parabolic shape.

Another parabola is shown: this one is not quite so high, and is wider. However, the rules are exactly the same – here we have simply another size of cone and another cut parallel to the side.

It is worth reiterating that the parabola is a mathematical curve and that the shape must, if required, be actually calculated from information available (diver's weight, force of take-off etc). Slicing the ice-cream cone is merely to illustrate the form of the flight arc and demonstrate that it is not circular.

Going over (fig. 27.40)
This is one of the basic and indeed dangerous faults of diving. The main cause of it is too severely generated rotation: the diver may be past the vertical even before her hands enter the water and hence she lands on her back. It has been established that the diver starts to rotate immediately from take-off and continues to rotate, with nothing to stop her until she hits the water. If her hands enter the water first and their rotation is arrested by the water, the body carries on rotating about a new centre – a point somewhere on her submerged arms. If the diver is near to being vertical and still rotating vigorously as her hands and lower arms are anchored by the water this is another reason for going over (although the basic cause is the same).

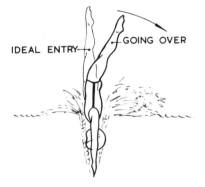

IDEAL ENTRY

GOING OVER

Fig. 27.40 The diver continues to rotate after her arms are anchored by the water. The centre of rotation is now in the water. If the entry is too steep and the rotation is severe, she goes over

The expert diver recognises this phenomenon. She therefore reduces her horizontal momentum and her entry angle so that, as her hands enter the water and become the pivot or rotation centre, the angle of her body to the vertical is such that continuing rotation just brings her upright as she fully enters the water.

Rotation (angular movement)
If a diver takes off from the standing position and enters the water head-first, he has rotated through 180 degrees in the vertical plane; or he may rotate completely (360 degrees) for a feet-first entry; or, in the case of multi-somersault dives, even more.

The first thing that must be understood about rotation during flight is that once the diver loses contact with the poolside or diving board, the fact that angular movement has been created (or not created) cannot be changed in any way. In other words, if he has not started to rotate before he leaves the take-off point, it is too late to start when he is in the air. Similarly, if he has started to rotate at take-off, he cannot change his mind while he is in flight and stop. He must use the take-off point to create rotation if rotation is required.

He can, however, change his speed of rotation during flight simply by altering the attitude of his body. To demonstrate how this is done, try sitting in an easy-moving swivel chair and stretching your legs and arms out horizontally as far as possible, and get someone to give you a spin. Then, try contracting yourself into a tucked-up attitude and you will find that the speed of rotation increases. Spread out again and you slow down. This is how the speed of rotation is controlled during flight; although you are rotating in the horizontal instead of the vertical plane, the principle is exactly the same. If the diver wishes to rotate quickly, he tucks up; if he assumes a pike or straight mode, the resulting rotation is slower (fig. 27.41).

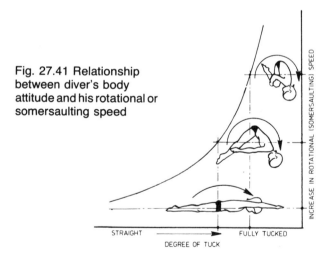

Fig. 27.41 Relationship between diver's body attitude and his rotational or somersaulting speed

STRAIGHT   FULLY TUCKED

DEGREE OF TUCK

INCREASE IN ROTATIONAL (SOMERSAULTING) SPEED

Rotation from the poolside, diving platform or springboard may be created by:

1. Leaning or over-balancing (see fig. 27.42)
2. Eccentric thrust (see fig. 27.43)
3. Transfer of momentum (figs 27.44 and 27.45). In fig. 27.44 the diver is seen to be transferring the momentum developed by swinging two filled bottles to his shoulders.

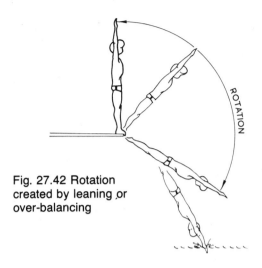

Fig. 27.42 Rotation created by leaning or over-balancing

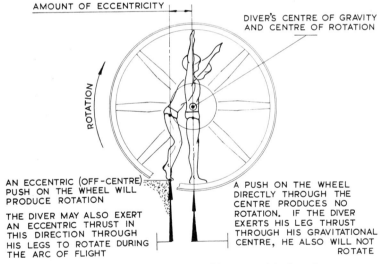

AMOUNT OF ECCENTRICITY

DIVER'S CENTRE OF GRAVITY AND CENTRE OF ROTATION

ROTATION

AN ECCENTRIC (OFF-CENTRE) PUSH ON THE WHEEL WILL PRODUCE ROTATION

THE DIVER MAY ALSO EXERT AN ECCENTRIC THRUST IN THIS DIRECTION THROUGH HIS LEGS TO ROTATE DURING THE ARC OF FLIGHT

A PUSH ON THE WHEEL DIRECTLY THROUGH THE CENTRE PRODUCES NO ROTATION. IF THE DIVER EXERTS HIS LEG THRUST THROUGH HIS GRAVITATIONAL CENTRE, HE ALSO WILL NOT ROTATE

Fig. 27.43 Rotation created by eccentric thrust

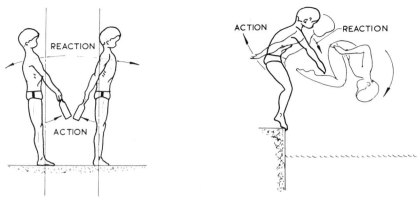

Fig. 27.44

Fig. 27.45 The diver's arms swing back and the resulting forward momentum of the body is transferred into rotation

Special Acknowledgement
Some of the activities that are mentioned in the foregoing text have originated from the extensive experience and expertise of Mr George Rackham, FSTA. These are as follows: variations on the sitting dives – the fall and spring; the squat fall and squat spring; and the spring header. I thank George for kindly allowing me to use these particular forms of entry first described in his book *Diving Complete* (Faber and Faber, 1975) in order to complete what would otherwise have been an incomplete diving programme.

28 An Introduction to Synchronised Swimming

This chapter is not a scientific treatise about the complex competitive sport of synchronised swimming, but is intended to provide the teacher with an elementary knowledge of the art of 'synchro' as a most useful addition to his or her repertoire. The skills described and illustrated here may serve to interest and encourage at least some of the pupils to partake further in this rather artistic and graceful activity outside the confines of the school. This can only be good for the sport of swimming in general. Synchronised swimming is, without doubt, the most elegant of the water-based activities, and, as far as pure aquatic excellence is concerned, it is probably the most demanding.

What is synchronised swimming? When two or more performers carry out a planned sequence of similar and co-ordinated swimming movements, the result is a demonstration of synchronised (synchro) swimming. The performance is often accompanied by music. The skill was first introduced as a team event, the various patterns of water work being regulated and synchronised by blasts from a whistle. Synchro owes its development as a competitive sport mainly to the USA and Canada, American national championships in the sport having been held regularly since 1945.

The competitive aspect has been mainly responsible for the development of 'solo synchro' (possibly a misnomer), in which there exists a syllabus of the basic figures for which various graded awards may be taken. It is from these basic patterns of movement that the choreographies of solo, duet and team routines are created.

Most of the skills illustrated here are of an elementary nature and an extension of the watermanship practices which appear elsewhere in this book, such as the push and glide, treading water and the surface dives. Most, if not all, the figures, both elementary and advanced, necessitate an ability to perform an efficient hand-sculling action. It is important for the teacher to realise that this skill forms the very foundation of synchronised swimming. The practices should therefore commence with a period of sculling exercises aimed at developing the basic movement pattern. The skill may then be utilised by the swimmers to support themselves in various postures in the water and to propel themselves in different directions on both the front and back.

PRINCIPLES OF SCULLING

An object may be propelled through the medium in which it exists by the rotation or oscillation of some kind of blade. For instance, a propeller, by rotating in either water or air, may be described as performing a 'uni-directional sculling action' (uni-directional because the propeller rotates in the same direction all the time rather than oscillating back and forth.) The thrust which is developed at right angles to the plane of propeller rotation serves to push, pull or support the object such as a boat in the water or a plane or helicopter in the air. Should the propeller and its source of power be prevented from moving forward or backward, the blade becomes that of a fan or turbine by moving the medium past it.

As we human beings are physically incapable of rotating our hands or feet propeller-fashion (we should probably swim faster if we could), we adopt the two-directional or oscillating hand/arm movement which we recognise as sculling.

One of the advantages of the oscillatory sculling motion is that, being continuous, it produces constant propulsion or support. The graceful appearance of synchro requires a non-fluctuating source of propulsion or support. Another advantage is that sculling may be used to augment a basic pull-and-push arm movement. This feature is also used in synchro where the aesthetic aspect requires a stroke to be elegant, slow and smooth.

It is worth noting that we use the uni-directional sculling movement during aquatic activities whenever we incline our hands or feet towards the direction of their movement. Examples of this can be seen in the 'weaving' arm-pull patterns of most of the swimming strokes and quite visibly in the soles of the feet during the breast-stroke leg kick.

Sculling should not be confused with 'feathering'. The former is a definite propulsive movement whereas feathering is merely 'finding the easiest way out'.

How are the propulsive and supporting forces of the scull generated? Figure 28.1 shows a section through an aircraft wing, fan or propeller blade. The profile is known as an aerofoil shape and is designed to produce, lift or move fluids by its movement. Lift can be produced by much simpler shapes but the principle which is now described still applies.

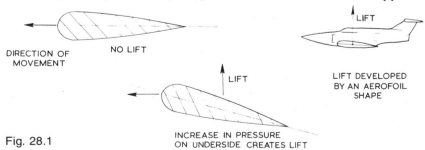

DIRECTION OF MOVEMENT   NO LIFT

LIFT

LIFT

LIFT DEVELOPED BY AN AEROFOIL SHAPE

Fig. 28.1

INCREASE IN PRESSURE ON UNDERSIDE CREATES LIFT

The direction of movement of the horizontal aerofoil through air (or water) is shown. The fluid passes over the top and underneath it at the same velocity and there is no lift created. However, when the aerofoil is tilted and becomes slightly more resistive, the velocity of the fluid passing underneath it is slowed down. When this occurs the underside pressure is increased above that of the upper surface where the velocity remains the same or else eddies of reduced pressure are formed. Whenever the velocity of a fluid passing over some object increases, the fluid pressure which is felt by the object falls. Likewise, when the velocity is slowed down, the local pressure increases.

The effect of the increased underside pressure is two-fold. It tends to drag the aerofoil backwards and, at the same time, it causes it to lift. Energy is required to overcome the resistive or dragging-back feature. But the lifting or propelling forces are utilised to make an aeroplane fly, push a boat along or, as we shall see, enable us to propel or support ourselves in the water by sculling.

This lifting effect may be demonstrated by the passenger of a motor-car travelling at 'town speed'. Ensuring it is safe to do so, one arm may be carefully extended through an open window. By facing the palm directly forward, full air pressure may be felt on the hand profile, forcing the arm backwards. If the hand is faced directly downwards the profile or frontal hand area is reduced, and consequently the pressure effect decreased. But if the leading part of the hand is now tilted so that the palm forms a slight angle with the horizontal, the lifting action will be felt which tends to force the hand and arm upwards. The drag effect will force the hand backwards as well. Tilting the hand while travelling forward clearly demonstrates in air how, by using the hand as an aerofoil, lifting or sculling forces may be generated.

If we now transfer our passenger from the motor-car to the swimming pool, the effect of tilting and moving the hands through the water may be observed.

The most effective method of utilising this phenomenon is for the swimmer to oscillate or scull both hands in unison, but in opposing directions to each other, at the same time facing the slightly tilted palms away from the direction of required movement or support. If a swimmer lying horizontally in the water wishes to move in a head-first direction by sculling, the palms of the hands should be tilted towards her feet. Similarly, if support is required, the palms should be directed towards the bottom of the pool (fig. 28.2).

The hand tilt should be such that the leading part (either thumb or little finger) should be slightly higher than the trailing part. This means that if the hand moves outwards, the little finger is higher than the thumb, and when travelling inwards, the thumb is elevated above the little finger (fig. 28.3).

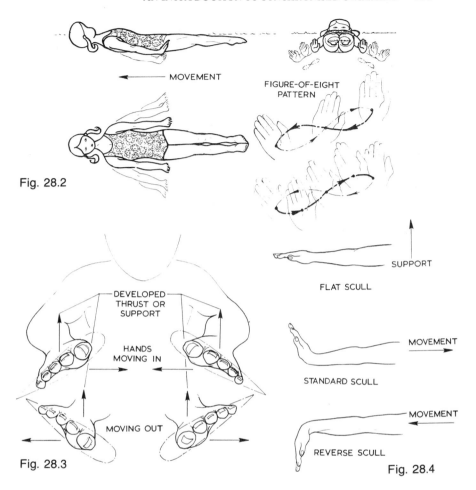

MOVEMENT

FIGURE-OF-EIGHT PATTERN

Fig. 28.2

SUPPORT

FLAT SCULL

DEVELOPED THRUST OR SUPPORT

HANDS MOVING IN

MOVEMENT

STANDARD SCULL

MOVING OUT

MOVEMENT

REVERSE SCULL

Fig. 28.3

Fig. 28.4

Types of scull (fig. 28.4)
There are three configurations of scull, namely:

Flat scull
The hand lies in line with the forearm and the sculling angle of the hand is created by axial rotation of the forearm.

Standard scull
The wrist is bent back so that the flat palm is inclined to the long axis of the forearm and faces away from the swimmer's head.

Reverse scull
With the wrist flexed forward in a mode similar but opposite to that described above, a reverse sculling action may be performed.

TEACHING THE SCULL

The technique of sculling may first be introduced as a land practice.

Land practices

The oscillating movement of the flat scull may be demonstrated by the teacher for the pupils to follow. Simplicity of movement is the essence of success, and before introducing the inclined hand (lift) technique, the teacher should ensure that the basic sideways oscillating movement with flat hands is correct.

The first, and probably the easiest way for the children to practise the movement, is by sitting on the poolside and placing both hands flat on the floor beside them (fig. 28.5). The oscillating motion may then be demonstrated and copied. By making suitable comparisons such as 'washing the floor' or 'wiping the windows', the children may use their imaginations to help them establish the oscillating movement.

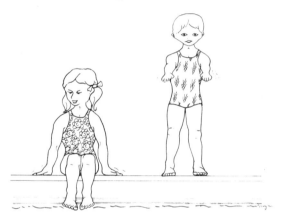

Fig. 28.5 Practising the scull on the poolside

For further poolside practice both arms should be stretched slightly forward. The fingers should be together, flat and in line with the forearm. Palms should face directly downwards. Sideways oscillation may now take place by moving the hand edgewise back and forth a distance of approximately 150 mm (6 in.) in either direction, using the shoulder as a central plane of oscillation. The rate of oscillation will eventually be related to the overall activity to be performed, but in the first instance, about one cycle per second will suffice.

As the hand pattern is established, the slight upward tilt of the little fingers (when the hands move outwards) or the thumbs (as they move inwards once more) may be added to the movement. An elongated figure-of-eight pattern, the wrist leading throughout the movement, should eventually be established (fig. 28.2).

Attempting the movements in other modes, as illustrated in fig. 28.6, may then be carried out: the girls are practising the scull while standing facing the wall, then on the pool surround where they pretend to be piling up and pushing apart imaginary sand, and then with hands actually in the water while flat on their tummies. (The piling and parting of imaginary sand is a useful descriptive comparison to adopt during the teaching of the scull, since most of the children have probably played with sand at some time or other.)

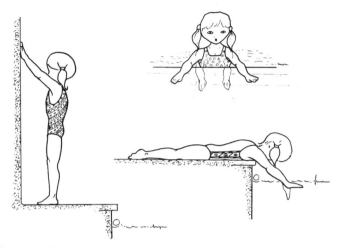

Fig. 28.6 Practising the scull on the poolside and in the water

Water practices
The effectiveness of the individual actions may now be demonstrated in shallow water by attempting the flat scull. The children may settle down into the water and try supporting themselves by the sculling motion while lifting their feet from the bottom of the pool.

We can now demonstrate the ability to become mobile. This may be achieved by hooking the feet under the rail, while a flat 'supporting' scull is established, then changing to a standard propelling scull across the pool (with a little help from the legs).

Deep-water sculling may be tried in the form of treading water in a vertical mode. The hands should oscillate by the sides or slightly ahead of the swimmer. The required support is upwards, therefore the palms will be inclined downwards in order to generate the lift.

Various hand positions and rates of scull may be experimented with. One favourite game is to see if, merely by sculling, the pupils can elevate their chests clear of the water! Directional movements may be developed by using the various individual sculls and combinations of the actions. For instance, a prone or supine head-first movement may be produced by a standard scull. A feet-first movement may be created by the opposing reverse hand movement. Merely floating in a horizontal mode requires a flat scull.

On the other hand a 'tub' may be performed while the hands scull in opposing modes, or while one hand propels to rotate and the other supports.

The art of sculling, together with the push-and-glide movements, must be regarded as one of the milestones in an aquatic career.

There are other methods of propulsion used in the art of synchro besides sculling and, of course, the normal swimming stroke action. These include:

Scoops
These arm movements are directed up the body, away from the feet. The path of the hand lies in front or at the side of the body or somewhere between these two planes (fig. 28.7). The effect of the movement is to propel the swimmer feet-first, if the body attitude is straight or arched or, if the swimmer assumes a tucked position, the scooping action will create forward rotation (somersault forward tuck).

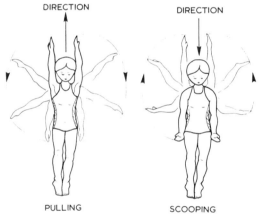

Fig. 28.7

Pulls
The hands start above the head and move down the body and towards the feet. As in the scoop, the path of movement may be in front or to the side of the body, or somewhere between the two (fig. 28.7). The effect is to direct the swimmer head-first if straight, or create backward rotation if tucked (somersault back tuck).

Lateral arm sweeps
These are arm movements used to rotate the swimmer about the long axis (rolling). They are fully described in the ensuing section.

SYNCHRO: THE INTRODUCTORY PRACTICES AND SKILLS

There follows a series of basic practices and skills which need to be performed with some dexterity if any degree of success in the art of synchronised swimming is to be attained. The exercises are versions of the basic watermanship practices, with the added refinements demanded by the disciplines of synchro.

Although the illustrations show the various stunts being performed by girls, boys too should be encouraged to try these early skills. Experience has shown that they will get much fun and satisfaction from their efforts. However, the teacher must realise that as the skills become more demanding, the less 'hip-buoyant' young males will find more difficulty in performing the movements. This applies particularly to the skills which require the leg(s) to be lifted and held above the water surface.

The swimmers will undoubtedly find the exercises more acceptable if nose clips are worn during their performance. The frequent submersive activities tend to allow some ingress of water up the nostrils, causing varying degrees of sinus discomfort. Nose clips are relatively cheap and the better-quality ones are quite effective.

Skill 1: The surface push and glide in both the front- and back-lay positions
The teaching practices and teaching points relating to these skills are to be found in chapters 11 and 14.

Skill 2: treading water
As a general rule, the 'egg-beater' type of kick is used during synchro swimming. This method of support and propulsion is described and illustrated in chapter 25.

Skill 3: various floating positions
PRONE Head down, arms and legs fully stretched and in the four-pointed star position
SUPINE Head in line with body – arms optional
PIKE Face in water, legs straight, hands holding or touching legs between knees and ankles
TUCK (MUSHROOM) Head down – full tuck, arms encircling knees, face as near to knees as possible

The prone, pike and tuck floating positions are illustrated in the shallow-water practices relating to diving (see chapter 27). The supine float is shown in fig. 5.9 which illustrates body-position control by the movement of the swimmer's arms.

Skill 4: gliding, reversing and swimming
ACTIVITY A (fig. 28.8)
Front glide with head up, then reverse direction by pulling the arms down

and back, and at the same time tuck up. Assume a back float for a brief instant and back paddle back to starting point. The face should be above the water surface throughout.

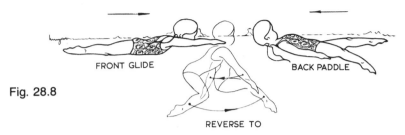

FRONT GLIDE

BACK PADDLE

Fig. 28.8

REVERSE TO

ACTIVITY B (fig. 28.9)
Back glide, then reverse direction by scooping the hands towards the water surface. Return to start using breast stroke. The face should be out of the water throughout. For teaching points, refer to the chapters relating to the various skills.

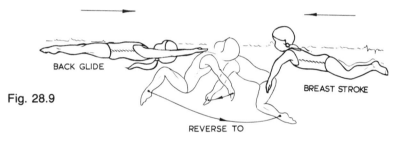

BACK GLIDE

BREAST STROKE

Fig. 28.9

REVERSE TO

Skill 5: rolling by using the arm-sweep technique (fig. 28.10)
Start in a front-lay position, face in the water, one arm extended beyond the head and the other stretched vertically downwards with palm facing inwards. By gently sweeping the downward-stretched arm across the body (the action), the swimmer will react by rolling in the opposite direction to the arm sweep to finish up in a back-lay position.

TEACHING POINTS
1. Head in line with the body throughout.

2. Arm movements controlled, but not too vigorous.

3. Whole movement to be smoothly executed.

4. Body to remain on the surface throughout.

5. Breath control by gently breathing out through the mouth as the face emerges (if a nose clip worn). If a nose clip is not being used, the swimmer should gently exhale through the nose on surfacing in order to clear the nostrils.

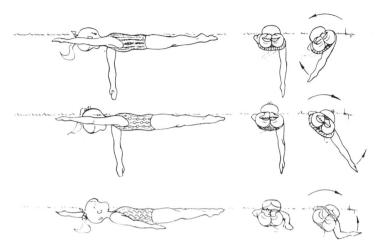

Fig. 28.10

A directional reverse of this exercise may be performed using the same arm and commencing in the same starting mode. The downward-directed arm is this time axially rotated through 180 degrees to face outwards. Then, by gently sweeping the arm outwards, the body roll will take place in the opposite direction to the arm sweep. Similar effects can, of course, be experienced by reversing the positions of the arms.

The axial-rotation exercise may be also carried out by starting in a back-lay position. Here both arms may be by the sides or one by the side and the other stretched beyond the head. Rolling is performed by sweeping one side-lying arm sideways and downwards in an arc with the little finger of the hand initially leading, then finally performing an upward and inward scoop. This arm action reacts the swimmer in the opposite direction enabling her to roll on to her front. As before, an outward-sweeping hand will produce reversal of rotation and again the rolling movements may be repeated using the opposite arm.

Skill 6: transitional stroke swimming by rolling
On the surface
ACTIVITY A (fig. 28.11)
Back paddle for a short distance then roll on to the front, still kicking and sculling. Continue for a short distance in this position then revert, by rolling over once more, to the back paddle. The exercise is a good width practice.

TEACHING POINTS
1. There should be no splash throughout the movement.

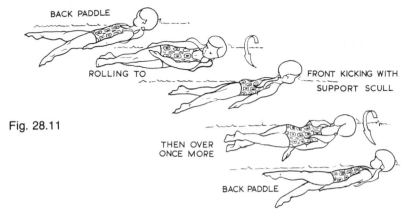

Fig. 28.11

2. The transitions from back to front and over again should be smooth and continuous.

3. The head and face should be clear of the water at all times.

ACTIVITY B (fig. 28.12)
Breast stroke for three cycles with prolonged glide, then change to front crawl. Swim with head up for a short distance then roll over on to the back and continue for a short distance using back crawl.

TEACHING POINTS
1. All movements should be unhurried and splash-free.

2. Stroke transitions should be carefully timed and smooth.

3. The swimmer's face should always be clear of the water.

4. The whole pattern of movement should be continuous.

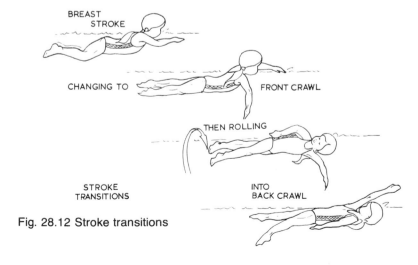

Fig. 28.12 Stroke transitions

Under water
ACTIVITY C (fig. 28.13)
From an underwater push and glide, perform two breast-stroke cycles then, by using the arm-sweep technique, roll over into a supine mode, back paddle to the surface and continue for a short distance.

TEACHING POINTS
1. Normal underwater push-and-glide technique as illustrated in chapter 14.

2. Normal breast-stroke action – head down otherwise there will be a tendency to re-surface too quickly.

3. Arm-sweep technique similar to that described in skill 5.

4. Slightly lift head in order to assist re-surfacing.

5. Breath control – gently exhale through mouth (with nose clip) or through nose (without nose clip) during re-surfacing.

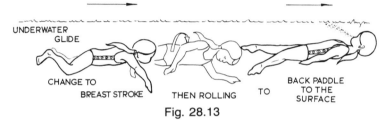

Fig. 28.13

Skill 7: surface sculling movements
ACTIVITY A: Head-first scull (fig. 28.14)

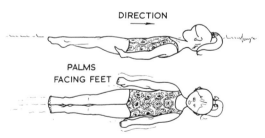

Fig. 28.14 Head-first scull

TEACHING POINTS
1. Minimum hand and arm movement.

2. Oscillating arm movement initiated from shoulders with minimal elbow bend, hand movement by axial arm rotation, palms facing or partially facing towards feet.

3. Arms close to the body throughout sculling cycle.

4. Sculling movement continuous and smooth.

5. Head in line with the body and face, chest, hips, legs and toes at the water surface.

ACTIVITY B: feet-first scull (fig. 28.15)

TEACHING POINTS

All teaching points as for head-first scull except that wrists should be fully flexed in order that palms face towards head, thus reversing direction of propelling forces.

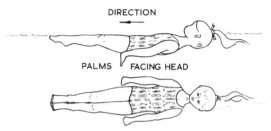

Fig. 28.15 Feet-first scull

ACTIVITY C: the tub – rotational sculling on the back, tucked (fig. 28.16)

Fig. 28.16 The tub

TEACHING POINTS

1. The movement starts and finishes in the back-lay position.

2. The tuck position is assumed by drawing the knees up towards the chin

so that the lower legs lie along the surface and the knees vertically above the hips. The feet should be plantar-flexed. This position should be maintained throughout the tub movement.

3. Rotation takes place either by supporting (scull) with one hand or propelling with both in opposite directions. The hands should be beside the body at an optional depth below the water surface.

4. The centre of rotation should be the swimmer's seat.

5. The head should be in line with the body throughout.

Skill 8: sculling variations
ACTIVITY A: torpedo or propeller – feet-first, sculling on the back (fig. 28.17)
TEACHING POINTS
1. The appropriate sculling technique applies.

2. The swimmer should be fully extended with the arms beyond the head. The origination of the scull should be from the shoulders with elbows straight.

3. The body, face and feet should be at the water surface.

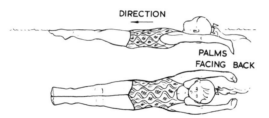

Fig. 28.17 Torpedo or propeller

ACTIVITY B: canoe – head-first, sculling on the front (fig. 28.18)

TEACHING POINTS
1. The appropriate sculling technique applies.

2. The swimmer's body is arched with the chin just clear of the water and the feet extended to the surface.

3. The hand scull should take place by the side of the body, between shoulders and hips. The actual position of the scull depends on the buoyancy of the swimmer's legs and hips. The palms should be directed backwards for the necessary forward propulsion.

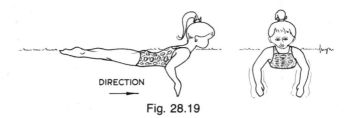

DIRECTION

Fig. 28.19

Skill 9: surface layouts
ACTIVITY A: back layout (fig. 28.19)
TEACHING POINTS
1. The approach to the layout should be slow, elegant and controlled.

2. The body and legs should be stretched and streamlined, with the face, thighs, legs and toes at the water surface.

3. Head should be in line with the body.

4. Arm position is optional, depending on the sculling efficiency and buoyancy characteristics of the swimmer.

5. The sculling movement should be effective and just adequate to maintain the desired mode.

6. Breathing should be shallow and controlled while the position is held, say, ten seconds.

BACK LAYOUT

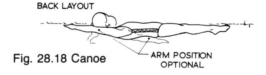

Fig. 28.18 Canoe   ARM POSITION
OPTIONAL

ACTIVITY B: front layout (fig. 28.20)
TEACHING POINTS
1. The approach to the layout should be slow, elegant and controlled.

2. The body and legs should be stretched and streamlined with head, shoulders, hips, lower leg and heels at the surface.

3. The face may be in or out of the water.

4. Arm position is optional, depending on the sculling efficiency and buoyancy characteristics of the swimmer.

5. The sculling movement should be effective and just adequate to maintain buoyancy and stability.

6. When the head is in the water, the breath should be held as the position is held, say ten seconds. Then gently exhale through mouth (with nose clip) or through the nose.

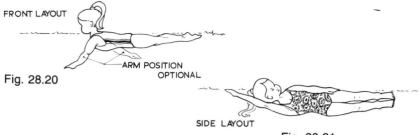

FRONT LAYOUT

ARM POSITION OPTIONAL

Fig. 28.20

SIDE LAYOUT

Fig. 28.21

ACTIVITY C: side layout (fig. 28.21)
This is rather a difficult position for the poor floater to maintain. It is taken up from a front or back layout, using the rolling technique as outlined in skill 5.

TEACHING POINTS
1. The swimmer should be directly on her side.

2. Her body should be fully extended and straight.

3. The head is slightly turned so that the face is above the water surface.

4. The head, one hip, one arm and one foot should be at the water surface.

5. One arm should be adjacent to the side in an 'attention' mode, the other stretched beyond the head.

ACTIVITY D: back layout with bent knee (fig. 28.22)
TEACHING POINTS
1. The swimmer assumes the basic stretched back-layout position as described in skill 7.

2. One leg is then slowly drawn up into a bent-knee position. The foot of the raised leg should be plantar-flexed and the toes should lie by the inside of the other knee or a short way up the thigh – not lower than the knee.

3. The effect of raising one leg out of the water changes the centre of gravity of the swimmer. Consequently a more vigorous sculling action and possibly a change in hand position (lower down the body) may be required.

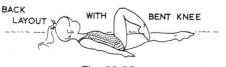

BACK LAYOUT   WITH   BENT KNEE

Fig. 28.22

ACTIVITY E: front layout with bent knee (fig. 28.23)
TEACHING POINTS
1. The swimmer assumes the basic front-layout position as described in skill 8.

2. Continue as for back layout.

Fig. 28.23

Skill 10: entries (fig. 28.24)
These should all be performed in deep water, i.e. not less than stretched-body height.

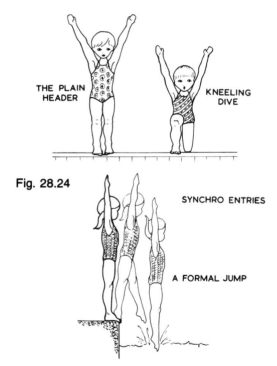

Fig. 28.24

ACTIVITY A: kneeling
Starting position is one-leg kneel, with foot of the upright leading leg on the edge of the pool, toes curled over poolside, trailing lower leg on pool floor; body erect, head up, eyes looking forward and slightly upward; arms in 'Y' position, palms facing forward. Take-off is originated by forward lean and extension of leading leg. Both legs are together as they

disappear below surface, arms converging to streamlined fully stretched mode just prior to entry, head maintained in line with body.

ACTIVITY B: formal jump
Similar to the formal jumps illustrated in the diving chapter. Start in 'Y' position, step forward, head up. Arms close together, stretched above head just prior to entry, the whole body straight and stretched or slightly arched on entry.

ACTIVITY C: diving – plain header
The technique is fully described and illustrated in chapter 27.

Skill 11: stroke variations (fig. 28.25)
The swimmers should be reasonably adept performers at this stage. They should be able to swim at least two of the competition strokes with some semblance of style and grace, displaying a minimum degree of water-surface disturbance from both arms and legs.

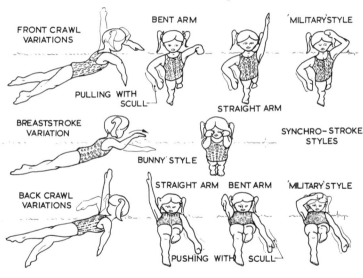

Fig. 28.25

Synchro swimming, however, demands a little showmanship beyond that of the normal 'get there as quick as you can' competition styles. We must therefore make some attempt to 'dress the strokes up a little' with an audience in mind. This is more difficult than it sounds and requires considerable practice. Sculling is again the foundation of the slow and controlled arm movements where the particular skill now becomes amalgamated with the basic patterns of movement.

In their new demonstrative guise, the arms should be recovered over the water with disciplined elegance and, if possible, the hands too should move to enhance the aesthetic impression. These prolonged and elevated recoveries require the underwater arm movements to be modified so that they provide body support as well as basic propulsion. Furthermore, the support is needed from both arms and legs as the synchro swimmer is required to swim with shoulders and head held high. This is contrary to the competition techniques. Anyone who has tried to swim in a head-up attitude will realise how vigorous the leg action needs to be in order to maintain even a semi-horizontal position, and also how important it is for the swimmer to establish an initial downward-pressing movement of the hands (not normal in the competition styles) in order to maintain the elevated shoulder mode. It is therefore aesthetically desirable and physically necessary that the synchro swimmer's legs lie rather lower in the water than when swimming for speed. The various stroke leg movements must help sustain the elevated swimming modes and at the same time contribute towards propulsion; they must be efficient, powerful and economic.

Some of the simplest variations in arm recovery are illustrated in fig. 28.25 and are described below. It should be noted that the leg action may be the regular, alternating, vertically-biased pattern or an 'egg-beater' action.

ACTIVITY: FRONT CRAWL

Variation 1: bent-arm recovery This is a near-normal type of arm-recovery movement with the emphasis on control rather than the forward throw normally associated with the stroke. The entry should be unhurried and free from splash.

Variation 2: straight-arm recovery This is a hand-elevated movement requiring slightly more control in order to achieve a splash-free entry. The arm is held straight from release to entry and traverses.an arc in the vertical plane.

Variation 3: 'military' style The military aspect is in the form of a saluting movement performed by the recovering hand before it re-enters the water. Control of the arm is obviously necessary throughout. The hand may touch the centre of the chest instead of the forehead during the actual salute.

ACTIVITY: BREAST STROKE

Variation 1: prolonged glide The stroke is performed in a near-normal fashion with an emphasis on maintaining an extended or prolonged glide.

Variation 2: bunny-style arm recovery The swimmer's recovery hands push forward together over the water surface in a rabbit-like posture; splash should be minimal.

ACTIVITY: BACK CRAWL

All the variations are similar to those of front crawl; the underwater movements should be accompanied by a sculling action.

Skill 12: somersault tucks

ACTIVITY A: backward rotation (fig. 28.26)

TEACHING POINTS

1. The swimmer should start and finish in a back-layout position and complete one full revolution.

2. The initial tuck should be controlled and complete before rotation commences.

3. Rotation is created by the action/reaction principle. The arms move in an arc about the shoulder joint, pulling towards the feet. The reaction of the swimmer is to somersault in an opposite or backward direction.

4. Throughout rotation the swimmer should maintain a fully tucked position, head close to the knees and body close to the surface.

5. The whole movement should be continuous and smooth.

6. Control of rotation should be such that the swimmer may re-attain the back layout smoothly and with minimal water-surface disturbance.

7. Breathing should be silent and unobtrusive.

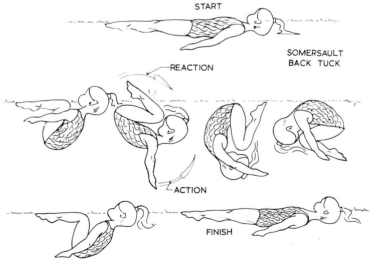

Fig. 28.26 Somersault back tuck

ACTIVITY B: forward rotation (fig. 28.27)
TEACHING POINTS
1. The swimmer should start and finish in a front-layout position and complete one full revolution.

2. The initial tuck should be controlled and complete before rotation commences.

3. Rotation is created by the arms scooping towards the head. The swimmer reacts in the opposite direction and somersaults forwards.

The rest of the teaching points are as for the back somersault, except that the final position is a front layout.

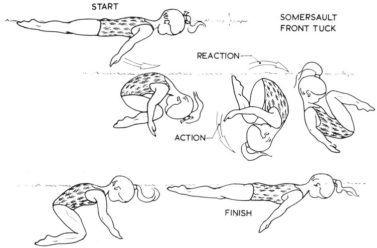

Fig. 28.27 Somersault front tuck

SIMPLE ROUTINES

When the individual skills are being performed with some style and elegance, the teacher may attempt to combine several different postures and movements, in order to compile a simple programme or routine.

The sequence of events should be practised in singular form, then gradually integrated to form a complete routine. Simplicity is the key factor initially, with an emphasis on smooth transitions from skill to skill. The gliding, rolling and stroke transitions described earlier are elementary examples of routine movements. These, when combined with the later skills such as the somersaults and layouts, can form quite an attractive pattern of movements.

A brief and simple routine, beginning with entry from the poolside, is illustrated in fig. 28.28. It combines simple movements which children should be able to perform quite satisfactorily.

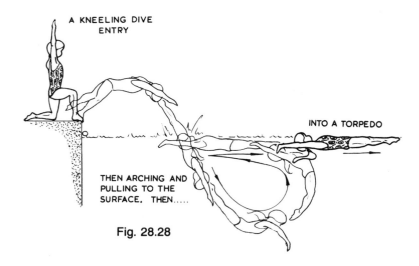

A KNEELING DIVE ENTRY

INTO A TORPEDO

THEN ARCHING AND PULLING TO THE SURFACE. THEN.....

Fig. 28.28

Further developments may be attempted by letting the children work in pairs to create short duets. Finally, a team may be formed in which simple but more extensive routines are attempted. This always goes down well at the annual school swimming gala, especially when accompanied by some contemporary musical theme.

This completes this brief introduction to synchronised swimming. It is hoped that the teachings and practices will encourage the children to find out more about the sport to develop their talents further. The teacher wishing to extend his or her knowledge of synchro is advised to contact the major organisations associated with the teaching of swimming, each of which has produced an excellent comprehensive teaching and award programme.

Special Acknowledgement
Some of the activities that are shown in the foregoing text have originated from the extensive experience and expertise of Mr George Rackham, FSTA. I thank George for kindly allowing me to use these particular activities, first described in his book *Synchronized Swimming* (Faber and Faber, 1968). These valuable skills have also been incorporated into the STA Synchro Awards Scheme.

29 An Introduction to Waterpolo

The standard of waterpolo would be much higher in this country if the game was fostered in the schools nationwide. This chapter is designed to provide the teacher with some basic information about the game, together with a few introductory activities with which to interest his or her charges should time, facilities and equipment be available.

As waterpolo is a game which involves the use of a ball, creating an interest among young swimmers should not be difficult.

Generally speaking, it is a boys' game, but I still carry scars gained while playing 'friendly' games against the 'gentle' sex in my youth. I remember thinking often that the boys would be far safer in the water if the girls concentrated on synchronised swimming. I have retained this view as I get older and more frail!

However, on with the game.

As with ice hockey, where the player requires to be an accomplished ice skater in order to participate, a waterpolo player needs to develop all his swimming and watermanship skills in order to take part successfully. In both games the necessary skills are considerably enhanced by actually playing the game.

Waterpolo possesses its own set of rules and regulations, some complex and some simple, and it is only intended that a few of these should be mentioned in this text. Perhaps the best way to introduce the game is to provide a suitable ball and start the action with a minimum of rules, like no biting, scratching or fighting! Let us call this simplified activity 'shallow ball', a title descriptive of the area of the pool in which it may be played.

Shallow ball

The ball should be soft, fairly light, made of either rubber or plastic and approximately 200 mm (8 in.) in diameter. It should be passed around by throwing from player to player.

Waterpolo teams consist of seven players actually water-borne at one time. But, providing there is enough pool space, shallow-ball teams may comprise a few more members so that all can join in. The participants are allowed to stand or walk about during play, as they are in shallow water and also to handle the ball with both hands. (All these actions constitute minor fouls in true waterpolo.)

The object in waterpolo is to score goals, but goal posts and nets are not always available for use and take time to set up. We must therefore devise some other form of goal. One good method is for two towels to be draped over the poolside to represent the goal posts. Another system is to use two plastic buckets or bowls into which the ball is landed in order to score a goal. The methods are many and varied and the teacher should use imagination within the scope of the facilities available to establish some easy and safe way of creating a scoring area.

There must be a referee (preferably the teacher) who should be equipped with a whistle in order to control the game should enthusiasm get out of hand. Infringements of the few rules the referee cares to impose should result in a free throw against the offending team. It may be advantageous to nominate a goalkeeper for each team but this is the only stipulated playing position necessary. The time of play should be short and teams should change ends after each nominated period of play. In a class all the pupils probably know each other, so that when the two sides are picked, everyone is aware who is playing for which side.

Water ball
Let us now proceed into deeper water with our soft plastic ball. With some players not able to touch bottom, walking and standing now become infringements of the game, but we shall still need to retain permission to handle the ball with two hands. As the players become more familiar with the game, there will be a tendency to throw the ball with one hand while using the other to fend off an attacker or remain afloat.

A few more rules and regulations will now be necessary as the game is taking place in deeper water. Holding on to each other, swimming over and ducking will need to be more rigidly controlled, although holding the handrail for a breather (another infringement of the rules of true waterpolo) will probably be necessary for most players.

With these refinements the game has changed slightly, so let us call this new activity by a different name – 'water ball'.

The players should now be restricted to seven per side, with replacements to order. Infringements, in addition to those already mentioned, should include pushing the ball under, swimming over and holding members of the opposing team.

The players may start the game waterpolo-style by lining up along the side of the pool. Then, at a signal from the referee, they swim to the centre of the field of play in order to gain possession of the ball which has been thrown into the water. (The field of play itself should be at least 10 m (11 yds) square and, if possible, part of the area should be in deep water.) The game should then consist of scoring goals by any fair means. After a goal, the re-start should be made from the centre of the field of play by one player passing the ball back to a team-mate. The teacher may invoke any extra rulings that become necessary as game skills and craft develop.

Having now revealed to the young swimmers some of the delights of playing a ball game in the water, let us examine some of the skills that are required for playing the parent game of waterpolo.

The waterpolo skills
Swimming
The game proper requires an ability to perform reasonable versions of both front and back crawls. Breast stroke is useful but not often used during play. The front crawl stroke should be practised mainly in a head-up swimming position, which is vital for observing play and dribbling the ball. This requires a definite and powerful leg kick. The waterpolo style also necessitates an arched body position and consequently is best performed as a complete movement rather than as a series of part-practices.

Short front-crawl sprints across the pool with the head elevated above the water surface are good starting exercises. Changing from front to back crawl and back again is often necessary during a game, so this is another skill to be developed. Changing direction while continuing to swim should become a natural movement. For these transitions, the young players should try swimming away in various directions on signals from the teacher.

Watermanship
Swimming, stopping, treading water, rotating, reversing and swimming away again, are all necessary skills of the game which must be taught and practised.

Handling the ball
The waterpolo ball is yellow with black panel-defining lines. It should be approximately 700 mm (27½ in.) in circumference; the resulting diameter will be in the region of 223 mm (8¾ in.) and it should weigh between 400 and 450 g (approximately 1 lb). It is inflated fairly hard.

Handling the ball in the water while attempting to remain afloat is rather difficult for novices. The difficult part, perhaps, is lifting the ball above the surface without 'wrapping it around the neck'. A worthwhile point to remember at the start is not to bring the ball too close to the body when handling it.

Treading water is vital when lifting the ball while in deep water, and it is an accentuated leg kick which serves to elevate the player's arm and shoulder clear of the water as he dispatches the 'missile' towards its target.

Picking the ball up (fig. 29.1)
There are several methods of picking the ball up off the water and all require a certain degree of skill. Using the full-size ball may be difficult for young swimmers with small hands. It may be expedient therefore to use a slightly smaller ball during the earlier practice games.

The art of handling is best practised initially in shallow water, where the ball may be lifted from the water in several different ways with the

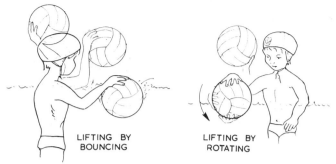

Fig. 29.1 (*left*) Lifting by bouncing and (*right*) lifting by rotating

exponents standing upright in chest-deep water, then settling down with shoulders submerged as dexterity improves. The easiest method of picking the ball up is by placing the hand under it and simply lifting it off the water. Once on the hand, it may be manoeuvred before shooting or passing. The second method is to place one spread hand on top of the ball and rotate it until the palm is underneath it, then simply lift once more. The third way is slightly more tricky than the others, but it is probably the most commonly used among waterpolo players. It demands that the ball is quickly *partially* submerged, then caught on the hand as the buoyancy forces are allowed to rebound it upwards. The movement is similar to that of the second method, whereby the hand is rotated under the ball as it rises.

Holding the ball
After picking the ball up off the surface, it must be controlled and held. The supporting hand should form a cup which is similar in shape to the contour of the ball and in which it may rest (rather like a golf ball on a tee). As previously mentioned, the ball is best kept away from the body where control is easier.

Throwing the ball (fig. 29.2)
When either passing or shooting at goal the tendency of the novice is to look at the ball. This is wrong. In each case the thrower's eyes should be fastened on the target, either a team-mate or the opponent's goal. The ball should, in a controlled fashion and with the throwing arm slightly flexed, be brought back behind the shoulder before being dispatched towards its target. The player's body should twist in a backward direction towards the throwing side in order to increase the 'winding-up' effect, and the throwing shoulder at least should be above the water surface.

In shallow water, with assistance from the bottom of the pool, this activity is quite easy. However, throwing the ball becomes more difficult in deeper water where the movement requires elevating assistance from a downward-directed leg kick and the free hand.

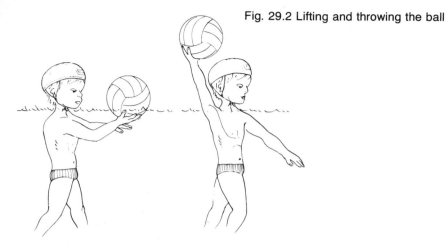

Fig. 29.2 Lifting and throwing the ball

Catching the ball

A good pass is one in which a player, on receipt of the ball, can easily control it with one hand and subsequently dispatch it to a team-mate or shoot at the opponent's goal with the minimum of fuss and bother. The ideal place for a player to receive a pass is squarely on his throwing hand. (Most players possess a 'throwing arm' although some members of the team may be able to use either hand with equal dexterity.)

A good position at which to receive a pass is approximately level with the top of the head and about 300 mm (12 in.) wide of the ear. The ball should be travelling on past the receiving player, whose hand should be slightly cupped and fingers spread wide. The most important point is that as the ball is caught the receiving arm should move in the same direction as that of the ball in order to absorb the impact of ball on hand. Players failing to carry this out find that the ball bounces straight out of their grasp as they try to control it.

Passes are not always what they should be and exercises in catching and controlling the ball in all positions should be practised.

A good throwing-and-catching practice for prospective waterpolo players is as follows: the players form a circle and, with one player in the centre, the ball is distributed and returned by each participant in turn using only one hand in the process. The number of circles usually depends on the number of practice balls available. The players may begin the practice in shallow water but should move to deeper water for short spells in order to improve the standard of the exercise.

Swimming with the ball (fig. 29.3)
This skill is an application of the earlier practice of swimming front crawl with the head up. The ball is placed in front of the swimmer who pushes it along in front of him as he swims.

Fig. 29.3 Swimming with the ball

Width practices are ideal for developing this skill, where one player takes the ball over from the previous one after each short swim. Passing the ball after a short swim is another facet of the game with which a young player must familiarise himself.

These few basic skills form the foundation of waterpolo and our young players may develop further by playing the game itself.

The rules of the game
There are quite a number of waterpolo rules and regulations but, during this introductory stage, the restrictions and possible infringements should be sensibly minimised, then gradually increased as the standard of play improves.

Minor or ordinary fouls
1. At the start, to move towards the centre of the pool before the referee's signal.
2. To walk when play is in progress or to stand when taking an active part in the game.
3. To hold on to the handrail except during the start or restart of the game.
4. To hold on to the sides of the pool or goal posts or push off from the wall or goal posts during play.
5. To take or hold the ball under water when tackled (fig. 29.4).
6. To strike the ball with the clenched fist (fig. 29.5).
7. Deliberately to impede or obstruct a player unless he is holding the ball (fig. 29.6).
8. Swimming on the back or shoulders of an opponent not holding the ball (fig. 29.7).
9. To splash water in the face of an opponent.
10. To jump from the bottom of the pool to play the ball or tackle an opponent.
11. To touch the ball with both hands at the same time.
12. To push off from or push an opponent.

These are some of the ordinary fouls which impose quite enough restrictions on our young players during their early practice games. The penalty

Fig. 29.4 Tackling

Fig. 29.5 Punching

Fig. 29.6 Obstructing an opponent   Fig. 29.7 Swimming over

for any of these infringements is a free throw to the other side, taken from where the foul was committed. The player may swim with the ball before passing, but the ball must be played by two players before a goal can be scored. Most players learn the rules by committing offences. This is one way of learning, but it is far more instructive for the teacher to hold a few brief rule-instruction sessions on the poolside with water demonstrations. During the initial stages of practice the referee will do well to 'go easy' on the whistle and instruct rather than penalise too harshly.

Major fouls

There are a series of infringements which are considered to be more serious; these are known as major fouls and some of these are listed below.

1. To hold, sink or pull back an opposing player not holding the ball.
2. To kick or strike an opponent.
3. To persist in an ordinary foul.
4. To interfere with a free throw, goal throw or corner throw.

The penalty for these offences is for the player to be ordered from the water for one minute or until a goal is scored.

Scoring a goal

A goal may be scored from anywhere within the field of play, providing that the scorer has received the ball outside the opponents' 2-m line. (See fig. 29.8 illustrating the field of play.) The ball must pass completely over the goal line for a goal to be registered. A corner throw should be awarded when the ball passes over the goal line outside the goal-scoring area, after being touched by a defender. If the ball is touched by an attacker, a goal throw is awarded.

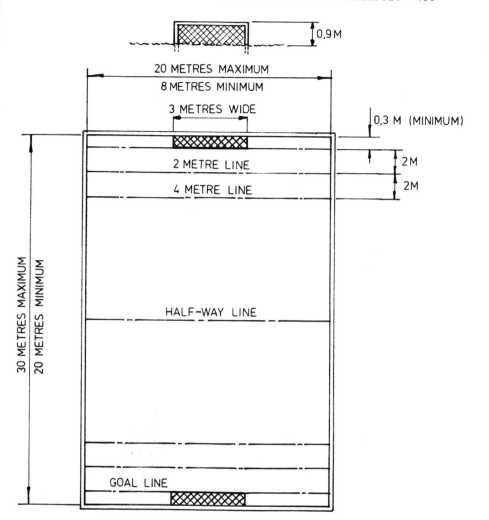

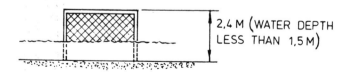

Fig. 29.8 Waterpolo: the field of play

Further information regarding the complete rules of the game can be obtained from the Amateur Swimming Association. Should the players wish to pursue the game beyond the confines of the school, there is a waterpolo section attached to most swimming clubs where young talent is usually welcomed.

Goalkeepers
The goalkeeper is subject to certain limitations but he is also allowed some privileges, such as:

1. Standing and walking during play.
2. Striking the ball with the fist.
3. Jumping from the bottom of the pool.
4. Using both hands to collect and distribute the ball.

The restrictions imposed on him are:

1. Not touching or throwing the ball beyond the half-way line.
2. Not holding on to any fittings at the end of the pool, including the goal posts.

A free throw against the goalkeeper is awarded for any of these offences.

Marking and tackling
The normal marking place for a defending player is between the opponent and the goal. There should be little distance between the two players, and it is up to the attacker to make space for himself by constantly swimming and manoeuvring, in order to establish a good shooting position when a pass is received. An opponent may only be tackled when he is actually holding the ball, *not* when he is swimming with it (fig. 29.3). The idea of a tackle is either to gain possession or to prevent the opponent from passing the ball or shooting at goal.

The team
There are eleven players in a waterpolo team, seven of whom are in the water at any one time. The remaining four members are substitutes, who may be called upon during the game. Substitutes may enter the water for several different reasons and at various times. In normal situations, the substitution time is during the intervals between play.

The usual line-up in the water takes the following form:

Goalkeeper	No. 1	Centre Forward	No. 6
Right Back	No. 2	Left Forward	No. 7
Left Back	No. 3	*with*	
Half Back	No. 4	Substitutes	Nos. 8, 9, 10 and 11
Right Forward	No. 5		on the poolside

Players often interchange positions during a game according to the standard and speed of play.

The field of play, equipment and officials
Figure 29.8 illustrates the layout and dimensions of the field of play, showing its maximum and minimum sizes.

Deviation from this dimensional standard is not important, however, where our early practice games take place. Remember, the object of this introductory chapter is to foster interest from which the game and its attendant skills may develop.

Polo caps are necessary for the game proper, but not essential for practising the skills. Light rubber caps may be used during practice games; however, where the players know each other, distinguishing precisely who is on which side becomes relatively easy. (There are only six other players at any given time to be remembered.)

The rules of waterpolo state that for each official game there should be a referee, two goal judges and a secretary. All these officials should be equipped with signal flags. There must also be a timekeeper who should possess a stop-watch and a whistle with which he should signal the end of the four five-minute periods.

However, for our introductory games, a referee should be quite sufficient. He should be provided with a wooden stick some 700 mm (27½ in.) long to which there should be fastened a dark blue flag at one end and a white flag at the other. A whistle is essential in order to signal an infringement during play and the team (blue or white) to which the free throw is awarded is indicated by displaying clearly the appropriate coloured flag.

The duration of a proper game is four periods of five minutes' *actual play*. The time is controlled by the timekeeper, who stops his watch at each signal for an infringement and restarts it as the ball is put into play once more. There are two-minute breaks between each period when the two sides change ends.

However, for our practice and friendly games, when water time may be at a premium, adjustments may be made by dividing the playing time, for instance, into two or four five-minute periods 'all in', i.e. not stopping the watch for each infringement. The game can become very exciting but, for the untrained, also very exhausting. The teacher, therefore, will be well advised to limit the periods of play to suit the standard of fitness, watermanship and polo-ability of the players concerned.

PART II

Anatomy and Physiology

The human body is the most complex and wonderful creation that exists. All swimming teachers and their charges are very fortunate indeed in that they each possess one. It is also useful to know how it works.

Individual bodies may be big or small, short or tall, and they may float quite readily or, again, they may sink steadily to the bottom of the swimming pool. Each body normally has two arms and two legs that may pull and push in order, hopefully, to propel itself through the water with ease and grace. Alternatively, the joints around which the limbs gyrate may be restricted in their movements and quickly grow tired. If muscular energy is seen to be lacking in swimmers, it is extremely useful for the teacher to know just why this is so and how vitality and energy may be restored and maintained. If the current activities concern the arts of muscular relaxation, an insight into the mysteries of how to develop these particular features can only enhance the quality of teaching.

When the limbs twist and turn in their many various ways, it is enlightening to know precisely how this happens and, with this acquired knowledge, be able to improve the efficiency and economy of such movements.

The essential life-supporting systems of respiration and blood circulation and their nervous supplies are all wonders in themselves and, if only in the name of safety, the teacher will indeed be wise to possess knowledge of their capabilities and their weaknesses. If they should accidentally fail, it is essential to know how to restore them to life once more.

The physical features of the human body are all supported by a strong and flexible bony frame which is known as the skeleton. The skeleton is a masterpiece in constructional technology in itself. It provides protection for the vital organs of the body and creates a foundation for the attachments of the skeletal muscles.

While being flexible as a whole, the components of the skeleton are extremely rigid and strong and able to support great loads and, in co-operation with the muscular system, exert tremendous forces. The ways in which these forces may be developed, and how the various muscles assist in their generation, is vital in understanding the mechanics of movement both on land and in the water.

The digestive system is the means by which food is transformed into energy. A knowledge of its function in relation to the production of this energy is yet another facet which should be explored.

The nervous system which is controlled by the brain is the most complex of all the systems. However, just a cursory insight into the central nervous system and its primary functions is useful in understanding the patterns of movement and why they occur.

The following chapters explain and illustrate but some of the many components of the human body, together with a brief description of their functions. In most instances these functions have been related to the swimmer. This is done in an attempt to provide the teacher with a deeper understanding of the physical aspects of the skills to be taught.

30 The Skeleton of the Human Body

The bony skeleton forms the rigid structure of the body (see fig. 30.1). It provides support and protection for some of the soft organs: the skull protects the brain and the rib cage serves to protect the vital organs of the thorax (the heart and lungs), and so on. The bones also serve as the rigid components of a mechanical leverage system. These levers also provide an integral surface on which the skeletal muscles, which provide the forces of movement, attach themselves. In certain parts of the skeleton, the bones are augmented by cartilage. The bones of the skeleton are also an abundant warehouse of calcium and phosphorus and play a major part in the metabolism of these minerals. The skeleton comprises two main groups of bones.

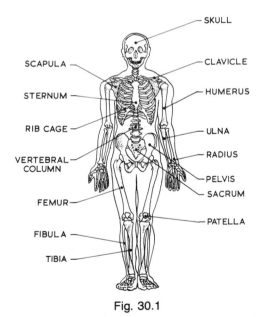

Fig. 30.1

    The axial skeleton is the basic structure to which the limbs are attached. It consists of the skull (fig. 30.2), the sternum and ribs – thoracic cage (figs 30.3 and 30.4), the vertebral column (figs 30.5 to 30.9) and the hyoid bone (see fig. 32.15). The skull is attached to the vertebral column by

441

means of the atlanto-occipital joint (that between the occipital bone of the skull and the uppermost vertebra, the atlas), which permits nodding movements of the head. The second vertebra, or axis, combines with the atlas to form the atlanto-axial joint, which enables head movement in a horizontal plane (shaking the head).

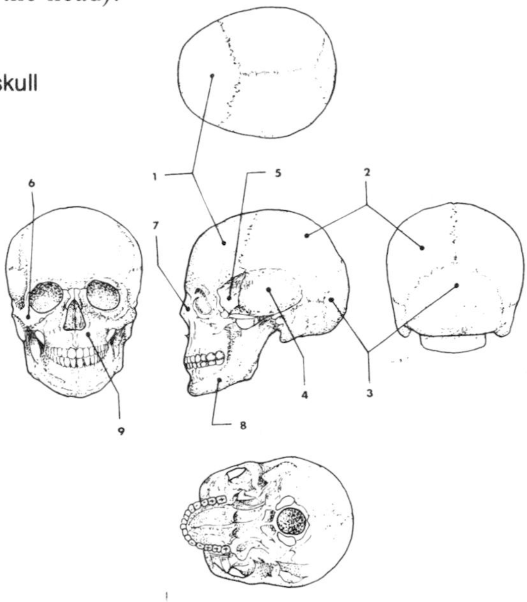

Fig. 30.2 The bones of the skull

The calvaria
1 frontal bone
2 parietal bones
3 occipital bone
4 temporal bone
5 sphenoid bone

The face
6 zygomatic (cheek bone)
7 nasal bone
8 mandible (lower jaw)
9 maxilla (upper jaw)

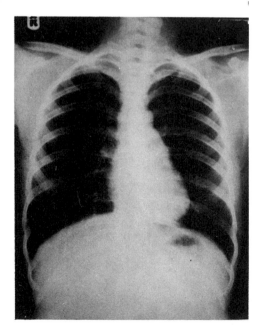

Fig. 30.3 X-ray photograph of thoracic cage, showing the ribs, clavicle and the outline of the heart

Fig. 30.4 The skeleton of the trunk and limb girdles (viewed from the front)

1–12 ribs
13–15 sternum
  13 manubrium
  14 body
  15 xiphoid process
16 vertebral column
17 hip bones forming the pelvic girdle
18 sacrum
19 coccyx
20 femur
21 scapula
22 humerus
23 pubis symphisis (anterior joint)

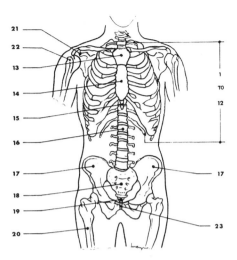

Fig. 30.5 The vertebral column

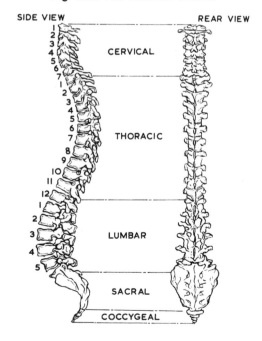

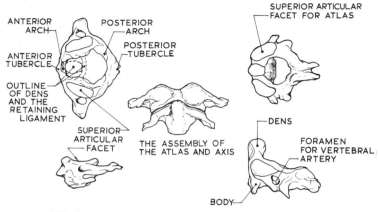

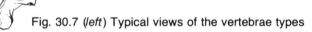

Fig. 30.6 The atlanto-axial joint

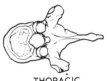

Fig. 30.7 (*left*) Typical views of the vertebrae types

CERVICAL

Fig. 30.8 X-ray photograph showing the cervical vertebrae and the atlanto-occipital joint

THORACIC

LUMBAR

A SECTIONAL VIEW
OF A
LUMBAR VERTEBRA

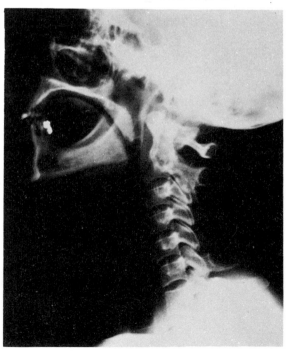

Fig. 30.9 X-ray photograph
of the lumbar vertebrae

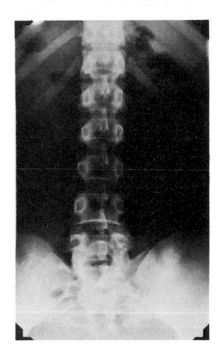

The appendicular skeleton is the formation of bone structures around which the limbs (including the hands and feet) and limb girdles are built up (see figs. 30.10 and 30.12 to 30.19).

There are, in addition to these, three small bones in each middle ear.

Fig. 30.10 The bones of the arm
and shoulder girdle

1 clavicle
2 scapula
3 humerus
4 radius
5 ulna
6 trochlea
7 capitulum
8 medial epicondyle
9 olecranon
10 lateral epicondyle
11 head of the humerus

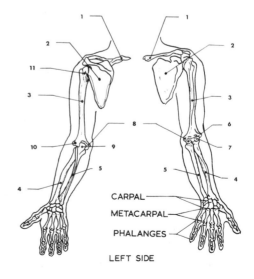

CARPAL

METACARPAL

PHALANGES

LEFT SIDE

FROM BEHIND   FROM THE FRONT

The structure of bone
Bone is the hardest connective tissue in the body. (Connective tissue is one of the various groups of elementary body-cell combinations.) It consists of about fifty per cent water, about thirty-four per cent calcium salts, and about sixteen per cent cellular matter. The section of most bones will reveal a *compact* outer layer and a spongy *cancellous* inner core. This spongy or cancellous structure is the means whereby the bulbous ends of bones are formed, while at the same time not introducing an increase in weight. If the inner layer of a bone were of the same material as the outer layer (compact), there would be a considerable increase in weight involved.

Classification of bones
Bones of the skeleton are classified, according to their shape, into the following groups:

LONG BONES Long bones consist of a long shaft with two extremities. They are found in the limbs and, acting as levers, they make movement possible.

SHORT BONES These are to be found in the hands and feet in the form of the carpal and tarsus groups. They are formed mostly of the cancellous bone tissue, covered by a thin compact layer. They are light, yet strong.

FLAT BONES Flat bones are of wafer-like construction, the spongy centre being sandwiched between the two layers of compact substance. These are to be found where protection is required, such as in the skull, ribs and scapula. Flat bones also provide for a large surface muscle attachment, as the scapula does.

Figure 30.11 shows how the scapula slides across the rib cage as the swimmer reaches forward on entry.

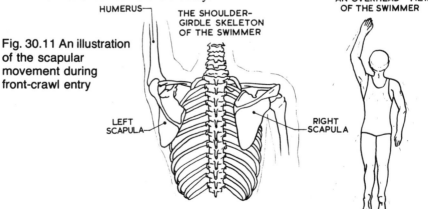

Fig. 30.11 An illustration of the scapular movement during front-crawl entry

AN OVERHEAD VIEW OF THE SWIMMER

HUMERUS

THE SHOULDER-GIRDLE SKELETON OF THE SWIMMER

LEFT SCAPULA

RIGHT SCAPULA

IRREGULAR BONES The irregular variety is the class of bony structures whose descriptions do not fall into the previous categories. Prime examples of these are the vertebrae.

SESAMOID BONES These are the bones which are developed in the muscular tendons and found in the regions of the joints. The patella, which assists in the articulation of the knee, is the largest of these.

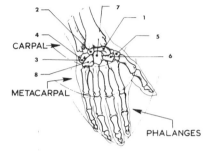

Fig. 30.12 The bones of the hand

1 scaphoid
2 lunate
3 triquetral
4 pisiform
5 trapezium
6 trapezoid
7 capitate
8 hamate

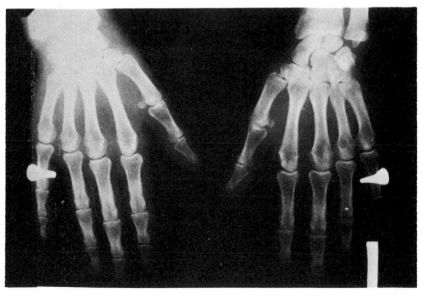

Fig. 30.13 X-ray photograph showing the skeleton of the hands (viewed from the back)

Fig. 30.14 The skeleton of the trunk
and limb girdles (viewed from behind)

1–12 ribs
13–15 hip bone
  13 ilium
  14 ischium
  15 pubis
16 vertebral column
17 pelvic brim
18 sacrum
19 coccyx
20 femur
21 scapula
22 humerus

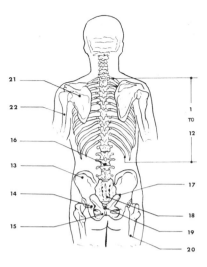

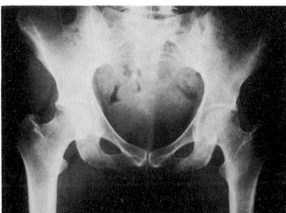

Fig. 30.15 X-ray
photograph of the
female lower limb
girdle

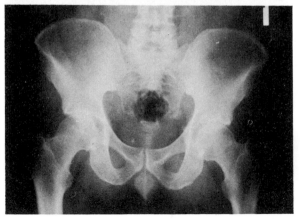

Fig. 30.16 X-ray
photograph of the
male lower limb
girdle

Fig. 30.17 The bones of the leg
and the lower limb girdle

1 femur
2 head of femur
3 neck of femur
4 great trochanter
5 lesser trochanter
6 medial condyle
7 lateral condyle
8 tibia (shaft)
9 lateral condyle of tibia
10 medial condyle of tibia
11 medial malleolus
12 fibula (shaft)
13 head of fibula
14 lateral malleolus
15 calcaneum
16 patella
17 hip bone
18 iliac fossa
19 iliac crest

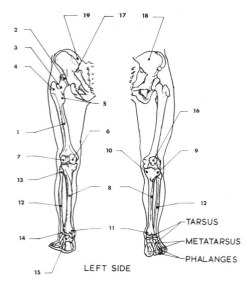

LEFT SIDE

FROM BEHIND   FROM THE FRONT

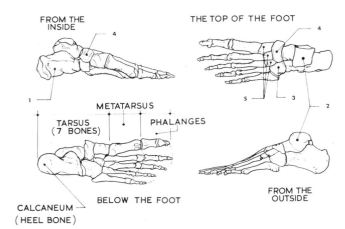

FROM THE
INSIDE

THE TOP OF THE FOOT

METATARSUS

TARSUS
(7 BONES)

PHALANGES

CALCANEUM
(HEEL BONE)

BELOW THE FOOT

FROM THE
OUTSIDE

Fig. 30.18 The bones of the foot

1 calcaneum
2 talus
3 cuboid
4 navicular
5 cuneiform

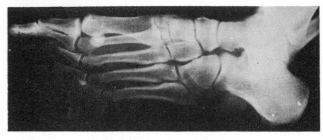

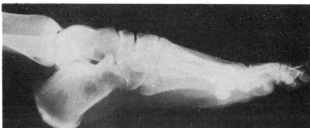

Fig. 30.19 X-ray photograph showing the skeleton of the foot in relaxed (*above*) and plantar-flexed position (*below*)

THE JOINTS OR ARTICULATIONS OF THE SKELETON

The movements of a swimmer's body and limbs are complex and variable, both in the water and during the many different forms of entry. It is therefore considered a useful aid to the teacher if he or she not only understands to some extent the mechanics of such movements, but also appreciates the capabilities and limitations of the various joint configurations of the body.

Joints or articulations are to be found in the body where bones communicate or unite with each other. Movements may be of differing modes and the related articulations are described as immovable, slightly movable, or freely movable.

The joints corresponding to these descriptions are classified respectively as fibrous, cartilaginous and synovial.

Fibrous joints (synthroses) (fig 30.20)
These are the immovable or fixed joints and may also include some slightly movable joints. The components of the joint are held adjacent to each other by fibrous tissue.

Sutures are confined to the skull and form a patterned joint wherever the broader surfaces of the bones articulate with each other.

A syndesmosis is a form of articulation which involves the binding together of adjacent bony surfaces by a membranous tissue. It affords a very slight movement and an example is the tibio-fibular joint.

A gomphosos (peg and socket) is a unique fibrous articulation restricted to the attachment of the teeth in the gums.

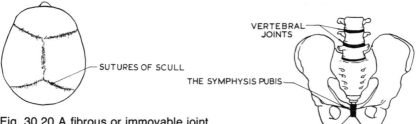

SUTURES OF SCULL

VERTEBRAL JOINTS

THE SYMPHYSIS PUBIS

Fig. 30.20 A fibrous or immovable joint

Fig. 30.21 Cartilaginous joints

Cartilaginous joints (amphiarthroses) (fig. 30.21)
These are wholly classified as slightly movable joints. The two adjacent surfaces of the articulations are covered by articular cartilage and connected by an intervening pad of fibrocartilage, then both surfaces are held together by ligaments. The pubic symphysis, whereby the two anterior articulations of the innominate bones are united, is an example. A further illustration of the cartilaginous joints occurs between the individual vertebrae.

Synovial joints (diathroses) (figs 30.22 and 30.23)
These are the freely moving joints and each displays a definite and similar set of characteristics as follows:

1. The end of the bones are covered with a layer of articular (hyaline) cartilage.
2. The components of the articulations are connected together by a fibrous capsule and often reinforced by accessory ligaments.
3. The capsule is completely lined with a synovial membrane.
4. The synovial membrane secretes a highly viscous synovial fluid which acts as a lubricant and also assists in maintaining the cell life in the articular cartilages.

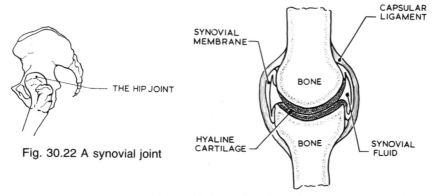

THE HIP JOINT

CAPSULAR LIGAMENT

SYNOVIAL MEMBRANE

BONE

HYALINE CARTILAGE

BONE

SYNOVIAL FLUID

Fig. 30.22 A synovial joint

Fig. 30.23 A section through a typical synovial joint

There are six varieties of joint in the synovial family:

Gliding joints (figs 30.12 and 30.18)
Two flat surfaces move in relation to each other while retaining contact,
e.g. the tarsus, carpus and articular processes of the vertebrae.

Hinge joints (figs 30.24 to 30.27)
In this type of joint, movement takes place when one articular surface fits
into another. The assembly is then constrained to allow movement in one
plane only, e.g. the elbow, knee, ankle, finger and toe joints.

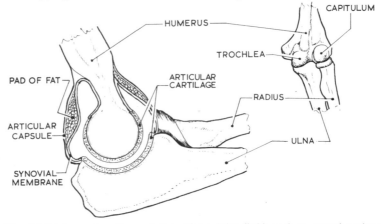

Fig. 30.24 A section through the elbow joint (*left*) and an exterior view

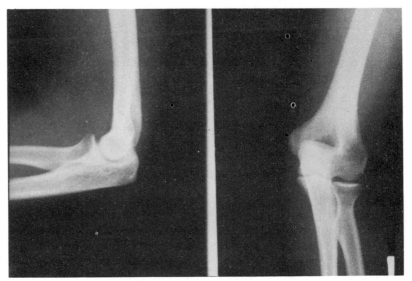

Fig. 30.25 X-ray photographs of the elbow joint

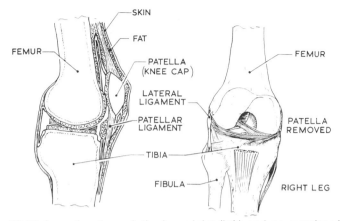

Fig. 30.26 A section through the knee joint (*left*) and an exterior view

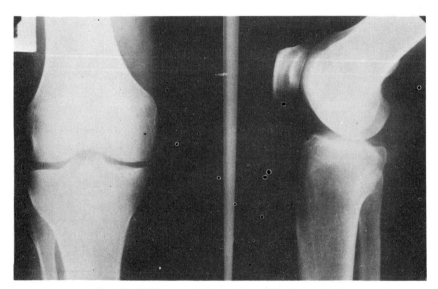

Fig. 30.27 X-ray photographs of the knee joint

Pivot joints (fig. 30.6)
Movement takes place also in one plane but about a central axis, e.g. the radio-ulnar and the atlanto-axial joints.

Condyloid joints (figs 30.12 and 30.13)
A convex inserted assembly or unit moves in relation to a stationary concave reception. This is similar to a hinge joint, but allows movement in two planes, i.e. forward-backward and sideways, but no rotation, e.g. the wrist joint.

Saddle joints (figs 30.12 and 30.13)
A concave unit moves in relation to a stationary convex bone. The movement is a reciprocal pattern of the condyloid articulation, e.g. the carpo-metacarpal joint of the thumb.

Ball and socket joints (figs. 30.28 to 30.30)
This is termed a spherical joint and allows freedom of movement to take place in three axes, e.g. the hip and shoulder joints.

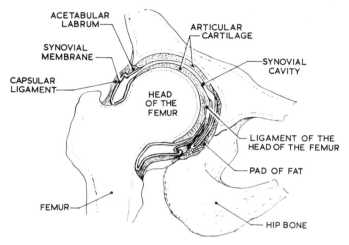

Fig. 30.28 A section through the hip joint

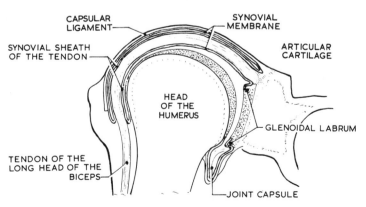

Fig. 30.29 A section through the shoulder joint

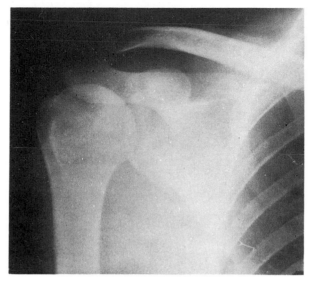

Fig. 30.30 X-ray photograph of the shoulder joint

DEFINITIONS OF MOVEMENT

The various forms of movement may be described by using the following terms:

Flexion

In the head, the spinal column, the hip, shoulder, elbow, wrist (supinated) and finger joints, flexion means to bend the limb in a forward direction. When the knee is bent, it is also flexed. When the ankle is plantar-flexed, the toes are moved away from the shin. Conversely dorsi-flexion means to move the foot in the direction of the shin. When the toes are flexed, they are moved towards the sole of the foot.

Extension

This is the opposed movement to flexion.

Abduction

Abduction is lateral movement away from the median plane. Where the digits of the hand and foot are concerned, however, abduction means spreading the fingers away from the second (middle) finger or moving the toes away from the second toe.

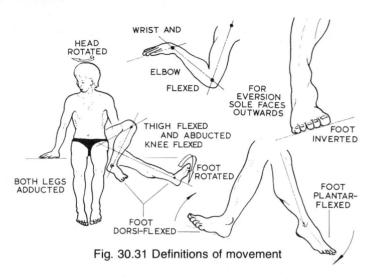

Fig. 30.31 Definitions of movement

Adduction
Adduction is the opposite movement to abduction.

Rotation
Rotation is movement around a longitudinal axis.

Circumduction
This is a (circular) combination of all the previously described movements.

Inversion
This is movement related to the feet and occurs when the inner border of the foot is raised and the sole directed inwards.

Eversion
This is the opposite movement to inversion.

31 The Muscles of the Human Body

Muscles make up the greater part of the soft tissue in the normal healthy human body, performing an enormous variety of voluntary and involuntary movements. There are three types of human muscle, each constructed of a different form of tissue and each performing a different function.

Skeletal muscle (fig. 31.1)
The muscles of the skeleton, namely the head, trunk and limbs, are known as voluntary muscles as their movement is controlled by the will. This particular muscle type is described as striped or striated because of the alternate light and dark bands which can be seen (under an electron microscope) on the long thin myofibrils which make up the muscle fibre. The bands contain two proteins, namely myosin and actin. When combined, these two proteins form a substance called actomyosin, the molecules of which contract in response to electrical impulses from the brain.

The tiny myofibrils are bound together by a thin membranous sheath called sarcolemma. The fibres, assembled thus, are then bundled together by a fibrous tissue called the perimysium. Finally, the individual bundles are bound together by a fibrous tissue called the epimysium to form the muscle.

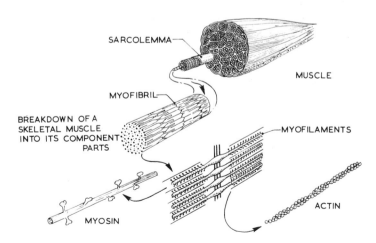

Fig. 31.1 Breakdown of a skeletal muscle into its component parts

457

Fig. 31.2 Unstriped muscle fibres

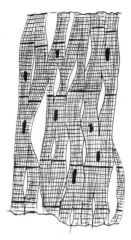

Fig. 31.3 Cardiac muscle

Unstriped muscle (fig. 31.2)
This type, which is also known as plain or involuntary muscle, cannot be controlled by the will and, in most parts of the body, its activity is under the control of the autonomic or involuntary nervous system. Involuntary muscle may be found in the digestive tract and in the blood vessels. It is also present in the trachea and the bronchi. The cells that form the muscle are long and flattened and without striations.

Cardiac muscle (fig. 31.3)
This is found only in the heart. It is striated in a similar fashion to that of voluntary muscle – but is involuntary. The fibres are shorter than those of the skeletal muscle and are branched. These anastomose with each other to form a network with adjacent fibres. The action of the cardiac contractions is rhythmical but the pulse rate is varied by signals which reach it from the vagus and sympathetic nerves. Branches from these nerves are fed to the sino-atrial node (the pacemaker), which is situated in the right atrium.

Muscle groups
The skeletal muscles may be divided into groups which have locations as follows: the head, the neck, the spinal column, the abdomen and thorax and the limbs. Each group may in turn be sub-divided according to their action and nerve supply. Each individual group is separated from the others by a formation of intermuscular septa.

The skeletal muscles are attached, in most cases, to two defined points. The more stationary attachment during the action of the muscles is termed the origin, while the moving point is known as the insertion. Muscle arises at its origin and passes to its insertion. Where the required movement is great in relation to the length of the muscle, the tendon is short and the muscle is long and fleshy. Where movement is short in relation to the muscle length, the tendon is long and the muscle belly is short. With very few exceptions, each muscle is able to act in such a way that the origin and the insertion can become reversed. For instance, in the simple act of opening a door, the brachialis muscle contracts to flex the forearm, thus pulling the door towards the person who is doing the opening. However, if the door is locked the person is, for an instant, pulled towards the door. In this case, the muscle attachments may be said to be reversed.

The act of swimming may be described as a partial reverse action, whereby, instead of the water being pushed back by the hand, the pressure build-up on the palm and lower arm is utilised to propel the swimmer forward. This action becomes more apparent as the swimmer increases his speed.

As already stated, the skeletal muscles tend to act in sub-groups, rather than individually, to perform movements of the limbs or body. Once a movement has been learnt, the same pattern of activity is reproduced every time this movement is carried out. The 'group movement' of the muscles is determined by the central nervous system and we are not conscious of the exact pattern of activity that is performed by the individual muscles.

In any particular movement, muscles may be programmed to act as prime movers, antagonists or synergists. These names relate to the function which the muscles actually perform during a movement.

Prime movers produce the movement which is determined by their physical attachments in relation to the neighbouring joint. For instance, contracting the brachialis produces flexion of the elbow because the mechanical link-up is such that the elbow joint is behind the muscle. In this instance, the prime mover is the brachialis muscle.

An antagonist is a muscle which acts in opposition to or in collaboration with a prime mover and can bring about the opposite movement when required. For instance, in the previous example of flexing the elbow, while the prime mover is the brachialis muscle, the antagonists are the triceps. Conversely, if the elbow is now straightened, the prime mover becomes the triceps, the antagonistic muscles now being the biceps.

When muscles act as synergists, they function as joint stabilisers or steadiers while other associations are moved. For example, the wrist may be steadied by its flexors while the fingers are extended. These wrist flexors are termed synergists.

Muscle relaxation

Total muscle relaxation only occurs when the fibres become bereft of life. However, for the purpose of this text, the pre-tension which is present in normal living muscles, giving them shape and firmness, is regarded as the condition of relaxation. This is the quality defined as 'muscle tone'.

It has been mentioned earlier that warm water is beneficial to relaxation and the learning-to-swim processes. Conversely, when cold water is in contact with the body, the sensory receptor nerve endings in the skin react and send signals to the central nervous system. Motor impulses are then generated which produce contractions in the muscle fibres, causing a state of general tension which hastens the onset of fatigue.

Muscle tension can also be of a psychological nature. Fear of the aquatic environment may also result in efferent motor impulses being transmitted from the brain to the muscles, thus causing unnecessary fibre contractions and premature tiredness. Muscle cramps may also be a result of such fear-induced tension.

Relaxation may take place in two ways. General relaxation is the condition of inactivity which takes place during rest and sleep, whereby the whole body is relaxed in a state of tranquillity. Specific relaxation is a local muscular condition which is brought about by the process of continual repetition of the same movement. It is this form of relaxation which is important to the swimmer.

It has been mentioned earlier that a prime mover muscle contracts in order to create a movement while the local antagonistic muscle assumes a relaxed state. Relaxation of the antagonistic groups is a natural function which develops with frequent practice and repetition of movement; it is also essential for prolonged activity.

Repetition of movement is also responsible for minimising the number of prime-moving muscles that are used during some particular skill. For instance, an untrained novice swimmer sometimes contracts *every single* muscle in his arms and shoulder girdle during a front-crawl recovery movement, and the tension may even spread right down to his finger-tips. This muscular effort is, of course, excessive. If we observe the trained and skilled swimmer, the same phase of the arm action will be seen to be relaxed and performed with dexterity and ease. He will have acquired the skill of specific arm- and shoulder-muscle relaxation by performing many repetitions of the same recovery movement.

Economy of effort goes hand in hand with specific muscle relaxation. Therefore, if the number of muscle fibres required to carry out a certain function can be minimised, the amount of oxygen and 'fuel' that is required will also be minimised. Consequently, fatigue will be delayed and longer periods of physical exertion will be possible. This does not mean that swimmers will necessarily swim faster, but it does mean that by repeated practice they will become fitter and develop the ability to swim for longer periods. This fact is important during the teaching of a skill, owing to the fact that a movement pattern tends to deteriorate as fatigue develops.

Muscle cramps

Most swimmers have experienced cramp either in the foot or leg. The condition, which is spontaneous and extremely painful, is brought about by the contraction of one or several muscles. Cramp may appear for no apparent reason, and it affects both the fit and the unfit. It often materialises after prolonged use of a certain muscle or group of muscles. The best method of relieving the painful contraction is by stretching the muscle. Cramp in the calf muscles is common in beginners and those attempting new leg-stretching movements relating to the different styles. Relief may be obtained by stretching or plantar-flexing the foot of the affected leg against something solid. Toe cramp may be relieved in a similar way. Firm kneading or rubbing sometimes helps.

'Stomach' or abdominal cramp is rare but to the swimmer it is serious and could prove fatal if experienced during aquatic exercise.

The cause of cramp is still subject to investigation but it is certain that the spasm is of a nervous or neuromuscular origin. Laboratory experiment has shown that an isolated muscle allowed to 'hypershorten' remains in the contracted state for some time unless forcibly stretched again. This situation is closely related to cramp.

Oxygen debt

The 'cellular warehouses' contain only enough ATP* to meet the demand of a relatively inactive body. The additional energy requirements are normally supplied by creatine P*, which is stored in the muscles. However, the swimmer, in performing some vigorous exercise, quickly exhausts the ATP which is stored in the muscle cells and the creatine P 'factories' cannot produce new ATP fast enough to replace that which has been used. But the swimmer keeps on swimming long, hard and fast.

Where does his extra supply of energy come from? The answer to this question is from the oxygen which is stored in the muscle fibres. Oxygen is most essential for the process of recovery after exertion while the immediate processes of a short (say, half-second) muscle contraction do not require it. It is therefore quite possible for muscles to perform quick spurts of activity in the absence of sufficient oxygen to assist in the chemical conversions. But, when the exertion is greater than normal, further supplies of glycogen are delivered to the muscles from the liver and, as this glycogen replenishes the creatine P supply, deposits of lactic acid are created. It is during this period of deprivation that the oxygen stored in the muscles is called upon to process the lactic acid into additional glycogen, and hence into creatine P, at a rate sufficient to sustain activity for a time. This discharging of the tissue-stored oxygen in order to sustain muscular effort is known as incurring an 'oxygen debt'.

---

* ATP (adenosine triphosphate) and creatine P are phosphates which make up the energy-rich compounds discharged during bodily exertion.

When such exertion is over, the swimmer goes through a period of heavy breathing and increased heart activity. This is in order to take in and subsequently distribute oxygen to the temporarily deprived cells and 'pay back the debt'.

Normal breathing will occur when the debt has been repaid and conditions return to normal. If for any reason the swimmer is unable to repay the oxygen debt, there will be a concentration of lactic acid and muscle fatigue will result. If the period of recovery phase lags too far behind the activity phase, the muscles will cease to respond in an efficient manner, thus forcing the swimmer to slow down or stop.

The amount of oxygen debt is approximately proportional to the severity of the exercise. For instance, during an energetic 100-m swim, an O_2 debt in the order 15–20 litres may be incurred. During a gentle and easy swim, a much smaller debt is incurred but will not be repaid until a rest is taken. The debt can always be repaid later, which is why a swimmer is able to hold his breath during a short sprint with no ill effects.

Levers

We have briefly reviewed the methods of construction of muscles and how they contract on signals from the brain; and how they are divided into groups in order to bring about movements of the limbs and parts of the trunk to which they are attached. We will now examine exactly how the skeletal muscles, acting as power sources, are able to pull on the bones via their tendonous attachments to create leverage. (Muscles are only able to pull by their contraction – they cannot push.)

Archimedes, when referring to the lever, is reputed to have said, 'Give me a firm spot on which to stand and I will move the earth.' He would, of course, have needed rather a long lever to carry out this task!

Getting back to reality, leverage is a mechanical term describing the action of one of the simplest machines known to man. A lever system consists of the lever itself, usually a rigid bar or something similar; two forces, one an effort, the other resisting the effort; and a fulcrum or pivot providing a supporting force. The distance from the effort to the fulcrum is known as the force arm and the distance between the fulcrum and resistive force (usually something to be moved), is known as the resistance arm. By dividing the length of the force arm by that of the resistance arm, we derive a factor known as the mechanical advantage (MA) of the lever system. The mechanical advantage of the system depends upon where the forces are located on the lever arm.

One of the advantages of the lever is that it may be used to shift heavier loads than would normally be possible by lifting or pulling and pushing. It can also effectively change the direction of the applied effort or alter the distance by which the resistive load is moved.

Certain physical laws which apply to levers become especially pertinent when considering their anatomical use.

One of these applications is the fact that an increase in the effort or force arm (fa in fig. 31.4) between fulcrum and applied effort *increases* the mechanical advantage but *decreases* the range of movement at the resistive end. The converse of this statement is also true. This means that if the biceps muscle which flexes the elbow (fig. 31.10) were inserted further along the radius towards the hand, for the *same* magnitude of muscular contraction, the swing of the forearm would be less. There would, however, be more force available at the hand.

Another feature is that the greatest effectiveness is gained when the effort is applied at right-angles to the lever. The gastrocnemius and soleus ankle flexors adequately demonstrate this quality.

When it is necessary to apply such effort at an acute angle or even in line with the lever itself, the mechanical advantage of the arrangement may be improved by the introduction of the pulley or guide which re-directs the applied force.

The knee joint is one such example (fig. 31.4). Here, the patella (knee cap) is seen to be sliding over the lower end of the femur during a leg-kick movement. At the same time it creates and maintains the patellar ligament insertion angle and the effort arm (fa). The bottom illustration shows how the mechanical advantage would diminish if no patella were present to improve the angle of insertion.

There is a simple set of relationships appertaining to the positions of the effort, resistance and fulcrum resulting in three types or classes of lever system. These apply to both mechanical and physical applications.

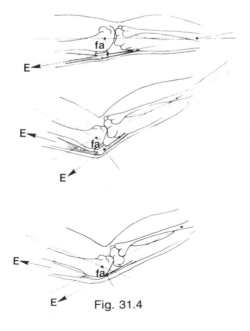

Fig. 31.4

First-class lever (fig. 31.5)
Here the fulcrum (F) lies between (but not necessarily in the centre of) the effort (E) and the resistive load (R). It is the most common and most versatile of the lever systems in which the direction of movement is changed. Thus, if the effort is downward, the tendency is for the resistive load to move upwards, see-saw fashion.

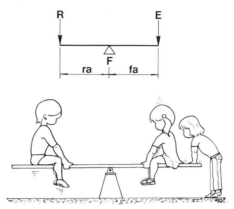

Fig. 31.5 First-class lever

The mechanical advantage of the first-class lever system may be greater than, equal to or less than 1.0. It should also be understood that when the effective or resistive load is increased by subtle repositioning of the fulcrum, the distance that it moves is reduced. Similarly, greater movement of a resistive load may be brought about by moving the fulcrum nearer to the effort, but more effort is needed in order to balance or shift it.

Common examples of the first-class lever are a pair of scissors or shears, a bottle opener or, as illustrated, the see-saw.

For equilibrum or balance, the following conditions apply in all three classes of lever.

$$\text{resistance} \times \text{resistance arm} = \text{effort} \times \text{force arm}$$
$$\text{or}$$
$$R \times ra = E \times fa \tag{1}$$
$$\text{also}$$
$$\frac{R}{E} = \frac{fa}{ra} = \text{mechanical advantage} \tag{2}$$

If we refer this formula to the children on the first-class lever system of the see-saw in fig. 31.5, for equilibrium:

boy's weight × his distance to fulcrum = girl's weight × her distance to fulcrum + the weight of the helping hand × its distance to fulcrum

If the boy moved nearer to the fulcrum, the helping hand would probably not be needed. If he moved back further, a little more assistance would be needed, and the girl who is standing would need to climb aboard behind her friend, using *all* her weight to help balance the see-saw.

An anatomical example of the first-class lever is shown in fig. 31.6. The human head pivots at the atlanto-occipital joint and its centre of gravity is normally in front of this joint. The head may be tilted by contraction of the splenius and trapezius muscles at the back of the neck.

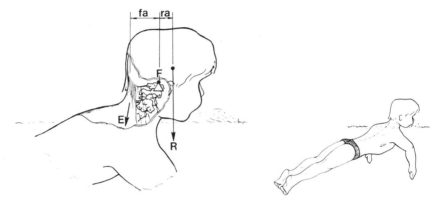

Fig. 31.6 Anatomical example of a first-class lever

In the example, the weight of the breast stroker's head (approximately seven and a half per cent of body weight) is 3 kg (R), and its centre of mass (CG) is approximately 2 cm (ra) forward of the atlanto-occipital joint (F); also, the neck extensor muscles attached to the back of the skull pull (E) at a distance of approximately 6 cm (fa) from the pivot, with a force of E which is derived:

$$E = \frac{R \times ra}{fa} = \frac{3 \times 2}{6} = 1.0 \text{ kg muscular force}$$

The head may be tilted back further until the centre of mass (R) passes over the top of the pivot where a new head-flexing set of neck muscles (longus capitis) comes into play.

Accepting the fact that, in a simple lever mechanism, the reactions of the effort force and the fulcrum are in some way physically connected, a further but more complicated anatomical example of the first-class lever is shown in fig. 31.7. The configuration is inverted but the basic principle remains the same. Here the swimmer is mounting the starting block and standing in 'tip-toe' fashion on one leg.

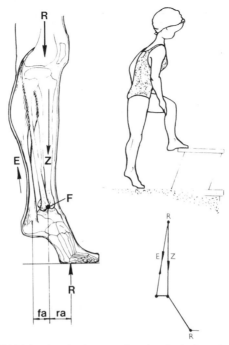

Fig. 31.7 Anatomical example of a first-class lever

The calf muscles (gastrocnemius and soleus) contract, providing the effort (E); the fulcrum (F) is the ankle joint formed by the lower end of the tibia and the talus. The weight of her body (R) is transmitted through the bony structure of the foot to the poolside. The ankle joint itself feels considerably more than just this body weight due to the contraction of the calf muscles pulling the joint together. The ankle-joint load (Z) may be *approximately* thus: assuming fa to be 3 cm (this remains fairly constant) and ra to be 4.5 cm (variable) and the swimmer's weight (R) to be 40 kg, then for equilibrium:

$$E \times fa \simeq R \times ra \qquad \therefore E = \frac{R \times ra}{fa}$$

also, by taking moments about the ball of the foot, we have:

$$\therefore Z \times ra \simeq \frac{R \times ra}{fa} \times (ra + fa)$$

$$\therefore \qquad Z \simeq \frac{R}{fa} (ra + fa)$$

Substituting the values of R, ra and fa, the ankle-joint load Z becomes approximately:

$$Z \backsimeq \frac{40}{3} \times (4.5 + 3) \backsimeq 100 \text{ kg}$$

which is two and a half times more than the swimmer's body weight. The calf muscles, in performing this lift, need to exert

$$E = \frac{40 \times 4.5}{3} = 60 \text{ kg}$$

which, although approximate, is one and a half times the body weight. The calf load however will tend to reduce as the swimmer raises herself higher on her toes because of the geometric reduction of ra.

Second-class lever (fig. 31.8)
In the second-class lever system, the resistance lies somewhere between the effort and the fulcrum. By this definition the resistance arm is *always* less than the force arm, hence the mechanical advantage is always greater than 1.0.

The conditions of equilibrium are exactly as before, whereby:

$$\frac{R}{E} = \frac{fa}{ra} = MA$$

However, it can probably be seen that, as the resistance is moved nearer to the fulcrum, the required effort to balance the system becomes less. If we insert some real values, we can illustrate the reduction in required effort to lift a load 20 kg when we shift it nearer to the fulcrum.

(Let ra = 50 cm and fa = 100 cm initially)

$$\therefore \text{from (1) R} \times \text{ra} = E \times \text{fa} \qquad \therefore E = \frac{R \times ra}{fa} = \frac{20 \times 50}{100} = 10 \text{ kg}$$

If we now shift R a little nearer to the fulcrum, say, 25 cm away from it (ra):

$$\text{from (1) } E = \frac{20 \times 25}{100} = 5 \text{ kg}$$

Thus any required lift is a little easier.

In fig. 31.8 the children are playing 'wheelbarrows' and it will be seen that if the boy 'tucked more leg under his arm' he would reduce fa and consequently take more of the girl's weight. The result would be that she would take less weight on her arms.

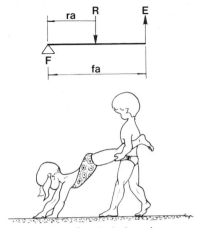

Fig. 31.8 Second-class lever

Third-class lever (fig. 31.9)
The third-class lever system has the effort (R) located between the fulcrum and the resistance. In this arrangement, the effort arm (fa) must always be less than the resistance arm (ra), resulting in a mechanical advantage of less than 1.0. Consequently, the effort to raise or balance a resistive load is always greater than the load itself, but moves less distance.

The third-class lever system may be seen in a pair of tongs or tweezers. The rod fisherman with a heavy strike uses this kind of leverage, as also do the pool staff occasionally – see fig. 31.9.

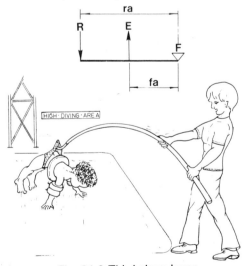

Fig. 31.9 Third-class lever

Anatomically, the forearm is an excellent example of a third-class lever system whereby contraction of the biceps muscle assists in flexing the elbow (fig. 31.10). Also illustrated is a swimmer performing a surface dive and, while the whole arm normally rotates about the shoulder, there is some flexing at the elbow. The resistance is in the form of water pressure which is created on the hand and lower arm by its downward movement.

A more conventional illustration of the forearm is also shown. One aspect of the arrangement is that the muscular insertion at the upper end of the ulna displays a short effort arm (fa). This produces a rapid forearm movement for a short muscular contraction. This contraction can take place very quickly, consequently the hand sweep may be very rapid.

Adding some real values to the system, let us assume that the average created water force felt on the arm is 10 kg (R) and that ra, the effective arm, is 25 cm; fa is small and in the region of 4 cm. The muscular effort is therefore calculated as

$$E = 10 \times \frac{25}{4} = 62.5 \text{ kg}$$

This means that due to the comparatively limited but variable magnitude of ra (it becomes a maximum when the forearm is at right-angles to the upper arm), quite a high muscular effort is required in order to counter a relatively small force.

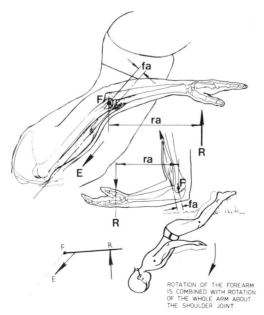

ROTATION OF THE FOREARM
IS COMBINED WITH ROTATION
OF THE WHOLE ARM ABOUT
THE SHOULDER JOINT

Fig. 31.10 Anatomical example of a third-class lever

32 The Muscles of the Body in Relation to the Swimmer

The energetic swimmer utilises almost every muscle in the body at some time or other. This is one reason why swimming is such a fine exercise. The following part of the text identifies, describes and illustrates most of these muscles; it explains how they act – muscles can only pull: they cannot push – and analyses patterns of movement. Finally it describes how the swimmer brings each particular muscle or group of muscles into use.

The major regions of muscles have been related to the movements of swimming and are as follows: the leg-kicking muscles (figs 32.1 to 32.6), the arm-stroke muscles (figs 32.7 to 32.10), the arm-stroke muscles of the chest and back (figs. 32.11 to 32.13), the muscles of the abdomen (figs 32.14 and 32.15), the muscles of the neck (fig. 32.16), and the respiratory muscles (fig. 32.17).

THE LEG-KICKING MUSCLES

1. Gluteus medius (fig. 32.3)

RELATED SWIMMING ACTIVITY: The breast-stroke leg kick is the only movement of the four competitive strokes which requires the legs to be spread (abducted), an action which is performed by the gluteus medius. Rotation of the feet can be increased when the legs are straight by medially rotating the thigh. This movement takes place during the front-crawl, back-crawl and butterfly leg kicks.

2. Piriformis (fig. 32.3)

RELATED SWIMMING ACTIVITY: The thighs are laterally rotated to some extent at the end of the breast-stroke whip-kick. Lateral abduction of the extended thigh is not a swimming function.

3. The gemelli muscles – gemellus superior and gemellus inferior (fig. 32.3)

RELATED SWIMMING ACTIVITY: The muscles are mainly active during the latter part of the breast-stroke leg kick as the flexed thighs are closing and straightening.

4. Obturator internus (fig. 32.3)

RELATED SWIMMING ACTIVITY: The muscle is mainly active during the latter part of the breast-stroke leg kick as the flexed thighs are closing and straightening.

5. Quadratus femoris (fig. 32.3)

RELATED SWIMMING ACTIVITY: During the latter part of the breast-stroke leg-recovery movement, when the swimmer's knees are opened, the activity continues until the termination of the kick, when the legs have assumed an athletically stretched mode and there is no lateral thigh rotation.

The iliopsoas muscles consist of two sets of muscles, the psoas and the iliacus:

6. Psoas (fig. 32.3)

RELATED SWIMMING ACTIVITY: The muscle contracts during the downbeat movements in both the front-crawl and butterfly leg kicks, in order to swing the upper leg downwards. In the back-crawl stroke, the muscle contracts to move the thigh upwards towards the water surface during the leg upbeat. The leg-recovery movement in the breast stroke requires the thighs to be flexed. Contraction of the psoas muscles assists in bringing about this movement.

7. Iliacus (fig. 32.3)

RELATED SWIMMING ACTIVITY: Assists the psoas muscles as previously described.

8. Gluteus maximus (fig. 32.3)

RELATED SWIMMING ACTIVITY: The upward movement of the thighs in both the front crawl and butterfly strokes is brought about by contraction of these powerful muscles. In the butterfly action, both muscles (one attached to each leg) contract simultaneously, while in the front crawl they act alternately. The back-stroke leg action requires the muscles to contract on the downbeats. The abduction of the thighs during the breast-stroke leg recovery is assisted by contraction of the upper fibres of the muscle. The lateral rotation of the thighs during recovery is also a gluteus maximus function. Additionally, the origination of the thigh extension throughout the propulsive movement is carried out mainly by the gluteus maximus muscle.

9. Tensor fasciae latae (fig. 32.3)

RELATED SWIMMING ACTIVITY: The muscle plays a minor roll in extending the lower leg during all the strokes. The abduction movement during the breast-stroke kick is assisted in a minor way by contraction of this muscle.

10. Gluteus minimus (fig. 32.3)

RELATED SWIMMING ACTIVITY: The muscle is comparatively inactive during the front- and back-crawl leg movements; there is also very little involvement during the butterfly kick. If feet inversion is magnified, however, by medial rotation of the thigh, then there will be a slight contraction of the muscles assisting those of the lower leg.

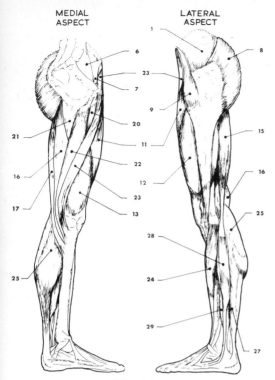

MEDIAL ASPECT · LATERAL ASPECT

The kicking muscles

1 gluteus medius
2 pirformis
3 gemelli
4 obturator internus
5 quadratus femoris
6 psoas
7 iliacus
8 gluteus maximus
9 tensor fascae latae
10 gluteus minimus
11 rectus femoris
12 vastus lateralis
13 vastus medialis
14 vastus intermedius
15 biceps femoris
16 semimembranosus
17 semitendinosus
18 pectineus
19 adductor brevis
20 adductor longus
21 adductor magnus
22 gracilis
23 sartorius
24 tibialis anterior

Fig. 32.1

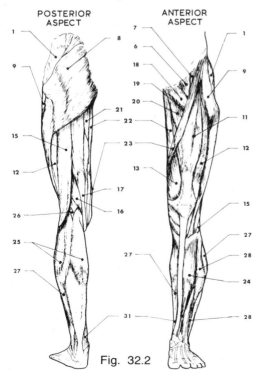

POSTERIOR ASPECT · ANTERIOR ASPECT

Fig. 32.2

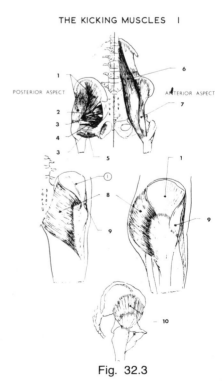

THE KICKING MUSCLES I

POSTERIOR ASPECT · ANTERIOR ASPECT

Fig. 32.3

25–26 triceps surae
  25 gastrocnemius
  26 soleus
27 popliteus
28 peroneus longus
29 peroneus brevis
30 tibialis posterior
31 flexor digitorum longus
32 flexor hallucis longus
33 extensor hallucis longus

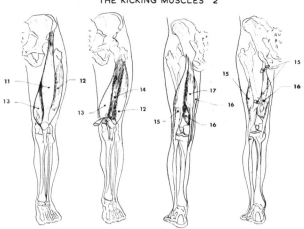

Fig. 32.4

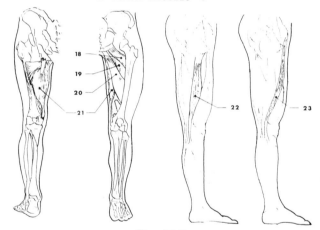

Fig. 32.5

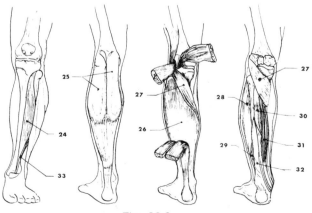

Fig. 32.6

11–14. The quadriceps group of muscles – quadriceps femoris (fig. 32.4)
This is formed by the rectus femoris, vastus lateralis, vastus medialis and vastus intermedius.

RELATED SWIMMING ACTIVITY: Whenever the flexed lower legs are straightened, the quadriceps group are the prime movers. This action applies to the downbeats of the front crawl and butterfly strokes and also to the back crawl upbeat. The final accelerating and whip-like propulsive breaststroke kick is also carried out mainly by these muscles. The rectus femoris is also active during the recovery action of the legs in breast stroke, when the thighs are flexed.

15–17. The 'hamstring' muscles (fig. 32.4)
Grouped together, the biceps femoris, semimembranosus and semitendinosus are more familiarly known as the 'hamstring' muscles.

RELATED SWIMMING ACTIVITY: This 'posterior femoral' group of muscles flexes the lower legs either together, as during the initial stage of butterfly downbeat, or singly, as at the start of the front-crawl downbeat. The upbeat of the back-crawl kick also initially utilises the action of all three flexors. Rotation of the leg to bring about the 'toeing-in' effect is carried out by contraction of the two medial muscles of the group (assisted by the popliteus, sartorius and gracilis). The breast-stroke leg kick demands that the lower legs be drawn up towards the bottom during their recovery. It is the action of the hamstrings which make this possible. When the feet are turned outwards, prior to performing the propulsive part of the kick, it is the action of the biceps femoris which makes this possible.

18. Pectineus (fig. 32.5)
RELATED SWIMMING ACTIVITY: In the front crawl and butterfly strokes, the pectineus assists the more powerful hip flexors during the downbeat part of the kick. In back crawl it is the upbeat which brings the muscle into play. The pectineal muscle, being an adductor, is used during the closing action of the breast-stroke kick.

19–21. Adductor brevis, adductor longus, adductor magnus (fig. 32.5)
RELATED SWIMMING ACTIVITY: The breast stroke would seem to be the main style to utilise these adductors, although as the closing action of the legs is not a common dry-land occurrence it is perhaps not advisable to submit beginner swimmers to too much of this particular muscular activity in the early stages of teaching. The breast-stroke leg kick needs to be moulded rather more than the others, and extensive repetition is necessary. The longus and magnus become active during all the kicks where flexion and extension of the thigh occur.

22. Gracilis (fig. 32.5)

RELATED SWIMMING ACTIVITY: The muscle acts in some way, during the leg-flexing movements of all the strokes. The inward rotation of the feet during the kicking movements in the vertical plane is assisted by this muscle. In breast stroke it assists the other adductors during the closing action of the legs, but acts in opposition to the outward feet rotators.

23. Sartorius (fig. 32.5)

RELATED SWIMMING ACTIVITY: Simultaneous or individual flexion of the hip and knee, as in the crawl and butterfly strokes, utilises the characteristics of this muscle. The abduction feature is used during the breast-stroke leg recovery, as also during the thigh- and knee-flexing movements. The lateral rotation of the thigh assists in establishing the essential outward-pointing of the feet during the propulsive movement.

24. Tibialis anterior (fig. 32.6)

RELATED SWIMMING ACTIVITY: The muscle is most important during the breast stroke, being one of the two dorsi-flexors of the foot. During the performance of the other strokes it is mainly an antagonist.

25. Gastrocnemius (fig. 32.6)

26. Soleus (fig. 32.6)

Together the gastrocnemius and soleus form a group which is sometimes termed the *triceps surae*.

RELATED SWIMMING ACTIVITY: In the crawl and butterfly strokes the triceps surae establish the streamlining and propelling features of the feet by plantar flexion. Breast stroke utilises the feature to a lesser extent. The triceps surae are very prominent during diving and push-offs from the wall.

27. Popliteus (fig. 32.6)

RELATED SWIMMING ACTIVITY: Assists in establishing the inward rotation of the feet (toeing-in) during the vertical-plane leg kicks. Also helps during knee-flexion movements in all strokes.

28. Peroneus longus (fig. 32.6)

RELATED SWIMMING ACTIVITY: The eversion qualities of the muscle are not often used in swimming. But the dorsi-flexion characteristics are, of course, used during the breast-stroke leg kick.

29. Peroneus brevis (fig. 32.6)

Relatively inactive during swimming activities.

30. Tibialis posterior (fig. 32.6)
RELATED SWIMMING ACTIVITY: Probably comes into play more during the diving and push-off activities than in swimming.

31. Flexor digitorum longus (fig. 32.6)
RELATED SWIMMING ACTIVITY: Dorsi-flexion activity during the breast-stroke leg kick.

32. Flexor hallucis longus (fig. 32.6)
RELATED SWIMMING ACTIVITY: Wherever 'toeing-in' occurs.

33. Extensor hallucis longus (fig. 32.6)
RELATED SWIMMING ACTIVITY: One of the dorsi-flexors of the foot during the breast-stroke leg kick.

THE ARM-STROKE MUSCLES
1. Supraspinatus (fig. 32.7)
RELATED SWIMMING ACTIVITY: Lateral rotation of the arm occurs in all the arm actions, especially sculling, and the muscle becomes active. As a joint stabiliser it is always active. The recovery actions of front and back crawl utilise the abduction qualities of the muscle.

2. Subscapularis (fig. 32.7)
RELATED SWIMMING ACTIVITY: The medial rotation feature occurs in most of the propulsive arm movements and is most prominent in the sculling action. Underwater swimming, whereby the arm is swept down the side of the body, utilises the adduction features. There is probably some action during the push phases of the crawl and butterfly strokes.

3. Teres major (fig. 32.7)
RELATED SWIMMING ACTIVITY: This is one of the pulling muscles and is active right through the catch, pull and push phases of crawl and butterfly strokes. In breast stroke it assists during the catch, pull and sculling phases.

3A. Teres minor (fig. 32.7)
RELATED SWIMMING ACTIVITY: Acts mainly as a joint steadier in all the arm movements.

4. Infra spinatus (fig. 32.7)
RELATED SWIMMING ACTIVITY: Mainly acts as a joint steadier with perhaps a little assistance during the initial stages of the front-crawl and butterfly arm recoveries.

5. Deltoid (fig. 32.7)

RELATED SWIMMING ACTIVITY: The over-the-surface recoveries of the crawl and butterfly strokes rely almost entirely on the action of the deltoid muscles, as do the latter stages of the push phases and release.

6. Triceps (fig. 32.8)

RELATED SWIMMING ACTIVITY: Wherever arm extension or partial extension is to be maintained, the muscle is extensively used. The propulsive movements of the front crawl and butterfly are examples of this, together with the initial stages of recovery. During the push phase of the back-crawl arm stroke, the muscle is active in the downward sweep of the arm. The outward and backward pull of the breast-stroke action utilises the muscle, as does the straightening action when the arms are recovered forward.

7. Anconeus (fig. 32.8)

RELATED SWIMMING ACTIVITY: Is closely allied to that of the triceps.

8. Brachialis (fig. 32.8)

RELATED SWIMMING ACTIVITY: Assists in flexing the forearm and maintaining it flexed, and is most prominent during the catch phases of the crawl and butterfly strokes. Active also during the breast-stroke arm scull and recovery.

9. Coracobrachialis (fig. 32.8)

RELATED SWIMMING ACTIVITY: The muscle is very active during the racing-dive arm swing. It assists also during the forward recovery movements of the breast-, front-crawl and butterfly strokes.

10. Biceps brachii (fig. 32.8)

RELATED SWIMMING ACTIVITY: Assists the brachialis in all its activities. The back-crawl catch movement utilises the lateral rotation features.

11. Flexor digitorum sublimis (fig. 32.9)

RELATED SWIMMING ACTIVITY: Flexion of the wrist is used during most of the various propulsive stroke phases, in order to direct the thrust forces backwards. These muscles are used for this task.

12. Flexor pollicis longus (fig. 32.9)

13. Flexor digitorum progundus (fig. 32.9)

14. Pronator teres (fig. 32.9)

RELATED SWIMMING ACTIVITY: The medial rotation or pronation of the forearm is necessary in all the strokes to assist in directing the hand backwards. This is carried out mainly by the pronator teres.

Fig. 32.7 The arm-stroke muscles (1)

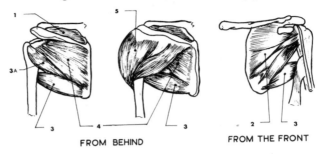

FROM BEHIND   FROM THE FRONT

Fig. 32.8 The arm-stroke muscles (2)

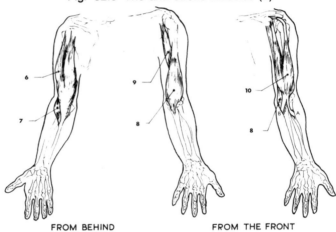

FROM BEHIND   FROM THE FRONT

Fig. 32.9 The arm-stroke muscles (3)

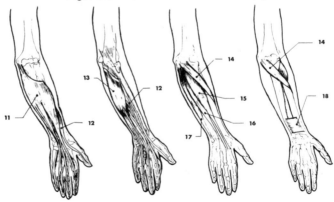

FROM THE FRONT

Fig. 32.10 The arm-stroke muscles (4)

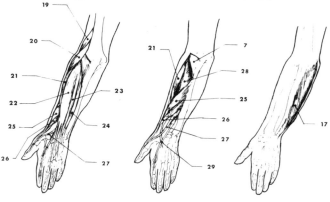

FROM BEHIND

The arm-stroke muscles

1 supraspinatus	16 palmaris longus
2 subscapularis	17 flexor carpi ulnaris
3 teres major	18 pronator quadratus
3A teres minor	19 brachioradialis
4 infraspinatus	20 extensor carpi radialis longus
5 deltoid	21 extensor carpi radialis brevis
6 triceps	22 extensor digitorum
7 anconeus	23 extensor digiti minimi
8 brachialis	24 extensor carpi ulnaris
9 coracobrachialis	25 abductor pollicis longus
10 biceps brachii	26 extensor pollicis brevis
11 flexor digitorum sublimis	27 extensor pollicis longus
12 flexor pollicis longus	28 supinator muscle
13 flexor digitorum profundus	29 extensor indicis
14 pronator teres	
15 flexor carpi radialis	

15. Flexor carpi radialis (fig. 32.9)

RELATED SWIMMING ACTIVITY: Assists the pronator teres in its activities.

16. Palmaris longus (fig. 32.9)

RELATED SWIMMING ACTIVITY: In all the propulsive phases of the strokes, the ability to flex the wrist is important. This muscle contracts to achieve this.

17. Flexor carpi ulnaris (fig. 32.9)

RELATED SWIMMING ACTIVITY: Assists the palmaris longus in its actions. Also, the pulling-towards-the-little-finger movement is used during the back-crawl hand entry.

18. Pronator quadratus (fig. 32.9)
RELATED SWIMMING ACTIVITY: The activity of the muscle is that of assisting the pronator teres in controlling the position of the hand during propulsion.

19. Brachioradialis (fig. 32.10)
Minimal usage during the swimming activity.

20. Extensor carpi radialis longus (fig. 32.10)
RELATED SWIMMING ACTIVITY: Extension of the wrist is required in many activities such as the push and glide and entry from a dive.

21. Extensor carpi radialis brevis (fig. 32.10)
RELATED SWIMMING ACTIVITY: Assists the previous muscle in its extending function.

22. Extensor digitorum (fig. 32.10)

23. Extensor digiti minimi (fig. 32.10)

24. Extensor carpi ulnaris (fig. 32.10)
RELATED SWIMMING ACTIVITY: Assists the other wrist extensors during the previously mentioned functions.

25. Abductor pollicis longus (fig. 32.10)

26. Extensor pollicis brevis (fig. 32.10)

27. Extensor pollicis longus (fig. 32.10)

28. Supinator muscle (fig. 32.10)
RELATED SWIMMING ACTIVITY: Used more in the back strokes where the sweep of the arms requires this supination movement.

29. Extensor indicis (fig. 32.10)

THE ARM-STROKE MUSCLES OF THE CHEST AND BACK
30. Subclavius (fig. 32.11)

31. Pectoralis major (fig. 32.11)
RELATED SWIMMING ACTIVITY: The catch, pull and push phases of the front crawl and butterfly strokes are closely allied to pull-up or climbing movements. It is here that these powerful chest muscles are used. Adduction is a characteristic of all the stroke arm movements and consequently trained swimmers display well-developed chests.

The arm-stroke muscles of the chest and back

30 subclavius
31 pectoralis major
32 pectoralis minor
33 serratus anterior
34 levator scapulae
35 rhomboideus major and minor
36 erectores spinae (sacrospinalis)
37 trapezius
38 latissimus dorsi

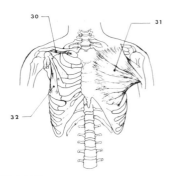

Fig. 32.11 The arm-stroke muscles
of the chest

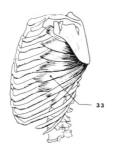
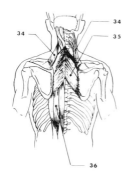
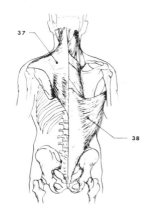

Fig. 32.12 The arm-stroke muscles
of the back

32. Pectoralis minor (fig. 32.11)

RELATED SWIMMING ACTIVITY: Working in conjunction with the levator scapulae and rhomboids, the muscle assists the swimmer in arm movements beyond the plane of the shoulder. This means that its activity becomes more pronounced during the push and release phases of the crawl and butterfly strokes.

33. Serratus anterior (fig. 32.11)

RELATED SWIMMING ACTIVITY: All the strokes require the arms to be stretched forward in the water prior to carrying out the catch movements. The serratus anterior is mainly responsible for this action.

34. Levator scapulae (fig. 32.12)

RELATED SWIMMING ACTIVITY: Assists in its steadying function throughout all the arm pulls, but becomes more active towards the end of the push and release in the crawl and butterfly strokes.

35. Rhomboidus major and minor (fig. 32.12)

RELATED SWIMMING ACTIVITY: The main function is that of controlling and fixing the scapular position during all the arm movements. Assists the other medially attached scapular muscles during the backward and sideways movement of the arms during underwater swimming. Also active during the initial recovery movements of front crawl and butterfly strokes.

36. Erector spinae – sacrospinalis (fig. 32.12)

RELATED SWIMMING ACTIVITY: These erector muscles do not contribute to the actual arm movements, but assist in maintaining the body in the flat mode which is so very necessary for speed swimming.

37. Trapezius (fig. 32.12)

This is so named because the two muscles of which it is composed together display a trapezium-like shape.

RELATED SWIMMING ACTIVITY: The muscle is very active during the scapular fixing and steadying activity and also during the various arm stroke movements. The latter end of the front-crawl push phase, then subsequent release and recovery over the water, see the muscle in full swing. The breast stroke utilises both the scapular and head-tilting features extensively. The back crawler uses the muscle during the early propulsive phases and, during butterfly recovery, the muscle becomes active in assisting the deltoid and tilting the head in order to breathe.

38. Latissimus dorsi (fig. 32.12)

RELATED SWIMMING ACTIVITY: Back-crawl arm action, its pull being of a lateral nature, utilises the muscle extensively, as do the back strokes with their sideways and inwards arm pull. During the front-crawl arm pull the muscle is very active and becomes more so when the swimmer rolls and digs deeply into the water. Both the butterfly and breast-stroke arm pulls call on the muscle, as also does the long backward sweep of the underwater swimmer.

THE MUSCLES OF THE ABDOMEN

1. Obliquus internus abdominis (fig. 32.13)

2. Obliquus externus abdominis (fig. 32.13)

3. Pyramidalis (fig. 32.13)

4. Rectus abdominis (fig. 32.13)

RELATED SWIMMING ACTIVITY: The downbeats of the front crawl and butterfly stroke and the upbeat of the back crawl place considerable strain on the abdominals. This is the result of the constraining or 'fixation' action to which they are subjected as the pelvis tends to pivot in a backward direction about the sacro-iliac joint (fig. 32.14). These backward-rotating forces are transmitted by the thigh flexors (psoas and iliacus muscles) as they contract to sweep the legs through the water. The trained swimmer usually displays a trim waist and a prominent abdominal muscular pattern. Land-based sit-ups and leg-raising exercises produce the same effect.

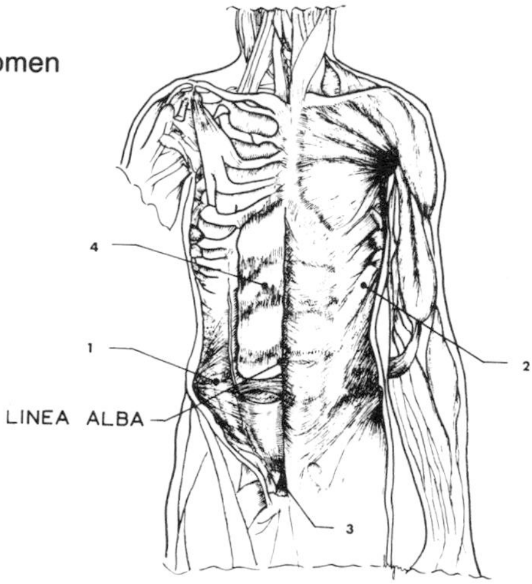

Fig. 32.13 The muscles of the abdomen

1 obliquus internus abdominus
2 obliquus externus abdominus
3 pyramidalis
4 rectus abdominus

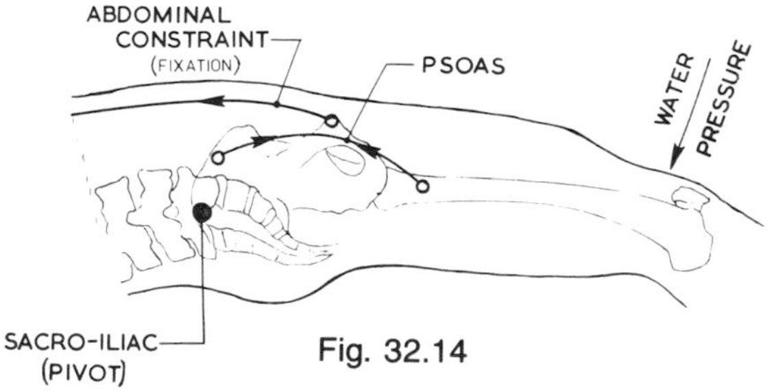

LINEA ALBA

ABDOMINAL
CONSTRAINT
(FIXATION)   PSOAS

WATER PRESSURE

SACRO-ILIAC
(PIVOT)   Fig. 32.14

THE MUSCLES OF THE NECK (fig. 32.15)
1. Sternomastoid

RELATED SWIMMING ACTIVITY: Very important during front-crawl breathing, where the muscle rotates the head to the side for inhalation. Its opposite number contracts to swivel the head once more to the central position. In breast-stroke and butterfly breathing, bilateral contraction helps to jut the chin forward. The back-stroke head position is largely controlled by bilateral contraction of the muscle.

Fig. 32.15 The muscles of the neck

1 sternomastoid
2 digrastic
3 stylohyoid
4 mylohyoid
5 sternohyoid
6 sternothyroid
7 thyrohyoid
8 omohyoid
9 scalenus anterior
10 scalenus medius

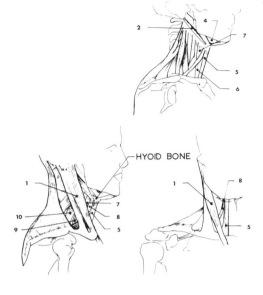

THE RESPIRATORY MUSCLES (fig. 32.16)

The principal breathing muscle is the diaphragm. It is assisted by the intercostal muscles which are attached between the ribs and combine to lift them during exhalation. During deep breathing, which may occur after exertion, certain accessory muscles are brought into action, namely the quadratus lumborum and erectores spinae, together with the abdominal, scalene and latissimus dorsi.

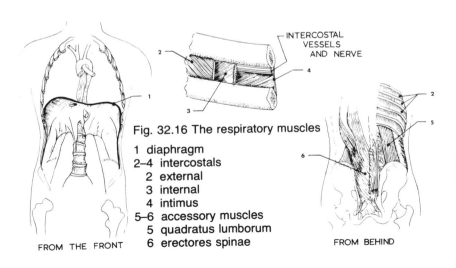

Fig. 32.16 The respiratory muscles

1 diaphragm
2–4 intercostals
   2 external
   3 internal
   4 intimus
5–6 accessory muscles
   5 quadratus lumborum
   6 erectores spinae

FROM THE FRONT   FROM BEHIND

A SUMMARY OF THE MUSCULAR MOVEMENTS FOR THE FOUR COMPETITION STROKES

FRONT CRAWL
Leg kick
The upbeat

LIMB MOVEMENTS	MUSCULAR ACTION
thigh extension	gluteus maximus, biceps femoris, semimembranosus, semitendinosus and adductor magnus
knee extension (aided by water forces)	quadriceps
foot extension (plantar flexion)	triceps surae
medial rotation	gluteus medius and minimus (anterior fibres), tensor fasciae latae and psoas

The downbeat

thigh flexion	psoas, iliacus, rectus femoris, gracilis and pectineus and sartorius
knee extension (finally)	quadriceps femoris
foot extension	triceps surae
medial rotation (slight)	gluteus medius and minimus

Arm stroke

LIMB MOVEMENTS	MUSCULAR ACTION

Catch and pull

arm extended forwards, elbow slightly flexed	latissimus dorsi, teres major, triceps and biceps, pectoralis major and minor, anterior deltoid, trapezius and pectoralis major and minor

Push

arm extended backwards, elbow extending	anterior deltoid, trapezius, teres major and minor and the pectoralis pair

Release

arm extended backwards	deltoid and trapezius

Entry

arm extended forward	deltoid and trapezius

BACK CRAWL
Leg movement

LIMB MOVEMENT	MUSCULAR ACTION

The upbeat (propulsion)

thigh flexion	psoas, iliacus, rectus femoris, gracilis, pectineus and sartorius
knee extension (finally)	quadriceps femoris
foot extension (aided by water forces)	triceps surae
medial rotation (slight)	gluteus medius and minimus (anterior fibres)

The downbeat

thigh extension	gluteus maximus
knee extension (aided by water forces)	quadriceps femoris
foot extension	triceps surae
medial rotation (slight)	gluteus medius and minimus (anterior fibres)

Arm stroke

LIMB MOVEMENTS	MUSCULAR ACTION

Catch and pull

| arm extended beyond the head, then moving sideways | anterior deltoid, pectoralis major and minor, latissimus dorsi, teres major and minor and biceps |

Push

| arm moving towards the feet | posterior deltoid, triceps brachii, palmaris longus and pronator teres |

Release

| arm and hand leaving the water | anterior, acromial and posterior deltoid and pronator teres |

BREAST STROKE
Leg kick

LIMB MOVEMENTS	MUSCULAR ACTION

Recovery

thigh flexion	psoas, iliacus, rectus femoris, sartorius
thigh abduction	gluteus medius and minimus, piriformis, sartorius and tensor fasciae latae
thigh lateral rotation	quadratus femoris, sartorius, biceps femoris
knee flexion	biceps femoris, semimembranosus. semitendinosus, gastrocnemius and sartorius
foot dorsi-flexed	tibialis anterior, extensor hallucis longus

Propulsion

thigh extension	gluteus maximus, biceps femoris
thigh adduction	adductors longus, brevis and magnus; and the pectineus
thigh medial rotation (to open the lower part of the legs)	gluteus medius and minimus (anterior fibres)
knee extension	quadriceps femoris
foot dorsi-flexed, and inverted . . .	tibialis anterior, extensor hallucis longus
. . . then plantar-flexed . . .	gastrocnemius and soleus, extensor digitorum, tibialis posterior and gracilis
. . . and the leg medially rotated	Semimembranosus and semitendinosus, gluteus medius, gluteus maximus, tensor fasciae latae and psoas

Arm stroke

LIMB MOVEMENTS	MUSCULAR ACTION

Propulsion

Arms extended in glide position with palms facing downwards	triceps, pectoralis major and anterior fibres of deltoid

Catch and pull

arms moving out and down, flexion of the wrist and rotation of the forearm	acromial and posterior fibres of the deltoid pectoralis major and minor

Scull

	latissimus dorsi, biceps, brachialis anticus, palmaris longus and flexor carpi radialis

Recovery to extended position

	triceps, pectoralis major and the anterior fibres of the deltoid

BUTTERFLY

The leg kick is essentially a double and simultaneous action similar to that of the front crawl.

Because there is no body roll, the arm adductors are not called upon to act so intensively. Otherwise the arm muscles act in much the same way as in the front crawl. This means that the back muscles which control scapular movement, namely the major and minor rhomboids and levator scapulae, act in unison on both sides of the trunk. The trapezius also acts as a 'complete' muscle rather than unilaterally.

33 Respiration

The mechanical process of breathing provides the means whereby the cells of the body receive their vital supply of oxygen and at the same time dispose of the waste products of oxidation. The tissues of each cell contain carbon and hydrogen and when oxygen is transported from the local environment it combines with these gaseous elements so that the metabolic processes within the body may proceed.

The chemistry of respiration

Air containing oxygen (20.94 per cent), nitrogen (79.02 per cent) and carbon dioxide (0.04 per cent) is drawn into the lungs during inspiration and expelled during expiration. The composition of the expired air is approximately oxygen 16.30 per cent, nitrogen 79.70 per cent and carbon dioxide 4.00 per cent. (There are other gaseous elements such as helium, argon and carbon monoxide in the atmosphere, but these are to be found only in small quantities.)

The respiratory passages

The respiratory passages originate at the mouth (oral cavity) and the nose (nasal cavity) – see fig. 33.1. Air may be drawn in or expelled via these orifices individually, or through both simultaneously. Further along their segregated tracks, the oral and nasal cavities meet up at the pharynx or 'back of the throat' to form one passage. The larynx, containing the vocal chords, is the 'next station' along the line. Guarded by the epiglottis, the larynx is made up of cartilage segments attached to each other by ligaments and membrane. It is the front part of the largest of these segments, the thyroid cartilage, which is known as the 'Adam's apple'.

Further along the respiratory passage is the trachea or wind pipe. This is a firm tube which is partially formed by crescents of semi-rigid cartilage arranged adjacent to each other. In section, the trachea takes the form of a 'D' with the flat side nearest to the oesophagus (gullet) being composed of fibrous tissue. This, the largest of the air passages, divides eventually into two smaller tubes, one each side of the chest cavity, which are known as the bronchi. These are similar in structure to the trachea, although the left bronchus is longer and slimmer than the right one. Further division now takes place into even smaller tubes, the bronchioles, and these terminate eventually in the tiny air sacs called alveoli.

Returning to the face once more, the nasal passage may be seen to be initially divided into two separate airways, by a partition formed partly of

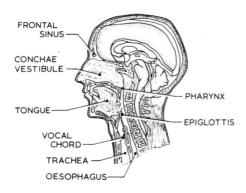

FRONTAL SINUS

CONCHAE VESTIBULE

TONGUE

VOCAL CHORD

TRACHEA

OESOPHAGUS

PHARYNX

EPIGLOTTIS

Fig. 33.1 Section of the face and neck showing the respiratory passage

bone and cartilage; this is known as the septum. The individual openings, the anterior nares, or nostrils, lead directly into an enlargement known as the vestibule of the nose which is lined with skin containing sebaceous glands and covered with coarse, downward-curving hairs. These hairs filter the incoming air as it passes on into the respiratory passage.

Another important part which the nose plays during inhalation is that of warming the air as it flows inwards. In fact, the nose may be described as the body's built-in air-conditioning plant, acting as filter, humidifier and warmer.

The surface of the nasal cavities, with the exception of the vestibules, is lined with the nasal mucous membrane, a continuation of the lining which covers the pharynx; it secretes a clear, slightly sticky fluid called mucus. The mucus, which may be evident on cold days in the form of a 'runny nose' or 'dew drop', serves several purposes. It enhances the air-filtration system by covering the nasal hairs causing foreign particles and bacteria to stick to them rather than pass on into the passages. The fluid also has properties which enable it to destroy certain species of bacteria. It is important that the mucous membrane remains moist at all times. If it should become dry while contending with a hot and stuffy atmosphere, its efficiency as a germ-trap is much depreciated. It is at these times that the common cold germ finds its way into the body.

The thoracic cage (fig. 33.2)
The thoracic cage, which consists of a bone and cartilage structure, surrounds the thoracic cavity. The structure is a compound one consisting of the following elements:

1. The sternum and costal cartilages (anterior)
2. The ribs and intercostal muscles (lateral)

3. The twelve thoracic vertebrae, together with their intervertebral discs (posterior)
4. The diaphragm (below)
5. The base of the neck (above)

The lungs completely fill the sides of the thoracic cavity. There is a space between them called the mediastinum and it is within this 'cavity within a cavity' that the heart, the great blood vessels, oesophagus, thoracic duct, descending aorta, superior vena cava, the vagi and phrenic nerves, together with numerous lymphatic glands, all exist.

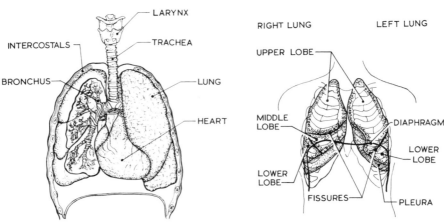

Fig. 33.2 the thoracic cage from the front

Fig. 33.3 The situation of the lungs within the thoracic cage

The lungs (figs 33.2 and 32.3)
The two lungs are the principal organs of respiration. They lie side by side within the thoracic cavity and are each encased by a very thin, glistening membrane called the pleura. This covering enables them to move freely and without friction against adjacent surfaces. Each lung lies freely in its particular pleural cavity, attached only to the heart, the root of the trachea and the pulmonary ligament. The pleura consists of two layers of membrane, the outer layer lining the rib cage and the adjoining intercostal muscles, and the inner one covering the pulmonary lobes. The two separate layers join together where the bronchi and blood vessels enter the lungs. The potential space between the two layers of adjacent membrane is known as the pleural cavity.

Normally, and in good health, the two layers remain pressed closely together and no cavity exists. But, if the outer or inner walls of the membranous sheath are punctured, air can enter between the two layers and the *potential* sub-atmospheric space becomes an *actual* pressure-created one. The consequent external pressure on the spongy and non-resistive lung tends to contract it. The 'collapsed' lung cannot be 'inflated' again until the external pressure source has been removed and the sub-atmospheric potential gap has been restored.

Pleurisy, a painful chest complaint, occurs when the two usually smooth and almost frictionless surfaces become inflamed and rough, and the consequent movements of the two rubbing surfaces causes pain and distress. If one lung collapses due to a failure of the pleura, the other one is capable of carrying out the respiratory function alone. This is because the two pleural cavities are distinct and separate.

As well as being light, spongy and porous the lungs are also extremely elastic. Because the heart is positioned to the left side of the thoracic cavity, the right lung is larger than the left. Each lung is divided into lobes by fissures, the right lung consisting of three lobes and the left of two. Each of these lobes is sub-divided into a number of lobules. Each individual lobule is a small polyhedral mass, receiving its own minute air tube (bronchiole), together with the tiny terminal blood vessels, the lymphatics and related nerves.

The trachea, bronchi and bronchioles (figs 33.2 and 33.4)
As already stated the trachea divides into two main branches called the principal bronchi. These in turn divide once again before they enter the substance of the lungs as the pulmonary bronchi, where they divide and sub-divide many times. The larger bronchi are of similar structure to the cartilaginous, fibrous and muscular trachea, and are lined with ciliated epithelium (cells with fine, hair-like processes attached to their free edge), but as they diminish in size and diameter the cartilage element gradually disappears.

After the repeated sub-division, the bronchioles finally enter their own allocated lung lobule to give off about six terminal bronchioles. These sub-divide further into the number of respiratory bronchioles after passing through a passage called the vestibule. It is at the vestibule that the ciliated epithelial lining starts to change its character to that of flattened epethelial cells. Directly branching from the vestibule are the infundibula, and it is in the walls of these minute structures that the alveoli (air sacs) are situated.

Each alveolus is constructed of a single layer of flat, epithelial cells forming the sac, and surrounding the tiny 'balloon' are the capillary blood vessels, where the interchange of gases takes place. Deoxygenated blood is carried from the right ventricle of the heart to the lungs by the pulmonary artery where, after repeated arterial sub-division, the blood continues to be transferred through the resulting tiny vessels called arterioles on towards the alveoli. When the arterioles finally reach the alveoli, they branch again to form a network of capillaries to surround

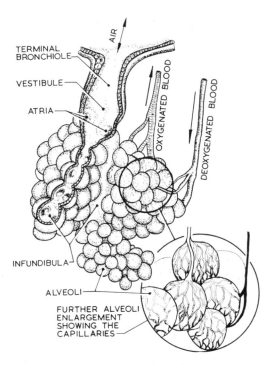

Fig. 33.4 The termination of a bronchiole into the alveoli

and be in contact with the tiny air sacs. These capillaries are so small in diameter that the red blood cells travel through them in almost single file.

The physiological process of interchange
The interchange of gases takes place by diffusion whereby the slow-moving venous blood in the capillaries arrives at the 'revitalising station' with an oxygen tension (partial pressure) of 40 mm Hg, and an oxygen saturation level of approximately 70 per cent. The accompanying carbon dioxide is 46 mm Hg. The freshly induced air retains an oxygen tension of 100 mm Hg, with only a slight and almost indistinguishable trace of carbon dioxide. With these great differential pressures present, the inter-change of oxygen to the capillary blood and carbon dioxide to air in the alveoli rapidly takes place.

When the process (which is, of course, continuous) has taken place, oxygenated blood (95 per cent saturation and 100 mm tension), with a carbon dioxide tension of approximately 40 mm Hg, leaves the lungs via the pulmonary veins for the left atrium of the heart.

The respiratory signals (fig. 33.5)
The control of the respiratory cycle originates from the respiratory centre

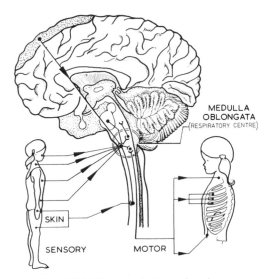

Fig. 33.5 The respiratory signals

of the brain. The area is known as the medulla oblongata and is situated in the hind brain. Signals from the centre travel down the spinal chord through the phrenic nerve, then on to the diaphragm. They also pass through intercostal nerves which eventually terminate in the intercostal muscles. The abdominal muscles also play a part in respiration and these are motivated by their own nerve supplies. Both lungs are supplied with signals via the vagus nerve which also arises out of the medulla. These signals, which are in the form of minute electrical impulses, cause reactions with the relevant muscles and organs, thus initiating the respiratory cycle.

These nervous impulses are emitted in a rhythmical pattern during normal breathing, causing contraction of the breathing muscles at the rate of approximately fifteen per minute. The major factor which controls the frequency of respiration is probably that of the various chemical changes which take place within the body. Carbon dioxide, an acidic product of metabolism, is the chemical which serves to stimulate the respiratory centre to send out its breathing-activity impulses. However, both nervous and chemical controls are vital in the breathing process.

There are, of course, other factors which affect respiration, such as vigorous exercise. The increased muscular activity creates a higher level of developed carbon dioxide wastes, and these need to be removed from the body. Increased respiration, coupled with a faster heart beat, serves to accomplish this within certain bounds. On the other hand, should there be a diminished amount of carbon dioxide in the bloodstream, the breathing rate decreases accordingly. Excessive and unnecessary deep breathing or artificially-induced pure oxygen in the respiratory system can have this effect (hyperventilation). The reduced activity can produce light-headedness or even unconsciousness. Other factors, such as fear, emotion or pain, can also serve to generate impulses that stimulate the respiratory centre and induce heavy breathing. Similar effects can be generated from the skin. For instance, when the body is suddenly plunged into cold water, a sudden inspiration (gasp) takes place.

Voluntary control of the respiratory movements is, of course, possible. The breath may be held, or forced respiration may take place, but only for short periods of time, because of the discomfort caused by the chemical unbalance in the respiratory system which it creates.

The mechanics of respiration (fig. 33.6)
Two movements occur during respiration, namely inspiration (breathing in) and expiration (breathing out). When the body is at rest, the inspiratory part of the cycle takes approximately one second and expiration is of about three seconds' duration.

During this quiet respiration, between 500 and 700 ml of tidal air is inhaled and exhaled at each complete cycle. About one-third of this air occupies what is known as the anatomical dead space, which stretches from the nostrils to the terminal bronchioles. Throughout this inactive region, there are no gaseous exchanges with the blood. (The process is not unlike a queue slowly entering a cinema, with people constantly joining on at the end of the line). During quiet inspiration, the principal and sometimes the only muscle involved in the process is the diaphragm. There may be other muscular activity, and if there is, it will be centred around the lower intercostal region.

During quiet expiration, the elastic recoil of the lungs and the thoracic cage is regulated by the comparatively slow relaxation of the inspiratory muscles. The movement may be described as a passive one whereby the relaxing muscles force the expired air out of the body. It has been demonstrated that both the diaphragm and intercostals continue decreasingly to contract well into the expiratory phase of the cycle.

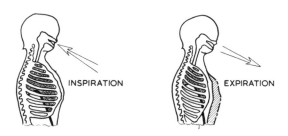

INSPIRATION   EXPIRATION

Fig. 33.6 The mechanics of respiration

If the ventilation rate remains below 40 litres per minute, there will probably be no active participation of the intercostal or abdominal muscles in the respiratory cycle.

During deep inspiration, the muscular movements previously described are magnified and additional breathing muscles are brought into action. The intercostals become very active to create movements of both the upper and lower ribs and sternum, thus enlarging the chest cavity from side to side and from back to front. The scaleri muscle also serves to elevate the first rib. Other muscles assist in holding and maintaining the rib structure rigidly while the process takes place. The pressure inside the lungs during deep inspiration rises to approximately 30 mm Hg (0.58 lb/ sq. in.) above atmospheric pressure.

During forced respiration (against a resistance), further muscles in addition to those already mentioned are brought into action. The forced expiration phase brings both the abdominal and latissimus dorsi muscles into play.

The bone structural changes in the chest cage which in turn bring about the changes in volumetric capacity are also shown in fig. 36.6.

34 The Circulatory System

The circulatory system consists of the blood, the heart, the blood vessels and the lymphatics.

The use of the circulatory system
Cells are the minute components from which all living organisms are composed. They consist of individual masses of protoplasm (semi-transparent, colourless semi-fluid containing oxygen, hydrogen, carbon and nitrogen). Cells of similar structure combine to form tissue. The thin, membranous boundary of the cell is a double layer of lipid (fatty) molecules sandwiched between two protein layers. It acts as a selective filter through which essential substances like oxygen and absorbed food materials can pass. If this inflow dries up, or if the waste materials, resulting from the metabolic processes, are impeded in their passage from the cell, the cell dies.

The maintenance of the cell life is the task of the blood circulatory system. It delivers energy supplies and oxygen to each unit and removes the waste products of the metabolism such as carbon dioxide and protein-breakdown products.

Functions of the blood
The functions of the blood are as follows:

1. To carry oxygen and foodstuffs to the tissues and their sub-structures.
2. To carry carbon dioxide and other waste products from the tissues and their sub-structures.
3. To provide fluid in the tissues.
4. To assist in the protection of the body from disease.
5. To clot when it is shed, thus protecting against excessive loss.
6. To carry away the secretions of the ductless glands, and hence transmit them to all parts of the body.

The fluid part of the blood takes up about fifty-five per cent of the overall volume, with the remaining forty-five per cent, known as the 'packed cell volume' or 'haematrocrit', being made up of solid elements or blood corpuscles. The volume of the blood is constant when a person is in good health.

The heart (fig. 34.1)
The heart is the automatic and computer(brain)-controlled central pum-

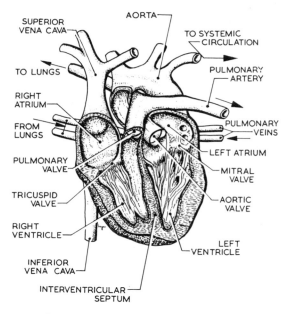

Fig. 34.1 An interior view of the heart

ping unit. It regulates the blood pressure and its rate of flow through the circulatory system. The heart is located in the thoracic cavity, between the lungs in the middle mediastinum (the central part of the partition between the lungs). It lies also to the left of the central plane of the chest, behind the sternum and costal cartilages and above the diaphragm.

The heart is approximately the size of a clenched fist and weighs (adult) about 250 g (9 oz). Its shape is more or less conical, with the apex pointing downwards; the base is uppermost and faces backwards and to the right.

The heart is divided into two separate chambers by a septum, and each chamber is itself divided again into two. The upper pair of chambers are called the left and right atria (auricles) and the lower pair (towards the apex of the heart) are termed the left and right ventricles. The septum is a solid divider, but each atrium is connected to its related ventricle by means of atrioventricular openings. Blood flows through these two orifices and its passage is controlled by valves. These two atrioventricular valves are individually termed the tricuspid valve on the right and the mitral valve on the left.

The valves allow the blood to flow freely in one direction only, from atrium to ventricle. When they close together, they form a seal through which the blood cannot flow in reverse from ventricle to atrium. The tricuspid valve consists of three flaps, and the mitral valve is made up of two. Both valves are provided with tendinous chords and papillary muscles which restrict their movement and prevent them from being turned inside out.

The nerve supply (fig. 34.2)
The action of the heart is normally of a rhythmic nature. The muscular contractions are produced by regular electrical impulses which originate in a tiny area of muscle called the sino-atrial node or pacemaker. The node activates spontaneously and electrically stimulates the muscular walls of the atria. From here, the impulses travel on to the atrio-ventricular node. Finally, the impulse is transmitted very quickly along a bunch of fibres called the bundle of his. These fibres in turn branch and intermingle with the ventricular muscles of the heart where the carried signal stimulates them into contraction.

The heart rate is dependent on signals from the sino-atrial node. However, if it fails for any reason, its function is taken over by the atrio-ventricular node. This secondary node signals at thirty-five to forty-five contractions per minute and is unaffected by external influences. The sino-atrial node is controlled by the vagus and sympathetic nerves. Stimulation of the vagus nerves will tend to slow the heart down and, conversely, stimulation of the sympathetic nerves increases the heart-beat rate. Under normal conditions, the heart is inhibited in its function by the vagus. But, when this controlling feature is withdrawn in situations such as exercise or emotional excitement, the heart rate increases.

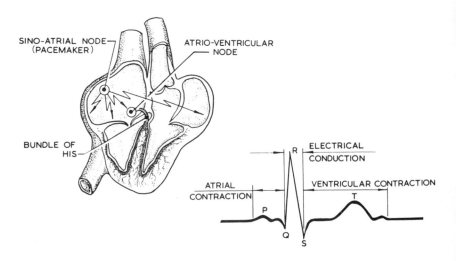

Fig. 34.2 Normal electrocardiogram (ECG) waveform

The cardiac activity can be recorded by means of an electrocardiogram (ECG). Electrodes, suitably affixed to the body, pick up and record the activity of the heart in the shape of a wave form. A normal read-out pattern is shown in fig. 34.2.

The blood vessels connected directly to the heart
The superior and inferior vena cava empty deoxygenated blood into the right atrium. The pulmonary artery carries this same blood from the right ventricle to the lungs. The four pulmonary veins bring the oxygenated blood to the left atrium. The left ventricle discharges blood to the body through the aorta.

The openings to both the aorta and the pulmonary artery are guarded by semilunar valves. Both these valves are of the flap type and prevent blood returning back into the respective ventricles.

The blood circulation (fig. 34.3)
The heart is the means whereby blood is pumped in a pulsating fashion around the body. The organ is in effect a *twin* pumping unit which supplies two distinct circuits. One circuit, which originates at the left ventricle, supplies blood via the arteries and their subsequent branches to all parts of the body except the lungs, then returns it to the right atrium. This is the systemic circulation. The second system, whereby blood is pumped from the right ventricle to the lungs, returning it eventually to the left atrium, is known as the pulmonary circulation.

Blood is supplied to the heart via the coronary circulation, and the liver receives its supply via the portal circulation.

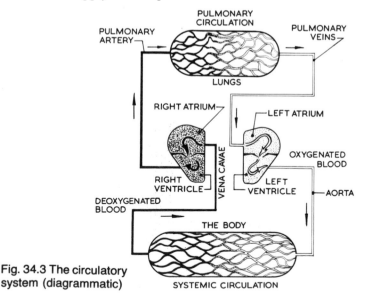

Fig. 34.3 The circulatory system (diagrammatic)

35 The Alimentary Canal and the Process of Digestion

The alimentary canal (fig. 35.1)
The alimentary canal is basically one long tube which is divided into various parts. Each part, besides channelling foods, liquids and waste products through the body, carries out its own digestive function.

The alimentary canal is about 9 m (29½ ft) long in an adult and consists of the following features: mouth, pharynx, oesophagus, stomach, small intestine and large intestine.

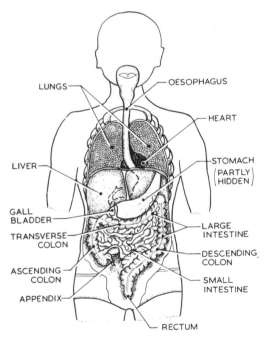

Fig. 35.1 The anatomy of the intestines

The mouth
The mouth or oral cavity consists of two parts, an outer small section termed the vestibule and an inner larger cavity. The vestibule of the mouth is bounded by the teeth and gums, together with the lips and cheeks. The second, larger space, is known as the oral cavity proper. It is surrounded by the hard (front) and soft (rear) palates in the roof of the

mouth, together with the tongue which lies in the floor attached to the hyoid bone. The forward part of the oral cavity is bounded by the gums and teeth and at the back by the pharynx. Saliva glands are also situated in this oral cavity below, beside and to the rear of the tongue.

The pharynx

The pharynx lies behind the nose, mouth and larynx and serves, by muscular control, to force the masticated food into the oesophagus (gullet). The organ is approximately 130 mm (5 in.) long and is divided into three parts:

1. The nasopharynx, which lies behind the nose and receives the eustachian tubes (see chapter 36).
2. The oral pharynx lies behind the mouth and stretches from the soft palate to the upper region of the epiglottis. The tonsils lie one on each side of this part of the pharynx.
3. The larangeal pharynx is the lowest part and is situated behind the larynx.

The oesophagus

The oesophagus or gullet is a muscular walled tube, approximately 250 mm (10 in.) long, which stretches from the pharynx to the stomach. It lies at the rear of the trachea and passes downwards behind the heart to pierce the diaphragm where it links up with the stomach.

At the upper end of the oesphagus, and at its juncture with the trachea, lies the epiglottis. This flap-like 'door' closes over the entrance to the larynx whenever food is swallowed, thus preventing its passage into the lungs.

The upper walls (approximately one-third) of the oesophagus are lined with voluntary muscle requiring conscious effort of the will to make them perform. The remaining two-thirds of the channel are covered with involuntary muscle. The passage of food through the oesophagus takes place by peristaltic action: the circular muscles ahead of the descending food relax, while those immediately behind contract to push the masticated food forward. The action is continuous and synchronised.

The stomach

The stomach is a muscular bag situated in the upper abdominal cavity and towards the left-hand side. It receives food from the oesophagus via the cardiac orifice and retains it for maybe several hours during which time various digestive functions are performed before despatching it into the small intestine via the pyloris. The pyloris is usually closed, but opens periodically during the passage of food into the intestine.

The stomach wall consists of four main layers (fig. 35.2):

1. The serosa or outer lining

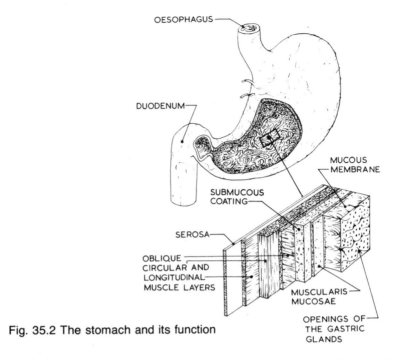

OESOPHAGUS

DUODENUM

MUCOUS MEMBRANE

SUBMUCOUS COATING

SEROSA

OBLIQUE CIRCULAR AND LONGITUDINAL MUSCLE LAYERS

MUSCULARIS MUCOSAE

OPENINGS OF THE GASTRIC GLANDS

Fig. 35.2 The stomach and its function

2. A three-layered muscular coat with longitudinal, circular and oblique fibres

3. A submuscous layer which contains the blood vessels and lymphatic vessels

4. The inner wall of the stomach which is lined with a mucous-secreting coating. This layer is thick and soft and is arranged in corrugated folds which disappear when the stomach is distended by food.

The stomach receives its blood supply from the gastric and splenic arteries.

The small intestine
The small intestine is a food-processing tube some 5 m (16½ ft) long in the adult. (A figure of 6–7 m (19½–23 ft) is often quoted for the length, but this is a post-mortem finding, when the muscular walls of the intestinal tube have lost their tone.) The tube is approximately 25 mm (1 in.) in diameter as it leaves the stomach, then decreases in size slightly as it travels towards its junction with the large intestine.

The small intestine lies in the umbilical region of the abdominal cavity and is bounded by the large intestine.

The duodenum (fig. 35.2) takes up the first 250 mm (10 in.) of the small intestine. It receives a common duct made up from two outer connecting ducts from the liver, the bile duct and the digestive juice-secreting pancreatic duct. This section is followed immediately by the jejunum (upper two-fifths) and the ileum (the remaining three-fifths). Both these latter sections are attached back to the abdominal wall by mesentary, which is thin membrane covered with a film of proteinaceous fluid. The muscular structure of the small intestine is very similar to that of the stomach.

The large intestine

The large intestine or colon is about 1.5 m (5 ft) long and is continuous with the small intestine. Its diameter is greatest at the junction of the ileum, a region termed the caecum, then gradually decreases towards the rectum.

It is to the caecum that the appendix is attached. This is a functionless organ which becomes inflamed and troublesome when filled with faecal material. The large intestine commences in the lower abdominal cavity and rises vertically; this section is known as the ascending colon. It then continues across the abdomen below the stomach and the liver, this horizontal part of the tract being termed the transverse colon. Finally, as the descending colon, it drops down on the left-hand side of the abdomen then into the central pelvic region, where it widens out for a short distance to form the rectum before decreasing in size to form the anal canal.

The colon is similar in structure to the small intestine, although the longitudinal fibres of the muscular coat are arranged in bands to give it a puckered appearance, rather than the tube-like appearance of its smaller counterpart. The inner walls are also smoother than those of the small intestine.

The liver (fig. 35.3)

The liver is the largest gland in the body, weighing about 1.8 kg (4 lb). It is situated below the diaphragm and to the right-hand side of the abdominal cavity. It is mainly protected by the rib cage.

The liver consists of two lobes and is enclosed by a tough fibrous capsule. The right lobe is six times larger than the left. The position of the right lobe is adjacent to the left and is sub-divided into two smaller lobes, termed the quadrate and candate lobes.

Functions of the liver

The liver may be described as the central chemical factory of the body. It has many functions, all of which are important to health and vitality.

It is a manufacturer of the greater part of the plasma proteins of the blood and also plays a role in the destruction of red blood cells. Forming the red cells during foetal life is another liver function related to the blood.

The major role of the liver, however, is in the processes concerned with the intermediate metabolism.

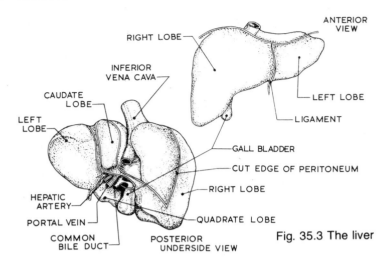

RIGHT LOBE

ANTERIOR
VIEW

INFERIOR
VENA CAVA

CAUDATE
LOBE

LEFT
LOBE

LEFT LOBE

LIGAMENT

GALL BLADDER

CUT EDGE OF PERITONEUM

RIGHT LOBE

HEPATIC
ARTERY

PORTAL VEIN

QUADRATE LOBE

COMMON
BILE DUCT

POSTERIOR
UNDERSIDE VIEW

Fig. 35.3 The liver

The pancreas (fig. 35.4)

The pancreas lies just behind the duodenum. It is a fleshy gland some 150 mm (6 in.) long.

The gland secretes pancreatic juice via the pancreatic duct into the duodenum. This juice, of which about 0.85–1.13 litres (1½–2 pints) are produced daily, breaks down starch, fats and fatty acids to form other substances necessary to the body functions.

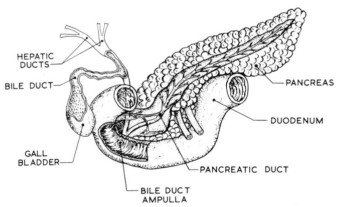

HEPATIC
DUCTS

BILE DUCT

PANCREAS

DUODENUM

GALL
BLADDER

PANCREATIC DUCT

BILE DUCT
AMPULLA

Fig. 35.4 The pancreas, bile duct and gall bladder

The gall bladder

The gall bladder is a small pear-shaped bag, some 75–100 m (3–4 in.) in length, with a volume of approximately 60 ml (¹/₁₀ pt). The function of the bladder is to act as a reservoir for the bile fluid secreted by the liver cells.

The urinary system (fig. 35.5)

The kidneys, of which there are two, form part of the urinary system. Each kidney weighs approximately 140 g (5 oz) in an adult and is bean-shaped. Due to the proximity of the liver, the right kidney is slightly lower than the left, which lies in the region of the first and second lumbar vertebrae. The right kidney is also shorter and thicker than its left-hand counterpart.

The functions of the kidneys are to regulate both the water balance and the concentration of blood salts within the body. They are also responsible for the excretion of fluid wastes.

The ureters are tubes which transfer urine from the kidney to the bladder. The bladder acts as a reservoir from which the urine is discharged by action of the urethra.

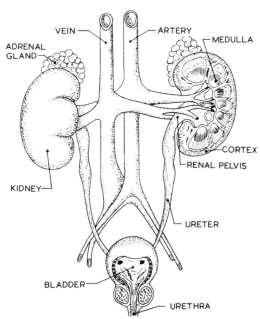

Fig. 35.5 The urinary system

ENERGY AND FOOD

Energy is required by the human body in order that it may live and move about. There is a certain similarity between the human body and an engine. An engine needs fuel, say petrol or coal, and when these are combusted or burnt, the heat energy is transformed into mechanical energy in order to drive the vehicle.

Food is the body's fuel, and when this is decomposed or burnt (oxidised), energy is released and absorbed by the body. When the food is oxidised, some of the energy is released as body warmth. The oxidisation process requires oxygen and this is where the respiratory, circulatory and digestive systems combine in order to convert and produce the energy needs of living. A simple diagrammatic illustration of the process is shown in fig. 35.6. The converted energy maintains such vital processes as breathing, blood circulation and the functioning of the brain together with all the other vital body organs.

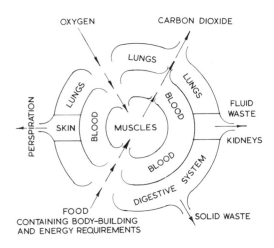

Fig. 35.6 Diagrammatic illustration of the body-maintenance systems

Energy is derived from foodstuffs by a process called metabolism. This is the biochemical process by which living tissue is created from basic food materials and energy is produced. The process involves the digestion of food in the intestines and the subsequent absorption of the constituents into the body tissues. This process is known as anabolism. The breaking-down process of the complex substances, whereby energy is released, is known as catabolism.

Energy and the swimmer
The human body is very inefficient in water, and the amount of energy used during swimming depends mainly on the stroke being used and the skill of the performer; other factors also come into the reckoning, such as water density and temperature. In the crawl stroke, for instance, the energy usage is approximately proportional to the square of the speed. Generally, the strokes may be arranged in descending order according to their energy usage in the following fashion:

1. Front crawl – the most efficient stroke but uses most energy
2. Back crawl
3. Butterfly, in excess of one metre/second
4. Breast stroke
5. Butterfly, when the speed is increased slightly
6. Side stroke
7. Butterfly, when performed slowly (below 0.76 metres/second)*

As previously stated, energy usage depends also on the *skill* of the performer. Swimming is essentially a cyclic effort/relaxation movement. Consequently, where the muscular effort is prolonged in the cycle due to an unskilled or badly executed recovery, the energy consumption is increased. Early stroke performances during the learning periods consume great quantities of energy, and it is worth noting that shivering can consume something like 250 calories per hour in a little 35-kg (5-st) swimmer, while an energetic swim may consume some 350 calories. This is another very good reason for teaching beginners in warm conditions.

* Karpovich and Sinning, *Physiology of Muscular Activity*, seventh edition (Saunders, 1971).

36 The Ear

The ear comprises three areas, namely the external, the middle and the inner ear (see fig. 36.1).

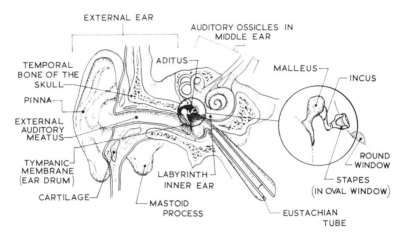

Fig. 36.1 Section of the ear

The external ear

The external or outer ear consists of the auricle or pinna (the visible part on each side of the head) and the channel leading to the ear drum. In some animals, the auricles may be rotated or directed in order to pick up sound waves. The channel or passage-way from the outer ear to the tympanic membrane (ear drum) is called the external auditory meatus and its function is to funnel sound waves to the ear drum which make it vibrate. It is in the walls of the meatus that the wax-secreting glands are situated. The secreted wax serves to line the walls of the meatus, in order to prevent maceration (softening due to soaking) by trapped water.

Over-production of wax can occur, which blocks the sound channel. Wax may be removed from the ear by careful softening and subsequent syringing. It is advisable, however, that this is carried out under qualified medical guidance, using the correct and specially designed equipment. Excess wax build-up can also trap water in the ear and, despite the protective qualities of the secretion, infection may be induced. It is therefore important that swimmers pay particular attention to ear care and, in the event of blockage or partial blockage, seek medical advice.

The middle ear

The middle ear or tympanic cavity is a small chamber beyond the tympanic membrane. The eustachian tube, which connects the cavity with the naso-pharynx tube, is normally closed but opens each time swallowing occurs. It is in this way that the air pressure in the tympanic cavity is equalised with environmental pressure, and no unnecessary strain is imposed on the ear drum.

The auditory ossicles are three small bones arranged in a chain across the inner ear. The malleus (hammer or mallet) has its 'handle' attached to the tympanic membrane and the 'head' articulates with the centre bone of the trio, termed the incus (or anvil). The stapes (or stirrup bone) is attached by its smaller end to the incus and by its oval cross-piece to the membrane covering the oval window of the cochlea (inner ear). The three bones form a mechanical linkage by which vibrations (sounds) are transmitted from the ear drum to the inner ear.

The inner ear

The inner ear consists of two parts, the bony labyrinth, which is a series of cavities, and the membranous labyrinth, consisting of a mass of communicating membranous sacs and ducts within the bony labyrinth. The vestibule is the central part of the bony labyrinth which communicates with all the other parts. It features an oval window to which the stirrup is attached and a round window covered with membrane.

Three semi-circular canals all communicate with the vestibule and, by nervous stimulations within the ends of these canals (ampulla), the brain is assisted in its sensory functions of position and balance.

The cochlea resembles the shell of a snail in shape. It is a fluid-filled tube coiled roughly two and three quarter times around a central bony area. It contains the actual organ of hearing known as the organ of Corti. This organ is a complex collection of specialised sensory nerve processes, positioned centrally on a fibrous layer called the basilar membrane.

Hearing

Sound waves are picked up at the outer ear and transmitted along the external auditory canal. When they impinge on the ear drum, it vibrates. The resulting tiny mechanical impulses are in turn transmitted via the malleus, incus and stapes (attached to the oval window) to the fluid in the cochlea, thus creating minute pressure waves. The pressure waves finally return to the middle ear at the round window, after spiralling around the cochlea and stimulating the organ of corti.

Different parts of the cochlea are receptive to different sound levels. It is these variations in frequency that affect different parts of the organ of Corti from which auditory signals are then transmitted to the brain.

The ears and swimming

The importance of *medically* maintaining the ears free from wax blockage cannot be over-stressed. Trying to remove wax or foreign objects by poking the ear with torturous implements such as matchsticks or pencils – even cocktail sticks have been used! – is very dangerous.

Cleaning and drying the ears after a swim should be regarded as most important. If excess wax is in evidence, the insertion of the corner of a towel or handkerchief may loosen it (and any loose tissue or scale which builds up in the tube) and drive it further along the meatus. This action will probably create a blockage even if there was none to begin with.

A clean handkerchief covering the middle finger will create restricted insertion into the outer ear, but when coupled with a sideways roll of the head to direct the ear downwards, it should be sufficient to remove most of the offending water. (The swimmer will feel the water emerge by a warm sensation in the outer ear and a sudden improvement in hearing.) Bashing the opposite ear does not help matters, although a *gentle* finger manipulation of the entrance to the meatus of the affected ear can sometimes release 'squelchy' trapped water while the swimmer's head is rolled to the side of the ear in question.

(This difficulty in removing ear-bound water raises doubts as to the wisdom of immersing tiny babies in chlorinated water.)

The swimmer's ear drum can become perforated. This can sometimes happen while in the water by collision with another swimmer. Alternatively, it can occur through infection. Waterpolo, gentle sport that it is, produces its share of perforation casualties, although caps are now designed to provide some degree of protection. When the ear drum becomes perforated, there is nothing to stop water seeping into the middle ear and such ingress will undoubtedly cause infection and severe pain. For this reason, sufferers are advised not to swim or in any way risk allowing water into the ear.

Earache and temporary deafness are products of the common cold. Nasal catarrh results from an infection of the mucous membrane accompanying such colds. In such a case secreted mucus builds up and tends to block the entrance of the eustachian tube. Consequently, the air which is trapped in the tympanic cavity is slowly absorbed and the air pressure in the middle ear drops below that of the outer ear. In other words, there is a differential pressure created across the ear drum which in turn deflects it inwards. Swallowing, in an effort to equalise the differing pressures, is ineffective because of the mucus blockage. For this reason, it is inadvisable for swimmers and divers to descend too deeply, because the external water pressure can cause the painful deflection of the tympanic membrane which the act of swallowing cannot relieve.

Protecting the ears during a swim should really be done only on medical advice. Ear plugs have limited use and should only be used after consultation with an ear, nose and throat specialist. Such items of equipment should be medically supplied and fitted. If there is excessive wax, ear plugs tend to act rather like ram rods, pushing the wax further into the meatus at each insertion until it contacts the ear drums, causing pain and temporary deafness. Water pressure, however slight, could push an ear plug further into the meatus. At 2½ m (8 ft) water depth, a plug could be subject to a water force of 122 g (0.25 lb), and a surface swimmer sometimes sinks this deep while carrying out various aquatic skills. Again, swallowing will be ineffective.

Rubber caps can offer some protection to the ears provided they fit closely to the head: the rim of the cap should make skin rather than hair contact which tends to allow water to seep in between the tufts.

Cotton wool and Vaseline, if properly inserted into the ears, can also afford a short-term barrier to the ingress of water. The important features in using this method are that the cotton-wool plug should be in one piece and large enough not to be lost from sight when inserted; and the Vaseline, when finally applied, should completely cover the plug on the outside only in order to form a water seal. The cotton-wool and Vaseline plug has been used by swimmers quite successfully for many years and, combined with the snug-fitting rubber cap, would seem to be favourite.

Discharge of any description from the ears should be taken seriously: swimming must be prohibited in such cases and the swimmer advised to seek medical advice as soon as possible.

37 The Nervous System

The nervous system is a highly complex arrangement by which signals are received, generated and transmitted to all parts of the human body. It consists of the brain and spinal chord and the nervous network. The nervous system has two basic functions: to detect and process information from both inside and outside the body, and to generate the signals which control and bring about muscular and body movement.

In order to facilitate description, the nervous system is divided into two main parts:

1. The central (or cerebro-spinal) nervous system which consists of the brain and spinal cord, together with the peripheral network, its function being related to the senses, thought processes and movement.
2. The autonomic nervous system which deals mainly with involuntary or automatic nervous control (heart, intestines, etc). It is divided into two functional parts:
(a) The sympathetic system
(b) The parasympathetic system

The central nervous system
The brain (fig. 37.1)
The brain, which is protected by the skull, is the origin of consciousness, and the mind is a reflection of its multitude of activities.

The adult brain weighs approximately 1.4 kg (3 lb) and is divided into various parts:

The cerebrum (forebrain), which is the largest part, fills the front and upper zone of the cranial cavity (the skull).

The surface of the cerebrum has a wrinkled appearance. This wrinkling creates a large surface area and allows many brain cells to be packed into a confined space. When dissected, the cerebrum is found to consist of the cortex (see fig. 37.2), an outer layer of grey matter (nerve cells) and an inner layer of white matter (nerve fibres). The functions and responsibilities of the cerebrum may be summarised as follows, various zones being responsible for their own unique commitments: mental behaviour, thought processes, consciousness, the will, language, speech, moral sense, intellect. The cerebrum is also responsible for the voluntary muscle movements.

Incoming signals from the skin, and the sensations of touch, pain, temperature, pressure, vibration, size, shape and texture, together with the muscle and joint senses, are also received and duly processed.

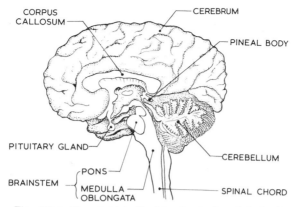

Fig. 37.1 The right half of the brain (medial view)

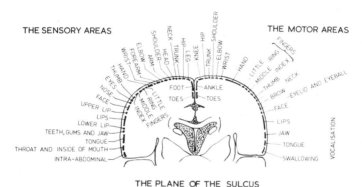

THE PLANE OF THE SULCUS

Fig. 37.2 The sensory and motor areas of the cortex

The brainstem, which joins up with the spinal column, contains in its upper reaches (the mid-brain) a number of movement co-ordinating centres. It is also concerned with the responsibilities of sleep and wakefulness and movements of the eyes. The middle portion of the brainstem is formed by the pons. Below this lies the medulla oblongata which forms the lower reaches of the brainstem and links the pons with the spinal cord.

The pons carries nerve fibres from the medulla to the spinal cord. The medulla is responsible for controlling such functions as respiration and blood pressure. It may be easily seen that injury to this part of the brain-stem is extremely serious.

The cerebellum sits behind the brainstem and below the cerebrum. It plays an important part in fine muscular co-ordination and the maintenance of balance.

It has a structure of grey and white matter similar to that of the cerebrum.

The hind brain consists of the pons, medulla oblongata and the cerebellum.

The spinal cord

The spinal cord originates at the medulla oblongata then passes down through the vertebrae, to end between the first and second lumbar vertebrae. The cord consists of grey and white matter from which the nerves emerge to travel to their various destinations. A section of the spinal cord is shown in fig. 37.3.

The function of the spinal cord is to provide communication between the brain and all parts of the body and to establish reflex-action circuits. A typical reflex arc is shown in fig. 37.4.

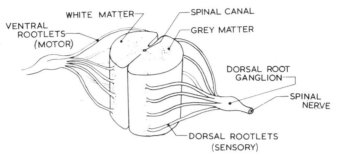

Fig. 37.3 Section of the spinal cord

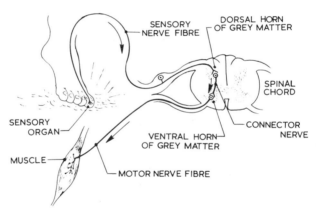

Fig. 37.4 A typical reflex arc

The autonomic nervous system

The sympathetic system innervates (supplies with nerve forces) the muscle of the heart, the involuntary muscle of all blood vessels and the organs of digestion. It also maintains the tone of all muscle. The parasympathetic system also innervates the various muscles, glands and organs of the body.

Where, however, a particular structure receives a supply from both the sympathetic and parasympathetic, the effects of the two systems are opposing. For instance, the sympathetic increases the heart beat while the parasympathetic slows it down. In the eye, the sympathetic dilates the pupil while the parasympathetic contracts it.

The nervous network

The whole complex nervous network is dependent on the ability of a nerve cell to carry out its function. This consists of transmitting a signal along its axon, or conducting central fibre.

The neurone, which is the nerve cell, complete with its attachments forms the structural and functional unit of the nervous system. It combines with other neurones to form nervous tissue. Neurones vary widely in both size and shape. However, virtually all types consist of the basic cell body, the signal-conducting axon, which may run a considerable distance as a nerve fibre, and the dendrites, which are the outlying branches which receive incoming messages (fig. 37.5).

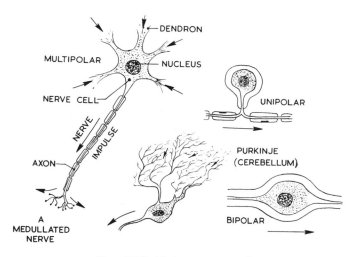

Fig. 37.5 Various nerve cells

Nerve cells, when massed together, form the grey matter which is to be found in the cortex of the brain and the inner part of the spinal cord.

Nerve fibres or axons constitute the white matter. The axon itself is the 'telephone line' which conveys information, in the form of minute electrical signals, to and from the cell body and, in the brain, ends by branching to meet the dendrites of other nerve cells at junctions which are termed synapses (fig. 37.6).

The central nerve fibre is covered by two sheaths and possesses the characteristics of conductivity and excitability. It is thus able to transmit an impulse along its length.

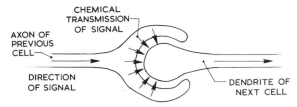

Fig. 37.6 Nerve synapse

Nervous impulses

A sensory nerve impulse is always conducted via a dendron (an individual nerve fibre) to a cell, then out once more via the axon. These sensory impulses are received by the nerve endings in the skin, then travel via the dendrons to the sensory cells in the dorsal root ganglion adjacent to the spinal cord (fig. 37.3). From here, they are transmitted via the axons of these cells into the spinal cord. They then rise to a nucleus in the medulla to be subsequently relayed to the relevant area of the brain.

A motor nerve impulse is generated in the motor area of the brain (fig. 37.7). The signals, which cause movement of the muscles, pass down the motor pathway which then controls movement on the opposite side of the body.

Sensory signals transmitted to the brain are termed afferent, and are carried by afferent nerves. Motor nerves carrying impulses away from the brain are termed efferent and the signals are known as efferent signals.

Further detailed analysis of the nervous system is beyond the scope of this text. However, the information and illustrations will, it is hoped, provide the teacher with a general idea of its fundamental structure and function.

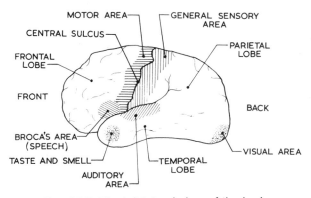

Fig. 37.7 The left lateral view of the brain

Index

pel van Salomo gevonden zouden hebben en die de kerk schade zouden kunnen toebrengen. Anderen denken dat de tempeliers het initiatief hebben genomen en Innocentius II hebben gechanteerd.

Irenaeus Invloedrijk theoloog en polemist. Zijn argumenten tegen **gnostische** sektes hebben in de laatste helft van de tweede eeuw een rol gespeeld bij het bepalen van de leerstellingen van het katholieke christendom: het credo, de erkende heilige boeken en de apostolische successie van bisschoppen. Irenaeus en andere kerkhistorici, zoals Eusebius en Tertullianus, worden er in *De DVC* van beschuldigd allemaal te hebben samengespannen bij het herschrijven van de christelijke geschiedenis en het creëren van de 'grote doofpotaffaire'.

Isis Een van de oudste en belangrijkste vrouwelijke godheden van het oude Egypte. In *DVC* wordt haar status als belichaming van het **heilig vrouwelijke** benadrukt. Isis werd beschouwd als beschermvrouwe van het gezin, de vrouwelijke vruchtbaarheid, de geneeskunde en de magie. Isis en haar tweelingbroer Osiris, kinderen van de God van de Aarde en de Godin van de Hemel, trouwden en regeerden als koning en koningin over de Egyptische kosmos.

Het valt Langdon op dat Saunière in het **Louvre** een grote collectie beel-

den van Isis heeft (het Louvre heeft inderdaad veel van die beelden), en er wordt gesuggereerd dat dat samenhangt met zijn geloof in het heilig vrouwelijke. Isis speelt ook een rol in Langdons betoog over de *Mona Lisa*. De naam is een anagram van de naam voor het oude pictogram van Isis, L I-SA, gecombineerd met de naam van haar mannelijke tegenhanger, de god Amon. LISA . AMON — MONA LISA. Er wordt wel beweerd dat Leonardo *Mona Lisa* oorspronkelijk heeft geschilderd met een lazuurstenen hanger met een afbeelding van Isis om haar hals, die hij later heeft overgeschilderd. Of dat nu waar is of niet, het lijdt geen twijfel dat de echo van Isis is blijven doorklinken in veel beroemde afbeeldingen van het heilig vrouwelijke.

De oudste bron voor het verhaal van Isis en Osiris zijn de piramideteksten, religieuze hiëroglyfen die dateren van 2600 voor Christus. Isis werd tot ver in de Romeinse tijd vereerd, en geleerden speculeren dat het romantische verlossingsverhaal dat de kern van haar mythe vormt in een grote behoefte voorzag, gezien de strenge en afstandelijke bijsmaak van de officiële religie van het keizerrijk. Ook geografisch was de verering van Isis wijdverbreid: de beelden van de 'zwarte Madonna' die in sommige Franse kathedralen werden aanbeden, stellen waarschijnlijk Isis voor. En er zijn oude tempels voor Isis ontdekt aan de oevers van de Donau en de Theems. Naar verluidt is er een tempel voor Isis geweest op de plek waar de Saint-Sulpicekerk in Parijs staat. Die kerk is door de **Merovingische** koning Childebert gebouwd om onderdak te bieden aan heilige relieken.

De mythe van Isis weerklinkt nog steeds door de mythologie en symboliek van het christelijke tijdperk. Ze is misschien wel het archetype van de hogepriesteres in het **tarot**spel. De manier waarop de Madonna met kind meestal wordt weergegeven, lijkt opvallend veel op de talloze afbeeldingen van Isis met Horus aan haar borst. Maria heeft ook vele van de benamingen van Isis overgenomen: Zetel der Wijsheid, Sterre der Zee en Koningin des Hemels. Ten slotte wordt de dood en verrijzenis van Osiris vaak gezien als een voorloper van de verrijzenis van Christus, zij het met een vrouwelijk tintje. Isis – het vroegste heilig vrouwelijke – is de macht die de god tot leven brengt en zijn geslacht voortzet.

Isis wordt nog steeds door veel new-age-adepten vereerd, wat betekent dat ze nu al vijfduizend jaar meegaat en nog steeds niet heeft afgedaan.

Jahweh De naam van God in het Oude Testament. Van de Hebreeuwse letters Yod, Heh, Vav en Heh (het tetragrammaton, zie **Adonai**). Bij de joden is het verboden de naam van God te noemen tijdens het bidden, en daarom zeggen ze in plaats daarvan Adonai. Deze beperking vloeit voort uit een interpretatie van het derde gebod, dat luidt: 'U zult de naam van de heer uw God niet lichtvaardig gebruiken.' In geschriften wordt Jahweh vervangen door HEER of G-d.

De weergave van het oude Hebreeuws als Jahweh is slechts gebaseerd op vermoedens over de manier waarop in een taal die al meer dan tweeduizend jaar niet meer wordt gesproken en niet over klinkers beschikt, de letters Yod, Heh, Vav en Heh zouden zijn uitgesproken. De vermoedelijke uitspraak is daarna getranscribeerd in het Nederlands (en in andere talen). Volgens de redenering in DVC was het Hebreeuwse JHWH een combinatie van oeroude mannelijke en vrouwelijke benamingen, het mannelijke *Jah* en de pre-Hebreeuwse naam voor Eva, *Havah*.

Jambische versvorm Een jambe is een eenheid van twee lettergrepen, waarvan de eerste onbenadrukt en de tweede benadrukt is. Het geheel heet een versvoet. Een jambische versregel is uit dergelijke elementen opgebouwd. Als er vijf achter elkaar staan, wordt het vers een vijfvoetige jambe genoemd. Dat patroon, met de nadruk steeds op de tweede lettergreep, wordt wel als typisch Engels gezien, maar de jambische versregel in de poëzie is van oorsprong Grieks. Sommigen denken dat deze versvoet zo algemeen wordt gebruikt vanwege zijn gelijkenis met de menselijke hartslag.

Katharen Een ketterse christelijke sekte die in de twaalfde en dertiende eeuw een bloeiperiode doormaakte. Het woord is afkomstig van het Griekse *katharos*, dat 'rein' of 'zuiver' betekent. De katharen waren in heel Zuid-Europa te vinden, vooral in de gebieden waar het gezag van de katholieke kerk het zwakst was, maar ze waren vooral goed vertegenwoordigd in de Provence, een rijk gebied in het zuiden van Frankrijk dat altijd bekend heeft gestaan om zijn politieke en religieuze onafhankelijkheid.

De oorsprong van de leer der katharen is onduidelijk, maar sommige deskundigen denken dat het dualisme dat de kern van hun geloof vormt, is geïntroduceerd door ketters uit het Byzantijnse Rijk, aan de oostrand van de christelijke wereld. Hoe dan ook, de katharen onderschreven een algemeen **gnostisch** denkbeeld, namelijk dat de wereld was geschapen door een kwade god, een god van de stoffelijke wereld, die zijn schepping van het begin af aan verdorven had gemaakt. Daarom waren alle stoffelijke zaken, waaronder het menselijk lichaam, kwaad; aan de gevangenis van het vlees ontsnappen en erbovenuit stijgen was de verlossing. De katharen geloofden dat de ziel of de geest gevangen zat tussen het spirituele goede en het stoffelijke kwade, en als het individu besloot zich over te geven aan de vulgaire verlokkingen van de materiële wereld, zou het steeds weer gereïncarneerd worden totdat het de juiste keuze maakte.

De katharen waren vroege feministen. Vrouwen konden net zo gemakkelijk tot de hoogste rang opklimmen als mannen. De ziel was geslachtloos en het stoffelijke lichaam slechts haar gevangenis. Spiritueel gezien was er geen natuurlijke superioriteit van de ene sekse aan de andere.

De ketterse overtuigingen van de katharen joegen de orthodoxe kerk angst aan, en die maakte de katharen dan ook zwart door hetzelfde soort geruchten te verspreiden als over de **tempeliers**: dat ze de duivel aanbaden, de as van verbrande baby's aten en verstokte homoseksuelen waren. Toen die lasterpraatjes de groeiende populariteit van het kathaarse geloof niet bleken te voorkomen, organiseerde Rome een kruistocht naar het plaatsje Albi en omgeving, waar een concentratie van katharen was gevestigd. De kruistocht tegen de Albigenzen, die van 1209 tot 1229 duurde, drukte het ontluikende geloof met geweld de kop in. Hele dorpen en steden die werden gezien als broedplaatsen van het ketterse geloof, werden geplunderd en vernietigd.

Kathedraal der Codes De bijnaam van **Rosslyn Chapel.**

Kelk In de christelijke kunst staat de kelk voor het Laatste Avondmaal, het offer van Jezus en het christelijk geloof. In het landhuis van Leigh Teabing legt Langdon de betekenis van de kelk aan Sophie uit. De kelk is het eenvoudigste symbool dat de mensheid heeft voor het vrouwelijke, het symbool voor de baarmoeder en vrouwelijkheid. De **heilige graal** is een  uitgebreidere symbolische variant op de kelk, die wordt geassocieerd met **Maria Magdalena** in haar rol van hoedster van het heilige geslacht.

Het tegengestelde, complementaire symbool, waarmee de kelk soms wordt gecombineerd, heet de kling. De kling wordt afgebeeld als een fallus, een mes of een speer. Het is het symbool van mannelijkheid en agressie. Als de kling en de kelk worden verenigd, vormen ze de davidster, door

Langdon gelijkgesteld aan de volmaakte verbintenis van het mannelijke en het vrouwelijke en het hoogste principe van het goddelijke.

De symbolen voor de kelk en de kling zijn nooit verdwenen, maar leven in verschillende vormen voort in de westerse cultuur.

'Koning der joden' Teabing, die altijd bereid is grote hoeveelheden informatie over de vroegste religieuze geschiedenis zoals hij die ziet over zijn toehoorders uit te storten, vertelt het verhaal waarin wordt gesteld dat Jezus Christus van koning Salomo en koning David afstamt, en daarom behalve de messias ook de werkelijke, rechtmatige koning der joden was. Toen Jezus met Maria Magdalena trouwde, trouwde hij volgens DVC met een vrouw van de stam Benjamin, een geslacht dat door Maria Magdalena en hun kind werd voortgezet en waaruit de Merovingische dynastie voortkwam. Volgens de legende van de Priorij van Sion is de huidige afstammeling van het geslacht van Jezus (wat dus Sophie zou zijn) ook de rechtmatige koning van Israël/Palestina (of van Frankrijk, dat hangt maar net af van wat men wil bewijzen aan de hand van deze geheimzinnige geschiedenis van tweeduizend jaar).

Koptisch De koptische taal stamt af van het oude Egyptisch en het Grieks. Ze ontstond in de derde eeuw voor Christus, na de Griekse verovering van Egypte, en werd door tot het christendom bekeerde Egyptenaren gebruikt om de bijbel en liturgische werken te vertalen. Het Evangelie van

Maria en het grootste deel van de zogenaamde gnostische evangeliën waren oorspronkelijk in het Grieks geschreven, maar de meeste bestaan nu alleen nog maar in de koptische vertalingen die bij Nag Hammadi zijn gevonden. De koptische taal wordt nog steeds gebruikt door de kopten, een christelijke sekte in Egypte.

Kruis De kunsthistorica Diane Apostolos-Cappadona zegt kort en bondig: 'Een zeer oud, universeel symbool van de combinatie van tegenpolen, waarbij de verticale balk staat voor de positieve krachten van het leven en de spiritualiteit, en de horizontale balk voor de negatieve krachten van de dood en het stoffelijke. Er bestaan ruim vierhonderd variaties van dit symbool.' In DVC wordt erop gewezen dat het kruis als belangrijk symbool al lang voor de kruisiging bestond, en wordt ingegaan op het verschil tussen het gelijkarmige kruis (zoals dat van de tempeliers) en het traditionele verlengde christelijke kruis.

Het Laatste Avondmaal De Mona Lisa en Het Laatste Avondmaal zijn de beroemdste werken van Leonardo. Leigh Teabing gebruikt Het Laatste Avondmaal ter verduidelijking van zijn betoog over de heilige graal en de symbolische verwijzingen ernaar in de westerse kunst, literatuur en geschiedenis. Teabing noemt een aantal eigenaardige kenmerken van het doek: de vrouwelijke gestalte van Maria Magdalena, die rechts van Jezus zit en gewoonlijk voor Johannes wordt aangezien, de dolk waar geen lichaam bij lijkt te horen en die dreigend naar Maria Magdalena wijst, en de symbolen van de kelk en de M die door de lichamen van Maria Magdalena en Jezus worden gevormd. Geen enkele gerespecteerde wetenschapper zou Teabings theorieën onderschrijven; Brown lijkt de onconventionele ideeën van Teabing uit twee boeken te hebben gehaald, *Het geheime boek der Grootmeesters* van Lynn Picknett en *De vrouw met de albasten kruik* van Margaret Starbird.

Leonardo da Vinci Schilder, beeldhouwer, architect, ingenieur, schrijver, natuurwetenschapper, wiskundige, geoloog, anatoom... allemaal woorden die van toepassing zijn op de verbazingwekkend veelzijdige Leonardo da Vinci. Maar de meeste roem heeft hij vergaard met zijn schilderijen, waar er eigenlijk maar heel weinig van zijn. Slechts dertien schilderijen worden algemeen aan Leonardo toegeschreven.

Er is maar weinig bekend over het leven van Leonardo, en vooral zijn jeugd is in nevelen gehuld. Hij is in 1452 geboren als de onwettige zoon van een boerendochter en de zoon van een middenstandsgezin in Florence. Hij ging in de leer bij de Florentijnse meester Andrea Verrochio en heeft daar mogelijk in dezelfde tijd gewerkt als een andere leerling die beroemd zou worden, Sandro **Botticelli**, de schilder van de *De geboorte van Venus* (net als Leonardo is hij in verband gebracht met de **Priorij van Sion** en zitten zijn schilderijen vol symboliek).

Leonardo overtrof zijn tijdgenoten in bijna alles waar hij zich mee bezighield. In de volgende veertig jaar werkte hij voor de talrijke edellieden van Milaan en Florence, de Franse koning en de kerk. Hij stierf in 1519, mogelijk aan een beroerte, toen hij in Frankrijk leefde en werkte.

Sommige beweringen van Dan Brown over Leonardo worden door deskundigen met kritische blik bekeken. Conventionele wetenschappers twijfelen aan de aanwezigheid van verborgen boodschappen in zijn werk, aan zijn banden met geheime genootschappen en zelfs aan zijn homoseksualiteit. Maar zijn genialiteit wordt door niemand betwist.

Het Louvre Het Louvre is het begin- en het eindpunt van DVC. Saunière wordt vermoord in de Grande Galerie van het Louvre. De stervende conservator verbergt aanwijzingen in een paar van de beroemdste kunstwerken van het museum. En uiteindelijk, na een dolle opeenvolging van steeds ingewikkelder complotten, cryptische aanwijzingen en nipte ontsnappingen, krijgt Langdon een openbaring over de grootste schat die het Louvre in huis heeft.

De geschiedenis van het Louvre is zeer gecompliceerd. Bijna achthonderd jaar lang hebben vorsten en regeringen hun sporen nagelaten in het gebouwencomplex, en behalve tijden van glorie heeft het ook lange periodes van verwaarlozing gekend. Het is in 1190 gebouwd als fort voor Filips II August. Filips gaf opdracht tot de bouw van een wal rond Parijs om de stad tegen invallen te beschermen, en op de oever van de Seine liet hij een kasteel bouwen, beschermd door een fort dat uitkeek over de rivier: het Louvre. De toren van het Louvre werd de koninklijke thesaurie, terwijl er ook gevangenen werden opgesloten. In de loop der eeuwen heeft het Louvre, zoals Catherine Chaine en Jean-Pierre Verdet beschrijven in *Le Grand Louvre*, gediend als

> gevangenis, arsenaal, paleis, ministerie... [het] heeft huisvesting geboden aan stallen, een drukkerij, een postdienst, de nationale loterij, ateliers en academies; het is het verblijf geweest van koningen, kunstenaars, commandanten, gevangenbewaarders, courtisanes, geleerden en zelfs paarden... Deze zalen, die zich door niets meer laten verrassen, zijn getuige geweest van het leven en zijn voortgang, festiviteiten, rechtszaken, complotten en misdrijven.

Een van de grote successen van president **François Mitterrand** was dat hij erin is geslaagd het enorme, verwaarloosde, labyrintische gebouw te veranderen in het nationale schathuis dat het al veel langer had moeten zijn. Toen hij ging nadenken over het opknappen van het complex, was de conditie van het Louvre slecht voor zo'n belangrijk cultureel instituut. Het bestuur was laks en er was weinig geld te besteden. Het museum had ruim 250.000 werken in bezit, maar de indeling in galerijen was dusdanig dat zelfs de meest frequente bezoeker er nog verdwaalde. Ook de kunstwerken hadden onder verwaarlozing te lijden. Schilderijen zaten dik onder het stof, werken kwijnden weg in de magazijnen en werden nooit tentoongesteld. De ramen van het Louvre waren zo vuil dat ze geen zuiver daglicht meer doorlieten; de reiniging van de buitenkant van de ramen viel onder een ander ministerie dan dat van de binnenkant, en de schema's waren niet op elkaar afgestemd!

Mitterrand veranderde dat allemaal, reorganiseerde het beheer en zorgde dat er geld kwam voor grote verbouwingen; een van de 'grote projecten' van zijn regeringsperiode, waarin hij zich concentreerde op het opknappen van culturele en stedelijke monumenten. Het ministerie van Financiën verhuisde van de noordelijke vleugel van het museum naar elders, zodat die vrijkwam als expositieruimte. De architect I.M. Pei werd aangetrokken, niet alleen om een nieuwe ingang voor het museum te maken (zie **La Pyramide**), maar ook om de bestaande museumzalen aan te passen en het totaal aan expositieruimte te vergroten. De kunstwerken worden nu in een begrijpelijke, logische volgorde aan het publiek getoond, zodat een bezoek aan het museum nu een aangename in plaats van een verbijsterende ervaring is.

Madonna in de grot De naam van twee schilderijen van **Leonardo da Vinci**, die letterlijk *De Maagd in de grot* heten. Met *Madonna in de grot* wordt gewoonlijk het exemplaar bedoeld dat in het Louvre hangt, terwijl het tweede, een 'afgezwakte' versie, in de National Gallery in Londen te vinden is.

Nadat Sophie het anagram '*so dark the con of man*' heeft opgelost (*Madonna of the rocks*, de Engelse naam van het schilderij), zoekt Sophie aan de achterkant van dit schilderij naar aanwijzingen die haar grootvader misschien heeft achtergelaten. Ze vindt de sleutel met een **Franse lelie** en de initialen PS erop, waarmee hij zijn belofte nakomt dat ze op een dag de sleutel tot vele mysteries zou krijgen. Nadat Sophie en Langdon, op de hielen gezeten door de bewaking, het Louvre zijn ontvlucht, springen ze in de **Smart** van Sophie en racen naar de Amerikaanse ambassade. Op weg daarheen mijmert Langdon over deze 'toepasselijke schakel in de keten van symboliek van die avond'.

Wat Langdon in het boek en geleerden in de echte wereld is opgevallen, is de complexe geschiedenis van het schilderij en de grote hoeveelheid mogelijke verborgen betekenissen, die bij elkaar de 'controversiële en schokkende details' vormen waar Langdon het over heeft. Enkele daarvan noemt hij: het feit dat het lijkt alsof Johannes Jezus zegent en het feit dat Maria een dreigend gebaar boven het hoofd van Johannes maakt.

Magdala Het plaatsje in de streek van Galilea waar volgens geleerden **Maria Magdalena** vandaan komt (ze wordt ook Maria van Magdala genoemd). Er bestaat geen overeenstemming over de locatie van het plaatsje, maar veel geleerden denken dat het een dorp is dat in de Talmoed Magdala Nunayya of Magdala van de Vissen wordt genoemd, waarschijnlijk vanwege de nabijheid van het meer van Galilea. Het Hebreeuwse woord *magdala* betekent 'toren' of 'fort'. Het is mogelijk dat Jezus zich na de vermenigvuldiging van het brood en de vis in Magdala heeft teruggetrokken.

Malleus Maleficarum Letterlijk de Heksenhamer. Het boek komt Langdon in gedachten als hij nadenkt over het anagram '*so dark the con of man*' ('zo duister de zwendel van de man'), dat op het plexiglas voor de **Mona Lisa** is geschreven. De *Malleus Maleficarum* is in 1486 verschenen en heeft voor ongelooflijk veel ellende gezorgd door de officieren van de inquisitie richtlijnen te verschaffen voor het identificeren van heksen (zie hoofdstuk 5). Mensen werden als heks bestempeld, vervolgd en meestal uitgeleverd aan de autoriteiten om op de brandstapel te eindigen.

Maltezer ridders De enige serieuze rivalen van de **tempeliers**. De Maltezer ridders (die ook johannieterridders van Jeruzalem en hospitaalridders worden genoemd) waren een militaire kloosterorde die in de elfde eeuw in het Heilige Land is gesticht. De orde legde zich toe op de verzorging van zieken en gewonden, en vestigde hospitalen voor pelgrims in het Heilige Land. De leden van de orde maakten zichzelf ondergeschikt aan hun patiënten: in sommige hospitalen sliepen de zieken op het fijnste linnengoed en aten ze van een zilveren servies. Opvallend genoeg verwierven ze ook een reputatie als geduchte krijgers, zowel te land als ter zee. Nadat het Heilige Land in handen van de mohammedanen viel, zwierven de hospitaalridders over de Middellandse Zee en stichtten ze nederzettingen op Cyprus, Rhodos en ten slotte op Malta. Vanuit hun vestingen op deze eilanden bestookten ze schepen en kustplaatsen van de mohammedanen.

Doordat er tijdens de Reformatie en de Franse Revolutie beslag werd gelegd op eigendommen van de hospitaalridders, verloren de ridders hun financiële onafhankelijkheid, en in 1798 moest de verzwakte orde Malta aan Napoleon afstaan. In de loop van de negentiende eeuw is de orde in verschillende vormen herrezen en teruggekeerd naar de oorsprong als hospitaalridders, die zieken en gewonden verzorging boden. Maltezer ridders bouwden operatiekamers, zorgden gedurende verschillende oorlogen voor verpleging en zetten in de Eerste Wereldoorlog veldhospitalen op. De orde bestaat nog steeds en is een soevereine staat, ongeveer zoals het Vaticaan. Hun hoofdzetel in Rome is exterritoriaal, wat betekent dat ze hun eigen paspoort kunnen uitgeven en ambassadeurs kunnen uitwisselen met andere landen (tot op heden veertig). Het is de kleinste onafhankelijke staat ter wereld.

Marcion Marcion, een ketter uit de tweede eeuw, was de zoon van de bisschop van Sinope. Hij verkondigde een leer waarin werd gesteld dat de god van het Oude Testament in werkelijkheid een demiurg was die de stoffelijke wereld had geschapen en er zijn eigen ingewortelde kwaad in had gebracht. Volgens de leer van Marcion was Jezus de zoon van een andere god, een grotere god dan degene die in zeven dagen de wereld had gemaakt. Deze grotere god had Jezus naar de mensheid gestuurd om haar te verlossen van het kwaad van de stoffelijke wereld; daarom kon Jezus geen mens zijn, maar was hij volledig onstoffelijk

en had hij geen vleselijke gestalte.

Om een oplossing te vinden voor de tegenstellingen tussen zijn overtuigingen en die van de algemeen aanvaarde evangeliën, paste Marcion het Nieuwe Testament grondig aan en schreef hij een verkorte versie van Lucas, waaruit alle verwijzingen naar de geboorte van Jezus waren verdwenen. In zijn canonieke werken nam hij ook tien zendbrieven van Paulus op, die hij beschouwde als de enige zuivere vertolker van het woord van Christus. Hij was een voorstander van het vegetarisme en volgens sommige bronnen van seksuele onthouding. Het marcionisme leefde tot in de vijfde eeuw voort, met een paar substantiële aanpassingen die het dichter bij de traditionele gnostiek brachten dan Marcion zelf had bedoeld.

Tertullianus, een van de kerkvaders die zich tegen ketterij verzetten, geeft ons een indruk van de woede die Marcion in zijn tijd opwekte. Hij schrijft: 'Immoreler dan de Scyth, erger dwalend dan de rondtrekkende Sarmaat, onmenselijker dan de Massageet, brutaler dan de amazone, kouder dan de winter, vergankelijker dan het ijs, verraderlijker dan de Ister, ontoegankelijker dan de Kaukasus. Welke muis van bij de Zwarte Zee heeft zulke sterke kaken gehad als degene die de evangeliën aan stukken heeft geknaagd?'

Maria Magdalena Volgelinge van Christus, door de hedendaagse wetenschap beschouwd als zijn 'metgezellin'. Wat dat woord precies betekent, is een terugkerend centraal thema van DVC. Door de conventionele kerk is Maria Magdalena altijd afgeschilderd als zondares, vaak als prostituee. In de modernere interpretatie van Maria Magdalena, die vooral is ingegeven door de **gnostische evangeliën** die bij **Nag Hammadi** zijn gevonden, is ze een invloedrijke en intieme metgezellin van Jezus, misschien zelfs wel zijn vrouw (zie hoofdstuk 1).

De mens van Vitruvius Een beroemde tekening van **Leonardo**. We zien een man, frontaal en gedeeltelijk in zijaanzicht, die zowel in een vierkant als in een cirkel staat. De eerste aanwijzing die de hoofdpersonen van DVC krijgen, is dat Saunière zich vlak voor hij stierf heeft uitgekleed en in dezelfde houding is gaan liggen als deze beroemde afbeelding van Leonardo. *De mens van Vitruvius* is genoemd naar Marcus Vitruvius Pollio, een Romeinse schrijver, architect en ingenieur uit de eerste eeuw na Christus. Hij had de leiding over de aanleg van de aquaducten van Rome en schreef *De architectura*, een werk in tien boeken, misschien wel het eerste werk over architectuur dat ooit is geschreven. Zijn studie naar de proporties van het menselijk lichaam stond in zijn derde boek, en dit is de richtlijn die hij voor kunstenaars en architecten heeft opgesteld:

De afmetingen van het menselijk lichaam zijn als volgt: 4 vingers zijn 1 palm, en 4 palmen zijn 1 voet, 6 palmen zijn 1 el; 4 ellen zijn de lengte van een man. En 4 ellen zijn 1 pas en 24 palmen zijn een man. De lengte van de gespreide armen van een man is gelijk aan zijn lichaamslengte.

Van zijn haargrens tot aan de onderkant van zijn kin is een tiende van de lengte van een man; van de onderkant van de kin tot de kruin is een achtste van zijn lengte; van de bovenkant van de borst tot de haarimplant is een zevende van zijn hele lengte. Van de tepels tot de kruin is een kwart van de man. De schouderbreedte beslaat een kwart van de man. Van de elleboog tot de vingertoppen is een vijfde van de man, en van de elleboog naar de oksel een achtste. De hele hand is een tiende van de man. De afstand van de onderkant van de kin tot de neus en van de haarimplant tot de wenkbrauwen is hetzelfde, en net zo lang als het oor: een derde van het gezicht.

De bijdrage van Leonardo was dat hij een eeuwenoud algoritme oploste dat bekendstaat als 'de kwadratuur van de cirkel', een meetkundig probleem waarbij met behulp van een passer en een liniaal wordt gepoogd een cirkel en een vierkant met een gelijk oppervlak te construeren. In theorie zou er een volmaakt geproportioneerd mens in de figuur passen, en hoewel de aanwijzingen van Vitruvius tamelijk ruw blijven, is Leonardo's tekening perfect; een werk dat zowel wiskundig als artistiek gezien geniaal is.

Merovingers De Merovingers zijn volgens Leigh Teabing in DVC de Frankische koninklijke familie waar de afstammelingen van Jezus en **Maria Magdalena** zich door middel van een huwelijk mee hebben vermengd, waardoor de heilige afstammingslijn werd voortgezet. Een latere telg uit die lijn was **Godfried van Bouillon**, de grondlegger van de **Priorij van Sion**.

De Merovingers zouden afstammen van Merovée, een fictief personage dat twee vaders had: een koning, Clodio genaamd, en een zeemonster dat zijn moeder had verleid toen ze in zee zwom. Door hun afstamming zouden Merovée en zijn nazaten over bovennatuurlijke krachten beschikken en uitzonderlijk lang leven. In andere legenden wordt hun oorsprong in verband gebracht met Noach en andere joodse stamvaders en met het Troje uit de oudheid. Andere beweringen – dat de Merovingers afstamden van buitenaardsen, dat ze het nageslacht van *nefilim* of gevallen engelen waren, en dat George en Jeb Bush afstammelingen zijn van Merovée – hebben minder aandacht gekregen. Eén eerbetoon aan de roodharige vorsten heeft van 'Merovinger' een bijna alledaags woord gemaakt: een personage in de succesvolle filmserie *The Matrix* heet '*the Merovingian*'.

Wat zeker is, is dat koning Clovis in het laatste deel van de vijfde eeuw de greep van de Merovingers over de Franken heeft verstevigd. Tijdens een veldslag met een andere stam zwoer Clovis dat hij zich tot het katholicisme zou bekeren als de overwinning hem gegund was. Dat was het geval, en zo won de katholieke kerk Frankrijk. Vanaf dat moment raakte de Merovingische lijn meer en meer verstrooid en regeerden de koningen over een groep kleine, oorlogvoerende landen. De onenigheid tussen die groepen bereikte een hoogtepunt met

de moord op **Dagobert II**, de laatste werkelijke Merovingische koning. Een paar generaties later kwam de troon in handen van het Karolingische geslacht, waarvan de beroemdste telg Karel de Grote was. In de beruchte *Dossiers secrets*, waarin geen steen op de andere blijft, zou worden beweerd dat Dagoberts kind in leven is gebleven en het Merovingische geslacht heeft voortgezet tot aan de hedendaagse familie van... **Pierre Plantard**.

Mirjam Een andere naam voor **Maria Magdalena**.

Mithras Teabing noemt Mithras een 'prechristelijke god' wiens bijbehorende mythologie veel overeenkomsten vertoont met de verhalen over Jezus. Mithras was een populaire god in het oude Rome, vooral van de tweede tot de vierde eeuw na Christus. Mithras is voortgekomen uit een oudere god uit het Midden-Oosten, die Mitra of Mithra heette en in Perzië en India werd vereerd. Oorspronkelijk was Mithra een lagere godheid die de Zoroastrische god Ahoera Mazda diende.

Mithras werd geassocieerd met het zonlicht en werd vaak vereerd samen met of als Sol Invictus, de onoverwinnelijke zon, een andere populaire Romeinse god. Vooral onder de Romeinse troepen en in de garnizoenen werd Mithras aanbeden. Doordat de soldaten lange periodes ver van huis waren, werden ze blootgesteld aan nieuwe ideeën en nieuwe godheden. Mithras was een van de meest succesvolle 'geïmporteerde' goden.

Veel tradities uit het christendom

en christelijke godsdienstoefeningen zouden afkomstig kunnen zijn van de verering van Mithras. De viering van het wintersolstitium, de terugkeer van de zon, die op 25 december plaatsvond, was zeer belangrijk in de Mithras-aanbidding. In veel gemeenschappen werd gedacht dat Mithras uit een maagd was geboren, en in sommige tradities maakte hij deel uit van een heilige drie-eenheid. Ook de rituele doop en het laatste avondmaal hadden een plaats in de verering van Mithras. Sommige geleerden denken dat het ontluikende christelijke geloof de gebruiken en overtuigingen van het mithraïsme heeft overgenomen, zodat de nieuwe religie gemakkelijker de plaats van de oude kon innemen.

Mitterrand, François Als hij tegen zijn zin met luitenant Collet naar het **Louvre** rijdt, laat Langdon zijn gedachten gaan over François Mitterrand, ex-president van Frankrijk. Volgens hem heeft Mitterrand zijn bijnaam 'de Sfinx' te danken aan zijn liefde voor de Egyptische cultuur. Later, in **La Pyramide**, twijfelt hij of hij *capitaine* Fache zal vertellen dat Mitterrand heeft verordend dat er 666 glazen ruitjes in de piramide gebruikt moesten worden. (Deze bewering wordt niet door feiten gestaafd; zie hoofdstuk 11. In werkelijkheid is de piramide van 698 ruiten gemaakt.)

Mitterrand, geboren in 1916, is een invloedrijke figuur geweest in de Franse politiek van de twintigste eeuw. Als infanterist raakte hij in de Tweede Wereldoorlog gewond en hij werd gevangengenomen door de Duitsers. Nadat hij was ontsnapt, keerde hij terug naar

Frankrijk en sloot zich aan bij het verzet. Na de bevrijding werd Mitterrand de jongste minister in de nieuwe regering van de Franse Republiek. Langzamerhand liet hij zijn conservatieve opvattingen varen en bij zijn derde poging, in 1981, werd hij de eerste socialistische president van Frankrijk.

Een van Mitterrands 'grote projecten', die waren gericht op het opknappen en aanpassen van culturele en stedelijke monumenten, was de verbouwing van het enorme **Louvre**.

Mitterrands bijnaam 'de Sfinx' lijkt hij te danken te hebben aan zijn ondoorgrondelijke en ongrijpbare karakter, en niet aan zijn liefde voor de Egyptische kunst. Zijn belangrijkste bijnaam was 'de Vos' en een andere was 'de Florentijn', vanwege de magistrale – sommigen zouden zeggen machiavellistische – manier waarop hij zijn tegenstanders manipuleerde. De alomtegenwoordige **Pierre Plantard** is verantwoordelijk voor de geruchten dat ook hij lid was van de **Priorij van Sion**.

Mona Lisa De *Mona Lisa*, misschien wel het favoriete meesterwerk van **Leonardo** zelf (hij hield het jarenlang bij zich), wordt door velen beschouwd als het beroemdste schilderij dat er bestaat. In DVC schrijft Jacques Saunière een anagram op de ruit van plexiglas die het schilderij beschermt. Terwijl Sophie en Langdon naar het schilderij lopen om de boodschap te lezen, mijmert Langdon over een lezing die hij eens voor een groep gevangenen heeft gegeven over het mysterie en de populariteit van het schilderij.

Veel eminente geleerden zijn het er-over eens dat het een afbeelding is van een jonge Florentijnse vrouw, ene Lisa Gherardini del Giocondo, de vrouw van een Florentijns koopman. Van de naam Giocondo (wat 'gelukkig' betekent) is de naam van het schilderij afgeleid: *La Joconde* of *La Gioconda*. Tegen het einde van Da Vinci's leven werd het schilderij verkocht of weggegeven aan koning Frans I van Frankrijk. Het is altijd in het bezit van de Franse koninklijke familie gebleven, die het in het Louvre heeft ondergebracht.

Langdon lijkt de kunstzinnige waarde van het schilderij te reduceren door de beroemdheid ervan toe te schrijven aan het geheim dat achter de glimlach zou schuilgaan. Vele kunsthistorici hebben gespeculeerd over de reden voor deze glimlach. Sommigen zijn van mening dat het geheim de identiteit van het model betreft: het schilderij zou een verhuld zelfportret van de schilder in vrouwenkleding zijn, een mogelijkheid die Langdon in zijn lezing noemt. Anderen denken dat Mona Lisa een prinses uit het geslacht van de Medici's, een Spaanse hertogin of een andere vrouw van historische betekenis is. Deskundigen zijn het over het algemeen niet eens met Langdons bewering dat *Mona Lisa* een anagram is van de namen van de Egyptische vruchtbaarheidsgod **Amon** en de Egyptische godin **Isis**. Misschien is het geheim van *Mona Lisa* wel haar geheimzinnigheid. Misschien heeft ze haar blijvende populariteit wel te danken aan het feit dat ze een geheim heeft, en zullen we nooit weten wat dat is. En iets niet weten is veel intrigerender dan iets weten ooit kan zijn.

In 1911 is de *Mona Lisa* gestolen als onderdeel van een geheim plan om reproducties te verkopen van een markante Argentijnse oplichter, Eduardo de Valfierno. Als het schilderij eenmaal verdwenen was, zou een getalenteerde kunstrestaurateur, Yves Chaudron, zo veel mogelijk kopieën maken; Valfierno zou die kopieën aan gretige kunstverzamelaars verkopen en het origineel daarna weer aan het Louvre teruggeven. Parijs was in rep en roer toen bekend werd dat *La Joconde* was verdwenen. Er werden vele verdachten opgepakt, onder wie het grootste deel van de staf van het Louvre en een verbaasde Pablo Picasso, op wie de verdenking was gevallen doordat hij twee gestolen beeldhouwwerken had gekocht van een vriend, die ze uit het Louvre had gestolen.

Het plan werkte een tijdje en er werden kopieën verkocht, maar een van de arbeiders die Valfierno in de arm had genomen om het origineel te stelen, probeerde het aan een Parijse kunsthandelaar te verkopen. De kunsthandelaar gaf hem aan bij de politie. De *Mona Lisa* werd teruggevonden in de dubbele bodem van een houten kist in de woning van de arbeider, niet ver van het Louvre. Valfierno, die zijn identiteit niet bekend had gemaakt aan zijn handlangers, stak het geld van zijn clandestiene zaakjes in zijn zak en leefde de rest van zijn leven tevreden in weelde, misschien een extra reden voor de *Mona Lisa* om te glimlachen.

Montanus Bekeerde zich in de tweede eeuw tot het christendom en vertelde zijn volgelingen rond het jaar 156 dat

hij een profeet was en de enige over-
brenger van goddelijke openbaringen.
Montanus profeteerde de wederkomst
van Christus en schreef een zeer strenge vorm van ascese en boetedoening
voor. Hij had veel volgelingen. Naar-
mate zijn populariteit groeide, werd
ook de tegenstand heftiger. Sommigen
dachten dat het montanisme door een
boze geest werd veroorzaakt en pro-
beerden die uit te drijven. Uiteindelijk
splitsten Montanus en zijn volgelingen zich af van de kerk.

Mozart, Wolfgang Amadeus Een ver-
maarde achttiende-eeuwse compo-
nist. Mozart (1756-91) was een en-
thousiast vrijmetselaar en in veel van
zijn werken zijn vrijmetselaarsele-
menten terug te vinden. Een van zijn
muziekstukken heet zelfs ronduit
Maurerische Trauermusik. Er wordt
ook beweerd dat Mozart banden onderhield met de **Priorij van Sion**, in
het bijzonder vanwege werken zoals
Die Zauberflöte. Velen zullen, terwijl
ze van de muziek genieten, niet besef-
fen dat de woorden thema's uit de
christelijke symboliek bevatten zoals
de strijd tussen licht en donker of
goed en kwaad, evenals Egyptische en
esoterische elementen.

Nag Hammadi De naam van de plaats
waar in 1947 enkele belangrijke teksten uit het vroege christendom werden gevonden (zie **gnostische evangeliën** en de hoofdstukken 1 t/m 5). De
teksten waren als pagina's gebonden
(in tegenstelling tot de meeste oude
geschriften, die op rollen waren geschreven, zie **Dode-Zeerollen**) en
hadden omslagen van leer, voor zover

we weten de eerste keer dat dat materiaal voor boekomslagen werd gebruikt. Deze **codices** hebben veel duidelijk gemaakt over die periode, maar
sommige geleerden schatten dat er
van alle teksten die in de vroege christelijke traditie hebben bestaan slechts
15 procent is teruggevonden. Wie
weet, misschien liggen er nog veel
meer interpretaties van Maria Magdalena's verhaal op ontdekking te wach-
ten en kunnen die opnieuw een bestseller opleveren.

Newton, sir Isaac Het enorme aantal
benamingen waar Newton (1642-1727)
rechtmatig aanspraak op kan maken –
wiskundige, natuurkundige, filosoof,
natuurwetenschapper, theoloog, politiek filosoof, om er maar een paar te
noemen – zou hem in elk tijdperk tot
een belangrijke figuur in het intellectuele leven maken. Maar de revolutie
in fysica en wiskunde die hij heeft veroorzaakt, geeft hem een wel heel bijzondere plek onder de grote denkers
uit de geschiedenis.

Newtons prestaties worden vaak gezien als de overwinning van de rede en
de wetenschap op de nog steeds do-
minante, 'bijgelovige', middeleeuwse
kijk op de natuurkunde. Ondanks deze vereenzelviging met de verstande-
lijke, wetenschappelijke waarden van
de Verlichting hield Newton zich in-
tensief bezig met esoterische kennis en
het occulte. Voordat hij omstreeks
1665 zijn doorbraken in de fysica bereikte, was Newton een geleerde van
zijn tijd: een alchemist die jarenlang
heeft geprobeerd de goddelijke geheimen van de natuurlijke wereld te
doorgronden met behulp van de ex-

perimentele chemie, een methode die in die tijd niet werd onderscheiden van magie. Het zal geen verbazing wekken dat hij zijn experimenten in het geheim deed.

In DVC wordt Newton een van de grootmeesters van de **Priorij van Sion** genoemd, waarschijnlijk gebaseerd op de omstreden *Dossiers secrets.* Hoewel deze bewering niet kan worden gestaafd, was het van Newton bekend dat hij contacten onderhield met vooraanstaande vrijmetselaars en komen zijn overtuigingen in veel opzichten overeen met de leer van de vrijmetselarij.

Hoewel hij formeel een ketter was die het heilige loochende, verleende koning Karel II hem een speciale ontheffing waardoor hij zijn onderzoek kon doen zonder directe betrokkenheid bij de anglicaanse kerk. Hij probeerde wel de in zijn ogen verborgen geheimen van de bijbel te doorgronden, en trachtte ook het grondplan van de **tempel van Salomo** te reconstueren, dat hij zag als een cryptische weergave van het universum. Intrigerend is de bewering van een onderzoeker dat hij verscheidene verborgen christelijke en ketterse symbolen heeft ontdekt in de diagrammen van de *Principia,* Newtons belangrijkste werk op het gebied van de natuurwetenschappen.

Geloofsbelijdenis van Nicea De korte verklaring die is opgesteld tijdens het **Concilie van Nicea** waarin de orthodoxe overtuigingen werden samengevat die de ruggengraat van de kerkleer vormden. In de geloofsbelijdenis wordt het arianisme expliciet verworpen (zie **Arius**):

En in één Here Jezus Christus, de eniggeboren zoon van God, geboren uit de Vader voor alle eeuwen; God uit God, Licht uit Licht, waarachtig God uit waarachtig God; geboren, niet geschapen, één van wezen met de Vader; door Hem zijn alle dingen geworden.

De geloofsbelijdenis van Nicea wordt nog steeds gebruikt in christelijke erediensten.

O'Keeffe, Georgia Als Teabing Sophie en Langdon vertelt dat de **roos** lang is beschouwd als 'het belangrijkste symbool voor de vrouwelijke seksualiteit', voert hij aan dat je het beste kunt zien hoe 'de bloeiende roos op de vrouwelijke geslachtsdelen lijkt' door naar het werk van Georgia O'Keeffe te kijken, die altijd met dit thema in verband wordt gebracht. O'Keeffe heeft zelf echter lang ontkend dat haar werk een symbolische lading had en heeft volgehouden dat de seksuele en vaak erotische associaties die haar werk wekten geheel toe te schrijven waren aan de fantasie van de toeschouwer.

Olympische Spelen De eerste olympiade begon in 776 v.C. als godsdienstig feest ter ere van de Griekse oppergod Zeus. De spelen, die oorspronkelijk plaatsvonden in Olympia, bij de tempel van Zeus, hadden duidelijk **heidense** wortels. In eerste instantie was de olympiade bedoeld als evenement om de saamhorigheid te stimuleren van de tamelijk verdeelde Griekse stadstaten. De eerste olympiades hadden slechts één onderdeel, maar er werd veel tijd besteed aan een religieus feest waarin onder andere offers werden gebracht aan een hele reeks hogere en lagere godheden. De olympiade bleef in deze vorm bestaan tot 393 n.C., toen de Romeinse keizer Theodosius een eind aan de spelen maakte. De moderne Olympische Spelen werden voor het eerst gehouden in 1896, op aandringen van de Franse baron Pierre de Coubertin. De Coubertin ontwierp in 1913 de vijf in elkaar grijpende ringen die het symbool van de hedendaagse Olympische Spelen zijn. De Coubertin zei dat de ringen voor de vijf deelnemende werelddelen stonden, en de kleuren voor alle nationale vlaggen ter wereld. Er zijn mensen die in het Olympische symbool een subtiel eerbetoon aan het polytheïstische voorchristlijke tijdperk zien.

Opus Dei Om zijn plot aan te scherpen heeft Dan Brown misschien wel de twee uitersten van de verschillende religieuze opvattingen sinds het leven van Jezus samengebracht. Aan de ene kant, vertegenwoordigd door Sophies grootvader en de mysteries die de hoofdpersonen proberen te doorgronden, staat de 'radicale' tak van de **gnostische** traditie, die gelooft in het huwelijk tussen Jezus en Maria Magdalena en die de lange **heidense** erfenis van de mensheid accepteert. Aan de andere kant staat het orthodoxe katholicisme, vertegenwoordigd door wat velen beschouwen als het meest conservatieve geluid, het Opus Dei. Beide zijden zijn op zoek naar de **heilige graal**, al is het om verschillende redenen.

De doelstelling van het Opus Dei is, in de woorden van de organisatie zelf: 'mee te werken aan deze evangelische zending van de kerk. Het Opus Dei moedigt christengelovigen in alle lagen van de maatschappij aan om in de gewone omstandigheden, en in het bijzonder door de heiliging van hun werk, een leven te leiden dat volledig overeenstemt met het geloof.' Het Opus Dei, dat in 1928 is opgericht door Josemaría Escrivá de Balaguer, is de gedachte toegedaan dat heiligheid ook bereikbaar is voor wereldlijke katholieken. Deze heiligheid behelst een heiliging en perfectie van het 'gewone' leven van de leek, die elke handeling vreugdevol aan God dient op te dragen. Leden van het Opus Dei dienen zich strikt te houden aan de restricties en leerstellingen van het katholicisme.

Het Opus Dei had een invloedrijke bondgenoot aan paus Johannes Paulus II, die de organisatie tot een persoonlijke prelatuur maakte: de leden staan onder gezag van een prelaat, die verantwoording aflegt tegenover de congregatie van bisschoppen, volledig onafhankelijk van geografische locatie of bisdom. Bovendien verklaarde de paus pater Escrivá in 2002 heilig. De aandacht die de organisatie krijgt, heeft niet alleen te maken met de conservatieve wortels die Johannes Paulus en St.-Josemaría deelden, maar ook met de groeiende populariteit en invloed van de groep. Geschat wordt dat het Opus Dei wereldwijd tussen de tachtigduizend en negentigduizend leden heeft, en de schattingen voor de Verenigde Staten lopen uiteen van drieduizend tot vijftigduizend leden.

Controverses blijven de organisatie

achtervolgen, meestal met betrekking tot het beoefenen van zelfkastijding en wat sommige critici beschouwen als de sekteachtige zeggenschap die de groep over haar leden zou hebben. Er zijn twee soorten Opus Dei-leden: surnumerair en numerair. Ongeveer zeventig procent van de leden is surnumerair; zij concentreren zich op de heiliging van hun werk en taken binnen het gezin. Numerairs wonen daarentegen vaak in leefgemeenschappen van het Opus Dei, geïsoleerd van leden van het andere geslacht. Ze beoefenen het celibaat en schenken hun inkomen aan de organisatie. Verder doen ze aan zelfkastijding, een geritualiseerde boetedoening die bedoeld is om verlost te worden van de zonden en de driften die daartoe leiden, met behulp van een boetekleed of -gordel (**cilice**) of een geselkoord.

Het Opus Dei vindt de manier waarop de geloofsopvattingen van de organisatie in DVC worden afgeschilderd ongefundeerd en heeft in verband daarmee op internet gezorgd voor links naar artikelen die kritisch zijn over Dan Browns interpretatie van de bijbel in het algemeen en de organisatie in het bijzonder.

Opus Dei Awareness Network (ODAN)
De anti-Opus Dei-organisatie die, zoals in DVC wordt geschreven, ernaar streeft het publiek te waarschuwen voor de 'angstaanjagende' activiteiten van het Opus Dei. Ook zij hebben hun eigen website.

Pentagram Het pentagram duikt in DVC voor het eerst op als een bloederig symbool dat door Jacques Sauniè-

re kort voor zijn overlijden op zijn buik is gekrabbeld. Langdon, die naar de plaats van het delict wordt gebracht, vertelt dat het een symbool is voor Venus, de godin van de liefde en seksualiteit, en dat het ook wordt geassocieerd met de natuurverering.

Het pentagram is een van de oudste symbolen die de mensheid kent. In de meest herkenbare vorm is het een vijfpuntige ster, die bestaat uit vijf elkaar snijdende lijnen van gelijke lengte en vijf punten die dezelfde hoek hebben. Als het in een cirkel wordt getekend, wordt het een pentakel genoemd. De pentakel was vroeger een symbool van Venus of Ishtar, afhankelijk van welke godin er werd vereerd.

De oorsprong van het pentagram is gehuld in de nevelen van het verre verleden van de mensheid, maar we weten wel dat het al in Soemerische tijden werd gebruikt. Naar de oorspronkelijke betekenis en ontwikkeling ervan kunnen we slechts gissen, maar geleerden hebben vastgesteld dat het een oud symbool is voor het menselijk lichaam, de vier elementen en de geest, en het universum zelf. De pythagoreeërs gebruikten het als herkenningsteken en associeerden het mogelijk met de godin Hygieia, de Griekse godin van de gezondheid.

Het pentagram is ook heden ten dage nog steeds in gebruik als symbool. Beoefenaars van wicca en andere esoterische groepen gebruiken het bij hun erediensten en rituelen. Verder

wordt het gebruikt om militaire on-
derscheidingen en rangen mee aan te
geven, als symbool voor de vijf pila-
ren van de islam en voor datgene waar
het het meest berucht om is: als symbool voor de aanbidding van de duivel en andere demonische krachten;
een gebruik dat, zoals Langdon opmerkt, historisch onjuist is.

Petrus de apostel Petrus heette Simon
toen hij Jezus voor het eerst ontmoet-
te, maar die gaf hem de naam Kefas
('rots'). De Latijnse versie van die
naam is Petrus. In de evangeliën van
het Nieuwe Testament lijkt Jezus een
voorliefde voor Petrus te hebben gehad. Hij is aanwezig bij enkele bepa-
lende gebeurtenissen in het leven van
Jezus. Een beroemde passage uit het
Nieuwe Testament zijn de woorden
waarmee Jezus zich tot Petrus wendt:
'En ik zeg je: jij bent Petrus, de rots
waarop ik mijn kerk zal bouwen.'
In DVC wordt Petrus genoemd in de
uitgebreide uiteenzetting van Teabing
over de aard van de **heilige graal.** Hij
haalt een passage uit het Evangelie van
Maria aan, waarin Peter zijn ongeloof
uit over het feit dat Jezus met **Maria
Magdalena** zou hebben gepraat zonder dat de andere **apostelen** dat wisten. 'Zou hij werkelijk buiten ons om
en niet openlijk met een vrouw gesproken hebben?... Heeft hij aan haar
de voorkeur gegeven boven ons?'
vraagt hij. Teabing zegt dat Petrus ja-
loers was op Maria Magdalena omdat
Christus de voortzetting van de kerk
aan haar had toevertrouwd, en niet
aan hem. Maar hoewel uit het Evangelie van Maria inderdaad blijkt dat
Petrus het niet leuk vond dat Jezus

met Maria Magdalena onder vier ogen
sprak, is er in deze tekst geen aanwijzing te vinden dat het gesprek van Jezus met Maria Magdalena iets te maken had met de voortzetting van de
kerk.

Phi Phi is het getal 1,6180339087... Het
heeft een oneindig aantal decimalen
achter de komma. Bij niet-wiskundi-
gen is het bekender onder de naam
'**gulden snede**'. In DVC vormt dit be-
grip het onderwerp van een college
dat Robert Langdon eens heeft gegeven en dat hij zich herinnert als hij een
trap af rent om samen met Sophie Ne-
veu het **Louvre** te ontvluchten. (Het is
geen toeval dat 'phi' ook de middelste
letters van Sophies naam zijn.)
Langdon legt zijn studenten uit dat
Phi een belangrijke rol speelt in de natuur en alomtegenwoordig is, in kolo-
nies honingbijen en in de spiralen van
nautilusschelpen, in zaadbollen van
zonnebloemen en in het menselijk lichaam (namelijk in de verhouding
tussen de totale lengte van het lichaam
en de lengte vanaf de navel tot aan de
vloer). En in navolging van die natuurlijke schoonheid en evenredig-
heid is Phi veel gebruikt in de kunst
(Dalí's *Laatste Avondmaal*), architectuur (het Parthenon) en muziek (Mozart, Bartok). Hoewel deze beschrij-
ving in grote lijnen op werkelijkheid
berust, zijn er een paar kanttekenin-
gen te plaatsen. Wiskundigen gebruiken 'Phi' voor de gulden snede en 'phi'
voor de omgekeerde waarde, maar
Dan Brown maakt dat onderscheid
niet. Een symboliekdeskundige als
Langdon zou het paar schrijven als Φ
en ϕ. Ook zegt Langdon dat 'het getal

phi was afgeleid van de **Fibonacci-reeks**', maar de geschiedenis leert dat het getal allang bekend was toen Fibonacci het afleidde uit zijn beroemde getallenreeks.

De eerste duidelijke definitie van wat pas veel later de gulden snede zou worden genoemd, werd volgens wetenschapper Mario Livio 'rond 300 v.C. gegeven door de grondlegger van de meetkunde als geformaliseerd deductiesysteem, Euclides van Alexandrië'. De Grieken duidden de verhouding aan met de letter *tau*. De naam 'gulden snede' wordt waarschijnlijk pas vanaf de negentiende eeuw gebruikt. De aanduiding 'Phi' verscheen pas aan het begin van de twintigste eeuw, toen de Amerikaanse wiskundige Mark Barr het gebruikte als eerbetoon aan de Griekse beeldhouwer en bouwmeester Phidias, die onder meer het Parthenon en de *Zeus* in de tempel van Olympia op zijn naam heeft staan.

De techniek van de gulden snede zou door **Leonardo** in sommige van zijn bekendste werken zijn gebruikt. Niet alle deskundigen zijn het daarover eens. Het wiskundige model voor de gulden snede werd in Italië pas bekend nadat het in het laatste decennium van de vijftiende eeuw door Pacioli werd gepubliceerd, en toen had Leonardo vele van zijn belangrijkste schilderijen en tekeningen al gemaakt.

Plantard, Pierre Pierre Plantard wordt niet genoemd in DVC, maar hij is van essentieel belang voor de mythologie waarvan het boek doortrokken is.

Pierre Plantard (1920-2000) heeft werkelijk bestaan. Hij was Fransman en de zelfverklaarde grootmeester van de **Priorij van Sion**, waartoe hij in 1981 was verkozen. De aandacht van het grote publiek werd op hem gevestigd door Michael Baigent, Richard Leigh en Henry Lincoln, die in hun bestseller *Het Heilige Bloed en de Heilige Graal* over hem schrijven. Hun boek was een inspiratiebron voor Dan Brown, en de rol die Plantard speelt in *Het Heilige Bloed en de Heilige Graal* wordt in DVC gespeeld door Jacques Saunière: de laatste grootmeester van de Priorij van Sion en afstammeling van de **Merovingische** koningen.

In een geval als dat van Plantard is het vaak moeilijk onderscheid te maken tussen feiten en fictie. Uit de *Dossiers secrets*, die hij hoogstwaarschijnlijk in de Bibliothèque Nationale in Parijs heeft gedeponeerd, zou blijken dat Pierre Plantard afstamt van Jean de Plantard, die zelf weer rechtstreeks afstamde van de Merovingische koningen.

Baigent, Lincoln en Leigh verklaarden dat in de loop van hun speurwerk naar de legende van de **heilige graal** 'alle sporen uiteindelijk naar [Plantard] leken te leiden'. Hij lijkt de belangrijkste informatiebron te zijn geweest voor allerlei verhalen rond **Rennes-le-Château** en heeft onderzoekers voorzien van vele raadselachtige details over de Priorij van Sion, die meestal meer vragen opriepen dan beantwoordden. Een sprekend voorbeeld hiervan is wat Plantard zei toen hij door het Franse tijdschrift *Le Charivari* werd geïnterviewd over de Priorij: 'het genootschap waartoe ik behoor is zeer oud. Ik volg slechts anderen op, ben niet meer dan een stipje in een reeks. We zijn hoeders van bepaalde zaken. En zonder publiciteit.' In *Het Heilige Bloed en de Heilige Graal* wordt hij omschreven als 'een waardige, hoffelijke man met een discreet aristocratische houding, zonder uiterlijk vertoon, met een vriendelijke, montere maar beschaafde manier van doen'. Hij nam in het openbaar afstand van de conclusies die Baigent, Lincoln en Leigh trokken, maar bood wel aan de Franse editie van het boek te corrigeren. Hij bleef echter onduidelijk over de kwestie of de Merovingers afstamden van het geslacht van Jezus.

Er lijkt ook een duistere kant aan het verhaal van Plantard te zitten. Plantard is beschuldigd van het hebben van nazi-sympathieën en antisemitische ideeën en is voor en gedurende de Tweede Wereldoorlog in verband gebracht met verscheidene rechtse publicaties en organisaties. Het kan zijn dat hij in de jaren vijftig in de gevangenis heeft gezeten wegens verduistering en fraude, het kan zijn dat hij het verhaal over **Bérenger Saunière** aan de schrijver heeft verteld die de raadselen van Rennes-le-Château – mogelijk als onderdeel van een financiële afspraak – algemeen bekend heeft gemaakt. Zijn beweringen over zijn afstamming van de Merovingers worden in twijfel getrokken; vele van de documenten die hij gebruikte om de afstamming te bewijzen, werden door hem of zijn medeplichtigen gefabriceerd en onder een andere naam in de Bibliothèque Nationale gedeponeerd.

Het lijkt alsof elke bewering van Plantard en de Priorij onmiddellijk weerlegd kan worden, waarna die weerlegging op haar beurt weer wordt ondermijnd door tegenbeschuldigingen. Codes binnen codes, verhalen binnen verhalen. De vraagtekens en onduidelijkheden van de mythe van Pierre Plantard zijn een toepasselijke basis voor DVC.

Pope, Alexander Een van de aanwijzingen die Sophie en Langdon krijgen, is een gedicht, geschreven door Sophies grootvader, waarin de volgende passage voorkomt: 'In Londen rust een ridder door wiens werk / in grote toorn ontstak de heilige kerk. Toch stond een paus te treuren aan zijn graf.'

In de bibliotheek van King's College ontdekken ze dat '*a Pope*' niet een katholieke paus was, maar de beroemde achttiende-eeuwse dichter Alexander Pope (1688-1744), en dat de ridder in kwestie **sir Isaac Newton** was. Brown zegt dat de begrafenis van Newton 'werd geleid' door de dichter, die 'een inspirerende grafrede hield voordat hij aarde over de kist strooide'. Het is waar dat Pope Newton kende en bewonderde, maar hoewel hij ongetwijfeld op de begrafenis was, is nergens terug te vinden dat hij die geleid zou hebben; Newton was zo'n prominente figuur dat er onder de baardragers een lord, twee hertogen en drie graven waren. De dienst werd geleid door de bisschop van Rochester.

Er bestaat echter geen twijfel over dat Pope een jaar of vier later, toen er een monument werd opgericht voor Newton, een grafschrift voor de wetenschapper heeft geschreven. Het is een van de beroemdste grafschriften uit de geschiedenis, gedeeltelijk in het Latijn en gedeeltelijk in het Engels. De vertaling van de Engelse regels luidt:

Natuur en natuurwet, zo duister, uit 't zicht.
God sprak: Er zij Newton, en ziet, er was licht.

Poussin, Nicolas Poussin wordt door velen als de grootste Franse schilder van de zeventiende eeuw beschouwd. Hij verwierf zijn bekendheid in Rome, waar hij romantische en poëtische voorstellingen schilderde, ontleend aan de klassieke mythologie. Sophie herinnert zich dat Poussin de op een na favoriete schilder van haar grootvader was, na Leonardo. Hij speelt een interessante rol in het bronnenmateriaal dat Dan Brown voor zijn boek heeft geraadpleegd. In DVC wordt gezegd dat Jacques Saunière een paar boeken over Poussin heeft geschreven die Langdon graag als lesmateriaal gebruikt. Ze gaan in het bijzonder over geheime codes in de schilderijen van Poussin en van de Nederlandse schilder **David Teniers**.

Op een van Poussins schilderijen, *Les Bergers d'Arcadie* (*De herders van Arcadië*), uit 1638, staat een groep herders voor een graf. Op het graf staat het Latijnse zinnetje *Et in Arcadia Ego*, in het Nederlands: 'En in Arcadië ik.' Het zinnetje is vaak geïnterpreteerd als een romantische zinspeling op de aanwezigheid van de dood, zelfs in het idyllische land van de herders. Er is echter een verband tussen het schilde-

rij en het mysterie van **Rennes-le-Château**. Een van de perkamenten die **Bérenger Saunière** gevonden zou hebben in de parochiekerk van Rennes-le-Château bevatte de volgende gecodeerde boodschap:

HERDERIN GEEN VERLEIDING DAT POUSSIN TENIERS DE SLEUTEL HEBBEN; VREDE 681 BIJ HET KRUIS EN DIT PAARD VAN GOD IK (VERNIETIG) DEZE DEMON VAN DE BEWAKER VOLLEDIG OP HET MIDDAGUUR BLAUWE APPELS

Er lijkt in de boodschap verwezen te worden naar *Les Bergers d'Arcadie*. Verschillende mensen die over het mysterie van Rennes-le-Château hebben geschreven, hebben beweerd dat er in de buurt van het gehucht een graf is dat grote gelijkenis vertoont met het graf op het schilderij. Had Poussin iets te maken met een verborgen geheim in Rennes-le-Château? Baigent, Leigh en Lincoln noemen in *Het Heilige Bloed en de Heilige Graal* een brief die abbé Louis Fouquet aan zijn broer heeft gestuurd, die beheerder van de schatkist was onder Lodewijk XIV. In de brief wordt een bezoek beschreven dat Fouquet in Rome aan Poussin had gebracht:

Hij en ik hebben bepaalde zaken besproken, die ik in detail aan je zal uitleggen; zaken die je, met de hulp van de heer Poussin, voordelen zullen bezorgen die zelfs koningen slechts met de grootste moeite aan hem zouden kunnen ontlokken, en waarvan het volgens hem mogelijk is dat niemand ze in de komende eeuwen opnieuw zal ontdekken.

Kort nadat hij deze overigens altijd onverklaard gebleven brief ontving, is Nicolas Fouquet gearresteerd en voor de rest van zijn leven in de gevangenis beland.

Priorij van Sion Op de eerste bladzijde van DVC vermeldt Dan Brown dat de Priorij van Sion een werkelijk bestaande organisatie is die in 1099 is opgericht, en dat er in perkamenten van de Bibliothèque Nationale een ledenlijst wordt gegeven waarop grote namen uit de literatuur, kunst en wetenschap figureren. De Priorij is ongetwijfeld een werkelijk bestaande organisatie, maar wat er verder met zekerheid over gezegd kan worden, is zeer de vraag. De Priorij kan zich beroepen op een gedocumenteerd bestaan vanaf 1956 (voor die tijd stond er niets op papier), toen de organisatie zich registreerde en statuten indiende bij de overheid. De woordvoerder van de organisatie is bijna dat gehele recente verleden **Pierre Plantard** geweest, een man wiens beweringen over zichzelf net zo verwarrend waren als de beweringen die de Priorij over zichzelf deed. Sterker nog, het is niet erg duidelijk wat het werkelijke verschil tussen Plantard en de Priorij van Sion eigenlijk was.

Uit de inhoud van de *Dossiers secrets* en de openbare verklaringen van Plantard en zijn kameraden rijst op zijn best een vaag beeld van de geschiedenis van de Priorij op. Er wordt beweerd dat de geheime organisatie in het laatste decennium van de elfde eeuw is opgericht door **Godfried van Bouillon**. Het lijkt algemeen aanvaard dat de Priorij opdracht gaf tot de vorming van de **tempeliers**, waarvan ze zich bijna honderd jaar later afscheidde om haar eigen lijn van grootmeesters te beginnen. Rond die tijd ging de Priorij zich ook 'l'Ordre de la Rose-Croix Veritas' noemen, de Orde van het Ware Rozenkruis, waarmee ze een verband legden met de **Rozenkruisers**. De organisatie zegt dat **Bérenger Saunière** de perkamenten die aanleiding gaven tot de controverse rond **Rennes-le-Château** heeft ontdekt nadat hij orders had ontvangen van de Priorij van Sion. En ze geeft een lijst van grootmeesters vanaf de afscheiding van de tempeliers in 1188 tot aan Thomas Plantard, de zoon van Pierre.

Op deze dunne schets, die werd gepresenteerd in poëtische, dubbelzinnige bewoordingen en in quasi-historische vorm, hebben honderden schrijvers hun speculaties en theorieën over de Priorij en haar plek in de geschiedenis geprojecteerd. Het zijn er te veel om op te sommen, maar DVC is gebaseerd op een van de beroemdste en hardnekkigste ideeën, dat tot op de bodem wordt uitgediept in *Het Heilige Bloed en de Heilige Graal*: de Priorij als eeuwenoude bewaker van het nageslacht van Christus en **Maria Magdalena**. Andere theorieën luiden dat de Priorij een dekmantel is voor verscheidene andere esoterische organisaties, en er zijn ook mensen die beweren dat de groep voorstander is van een theocratische 'Verenigde Staten van Europa'.

Elke bewering over de ware aard of oorsprong van de organisatie, van doorsnee tot hatelijk, is beantwoord met tegenbeschuldigingen van de Priorij en haar verdedigers. Het lijkt erop dat de Priorij bestaat in wat door één commentator 'een hermeneutische hel' wordt genoemd, een schimmenrijk van botsende interpretaties, hypothesen en aanwijzingen, dat juist door de draagwijdte en veelomvattendheid de mogelijkheid om ooit de waarheid te achterhalen lijkt te ondermijnen. Misschien vormt dat wel de blijvende aantrekkingskracht van de Priorij: het wezen van de organisatie is, voorzover we weten, zo onbestemd dat iedereen zijn eigen hoop, angst en verbeelding mee kan laten wegen bij zijn of haar interpretatie.

La Pyramide La Pyramide is de glazen piramide die I.M. Pei heeft ontworpen als nieuwe ingang van het **Louvre**. Het is een van de eerste dingen die Langdon ziet als hij naar de plaats van de moord wordt gebracht. La Pyramide heeft ook een omgekeerde tegenhanger, La Pyramide Inversée, die met de punt naar beneden steekt en zich onder de andere bevindt; dit is de piramide die een belangrijke rol speelt aan het eind van Browns boek.

La Pyramide is het duidelijkste kenmerk van de verbouwing van het Louvre en symboliseert de verstrekkende bouwkundige veranderingen die aan het gebouw zijn aangebracht onder leiding van de Chinese architect I.M. Pei. La Pyramide bracht alle verschillende ingangen op één plek samen en leidt naar een nieuwe ondergrondse hal die toegang biedt tot de tentoonstellingsruimten, maar ook tot restaurants, winkels en nieuwe ruimten voor

opslag en ondersteunende diensten die het museum zelf nodig had. Het bouwwerk van Pei is inmiddels algemeen aanvaard en wordt door veel Parijzenaars zelfs bewonderd, maar toen de plannen ervoor werden aangekondigd, werden die onthaald op een tumultueus openbaar debat en scherpe kritiek in de Parijse pers.

La Pyramide is vervaardigd van 698 panelen van gehard, zeer licht, transparant glas, en niet van 666, het zogenaamde 'satansgetal', zoals Brown/Langdon en veel liefhebbers van complottheorieën beweren. De lichtgewicht ruiten, die met elkaar verbonden zijn door eveneens lichte stalen steunen, vormen met elkaar een zeer krachtige vorm, een gedrongen piramide van niet meer dan een dikke twintig meter hoog, die tegelijk luchtig en indrukwekkend is. Het glas reflecteert de hemel boven Parijs, een weerspiegeling van de stemming in de Franse hoofdstad.

'Q'-document Als Teabing Sophie en Langdon in zijn werkkamer vertelt over de geheime geschiedenis van het christendom en hoe er zaken in de doofpot zijn gestopt, heeft hij het over 'het legendarische Q-document', 'een manuscript waarvan zelfs het Vaticaan toegeeft dat het bestaat. Dat zou een boek met de leer van Jezus moeten zijn, misschien wel door Hemzelf geschreven.' Dan laat hij zijn slag om de arm varen en stelt Sophie een retorische vraag: 'Waarom zou Hij zelf geen kroniek hebben bijgehouden van Zijn leven?'

Of hij dat heeft gedaan of niet, heeft geleerden beziggehouden sinds Herbert Marsh, een Engelsman, in 1801 voor het eerst de hypothese lanceerde dat er een Q-achtige bron bestond, waarbij hij zich baseerde op de overtuiging dat iemand de woorden van Jezus in het Aramees had vertaald. Hij noemde die vertaling *beth*, een Hebreeuwse letter die de vorm van een huis heeft. Later in die eeuw hebben verscheidene Duitse geleerden het onderwerp opgepikt en grote beroering veroorzaakt: zou het, gezien het feit dat de evangeliën van Matteüs en Lucas enigszins van elkaar afwijken, mogelijk zijn dat er nog een andere bron is voor de woorden van Jezus dan de synoptische evangeliën? En zo ja, wat was dan de 'juiste'? Aangezien er enige twijfel rees over de authenticiteit van de woorden van Jezus zoals wij die kenden, bedacht de Duitse geleerde Johannes Weiss de neutralere aanduiding Q, naar het Duitse woord *quelle*, wat 'bron' betekent. Zo was de stand van zaken in de jaren zestig van de vorige eeuw: wetenschappers die laag na laag aan reconstructies toevoegden. Toen leverde de vertaling van de documenten die in 1947 bij **Nag Hammadi** werden gevonden een Evangelie van Tomas op.

Blijkt uit het Evangelie van Tomas inderdaad dat het de directe bron van de woorden van Jezus is? Het antwoord is gedeeltelijk gelegen in de datering van de documenten, een kwestie die nog niet is afgedaan. Als ze dateren van halverwege de eerste eeuw, kan dat als een sterk argument worden beschouwd. Als, zoals de wat behoudender geleerden van mening zijn, het Evangelie van Tomas na de eerste eeuw is geschreven, is de kans groter dat het is samengesteld uit bijeengebrachte herinneringen (en dan is er dus niet echt sprake van geschiedenis uit de eerste hand).

Professor Robinson, de 'oervader' van dit debat, beantwoordt de vraag als volgt: 'De verwijzing naar Q en de kwestie of Jezus dat zelf heeft geschreven? Natuurlijk heeft Jezus dat niet geschreven. Dat is weer een van de punten waarop Dan Brown een beetje knoeit met het bewijsmateriaal, zodat het sensationeler lijkt dan het is.' Het debat zal voortduren, en we kunnen alleen maar hopen dat er meer teksten uit het vroege christendom gevonden zullen worden, zodat deze en andere controverses kunnen worden opgehelderd.

Rennes-le-Château Er zijn maar weinig plekken op aarde, van Stonehenge tot de Bermudadriehoek, die de achtergrond zijn geweest van zo veel complottheorieën als Rennes-le-Château, een Frans dorpje op een bergtop aan de oostrand van de Pyreneeën. Hoewel het in DVC niet wordt genoemd, vormt het de kern van de samenzwering waar het boek over gaat.

De geschiedenis van Rennes-le-Château gaat ver terug. In de prehistorie woonden er al mensen, daarna was er een Romeinse nederzetting en later een middeleeuwse vesting. Aan de vooravond van de Franse Revolutie was het dorp, als gevolg van een ingewikkelde reeks huwelijken, in handen gevallen van de familie Blanchefort. Er gaan geruchten dat markiezin Marie d'Hautpol de Blanchefort, die in elk geval dezelfde adellijke titel had als een grootmeester van de **tempeliers**, vlak voordat ze stierf een geheim heeft doorgegeven aan haar pastoor. Deze pastoor, ene abbé Bigou, die kort na haar overlijden vanwege de Revolutie een veilig heenkomen moest zoeken in Spanje, was in zijn functie als pastoor de voorganger van de intrigerendste inwoner die Rennes-le-Château heeft gehad: **Bérenger Saunière.**

Roos De roos heeft een grote symbolische waarde en in DVC komen een aantal aspecten ter sprake. Het rozenhouten kistje waarin de cryptex zit en dat Sophie op haar schoot houdt als zij en Langdon met een gewapende vrachtwagen uit de Zwitserse bank ontsnappen, heeft een roos op het deksel. Ze associeert die bloem met grote geheimen, en Langdon legt onmiddellijk verband met de Latijnse uitdrukking *sub rosa* (letterlijk: 'onder de roos'), die betekent dat alles wat wordt gezegd vertrouwelijk moet blijven. Ook is de roos door de **Priorij van Sion** gebruikt als symbool voor de **graal.** Er bestaat een soort die vijf bloemblaadjes en daarmee een pentagonale symmetrie heeft, wat hem in verband brengt met de baan van Venus langs de hemel en het **heilig vrouwelijke.** En dan is er nog het gebruik als kompasroos, die in de 'juiste richting' wijst.

Terwijl hij dit allemaal uitlegt, krijgt Langdon een ingeving. Hij begrijpt plotseling dat de graal waarschijnlijk *sub rosa* is verborgen, dat wil zeggen, onder het teken van de roos, in een kerk met roosvensters, rozetten en vijfbladen, 'de vijfbladige bloemversieringen die vaak boven een poort werden aangebracht, recht boven de sluitsteen'.

Verderop in het boek brengt Teabing de roos in verband met de vrouwelijke seksualiteit, waarbij de vijf bloemblaadjes staan voor 'de vijf stadia van het vrouwenleven: geboorte, menstruatie, moederschap, menopauze en dood'. Hij vertelt Landon en Sophie ook dat het woord 'roos' in heel veel talen, waaronder het Engels, Frans en Duits, 'rose' is, en Langdon meldt dat dat een anagram is van Eros, de Griekse god van de lichamelijke liefde.

Er zijn veel andere betekenissen aan de roos toegekend: een zinnebeeld van Christus, een symbool voor de geboorte van Christus en de Messiaanse profetieën. In de Grieks-Romeinse cultuur stond de roos voor schoonheid, lente en liefde. De roos verwees ook naar het snelle verstrijken van de tijd, en daarmee naar de naderende dood en de volgende wereld. Het Romeinse feest Rosalia was een feest voor de doden. Gothische kerken hebben roosvormige glas-inloodramen boven de drie ingangen, met Christus in het midden van elk venster. In deze context zou de roos staan voor de verlossing die in de kerk te vinden is en die door God is geopenbaard. In de latere christelijke kunst, vanaf de dertiende eeuw, wordt Maria vaak afgebeeld met een roos in haar hand, in een rozentuin of voor een wandtapijt met rozen. De roos verwijst symbolisch naar de eenheid van Christus met zijn kerk en God met zijn volk.

En ten slotte heeft de roos dezelfde kleur als de **appel**, wat haar weer in verband brengt met de plot van DVC. In het gedicht van Sophies grootvader dat de hoofdpersonen naar het graf van Newton brengt, lezen we:

Zoek nu de bol die aan zijn graf ontbreekt,
van rozig vlees, gevuld met zaden, spreekt.

Langdon beschouwt die laatste zin als een duidelijke verwijzing naar **Maria Magdalena**, 'de roos die het zaad van Jezus had gedragen'.

Rosslyn Chapel Tegen het einde van DVC brengt Saunières tweede cryptex Robert Langdon en Sophie Neveu naar Rosslyn Chapel, in de buurt van de Schotse plaats Edinburgh. Talrijke scribenten over het occulte en het new-agegebeuren zijn er jarenlang van overtuigd geweest dat de **heilige graal** zich in of bij Rosslyn Chapel bevindt, waar hij na de afslachting van de **tempeliers** in het Frankrijk van de veertiende eeuw naartoe zou zijn gebracht. De Schotse vrijmetselaars werden beschouwd als erfgenamen van de tempelierstraditie.

De bouw van Rosslyn Chapel – die ook de Kathedraal der Codes wordt genoemd – begon in 1446, in opdracht van sir William St. Clair of Sinclair, die de titel van grootmeester van de Schotse vrijmetselarij had geërfd. Ook zou hij van de **Merovingers** afstammen. Sir William hield persoonlijk toezicht op de bouw van de kapel, die kort na zijn dood in 1484 werd stopgezet. Alleen het koor – het deel van de kerk waar tijdens de dienst het koor en de geestelijken zich bevinden – is voltooid. Het wemelt in de kapel van de codes, symbolen, lettertekens in allerlei alfabetten en beeltenissen die doen denken aan een soort universele symbolische taal. Christelijke en joodse symbolen zijn naast elkaar gebruikt, net als Griekse, Latijnse, Hebreeuwse en andere alfabetten en verwijzingen naar de Noorse, Keltische en tempeliersgeschiedenis. Aan het eind van hun bezoek aan Rosslyn lijken Robert en Sophie tot de conclusie te komen dat de heilige graal, als die zich al ooit in Rosslyn Chapel heeft bevonden, daar nu in elk geval niet meer is.

Rozenkruisers De leer van de Rozenkruisers werd voor het eerst uiteengezet in *Allgemeine und General-Reformation der ganzen weiten Welt*, dat in 1614 werd gepubliceerd. Hierin wordt verteld dat Christian Rosencreutz, een Duitse edelman die als jongeman naar het Oosten was getrokken, daar kennis had verzameld en was ingewijd in geheime wijsheid. Deze wijsheid kwam neer op een oecumenische benadering waarin werd aanbevolen eenvoudig en deugdzaam te leven en in gemeenschappelijkheid een opperwezen of god te vereren. Er werden alchemistische metaforen gebruikt om de magische transformatie van de menselijke ziel te symboliseren.

Er zijn geleerden die menen dat Rosencreutz slechts een verzinsel was van de Duitse theoloog Johann Valentin Andreae, die volgens de **Priorij van Sion** van 1637 tot 1654 grootmeester van die organisatie is geweest. Velen denken dat Andreae een van de Rosencreutz-boeken, *De Chymische Bruiloft van Christian Rosencreutz*, heeft geschreven bij wijze van satire op de obsessie met het occulte die in dat tijdperk heerste. Maar of hun naamgever nu fictief was of niet, de Rozenkruisers gedijen vandaag de dag nog steeds als esoterisch genootschap dat zich baseert op de geschriften van Rosencreutz. De leer van de Rozenkruisers werd in de achttiende eeuw populair bij de vrijmetselaars, die toen veel symbolen van de Rozenkruisers overnamen, met name de **roos** en het **kruis**. (Vóór die tijd was de opvallendste plek waar die twee symbolen samen waren gebruikt, waarschijnlijk het wapenschild van Martin Luther.) De orde bestaat nog steeds, zij het in allerlei zeer uiteenlopende vormen.

Sangreal/Sangraal Sangreal is het woord dat Langdon noemt als de verzamelnaam die al eeuwenlang wordt gebruikt voor de documenten en relikwieën die met elkaar vormen wat we tegenwoordig de **heilige graal** noemen. Later legt Teabing uit dat het woord in de loop der tijden gesplitst werd in de woorden 'San' en 'Greal': heilige graal. Maar als de splitsing op een andere plek was gevallen – *sang real* – zouden de woorden 'koninklijk bloed' hebben betekend. De schrijvers van *Het Heilige Bloed en de Heilige Graal*, Baigent, Leigh en Lincoln, stellen dat de graal de Sangreal of de Sangraal wordt genoemd. Splitsing van deze woorden kan San Greal of San Graal opleveren (heilige graal), of sang real of sang raal (koninklijk bloed). Sir Thomas Malory, de schrijver van *Le Morte d'Arthur* en de eerste van wie we het woord in het Engels kennen, gebruikt Sangreal en *sang royal* (afgeleid van het Middelengelse real of rial) echter in twee verschillende betekenissen: Sangreal voor de heilige graal en *sang royal* voor heilig bloed, dus het is mogelijk dat dit de etymologische redenering van Teabing en Langdon ondermijnt.

Volgens de *Oxford English Dictionary* is de etymologie met de dubbele betekenis, die in de zeventiende eeuw is geïntroduceerd, onjuist.

Saunière, Bérenger Vanaf 1885 de pastoor van **Rennes-le-Château**, en het historische voorbeeld naar wie Jacques Saunière uit DVC is gemodelleerd. Tijdens een opknapbeurt van de dorpskerk zou Saunière (1852-1917) in een pilaar onder het kerkaltaar vier perkamenten met gecodeerde boodschappen hebben gevonden. Toen de boodschappen ontcijferd waren, bleken ze onduidelijke verwijzingen naar mensen en dingen te bevatten die niets met elkaar gemeen leken te hebben: de schilders **Poussin** en **Teniers**, de **Merovingische** koning **Dagobert**, Sion en 'blauwe **appels**'. Geïntrigeerd liet hij de documenten aan zijn superieuren zien, die hem opdroegen naar Parijs te gaan en de perkamenten aan andere kerkelijke hoogwaardigheidsbekleders te laten zien, onder wie abbé Bieil, de directeur van het seminarie van Saint-Sulpice.

Er is weinig bekend van wat er gebeurde gedurende Saunières bezoek aan Parijs (velen betwijfelen of hij er inderdaad wel is geweest), maar na zijn terugkeer in Rennes-le-Château zou hij buitensporig veel geld zijn gaan uitgeven aan restauratiewerkzaamheden en de bouw van een groot nieuw huis voor zichzelf. Zijn projecten namen bizarre vormen aan. Hij liet de inscriptie op de grafsteen van markiezin Marie d'Hautpol de Blanchefort verwijderen (die was door abbé Bigou voor haar graf ontworpen, en de inscriptie was een volmaakt anagram van een van de gecodeerde boodschappen die Saunière in het altaar had gevonden). Hij gaf opdracht tot de bouw van een toren die hij de Tour Magdala noemde, naar **Maria Magdalena**. Hij liet een luxueus landhuis bouwen, de Villa Bethania, waar hij nooit heeft gewoond. Hij liet ook de kerk verbouwen en opknappen, maar zijn nieuwe kunstzinnige aanpassingen waren enigszins onconventioneel: het wijwatervat wordt gedragen door een demon, boven de kerkdeur zijn de woorden 'Deze plek is verschrikkelijk' gegraveerd, en de kruiswegstaties die op de muren van de kerk zijn geschilderd, wemelen van de ongerijmde en verontrustende details.

Rennes-le-Château was een provincieplaatsje en Saunières salaris als pastoor was bescheiden. Waar haalde Saunière het geld vandaan voor zijn renovaties en bouwwerkzaamheden? Waarom gaf hij het op die manier uit? De antwoorden op die vragen heeft hij meegenomen het graf in, en daarna zijn de speculaties alleen maar wilder geworden.

Saunière, zo gaat het verhaal, zou zijn rijkdom te danken kunnen hebben aan de ontdekking van een oude schat van de Visigoten; aan steekpenningen van een geheim genootschap dat iets te verbergen had; aan de geheime locatie van de **heilige graal**; aan

de beroemde schat van Oak Island in Nova Scotia. Er zijn verbanden gelegd tussen Saunière, de **Priorij van Sion**, de vrijmetselaars en de **tempeliers**. Astronomen en landmeters hebben een ongelooflijk aantal figuren – driehoeken, **pentagrammen**, vijfhoeken – in en om Rennes-le-Château opgetekend, stuk voor stuk met een esoterische betekenis. Er is een relatie verondersteld tussen Rennes-le-Château, Stonehenge en talloze locaties van megalieten op het vasteland van Europa en in Groot-Brittannië, en er is beweerd dat er in het dorp een soort mathematische poort naar een andere dimensie verborgen is.

De perkamenten die aanleiding hebben gegeven tot al deze speculaties zijn nooit teruggevonden, hoewel één persoon – **Pierre Plantard**, de overleden grootmeester van de Priorij van Sion – beweerde dat hij ze in een kluis in Londen had opgeborgen. Saunière en zijn mysteries zijn voer geweest voor schrijvers van historische bespiegelingen en fascinerende verhalen, zoals Michael Baigent, Richard Leigh en Henry Lincoln (zowel individueel als gedrieën, in boeken als *Het Heilige Bloed en de Heilige Graal*), Lynn Picknett en Clive Prince, en Tim Wallace-Murphy.

Het is duidelijk dat er iets raadselachtigs in de lucht hangt rond Rennes-le-Château, maar is het echt een complot, of zijn het de complottheorieën zelf? Komt er een moment dat de kennis van de werkelijke gebeurtenissen die we hadden kunnen vergaren bedolven raakt onder complottheorieën? Bérenger Saunière zwijgt als het graf.

Sénéchaux Meervoud van het Franse woord *sénéchal*, in het Nederlands 'seneschalk', een hoge beambte aan wie belangrijke taken worden toevertrouwd, meestal in kringen van de geestelijkheid of het hof. In *DVC* zijn de *sénéchaux* drie personen met een hoge positie in de **Priorij van Sion** die ondergeschikt zijn aan Jacques Saunière, de grootmeester van de Priorij. Ze lijken een kring van ingewijden te vormen. De sénéchaux worden een voor een vermoord door Silas, de monnik van het **Opus Dei**. De drie sénéchaux waren, evenals Jacques Saunière, op de hoogte van de geheime bergplaats van de heilige graal. Ze wisten ook dat ze eventuele ondervragers moesten bedriegen met een gecoördineerde leugen over de plek waar de graal zich bevond, om er zeker van te zijn dat de graal veilig was, zelfs als hun identiteit bekend werd en ze werden uitgehoord. Zuster Sandrine probeert hen alle drie te bellen als ze beseft dat Silas naar de **Saint-Sulpice** is gekomen om de **sluitsteen** te vinden, maar tot haar schrik blijkt uit elk van haar telefoontjes dat de sénéchaux dood zijn. Het idee van de sénéchaux is afkomstig van de twijfelachtige lijst die door **Plantard** is geleverd en via websites is verspreid.

Sesach In *DVC* past Sophie haar kennis van de **Atbash-code** toe, een substitutiesysteem waarin de eerste letter van het alfabet wordt vervangen door de laatste, de tweede door de op een na laatste, enzovoort. De Hebreeuwse letters die het woord vormen dat in transcriptie 'Sesach' is, leveren een woord op dat, na invoeging van de klinkers (die het Hebreeuws niet kent) kan worden geschreven als 'Babel'.

Shekinah Shekinah is een Hebreeuws woord dat 'Gods aanwezigheid' betekent, en velen zijn van mening dat het betrekking heeft op het vrouwelijke aspect en de vrouwelijke eigenschappen van die aanwezigheid. Het christelijke concept dat er het dichtst bij in de buurt komt, is de Heilige Geest. Shekinah werd gezien als de fysieke manifestatie van Gods aanwezigheid in de tabernakel en later in de **tempel van Salomo**. Toen de Heer de Israëlieten wegleidde uit Egypte, ging hij voor hen uit 'in een wolkkolom': shekinah.

Sluitsteen Volgens Langdon behoort de sluitsteen 'tot de best bewaarde geheimen van de vroege broederschap der vrijmetselaars', en dat bedoelt hij zowel letterlijk als figuurlijk. Letterlijk is de sluitsteen een wigvormige steen boven in een gewelf die de andere stenen bijeenhoudt en het gewicht draagt (zie **clef de voûte**). Symbolisch staat hij voor de sleutel tot de geheimen van de **Priorij van Sion**.

Sophia Van het Griekse woord voor wijsheid. Het wordt in verband gebracht met de maagdelijke godinnen, zoals Athene, met de zinnebeeldige uitdrukking van wijsheid in de Heilige Geest en met **Maria Magdalena**.

Stam Benjamin Een van de twaalf stammen van Israël, voortgekomen uit Jacobs zoon Benjamin. Volgens de bijbel is de stad Jeruzalem zijn erfdeel. De stam speelt een rol in Teabings betoog als hij Sophie vertelt wat de **hei-**

lige graal eigenlijk is. Maria Magdalena, zegt hij, is afkomstig uit de stam
Benjamin, en daarom was haar verbintenis met Jezus – een afstammeling
van het koninklijk geslacht van David
en de stam Juda – van groot politiek
belang. In het boek Rechters staat dat
de stam Benjamin door de andere
stammen van Israël werd aangevallen
vanwege de bescherming die hij bood
aan bepaalde misdadigers. De gedeci-
meerde stam overleefde, maar volgens
de *Dossiers secrets* is een deel van de
stam naar het oosten van Europa getrokken, heeft zich eerst in de Griekse
provincie Arcadië gevestigd en is later
via de Donau en de Rijn naar het
noorden getrokken. In *Het Heilige
Bloed en de Heilige Graal* wordt gesuggereerd dat de stam de voorvader
zou kunnen zijn van de Franken, en
daarmee van de **Merovingers.**

Sub rosa Letterlijk 'onder de roos'. Deze uitdrukking stamt waarschijnlijk
uit de tijd van de Romeinen, toen bij
een officieel diner de tafels in een u-
vorm werden gezet, met de eregast en
zijn gastheer aan de kant tegenover de
opening. Boven het midden van de u
werd een roos gehangen. Die moest de
aanwezigen eraan herinneren dat Eros
een roos aan Harpocrates, de god van
de stilte, had gegeven om hem ervan
te weerhouden te praten over de on-
bezonnenheden van Venus, de moeder van Eros. Alles wat *sub rosa* (onder de roos) werd gezegd, moest
geheim blijven.

Symboliek Symbolen werden door
wijlen Leslie White, een antropoloog,
omschreven als 'de willekeurige toe-

kenning van betekenis aan vorm', en
een van de weinige dingen die de mens
echt van andere dieren onderscheidt.
Symbolen zijn abstracties. De bijbel
en natuurlijk DVC staan bol van symboliek: van *De mens van Vitruvius,*
wiens houding Saunière in de dood
aanneemt, tot het **kruis** en de **appel.**
Stoffelijke voorwerpen verwijzen naar
onstoffelijke en soms ingewikkelde
begrippen.

Door middel van symbolen kun je
sneller communiceren. Zoals de **roos**
boven de Romeinse tafel een symbool
van het geschenk van Eros aan Harpocrates was en overbracht dat geheimen geheim moesten blijven, is ook
een symbool als het kruis een bondi-
ge manier om mensen te herinneren
aan een ingewikkelde werkelijkheid.

In DVC werkte Langdon aan een artikel over de symbolen voor het **heilig
vrouwelijke.** Aan het eind van het
boek buigt hij zich samen met de we-
duwe van Saunière, Marie, bij **Rosslyn
Chapel** over de papyrusrol met de
tekst:

> Diep onder Roslin ligt de graal
> nu daar,
> waar kelk en kling steeds waken
> over haar.

Marie tekent met haar vinger een
driehoek, met de punt naar boven, in
haar handpalm. Een oud symbool
voor de kling en het mannelijke. Dan
tekent ze een driehoek met de punt
naar beneden. Een oud symbool voor
de kelk en het vrouwelijke. Ze neemt
Langdon mee de kerk in, waar hij eindelijk in de davidster de combinatie
van kling en kelk ziet, van mannelijk

en vrouwelijk. De davidster is ook het zegel van Salomo, dat het heilige der heiligen aangaf, waar de mannelijke en vrouwelijke godheden – **Jahweh** en **Shekinah** – zouden wonen.

Tarotkaarten De oorsprong van het tarotspel is onderwerp van discussie. Er zijn geleerden die een heel specifieke tijd en plaats aangeven waarop ze voor het eerst zouden zijn gebruikt: in het begin van de vijftiende eeuw, in Noord-Italië. De eerste praktische toepassing van de kaarten is waarschijnlijk een spel geweest dat een beetje op ons huidige bridge leek. Aangezien alchemistische, astrologische en esoterische filosofieën een belangrijke plek hadden in het middeleeuwse intellectuele leven, hebben de illustratoren van de eerste spellen misschien verborgen betekenissen in de beeldtaal van de kaarten gestopt. De vele verschillende interpretaties waartoe tarotkaarten aanleiding hebben gegeven, wijzen erop dat tarot meer is dan gewoon bridge.

Occultisten, liefhebbers van esoterie en zelfs hedendaagse bestsellerschrijvers denken echter dat de kaarten een veel langere geschiedenis hebben (met een oorsprong in het oude Israël of het oude Egypte), en ook een veel diepere betekenis. Er zou een verband zijn met de kabbala, de joodse mystieke leer. Robert Langdon beweert dat de tarot 'oorspronkelijk [was] bedacht als een verborgen manier om ideologieën door te geven die door de kerk verboden waren' en dat de kleur pentakels uit het tarotspel staat voor 'vrouwelijke goddelijkheid'. Critici wijzen dit soort theorieën van

de hand en zijn ervan overtuigd dat de tarot is bedoeld om 'onschuldige spelletjes' mee te spelen. 'Het idee dat ruiten voor pentakels staan, is een onjuiste voorstelling van zaken,' betoogt Sandra Miesel, die een lang en zeer kritisch artikel heeft geschreven over de 'zogenaamde feiten' in DVC.

Er lijkt geen hard bewijs te zijn voor het verband tussen de oorsprong van de spellen en oude tradities. De geschiedenis leert ons dat de tarotkaarten pas aan het einde van de achttiende eeuw in Frankrijk een rol gaan spelen als systemátisch occult stelsel. Traditie kan uiteraard zegevieren over geschiedenis, en het is niet moeilijk om weer helemaal opnieuw te gaan speculeren over 'toevalligheden' als de rangschikking van de Grote Arcana: de kaart van de Hogepriesteres (**vrouwelijke paus**) krijgt gewoonlijk het getal twee en de kaart met het getal vijf, de Paus, is de logische tegenpool ervan, zoals ook de Keizerin en de Keizer (respectievelijk drie en vier) elkaars tegenhanger zijn.

Tempeliers De tempeliers worden in DVC voor het eerst genoemd als Sophie en Langdon door het **Bois de Boulogne** rijden. Langdon geeft een korte samenvatting van hun geschiedenis en vertelt over het verband met de **Priorij van Sion**. De tempeliers spelen een centrale rol in het boek als een van de historische organisaties waarom de plot draait. Volgens DVC heeft de Priorij de tempeliersorde gesticht als een militaire tak die belast was met het vinden en beschermen van de documenten en relieken waaruit de heilige graal bestond.

In 1119 beloofden negen ridders, die zichzelf de 'Arme Soldatenbroeders van Jezus Christus' noemden, plechtig dat ze de pelgrims zouden beschermen die af en aan reisden naar de verscheidene heilige plaatsen in en rond Jeruzalem. Dit was een nieuw soort orde: geestelijken die tegelijk krijger en monnik waren en voor wie bloedvergieten in dienst van God een vreugde was.

Koning Boudewijn II gaf hun toestemming in de al-Aksamoskee te gaan wonen, die volgens de kruisvaarders was gebouwd op de ruïne van de vroegere **tempel van Salomo** (er bestaat nog steeds meningsverschil over de vraag of de moskee nu wel of niet op de tempel van Salomo staat). Van hun verblijfplaats boven de tempel is hun naam afkomstig: de ridders van de tempel van Salomo, of de tempelridders.

Zoals Langdon opmerkt, is de opkomst van de tempeliers gezien hun ongunstige start zeker verrassend. Traditionele historici schrijven dat echter niet toe aan geheimen of schatten die ze onder de al-Aksa hebben gevonden; de heersende opvatting is dat zowel wereldlijke als kerkelijke autoriteiten vanuit hun oprechte wens het Heilige Land in christelijke handen te houden de tempeliers grote geldbedragen hebben geschonken. Bovendien vaardigde paus **Innocentius** II een bul uit waarin werd bepaald dat de tempeliers alleen de paus verantwoording schuldig waren. Door deze immuniteit voor alle seculiere en kerkelijke machten – waaronder vrijstelling van belastingen – werden de tempeliers niet alleen rijker, maar kregen ze ook meer invloed.

Het lot van de tempeliers was verbonden met dat van het Heilige Land, dat voortdurend werd bedreigd door de legers van de mohammedaanse koninkrijken ten oosten ervan. Toen het Heilige Land in 1291 in handen van de mohammedanen viel, slonk het fortuin van de tempeliers. Zestien jaar later werden in Frankrijk leden van de tempeliersorde in groten getale opgepakt en door koning **Filips de Schone** beschuldigd van ketterij, blasfemie, homoseksualiteit en andere zonden tegen de kerk en God. Hoewel de beschuldigingen waarschijnlijk onterecht waren, legden de tempeliers, al of niet door marteling gedwongen, bekentenissen af. Degenen die hun bekentenis introkken, werden levend verbrand. In 1314 betekende de verbranding van de laatste grootmeester, Jacques de Molay, het feitelijke einde van de orde. Hij had zijn eerdere bekentenis ingetrokken en moest daarvoor boeten.

Tempel van Salomo David, de eerste koning van Israël, wilde een tempel bouwen voor de Koning der koningen, zijn God. In een droom vertelde God David dat de tempel niet door hem gebouwd kon worden, omdat hij een man van oorlog was en te veel bloed had vergoten. De tempel zou worden gebouwd door zijn zoon, Salomo, die een vredige regeringstijd zou kennen, zodat de tempel gebouwd kon worden.

Hoewel hij de tempel niet bouwde, heeft koning David er wel plannen voor gemaakt en bouwmateriaal voor verzameld. Na de dood van David gaf Salomo opdracht tot de bouw van de eerste tempel. Hij riep de hulp in van de Feniciërs, die vakkundige bouwers waren, en de tempel werd gemaakt naar het voorbeeld van de Fenicische tempels uit die tijd. De bouw van de tempel van Salomo op de berg Moria in het huidige Jeruzalem was een enorm karwei, waar tienduizenden mensen zeven jaar mee bezig zijn geweest. In 953 v.C. was hij af.

De tempel van Salomo was anders dan andere tempels in de oude wereld: hij had geen afgodsbeeld. Dat kwam voort uit de overtuiging dat er geen afgodsbeeld nodig was voor de aanwezigheid van God; de tempel was gebouwd om aan de behoeften van de mensen te voldoen, niet aan die van God.

In de loop van de geschiedenis werd de tempel regelmatig verwoest. De oorspronkelijke tempel werd in 586 v.C. door Nebukadnezar vernield. Zeventig jaar later werd op dezelfde plek de tweede tempel gebouwd, die in 19 v.C. door koning Herodes werd uitgebreid. Deze werd in 70 n.C. door de Romeinen verwoest.

En dan DVC. Langdon vertelt Sophie dat de primaire taak van de **tempeliers** in het Heilige Land niet was de pelgrims te beschermen, maar zich in de tempel te vestigen, zodat ze 'de [geheime] documenten onder de ruïne van de tempel vandaan [konden] halen'. Daarna zegt hij dat niemand zeker weet wat ze hebben gevonden, maar dat het in elk geval iets was 'waar ze rijker en machtiger door zijn geworden dan iemand zich in zijn stoutste dromen had kunnen voorstellen'.

Tegenwoordig staat op dezelfde plek de al-Aksamoskee, de op twee na heiligste plek van de islam.

Teniers, David II Vlaams schilder, de zoon van David I, die ook schilder was. Hij is in 1610 geboren en heeft historische, mythologische en allegorische onderwerpen geschilderd, waaronder een serie schilderijen van St.-Antonius. In het begin van DVC wordt hij genoemd, omdat Jacques Saunière een paar boeken over hem en over de schilder **Poussin** heeft geschreven.

Deze boeken behoren tot Langdons favoriete lesmateriaal; ze gaan over geheime codes in het werk van de beide schilders. Hier verwijst Dan Brown rechtstreeks naar gecodeerde boodschappen die Saunières historische naamgenoot heeft gevonden: **Bérenger Saunière**, de pastoor van **Rennes-le-Château**. Een van de gecodeerde boodschappen die Bérenger Saunière in een pilaar van het altaar van zijn parochiekerk heeft gevonden, luidt als volgt:

HERDERIN GEEN VERLEIDING DAT POUSSIN TENIERS DE SLEUTEL HEBBEN; VREDE 681 BIJ HET KRUIS EN DIT PAARD VAN GOD IK (VERNIETIG) DEZE DEMON VAN DE BEWAKER VOLLEDIG OP HET MIDDAGUUR BLAUWE APPELS

Nadat hij deze documenten had gevonden, zou Bérenger Saunière naar Parijs zijn gegaan, en naar verluidt zou hij op die reis reproducties hebben gekocht van een werk van Teniers, een portret van paus Celestinus v, en van Poussins *De herders van Arcadië.*

Tertullianus De eerste grote Latijnse schrijver van het christendom. In zijn veelomvattende werken wordt het hele theologische spectrum van die tijd bestreken: heidendom en jodendom, polemiek, staatsvormen, ethiek en de hele reorganisatie van het leven volgens zijn interpretatie van de christelijke leer. Hij was een toegewijd voorstander van strikte discipline en een sobere levensstijl. Hij vond dat vrouwen kostbare sieraden weg moesten bergen, omdat die mannen tot zonde konden verleiden, en beschouwde ongetrouwd zijn en celibatair leven als de hoogste staat van zijn.

Vaticaanse Bibliotheek Bisschop Aringarosa bezoekt **Castel Gandolfo** en komt langs de Biblioteca Astronomica, de bibliotheek van het Vaticaanse Observatorium. Er zijn aanwijzingen dat er al in de vierde eeuw een bibliotheek was, maar de Vaticaanse Bibliotheek zoals we die tegenwoordig kennen, is ontstaan in de tijd van Nicolaas v, die in 1447 paus werd. Nicolaas breidde de bibliotheek uit van een paar honderd boeken tot meer dan vijftienhonderd, waarmee ze in die tijd de grootste bibliotheek van Europa was. Tegenwoordig zijn er meer dan een miljoen boeken en honderdvijftigduizend manuscripten ondergebracht, waaronder de oudst bekende Griekse versies van het Oude en Nieuwe Testament en vroege uitgaven van werken van Dante, Vergilius en Homerus.

Venus-pentagram Een van de intrigerendste theorieën rond de oorsprong van het **pentagram** is astronomisch: de planeet Venus beschrijft een pentagram aan de nachtelijke hemel. Hoe? Als de bewegingen van de planeet worden afgezet tegen de sterren, lijkt ze in een regelmatig patroon tegen ze in te bewegen. In de oudheid werd gedacht dat de sterren die de mensen langs de hemel zagen trekken, 'vastzaten' op een bol met de aarde als middelpunt. Ze gebruikten deze vaste sterren als referentiepunt voor de bewegingen van de planeten, die onafhankelijk van de vaste sterren bewogen en op verschillende tijden tegen verschillende delen van de bol verschenen. Als een waarnemer zes jaar lang op dezelfde dag de positie van Venus ten opzichte van de vaste sterren vastlegt, en deze punten in volgorde met elkaar verbindt, levert dat een pentagram op. (In het zesde jaar keert Venus terug naar haar uitgangspositie en begint de cyclus opnieuw.) Deze observatie heeft de toets der kritiek van de latere astronomische wetenschap niet doorstaan: het is waar dat het volgen van de planeet vanuit een plaats ergens in het Nabije Oosten een soort pentagram oplevert, hoewel je er wel wat fantasie voor nodig hebt om dat erin te zien. Vanuit andere delen van de wereld ziet het er heel anders uit, en inmiddels is het idee dat de aarde het middelpunt van het heelal is reeds lang achterhaald.

Vrijdag de dertiende In DVC vertelt Dan Brown over een incident rond de **tempeliers** dat de oorsprong zou zijn van het wijdverbreide bijgeloof dat vrijdag de dertiende een ongeluksdag is. Op vrijdag 13 oktober 1307 'vaardigde **paus Clemens** geheime, verzegelde orders uit die door zijn soldaten in heel Europa tegelijk moesten worden geopend', schrijft Brown. De noodlottige orders luidden dat God de paus in een visioen had bezocht en hem had verteld dat de tempeliers ketters waren die zich schuldig maakten aan duivelsverering, homoseksualiteit, sodomie, ontheiliging van het **kruis** en allerlei andere zonden. De soldaten van de Franse koning **Filips de Schone** kregen de opdracht de tempeliers op te pakken en te martelen om de ware omvang van hun zonden tegen God duidelijk te maken. Hoewel Brown de gevangenneming, marteling en dood op de brandstapel van de tempeliers beschrijft alsof alles in één zeer hectisch etmaal gebeurde, vonden deze gebeurtenissen in werkelijkheid in de loop van de volgende jaren plaats, en niet 'op die dag'.

De werkelijke zonde van de tempeliers lijkt te zijn geweest dat ze te veel macht hadden. Door de combinatie van de pauselijke bescherming en hun financiële activiteiten waren de tempeliers vermogend en invloedrijk geworden, en er werd beweerd dat ze over geheimen beschikten die iets met de **heilige graal** te maken hadden. De paus beschouwde de tempeliers als een gevaar voor zijn macht en vond dat ze moesten verdwijnen, dus de meeste van hen – maar niet allemaal – werden op die vrijdag de dertiende gearresteerd. De overlevenden zouden de geheimen van de heilige graal zijn blijven bewaken.

Brown noemt dit incident als dé reden voor het bijgeloof rond die bewuste dag en datum, maar er zijn meer dingen die tegen vrijdag de dertiende pleiten, en sommige daarvan gaan terug tot honderden jaren voordat de paus deze orders uitvaardigde. In de Noorse mythologie zaten er dertien goden aan aan een banket in het Walhalla toen Balder (de zoon van Odin) werd vermoord, wat tot de val van de goden leidde. Rond 1000 v.C. schreef Hesiodus in zijn *Werken en Dagen* dat het ongeluk brengt om op de dertiende dag te zaaien, maar geluk om op die dag te planten. Vrijdag is de ongeluksdag voor christenen, want sommigen geloven dat Jezus op die dag is gekruisigd. Ze beschouwen dertien ook als ongeluksgetal omdat er dertien aanwezigen waren bij het Laatste Avondmaal, onder wie de dertiende apostel, die verraad pleegde.

Vrouwelijke paus In een gesprek met Sophie over **tarot** noemt Langdon het middeleeuwse kaartspel 'doordrenkt van verborgen ketterse symboliek' en verwijst hij onder meer naar een kaart die de Hogepriesteres of de Vrouwelijke paus heet. In het tarotspel staat ze voor verborgen of esoterische kennis en wordt ze meestal afgebeeld als een zittende vrouw, die een soutane en een driekroon draagt en een open boek op haar schoot heeft.

De belangrijkste bron voor het weinige dat we weten over de vrouwelijke paus is een dominicaner monnik, Martin Polonus, die beweerde dat een zekere paus Johannes uit de dertiende eeuw in werkelijkheid paus Johanna was, wat pas werd ontdekt toen ze te midden van een pauselijke processie

van de Sint-Pieter naar het Lateraan-
paleis een kind baarde. Polonus zegt
dat kerkhistorici later haar naam hebben verdoezeld 'zowel vanwege haar
vrouwelijkheid als vanwege de obsce-
niteit van het gebeurde'. Volgens andere verslagen is ze door de menigte
ter plekke gestenigd toen het bedrog
werd ontdekt. In sommige verhalen
was ze een Engelse die een opleiding
had genoten in Duitsland en zich als
man kleedde om monnik te kunnen
worden, in andere verhalen kwam ze
uit Athene, waar ze blijk had gegeven
van een grote kennis van theologie en
talen. Er zijn nooit historische documenten gevonden die het verhaal van
paus Johanna ondubbelzinnig beves-
tigen, en halverwege de zeventiende
eeuw schijnt het door een protestants
historicus te zijn weerlegd. Deze legende kan van oorsprong ook een an-
tipauselijke satire zijn geweest die gericht was op de angst van de kerk voor
misleiding, vrouwen die te veel gezag
hadden en de mogelijkheid dat een
paus seksueel actief zou zijn. Hoe dan
ook, er is nog steeds een tarotkaart ter
ere van paus Johanna. Rosemary en
Darroll Pardoe hebben er een uitgebreide studie over geschreven.

Bronnen op het web

Dieper graven in De Da Vinci Code

Door Betsy Eble

Steek je hand op als je een afbeelding van *Het Laatste Avondmaal* hebt opgezocht om te zien wie er nu echt aan Jezus' rechterzijde zat. Vinger omhoog als je nooit eerder van het Opus Dei had gehoord. Een koninklijke stamboom? De Priorij van Sion? Ben ik de enige die van al die zaken niets afwist? Hoe dan ook, de antwoorden op al deze en dergelijke vragen zijn met zoekmachines geïndexeerd, uitgeplozen en gewaardeerd door honderden gebruikers die je voorgingen. Voor het verkennen van onderwerpen en invalshoeken die nieuw voor je zijn is het web de uitgelezen plaats om er kennis mee te maken.

Toen ik vanochtend 'Da Vinci Code' intypte, wist Google bijna een half miljoen treffers op te hoesten. In die reusachtige hoeveelheid informatie vind je voor elke denkbare bewering zowel een overweldigende hoeveelheid bevestigingen als weerleggingen.

De zomer van 2003 heb ik besteed aan het onderzoeken van de literaire, artistieke en historische verwijzingen in *De Da Vinci Code*. Vervolgens heb ik het materiaal dat uitsluitend op het web te vinden is samengebracht en gepubliceerd onder de titel *Depth & Details, A Reader's Guide to Dan Brown's* The Da Vinci Code. In *Depth & Details* verwijs ik naar interessante sites die verband houden met de afzonderlijke hoofdstukken van het boek, zodat de lezer zich tijdens het lezen van het boek nader kan oriënteren. Het onderstaande geeft een samenvatting van enkele van de boeiendste sites die op het web te vinden zijn.

Cryptologie

Voor wie meer wil weten over cryptologie en geheimschrift is er een fraaie inleiding te vinden op www.murky.org/cryptography/index.shtml. Je treft er informatie aan over klassieke en moderne cryptologie, maar ook boeiende vraagstukken en raadsels. Als je zelf anagrammen of cryptogrammen wilt maken, probeer dan deze sites: www.wordsmith.org/anagram/advanced.html en www.wordles.com/getmycrypto.asp.

Da Vinci

Hoewel de meeste onderwerpen die in *De Da Vinci Code* aan bod komen nogal controversieel zijn, worden zaken die met Leonardo da Vinci verband houden al eeuwenlang op ruime schaal bestudeerd en gepubliceerd. Een aantal jaren geleden heeft Bill Gates de zogenoemde *Codex Leicester* aangekocht – een boek met door Leonardo da Vinci vervaardigde tekeningen – een werk dat in de loop der eeuwen steeds in handen van zeer welgestelden is geweest. Da Vinci's kunst, architectuur, beeldhouwwerken, machines en toestellen zijn ook op het web zeer goed gedocumenteerd. Een zeer uitvoerige site over Da Vinci's leven en werken is te vinden op www.lairweb.org.nz/leonardo. Er wordt ingegaan op onderwerpen als zijn leertijd bij Verrocchio, zijn seksuele geaardheid, zijn werk en zelfs zijn overlijden op 2 mei 1519 op zevenenzestigjarige leeftijd. De site staat vol interessante feiten en speculaties, zoals de bewering dat Da Vinci de uitvinder was van de schaar en dat hij er tien jaar over deed om Mona Lisa's lippen te schilderen.

De Da Vinci Code-websites

Er zijn in de afgelopen tijd tal van websites aan *De Da Vinci Code* gewijd. Sites die in elk geval genoemd moeten worden zijn www.danbrown.com en www.randomhouse.com/doubleday/davinci/. Op www.danbrown.com tref je onder andere links aan naar afbeeldingen en historische studies. Een website die chaotischer is maar wel veel afbeeldingen en links heeft naar allerlei boeiende aspecten die verband houden met *De Da Vinci Code*, is www.darkprotocols.com/.

Kerken

De plaats van handeling in *De Da Vinci Code* is vaak een kerk, zoals de Saint-Sulpice, Rosslyn Chapel, de Tempelkerk en Westminster Abbey. De meeste van die kerken hebben een eigen website met plattegronden, foto's en historische achtergronden. De Rosslyn Templars hebben een site gemaakt met afbeeldingen en gedetailleerde informatie over de architectuur en de symboliek van Rosslyn Chapel (www.rosslyntemplars.org.uk/rosslyn.htm). De even fascinerende als vindingrijke hypothese dat de Tempel van Salomo de vorm had van een menselijk lichaam (zoals met schematische voorstellingen wordt aangetoond) is te vinden op home.earthlink.net/~tonybadillo/. Hoewel de afbeeldingen iets te klein zijn om de graven van de ridders te zien die in *De Da Vinci Code* worden genoemd, heeft de site van de Tempelkerk in Londen – www.templechurch.com/ – interessante webpagina's gewijd aan de geschiedenis en de oorsprong van de kerk. De Saint-Sulpice is uiteraard een kerk waarvan veel beeldmateriaal te vinden is, onder andere op www.pbase.com en www.picsearch.com.

Koninklijke bloedlijn – de Merovingers

Volgens de esoterische versie van de geschiedenis die wordt uitgewerkt door Michael Baigent, Richard Leigh en Henry Lincoln in hun boek *Het Heilige Bloed en de Heilige Graal*, waren de Merovingische koningen nazaten van Maria Magdalena en Jezus Christus. De auteurs beweren verder dat de kerk van Rome tijdens de inquisitie alle sporen van deze dynastie – de kathaarse ketterij van de Languedoc en de tempeliers – zou hebben uitgeroeid om macht te verwerven via de 'spirituele' dynastie van Petrus in plaats van het 'heilige bloed' (*sangreal*) van de nakomelingen van Maria Magdalena. Deze theorieën worden door de meeste historici van de hand gewezen. De Merovingers vormden een dynastie van Frankische koningen die tussen de vijfde en de achtste eeuw aan de macht waren. De website van de tempeliers presenteert een stamboom van de Merovingische koningen: www.ordotempli.org/the–merovingians.htm.

Het Louvre

Als je na het lezen van *De Da Vinci Code* toch al van plan was je Frans op te halen, laat je dan eens meevoeren naar www.louvre.org. Hoewel mijn beperkte kennis van de Franse taal toereikend was om me door de meeste Franse passages in het boek te worstelen, moet ik toegeven dat de web-site van het Louvre voor mij onoverkomelijke moeilijkheden opleverde. Gelukkig is er behalve een Spaanse en een Japanse ook een Engelse versie beschikbaar: www.louvre.org/louvrea.htm. Vergeet beslist niet gebruik te maken van de mogelijkheid om een virtueel kijkje te nemen in en rond het museum. De Salle des Etats en de *Mona Lisa* zijn allebei op de site te bezichtigen. Je ziet helemaal voor je hoe Robert Langdon en Sophie Ne-veu in het donker door de zalen sluipen om de aanwijzingen te zoeken die door Jacques Saunière werden achtergelaten.

Ga na het Louvre bezocht te hebben naar een andere website, waar je de rechtstreekse beelden van vijfentwintig webcams kunt bekijken die op verschillende plaatsen in Parijs staan opgesteld, waaronder ook enkele plaatsen die in *De Da Vinci Code* ter sprake komen: www.parispourvous.net/index.php3?=c3 is de Engelse versie van de Fran-se site parispourvous.com.

Maria Magdalena

Margaret Starbird, de schrijfster van het boek *De vrouw met de albasten kruik* waarnaar in *De Da Vinci Code* wordt verwezen, schrijft ook veel ar-tikelen voor de populaire website www.magdalene.org. Op die site zijn be-halve artikelen ook stichtelijke teksten, gedichten en allerlei andere zaken te vinden die aan Maria Magdalena zijn gerelateerd. www.beliefnet.com voorziet eveneens in specifiek aan Maria Magdalena gewijde pagina's: www.beliefnet.com/index/index–10126.html, met teksten over en bijbel-verwijzingen naar Maria Magdalena. De link naar een pagina met kunst-werken waarop Maria Magdalena is afgebeeld is een bijzondere vermel-ding waard. Ook zijn er pagina's over de gnostiek en *De Da Vinci Code*. Beliefnet verdient lof omdat er ruimte wordt gegeven aan onderling on-verenigbare opvattingen, zowel over de rol van Maria Magdalena in de christelijke geschiedenis als over de inhoud van *De Da Vinci Code*.

Olga's Gallery

Dit is een virtueel kunstmuseum, www.abcgallery.com. Wie kwalitatief goede afbeeldingen van kunstwerken zoekt, is op deze site aan het goede adres. Het enige minpuntje is dat je op enkele pop-ups wordt getrakteerd, maar die neem je, vanwege de omvangrijke verzameling hoogwaardige kunst die je te zien krijgt, moeiteloos op de koop toe. De meeste kunstwerken zijn voorzien van verklarende aantekeningen en verwijzingen naar andere bronnen. Behalve de werken en biografieën van Monet, Caravaggio, Picasso en Bosch tref je ook alle schilderijen van Leonardo da Vinci aan die in *De Da Vinci Code* worden genoemd, waaronder *Madonna in de grot*, *Het Laatste Avondmaal* en de *Mona Lisa*.

Het Opus Dei

Het Opus Dei is een prelatuur van de katholieke kerk die een belangrijke rol speelt in *De Da Vinci Code*. De eerste plek waar je – ook in het Nederlands – nadere informatie kunt vinden over het controversiële Opus Dei is op de eigen website van de organisatie: www.opusdei.org en www.opusdei.nl. De lijst van veelgestelde vragen (FAQ) helpt je de onderwerpen waar je meer over wilt weten snel te vinden. Om te achterhalen hoe en waarom het Opus Dei in het leven werd geroepen kun je de werken raadplegen die door de oprichter van de organisatie, Josemaría Escrivá, zijn geschreven. Ook die zijn beschikbaar in meerdere talen, waaronder het Nederlands, via www.escrivaworks.nl.

Ga voor een onafhankelijke en kritische beschouwing van de rol van het Opus Dei naar de site www.rickross.com/groups/opus.html. Het Rick A. Ross Institute heeft tal van verhalen en artikelen samengebracht die over het Opus Dei zijn verschenen in onder andere *U.S. News*, *New York Daily News*, *The Guardian* en bij Associated Press.

De biografie van Opus Dei-lid en spion Robert Hanssen, die ook in *De Da Vinci Code* wordt genoemd, is te vinden op www.crimelibrary.com/terrorists–spies/spies/hanssen/5.html?sect=23.

De Priorij van Sion

De Priorij van Sion is een quasi-geheime organisatie, met haar basis in Europa, die beweert machtige geheimen te bewaken over de oorsprong van het christendom. De organisatie zou aan de wieg gestaan hebben van de tempeliers en mogelijk de vrijmetselaars. Tot de illustere grootmeesters zouden onder andere Isaac Newton en Leonardo da Vinci behoord hebben. Er is veel informatie over de tempeliers en de Priorij van Sion te vinden op www.ordotempli.org/priory–of–sion.htm, de website van de International Knights Templar.

Symbolen

www.symbols.com leent zich uitstekend om met een kop koffie in de hand
te bekijken en de fraai gepresenteerde resultaten van gedegen onder-
zoekswerk in je op te nemen. Hoewel ik niet weet welke bezoekers naar
symbolen zoeken aan de hand van typeringen als 'symmetrisch' en 'rech-
te, gebogen en/of kruisende lijnen', is het toch aardig een poging te wa-
gen, om te zien waar symbols.com mee voor de dag komt. De bezoeker
die meer woordgericht is hoeft slechts op een woord in de alfabetische lijst
te klikken om meegesleept te worden op een urenlange tocht van gega-
randeerd leesplezier. In verband met *De Da Vinci Code* vind je er symbolen van de *chalice* (kelk), van Venus, het pentagram, van heidense en christelijke kruisen, van de vrijmetselaars en ga zo maar door.

Tempeliers

De makers van *Templar History Magazine* hebben een zeer lezenswaardi-
ge website ontwikkeld: www.templarhistory.com. Hier kun je diepgra-
vende artikelen vinden over de tempelridders. Je kunt je nader verdiepen
in uitsluitend op historisch feitenmateriaal gebaseerde onderzoek, maar
ook kennis nemen van de talloze mythen en verhalen die over deze organisatie de ronde doen. De site bevat ook recensies van boeken die nog altijd over de tempeliers verschijnen.

Wiskunde, kunst en architectuur

Op Fibonacci, de vader van de Fibonacci-reeks – de code bij de plek van
de moord in *De Da Vinci Code* – wordt zeer gedetailleerd ingegaan op
www-groups.dcs.st-and.ac.uk/~history/Mathematicians/Fibonacci.html.
Zeer veel sites met informatie over wiskundige onderwerpen bevatten
links naar deze site. Dat is gewoonlijk een goede incator dat de inhoud ac-
curaat en waardevol is.

Ook de *sectio divina* of gulden snede (Phi) wordt uitgebreid op het web
gedocumenteerd. Elke studie kunstgeschiedenis of architectuur gaat nader in op de gulden snede in het ontwerp van het Parthenon en in de schilderijen van Da Vinci en Dürer. Een goede website waar je tientallen links
vindt naar Phi, kunst en architectuur is www.mcs.surrey.ac.uk/Person-
al/R.Knott/Fibonacci/fibInArt.html. Visueel beschouwd is de site geen
hoogstandje, wat gezien het onderwerp – de gulden snede in kunstwer-

ken – enigszins ironisch is, maar de teksten zijn zeer lezenswaardig en de links zijn allemaal uiterst informatief.

Over de auteurs

Dan Burstein (samensteller) is oprichter en directielid van Millennium Technology Ventures Advisors, een in New York gevestigd bedrijf dat investeert in nieuwe innovatieve technologiebedrijven. Hij is ook een bekroond journalist en auteur van zes boeken over wereldeconomie en technologie.

Zijn boek *Yen!* uit 1988, dat gaat over de opkomst van Japan als financiële grootmacht, was in meer dan twintig landen een bestseller. In 1995 was zijn boek *Road Warriors* een van de eerste studies naar de invloed van internet en de digitale technologie op het bedrijfsleven en de samenleving. In zijn in 1998 gepubliceerde boek *Big Dragon*, dat hij samen met Arne de Keijzer schreef, schetst hij de rol die in de eenentwintigste eeuw voor China is weggelegd. Burstein en De Keijzer richtten onlangs hun eigen uitgeverij op, Squibnocket Press, en werken momenteel aan een serie, *The Best Things Ever Said*, die onder andere boeken zal bevatten over de toekomst van internet, weblogs en nanotechnologie.

Burstein werkte in de jaren tachtig als journalist en publiceerde meer dan duizend artikelen in meer dan tweehonderd periodieken, waaronder *The New York Times*, *The Wall Street Journal*, de *Los Angeles Times*, *The Boston Globe*, de *Chicago Tribune*, *New York Magazine*, *Rolling Stone* en vele andere kranten en tijdschriften in Amerika, Europa en Azië. Daarnaast was hij adviseur van ABC News, CBS News, *Time* en andere toonaangevende mediabedrijven.

De afgelopen tien jaar heeft Burstein financieel en anderszins bijgedragen aan het opzetten van meer dan vijfentwintig technologiebedrijven. Van 1988 tot 2000 was hij adviseur van The Blackstone Group, een van de prominentste handelsbanken van Wall Street. Burnstein is voorts een vooraanstaand bedrijfsadviseur van ondernemingen als Sony, Toyota, Microsoft, Boardroom Inc. en Sun Microsystems.

Arne de Keijzer (hoofdredacteur) is auteur, voormalig bedrijfsadviseur met betrekking tot China en Dan Burnsteins partner in Squibnocket Press. Hij heeft vijf boeken geschreven, waaronder een populaire reisgids voor China en twee boeken die hij samen met Dan Burstein schreef: *The Rise, Fall and Future of the*

Internet Economy (uit de *Best Things Ever Said*-reeks van Squibnocket Press) en
*Big Dragon: China's Future – What It Means for Business, the Economy, and the
Global Order.* Verder heeft hij geschreven voor uiteenlopende publicaties, van
The New York Times tot *Powerboat Reports.*

Diane Apostolos-Cappadona is docente religieuze kunst- en cultuurgeschiedenis aan het Center for Muslim-Christian Understanding en aan de kunst- en
cultuurfaculteit van Georgetown University. Dr. Apostolos-Cappadona was
gastcurator en auteur van de catalogus voor *In Search of Mary Magdalene: Images and Traditions* (2002). Momenteel schrijft ze de inleiding bij de herdruk van
Sacred and Profane Beauty: The Holy Art van Gerardus van der Leeuw, dat bestaat uit de delen *Sources and Documents in the History of Christian Art* en *Sources and Documents in the History of Religious Art in 19th-century America,* en een
studieboek, *The Art of the World's Religions.* Ze geeft diverse vakken, waaronder
Kunst, creativiteit en het sacrale, Oosters-orthodox christendom: geschiedenis
en theologie en De middeleeuwse synthese: kunst en religie in de Middeleeuwen. Samen met Deirdre Good gaf ze een reeks workshops en lezingen over de
waarheid van *De Da Vinci Code.*

Michael Baigent werd in 1948 in Nieuw-Zeeland geboren. Hij studeerde psychologie aan Canterbury University in Christchurch. Sinds 1976 woont hij in
Engeland. Hij is de auteur van *Sporen uit de oude tijd* (Tirion, 1999) en *From the
Omens of Babylon.* Samen met Richard Leigh en Henry Lincoln schreef hij twee
internationale bestsellers, *Het Heilige Bloed en de Heilige Graal* (Tirion,
1999/2004) en *De Messiaanse erfenis* (Tirion, 1998). Samen met Richard Leigh
schreef hij *De Tempel en de Loge: van tempelridders tot vrijmetselarij* (Tirion,
1990), *De Dode-Zeerollen en de verzwegen waarheid* (Tirion, 1991/1997/2004),
Claus von Stauffenberg en zijn mystieke kruistocht tegen Hitler (Tirion, 1994), *Het
Elixer en de Steen* (Tirion, 1997) en *De Inquisitie* (Tirion, 2004).

Amy D. Bernstein is als schrijfster en academica gespecialiseerd in de renaissanceliteratuur. Ze bezorgde een nieuwe editie van de sonnetten van Jacques de
Billy de Prunay, een benedictijner monnik en een populaire schrijver en vertaler van Gregorius van Nanzianze en andere patristische auteurs.

Peter W. Bernstein geeft samen met Annalyn Swan leiding aan A.S.A.P. Media
en was adviserend redacteur voor dit boek. Bernstein werkte als redacteur bij
U.S News & World Report en *Fortune.* Hij was ook uitgever bij Times Books en
Random House. Hij is de bedenker, redacteur en uitgever van *The Ernst & Young
Tax Guide* en was medeauteur van *The Practical Guide to Practically Everything.*
Samen met zijn vrouw Amy verzorgde hij de uitgave *Quotations from Speaker
Newt: The Red, White and Blue Book of the Republican Revolution.*

Esther de Boer bestudeerde het Nieuwe Testament en de gnostiek aan de Vrije Universiteit in Amsterdam. Vanaf 1988 is ze gereformeerd predikante en werkte ze als legerpredikante in het Duitse Seedorf. Van 1992 tot 2003 was ze predikante van de gereformeerde kerk van Ouderkerk aan de Amstel. Van 1998 tot 2002 was ze ook verbonden aan de Theologische Universiteit van Kampen, waar ze haar dissertatie schreef. Sinds 2003 is ze thuis bij haar drie kinderen en werkt ze aan een boek over Moeder Marcella (vierde eeuw, Rome) en aan een bundel vroeg-christelijke teksten over Maria Magdalena.

Esther de Boer schreef de boeken *Maria Magdalena: de mythe voorbij* (Meinema, 1997), *The Gospel of Mary: Beyond a Gnostic and a Biblical Mary Magdalene* (2004, proefschrift) en samen met Marvin Meyer *The Gospels of Mary: The Secret Tradition of Mary Magdalene, the Companion of Jesus* (2004).

Serge Bramly woont in Parijs en is de auteur van diverse romans en essays. Hij won in Frankrijk voor zijn historische roman *De dans van de wolf* (1982, de vertaling verscheen in 1986 bij Sijthoff) de prestigieuze Prix des Librairies. Zijn *Leonardo* (1982) stond in Frankrijk wekenlang op de bestsellerlijsten en werd in vijftien landen ontvangen als een uitstekende biografie. De vertaling verscheen oorspronkelijk in 1990 bij Ambo en in 2005 bij Luitingh in een herziene vertaling met fraaie kleurenillustraties.

Denise Budd studeerde aan Rutgers University in New Brunswick en promoveerde aan Colombia University. In 2002 voltooide ze haar proefschrift over Leonardo da Vinci, een herinterpretatie van het documentair bewijs van de eerste helft van de carrière van de kunstenaar. Dr. Budd doceerde het kerncurriculum aan Columbia University. Momenteel zet ze haar onderzoek voort en doceert ze aan Rutgers University.

David Burstein zit op de middelbare school, waar hij onder andere Latijn doet, en is auteur van het nog te verschijnen boek *Harry Potter and the Prisoner of the New York Times Bestseller List*. Hij schreef een dichtbundel en zeven avondvullende toneelstukken en speelde de hoofdrol in schooluitvoeringen van *Noises Off, The Wind in the Willows, Much Ado About Nothing, Cinderella* en *Fiddler on the Roof*. Voorts is hij hoofd fondsenwerving van het Westport Youth Film Festival.

John Castro is een in New York woonachtig schrijver, redacteur en onderzoeker. Hij was betrokken bij publicaties van burgerrechtenactivist Jesse Jackson, journalist Marshall Loeb en internetondernemer Charles Ferguson. Daarnaast is Castro theaterdirecteur, acteur en toneelschrijver met een grote voorliefde voor Shakespeare. Hij studeerde aan het St. John's College in Annapolis, Maryland.

534 GEHEIMEN VAN DE CODE

Michelle Delio schrijft over de meest uiteenlopende technologische ontwikkelingen en er verschijnen met grote regelmaat artikelen van haar in het tijdschrift *Wired*. Ook schreef ze voor Salon.com over allerlei onderwerpen, van het blokkeren van spam tot Harley-Davidsons.

Jennifer Doll deed onderzoeks- en redactiewerk voor dit boek, een taak die ze al voor een reeks andere boeken en tijdschriften vervulde. Ze is momenteel actief als redactieconsultant bij *Reader's Digest*. Verder werkte ze voor McKinsey & Company, het tijdschrift *Continental* en The Teaching Commission. In haar vrije tijd werkt ze aan haar eerste roman.

David Downie woont en werkt in Parijs en is schrijver, redacteur en vertaler. De afgelopen twintig jaar schreef hij over Europese cultuur, reizen en de Europese keuken voor Amerikaanse en Britse kranten en tijdschriften en soms voor Franse, Italiaanse en Nederlandse publicaties. Zijn werk is wereldwijd verschenen. Zijn laatste met groot enthousiasme ontvangen boek, *Cooking the Roman Way: Authentic Recipes from the Home Cooks and Trattorias of Rome*, gaat over de gerechten en culinaire cultuur in het huidige Rome. Momenteel werkt hij aan een verzameling reisverhalen getiteld *Paris, Paris*.

Betsy Eble is zolang ze zich kan herinneren scheppend bezig – in ieder geval sinds ze als klein kind haar eigen babypoppen maakte. Overdag ontwikkelt ze informatiesystemen en online-gebruikersinterfaces. 's Avonds en in het weekend schildert ze, schrijft ze artikelen voor haar weblog en verzamelt ze onderzoek naar historische romans. Ze is de auteur van *Depth & Details: A Reader's Guide to Dan Brown's* The Da Vinci Code. Dit was de eerste gids die verwees naar onderzoek dat relevant is voor het boek.

Bart D. Ehrman is James A. Gray Distinguished Professor of Religious Studies aan de University of North Carolina in Chapel Hill, waar hij vanaf 1988 doceert. Als autoriteit op het gebied van het Nieuwe Testament en de geschiedenis van het vroege christendom was hij aan het woord op CNN, The History Channel, A&E en andere tv- en radiozenders. Hij heeft diverse videovoordrachten gemaakt voor The Teaching Company en was als auteur of redacteur betrokken bij de publicatie van dertien boeken, waaronder *Lost Christianities: The Battles for Scripture and the Faiths We Never Knew* en *Lost Scriptures: Books that Did Not Make It into the New Testament*.

Raine Eisler is sociologe, cultuurhistorica en evolutietheoretica. Tot de boeken die ze publiceerde behoort de bestseller *De kelk en het zwaard* (Entheon, 1997), een multidisciplinaire studie van de menselijke cultuur. Andere boeken van haar hand zijn *Sacred Pleasure, Tomorrow's Children* en *The Power of Partnership: Seven Relationships That Will Change Your Life*. Eisler leidt het Center for Partnership Studies, doceerde aan UCLA en heeft lezingen gegeven op conferenties in de hele wereld.

Glenn W. Erickson doceerde filosofie aan Southern Illinois University, Texas A&M University, Western Carolina University en de Rhode Island School of Design, plus aan vijf nationale universiteiten in Brazilië en Nigeria, soms met een Fulbright-beurs. Hij is auteur van een tiental werken over filosofie (*Negative Dialectics and the End of Philosophy*), logica (*Dictionary of Paradox*, met John Fossa), literatuurkritiek (*A Tree of Stories*, met zijn vrouw Sandra S.F. Erickson), poëzie, korte verhalen, kunstgeschiedenis (*New Theory of the Tarot*) en de geschiedenis van de wiskunde.

Timothy Freke studeerde filosofie en is de auteur van meer dan twintig boeken. Hij is een autoriteit op het gebied van de spiritualiteit. Samen met Peter Gandy schreef hij vijf boeken, waaronder *The Jesus Mysteries* en *Jesus and the Lost Goddess*. Hij verzorgt lezingen en internationale seminars over gnosis of spirituele verlichting. Meer informatie over de boeken en seminars van Timothy Freke en Peter Gandy is te vinden op de website www.timfreke.demon.co.uk.

Peter Gandy bestudeerde klassieke beschavingen en specialiseerde zich in de oude heidense mysteriegodsdiensten. Hij is vooral bekend door zijn werken over Jezus, geschreven met Timothy Freke, waaronder *Jesus and the Lost Goddess* en *The Jesus Mysteries*.

Willem Glaudemans promoveerde in Utrecht op een proefschrift over W.F. Hermans. Bij Ankh-Hermes verschenen o.a. van zijn hand *Het Evangelie der Waarheid* (1997), *Het Nachtblauwe boek* (2000) en *Het wonder van vergeving* (2002). Voorts was hij vertaler/eindredacteur van *Een cursus in wonderen* (1999) en de bijbehorende titels. Met Jacob Slavenburg verzorgde hij in 1994 en 1995 de eerste volledige Nederlandse vertaling van de Nag Hammadi-codices en de Berlijnse Codex, getiteld *De Nag Hammadi-geschriften*, waarvan in 2004 een geheel herziene en uitgebreide versie verscheen.

Deirdre Good is Professor of New Testament aan het General Theological Seminary van de episcopale kerk in New York. Ze heeft veel gepubliceerd en veel lezingen gegeven over de traditie van Mirjam en het vrouwelijke in koptische en gnostische teksten. Haar recentste boek is *Mariam, the Magdala, and the Mother*.

Susan Haskins is schrijfster, redactrice, onderzoekster en vertaalster. Ze gaf over de hele wereld lezingen en verscheen in diverse televisieprogramma's waarin ze sprak over Maria Magdalena. Momenteel vertaalt en redigeert ze *Three Marian Writings* (teksten over het leven van de Maagd door drie zestiende-eeuwse Italiaanse schrijfsters). Ze schreef ook het boek *Mary Magdalen: Myth & Metaphor.*

Collin Hansen werkt op de redactie van het tijdschrift *Christian History.* Met een academische achtergrond in journalistiek en kerkgeschiedenis schreef Hansen over onderwerpen als het Europese secularisme, de oorlog in Irak en christelijk hoger onderwijs.

Stephan A. Hoeller heeft een doctorstitel en is bisschop van de Ecclesia Gnostica en hoofd van de English Gnostic Transmissions in Amerika. Hoeller schreef diverse boeken, waaronder *Gnosticism, Jung and the Lost Gospels* en *Freedom: Alchemy for a Voluntary Society.* Hoeller bekleedde zestien jaar de leerstoel vergelijkende godsdienstwetenschappen aan het College of Oriental Studies in Los Angeles.

Katherine Ludwig Jansen is docente geschiedenis aan de Catholic University. Ze is schrijfster van het boek *The Making of the Magdalen: Preaching and Popular Devotion in the Later Middle Ages.*

Karen L. King is Winn Professor of Ecclesiastical History aan Harvard University Divinity School. Ze studeerde vergelijkende godsdienstwetenschappen en geschiedenis en heeft zich gespecialiseerd in de geschiedenis van het christendom en in vrouwenstudies. Haar recentste boeken, *What is Gnosticism?* en *The Gospel of Mary of Magdala: Jezus and the First Woman Apostle,* kregen veel lof. Haar theoretische belangstelling gaat vooral uit naar religieuze identiteitsformatie, discoursen over normativiteit (orthodoxie en ketterij) en *gender studies.*

David Klinghoffer is de schrijver van *The Lord Will Gather Me In* en *The Discovery of God: Abraham and the Birth of Monotheism.* Hij levert ook regelmatig bijdragen aan *National Review.*

Richard Leigh schrijft romans en korte verhalen. Met Michael Baigent schreef hij diverse boeken, waaronder *Het Heilige Bloed en de Heilige Graal* (met Henry Lincoln, Tirion, 1999/2004), *De Dode-Zeerollen en de verzwegen waarheid* (Tirion, 1991/1997/2004), *De Messiaanse erfenis* (Tirion, 1998), *De Tempel en de Loge: van tempelridders tot vrijmetselarij* (Tirion, 1990), *Claus von Stauffenberg en zijn mystieke kruistocht tegen Hitler* (Tirion, 1994), *Het Elixer en de Steen* (Tirion, 1997) en hun recentste boek: *De Inquisitie* (Tirion, 2004).

Henry Lincoln begon zijn carrière als acteur, maar schreef vanaf het begin van de jaren zestig meer dan tweehonderd televisiedrama's. Zijn vroege fascinatie voor egyptologie (hij leerde door zelfstudie hiërogliefen lezen) leidde tot verdere studie van historische mysteries, mythologie en vergelijkende theologie.

Nadat hij in de ban raakte van het mysterie van Rennes-le-Château presenteerde hij voor de BBC diverse documentaires over andere historische mysteriën, waaronder *De man met het ijzeren masker, Nostradamus* en *De vloek van Toetankhamon.* Samen met Michael Baigent en Richard Leigh schreef hij *Het Heilige Bloed en de Heilige Graal* (Tirion, 1999/2004).

James Martin, S.J. is pater jezuïet en redacteur van het katholieke tijdschrift *America.* Hij schreef diverse boeken over religie en spiritualiteit, waaronder de autobiografie *In Good Company: The Fast Track from the Corporate World to Poverty, Chastity and Obedience.*

Richard P. McBrien is Crowley-O'Brien Professor of Theology en een voormalig voorzitter van het Theologisch Instituut (1980-1991) aan de University of Notre Dame. Hij was ook voorzitter van de Catholic Theological Society of America. Tot zijn wetenschappelijke interessegebieden behoren de kerkleer, de verhouding tussen religie en politiek, en de theologische, leerstellige en spirituele dimensies van de katholieke traditie. Zijn recentste boek is *Lives of the Saints: From Mary and St. Francis of Assisi to John XIII and Mother Teresa.* Hij is priester in het aartsbisdom van Hartford, Connecticut.

Graig M. McDonald is een bekroonde journalist en redacteur. Hij interviewde talloze auteurs, waaronder James Ellroy, Anne Rice, Dennis Lehane, Walter Mosley, Alistair Macleod en Dan Brown. Zijn interviews zijn opgenomen in *Writers on Writing* dat te vinden is op: www.modestyarbor.com.

Brendan McKay doceert computerwetenschappen aan de Australian National University. Hij verwierf enkele jaren geleden bekendheid toen hij in *De Bijbelcode* (Strengholt, 1999) die theorie naar het rijk der fabelen verwees.

Laura Miller schrijft voor dagbladen en tijdschriften over film, boeken, theater, digitale cultuur en sociale kwesties. Haar werk verscheen in *The New York Times, San Francisco Chronicle, Harper's Bazaar* en *Wired.* Ze levert ook regelmatig bijdragen aan Salon.com.

Sherwin B. Nuland is de auteur van *Leonardo da Vinci* (Balans, 2002) en van de bestseller *How We Die,* die in de VS in 1994 de National Book Award for Nonfiction won. Tot zijn andere boeken behoren *The Mysteries Within: A Surgeon Reflects on Medical Myth, Doctors: The Biography of Medicine* en *The Wisdom of the Body* dat als paperback de titel *How We Live* kreeg. Hij is Clinical Professor of Surgery aan Yale University, waar hij ook bio-ethiek en geschiedenis van de geneeskunde doceert.

Lance S. Owens, M.D. is zowel praktiserend arts als priester van een parochie van de Ecclesia Gnostica. Hij studeerde geschiedenis aan Georgetown University en Utah State University en promoveerde aan Columbia University. Owens beheert ook de website www.gnosis.org.

Elaine Pagels is de auteur van de bestseller *De Gnostische Evangeliën* (Servire, 1980), waarvoor ze in de vs de National Book Critics Circle Award en de National Book Award ontving en waarvan in 2005 bij Servire een herziene editie is verschenen. Ze studeerde geschiedenis en oudheidkunde aan Stanford University en promoveerde aan Harvard University. Daarnaast schreef ze de bestseller *Ketters en rechtgelovigen* (Servire, 2003), *Adam, Eva en de slang* (Servire, 1989) en *The Origin of Satan*. Ze is momenteel de Harrington Spear Paine Professor of Religion aan Princeton University.

Lynn Picknett en Clive Prince zijn onderzoekers, auteurs en sprekers over het paranormale, het occulte en over historische en religieuze mysteriën. Ze schreven de bestseller *Het geheime boek der Grootmeesters* (Tirion, 1998), een belangrijke bron voor *De Da Vinci Code*. Picknett en Prince schreven ook *Turin Shroud: In Whose Image? The Truth Behind the Centuries-Long Conspiracy of Silence* waarin wordt gesteld dat de aanbeden lijkwade een practical joke van Leonardo was. Picknett en Prince wonen in Londen.

Gilles Quispel studeerde klassieke letteren en theologie in Leiden en Groningen en promoveerde in Utrecht op een proefschrift over de boeken van Tertullianus tegen de gnosticus Marcion. Aan de theologische faculteit van de Rijksuniversiteit Utrecht was hij 32 jaar hoogleraar in de geschiedenis van de vroege kerk. Op 10 mei 1952 kocht hij in Brussel de *Jung Codex* met vijf onbekende geschriften uit de school van de gnosticus Valentinus. Deze codex keerde na uitgave terug naar Egypte, op voorwaarde dat eindelijk alle 52 bij Nag Hammadi gevonden geschriften zouden worden uitgegeven. In 1956 smokkelde Quispel tijdens de Suezcrisis een fotokopie van het Evangelie van Thomas Egypte uit, dat hij met anderen uitgaf. Recentelijk boekstaafde hij een synthese van zijn levenswerk. Hij schreef *Valentinus de gnosticus en zijn Evangelie der Waarheid* (In de Pelikaan, 2003) en *Het Evangelie van Thomas* (In de Pelikaan, 2004), waarin hij antwoord probeert te geven op de vraag wie en wat Jezus werkelijk was en is.

James M. Robinson is emeritus hoogleraar religie van Claremont Graduate University en hoofdredacteur van de *Nag Hammadi Library*. Als een van 's werelds grootste autoriteiten op het gebied van het vroege christendom gaf hij leiding aan een team geleerden en vertalers die de Nag Hammadi-vondsten beschikbaar maakten.

David A. Shugarts kan bogen op dertig jaar ervaring als journalist en werkte als verslaggever, fotograaf, bureauredacteur en hoofdredacteur voor kranten en tijdschriften. Tot zijn specialismen behoren de lucht- en scheepvaart. Hij is vijf keer bekroond door de Aviation/Space Writers Association. Shugarts stichtte zelf ook twee tijdschriften: *Aviation Safety* in 1981 en *Powerboat Reports* in 1988.

Jacob Slavenburg is cultuurhistoricus en schrijver over het vroege christendom, mystiek, esoterische stromingen, gnosis en hermetisme. Tot zijn boeken daarover behoren o.a. *Gnosis* (1993), *De geheime woorden* (1999), *Een sleutel tot gnosis: inzicht in de betekenis van de Nag Hammadi-vondst voor de mens van nu* (2000) en *De Hermetische schakel* (2004). Over het vroege Christendom en de apocriefe bijbelboeken schreef hij o.a. *Een ander testament* (1991), *De verborgen leringen van Jezus* (1992), *De verloren erfenis* (1995), *Het evangelie van Maria Magdalena* (1994), *Het Thomas-Evangelie, tekst en toelichting* (1996), *De mislukte man* (1996), *Valsheid in geschrifte* (1997), *50 jaar Nag Hammadi en nu?* (1996), *Het openvallend testament: nieuwe teksten over Jezus en de vrouw uit Magdala* (2001) en *De 'logische' Jezus* (2002). Met Willem Glaudemans bezorgde hij de eerste volledige Nederlandse vertaling van de bij Nag Hammadi gevonden teksten, *De Nag Hammadi-geschriften*, waarvan in 2004 een volledig herziene en uitgebreide versie verscheen. De genoemde titels verschenen bij Ankh-Hermes, behalve *Valsheid in geschrifte* (Walburg Pers).

Margaret Starbird studeerde aan de University of Maryland, aan Christian-Albrechts Universität in Kiel en aan de Vanderbilt Divinity School. Ze heeft veel gepubliceerd over het concept van het heilig vrouwelijke. Tot de boeken die ze schreef behoren *Magdalen's Lost Legacy: Symbolic Numbers and the Sacred Union in Christianity*, *The Goddess in the Gospels: Reclaiming the Sacred Feminine*, *The Feminine Face of Christianity* en *De vrouw met de albasten kruik: Maria Magdalena en de betekenis van de graal* (Ankh-Hermes, 1995).

Kate Stohr werkte als onderzoekster en redactrice mee aan dit boek. Ze is journaliste en maakt documentaires. Haar artikelen verschenen in *The New York Times*, *U.S. News & World Report*, de *Christian Science Monitor*, *Time Digital*, *People*, *Rosie* en *In Style*. Recente reportages van haar hand gingen over de bioindustrie, pensioenmigratie, afvalverwerking, arbeidsomstandigheden en milieucriminaliteit.

Annalyn Swan was als adviserend redactrice betrokken bij dit boek en leidt samen met Peter Bernstein A.S.A.P. Media. Ze werkte als schrijfster en redactrice voor *Time*, als muziek- en kunstcritica voor *Newsweek* en ze was hoofdredactrice van *Savvy*. Met kunstcriticus Mark Stevens schreef ze de biografie *De Kooning: An American Master*.

David Van Biema schrijft voor het tijdschrift *Time* en is gespecialiseerd in religie.

Brian Weiss schrijft al bijna dertig jaar boeken en artikelen over uiteenlopende onderwerpen als technologie, handel, luchtvaart en geneesmiddelen. Hij was als eindredacteur verantwoordelijk voor diverse publicaties, schreef columns die in diverse dagbladen verschenen en leverde bijdragen aan vele boeken. Zijn succesvolle marketing- en adviesbureau Word'sworth is gevestigd in Pasadena in Californië.

David Wilk was als adviserend redacteur betrokken bij dit boek. Hij verdiende in vele hoedanigheden zijn sporen in de boekenbranche, onder andere als auteur, redacteur, uitgever en distributeur. Hij was hoofd van de afdeling literatuur van de National Endowment for the Arts en is tegenwoordig directielid van CDS in New York City.

Kenneth L. Woodward schrijft voor het tijdschrift *Newsweek* artikelen over godsdienst en religie. Zijn recentste boek is *The Book of Miracles: the Meaning of the Miracle Stories in Christianity, Judaism, Buddhism, Hinduism and Islam.*

Nicole Zaray was als onderzoekster en redactielid bij dit boek betrokken. Zaray is schrijfster en filmmaakster en regisseerde en produceerde de documentaire *Work Life and The Unknowable.* Ze was co-scenarist van de nog niet verschenen film *Monopolis* en de off-Broadway show *Bread and Circus 3099.*